In Her Own Words

Women Offenders' Views on Crime and Victimization

An Anthology

Leanne Fiftal Alarid
University of Missouri–Kansas City

Paul Cromwell
Wichita State University

Roxbury Publishing Company
Los Angeles, California

Library of Congress Cataloging-in-Publication Data

In her own words: women offenders' views on crime and victimization / edited by
Leanne Fiftal Alarid and Paul Cromwell.
    p. cm.
Includes bibliographical references
ISBN 1-933220-03-1
1. Female offenders—United States 2. Criminal behavior—United States 3. Women
with social disabilities—United States I. Alarid, Leanne Fiftal, 1967– II. Cromwell, Paul
F.
HV6046.I44 2006
364.3'74—dc22   2005012805

Publisher: Claude Teweles
Managing Editor: Dawn VanDercreek
Production Editor: Monica K. Gomez
Copy Editor: Ann West
Typography: Jerry Lenihan
Cover Design: Marnie Kenney

Printed on acid-free paper in the United States of America. This book meets the standards for
recycling of the Environmental Protection Agency.

ISBN 1-933220-03-1

ROXBURY PUBLISHING COMPANY
P.O. Box 491044
Los Angeles, California 90049-9044
Voice: (310) 473-3312 • Fax: (310) 473-4490
E-mail: roxbury@roxbury.net
Website: www.roxbury.net

Contents

Section I: Women's Pathways to Crime: Linking Victimization and Criminalization

   ### Mary E. Gilfus

   Gilfus constructs a framework for understanding women's progression from victim to offender through a variety of pathways, including childhood abuse, neglect, addiction, and homelessness.

   ### Lisa Maher, Eloise Dunlap, and Bruce D. Johnson

   Maher and colleagues consider how exposure to various factors limits economic options available to women in certain socioeconomic areas, creating a pathway to drug use.

   ### Elizabeth Comack

   Comack shows how physical and sexual abuses play a role in women ending up in prison.

   ### Brenda Geiger and Michael Fischer

   The authors compare how women and men offenders are able to rationalize a favorable identity of themselves and justify criminal behavior.

Section II: The Nexus Between Criminal Behavior and Family

   ### Geoffrey P. Hunt, Kathleen MacKenzie, and Karen A. Joe-Laidler

   Hunt and colleagues illustrate the complexities of family ties with adolescent Latina gang members.

Section III: Crime Partnerships, Networks, and Gangs

Section IV: Economic Marginality and Survival Crimes

Section V: Women's Crime as Rational Choice

Acknowledgments

We would like to thank Christy Circle for assistance in article preparation and scanning. Kristi Holsinger, Leanne's colleague at the University of Missouri–Kansas City, was helpful at providing a second opinion to what may have seemed at the time to be unrelated questions and e-mails. We are also grateful to the reviewers of the text who provided us with helpful comments: Mary Atwell (Radford University), Suzette Cote (California State University, Sacramento), Venessa Garcia (Keane University), Angel D. Geoghagan (University of Tennessee–Chattanooga), Phoebe Godfrey (Texas A&M International University), Jessie L. Krienert (Illinois State University), Celia Lo (University of Alabama at Tuscaloosa), and Sharon Redhawk Love (Pennsylvania State University–Altoona). Finally, we appreciate Claude's support to make it all happen. ✦

Leanne Alarid and Paul Cromwell

Preface

This anthology provides the opportunity for the reader to view firsthand accounts of women's experiences with crime as they are embedded within victimization. These personal accounts are interpreted and illuminated through a social scientific lens. Model examples in the field of criminology that reflect this approach include Lenore Walker's (1979) *The Battered Woman*, Marsha Rosenbaum's (1981) research on female heroin addicts, Anne Campbell's (1984) work with gang girls, and Eleanor Miller's (1986) ethnography entitled *Street Woman*. In these works, the researchers befriend, observe, and interview marginalized individuals who are victims of abuse, or may be involved in lawbreaking behavior, or both. The researchers provide detailed qualitative descriptions for criminal events and their personal reaction and construction of these events from a feminist social science viewpoint.

A *feminist view* as defined in this text is "a way of conceptualizing reality from the vantage point of women's lives" (Hennessy 1993, 14). Gender identity and experiences with crime and victimization are socially constructed, from how women offenders see themselves to how they view their involvement in crime and deviance. In the criminological sense, a feminist viewpoint is placing women at the center as a "way of making sense of their [women's] lives, that is capable of shedding light on the factors and conditions which brought them into conflict with the law" (Comack 1996, 34). The use of feminist research methodology (e.g., face-to-face interviews, life histories, participant observation, and other ethnographic or field research methods) central to this text. Although interviews are valuable self-reported accounts of criminal behavior, there is little way for the researcher to check accuracy. Thus, the reader should be mindful that while sample sizes vary widely in each chapter (ranging from one person to over 300 women), these nonrandom samples are not necessarily generalizable to larger groups of women offenders. Also, the quotes presented by the authors are used to illustrate typical experiences and perceptions of only the largely economically marginalized women who come to the attention of the criminal justice system. Moreover, part of constructing these firsthand accounts requires us to be mindful of how only some of society defines criminal behavior.

Criminal behavior is defined as illegal conduct that requires government intervention. But who defines what behavior is illegal? Functionalists would say that laws represent the will and moral values of the majority of the populace. Perhaps for some behaviors (e.g., premeditated murder and felony theft) this might be true. Conflict theorists would counter by arguing that laws are made by the "haves" to control the "have nots." In other words, wishes of the dominant power elite (i.e., overwhelmingly white, upper-class males) define what is considered illegal, immoral, or in need of government intervention to draw attention away from themselves and toward the less powerful. For example, increases in punishments for drug offenses have led to more criminalized women, particularly poor women of color.

When assessing responsibility, criminal laws make two assumptions. First, the law presumes that at some level, people who are not deterred by punishment make rational choices to commit crime. The second assumption is that defendants have similar backgrounds, experiences, knowledge, skills, and abilities to make these choices. Although the law attempts to compensate for these assumptions through providing defenses, justifications, and excuses for some types of criminal behavior, the law tends to criminalize individuals who face victimization from domestic abuse or drug and alcohol addiction or who are marginalized in some way through poverty or discrimination. When someone's behavior comes to the attention of police through arrest or the person is ultimately convicted, he or she becomes *criminalized*. The criminal charge or conviction describes official versions by police or prosecutors of what type of criminal behavior occurred that led to the initial arrest.

In turn, some criminologists tend to gather arrest and conviction data and to interview groups of people according to their conviction, their crime categories (e.g., violent crime, drug crime, and property crime), or both. Sometimes, due to prosecutorial discretion or plea bargaining, the conviction (or crime category) may not match what actually happened.

Women's law violations may be viewed more accurately as legal constructions or typologies of behavior that are "an outgrowth of the problems, conflicts, and dilemmas which they confront in everyday life" (Comack 1996, 20). In effect, a criminalized woman may share many commonalities of women who are victimized, such as a feeling of powerlessness or learned helplessness and an involvement in oppressive relationships (Thornburg and Trunk 1992). To fully understand the nature of female criminality and how offending behavior is intimately linked to prior victimization and a host of current challenges that women face, we must be careful not to categorize women offenders solely on the basis of these crime typologies. Rather, we should view crime as an outcome, or view the conviction as one of many possible consequences, of women's lives that are embedded in various pathways to crime.

In Her Own Words brings together a variety of field research and personal interviews of marginalized women who have offended and who may or may not be labeled as criminals by the justice system. These firsthand accounts are placed in a theoretical and social scientific context so that the reader can better understand their broader meaning. We believe that the text has utility in crime control policy strategies because factors that determine paths to crime must first be understood before our society can respond intelligently and effectively to crime reduction.

In making our selections for this anthology, we struggled with how to organize them in a manner that best expresses women's experiences with crime and victimization. In our view, women's experiences largely differ from traditional paradigms, and therefore we have structured the readings according to various explanations of female crime, knowing full well that these explanations overlap and that various readings could have been placed in more than one section. Ultimately, the interpretations, perceptions, and definitions of each woman's situation within the readings is, in our minds, more important to note than where the reading appears within the book.

We also took great pains to include as wide a range of criminal behaviors as possible. Most studies in this area have been done by only a handful of social scientists, and their work has focused largely on vice offenses, drugs, and violent crime. We were successful at locating research that captured criminal offending by women of different age-groups and who are members of different racial or ethnic groups. However, there is a dearth of recent qualitative pieces that capture women's involvement in white-collar offending, computer crime, petty property crimes, and crimes of middle and privileged socioeconomic statuses.

To create this book in a format that is conducive to teaching pedagogy, we prepared an introduction to each section and discussion questions at the end of each chapter. To make the text more readable and to maximize the number of articles included, we reduced the length of the literature reviewed in each article and summarized the methods section in our editorial summary at the beginning of each chapter. The section introductions bring the essence of each group of readings together for a general understanding of how the various chapters fit within the book.

References

Campbell, A. 1984. *The Girls in the Gang.* Oxford, UK: Basil Blackwell.

Comack, E. 1996. *Women in Trouble.* Halifax, Nova Scotia: Fernwood.

Cromwell, P. 2005. *In Their Own Words: Criminals on Crime*, 4th ed. Los Angeles: Roxbury Publishing.

Hennessy, R. 1993. "Women's Lives/Feminist Knowledge: Standpoint as Ideology Critique." *Hypatia: A Journal of Feminist Philosophy* 8 (1): 14–34.

Miller, E. M. 1986. *Street Woman.* Philadelphia: Temple University Press.

Rosenbaum, M. 1981. *Women on Heroin.* New Brunswick, NJ: Rutgers University Press.

Thornburg, T., and D. Trunk. 1992. "A Collage of Voices: A Dialogue With Women in Prison." *Southern California Review of Law and Women's Studies* 2 (1): 155–217.

Walker, L. 1979. *The Battered Woman.* New York: Harper and Row. ✦

About the Editors

Leanne Fiftal Alarid is an associate professor and program coordinator of the criminal justice program in the Department of Sociology/Criminal Justice at the University of Missouri–Kansas City. She received her Ph.D. in Criminal Justice from Sam Houston State University in 1996. She has authored or edited 5 books and 25 journal articles and book chapters in the area of corrections, gender and crime, and policing. Dr. Alarid is experienced in survey methodology, focus groups, and interviewing techniques within institutional and community-based correctional settings. Dr. Alarid received the UMKC Board of Trustees Faculty Scholar Award for 2001–2002 for excellence in research.

Paul Cromwell is a professor of criminal justice and director of the School of Community Affairs at Wichita State University. He received his Ph.D. in Criminology at Florida State University in 1986. He has taught previously at the University of Miami and the University of Texas–Permian Basin. He is the author or editor of 16 books and 50 articles and book chapters. He has extensive experience in the criminal justice system, including service as chairman of the Texas Board of Pardons and Paroles, as a chief juvenile probation officer and director of juvenile services, and as a United States probation officer. He is an ethnographer who has conducted field studies of burglars, shoplifters, and graffiti artists. ✦

About the Contributors

Leanne Fiftal Alarid, Ph.D., is an associate professor and program coordinator of the criminal justice program in the Department of Sociology/Criminal Justice at the University of Missouri–Kansas City.

Dorothy Allison is the best-selling author of *Bastard Out of Carolina, Cavedweller,* and a memoir, *Two or Three Things I Know for Sure.* She currently lives with her partner and her son in Northern California.

Deborah R. Baskin, Ph.D., is a professor in the Department of Criminal Justice at California State University–Los Angeles.

David C. Brotherton is an associate professor of sociology and criminal justice at John Jay College in New York.

Henry H. Brownstein, Ph.D., is director of Abt Associates Center on Crime, Drugs and Justice.

Velmer S. Burton Jr., Ph.D., is a professor in the administration office at the University of Minnesota–Crookston.

Elizabeth Comack, Ph.D., is professor in the Department of Sociology at the University of Manitoba in Canada.

Susan M. Crimmins, Ph.D., is a professor in the Department of Criminal Justice at California State University–Los Angeles.

Francis T. Cullen, Ph.D., is a distinguished research professor in the Department of Criminal Justice at the University of Cincinnati in Ohio.

Steven J. Cuvelier, Ph.D., is a professor in the George Beto College of Criminal Justice at Sam Houston State University in Huntsville, Texas.

Scott H. Decker, Ph.D., is Curator's Professor in the Department of Criminology and Criminal Justice at the University of Missouri–St. Louis.

Barbara Denton, Ph.D., is a research fellow in the School of Law and Legal Studies at La Trobe University in Melbourne, Australia.

Eloise Dunlap, Ph.D., is employed at the Institution for Special Population Research, National Development and Research Institutes, Inc., in New York City.

Jeffrey Fagan, Ph.D., is a professor at Columbia University's School of Law in New York City.

Kathleen J. Ferraro, Ph.D., is an associate professor in the Sociology Department at Northern Arizona University.

Michael Fischer, Ph.D., teaches in the Department of Justice Studies at Pittsburg State University, in Kansas.

Brenda Geiger, Ph.D., teaches in the Department of Criminology at Bar-Ilan University in Israel.

Mary E. Gilfus, Ph.D., is associate professor of social work at Simmons College in Boston.

Ansley Hamid, Ph.D., is a former John Jay professor of criminal justice. He writes and researches independently.

Geoffrey P. Hunt, Ph.D., is a senior research associate at the Institute of Scientific Analysis in San Francisco.

James A. Inciardi, Ph.D., is the director of the Center for Drug and Alcohol Studies and a professor in the Department of Sociology and Criminal Justice at the University of Delaware.

Karen A. Joe-Laidler, Ph.D., is an associate professor of sociology at the University of Hong Kong.

Bruce D. Johnson, Ph.D., is employed at the Institution for Special Population Research, National Development and Research Institutes, Inc., in New York City.

Marion C. Kiley, M.P.A., is the intervention site director for Women Protecting Women in Miami, Florida.

Steven P. Kurtz, Ph.D., is an associate scientist with the Center for Drug and Alcohol Studies at the University of Delaware.

Sandra C. Langley is a researcher at the Medical and Health Research Association of NYC, at the National Development and Research Institutes, Inc.

Nikki Levine is a high school dropout and was previously incarcerated in Washington, DC. She is a self-taught UNIX engineer.

Kathleen MacKenzie, M.A., holds a research position at the Institute for Scientific Analysis in San Francisco.

Lisa Maher, Ph.D., is an associate professor of the Viral Hepatitis Program at the National Centre in HIV Epidemiology and Clinical Research in Sydney, Australia.

James W. Marquart, Ph.D., is a professor in the George Beto College of Criminal Justice at

Sam Houston State University in Huntsville, Texas.

Jody Miller, Ph.D., is an associate professor in the Department of Criminology and Criminal justice at the University of Missouri–St. Louis.

Angela M. Moe, Ph.D., is an assistant professor in the Department of Sociology at Western Michigan University, in Kalamazoo, Michigan.

Pat O'Malley, Ph.D., is a professor in the Department of Sociology/Anthropology at Carleton University in Ottawa, Ontario, Canada.

Allison Redfern is a former graduate student in the University of Missouri–St Louis' criminology and criminal justice program.

Lisa E. Sanchez, Ph.D., is an assistant professor in the Department of Ethnic Studies at the University of California, San Diego

Dietrich Smith is a former graduate student of University of Missouri–St Louis's criminology and criminal justice program.

Ira Sommers, Ph.D., is a professor in the Department of Criminal Justice at California State University–Los Angeles.

Barry J. Spunt, Ph.D., is associate professor and chair in the Department of Sociology at John Jay College in New York.

Hilary L. Surratt, M.A., M.Phil., is an associate scientist with the Center for Drug and Alcohol Studies at the University of Delaware.

Richard Wright, Ph.D., is a Curator's Professor in the Department of Criminology and Criminal Justice at the University of Missouri–St. Louis. ✦

Section I

Women's Pathways to Crime: Linking Victimization and Criminalization

To understand female criminality, it is important to begin with possible origins or sources that led to criminal acts or a pattern of law-violating behaviors. Criminologists have called these origins "pathways to felony court" (Daly 1992), "routes of entry" (Gilfus 1992), "paths to crime" (Richie 1996), and "pathways to imprisonment" (Owen 1998). These routes make two important assumptions. First, that we live in a patriarchal society that structurally devalues the status of women compared with men. Raising and socializing girls is, for most people, different than raising boys. Early childhood experiences in turn affect how young girls view themselves. This continues throughout adulthood and affects how women view their relationships with other people and with organizations and social systems outside the family.

There is not just one entry route that purports to explain all types of female criminality. Paths to crime are not neatly divided or clear-cut to explain each specific type of female crime. Instead, criminal behavior and paths to those crimes overlap, embedded like a spiderweb in women's lives. The readings in this section illustrate the process and types of victimization that many offending women experience, thus obscuring the boundaries between that of a victim and a criminal. Daly (1992) identified three main paths to crime: (1) survival; (2) resistance to oppressive relationships; and (3) economic and/or physical victimization. Gilfus (2002, 3) identified a total of six paths and noted that

> the first three pathways best reflect the process of criminalization by which girls' and women's resources for escaping and surviving abuse are so limited that they must depend on illegal activity for income.

These pathways include abused and runaway girls, homeless women, and women addicted to drugs.

The next three pathways are

> . . . more reflective of the process of entrapment by which battered women are forced into crime by abusers and/or poverty and are forced into the criminal justice system by laws and practices that entrap battered women." (Gilfus 2002, 4)

These situations include women arrested for economic crimes who are coerced by batterers, women arrested for harm to children or abusers, and women affected by discriminatory and coercive welfare or immigration policies. However, criminalization and entrapment are influential in all six paths.

Women's criminal behavior may thus be seen as coping mechanisms or resistance to childhood sexual and physical victimization, childhood neglect, economic marginalization, and domestic violence. Still, a large percentage of women prisoners take responsibility for their actions that ultimately led to their incarceration (Owen 1998). **The first reading in this section, by Mary Gilfus,** is a classic, and it is included here because it accurately illustrates a broad overview of situations that precede lawbreaking behavior, such as poverty, childhood abuse, running away from home, and battering and other forms of intimate abuse. These themes form the basis of girls' and women's responses to victimization and are therefore discussed in more detail here.

Childhood Abuse, Incest, and Neglect

Traumatic childhood experiences for many juvenile girls play a significant role in both female juvenile delinquency and, later, in various forms of adult lawbreaking behavior. Childhood abuse in the home, in the form of sexual assault, incest, and/or parental neglect, is more likely to happen to juvenile girls than to boys (Belknap, Holsinger, and Dunn 1997). Longitudinal studies of girls who have been abused or neglected compared with girls who were not abused indicate that over 70 percent of abused and neglected girls do not become juvenile or adult offenders. However, of the girls who come to the attention of the juvenile justice and criminal justice system, abused and neglected girls are twice as likely as girls who have not been abused to be arrested as a juvenile or an adult, and over twice as likely to commit a violent crime (Widom 2000). Abused girls are more likely to run away from home, and they are also more likely to later be arrested for drug offenses and violent crimes as adults (Siegel and Williams 2000).

Childhood abuse and neglect has a negative impact within all socioeconomic classes. According to other studies, middle-class girls who engage in fighting at school are significantly more likely than assaultive boys and nonassaultive boys and girls to have been physically and sexually abused at home (Artz 1998). Other than this main difference, assaultive girls more closely resembled assaultive boys than they do girls who do not engage in violence, in terms of delinquent behavior, drug use, and other status offenses (e.g., gang membership, curfew, skipping school, petty theft, smoking cigarettes, underage drinking).

Running Away

Most girls run away from home to escape childhood abuse or family problems. If picked up by police, many runaways are placed in an alternative living arrangement, such as extended family networks, foster care, or group homes. Underage girls who avoid being detected by police or are able to survive on the streets support themselves by criminal activities such as theft, shoplifting, or panhandling, or they are supported by another adult male, who may introduce them to drugs and prostitution. Although some young Latina women tend to be more insulated from involvement in prostitution, Latinas may later become involved in criminal networks through men. Thus, running away and drug use are two main routes to deviant networks (Miller 1986). It is no accident that arrest data show adult prostitution and juvenile runaways are the only two offenses for which there are more females than males that come to police attention (Federal Bureau of Investigation 2003).

Limited Economic Opportunities

Another assumption of pathways to crime is that many women, particularly women of color in the inner city, have limited economic opportunities. Many impoverished and undereducated people find other sources of income or "hustles" to supplement their legitimate income to support their families. **The second reading, by Lisa Maher, Eloise Dunlap, and Bruce Johnson,** explains how drug dealing is a lucrative form of hustling as an alternative income source, mainly due to lack of legitimate job opportunities and recognition of social marginality. Early age immersion in neighborhood street life and relationships, to the exclusion of outside relationships and activities, seems to limit opportunities for mainstream exposure to educational and employment institutions that, in turn, would expand choices.

Women as Victims of Violence

Tied to the themes of childhood abuse and neglect and women's decreased economic opportunities is the theme of adult women as victims of violence. Across the country in one year, between 1 and 1.5 million adult women in the general population are victimized by a violent crime, which includes battering, assault, rape, robbery, and homicide (Tjaden and Thoennes 2000). Women who are young and have never been married, or who have recently separated or divorced, are more likely to be victimized by someone they know than are older and/or married women. Age and marital status are stronger predictors than socioeconomic status and race/ethnicity, particularly for intimate partner violence (Lauritsen and Schaum 2004). Women who lack social support networks, either from being a single female-head of household, being new to a community, or having gone through a recent divorce, are more likely to be targets for violent behavior. Violence against women is proportionately higher for women who are incarcerated in jail or prison—about half of imprisoned women were physically or sexually assaulted prior to their arrest (Harlow 1999). One reason may be that women who react to recurrent abuse with violence are criminalized. Another reason for this difference is that many incidences of victimization by violent crime go unreported, particularly by women who feel the need to protect their abuser, or who are themselves involved in illegal activity. Researchers have suggested the possibility of a stronger causal relationship between some forms of victimization and criminal behavior of marginalized women, whereby women view violence as a protective measure, a way to postpone a violent episode, or a way out of the abusive relationship (Richie 1996, 2000). Some women, even after imprisonment, return to abusive relationships because of "fear, familiarity, the desire not to be alone, or a sense of loyalty" (Henriques and Manatu-Rupert 2001, 16).

Resisting Violence and Abuse

Elizabeth Comack's reading, the third selection, addresses various forms of female criminality that are a result of coping with or resisting an abusive or violent relationship. The prevalence of women who are abused crosses racial, educational, age, and class lines. Many adult women who remain in abusive relationships feel a sense of learned helplessness and powerlessness over their own actions. This learned helplessness creates an inability to make choices and feel in control of one's actions (Thornburg and Trunk 1992). Low self-esteem and learned helplessness are precisely the ways that abusers effectively control another person. The battered woman typically has fabricated her own ideas of what she believes a traditional family should be and will maintain this role or image at all costs. This initial belief—together with pressure to stay together from other family members (e.g., parents, children), threats of bodily harm (or even death) from her partner if she leaves the relationship, and lack of a solid escape plan—makes leaving an abusive relationship nearly impossible.

According to official statistics, women are significantly more likely to be killed by their male partner or spouse than men are to be killed by a female partner. Murder committed by female offenders has declined consistently over the last 45 years (Heimer 2000). When women kill, it is most often a result of being powerless. There is a distinct difference between women who kill their abusers and battered women who do *not* kill their abusers. In one study, battered women who killed their male abusers endured more physical injury and more frequent threats, and were more likely to be sexually assaulted. Male abusers who were killed were also more likely to use drugs or alcohol and to abuse both women and children (Browne 1987). Of course, battered and abused women rarely kill in response to their abuse. Of the battered women with a partner involved in crime, it is more likely that they may commit crimes under duress or agree to commit crimes as a show of loyalty or to delay the abuse.

Among women as a group, African-American women are arrested for crimes of violence at much greater and disproportionate rates than Caucasian women and women of other ethnic groups (Steffensmeier and Allan 1988). Various explanations have been proposed, including increased attention to violence by researchers, differences in socialization (Holsinger and Holsinger 2005), and a racially biased perception by police and prosecutors. A general correlation between economic inequality and violence exists for men and women. Applying this correlation to white and black women's rates of violence, women who are African-American are more likely to be members of the economic underclass. White women can mitigate their powerlessness in a sexist and racist system by attaching themselves to white men. Black women face both sexism and racism in their daily lives and cannot merely attach themselves to black men, who also face economic hardships and racism. Violence may be a form of gender resistance (Lorde 1988), in which women act to protect themselves from further victimization by men. However, most women who have had experiences with abuse, neglect, sexual assault, and economic marginality turn their frustration and despair inward, and this has a profound effect on their self-esteem and how they ultimately view themselves. The **final selection, by Brenda Geiger and Michael Fischer**, explains why women (when compared with men) have a more difficult time resisting stigmatizing criminal labels and empowering themselves to reconstruct a positive identity.

In summary, in this first section we wish to establish the link between women's victimization, their identity of themselves, and their involvement in lawbreaking behaviors. We also wish to emphasize that there is not just one pathway to crime but many overlapping, yet complicated reasons for women's involvement in criminal behavior.

References

Artz, S. 1998. *Sex, Power, and the Violent School Girl.* New York: Teachers College Press.

Belknap, J., K. Holsinger, and M. Dunn. 1997. "Understanding Incarcerated Girls: The Results of a Focus Group Study." *The Prison Journal* 77 (2): 381–404.

Browne, A. 1987. *When Battered Women Kill.* New York: Free Press.

Daly, K. 1992. "Women's Pathways to Felony Court: Feminist Theories of Lawbreaking and Problems of Representation." *Southern California Review of Law and Women's Studies* 2 (1): 11–52.

Federal Bureau of Investigation. 2003. Uniform Crime Reports, 2002. Accessed on September 1, 2004, at: *http://www.fbi.gov/ucr.*

Gilfus, M. E. 1992. "From Victims to Survivors to Offenders: Women's Routes of Entry and Immersion Into Street Crime." *Women and Criminal Justice* 4 (1): 63–89.

——. 2002. "Women's Experiences of Abuse as a Risk Factor for Incarceration." Retrieved on February 21, 2005, from: *www.vawnet.org/DomesticViolence/Research/VAWnetDocs/AR_Incarceration.pdf.*

Harlow, C. W. 1999. *Prior Abuse Reported by Inmates and Probationers* (NCJ 172879). Washington, DC: U.S. Department of Justice.

Heimer, K. 2000. "Changes in the Gender Gap in Crime and Women's Economic Marginalization." *Criminal Justice 2000: The Nature of Crime: Continuity and Change.* Washington, DC: National Institute of Justice, Office of Justice Programs.

Henriques, Z. W., and N. Manatu-Rupert. 2001. "Living on the Outside: African American Women Before, During, and After Imprisonment." *The Prison Journal* 81 (1): 6–19.

Holsinger, K., and A. Holsinger. 2005. "Differential Pathways to Violence and Self-Injurious Behavior: African-American and White Girls in the Juvenile Justice System." *Journal of Research in Crime and Delinquency* 42 (2): 211–242.

Lauritsen, J. L., and R. J. Schaum. 2004. "The Social Ecology of Violence Against Women." *Criminology* 42 (2): 323–357.

Lorde, A. 1988. "Age, Race, Class, and Sex: Women Redefining Difference." In *Racism and Sexism: An Integrated Study* (Paul S. Rothenburg, ed.). New York: St. Martin's Press.

Miller, E. M. 1986. *Street Woman.* Philadelphia: Temple University Press.

Owen, B. 1998. *In the Mix: Struggle and Survival in a Women's Prison.* Albany: State University of New York Press.

Richie, B. E. 1996. "Six Paths to Crime." Pp. 101–131) in *Compelled to Crime: The Gender Entrapment of Battered Black Women.* New York: Routledge.

——. 2000. "Exploring the Link Between Violence Against Women and Women's Involvement in Illegal Activity." *Research on Women and Girls in the Justice System: Plenary Papers of the 1999 Conference on Criminal Justice Research and Evaluation—Enhancing Policy and Practice Through Research, Volume 3* (NCJ 180973). Washington, DC: National Institute of Justice, Office of Justice Programs.

Siegel, J. A., and L. M. Williams. 2000. "The Relationship Between Child Sexual Abuse and Female Delinquency and Crime: A Prospective Study." *Journal of Research in Crime and Delinquency* 40 (1): 71–94.

Steffensmeier, D. J., and E. A. Allan. 1988. "Sex Disparities in Arrest by Residence, Race, and Age: An Assessment of the Gender Convergence/Crime Hypothesis." *Justice Quarterly* 5: 53–80.

Thornburg, T., and D. Trunk. 1992. "A Collage of Voices: A Dialogue With Women in Prison." *Southern California Review of Law and Women's Studies* 2 (1): 155–217.

Tjaden, P., and N. Thoennes. 2000. *Full Report of the Prevalence, Incidence, and Consequences of Violence Against Women: Findings From the National Violence Against Women Survey* (NCJ 172837). Washington, DC: National Institute of Justice, U.S. Department of Justice.

Widom, C. S. 2000. "Childhood Victimization and the Derailment of Girls and Women to the Criminal Justice System." Pp. 27–36 in *Research on Women and Girls in the Justice System: Plenary Papers of the 1999 Conference on Criminal Justice Research and Evaluation—Enhancing Policy and Practice Through Research, Volume 3* (NCJ 180973). Washington, DC: National Institute of Justice, Office of Justice Programs. ✦

1

From Victims to Survivors to Offenders

Women's Routes of Entry and Immersion Into Street Crime

Mary E. Gilfus

This study explores the patterns by which women enter into crime by drawing on in-depth life history interviews with a sample of 20 incarcerated women. The author constructs a conceptual framework for understanding the progression from victim to survivor to offender in the subjects' life histories. This framework shows that the best available options for escape from physical and sexual violence are often survival strategies that are criminal (i.e., running away from home, drug use, and the illegal street work required to survive as a runaway). The women's own narratives are used to illustrate their views of themselves as survivors, not as victims, and their commitments to important relationships in their lives that explain their entry into and commitments to criminal activities. Women's responses to victimization and women's relational identities are seen as factors that both motivate and restrain women's criminal activities. The term "immersion in street crime" is more accurate than "criminal career" in describing women's criminal histories.

Criminology literature has recently begun to focus on concepts such as "criminal career" and "career offender" suggesting that there may be discernible patterns in the criminal histories of offenders (Gottfredson & Hirschi, 1986; Gottfredson & Hirschi, 1988). Yet this literature, thus far, centers almost exclusively about *male* offenders. Little attention has been paid to questions such as *whether* there is such a thing as a *female* "criminal career" pattern and if so, how that career begins and what shapes its contours and how they define their commitments and identities in relation to criminality. This study will focus

on women's personal accounts of the life events and socializing experiences which they perceive to be connected to their entry into and immersion in illegal activity. Special attention will be given to men's interpretation of sex roles and the role of victimization, as well as poverty and racism, in setting up the conditions which both compel and constrain women's criminal activities.

Gender, Race, and Crime

Women's patterns of criminal activity differ markedly from those of men both in the types and the amounts of crime they commit. A major gender difference is the very low rate of violent crime committed by women. The offenses for which women are arrested and incarcerated are primarily non-violent and minor property offenses: shoplifting, larceny, check or credit card fraud, prostitution, and drug possession. When women do commit acts of violence, it is most likely against family members and in a context of self defense. Women's arrest and incarceration rates vary by race. For example, women of color are somewhat more likely than white women to be arrested for crimes against persons and are more likely to be sentenced to jail or prison; resulting in minority group women representing more than half of the adult female inmate population nationwide. The majority of incarcerated women are young, poor, single mothers, and are disproportionately from minority groups (American Correctional Association, 1990). These groups of women are also disproportionately the *victims* of crime, particularly violent crimes such as rape. Economic, social, and political marginality, may well account for the overlap in membership in high-risk groups among women who are at risk of becoming both victims and offenders.

Daly and Chesney-Lind (1988) argue that before we can address the question of what explains the gender gap in crime rates, and in order to understand race and class differences among women offenders, we need much more in-depth descriptive information about women who engage in crime. While in recent years there has been a burst of scholarly attention to women and crime, very few studies have been based on data obtained first hand from the women themselves in order to explore their own perceptions, experiences, and motivations for engaging in illegal activity. Nor have any studies focused specifically on women's criminal "careers," how women enter into illegal activities and what kind of progression occurs over time.

Miller (1986) concludes that economic marginality is strongly connected to women's motivations to enter illegal activity, and that black and white women enter illegal "street work" through somewhat different routes. She found family violence and runaway status more related to white women's entry patterns, while black women were more likely to be introduced to illegal activity through kin and neighborhood networks.

Miller (1986) and Romenesko and Miller (1989) document that once women become involved in street work, they become part of a highly gendered division of labor in the male-dominated world of street hustling. The male heads of the "pseudo-families" which are organized around street hustling activities keep women in subordinate positions by fostering competition among "their women," keeping the women economically dependent, and by physical and psychological abuse (Romenesko and Miller, 1989).

Chesney-Lind and Rodriguez's (1983) in-depth interviews with women incarcerated in Hawaii also reveal life histories which are characterized by high rates of victimization. Chesney-Lind and Rodriguez (1983; 62–63) conclude that victimization results in a "process of criminalization unique to women" in which

> young girls faced with violence and/or sexual abuse at home . . . became criminalized by their efforts to save themselves (by running away) from the abuse. . . . Once on the streets, the position afforded these women in the criminal world indicates that, again, it was not liberation but lack of formal education and genuine employment options that forced them to continue committing crimes.

Chesney-Lind (1989) argues that the criminalization of girls' survival strategies is the process by which young women who are victims of violence become transformed into offenders. This study illustrates that process of criminalization of girls' survival strategies and shows when and how a small sample of women entered into illegal activities. The study also explores how women's relational identities and socialization into nurturing and caretaking roles shape the ways in which women approach criminal activities.

Childhood: Themes of Violence and Caring for Others

Thematic coding of the childhood segments of the interviews were organized around the predominating themes by which each woman described her childhood memories. For most of the women the dominant themes were of violence, loss, and neglect with a strong sub-theme

in which they portrayed themselves as caring for and protecting other family members.

Family Backgrounds

Four of the 20 women interviewed reported that they grew up in middle class families, 12 in working class families, and four in poor families which periodically received welfare benefits. The black women in the study were generally from more economically disadvantaged backgrounds than the white women.

Five women (two black and three white) reported growing up in families in which both parents were present throughout childhood but four of those five families were characterized by parental substance abuse and family violence. The remaining 15 women were from families disrupted during childhood by divorce, death, or desertion. Four women lost a parent during childhood due to death, two of those by suicide. Four of the eight black women had been cared for during some or all of their childhoods by grandparents or other members of their extended families, and two of the white women had spent some time in foster homes.

Eleven of the women felt that one or both parents (or guardians) had significant problems with drugs or alcohol, and ten women had seen their mothers battered by male family members. These patterns of family substance abuse and violence were similar for both the black and the white women.

Thirteen of the 20 women reported experiences of childhood sexual abuse. They reported an average of two different perpetrators each, with ten women reporting sexual abuse (incest) by a male family member. Fifteen of the women reported recurrent episodes of physical abuse by family members which resulted in bodily injuries and could be classified as severe child abuse. There were no differences between the black women and the white women either in the proportion who reported childhood physical and sexual abuse, or in the types of abuse reported.

Sexual Abuse and Incest

Five women's childhood memories were organized almost completely around sexual abuse experiences. These women explained their involvement in illegal activities as a direct result of childhood sexual abuse. For example, Janet, a 28-year-old, black woman incarcerated for breaking and entering, was sexually victimized repeatedly during childhood. Her first memory of sexual abuse was by a female babysitter around the age of three or four, then by a group of male and female cousins from age five to seven, then by her grandfather at the age of ten, by another male cousin at age twelve, and finally by her step-father from the age of twelve to fourteen. She never told anyone of these experiences. Janet left home at age 14 to escape her stepfather's sexual abuse and became involved in prostitution as a teenage runaway. The resulting drug addiction and abusive domination by her male partner kept Janet immersed in a variety of street crime activities.

Sarah, a 26-year-old white woman, was incarcerated for writing illegal prescriptions for drugs. She was sexually abused by her step-father from the age of nine to fifteen. Her step-father gave her drugs, money, and other gifts in order to secure her silence and cooperation in his sexual abuse. She became addicted to drugs while still living at home and being sexually abused by her stepfather. All of her criminal activity involved forging prescriptions in order to obtain drugs to maintain her habit.

Multiple Types of Abuse and Neglect

Ten other women organized their childhood memories around multiple forms of abuse and neglect. Marcia, a 28-year-old white woman, was one of ten children. Her parents were both alcoholics. Her father battered her mother, both parents battered the children and neglected their basic needs, and the two oldest sons sexually abused Marcia. She graphically portrayed herself as a "guinea pig," a "gopher," and "not human" in the following interview excerpts. At the same time, she minimized the extent of her parents' violence.

Interviewer: Did either of your parents abuse you?

Marcia: No. As far as, what do you mean, sexually? No.

Interviewer: Physically or in any way.

Marcia: No, I just got hit a lot. 'Cause of the lies they used to tell. It was just like I was a guinea pig. You know, I was a gopher, out of ten kids, anything that used to happen, they said "she did it." I used to get beat up all the time from this one and that one.

Interviewer: So your parents both would hit you?

Marcia: 'Cause they both would drink and they wouldn't know the difference. Mmm, picked up, thrown against walls, everything. You name it.

Interviewer: Did you ever have to go to a doctor or hospital for any injuries?

Marcia: No, never went. I always hid it. Bruises and welts all over me. Teachers used

to ask me what's wrong with ya? I'd say I fell down.

Marcia, perhaps not unlike other abused children, protected her parents from discovery by covering up the signs of abuse. Next she described the neglect which accompanied the abuse. In doing so, she focused on the embarrassment she felt about going to school in dirty, ragged, and inappropriate clothing and described a number of strategies she used for coping with the neglect and the embarrassment: hiding, skipping school, daydreaming and fantasizing, and finally giving up.

Interviewer: Do you remember what it was like when you started school? How did it feel to you?

Marcia: Weird. 'Cause I wasn't dressed right or nothin', I didn't feel comfortable, I felt like a black sheep. Didn't have proper care. You know.

My mother would say "Go to school like you are, get your own clothes." You know odd socks, the whole bit. Oh god, I used to dread that.

So I never went, I hated it. Used to hide. Hated bein' laughed at. Teased. . . . Felt like I wasn't a human, like I was a creature or something all dirty and you know. . . . I don't know . . . just didn't like it. And I used to get hit for that too, and I didn't care. My father would hit me and say: "Why wasn't you in school today?" But he wouldn't find out until about six months later. 'Cause they never went to any events or anything like that.

I couldn't do home work, I couldn't concentrate, I couldn't do none of it. It was never quiet enough. And I had to sleep in a room with me and four brothers. . . .

I failed quite a few grades 'cause I used to day dream, and I didn't do the work. I didn't give a shit. I was in a fantasy land. I said: "I'm just going to be a movie star when I grow up, I don't need this homework shit." I didn't care. I didn't have nothin' to care about.

Caring for Others

In spite of the violence and neglect the women recalled in childhood, they often framed their presentations of themselves as protectors and caretakers of others. The following narrative by Denise, a 31-year-old black woman recalling events when she was ten years old, illustrates this point.

When my mother was going with this guy she really started drinking a lot and she started staying away from home a lot. So we had to get ourselves up for school, get ready, clean the house, fix ourselves something to eat. Me, my older sister and my brother, we looked out for the little ones. And we learned to cook, and we knew how to wash clothes with a rub board and a bucket. We used to get this stool and stand on it to reach the stove and cook. But we knew how to cook, we could cook anything.

And we didn't like to see her like that. She would be sick, and she would piss on herself and throw up on herself. And we used to clean her up, fix her hair, and try to get her to eat something. But she couldn't keep anything down, so we would get her some liquor, because we thought that would help her. Or if we refused to go get her some liquor, she would hit us. We would get mad at her and threaten to tell our father, but she threatened to flush our heads down the toilet, and we really believed that, so we never told, and we just did what we had to do.

In this narrative Denise recalled very actively trying to cope with her mother's alcoholism. She and her siblings took over all of the household tasks and began acting as parents toward their mother. They tried to intervene to stop their mother's drinking, but were eventually defeated by her threats and abusive behavior. Denise took pride in her ability to nurture the younger children and in spite of her anger at her mother, remained loyal to her and very lovingly cared for her. This sense of self as a caretaker of others was a positive part of Denise's identity, as it was for many of the other women interviewed. Yet this ability to care for others who are abusive and neglectful caused Denise much trouble throughout her life. The first man she fell in love with was a pimp and an addict who beat her and lived off of her earnings as a prostitute, yet her loyalty to him allowed her to serve an earlier prison sentence for a crime which she now claims he had committed.

Educational Neglect and Racial Violence

Another set of themes in the childhood memories of many of the women, but particularly the black women and the white women who grew up in poor inner-city neighborhoods, were themes of educational neglect and racism. Many of the women attended public schools during the turbulent years of school desegregation.

Three of the black women directly experienced racial violence as children. Denise had seen her uncle murdered by two white men, Karen had been constantly taunted by white students in her school, and Tina had been insulted and slapped in school by white teachers. The remaining five black women attended predominantly black schools where they were not so directly exposed to white racism, but they were aware that they were receiving a segregated and inadequate education. Some of their parents spent scarce family resources sending the children to private Catholic schools, but the young women again encountered hostility and insult from students and teachers with low expectations and condescending attitudes toward black children. Many of the women recalled that they had once dreamed of going to college and entering professional careers, but had found no support for those aspirations.

Other complaints about school which were echoed by most of the women included teachers who failed to notice the signs of their abuse and the easy availability of drugs in the schools: Feeling like failures and misfits, unable to concentrate on school work, and their pain unacknowledged, the availability of drugs was too easy a temptation to turn down. Many of the young women found their first feeling of acceptance and belonging in the drug subculture of their schools.

Adolescence: Survival Strategies and Delinquency

With the onset of adolescence themes of violence and caring for others, as well as the dreams for a successful future, gave way to questions of survival and escape.

Survival Strategies

Escape from an intolerable home situation may sometimes be the only sane solution for an abused child and the only way to end the violence. But when children or adolescents run away and seek sanctuary wherever they can find it, usually with "street people" and other runaways, they become delinquents in the eyes of law enforcement rather than children in need of protection from the recruiters for the sex and drug industries who prey on runaway children. This was exactly what happened during adolescence for many of the women interviewed.

Yvonne, a 20-year-old white woman incarcerated for drug possession, began running away from home at age 13 because she was being sexually molested by an uncle, occasionally physically abused by her mother, and emotionally taxed by her mother's episodes of depression and suicide attempts. On one of her first escapes from home she packed a suitcase full of stuffed animals and tried to hitchhike to where she thought a boyfriend lived, only to be picked up by the police and returned home. She continued to run away and was placed in several foster homes. She was raped by a foster brother in one of those homes, and while she was in foster care her mother gave away her dog. Feeling that she had nothing left to care about at home, she went to New York City with a boyfriend. She described the plight of a runaway with no money.

> The third night came, we had no more money. He said "get some money." I didn't understand what he was talking about. But he was talking about being a prostitute. . . . We didn't have a place to stay, we slept on trains. . . . I had to steal food. Times I went two, three days without eating, I'd have to steal something.

Yvonne began working as a prostitute and shoplifting to insure that she and her boyfriend had food and a place to stay.

Janet, who had been sexually abused multiple times as a child, engaged in a long narrative detailing the events leading up to the day she left home and the experiences which followed. At age 14 Janet felt pressured to have intercourse with her boyfriend in order to prove that she loved him. After their first sexual experience, her boyfriend left for summer camp. She described in great detail the day he returned from summer camp, and how she baked a cake for him and waited all day for him. He finally arrived at her house and announced that he was breaking up with her because she had not been a virgin for him. She was mortified that he had been able to tell that she was sexually "experienced" as a result of having forced intercourse with her stepfather.

After the rejection by her boyfriend she went to her father's nearby home and waited for him to return home from work. Just as he pulled into the driveway, teenage boys in a passing car yelled and waved at Janet, and she responded by waving back at them. Her father got out of his car, slapped her on the face and called her a "whore." Taking this as another rejection, Janet went home and tried to commit suicide by taking a bottle of aspirin. She slept for several hours and awoke to discover that no one had even noticed her suicide gesture, so she ran away. (Suicide was seriously considered as an escape by many of the women, and ten women made suicide attempts during adolescence).

Janet ran away to a nearby city where she was kidnapped, raped, and injected with drugs by a man who told her he was planning to sell her as a slave to a pimp. She escaped from her kidnapper and eventually returned home, but was once again faced with her stepfather's sexual demands and her mother's lack of concern. She ran away again and lied about her age in order to get a waitress job, only to be sexually harassed by her employer. This was the final straw for Janet; she decided that if everyone expected her to be a "whore" she might as well make some money at it. She went out on a street corner in the downtown prostitution district and tried soliciting customers on her own. Within minutes she was befriended by a man who offered to be her pimp, and she readily accepted. Janet had begun experimenting with drugs at age 12, began intravenous use of heroin shortly after entering prostitution, and reported that she was addicted by the age of 16 when she became pregnant with her first child.

Janet presented the above events as a way of explaining her entry into illegal street work, the best survival strategy she could find as a 14-year-old incest victim and runaway.

Onset of Delinquency

Chronologically the first "delinquent" event experienced by 13 of the 20 women was running away from home. When we consider the fact that most of the young women were being abused at home, running away seems to have been a sane and logical response. That logical act of self-protection, however, pushed the young women into finding illegal ways of supporting themselves.

Onset of drug use, truancy and stealing were closely associated with early runaway attempts. The women talked about how impossible it was to stay in school when on the run, sleeping in cars, parks, or "crash pads," and "hustling" money for food by panhandling and petty shoplifting. The first use of drugs or alcohol was reported at a mean age of 12.7 years old. The average age at leaving home for the whole sample was 16 years old, a very young age to be fending for oneself. Seven of the 17 women who had worked as prostitutes began as juvenile prostitutes, four of them having been coerced into prostitution while young runaways.

The Transition to Adulthood

Leaving home at an early age, often coupled with teenage pregnancy meant that adulthood began early for these women. Patterns of repeated victimization, drug addiction, street work, relationships with men involved in street crime, and the demands of mothering are the themes that mark their transitions from childhood to adulthood. The survival strategies which had helped the women escape from early victimization contributed to revictimization and their adult status as offenders. Yet, much like their childhood identities, the women presented themselves as adults committed to caring for others and organizing their lives around relational commitments. It was usually their relational commitments and their addiction to drugs which they described as creating the conditions which necessitated their continued involvement in criminal activity.

Street Work and Revictimization

Survival on the streets of any city is dangerous for a young woman. If she is too young to look for legal work or has too few skills to find work at a living wage, she has few choices other than to find a "hustle" which will generate income for food and a place to sleep. Whether looking for shelter, panhandling, shoplifting, selling drugs, or turning tricks, a young woman alone on the streets is often "fair game" for male violence (see Weisberg, 1985; Delacoste and Alexander, 1987). Rape, assault, and even attempted murder were experiences reported by 16 of the 20 women, with an average of three rapes or violent rape attempts per woman as adolescents or adults. Many of the rapes and assaults occurred while the women were working as prostitutes. A common scenario was for a trick to pick up the woman in his car, drive her to a remote location, rape and torture her, and leave her perhaps to die. The women who reported these crimes to the police were ridiculed and/or threatened with arrest for prostitution. Sometimes police officers would demand sexual services in exchange for not arresting the woman.

Battering Relationships

Sixteen of the women had been in battering relationships as adults, some as many as five different battering relationships. These were typically co-addict relationships in which the couple shared the activities of securing and injecting drugs, but had a gendered division of labor for illegally obtaining money for drugs. The female partner was often expected to supply money from her work as a prostitute and from shoplifting. Male partners, if they did any work other than pimping, were likely to commit robberies or did the fencing of the goods the women shoplifted. Severe battering episodes were likely to occur if the male partner felt the woman was using more than her "share" of the money on drugs, or if she was not producing "enough" income, or if he felt like punishing her for working as a prostitute.

Marcia, whose childhood narrative of abuse and neglect was presented above ran away at age 13 to the streets of a nearby city. There she met Charlie, a pimp for whom she worked from the age of 13 to 18, whenever she was not in juvenile detention halls. Charlie employed the techniques pimps often use to "season" young women into dependent and loyal prostitutes (Barry, 1984): isolation, physical violence, occasional indulgences of presents (usually drugs), and romantic vows of love. Marcia described being kept in darkened hotel rooms, heavily drugged, turning tricks, and being beaten periodically. At the time she was interviewed, Marcia had served a sentence for a crime which took place while Charlie was recruiting a new runaway to work for him, yet she still felt a strong bond of loyalty and affection for Charlie.

Addiction

Substance abuse has repeatedly been found to be one of the major long-term psychological effects of childhood sexual abuse (Briere & Runtz, 1988; Peters, 1988; Russell, Sherman, & Trocki, 1988; Stein et al., 1988). Nearly all of the 15 women who reported intravenous drug abuse histories began experimental drug or alcohol use prior to engaging in illegal activity (other than running away from home), on average by age 13. Accounts of why they started using drugs were strikingly similar, using terms such as "wanting to be obliterated" and describing their initial work as prostitutes as so "disgusting" that they "had to be high to do it." Additional reasons for beginning drug use included acceptance by peer groups and feelings of greater self-confidence when high. But the primary pattern of shifting from experimental use to intravenous use of opiates and/or cocaine typically occurred after entry into illegal activity, primarily prostitution. Many of the women attributed their continuing motivation for illegal activities to their deepening addiction to drugs. They also described numerous efforts to give up drugs, efforts which were often motivated by pregnancy or by the fear of losing custody of their children.

Mothering

Thirteen women became pregnant as teenagers; only four of them kept their first baby, struggling to survive as single teen parents. The nine women who miscarried, aborted, or gave their babies up for adoption deeply mourned the loss and felt that the loss had pushed them further into drug abuse and illegal activity. It was not long before some of the women became pregnant again and tried to keep their children in spite of their worsening addiction. Fifteen of the women had custody of their children prior to incarceration. All of the women whose mothers were still alive were in regular, nearly daily, contact with their mothers prior to incarceration, and most of the women had placed their children with their mothers while incarcerated. Even the mothers who had been physically and emotionally abusive toward them were entrusted with the care of their children. This arrangement was preferable to giving custody over to the state and risking permanent loss of one's children. One of the recurring themes expressed by the women was the pain and guilt they felt about their children. Most of the women saw themselves as good and loving mothers who tried very hard to protect their children from the negative effects of their own illegal activities, but who were increasingly torn between the competing demands of addiction, mothering, and hustling.

Relational Patterns of Entry and Immersion in Illegal Activities

Most of the women attributed some relational components to their reasons for entry into delinquent and illegal activity, either in response to childhood family violence, or death of a parent, or in response to adult marital or family issues. It should be noted that the women presented these connections not as excuses for their crimes, in fact, most of the women were quick to take responsibility for their actions, but rather as a constellation of problems which led them to "the street life."

Fourteen women had established patterns of serial relationships with men who shared and encouraged their drug abuse and illegal work and who used violence to keep the women "in line." Those 14 women presented themselves primarily in terms of their relational identities, organizing their legal work around caretaking responsibilities, and often *defining* their illegal work as a part of their caretaking roles. Thus these women had spent most of their adult years involved in a series of relationships in which mutual drug abuse and illegal activity were an integral part of the relationship. Interestingly, while the women defined their caretaking roles to include economic support of their partners, they did not define or expect their partners' roles to include childcare responsibilities. Seven women were currently incarcerated for offenses which they reported were committed with or by the male partner. All but one of the women who typically worked and lived in partnerships with men had been battered in those relationships.

Five women remained relatively independent of male partners after leaving their families of origin. One woman entered a long-term lesbian relationship, but was evasive about whether as a couple they shared a pattern of addiction and illegal activity. These five women seemed more independently committed to illegal activity and continued such activity

whether or not they were in relationships with partners who supported or disapproved of their activity. Their illegal activity was still well within the traditional realm of women's street crimes: prostitution, petty drug trafficking, and shoplifting. What appeared to distinguish these women from the more traditional women was their obvious pride in their abilities at performing illegal work and the benefits which attracted them to it (fast money and the excitement and glamour of a "party" lifestyle). It is possible that these women were in fairly early stages of illegal street work, a time when the benefits appear to outweigh the risks and the costs (Rosenbaum, 1981; Romenesko and Miller, 1989). Three of these five women expressed a desire (without much optimism of successfully fulfilling it) to eventually marry, have children and leave behind their illegal work. Thus even the most independent of the women in this study were traditional in their views on women's roles and in the types of illegal activities in which they participated.

Caretaking Roles

A central theme in the ways the women presented themselves was as caretakers. Sometimes caretaking was a reason for initial entry into illegal work, other times illegal work was perceived as an integral component of a caretaking role.

Lois, a 37-year-old white woman, is an example of a woman who clearly defined her illegal work as one aspect of traditional female role responsibilities. Lois was violently abused as a child and sexually assaulted by her father at age 14. By age 17 she fell in love with a male addict and left home. She began using heroin just to be with him and continued using it, even though she disliked it, until she was also addicted. She had initially supplied the couple's drug money by stealing from her family, but when she could no longer get away with that, she took responsibility for finding a way to support their shared addiction. She described feeling especially nurturing toward her partner when he was experiencing withdrawal symptoms. She thought about her money-earning capabilities and options, realizing that she could not earn enough money through legal employment. She thought about robbery, but ruled this out on ethical grounds fearing that she might hurt someone. She then decided on prostitution thinking that "this way I was only hurting myself." At the age of 37 Lois was in her fifth addicted and battering relationship, again supplying money for her partner's drugs from her illegal work. By now she had abandoned her ethical stance and had resorted to breaking and entering because of her dwindling earning power as a prostitute. This caused her to begin examining the reasons for her vulnerability to abusive partners, and she had just begun to regain memories of being sexually assaulted by her father.

Ann, a 37-year-old black woman, was serving six months for disorderly conduct (a prostitution-related offense). Ann was violently abused by her stepfather from the ages of ten to 16. Whenever she had to be taken to the hospital for treatment of her injuries, her mother would lie about the source of the injuries, and Ann would collaborate in the lies, explaining: "I loved my mother, and I knew they would take me away from her if I told the truth." At age 16 she moved into her own apartment and worked for a year in a low-paying clerical job. That year she was raped by the first boyfriend she had ever dated. Feeling alone and betrayed, struggling economically, Ann was convinced by a girlfriend to go "downtown" to get a job as a go-go dancer. Ann enjoyed the money she began making and was enthralled by the glitter of "downtown" life. She soon met and fell in love with Joe, a flashy pimp who made no effort to conceal his plans for Ann. She readily agreed to work as a prostitute for him, explaining in retrospect: "I was a fool for love."

Joe already had a wife and children. Ann moved in with Joe, Carol, and the children. Both women took turns working as prostitutes for Joe and caring for the children. Joe battered both women regularly, but Ann felt that she was his "number one" woman since he beat Carol more severely. Ann described herself as the mother of the family, looking after Carol when she was injured or drug sick, making sure the children were properly clothed and fed, and serving as Joe's helpmate in his illegal operations. Ann bragged about obtaining a gun so she could return home periodically to threaten her stepfather that she would kill him if he ever hurt her mother or her younger sister. After 14 years in this family style arrangement, Joe replaced Ann with another "number one" woman, and Ann left. Ann had spent the last five years in what she described as an often-faltering effort to remain drug and arrest-free, going back to school, and living with a series of partners, but vowing not to fall in love again the way she had with Joe. Ann's narrative about her years with Joe focused heavily on the sense of fulfillment she derived from her caretaking roles which were rather androgynous: protector to her mother and sister, breadwinner and protector to Carol, and sometimes co-equal partner in crime with Joe, yet also stereotypically feminine in her nurturing, loyalty, and acceptance of Joe's domination in the family.

Some of the women interviewed began their illegal activities independently, usually as a means of obtaining drugs, but later organized their illegal work around their caretaking roles. Ellen, a 32-year-old white woman and mother of four young children, was serving a ten year sentence for distribution of narcotics. Ellen's father died when she was five years old; as an only child she grew up with a close bond with her mother who was severely depressed and abused prescription drugs. When Ellen was 18 years old her mother committed suicide, and Ellen began using heroin to deal with her own depression. She worked as a street prostitute and occasionally shoplifted to support her addiction. She eventually met Bill, a heroin addict, and they had four children together. Ellen tried from time to time to give up her heroin habit, but each time she was drug-free she became depressed and suicidal.

Ellen's identity revolved around her children, but unable to control her addiction, she organized her illegal work to accommodate her caretaking responsibilities. She did this by turning her home into a "shooting gallery," a place where other addicts could come to purchase and inject heroin. She described in careful detail the ways she managed her "business," operating only while the children were asleep or at school, so that her children would be sheltered from any knowledge of her activities. Of course this careful arrangement fell apart when she and Bill were arrested; the state took custody of their children and was petitioning for permanent adoptive homes for them. Ellen, having been unable to juggle the competing demands of her addiction and her mothering responsibilities, was seriously considering suicide if the state succeeded in removing her parental rights.

Conclusions and Implications

The life histories examined here suggest that the nature of the violence to which some women have been exposed serves as a strong force in the "criminalization" of women, that is, the survival strategies selected by (or which are the only options available to) some women are the beginning of a process of transition from victim to offender.

The women in this study were victims of an overwhelming amount of violence as children and adults, yet they were on the whole committed to not harming others in their criminal activities. In spite of, or perhaps because of, those early experiences of violence, the women adopted roles and identities as caretakers and protectors, often remaining loyal to parents (and later to partners) who abused and exploited them. During adolescence the young women responded to those violations by striking out on their own, running away literally as well as symbolically through the use of drugs, but in doing so, their chances of achieving normative transitions to adult roles and responsibilities were derailed. What may have appeared to be the best available means of escape from violence meant that as young runaways they had to begin illegal "work" simply in order to survive, thus linking victimization to "criminalization" and blurring the boundaries between victim and offender. Those early experiences of violence may have had a strong socializing impact on the women's development of highly gender stereotyped identities centered around distorted notions of relational and caretaking obligations. Constant and repeated victimization by violence from early childhood into adulthood apparently seasons women well for the world of illegal street work where women's work is still highly exploited.

It is apparent that the women in this study consider their illegal activities to be a form of *work* which is undertaken primarily out of economic necessity to support partners, children, and addictions. Yet it is not so clear that terms such as "criminal careers" or "career criminals" are accurate descriptions of the women's activities or identities. At this stage of our thinking about women and crime, a more accurate conceptualization may be that of "immersion," a concept which takes into account the slide into criminality by way of survival strategies and which reflects the difficulty women have in extricating themselves from the relationships, addictions, and economic necessities which arise once they are immersed in "street work." However, further research is needed to test and elaborate upon the preliminary conceptualizations offered here.

The women studied here, similar to those studied by Romenesko and Miller (1989), Miller (1986), and Chesney-Lind and Rodriguez (1983), entered criminal activity which was itself highly sex-role stereotyped, suggesting that the division of labor remains highly sex-segregated whether in the world of legal or illegal work, and that such sex-segregation is enforced through physical and sexual violence. These findings also support the conclusions drawn by Chesney-Lind and Rodriguez (1983) that the process of criminalization for women is indeed intricately connected to women's subordinate position in society where victimization by violence coupled with economic marginality related to race, class, and gender all too often blur the boundaries between victims and offenders.

When women have been violated and exploited as harshly and as often as the women in this study, one must ask how those experiences of violence affect women's development and women's moral orientation to the world. When extreme victimization is accompanied by poverty and racial discrimination, women may have very few options for survival by legal avenues and may find a sense of belonging and relational commitment in the world of street crime when it is unattainable elsewhere.

Exposure to such extreme violence may socialize women to adopt a tenacious commitment to caring for anyone who promises love, material success, and acceptance, such that it represents an extreme liability for self survival and places some women at risk for becoming offenders. While women's moral orientation to caring (Gilligan, 1982), in the abstract, may appear to be an asset, in a social context of violence and an absence of the right to protection, the ethic of care (Gilligan, 1982) can be fatal. For the women in this study, the ethic of care appears to constrain them from initially engaging in more violent and serious crime, yet it is also that ethic coupled with the strength of women's commitment to relationships which seasons the women for recruitment and entrapment in illegal street work and ultimately leads to incarceration. Perhaps at later stages of their involvement in street work, the ethic of care gives way once again to questions of sheer survival, pushing some women into more serious forms of illegal activity. Future research should examine those later stages of women's immersion in street crime.

As we continue to investigate and understand the lives of women engaged in street crime, we can begin to call for criminal justice policies and programs which recognize the relationship between victimization and offending among women. We must begin to offer women realistic alternatives to illegal street work as a means of economic and emotional survival.

Discussion Questions

1. Is criminal behavior higher among abused/neglected girls and women than among girls who have not been abused? Discuss why this may or may not be the case.

2. Why does running away play such a major part in girls' delinquency but a minor part in boys' delinquency?

3. How do men keep women street hustlers dependent on them for survival?

4. Out of all the pathways and experiences of women in Gilfus' study, which factor is most strongly correlated to the *victimization* of women?

5. Which factor is most responsible for the *criminalization* of women and why? How do these criminalization experiences overlap with victimization?

References

American Correctional Association. 1990. *The female offender: What does the future hold?* Laurel, MD: American Correctional Association.

Barry, K. 1984. *Female sexual slavery.* New York: NYU Press.

Briere, J. and M. Runtz. 1988. Post sexual abuse trauma. In *Lasting effects of child sexual abuse,* edited by G. Wyatt and G. Powell. Beverly Hills: Sage.

Browne, A. 1987. *When battered women kill.* New York: The Free Press.

Bureau of Justice Statistics. 1989. *Prisoners in 1988.* Washington, D.C.: U.S. Department of Justice (#NCJ-116315).

Chesney-Lind, M. 1986. Women and crime: The female offender. *Signs: Journal of Women in Culture and Society,* 12: 78–96.

———. 1989. Girl's time and women's place: Toward a feminist model of female delinquency. *Crime and Delinquency,* 35: 5–29.

Chesney-Lind, M. and N. Rodriguez. 1983. Women under lock and key: A view from the inside. *The Prison Journal,* 63: 47–65.

Crites, L. 1976. *The female offender.* Lexington, MA: Lexington Books.

Daly, K. 1989. Neither conflict nor labeling nor paternalism will suffice: Intersections of race, ethnicity, gender, and family in criminal court decisions. *Crime and Delinquency,* 35: 136–168.

Daly, K. and M. Chesney-Lind. 1988. Feminism and criminology. *Justice Quarterly,* 5: 497–535.

Delacoste, F. and P. Alexander. 1987. *Sex work: Writings by women in the sex industry.* Pittsburgh: Cleis Press.

Emerson, R. 1983. *Contemporary field research.* Boston: Little, Brown.

General Accounting Office. 1979. *Female offenders: Who are they and what are the problems confronting them?* Washington, D.C.: U.S. Government Printing Office, #GGD-79-73.

Gilligan, C. 1982. *In a different voice.* Cambridge, MA: Harvard University Press.

Glaser, B. and A. Strauss. 1967. *The discovery of grounded theory: Strategies for qualitative research.* New York: Aldine.

Glick, R. and V. Neto. 1977. *National study of women's correctional programs.* Washington, D.C.: U.S. Government Printing Office.

Gottfredson, M. and T. Hirschi. 1986. The true value of lambda would appear to be zero: An essay on career criminals, criminal careers, selective incapacitation, cohort studies, and related topics. *Criminology,* 24: 213–233.

———. 1988. Science, public policy, and the career paradigm. *Criminology,* 26: 35–55.

Lewis, D. 1981. Black women offenders and criminal justice. In *Comparing female and male offenders,* edited by M. Warren. Beverly Hills: Sage.

Miller, E. 1986. *Street Woman.* Philadelphia: Temple University Press.

Mishler, E. 1986. *Research interviewing: Context and narrative.* Cambridge, MA: Harvard University Press.

Nesbitt, C. 1985. Female offenders. *Network,* 1: 3–8.

Peters, S. D. 1988. Child sexual abuse and later psychological problems. In *Lasting effects of child sexual abuse,* edited by G. Wyatt & G. Powell. Beverly Hills: Sage.

Romenesko, K. and E. Miller. 1989. The second step in double jeopardy: Appropriating the labor of female street hustlers. *Crime and Delinquency,* 35: 109–135.

Rosenbaum, M. 1981. *Women on heroin.* New Brunswick, NJ: Rutgers University Press.

Russell, D., R. Sherman, and K. Trocki. 1988. The long-term effects of incestuous abuse: A comparison of Afro-American and white American victims. In *Lasting effects of child sexual abuse,* edited by G. Wyatt and G. Powell. Beverly Hills: Sage.

Sarri, R. 1987. Unequal protection under the law: Women and the criminal justice system. In *The trapped woman: Catch 22 in deviance and control,* edited by J. Figueira-McDonough and R. Sarri. Beverly Hills: Sage.

Steffensmeier, D. 1982. Trends in female crime: It's still a man's world. In *The criminal justice system and women,* edited by B. Price and N. Sokoloff. New York: Clark Boardman.

Stein, J., J. Golding, J. Siegel, M. Burnam, and S. Sorenson. 1988. Long term psychological sequelae of child sexual abuse. In *Lasting effects of child sexual abuse,* edited by G. Wyatt and G. Powell. Beverly Hills: Sage.

Uniform Crime Reports. 1989. *Crime in the United States.* Washington, D.C.: U.S. Department of Justice, Federal Bureau of Investigation.

Ward, D., M. Jackson, and R. Ward. 1980. Crimes of violence by women. In *Women, crime, and justice,* edited by S. Datesman and F. Scarpitti. New York: Oxford University Press.

Weisberg, D. K. 1985. *Children of the night: A study of adolescent prostitution.* Lexington, MA: Lexington Books.

2

Black Women's Pathways to Involvement in Illicit Drug Distribution and Sales

Lisa Maher
Eloise Dunlap
Bruce D. Johnson

What factors in black women's backgrounds lead them toward crack (and other drug) sales as a primary economic activity in adulthood? This chapter is an exploratory analysis designed to identify common pathways during adolescence and early adult years reported by African-American women involved as crack and other drug distributors. The data are derived from a larger NIDA-funded study, whereby 250 male (primarily African-American) and 107 female (87 African-American, 15 Latina, 5 Caucasian) cocaine and crack dealers and distributors from a wide range of socioeconomic statuses were studied over a period of three to five years on the structure, functioning, and economics of cocaine and crack distribution in low-income, minority communities in New York City. The data for this chapter are limited to the 87 African-American women who were contacted and observed during the course of the research and whose activities were recorded in the form of detailed field notes. Quotations are derived from in-depth tape-recorded interviews that cover familial and personal histories and how the women became involved in crack sales and distribution activity. The participants provided information reflecting a range of experiences and factors associated with their entry into drug use and crack selling. The pathways identified in this chapter show how the impact of structural and cultural disinvestment constrained the family backgrounds and labor market opportunities of these women so as to effectively exclude them from

the formal economy. At the neighborhood level, their early investment in street life and continuing exposure to informal sector activity, including criminality, meant that drug selling was one of the limited economic options available to these women, many of whom were concentrated at the lower levels of the drug distribution network.

Drug research has rarely depicted women as economic agents, actively involved in the purchase, sale and consumption of illicit substances. Rather, the literature has been primarily focused upon prescription drug use, prostitution and female sexuality, and the effects of illicit drug use on women's reproductive functioning. Studies also suggest that women's initial experiences of illicit drug use, and heroin use in particular, are strongly mediated by males (Rosenbaum, 1981a; Blom and van den Berg, 1989; Stephens, 1991). Heroin use results in a 'narrowing of options' for women (Rosenbaum, 1981a; Maher and Curtis, 1992) whereby women generate income through sex work and other gendered forms of lawbreaking such as shoplifting and fraud and are only rarely involved in violent interpersonal crimes such as robbery or the distribution and sale of illicit drugs (for example, Adler, 1985; Johnson et al., 1985; Williams, 1989; Maher and Curtis, 1992). Within the heroin economy, women appeared confined to low-status, passive and peripheral roles such as 'bag followers' and 'holders' (Goldstein, 1979).

However, by the 1990s research highlighted the salience of crack distribution and sales as a source of income generation among drug users in the inner city (for example, Bourgois, 1989, 1995; Hamid, 1990, 1991a, 1991b; Mieczkowski, 1990). During this period, crack was clearly the most lucrative and frequently sold drug in street-level markets in New York City and even drug users active in other forms of lawbreaking were unable to generate income from these activities which rivaled that received from crack sales (Johnson et al., 1994). While little was known about the participation of women, early studies pointed to new opportunities in the wake of the crack-propelled expansion in street-level drug markets. In a study of women crack users in Miami, Inciardi et al. (1993) found that drug business offences represented a much greater proportion of total crime (94 per cent) than that found among two earlier cohorts of female heroin users (28 per cent and 34 per cent respectively) and women were less likely to engage in prostitution than the female heroin users studied previously. In New York

City, Fagan (1994) found 36 per cent of women drug users reported having sold drugs more than 50 times, concluding that,

> the size and seemingly frantic activity of the current drug markets has made possible for women new ways to participate in street networks. Their involvement in drug selling at high income levels defies the gendered norms and roles of the past, where drug dealing was an incidental income source often mediated by domestic partnerships. . . . The expansion of drug markets in the cocaine economy has provided new ways for women to escape their limited roles, statuses and incomes in previous eras. (Fagan, 1994: 210)

Similarly, 'The high incidence of incarceration and homicide among young, inner-city minority males, in the wake of the expanded demand for drugs, has provided an opportunity structure for female entry into the informal drug economy' (Baskin et al., 1993: 410–11; Mieczkowski, 1994). However, ethnographic research cautions that while crack has prompted shifts in the gender patterns of crime, these shifts have not necessarily strengthened the position of women (Bourgois and Dunlap, 1993; Maher and Daly, 1996; Maher, 1997). Where women are involved in crack distribution, they tend to be concentrated in secondary roles and/or low-level distribution activities (Dunlap, 1992, 1995; Dunlap et al., 1997; Inciardi et al., 1993; Fagan, 1994: 202). 'Life in criminal subcultures is dynamic, and much suggests that, with the ascendancy of crack, the lot of black women who engage in deviant activity has taken a turn for the worse' (Austin, 1992: 1794).

The Pathways Approach

Feminist research has highlighted the importance of several factors identified as pathways to criminal activity for women. This approach is perhaps best represented by Miller's (1986) pioneering study of Milwaukee 'street women.' Miller suggests three analytically distinct pathways that characterize women's entry to 'deviant street networks' and participation in criminal activity: drug use, membership of domestic networks, and running away from or being 'pushed out' of home.

While the drug use 'causes' crime hypothesis remains one of the 'highly cherished beliefs' (Inciardi and Pottieger, 1986: 101) of drug research, a growing body of literature suggests that involvement in lawbreaking may precede regular drug use (for example, Anglin and Speckart, 1988; Anglin and Hser, 1987; Chaiken

and Chaiken, 1990). Inciardi and Pottieger found that criminal activity emerged concomitant with drug experimentation, and regular use of heroin and other narcotics began only several years after the onset of crime (1986: 104; see also Inciardi et al., 1993, on female crack users).

Similarly, Miller (1986: 108) found 'The overwhelming majority of women with serious substance abuse problems developed them *after* they were already immersed in the fast life.' Substance abuse served as a pathway for only 10 out of a sample of 64 women (Miller, 1986: 109). Miller argues that young black women are more likely to be recruited to 'street life' and criminal activity via the interface between black domestic networks comprised of kin, non-kin and pseudo-kin, and deviant street networks. Compared to white and Hispanic women, for whom household *disorganization* (expressed by conflict between young women and their caretakers) propels recruitment into deviant street networks as a result of running away and drug use, 'It is the organization of households among poor blacks into domestic networks that promotes the recruitment of young black women directly to deviant street networks' (ibid.: 117; emphasis in original).

Cultural practices within the black community, such as other mothering and involvement of the extended kin network in the caring and rearing of children, are also implicated in this process:

> the very system that may be responsible for household survival then, may promote the initiation of young adults into a generally disapproved way of life simply by exposing them to more possible recruiters to deviant street networks. A very striking example of this has to do with the cultural pattern of 'child-keeping'. . . . On the one hand, this pattern clearly promotes the care and nurturing of children in an environment of scarce and uncertain resources. . . . On the other hand, this pattern may maximize exposure to deviant networks. (ibid.: 79)

Miller's work calls attention to the organization of domestic networks (which were primarily law-abiding in Milwaukee in the early 1980s) and to running away from home as female pathways to deviant street networks. Miller (1986) found that running away served as a pathway to involvement in deviant street networks and criminal activity for young women regardless of race/ethnicity and social class. The sexual victimization of young women is believed to play a prominent part in this process.

[Sexual abuse] is a much more important factor in patterns of running away and drug use and, thus, in recruitment to deviant street networks than is generally acknowledged. It is also my belief that the experience of emotional distancing during sexual contact that incest victims often describe is too like the psychological state described by prostitutes when they are servicing a trick for one not to be a sort of rehearsal for the other. In those cases, sexual exploitation on the street seems but an extension of sexual exploitation in the family. (ibid.: 115)

Indeed, much feminist research has explored the apparent links between childhood victimization and abuse and adult female lawbreaking (for example, Widom, 1989, 1990; Gilfus, 1992). As Chesney-Lind and Rodriguez (1983: 62) have argued, 'young girls faced with violence and/or sexual abuse at home . . . became criminalized by their efforts to save themselves (by running away) from the abuse.' Similarly, in a study of 50 black women imprisoned in New York City, Arnold (1990) proposes a trajectory from gender victimization to imprisonment in accounting for Black women's criminalization. Drug use plays a prominent role in this process whereby young Black women respond to or resist their victimization, both in terms of 'dulling the pain' and in providing a 'pseudo-family' (ibid.). Daly has constructed a composite of women's pathways to involvement in lawbreaking which she terms the 'street woman scenario';

Whether they were pushed out or ran away from abusive homes, or became part of deviant milieu, young women begin to engage in petty hustles or prostitution. Life on the streets leads to drug use and addiction, which in turn leads to more frequent lawbreaking to support a drug habit. Meanwhile, young women drop out of school because of pregnancy, boredom or disinterest in school or both. Their paid employment record is negligible because they lack interest to work in low-paid or unskilled jobs. Having a child may facilitate entry into adult women's networks and allow a woman to support herself in part by state aid. A woman may continue lawbreaking as a result of relationships with men who may also be involved in crime. (Daly, 1992: 14)

This chapter examines Black women's pathways to involvement in drug distribution in light of recent feminist research and theorizing which strongly implicates the 'street woman scenario' in women's lawbreaking and participation in the criminal economy. Utilizing ethnographic data from a small sample of women engaged in street-level drug distribu-tion, it provides insights into the lives of a 'hidden' group of women participating in what has historically been regarded as a male-dominated labor market. By exploring the role of domestic networks and neighborhood contexts, women's experiences of the formal sector workforce, drug use and 'street life' itself, the chapter attempts to identify key factors shaping black women's involvements in the drug economy. . . .

The case history of Rachel (summarized in this paragraph only) provides a direct contrast to the more common pathways and selling patterns documented later in this chapter. Rachel was a successful crack-selling, African-American woman living in Harlem. With no arrests for any crime, her success depended primarily upon selling crack to a small number of working/middle class people who were older cocaine and crack users from her apartment; she avoided sales to street crack users (Dunlap, Johnson, and Manwar, 1996). Rachel also experienced a very different pathway into crack selling (Dunlap and Johnson, 1996) than the pathways documented below for the more typical African-American female crack sellers. Her career path to, and success as, a crack seller was primarily due to the importance of Rachel's powerful grandmother (despite an alcoholic mother) who provided Rachel with many critical skills in household and interpersonal management; Rachel made critical choices to limit her drug consumption and business operations that effectively prevented her from becoming enmeshed as a street-level seller or sex worker. . . .

Domestic Networks and Neighborhood Contexts

Low-income urban communities in the United States have a long history of reliance on the informal sector (Whyte, 1943; Liebow, 1967; Stack, 1974; Valentine, 1978). These informal trading and exchange systems, based on social and kin networks, serve to meet the survival needs of the urban poor (Susser, 1982; Sharff, 1987). Within such communities, the informal economy provides opportunities for income generation and access to goods and services for populations that are denied access to formal sector mechanisms because of the inadequate division of labor in advanced industrial economies (Pahl, 1980). In addition to providing an alternative market for jobs, goods and services, these activities may also serve as a kind of 'glue' which gives both 'form and stability to social life' (Ferman, 1985; Folb, 1980).

Within many inner-city 'ghetto' neighborhoods, 'everyone beyond early childhood has knowledge of or at least indirect contact with "hustling" as a possible alternative source of income' (Valentine, 1978: 23). All women in this study grew up in impoverished inner-city minority communities characterized by the presence of a strong informal economy, including the drug trade. Drug distribution and sales activity were an institutionalized aspect of the local economy, providing opportunities for income generation and redistribution of the limited wealth.

Queen Bee is a 35-year-old African-American woman, born in the south and raised in New York City. Queen Bee's recollections of her childhood indicate that both her domestic network and the wider community in which she grew up were deeply involved in the pursuit of income through informal opportunities. Queen Bee was raised by an aunt from the age of nine months. Queen Bee's aunt worked in a restaurant. Although she received a small supplement for Queen Bee through the foster care administration, formal sector income was inadequate to ensure the economic survival of the household. In order to make ends meet, Queen Bee's aunt sold food (dinners and sandwiches) and hosted card games or 'parties' in her apartment, during which she also sold liquor.

As a child, Queen Bee held mixed feelings about these ventures. Aware of the struggle to survive from an early age, she did not view them as iniquitous. However, her aunt's negative teachings against her mother and father prompted Queen Bee to develop a degree of animosity towards her aunt. As an adolescent, Queen Bee's desire for interaction with her peers and certain social activities were curtailed by her aunt's insistence that she help out with these enterprises. She began to view her aunt as greedy and as having too many parties. As she put it, her aunt took advantage of 'a good thing' (her free labor).

Today, what Queen Bee remembers most about her aunt is her entrepreneurial abilities and her constant efforts to generate income through card games, illicit liquor sales, home-cooked food and other informal sector activities. Queen Bee's aunt clearly provided an important role model for the adolescent girl, instilling in her a desire for economic independence and teaching her to think in business terms. Talking about her aunt's dinners and parties Queen Bee recalled,

> we used to sell food outside, right in front of the store—fried chicken, uh, rice and beans, macaroni and cheese, cakes, and dinners on

the weekend. . . . We made money. It wasn't like a waste of time. Yeah, we sold food and liquor. We made money. We made what you cut out you double it and you triple it.

While Queen Bee's family of orientation illustrates how inadequate wages forced many minority women to look for other sources of income to support their families, it also suggests that such involvements extend beyond domestic networks into the community. Indeed, individual or household participation is only made possible by the availability of such options at the neighborhood level. Queen Bee's experiences of the informal economy clearly extended beyond her domestic or kinship network, serving to reinforce the role of the informal economy, and the drug industry in particular, as a source of alternative institutions for the fulfillment of community needs (see also Hamid, 1991a, 1991b). Growing up, Queen Bee remembers 'number runners' and 'drug dealers' serving as a banking system for the community. Because many people could not go to a bank and expect to receive a formal loan, alternative institutions arose to provide this service. As she explained,

> Well, at the time like that around there, the people from the number hole and the block were wrapped so together if I, I had a pair of sneakers, and I had holes in them, then, you know she [Queen Bee's aunt] went to—in there, and he gave her the money. But no strings attached to it, because she plays her numbers there.

Nor was it necessary to be a drug user or a numbers customer in order to get a loan from these sources.

> Even if, they didn't use drugs—and they went to one of those drug dealers for food money, for food, or whatever, they have one of they workers to go shoppin' and bring you food. I'm tellin' you what I know for a fact. All right. I remember Nicky Barnes bought my outfit for school. Because we had had a fire in the building. And it was around school time, you know for school to start back in September? . . . And a lotta, uh, you know, my clothes and stuff got messed up. And he gave my mother some money, and they just throw us some money, and we still went to school on that first day like we would usually do.

The local-level informal economy played an important role in Queen Bee's childhood and had a profound effect on her. Her experience indicates how larger social structures and economic conditions, in addition to prompting individual adaptations, served to promote the development of alternative institutions in impoverished inner-city communities. Although their activities were illegal, 'number runners' and 'drug dealers' performed valuable economic and social functions for this community.

> They used to give us bus rides, in the summer time they went to block parties. Even the drug dealers. They had free bus rides. They made sure it was enough buses so that all the kids could go free—babies on up. And if it wasn't enough buses, they order another bus, or they cars would take you. Yes, those are the days that I'll never—it's just a fact, they have to do it, but they kept that money in their community.

Denied access to legal avenues and formal institutions, inner-city residents were forced to rely on the informal sector. For children like Queen Bee, illegal activities, especially number games and drug dealing, were cast in a positive light at an early age.

Similarly, Sha, a 32-year-old African-American woman, grew up in an adjacent community with a long history of informal economic institutions. Although her family of origin was engaged in a wide variety of informal-sector activity, Sha's kinship network was also heavily immersed in drug distribution and sales.

> My people didn't do nothing. All my people know about is drugs, eatin' and livin', that's all they know about. They didn't never get involved [in my schooling]. The only time my mother came up to the school if I got a call from the teacher and then she'd be there—you know what I'm sayin'—Church? shoot. I'm a Baptist, man. My moms didn't know nothin' about no church.

Nor is participation in the informal sector confined to single-parent families. Sha's family of origin indicates the bind that many two-parent black families are caught in when the man is unable to earn enough to support the household. Despite the presence of a husband, Sha's mother, like Queen Bee's aunt, was an active participant in the informal economy, hosting card games most Friday nights and selling liquor on the side.

> She'd sell drinks at the card games to keep the people, you know keep the money goin'. . . . I guess she was doin' it for a while until my father got a promotion and enough money to, you know. She did it for a while.

Even though this was a two-parent household, Sha's family of orientation struggled to survive. In the wake of regional economic restructuring in the 1970s (Kasarda, 1992), blue collar workers like Sha's father were rendered increasingly marginal to the formal labor force.

Denied access to the growing service sector and confronted with the prospect of severe impoverishment, Sha remembers her mother and father as increasingly willing to do anything that would enable the family to survive. This included participation in drug selling.

> My uncles, they stay in drugs, you know, I was in that type of situation all my life . . . they drug dealers and stuff like that. And I was around, my mother was around at that time so it affected my family too. My mother too at that time cause we was in there, you know, cause I guess that they was the only people that she could turn to at the time when she had us, so we was there involved with this and I was there seein' it.

During Sha's adolescence, her parents' gradual immersion in drug dealing prompted considerable residential instability and a series of short-term accommodations, including stays in abandoned buildings and, at one stage, relocation to Florida:

> you know we couldn't stay in one apartment too long . . . like they made a certain amount of money and we had to move outta there before they get busted for some old wild shit. But I knew I was movin' so everywhere I went it was home.

Sha's life history suggests how the labor market marginality of her father reinforced the lure of alternative opportunities for income generation offered by the drug industry. However, as Preble and Casey (1969: 19) noted more than 30 years ago, the drug economy existed to service the needs of a broader community beyond drug users and those unwilling, unable or denied access to formal labor market participation. Heroin users, in particular, have long been regarded as 'important figure[s] in the economic life of the slums' and have typically received support for their income-generating activities in return for providing a supply of cheap goods. Crime—as a form of redistribution—produces 'complex chains of interaction resulting in local tolerance and shelter . . . for illegal activities' (Sullivan, 1986: 386, 1989). In many low-income inner-city neighborhoods, the drug economy is firmly embedded in a local context whereby a range of illegal activities are both possible and 'tolerated' because of the functions they perform in providing alternative economic institutions and redistributing scarce resources.

The expansion of the drug economy and, in particular, the rapid growth in street level crack markets must be viewed in the broader context of a long history of informalization, exacerbated by recent processes of economic restructuring and the increasing polarization of economic and social life in the inner city (Wilson, 1987, 1991; Bailey and Waldinger, 1991; Mollenkopf and Castells, 1991). The simultaneous expansion of the informal sector and, in particular, the crack economy in large urban centers, created significant opportunities for participation in illegal work. However, there is almost no evidence to suggest that the street drug economy has attracted many well-educated or skilled participants from the formal economy; rather, most crack sellers have been drawn from the underemployed and unemployed earning low wages and/or with histories of participation in drug use and sales (Fagan, 1992, 1994). In the context of distressed inner-city minority neighborhoods where persistent poverty, structural unemployment and urban dispossession already supported a thriving informal sector, this combination provided many minority women with increased opportunities and motivation for participation in the informal economy (Sassen-Koob, 1989; Sassen, 1991).

Limited Formal Labor Force Participation

Previous studies of heroin users indicated that Black women were more likely to be unemployed than white women (Covington, 1988). More recently, ethnographic research conducted among women crack users in New York City found that minority women were less likely than European-American women to have experience of the formal sector workforce (Maher, 1997).

Debbie was a 27-year-old African-American woman. Born and raised in New York City of a Panaman mother and an African-American father, Debbie was the youngest in a family of four children. Although she had begun to smoke and sell marijuana while still in high school, peer pressure in the form of her friends 'studying and doing their homework' prompted Debbie to stop and concentrate on her studies. Upon high school graduation however, she resumed selling marijuana until she acquired a legal job as a detective in a department store, which she held for a few years. Her brief and unsatisfactory work experience demonstrated the ways in which racism shaped the formal labor market experiences of many black women. In Debbie's case, doing the job she was hired to do resulted in her being fired.

> I lost the job in [department store]—they sent me out to Wildlife. I was the youngest so, and I made a bust out there on some employee. And it seemed like the employee

was a, uh, some big time people. I was all the way out in, uh, Far Rockaway. They was sellin', uh, it was records. And the girl had rang up 88 cents on about—it was at least $300 worth of records. And I was in there dancing. They didn't know who the hell I was cause I used to come in to work bummy and stuff. And that's what they sent me out there for to watch the record shop. And I caught them—I caught it. Three people got fired, yup. Three White people got fired. Uh, a week later they told me they had to let me go cause, uh, somethin' was wrong with they, uh, it was a silly—it was a lie anyway. Yeah. I didn't get no pink slip. I was there for a while and never got an appointment or anything. I found out afterwards that I had busted some of the top people.

Without a job and lacking a good reference, the subsequent legal work experience of this bright young woman was confined to menial labor such as door-to-door sales and waitressing. Exploited by a magazine company who gathered crews of young people and took them throughout America selling magazines, Debbie was eventually forced to get money from her family to return to New York. Back in New York, she worked as a waitress in various after-hour clubs where she became entrenched in drug consumption/sales.

Unlike most women in this study, Debbie acquired a high school education and had several years of legal employment. However, her experiences suggest that the attainment of formal qualifications did little to enhance her labor market opportunities. Her high school education was no longer sufficient in the job market. Debbie's job as a store detective was a low-wage entry-level position with few prospects of advancement; her experience illustrated the additional obstacles minorities faced in the workplace. Debbie's desire to work and the lack of opportunities for minority women were evident in her willingness to take the below minimum wage magazine-selling job which took her thousands of miles away from her home and family, as well as in her subsequent waitressing positions. Her experience attested to the considerable motivation and persistent efforts expended by many minority women in attempting to penetrate the legal employment sector, albeit with limited or no success.

For other women, however, the effects of macro forces (Dunlap and Johnson, 1992a) of structural and cultural disinvestment, and the lack of viable economic alternatives in the formal sector, led most to conclude that the informal economy had more to offer. For a small group of women, participation in the drug economy clearly represented a crude cultural adaptation to their poor job prospects. Not unlike the minority males described by Bourgois (1989, 1995), Sullivan (1989), Moore (1991) and others, these women decided at a young age to substitute investment in the informal economy for allegiance to the dominant culture and the prospect of minimum wage jobs and workplace racism.

Although Mena, a 39-year-old African-American woman, did not complete high school, her labor market position was similar to that of Debbie in that they both faced a lack of economic opportunities. While Mena perhaps realistically saw her choices as being between drug dealing and menial labor, her mother remained convinced that a high school education would provide her daughter with the opportunities she herself had been denied. Indeed, Mena's mother resorted to drastic measures to encourage Mena to complete high school education; Mena recalls having been 'beat' by her mother and forced to attend school. Mena's mother struggled to keep her daughter at school and 'off the streets' demonstrating the enormous task faced by many Black women in their roles as economic providers and female heads of households. Despite her mother's best efforts, Mena dropped out of school in the tenth grade.

Upon leaving school, she held a short-lived succession of legal jobs—in the garment industry, the parks department and as a messenger—before deciding that she could earn more money in the drug industry. As her drug consumption increased and her options narrowed, the viability of a distribution career was confirmed. As she put it, 'I could see myself dealing more with selling drugs rather than somebody else selling my body.'

For many of the families of orientation in this study, the combination of economic marginality and low social status meant that they were unable to pass on much in the way of cultural capital to their children. These women's parents' employment histories revealed that, while they had been relegated to low-paying menial jobs (Dunlap, 1995; Dunlap and Johnson, 1992b, 1996; Dunlap, Johnson and Manwar, 1996; Dunlap, Johnson and Rath, 1996), most had at least been able to find and hold legal employment. Many of their children, however, were unable to find any employment at all. The rapid expansion of the drug industry in the 1970s and 1980s meant that illegal work offered not only alternative opportunities for income generation, but in some cases provided the only 'work' opportunities. As Sha indicated, given the disjuncture between her aspirations and the options open to her, participation in the drug economy was a rational choice.

I like a lot of things. I like to travel. That's what I told you. I like to get that fast money, and I don't like the white man tellin' me what to do all the time, breathin' and holdin' over my neck. So this is the way I do it.

Although all the women were engaged in crack selling to support their consumption, some women were not drug users when they began selling drugs. Moreover, even those women who entered the market as consumers reported motivations that extended beyond simply supporting their consumption. For many of these women, then, drug selling was a profession which, in addition to income, provided them with a sense of security and self-esteem (Dunlap et al., 1997). For some, it was the only profession they had ever had. Being able to sell large quantities of drugs made them feel they could do something well. Many of the women in this study were proud of their ability to sell and considered themselves excellent saleswomen. As Sha noted,

> It gave me a whole lot of self-esteem. I felt good about myself. I had everything I had on was brand new. I could do whatever I want, eat whatever I want . . . it felt damn good.

Just as importantly, being a good seller also allowed women to differentiate themselves from other crack consumers. Women user/sellers often sought to distinguish themselves from other users insofar as they perceived that, while they 'could hold down a job,' they still had control over at least one aspect of their lives. This may be particularly significant for women who have lost or are at risk of losing their children and are often estranged from their families of orientation or procreation (ibid.). The feelings of independence and self-assurance that involvement in drug distribution brought some of these women provided them with a rare opportunity to feel that they were in control of at least one aspect of their lives.

Drugs and Crime

While women's attitudes and experiences of the informal sector were influenced by family and community participation, as young adults their exposure to experiences of racism and sexism in the formal sector workplace served to confirm their own labor market marginality. For many women, this realization encouraged them to utilize alternative avenues of income generation. For most young women growing up in impoverished inner-city neighborhoods, this may simply mean participation in the kinds of relatively innocuous 'off-the-books,' informal sector activities their mothers and female kin before them had done, such as selling food, hosting card games and babysitting. For other young women, their own drug use was an intervening variable which structured informal sector participation of a more serious, criminal nature.

Both the drug use and criminal careers of these women typically started in their early and mid-teens, usually while they were still in school. However, while all of the women were able to recount clearly, and in some instances vividly, their initial drug use experiences, most did not view their first forays into lawbreaking as significant and in fact, many could not even remember their first 'crime.' Moreover, it is important to note that the majority of the women maintained that drug sales, typically crack sales, were the most serious offences they had committed.

Their initial foray into drug selling was typically linked with a recognition of their social marginality (for example, no legal job/legal income, no clear options), their growing drug consumption, and participation in informal networks of drug sellers. A key linkage was direct interaction with specific persons from whom they bought drugs. It was often not clear that a woman's initial involvement in a drug sales role occurred because the woman 'sought out' or 'asked for' some role in drug selling, or whether it was 'suggested' or 'offered' as an opportunity by a supplier (a seller). The informal give-and-take between sellers and customers, and especially steady customers who wanted 'free' (for example, no cash payment) drugs, often led a woman to do 'favors' for a seller, by transporting drugs or money (but rarely both at the same time) to a buyer or to other sellers, or by acting as a lookout for a seller, or by providing other services (see Dunlap et al., 1997, for details of various drug distribution roles).

Debbie (who lost legal employment—see above) recognized the importance of her marginality as instrumental in seeking employment with sellers, but she was initially confronted by one crack seller who at first resisted employing women.

Interviewer: What made you take your first hit?

Debbie: I ain't had nothing better to do. I was homeless. [Laughs] She just drops it off; and, she goes and I call her when I am finished.

Interviewer: She drops it off. Who drops it off?

Debbie: Me. Anyway um . . . I use to just run around the corner. I use to run around the

corner and cop. From the same guy I am selling for right now. And there was some other guys who had a spot upstairs that was Thomas. That had that spot upstairs and I use to go up there and buy.

So one day Gregory sat right in front of the spot in a chair. And started selling capsules [crack vials] right in front of the spot. So I asked Gregory could I sell for him?

He told me, 'No Mama.' 'We don't want no women work for me.' He didn't want me to work for him. So I asked Tuffy could I sell. Tuffy said, 'Do you think you could sell?' 'Because if you can't sell my things, don't tell me you can sell my things if you can't sell my things.'

I said, 'Yeah, Man, I could sell. I could sell.' So they gave it a little while. It took me about a month before I . . . they would even trust me to sell something for them. They use to tell me go upstairs and get the money from who ever they had up there selling.

Interviewer: You were kind of a runner?

Debbie: Yeah. I use to be like um . . . I use to drop off the stuff [drugs] and come back and pick up the money. You know. I'd use to accept a lot of money from them; it was just little chicken fee . . . I was still smoking it [crack]. They knew I was smoking that shit.

Once Debbie established her value as a reliable go-between and seller Gregory (who was supplying Tuffy) relented and set her up with 'too much' crack.

Debbie: They said, 'Deb, we can't even deal with it. You going to have to stay up there and sell it.' I started juggling for the both of them. As matter of fact, I started working for Tuffy. . . . It wasn't Gregory I was working for because Gregory kept insisting I couldn't. . . .

But after he saw . . . that I was making so much good money for a, for Tuffy, he started getting jealous and saying how I worked for him first. And he is the one who took Tuffy upstairs and it was a whole big scene with us . . . with this.

Tuffy said, 'I can't get you to work for me no more, you got to work for Gregory.' I said, 'No. I could work for the both of you.'

You know. The first package Gregory gave me I thought I was going to shit myself. He gave me a thousand dollars' worth of coke, crack vials. Yeah. You know how much crack, that's two hundred capsules. . . . When I thought he said two hundred. . . . I thought he meant two hundred dollars. He gave me two hundred capsules. And I am like. You should of seen I was like in a panic man. I flew home. [laughs] Flew home with them. Dug I dug a hole in my mother's yard. [laughs] And put, put a certain amount down there. Took a certain amount in the house so that I could just come in the house and snatch it up. . . .

Interviewer: How long did it take you to sell that?

Debbie: Not long, after the clientele started getting really big. It took us a while to get in, in the money. But I'd say about no more than a month for business to really start rolling.

Interviewer: You were selling how much a day?

Debbie: I was selling like sometime five, six hundred a day.

Interviewer: Six hundred capsules a day or six hundred dollars a day?

Debbie: A day . . . Capsules. I mean dollars.

Interviewer: Six hundred dollars a day?

Debbie: Six hundred dollars a day that's for only one person. I was working for two people. See it was easy to keep track of Gregory's money because Gregory would only give you like five hundred or a thousand at a time. You know. I told him never bring me two hundred capsules again . . . please.

Although Debbie was selling about 200 vials each day, she did not wish to be in possession of so many vials at one time. Almost all the other women experienced similar 'trial' periods where they functioned in and demonstrated reliability and competence in performing various low-level distribution roles (Johnson et al., 1991) prior to engaging in direct sales, as street sellers, or in upper level roles (Dunlap et al., 1997). However, for the women in this study, drug use neither initiated nor served to 'drive' their participation in criminal activities (also see Elliott et al., 1983; Waterston, 1993). For these women, drug distribution was much more than a means to an end and, as noted in the previous section, women felt that it offered them control over their economic lives and additional benefits beyond supporting personal consumption. Experimental drug use and criminal activities occurred almost simultaneously during adolescence and well prior to problematic use (Inciardi and Pottieger, 1986; Inciardi et al., 1993).

Nonetheless, like heroin, crack use appeared to amplify women's lawbreaking to incorporate not only income generating activities such as drug distribution and prostitution, but involvement in violence (see also Anglin and Hser, 1987; Fagan, 1994; Johnson et al., 1995). For example, Mena began drug consumption earlier than many of these women. At age 12 she began to smoke marijuana and use alcohol. At 15 she sniffed glue, at the age of 16 she went to a friend's house where she received her first shot of heroin. She continued to shoot heroin for over 20 years. At 20 she started shooting cocaine, sampling angel dust (which she did not like) at the age of 34. Mena added crack to her drug consumption when she was 38 years old, and was a current crack user and seller in her early 40s.

Mena was well versed in street life and in addition to her current crack selling activities, she had participated in various types of lawbreaking, including robbery (in which her friend was killed when they tried to rob a store to get money for heroin) and drug-related burglaries. Mena's drug career also prompted involvement in violent incidents including one occasion where she stabbed a man in the chest as he attempted to rob her and again during a bar quarrel where a man attempted to cut her throat. Mena carried the scars from the many stitches she received following these episodes. Crack use, then, while not functioning as a pathway to lawbreaking *per se*, exacerbated involvement in and commitment to the drug economy, bringing women into situations not only where they were at risk of more serious offending, but which increased their likelihood of violent victimization.

The relationship between drug use and crime is clearly complex. The interactive nature of this relationship over time was mediated by the social and economic environments in which both drug use and criminal activity occurred. While most of the women had a history of concomitant minor lawbreaking/illicit drug consumption, our research revealed that, for the women in this sample, participation in the crack economy as adults was strongly preceded by an active street life in adolescence.

Street Life

In the inner city, the 'street' is not normally conceived of as 'something we walk or drive along, or that chickens cross' (Connell, 1987: 132). For drug users and inner city residents in large urban centers, the notion of the 'street' encapsulates a complex of meanings. In the Black vernacular, the 'street' functions as a 'source of practical experience and knowledge necessary for survival' (Folb, 1980: 256). Immersion in street life, or being 'out there,' includes elements of risk and excitement not always present in everyday life. Within this context, street life provided some women with 'opportunities to feel a sense of mastery, independence, individual accomplishment, and immediate reward' (Miller, 1986: 140).

An important element of street life was 'partyin,' (ibid.: 139). For the women in this study, 'partyin,' meant 'good times.' Kiki's story emphasizes the pull of street life—the fast pace and 'good times' that it appeared, at least initially, to offer young women (Gilfus, 1992). After dropping out of school and getting married at the age of 16, Kiki began street life by 'partyin' during her husband's extended work-related absences.

> I remember very good, the first day that I had to myself in the house, I partied, didn't I call all the brothers over, we had our drinks, we had our liquor. You see we had a room under my apartment, that my husband painted the ceiling black and with what you call the colors the bright colors that go on the light . . . and all the flat paint and then he used the ultra violet colors and there was the stars and the moon, there was Jupiter shooting across, you know.

Kiki's account emphasizes the 'partying' and the 'good times' that many women perceived enticed them into street life. Street life proceeded at a fast pace involving a constant round of parties, drug consumption, sexual experimentation and an influx of new friends and acquaintances. This was a lifestyle that kept women busy and some women enjoyed the 'fast money' and frantic pace of life on the street and clearly felt that they were too young to stop participating. However, while many women were clearly ambivalent about traditional gender roles and expectations, most simultaneously dreamed of a future which involved settling down in a stable residence.

> I would consider a good life, like settlin' down, gettin' out of the streets, you know. I'm still kind of young now, so basically I still want to run around, and have fun. You know . . . I guess when I get older, I'll, you know, have to settle down—you get old you have to slow down, to like think about life, what you're gonna do when you get to senior citizen age. You know, stuff like that.

However the downside, as related by Mena, was that before they realized it, women had nowhere else to go. Immersion in street life had a high cost in terms of forgone opportunities for participation in mainstream social and economic life. Even if initially acquired, the social and economic skills necessary to compete in the legitimate job market were soon obsolete. While women were busily acquiring much-needed knowledge and skills in street life and the drug economy, they were simultaneously reducing or

eliminating their chances of finding even the most menial of employment in the legitimate job market. As Mena noted,

> See it's just mainly the environment down this road, you know. Like you say it's nothing to do with, I am bored, and it's other people around that's doing it [drugs and partying], you know . . . so that's what make me just say chuck it in, just go along with the program, you know.

Similarly, Renee, a 26-year-old woman, who retailed crack out of the apartment she shared with her female partner, dropped out of school in the 12th grade and began 'hangin' out in the street.' Looking back on her adolescence, Renee related that,

> I started hangin' out with the wrong group, got into drugs, and now I regret it cause I had so much. My family gave me and I really regret it. I was doin' cocaine, I was doin' crack, I was smokin' reefer, drinkin' and now I realize this is the wrong mother fuckin' move.

Renee's involvement in street life and 'partyin,' led her further and further into drug consumption. Although she managed to acquire an apartment in the projects for herself and her daughter and was working in a security job and collecting welfare, Renee found that her income was increasingly being expended on drugs. She eventually lost her apartment and became homeless. Indeed, it was in the city shelter system that Renee met her present girlfriend, also a crack user. Like Mena and Renee, most women crack users realized that the 'partyin,' was rapidly replaced by the 'mission'—the intense, constant and neverending search for crack. So, although it might offer a 'good life' initially, as crack consumption increased and resources were depleted, street life also functioned (more predictably) as a route to chronic impoverishment, homelessness and despair.

Ironically, vigorous participation in street life was an occupational prerequisite for women who wished to become involved in street-level drug distribution. A dynamic street life provided women with contacts and customers as well as street knowledge or 'smarts,' and a broad range of skills crucial to occupational health and safety in this hazardous workplace. Most of these women had large networks of acquaintances and associates. An early exposure to street life and the subsequent development and fine tuning of survival skills combined with a pool of existing and potential customers to provide the women in this sample with access to drug distribution careers. As Dee noted, watching others make money through drug distribution, she began to think about 'earning some money.'

> People I used to go to school with and I was hangin' around with them. I had nothing else to do, so I was like, let me get a package . . . let me start . . . I asked for a package and they told me the guy they was gettin' it from and they let me start sellin' . . . there was other people around me, it was all girls . . . a all girl crew, about ten of us, you know . . . I saw the fast money . . . the money made me interested, you know.

Similarly, Ninety-Nine, 30 years old, grew up in a large inner-city housing project. Most of the people she grew up with were involved in street life and her own network expanded rapidly as she herself began to participate during adolescence. Like the other female dealers presented here, Ninety-Nine knew most of the people in her area. These were essential credentials in street life for both men and women. Likewise, Queen Bee, in talking about her freelance dealing career—how she developed her contacts, learnt to make certain drugs, found out about where to get equipment—summarized the significance of an active street life.

> You gonna find somebody that know something that you wanna know . . . well I can't explain it no further than that but in the street you'll find somebody that, you know, whatever you lookin' for they help you.

However, street life can only be participated in to its full extent when one does not accept one's responsibilities for conventional adult roles. Most of these women had children in their teens and twenties. Their children were being (or had been) raised by kin or fictive kin or had been placed in foster care. For the majority of these female dealers, family responsibilities were secondary to participation in a vigorous street life which provided opportunities for income generation and crack consumption. Indeed, crack consumption encouraged them to act from a stance of immediate gratification. Although these women repeatedly expressed their love for their children, and some vowed that they intended to quit street life and drug use because their children were getting older, street life was hard to leave because such participation further narrowed the options available to women drug users (see Dunlap et al., 1997; Maher et al., 1996).

Discussion

As noted by Miller in relation to her analysis of Milwaukee street women, 'The separate consideration of each route is not meant to suggest that in every case one can say without hesitation which particular path was followed . . . there may be more overlap in the behaviors actually exhibited and the structural conditions that appear to have promoted them than the separate treatments offered here suggest' (Miller, 1986: 116). Indeed, the factors identified here—positive exposure to the local level informal economy during childhood, the historical positioning of Black women as producers and consumers within the informal sector, the impact of structural and cultural disinvestment, drug use and importantly, early recruitment to and extensive participation in street life—point to the difficulties in isolating anyone 'causally dominant route' (ibid.).

However, while these women's pathways to involvement in drug distribution exhibit considerable overlap, this analysis indicates the critical importance of structural conditions in shaping the nature and extent of Black female participation in the drug economy (Dunlap and Johnson, 1992a). In doing so, it points to the need for research which explores the impact of structural and cultural disinvestment (reduced governmental and private spending on education, job development, placement and other investments primarily benefiting inner-city low-income Americans) on the lives of Black women and, in particular, how this relates to women's involvement in lawbreaking and female participation in the drug economy.

All of the women in this sample grew up in impoverished inner-city communities characterized by the presence of a strong informal economy and a history of institutionalized drug distribution and sales. Within these communities, existing disincentives to formal labor force participation were exacerbated during the 1970s and 1980s. Regional economic restructuring (primarily a striking decline in stable low-wage manufacturing jobs, declining purchasing power of welfare grants, and deterioration and escalating cost of rental housing for low income persons) and the resultant social and economic dislocation combined with the rapid expansion of the drug economy in the late 1980s to provide powerful incentives for participation in drug distribution and sales by large numbers of inner-city residents. However, for the most part these opportunities were created by and utilized among young minority males who, by virtue of their spatial and skill mismatches, have been excluded from formal sector opportunities for income generation (Bourgois, 1989, 1995; Williams, 1989, 1992; Fagan, 1992).

Although minority women have a long history of informal-sector participation, historically relatively few women participated directly in drug distribution and sales activities. Almost all of the women in this study began drug consumption at an early age. Their decisions to initiate drug use took a variety of different forms, occurred in a number of different settings and took place in the context of varied relationships—although almost all women first used illicit drugs in the presence of an older experienced user. Some women initiated drug use in concert with males, some with another female, others in a group, and still others alone (Maher, 1995).

Both kinship networks and community level opportunity structures also exerted considerable influence over women's attitudes towards drug use and distribution activities. All of the women grew up in neighborhoods where participation in the formal economy was limited and the informal economy provided a crucial and well recognized means of income generation and survival. These women's lives and communities were steeped in participation in the informal economy long before they themselves actually engaged in drug use or selling activity.

However, this research has also suggested that, while the individual career trajectories of the female dealers presented here exhibited considerable variation, all acquired an early start in street life and an early introduction to ways of making 'fast' money. For these women, street life presents as a critical variable, mediating their involvement in drug distribution. Rather than exposure to deviant domestic networks or a history of serious criminality, the women in this study evinced extensive involvement in street life during adolescence which may or may not have involved lawbreaking, but which brought women into situations and circumstances wherein they acquired the various skills and networks of associates that enabled them, not only to generate income, but also to survive in hostile and often dangerous environments.

Over time, participation in 'partyin' and street life enabled these women to amass a significant amount of social capital in the neighborhood street networks. In addition to cultivating extensive street knowledge, broad social networks and a variety of potential distribution channels, most of these women developed a 'rep' for, among other things, toughness or a certain amount of 'juice,' and a capacity for diffusing potentially dangerous situations. In addition, a vigorous street life provided women with important information and opportunities for the sale and exchange of drugs and stolen goods. Per-

haps just as significant, street life and, in particular, the element of 'partyin,' while promoting and legitimizing both drug use and lawbreaking, also provided women with a social organization that enabled them to alleviate the strain, frustration and boredom of being poor, black and female in the inner-city context.

This study found little evidence to support Miller's (1986: 109) claim that 'The social world of deviant street activity and the social world of the addict are to a certain extent distinct and incompatible. The chaos that can pervade the lives of addicts, at least episodically, precludes their ever being more than peripheral members of deviant street networks.' (While that statement may have been true when Miller conducted her research in Milwaukee during the early 1980s, it was not true in New York, as Johnson et al. (1985) documented in their study of the central role of addicts in street life during the same time period.) In the context of crack selling in New York, at least, street life, drug use and drug selling have become so intertwined as to be nearly impossible to disentangle.

For a minority of women in the present study, family life was also characterized by intergenerational and intragenerational drug use and participation in the drug economy (Dunlap, 1992, 1995; Dunlap and Johnson, 1992b, 1996; Dunlap, Johnson and Rath, 1996). Using Miller's (1986) terminology, the 'domestic' networks (households and kin) of many inner-city women in the 1980s and 1990s consisted of several (often interchangeable) adults whose primary economic activities included heroin, crack or other drug sales and/or non-drug users' criminality. Few household adults were employed or had a legal income other than welfare. Rather, in such households, the 'street' and 'deviant' networks have effectively been incorporated into the 'domestic' networks. Girls (and boys) growing up in such households in the 1990s learned about street culture within their households, from their parents, guardians and kin networks, but had limited opportunities to learn conventional living patterns. Indeed, many adolescent girls no longer need to 'run away' from home to engage in street life, as they grow up in households permeated by 'street people' (often their relatives) seeking respite from street life, but who also bring street behaviors into the household (Dunlap, 1995; Dunlap et al., 1997).

Examining these women's street lives also extends the picture of female participation in drug dealing beyond that of simply being adjuncts to males. While the results of this examination were consistent with other studies indicating that drug use leads women into dealing (for example, Rosenbaum, 1981a; Anglin and Hser, 1987; Hunt, 1990), these women demonstrated considerable agency in the negotiation of pathways into the drug industry. Their participation extended beyond either pharmacological enslavement or connectedness to some male. Indeed, for most of these women, the decision to engage in drug distribution can be seen as rational and intelligible, given their lack of social capital, limited options for formal sector participation and the increasing constraints of their personal consumption.

Conclusion

The structural and economic contexts in which women's involvement in drug use and distribution are situated have altered significantly since the mid-1970s. In contrast to the research literature prior to the 1990s, this study highlights the declining significance of intimate involvement with males in facilitating women's pathways to drug use and distribution. Nor was there evidence to suggest that these women had run away from home to begin their drug consumption and dealing careers. While drug use was a crucial variable in determining their subsequent involvements in distribution activities, our research indicates that most women sellers were engaged in lawbreaking prior to commencing regular involvement in illicit drug use.

These women's experiences also reveal the inadequacy of explanations which depict female lawbreaking through a single gendered lens. Sex/gender clearly does not operate in a vacuum isolated from race and social class and their effects on women's lives. These results suggest that black female participation in drug distribution and other forms of lawbreaking is closely related to structural forces and that the antecedents of Black female criminality may be located within a different set of experiences and contexts than that of either white females or other women of color. Raised in low-income inner-city communities, these women gained early exposure to an opportunity structure which implicitly sanctioned the use of criminal means to achieve not only culturally approved goals, but perhaps more importantly, day-to-day survival. While they were all disadvantaged in relation to education, vocational training and opportunities for legitimate work, for many women, prospects of legal employment were further compromised at a young age by the existence of racism, sexism and criminal records.

However, unlike Miller's (1986) findings, these women's accounts strongly suggest that it was not domestic networks per se which served as conduits to the street for young Black women. Rather, the concept of 'domestic networks' may be somewhat misleading in this context. Focusing on individual household units and kinship groupings such as domestic networks serves to deflect attention away from the broader macro-level structural forces which constrain participation in legal labor markets and the role of the institutionalized informal economic activities at the neighborhood level. Within such contexts, individual women's domestic networks can only be understood by reference to the enduring structural features of the global and regional economies which ensure the maintenance of alternative economic institutions at the local level.

These women's experiences strongly suggested that it was not merely the involvement of the domestic network or kinship group in extra-legal and illegal activities but, rather, the lack of social and economic infrastructure and the absence of legitimate opportunity structures and employment at the neighborhood level, that prompted women to seek alternative avenues of income generation. For many minority women, this meant utilizing the opportunities they had grown up with and had always known were there. As Edin's (1989) multi-ethnic research on women in receipt of AFDC (Aid to Families with Dependent Children) benefits in Chicago found, women's involvement in unreportable (illegal) income generation was conditioned by an opportunity structure which included the neighborhood milieu, as well as a woman's family and friends, and individual variations in human capital. For the women in this study, an early investment in street life yielded social capital which was valuable, but only within street networks and drug markets. Their experiences suggest that, despite the concomitant risk of problematic drug use, this capital was put to opportunistic use in gaining access to a male-dominated labor market. Cognizant of the fact that the dominant culture had failed to make sufficient investment in their futures, these women generated their own social capital by cultivating an active and vigorous street life.

Finally, these women's accounts indicate that experiences within the drug economy, while clearly gendered in important respects (Maher, 1997), are diverse and cannot be captured by a singular perspective. As in the legitimate world, a combination of life events and experiences, including what had been identified here as significant social capital accruing from participation in street life, facilitated the entree of a small number of women into a male-dominated enclave. Theirs was, above all, a participation rooted in, and made possible by, the social and economic structure of the neighborhood and the interrelation of gender, race and class at the local level. While their experiences attest to the fact that the drug economy cannot simply be characterized as patriarchy writ large, the overwhelming concentration of women at the lowest levels of the distribution hierarchy is hardly suggestive of an equal opportunity marketplace. Moreover, there are indications that the halcyon days of the street-level crack market may be a thing of the past (Golub and Johnson, 1994c). While the rapid expansion of street-level drug markets in the previous decade may have provided limited opportunities for participation by women drug users, the current declining market and shrinking pool of consumers suggests that as street-level markets consolidate, women drug users, among the last hired, will surely be the first to go.

Discussion Questions

1. What structural factors contribute to women's involvement in crack and other drug sales as a primary economic activity in adulthood?

2. How have pathways to female crime changed over time (e.g., compare Miller's 1986 study of Milwaukee "street women" with the current study)?

3. Discuss the intertwining relationship between drug use and crime. Does one cause or contribute to the other? If so, how?

4. If gender patterns of drug dealing have changed over time, why haven't they strengthened the position of women's equality in drug networks?

5. How does the government's reduced spending on welfare programs, early education, and job development influence participation in the drug economy?

References

Adler, P. A. (1985), *Wheeling and Dealing: An Ethnography of an Upper-Level Drug Dealing and Smuggling Community*, New York: Columbia University Press.

Anglin, M. D. and Hser, Y. (1987), 'Addicted women and crime,' *Criminology*, 25 (2), 359–97.

Anglin, M. D. and Speckart, G. (1988), 'Narcotics use and crime: a multisample multimethod analysis,' *Criminology*, 26 (4), 197–234.

Arnold, R. A. (1990), 'Processes of victimization and criminalization of Black women,' *Social Justice*, 17 (3), 153–66.

Austin, R. (1992), 'The Black community, its lawbreakers and a politics of identification,' *Southern California Law Review*, 65, 1769–1817.

Bailey, V. T. and Waldinger, R. (1991), 'The Changing Ethnic/Racial Division of Labor,' in J. H. Mollenkopf and M. Castells (eds.), *Dual City: Restructuring New York*, New York: Russell Sage Foundation, pp. 43–78.

Baskin, D., Sommers, I. and Fagan, J. A. (1993), 'The political economy of violent female street crime,' *Fordham Urban Law Journal*, 20, 401–17.

Blom, M. and van den Berg, T. (1989), 'A Topology of the Life and Work Styles of "Heroin Prostitutes:" From a Male Career Model to a Feminized Career Model,' in M. Cain (ed.), *Growing up Good: Policing the Behavior of Girls in Europe*, Newbury Park, CA: Sage, pp. 55–69.

Bourgois, P. (1989), 'In search of Horatio Alger: culture and ideology in the crack economy,' *Contemporary Drug Problems*, 16 (4), 619–49.

——. (1995), *In Search of Respect: Selling Crack in El Barrio*, New York: Cambridge University Press.

Bourgois, P. and Dunlap, E. (1993), 'Exorcising Sex-for-Crack: An Ethnographic Perspective from Harlem,' in M. S. Ratner (ed.), *Crack Pipe as Pimp: An Ethnographic Investigation of Sex-for-Crack Exchanges*, New York: Lexington Books, pp. 97–132.

Chaiken, J. and M. R. Chaiken (1990), 'Drugs and Predatory Crime', in M. Tonry and J. Q. Wilson (eds.), *Drugs and Crime, Crime and Justice*, Chicago: University of Chicago Press, 13, 203–40.

Chesney-Lind, M. and Rodriguez, N. (1983), 'Women under lock and key: a view from the inside,' *The Prison Journal*, 63, 47–65.

Chesney-Lind, M. and Sheldon, R. (1992), *Girls, Delinquency and Juvenile Justice*, Pacific Grove, CA: Brooks/Cole Publishing.

Connell, R. W. (1987), *Gender and Power*, Stanford, CA: Stanford University Press.

Covington, J. (1985), 'Gender differences in criminality among heroin users,' *Journal of Research in Crime and Delinquency*, 22 (4), 329–54.

——. (1988), 'Crime and heroin: the effects of race and gender,' *Journal of Black Studies*, 18, 486–506.

Daly, K. (1992), 'Women's pathways to felony court: feminist theories of lawbreaking and problems of representation,' *Southern California Review of Law and Women's Studies*, 2 (1), 11–52.

Dunlap, E. (1992), 'Impact of Drugs on Family Life and Kin Networks in Inner-city African American Single Parent Households,' in A. Harrell and G. Peterson (eds.), *Drugs, Crime and Social isolation: Barriers to Urban Opportunity*, Washington, DC: Urban Institute Press, pp. 181–207.

——. (1995), 'Inner-City Crisis and Drug Dealing: Portrait of a Drug Dealer and His Household,' in S. MacGregor and A. Lipow (eds.), *The Other City: People and Politics in New York and London*, Atlantic Island, NJ: Humanities Press, pp. 114–31.

Dunlap, E. and Johnson, B. D. (1992a), 'The setting for the crack era: macro forces, micro consequences (1960–1992),' *Journal of Psychoactive Drugs*, 24 (3), 307–21.

——. (1992b), 'Structural and economic changes: an examination of female crack dealers in New York City and their family life,' paper presented at the Annual Meeting of the American Society of Criminology, New Orleans, November.

——. (1994), 'Gaining access for conducting ethnographic research among drug dealer/sellers,' paper presented at Society for Applied Anthropology, Cancun, Mexico.

——. (1996), 'Family/resources in the development of a female crack-seller career: case study of a hidden population,' *Journal of Drug Issues*, 26 (1), 177–200.

Dunlap, E., Johnson, B. D. and Maher, L. E. (1997), 'Female crack dealers in New York City: who they are and what they do,' *Women and Criminal Justice*, 8 (4), 25–55.

Dunlap, E., Johnson, B. D. and Manwar, A. (1996), 'A successfull female crack dealer: case study of a deviant career,' *Deviant Behavior*, 15, 1–25.

Dunlap, E., Johnson, B. D. and Rath, I. (1996). 'Aggression and violence in households of crack sellers/abusers,' *Applied Behavioral Science Review*, 4 (2), 191–217.

Dunlap, E., Johnson, B. D., Sanabria, H., Holliday, E., Lipsey, V., Barnett, M., Hopkins, W., Sobel, L., Randolph, D. and Chin, K. (1990), 'Studying crack users and their criminal careers: the scientific and artistic aspects of locating hard-to-reach subjects and interviewing them about sensitive topics,' *Contemporary Drug Problems*, 17 (1), 121–44.

Edin, K. J. (1989), 'There's a lot of month left at the end of the money: how welfare recipients in Chicago make ends meet,' unpublished PhD thesis, Northwestern University.

Elliot, D. S., Ageton, S. S., Huizinga, D., Knowles, B. A. and Canter, R. J. (1983), 'The prevalence and incidence of delinquent behavior: 1976–1980,' *The National Youth Survey Project Report No. 26*, Boulder, Colorado: Behavioral Research Institute.

Fagan, J. A. (1992), 'Drug Selling and Licit Income in Distressed Neighborhoods: The Economic Lives of Street-level Drug Users and Dealers,' in A. Harrell and G. Petersen (eds.), *Drugs, Crime and Social Isolation: Barriers to Urban Opportunity*, Washington, DC: Urban Institute Press.

——. (1994), 'Women and drugs revisited: female participation in the cocaine economy,' *Journal of Drug Issues*, 24 (2), 179–225.

Fagan, J. A. and Chin, K. (1989), 'Initiation into crack and cocaine: a tale of two epidemics,' *Contemporary Drug Problems*, 16 (4), 579–617.

——. (1991), 'Social processes of initiation into crack,' *Journal of Drug Issues*, 21 (2), 313–43.

Ferman, L. A. (1985), 'The Role of the Informal Economy in the Economic Development of Low Income Neighborhoods,' unpublished Monograph, The Institute of Labor and Industrial Relations, The University of Michigan, Ann Arbor.

Folb, E. A. (1980), *Runnin' Down Some Lines*, Cambridge, MA: Harvard University Press.

Gilfus, M. E. (1992), 'From victims to survivors to offenders: women's routes of entry and immersion into street crime,' *Women and Criminal Justice*, 4 (1), 63–88.

Goldstein, P. J. (1979), *Prostitution and Drugs*, Lexington, MA: Lexington Books.

Golub, A. and Johnson, B. D. (1992), 'Crack and the developmental progression of substance abuse,' paper presented at the Annual Meeting of the American Society of Criminology, New Orleans, LA, November.

——. (1994a), 'The shifting importance of alcohol and marijuana as gateway substances among serious drug abusers,' *Journal of Alcohol Studies*, 55 (5), 607–14.

——. (1994b), 'Cohort differences in drug use pathways to crack among current crack abusers in New York City,' *Criminal Justice and Behavior*, 21 (4), 403–22.

——. (1994c), 'A recent decline in cocaine use among youthful arrestees in Manhattan (1987–1993),' *American Journal of Public Health*, 84 (8), 1250–54.

Hamid, A. (1990), 'The political economy of crack-related violence,' *Contemporary Drug Problems*, 17 (1), 31–78.

——. (1991a), 'From ganja to crack: Caribbean participation in the underground economy in Brooklyn, 1976–1986, Part 1, Establishment of the marijuana economy,' *International Journal of the Addictions*, 26 (6), 615–28.

——. (1991b), 'From ganja to crack: Caribbean participation in the underground economy in Brooklyn, 1976–1986, Part 2, Establishment of the cocaine (and crack) economy,' *International Journal of the Addictions*, 26 (7), 729–38.

Hunt, D. (1990), 'Drugs and Consensual Crimes: Drug Dealing and Prostitution,' in M. Tonry and J. Q. Wilson (eds.), *Drugs and Crime, Crime and Justice*, Chicago: University of Chicago Press, 13, 159–202.

Inciardi, J. A. and Pottieger, A. E. (1986), 'Drug use and crime among two cohorts of women narcotics users: an empirical assessment,' *Journal of Drug Issues*, 16, 91–106.

Inciardi, J. A., Lockwood, D. and Pottieger, A. E. (1993), *Women and Crack Cocaine*, New York: Macmillan.

Johnson, B. D., Golub, A. and Fagan, J. A. (1995), 'Careers in crack, drug-use distribution and non-drug criminality,' *Crime and Delinquency*, 34 (3), 251–79.

Johnson, B. D., Hamiel, A. and Sanabria, H. (1991), 'Emerging Models of Crack Distribution,' in T. Mieczkowksi (ed.), *Drugs and Crime: A Reader*, Boston: Allyn-Bacon, pp. 56–78.

Johnson, B. D., Natarajan, M., Dunlap, E. and Elmoghazy, E. (1994), 'Crack abusers and noncrack abusers: profiles of drug use, drug sales and nondrug criminality,' *Journal of Drug Issues*, 24 (1), 117–41.

Johnson, B. D., Goldstein, P. J., Preble, E., Schmeidler, J., Lipton, D. S., Spunt, B. and Miller,

T. (1985), *Taking Care of Business: The Economics of Crime by Heroin Abusers*, Lexington, MA: Lexington Books, D.C. Heath.

Kasarda, I. (1992), 'The Severely Distressed in Economically Transforming Cities,' in A. Harrell and G. Peterson (eds.), *Drugs, Crime and Social Isolation: Barriers to Urban Opportunity*, Washington, DC: Urban Institute Press, pp. 45–98.

Lewis, C., Johnson, B. D., Golub, A. and Dunlap, E. (1992), 'Studying crack abusers: strategies for recruiting the right tail of an ill-defined population,' *Journal of Psychoactive Drugs*, 24 (4), 323–36.

Liebow, E. (1967), *Tally's Corner: A Story of Streetcorner Men*, Boston: Little, Brown and Company.

Maher, L. (1995), 'In the name of love: women and initiation to illicit drugs,' in R. E. Dobash, R. P. Dobash and L. Noaks (eds.), *Gender and Crime*, Cardiff: University of Wales Press, pp. 132–66.

——. (1996), 'Hidden in the light: discrimination and occupational norms among crack using street-level sexworkers,' *Journal of Drug Issues*, 26 (1), 145–75.

——. (1997), *Sexed work: Gender, Race and Resistance in a Brooklyn Drug Market*, Oxford: Oxford University Press.

Maher, L. and Curtis, R. (1992), 'Women on the edge of crime: crack cocaine and the changing contexts of street-level sex work in New York City,' *Crime, Law and Social Change*, 18 (3), 221–58.

Maher, L. and Daly, K. (1996), 'Women in the street-level drug economy: continuity or change?,' *Criminology*, 34 (4), 465–91.

Maher, L., Dunlap, E., Johnson, B. D. and Hamid, A. (1996), 'Gender, power and alternative living arrangements in the inner-city crack culture,' *Journal of Research on Crime and Delinquency*, 33 (2), 181–205.

Manwar, A., Johnson, B. D. and Dunlap, E. (1994), 'Qualitative data analysis with hypertext: a case of New York City crack dealers,' *Qualitative Sociology*, 17 (3), 283–92.

Mieczkowski, T. (1990), 'Crack dealing on the street: an exploration of the YBI hypothesis and the Detroit crack trade,' paper presented at the Annual Meeting of the American Society of Criminology, Baltimore, November.

——. (1994), 'The experiences of women who sell crack: some descriptive data from the Detroit crack ethnography project,' *Journal of Drug Issues*, 24 (2), 227–48.

Miller, E. (1986), *Street Woman*, Philadelphia: Temple University Press.

Miller, J. (1993), 'Gender and power on the streets: the ecology of street prostitution in an era of crack cocaine,' unpublished paper.

Mollenkopf, J. H. and Castells, M. (eds.) (1991), *Dual City: Restructuring New York*, New York: Russell Sage Foundation.

Moore, J. W. (1991), *Going Down to the Barrio: Homeboys and Homegirls in Change*, Philadelphia, PA: Temple University Press.

Pahl, R. E. (1980), 'Employment, work and the domestic division of labor,' *International Journal of Urban and Regional Research*, 4, 1–20.

Preble, E. and Casey, J. (1969), 'Taking care of business: the heroin user's life on the street,' *International Journal of the Addictions*, 4, 1–24.

Rosenbaum, M. (1981a), *Women on Heroin*, New Brunswick, NJ: Rutgers University Press.

——. (1981b), 'Sex roles among deviants: the woman addict,' *International Journal of the Addictions*, 16 (5), 859–77.

Sassen-Koob, S. (1989), 'New York City's Informal Economy,' in A. Portes, M. Castells and L. A. Benton (eds.), *The Informal Economy: Studies in Advanced and Less Developed Countries*, Baltimore, MD: The Johns Hopkins University Press, pp. 60–77.

Sassen, S. (1991), 'The Informal Economy,' in J. H. Mollenkopf and M. Castells (eds.), *Dual City: Restructuring New York*, New York: Russell Sage Foundation, pp. 79–101.

Sharff, J. W. (1987), 'The Underground Economy of a Poor Neighborhood,' in L. Mullings (ed.), *Cities of the United States: Studies in Urban Anthropology*, New York: Columbia University Press, pp. 19–50.

Stack, C. B. (1974), *All Our Kin: Strategies for Survival in a Black Community*, New York: Harper & Row.

Stephens, R. C. (1991), *The Street Addict Role: A Theory of Heroin Addiction*, Albany: University of New York Press.

Sullivan, M. L. (1986), 'Getting over: economy, culture and youth crime in three urban neighborhoods,' unpublished PhD thesis, Columbia University, New York.

——. (1989), *Getting Paid: Youth Crime and Work in the Inner City*, Ithaca, New York: Cornell University Press.

Susser, I. (1982), *Norman Street: Poverty and Politics in an Urban Neighborhood*, New York: Oxford University Press.

Valentine, B. (1978), *Hustling and Other Hard Work: Life Styles in the Ghetto*, New York: Free Press.

Waldorf, D. (1973), *Careers in Dope*, Englewood Cliffs, NJ: Prentice Hall.

Waterston, A. (1993), *Street Addicts in the Political Economy*, Philadelphia: Temple University Press.

Whyte, W. F. (1943), *Street Corner Society*, Chicago: University of Chicago Press.

Widom, C. S. (1989), 'Child abuse, neglect and violent criminal behavior,' *Criminology*, 27, 251–71.

——. (1990), *The Cycle of Violence*, National Institute of Justice Research in Brief, Washington, DC: U.S. Department of Justice.

Williams, T. (1989), *The Cocaine Kids*, Reading, MA: Addison-Wesley.

——. (1992), *Crackhouse: Notes From the End of the Line*, New York: Addison Wesley.

Williams, T., Dunlap, E., Johnson, B. D. and Hamid, A. (1992), 'Personal safety in dangerous places,'

Journal of Contemporary Ethnography, 21 (2), 343–74.

Wilson, W. I. (1987), *The Truly Disadvantaged,* Chicago: University of Chicago Press.

——. (1991), 'Studying inner-city social dislocation: the challenge of public agenda research,' *American Sociological Review,* 56 (1), 1–14.

3

Coping, Resisting, and Surviving

Connecting Women's Law Violations to Their Histories of Abuse

Elizabeth Comack

The vast majority of the selected readings are about the experiences of lawbreaking women in the United States. We thought it important to include research on women in neighboring Canada to emphasize the similarities of women in cultures outside of the United States, particularly with respect to two points. First, the overlap of women's abuse histories to their criminal behavior is present in countries around the world and is not just an American phenomenon. Second, we recognize the disproportionately high number of women of color and indigenous women incarcerated in countries outside the U.S.; Canadian prisons, for example, incarcerate a high number of Aboriginal women native to the area, compared with people who migrated or moved to Canada from Europe and elsewhere. This lends further credibility to the main issues presented in this book: women's overlap of crime and victimization and the differential treatment of these lawbreaking behaviors according to cultural and ethnic differences.

One of the key projects of feminist criminologists has been to remedy the invisibility of women in prison. We need to hear their stories. Who are these women? What have their lives been like? In the fall of 1992, I interviewed 24 women who were incarcerated at a provincial prison.[1] My previous research had uncovered that the majority (78 percent) of women admitted to this prison had histories of physical and sexual abuse.[2] I was interested in exploring this issue further in terms of the (inter)connections between the women's abuse experiences and their law violations. These interviews—and the lessons I learned from the women—formed the basis of a book entitled *Women in Trouble* (Comack 1996).

The women I interviewed were representative of most women who end up behind bars in Canada (Adelberg and Currie 1993; Faith 1993; Hannah-Moffat and Shaw 2000). As a group, they were young (over half of the 24 women were under 30 years of age), undereducated (20 of the women had less than a Grade 12 education), and unemployed (20 of the women were without jobs at the time of arrest). Like the population of women prisoners on the Canadian prairies generally, the majority (19) of the women were of Aboriginal ancestry.

Traditionally, criminologists interested in theorizing women's crime have started from the observation that women in prison have been suspected (in the case of those held on remand) or judged to have committed a criminal offence. "Women offenders" is taken to be a separate and distinct category, and this distinctiveness is the basis on which the investigator formulates his or her theoretical explanation. Following this approach, women's patterns of offending are attributed to some personal deficiency, susceptibility to alcohol and other drugs, dysfunctional families, or even unwise choices for the men in their lives. Alone or in combination, such factors are then used not only to explain women's law violations but also to devise appropriate therapeutic remedies that will transform the woman offender into a law-abiding citizen.

The approach I adopted for my investigation starts from a different place. Rather than taking crime categories as a given, and proceeding to treat women in prison as "Other," I maintain that the line that separates criminalized women from law-abiding women is neither straight nor clear-cut. Criminalized women are in very many ways no different from the rest of us: they are daughters, sisters, girlfriends, wives, and mothers, and they share many of the experiences of women collectively. In particular, while abuse has been a prevalent feature in the lives of the majority of women in prison, they are not unique in this respect. Sadly, as many as half of all Canadian women have experienced child abuse, rape, beatings at the hands of their partners, and the other manifestations that abuse can take (Johnson 1996; Canadian Panel on Violence Against Women 1993).

Rather than focusing on women who have been criminalized as a separate and distinct category, I argue that women's law violations can be understood as an outgrowth of the problems, conflicts, and dilemmas that they confront in their everyday life. Moreover, these problems, conflicts, and dilemmas have a distinctly *social* basis; they emanate from women's experiences of living in a society that is structured by class, race, and gender inequalities. For instance, like their male counterparts, women in prison constitute an extremely marginalized group. In class terms, they are largely drawn from the ranks of the undereducated and under- or unemployed. In racial terms, many of the women who have been criminalized come from Aboriginal communities where colonization has left such deep scars that violence and alcohol abuse are now common features of life in these communities (York 1989; Hamilton and Sinclair 1991; Royal Commission on Aboriginal Peoples 1996). Just as significant as class and race is the fact that social relations are gendered. In this respect, many of the problems, conflicts, and dilemmas that criminalized women encounter, they encounter as women and because they are women. Abuse is one of the ways in which the women's lives are gendered. While abusive relationships can take different forms and occur in different contexts, they ultimately boil down to issues of power and control. In these terms, the ability of a woman to manage the problems, conflicts, and dilemmas that abuse generates will be very much contoured and conditioned by other factors in her life situation, including her age, her race, and her class positioning in society.

Once women's law violations are situated within the broader structural context in which women find themselves, the task then becomes one of uncovering how these structures are worked out in the women's everyday lives. I argue that to do so involves learning about the standpoint of the women, exploring what each woman's life has been like to this point in her history.

In the following pages, I recount some of the stories of the women I interviewed to reveal how their law violations can be understood by situating them in the context of the women's abuse histories. My intention, however, is not to argue that abuse provides the basis for a general theory of women's crime. I have learned from speaking with the women that their lives and the circumstances that brought them into conflict with the law are far too complex to be captured in some monocausal or reductionist fashion. Nevertheless, by listening to the details of the women's stories, we can begin to grasp the patterns and connections existing between abuse and law violation. To grasp these patterns and connections, I have relied on the work of Liz Kelly (1988). In her work, Kelly uses the concepts of coping, resisting, and survival to explore the strategies that women adopt to deal with sexual violence. While Kelly's purpose was to understand the impact of abuse on the woman who experiences it, mine is to use the concepts of coping, resisting, and surviving to reveal the (inter)connections between a woman's abuse history and her law violations.

Coping With Abuse

Kelly (1988: 160) defines coping as "the actions taken to avoid or control distress." For several of the women in the prison, it would appear that their law violations become understandable when placed within this context. More specifically, if "to cope" means "to contend with," then law violation can be located as one of the ways in which a woman contends with the abuse and its effects on her life. One of the women's stories will be told here to explore these connections.

Merideth's Story[3]

Merideth is a woman in her early thirties. She is different from the other women I spoke with in that she comes from a relatively privileged background and has a university degree. At the time of our meeting, she was serving a sentence for fraud charges and had been in prison once before, also for fraud.

Merideth was sexually abused by her father beginning at the age of four or five.

> When I was a kid, it was just like fondling and stroking and touching, and when I was, like, 11, it got into, umm, oral sex. And when I was 12 it was vaginal, and that's when I left. And when I came back, it was out and out rape. And so, umm, yeah, that was up until I was 17. . . .

The abuse had resulted in a pregnancy when Merideth was 14.

> I remember my mom taking me to the doctor and saying that I had been raped by a bunch of boys. And I remember wanting so badly to say "That's not true." But I couldn't. Because our home was a very respected home. . . . It was, like, heaven forbid, you just don't do that! It would never have been, it was almost like I always believed it would not have been believed? Because of the lifestyle, you know?

I asked Merideth how she was able to deal with the abuse at the time:

> I know I learned really early on to take myself out of myself? Like, if there was something I could focus on—if this tree (pointing to a picture on the wall)—although I'm here in the time of the abuse, I would be, let's say, on that post, you know? I would put myself somewhere else. So, that's basically how I

coped—was learning not to put myself there. And also, I have a younger sister who's four years younger, so fear for my sister made me cope . . . it was rather me than her. . . . I've never, I was never aggressive or violent or anything like that? But I learned to lie because of it. I learned (pause) well, you learn a lot. You learn to hide things well, some of those were coping skills. Um, being an overachiever, that was a coping skill because you'd feel something horrible was happening to you, you have to cope and compensate, so reward yourself. Getting an A on a test, winning a competition, that was a reward to me, something that would help.

Merideth also spoke about the effects her father's abuse had on her as she was growing up:

You lose all concept of right from, of right and wrong. You lose a lot of perception of life altogether. You look at people and you don't trust anybody. . . .

At another point she commented: "You don't cry after a while, you just don't give a damn."

By the time Merideth was 18, she says, "I didn't know who I was." She was using drugs—which her father had started her on at the age of 13 (first mescaline, then pot, hash, acid, and cocaine)—and she worked as a stripper and a prostitute in an escort service. Looking back, Merideth remarked:

Those are all self-destructive things. But I think now, looking at it, I don't think I could have made the progress I have had unless I had done those things. . . . I had to reach my absolutely lowest that I could get before I could get better.

Merideth's relationships with young men were abusive as well: "I went from one abusive relationship to another until I was 20." At the age of 20, she married. Merideth describes the relationship as "horribly abusive"—not so much physically (there were two incidents in the six years of the marriage), as emotionally.

I had gotten to the point where . . . nobody's gonna be physical with me anymore. But mentally, I'm the doormat. Emotionally, I was a basket case. I was abusive to myself. Uh, I had no respect for myself, my body, my person. The only thing that I would not let anybody fuck with basically was my brain. . . . I knew I was smart. I was on the honor roll. I was going to school—I was going to university. You can go ahead, you can do whatever you want to me, but you can't fuck with my head. Because I knew that was the only place, that was the only thing that belonged to me, personally.

Nobody had touched it. It was virgin still. It was mine. Nobody was gonna touch it. But emotionally I was a wreck. Physically I was abusive to myself, but as other people were.

Merideth's husband was an alcoholic. It was during times when he drank that things would get abusive:

He did some pretty wild things. He, like, things, or things for me that was too much. . . . Number one, he slept with our babysitter. And to me it was just like reliving my childhood. She was too young. And two, he had, um, a bisexual relationship.

After the marriage ended, Merideth was involved in a number of other abusive relationships, one of which resulted in the man breaking into her apartment, destroying her possessions, attacking her with a butcher knife in front of her terrified children, and then raping her. It was shortly after this that Merideth started dealing with everything.

I'd had enough of it, I couldn't take it anymore? Um, I've never felt suicidal or anything like that in my life, but I had really—like I couldn't feel anything anymore? I didn't feel. I just didn't feel. You could've hit me in the head with a brick. Oh, well, you know, at least it'd be pain, at least that was something. You know, up to that point, it's like, pain is better than nothing?

Merideth was unaware of the existence of self-help or support groups. In keeping with her academic background, she headed to the library.

So I started reading and I found a book about dysfunctional families. And I started reading that book and I realized, "Hey, now I'm on to something!" And I started reading, and I'm just thankful every day that I have the ability, for one, that I was intelligent, that I could read, and that I had the ability to work on my own.

Merideth also began seeing a counselor at a local crisis center, but when they "got into some really touchy issues," she stopped seeing her. It was around that time that she started taking drugs again—and doing fraud.

I've never had any kind of conflict with the law. (long pause) When I started dealing with all these different things, then I started having problems. And then I took it out in the form of fraud.

Merideth's fraud involved writing checks on her account when she did not have the money to cover them.

Like, I think, I think society as a whole looks at it that we're doing this strictly out of ignorance, and I swear if I could have stopped myself from doing that I would have done it. But at the time it was like "Fuck the world." That's how I felt. 'Cause like, no. And this was my only way. Some people are violent, some people take it out in other ways, but that was my only way to release it. It was like, it's almost orgasmic, you know, you'd write the checks, and you'd get home and you'd go through all these things and it's like "There's so much there. I have all these new things to keep my mind off. I don't have to deal with the old issues." And so you do it. And it becomes an escape. You don't know what else to do. But you keep doing it time and time and time and again. I've tried other things like drugs. All it did was give me track marks, 'cause I was using drugs intravenously. And—what more can you do?

She was eventually charged with fraud regarding 21 outstanding checks, and received a six-month prison sentence. Ironically, Merideth describes her prison experience as "probably the best thing that's happened to me," as it was during this time that she worked intensively with the abuse counselor at the prison. Things began to look up. Two days after her release, however, her father showed up at her apartment:

My dad walked into my apartment—I have a problem with locking the doors—but my dad came in the apartment, which blew me away 'cause I hadn't talked to my dad for over a year, 'cause I started dealing with things. I didn't want to talk to him no more. Anyway, he walked into my apartment, and um, I was upstairs. I say, "Who is it?" . . . He came upstairs and he'd been drinking, and he grabbed me, he grabbed me by the breasts, and I just flipped. I just turned around and I said, "Don't touch me!" and I pushed him. And he grabbed me and he threw me and I went down some stairs. I wasn't too happy with that! So then (sigh, pause) I told him he had two minutes to get out of my apartment or I was going to phone the police on him. My dad's never been in trouble before. Well, it's—I did charge my dad once, but my family, my mom talked me out of it. I charged my dad with assault and abuse when I was 15 years old, and I wish to this day I had left them, but that's another story. Anyway, I told him he had two minutes to get out of my apartment. And my dad left. And it just, I just felt like he had taken everything that I had worked so hard for. I felt like he had taken that away from me. And in two weeks, I offended, got charged, and, and—(long pause).

Merideth ended up with another prison sentence, this time for 10 months. She has continued to work at healing and believes things have changed for her. Finding her own anger has been important to Merideth's ability to survive:

Before, I've never been one to cuss and swear or, it's just not part of me, but um, I was, like, I never vented my anger, okay? You could get me so angry, and I would just take it. I was so used to just being, taking things from people, garbage other people give out? Just taking it and taking it and taking it. And then just taking it out on myself, you know? Now, you piss me off I'm gonna tell you, "Hey, I don't like what you're doing. I don't like it and I'm gonna stand up for myself now." And I wouldn't have done that before.

While Merideth had been previously involved in illicit activities (namely, drugs and prostitution), it was fraud that brought her into conflict with the law. The check writing appears to be bound up with her struggle to cope with her abuse history.

I can't understand why we do, why we even go to fraud, but it's something that gets you out of the house for once and gets you away from the situation. It gives you a sense of power, and you're doing something for yourself—as a woman, you know? Most women who'd do fraud would be buying something personal. You're doing something for yourself.

***

In Kelly's (1988) terms, a woman's coping responses are "active, constructive adaptations to experiences of abuse." For Merideth, incestuous experiences initiated a lengthy process of coping and adapting. In this respect, it is worth noting that the options available to children for coping with abuse are limited. For Merideth, coping took the form of "taking herself out of herself" at the time the abuse was happening. Becoming an overachiever in school helped to compensate for what was happening to her at home. As an adult, Merideth has thought through the effects of abuse on her life and on her conception of self. It led to getting involved in "self-destructive things" like drugs and prostitution. At the same time, Merideth relied on her own inner strengths to contend with the abuse. In particular, it was her faith in her brain, her intelligence that gave her the wherewithal to begin to eventually deal with the abuse and its effects on her life.

Merideth's law violations can also be located within this broader context of "coping." She seems to have turned to writing bad checks around the time that she began to deal with her abuse. Much like her drug use, it was an escape, a way of trying to cope with her feelings. As Merideth explained it, fraud "gives you a sense of power . . . you're doing something for yourself." In this sense, as a coping strategy, committing fraud was not all that different from being an overachiever in school as a child. It was a reward, something she could do to try to make herself feel better (although obviously with different results).

Merideth continues to struggle with the impact that the abuse has had on her life and on who she is. In listening to her story, it becomes clear that coping with abuse is a lifelong process. Nevertheless, Merideth is optimistic. As she told me, "you can't ever forget where you come from, but you can decide where you're gonna go."

Resisting Abuse

According to Kelly (1988: 161), the verb "to resist" can mean "to oppose actively, to fight, to refuse to co-operate with or submit." While Kelly delineates resisting as a particular form of coping strategy, I use it to refer to those actions that a woman takes at the time to oppose the abuse. In this respect, for some women, *law violation can be located in terms of their specific efforts to resist the abuse at the time it is happening.* Indeed, for some of the women I spoke with, law violation was a much more direct outcome of the abuse. Two of their stories will be told here.

Janice's Story

Janice is an Aboriginal woman who is in her early twenties. She was adopted into a white family as a child. Her conflicts with the law started when she was 17 and were typically associated with drinking and "rowdy" behavior. At the time we spoke, however, Janice was serving a federal sentence for manslaughter.

At the age of 14, Janice was raped by her brother-in-law. She told her mother what had happened:

My mother charged him and, (pause) what (sigh) ended up happening is I dropped the charge against him. Because I felt sorry for my sister. . . . I felt sorry for her 'cause she was pregnant at the time plus they had a little boy already. And, I didn't want to ruin that, their family.

While Janice received counseling from a psychologist at the time, she says that she "didn't really deal with it then. . . . I hid it. I kept it in-

side." By the time she turned 17, Janice was drinking regularly.

Like, most women, like, there's men too that are, that are being abused, that, um, (pause) like they don't really have nobody to turn to? So they go to the bottle, or to drugs, whatever drug—and that's how they coped with it. That's how I did it.

[I asked Janice to tell me what happened that led to the manslaughter charge.]

Um, okay, well I was at a party, and this guy, older, older guy, came, came on to me. He tried telling me, "Why don't you go to bed with me. I'm getting some money, you know." And I said, "No." And then he started hitting me and then he raped me and then (pause) I lost it. Like I just, I went, I got very angry and I snapped. And I started hitting him. I threw a coffee table on top of his head and then I stabbed him, and then I left.

(Where'd you get the knife from?)

In the kitchen. We were alone.

(What did you do when you left?)

I went, I went out drinking. That's what we were doing, we were drinking and then, that's when he asked me to have sex with him for money. And I said no.

(Why do you think you got so angry?)

Okay, well, um, well, when he was (pause) having his way with me, I had flashbacks of my brother-in-law—when I was 14. (pause) And uh, I just, (pause) yeah.

(So what happened then, you went out drinking and then—?)

And they, the cops, they, they found me and they came and got me. And then they charged me with second degree and then, then, they, they dropped it to manslaughter.

(So what kind of sentence did you get?)

I got three years.

(Did all this stuff come out in the trial?)

Um, no. Just what happened at that—I gave my statement.

(Do you think it would have helped at all if you were at all prepared to tell them about your brother-in-law?)

No. I didn't (pause) say anything about that.

Eileen's Story

Eileen is an Aboriginal woman in her early thirties. She comes from an isolated reserve in the northern part of the province. She has been married for 13 years and has five children. Eileen has a series of charges dating back seven years. All of them are in relation to conflicts with her husband.

When asked about her abuse experiences, Eileen responded: "My husband beats me a lot." The abuse started shortly after her first child was born 12 years ago. When I asked her how often it happened, she replied, "Every day."

Eileen has tried a number of strategies for dealing with the abuse. She has sought shelter at a crisis center in a nearby town and has gone to the police for help:

> One time the cops said to me, "Go patch things over." The second time when I went down to the cops . . . I had to knock on the door. They didn't answer. My husband was following me, he was really catching up on me, so I went to the cops. I was standing there for a long time, waiting for the cops to answer the door. And when they did they said that, because I didn't go see some place else, that they couldn't do nothing. And another time, when I charged him, there were two cops and they'd seen him hitting me—it was outside my brother's house one time. And when we went to court, they threw that thing out.

In the last seven years, Eileen has started to fight back. I asked her what happens when she does and she replied, "I always end up in court." Eileen has been charged four times in the past seven years. The charges include careless use of a firearm and assault. On the first two occasions, she received probation and a fine. The third charge came after Eileen hit her husband with an axe. She received a six-month prison sentence. When I spoke with her, she was serving a sentence for the fourth charge:

> The reason why I'm here is the same thing. Last December—January—we were walking on the road. . . . [M]y husband hit me. . . . Then my mom came out. . . . I went back to my house, I didn't go back there. Then he came home. . . . "He was just fooling around. . . ." I told them to call the cops. . . . They didn't. I was sitting on the chesterfield—he kicked right where I was sitting. . . . And I just turned around and I hit him. I didn't know how hard I hit him. . . . And I got charged for that.

Eileen received an eight-month sentence. Her husband was also charged with assault. He received 30 days. Eileen attributes this disparity in sentences to the fact that her husband is somewhat of a "role model" on the reserve:

> When I say something to them about him, that's when people back him up. They don't want to believe that he's doing that to me.

Sometimes I feel so alone out there. Like everybody is against me. . . . A lot of times I ask for help and nobody responds. They'd rather listen to him than listen to me.

I asked Eileen how she felt about the fact that she was the one being beaten up, yet she was also the one being charged:

> I don't know how to describe it. (pause) . . . It's as if they're saying to me, "She's not going through those things." The way I feel 'cause if they're calling me a liar. Like, I remember telling my lawyer that—after that sentence—"Who's gonna believe me now?" (pause) . . . It's hopeless (long pause; she's crying).

Eileen's options are extremely limited. I asked her if it was possible to leave the relationship:

> I've tried that many times.

(What happens when you do?)

> My kids want to go back. 'Cause they're—I don't know, they're just too young to understand what's going on—'cause I know they've seen it.

***

In their stories, Janice and Eileen talk about a different pattern from the one described by Merideth. This difference, in large part, resides in their use of force to oppose the abuse at the time it was happening. While Janice and Eileen engaged in specific coping strategies to deal with the abuse (like using alcohol or seeking shelter at a crisis center), the way in which law violation becomes connected to their abuse histories can best be understood in terms of resisting.

For Janice, resisting took the form of killing her abuser with a kitchen knife. At the time, she was dealing not only with the assault and rape but with her memory of being raped by her brother-in-law at the age of 14. Clearly, when placed in the context of her abuse history, Janice's use of force becomes more understandable. While the initial charge of second-degree murder was reduced to manslaughter (presumably because the deceased had committed rape), one wonders what the court's response would have been had Janice been in a position to disclose her past experience to the police. The fact remains, however, that resisting has meant a federal term of imprisonment for Janice.

Resisting, for Eileen, occurred in a different context. The daily beatings from her husband had been going on for 12 years. Eileen's location on an isolated reserve gave her few options from which to choose. Whatever options she did try (such as seeking shelter or going to the police for help) did not bring an end to the abuse. Because of her husband's position of influence on the reserve, Eileen feels that no one wants to believe or support her. Her calls for help have gone unanswered. In her words, the situation is "hopeless." Over the last seven years, Eileen has started to fight back. This decision is one that emanates from her own sense of danger. As Eileen told me, "There's a time for me to know when I'm really in danger—that's when I do something." The irony is that, when she does resist the beatings, Eileen is the one who ends up in jail.

Locating Janice's and Eileen's law violations as direct outcomes of abuse raises significant questions about the criminal justice system and how it has responded in cases involving abused women and women's self-defense. So long as the courts fail to adequately explore the social context in which law violation occurs, and the often blurred boundaries between victim and offender, women like Janice and Eileen will continue to find themselves in prison for resisting their abusers.

Surviving

For women who have been abused, surviving is very much a process. Their struggle to contend with the effects of abuse experiences will be especially compounded when the abuse in their lives is ongoing. This is especially the case for women who end up on the streets. These women have been relegated to the margins of society. For them, surviving is an almost daily concern, as their social circumstances place them in a situation of constant endangerment. I use the term "surviving," therefore, to capture *how the connections between abuse and law violation become intertwined in a woman's struggle to live through and with her endangerment.*

Brenda's Story

Brenda is in her midtwenties. Brenda's life to this point in time has been marked by being in and out of foster care, juvenile institutions, and prison, and being involved in a life on the streets that includes drugs and prostitution. Abuse and law violations have been part and parcel of her life. When I spoke with Brenda, she was serving a sentence for armed robbery.

Brenda's childhood can best be described as unstable. She comes from a very large family. Both of her parents are alcoholics. Brenda spent from age three to nine in foster care. At 10, she was sent back to live with her family:

I was always looking after my little brother and my little sister, cleaning up the house, doing the laundry, you know? Taking my brother to day care, my sister to school with me and, you know, coming home. And I'd have to go see my parents at the hotel all the time to get money for food and stuff, you know? And, you know, they'd get upset because I'd always show up at the hotel with my, my brother and sister and, you know, "Well wait 'til we get home" sort of thing. So, you know, I'd always hide my little brother and sister just in case, you know? And I would hide myself because I knew, once my dad walked in it'd be all over with because he'd always get his belt out, or a cord or even a stick or whatever he could find to hit. I went through a lot of abuse with him.

Brenda had difficulty getting anyone in authority to help her to deal with the abuse at home:

I would even tell my schoolteacher that my dad's always hurting me, and—I'd tell her what was going on at home. I tried to express, you know, how I was feeling and stuff, and then she got a worker involved and I would tell the worker what was going on at home and the worker didn't believe me! . . . So she kept sending me back home, you know? And I would, at that time I just felt like, "Shit, you know, nobody cares," you know? 'Cause I figured I could trust my teacher, you know, that she wouldn't tell nobody. And then she got all these other people involved and then what happens is they go to my parents and they don't, they don't even believe me. They, they say that I was lying about it. You know, and they, even the worker said, "Maybe your parents upset you in some way, you know, and you want to get away from home" and stuff like that, you know? It went on like that for a long time. For about a year and a half. Two years it went like that, before they even believed that there was even abuse.

To get away from the abuse, Brenda decided to set a neighbor's house on fire:

I was so angry and I was trying to figure out a way to get away from home. And I saw it on T.V., you know? I saw it on a, it was a western movie. Some guy was getting mad at another guy and he threw the gasoline on the house. So I uh, I went and got my dad's gasoline tank out of the back—what he uses for his boat. And I poured gas in the house and lit it on fire.

Brenda ended up in the juvenile detention center and was subsequently sent to foster homes. Not feeling comfortable in these settings, she ran away. Before long, she was back in detention

> 'cause I used to fight, do stupid things for attention . . . I ran away from [the detention center] when I was 13. I was raped.

> I was uh, me and my girlfriend were hanging around [street name] because we were on the run and stuff. I didn't want to go to my parents because I knew if I went to my parents I would just, you know. So, uh, I started hanging out with my girlfriend's sister and she's older. She took us down to [street name] drinking.

> And this guy was uh, wanted me to go home with him for money. But I, at that time I didn't even know what, you know, he was talking about, sort of thing. And my girlfriend said, "Go with him." So I went with him. And um, (pause) he raped me behind this one hotel, and um (pause), I phoned the Rape Crisis. (pause) And I, I didn't feel good about phoning them because, once I got on the phone they wanted to know everything, you know, "What happened? What did he do?" You know? It was just like, uh, I didn't feel like explaining what he did. I just wanted to see somebody that's all, you know. And the woman wouldn't let me speak to anybody else unless I told her exactly what went on. So I was pissed off, I just told her to "F off" and hung up the phone, you know, I don't need this, you know?

> And then I became involved in heroin. Because at that time I figured, "Well, shit." I was on the run. So I figured nobody'd care. So I'd start doing heroin, cocaine. (pause) I did a lot of drugs. Started hooking, you know, because I wasn't ashamed no more.

I asked Brenda how she was able to deal with the rape and the fact that the rape crisis center did not help her:

> At that time I just thought it was supposed to happen, you know? Because you're a woman, so one day it's gonna happen sort of thing. 'Cause that's the way I was brought up, you know? One day it's gonna happen, you're gonna have a baby or whatever, you know. My mom never really explained anything to us, you know? (pause)

> But after that um, I lived at my parents' place, so I told my mom what happened, so I stayed at my mom's place, and I would clean up her house and stuff for money just so I could buy my cigarettes and stuff. But see I would clean up the house and that and my parents would kick me out after seven o'clock, and I'd have to go stay somewhere else. They didn't want the cops bugging them.

> And uh, this one night they let me sleep over and um, my cousin [his name] came over. And he raped me, and I charged him. And uh, when I, I was going to testify against him and stuff (pause) I found out I was pregnant. So that's what convicted him was 'cause I was pregnant, and they found semen inside of me.

Brenda had a difficult time dealing with the resulting pregnancy:

> I tried to kill myself. I would slash my wrists, I would shoot heroin into my arm when I was pregnant. Because I didn't want this baby, you know? I didn't want, I didn't want this living thing in me, you know? 'Cause I thought I was too young. And it pissed me off because my parents just, didn't—I was under the Child and Family Services at that time and, and, uh, Child and Family Services wanted me to get an abortion. My parents didn't want to sign the paper for me to get an abortion. So I'd have to have this, this, creature living inside me. And it freaked me out because I was so young, you know? So I'd start doing weird things like jumping off of, like, you know, second story windows, just so I can get rid of it, you know? And no matter how hard I tried, I just couldn't get rid of it (laughing), you know what I mean? I just wasn't doing something right or, I don't know. I was young too, so it was just in my mind to get rid of this baby. And uh, my cousin only got, uh, three months for raping me. (pause) And then I had the baby and I gave the baby up. (pause)

Brenda went after her cousin on a number of occasions:

> I remember I always used to go after my cousin every time I was home after that—I went after him with a knife one time. This was years later, like I was about 17, 18 when I saw him again. And I remember I went after him with a, you know, a knife, trying to stab him. And I was charged for assaulting him. And uh, I walked, like this time I went to his house with a gun to blow his head off. And I was charged with dangerous weapons. (pause) But when I see my abusers I cannot handle it because I feel like, uh, I feel like, you know, they can do this, they can do this to anyone and get away with it. Because, you know, (pause) a lot of people do.

When she was not in detention, Brenda was on the streets. I asked her whether she experienced abuse from the johns when she was hooking:

> No, I didn't get a lot of abuse from the johns 'cause I always carried my gun, you know? (pause) And I was brought up that way from living on the streets, you know, you just don't walk the streets without a weapon. So

I always, you know, when I first went to work I invested and bought a gun, you know. And that was my weapon, you know? And uh, being a prostitute, you know, it's taught me a lot because I know how men are, you know? You know, once they give you that money, it's, they, they're in control. You do anything they say, sort of thing. And some guys are just really bizarre, you know, they do start getting abusive. Once they hand that money to you they figure they can throw you out of bed, slap you around, whatever, you know? You're their bitch for the night, sort of thing. That's how they look at it. But I didn't put up with that.

While she never had occasion to use her gun, Brenda did run into situations where she had to defend herself:

> I've stabbed a couple guys. Because this one guy, we were drinking and uh, this one guy kept telling me to come lie down. And I didn't want to lay down, you know? We'd already finished what we were doing and I got paid and I was just having a drink and I was gonna go. But he figured, you know, I should stay with him for the, the whole night for, you know, 60 bucks. Well, "You're gonna stay with me all night" and make me do this for him. And I told him, I said, "I'm not staying with you, no." You know, "You got your money's worth, I'm gone" sort of thing. So he was throwing me on the bed, and trying to rip off my clothes. So I stabbed him.

She also talked about what life on the street was like:

> Street life is a, it's a power game, you know? Street life? You have to show you're tough. You have to beat up this broad or you have to shank this person, or, you know, you're always carrying guns, you always have blow on you, you always have drugs on you, and you're always working the streets with the pimps and the bikers, you know? That, that alone, you know, it has so much fucking abuse, it has more abuse than what you were brought up with! You know? That crowd. You know, 'cause you have to deal with, "Oh, this person said that" and "Fight this person" and, you know. And it goes on—that cycle never stops. That's worse than, I find living on the street I went through more abuse than I did at home.

***

While all of the women I interviewed are survivors, Brenda's story reveals how interconnected abuse and law violations have been in her ongoing struggle to survive. Unlike coping (where law violation becomes a way of dealing with the abuse) or resisting (where the woman takes action to oppose the abuse, which brings her into conflict with the law), surviving suggests that both the abuse and law violation are pervasive features of the woman's life. Trying to understand Brenda's life, then, involves understanding the conditions of her endangerment.

Seeing the Patterns

Listening to the women's stories allows us a better appreciation of the complex ways in which a woman's law violations become connected to her abuse history. Sometimes those connections are direct, as in the case of women like Janice and Eileen, who were serving prison sentences for resisting their abusers. Sometimes the connections only become discernible once a woman's law violations are located in the context of her lifelong struggle to deal with the abuse and its effects. For women like Merideth, the decision to commit fraud becomes more understandable once situated as a coping response to her abuse experiences. Sometimes the connections are even more entangled, as in the case of women like Brenda, where abuse and law violation become enmeshed in the ongoing, everyday struggle to survive.

While abuse has been located as a gender-related factor, I suggested earlier that the ways in which abuse plays out in a woman's life will be very much conditioned and contoured by other factors related to her structural position in society, specifically, her age, her race, and her class positioning. These interconnections cannot be ignored, especially in terms of their impact on the kinds of choices and options available for coping with, resisting, or surviving abuse experiences. But these factors become determining in other ways. Indeed, while the analysis presented here offers one way of making sense of the factors and conditions that bring women into conflict with the law, the connections I have drawn between abuse and law violation do not hold purchase for every woman. In some of the women's stories, it would appear that race and class factors were more determining of the kinds of troubles a woman encounters.

For many of the women included in this study, law violations are intricately bound up with the problems, conflicts, and dilemmas associated with being Aboriginal in Canadian society. Listening to the stories of women like Janice and Eileen gives us only a glimpse of what their lives have been like. We cannot fully grasp their experiences without maintaining a sensitivity to the historical forces that have shaped contemporary Aboriginal communities: the processes of colonization, of economic, social, and political marginalization, and of forced dependency on a so-called benevolent state.

In some of the women's stories, it would appear that factors associated with their class position had a more determining effect on their law violations than did the presence of an abuse history. For instance, similar to Merideth, another woman I interviewed was serving a prison sentence for writing fraudulent checks on her own bank account. Whereas Merideth's fraud charges appear to have emerged as a coping response to her abuse experiences, this woman's law violation stemmed more directly from her class positioning. Being without financial means, she made the "choice" to commit fraud in order to secure the funds she needed to visit her dying father in a hospital some distance away.

The category "women's law violations" is not homogeneous. It includes a diverse number of actions and behaviors that range in seriousness from shoplifting to murder. What binds all of the women together, though, is the fact that their violations of law have resulted in their incarceration, sometimes for only a few days or months, sometimes for many years. Locating the women's law violations within the context of their abuse histories, however, does not automatically lead to the conclusion that women are merely "victims" who have been falsely accused and punished for alleged wrongdoings. Ultimately, as the women themselves acknowledge, they must accept responsibility for their actions and behaviors. Yet, drawing out the social context in which those actions and behaviors occur does make them more understandable. Even more than this, such an analysis generates questions about the incarceration of women in trouble.

Endnotes

1. In Canada, provincial prisons normally hold people who are given sentences of up to "two years less a day." Sentences of two years or more are served in federal institutions.

2. Research on federally sentenced women in Canada has uncovered similar findings. The Canadian Task Force on Federally Sentenced Women, for example, found that of the 191 women interviewed, over two-thirds (68 percent) said they had been physically and sexually abused as children or adults, and half of them (53 percent) sexually abused at some stage of their lives. Among Aboriginal women, these figures were considerably higher: 90 percent (35) said they had been physically abused during their lives, usually regularly over long periods, and 61 percent (24) sexually abused (Shaw et al. 1991).

3. Pseudonyms are used throughout this discussion to maintain confidentiality. I have used the names of women with whom I share close relationships (my daughter, mother, sisters, friends) in an effort to combat the "othering" of women in prison.

Discussion Questions

1. Discuss women's experiences of living in a society that is structured by class, race, and gender inequalities.

2. How might the experiences of being Aboriginal in Canadian society be similar to being Latina, Native American, or black in American society?

3. How do race and ethnicity intersect with gender in pathways to crime?

4. What common threads do the first three articles in this section (i.e., by Gilfus, Maher et al., and Comack) all share?

5. How does Comack's article differ from the first two articles?

References

Adelberg, Ellen, and Claudia Currie (eds.). 1993. *In Conflict With the Law: Women and the Canadian Justice System*. Vancouver: Press Gang Publishers.

Canadian Panel on Violence Against Women. 1993. *Changing the Landscape: Ending Violence—Achieving Equality*. Ottawa: Minister of Supply and Services Canada.

Comack, Elizabeth. 1996. *Women in Trouble: Connecting Women's Law Violations to their Histories of Abuse*. Halifax: Fernwood Publishing.

Faith, Karlene. 1993. *Unruly Women: The Politics of Confinement and Resistance*. Vancouver: Press Gang Publishers.

Hamilton, A. C., and C. M. Sinclair. 1991. *The Justice System and Aboriginal People: Report of the Aboriginal Justice Inquiry of Manitoba*. Winnipeg: Queen's Printer.

Hannah-Moffat, Kelly, and Margaret Shaw (eds.). 2000. *An Ideal Prison? Critical Essays on Women's Imprisonment in Canada*. Halifax: Fernwood Publishing.

Johnson, Holly. 1996. *Dangerous Domains: Violence Against Women in Canada*. Toronto: Nelson Canada.

Kelly, Liz. 1988. *Surviving Sexual Violence*. Minneapolis: University of Minnesota Press.

Royal Commission on Aboriginal Peoples. 1996. *Bridging the Cultural Divide: A Report on Aboriginal People and the Criminal Justice System in Canada*. Ottawa: Supply and Services Canada.

Shaw, M., K. Rogers, J. Blanchette, T. Hattem, L. S. Thomas, and L. Tamarack. 1991. *Survey of Federally Sentenced Women: Report to the Task Force on Federally Sentenced Women. User Report 1991-4*. Ottawa: Ministry of the Solicitor General.

York, Geoffrey. 1989. *The Dispossessed: Life and Death in Native Canada*. Toronto: Lester and Orpen Dennys.

4

Naming Oneself Criminal

Gender Differences in Offenders' Identity Negotiation

Brenda Geiger
Michael Fischer

The goal of this research is to comprehend gender differences in the way female and male offenders are capable of accounting for or casting off stigmatizing labels in the process of negotiating a favorable identity. More specifically, the researchers were interested in examining the role played by street and conventional norms and that of human strengths in empowering offenders to reject or resist pejorative roles and labels of condemnation. In-depth semistructured, focused interviews were conducted with a purposeful sample of eight male and eight female offenders who were about to be released or had recently been released from prison. All 16 offenders had extensive criminal histories, primarily those of nonviolent property and drug crimes. Only two offenders (one male and one female) had convictions for murder or attempted murder. All offenders came from economically deprived homes.

Findings reveal that males were much more adept than female offenders at juggling conventional and street norms to justify and/or resist stigmatizing labels in order to construct a favorable identity. Even though female offenders were able to justify the labels of drug dealer, prostitute, and thief by appealing to higher loyalties, all their justifications collapsed when they were to negotiating the identity of incompetent mother. Female offenders' negative internal attributions and deprivation of the normative center of motherhood resulted in apathy, anomie, and lack of confidence in their ability to do something worthwhile.

Naming offenders criminals, prostitutes, drug addicts, drug dealers, or incompetent parents casts offenders into pejorative roles and deviant identities. Whether attached by others or self, these labels initiate a process of identity negotiation during which accounts and attributions are provided and autobiographies reconstructed in order to establish a socially acceptable identity.

From a symbolic interactionist perspective, societal reaction of condemnation evidenced by the application of stigmatizing labels may change the way the so-labeled individuals perceive and define themselves. They may be pushed to engage in secondary deviance, that is, forced to organize their life and identity around those deviant labels and ultimately withdraw from conventional groups and activities (Lemert, 1972). Becker (1963, 1973), however, stresses that the stigmatizing process is not always successful in reaching its goal. "The deviant is one to whom that [*deviant*] label has successfully been applied" (Becker, 1963). It is only to the extent that the deviant labels applied by others onto offenders cannot be neutralized, resisted, and cast off as alien to the self that they will stick and become an essential trait of the offenders' identity.

According to Scott and Lyman (1968), accounts are provided and identities switched, constructed, and deconstructed against a background of normative expectations. Within a conventional normative framework, incarceration and consequent separation from the children and family imply that offenders have deviated from lawful behaviors and basic gender-role expectations. The labels of criminal, drug addict, prostitute, and incompetent parent doubly condemn the offenders, once for transgressing the law, and another time for failing to fulfill the essential duties attributed to males and females in society. For female offenders, these duties are related to the master status of motherhood, that is, to take care of children (Henley & Freemen, 1979; Ker-Conway, 1994; Nagel & Hagen, 1983; Schur, 1984). Comparable roles for male offenders would be those of father, breadwinner, and husband.

The street culture is another normative framework within which offenders' departure from lawful behavior and traditional familial roles and duties may be judged or justified. Within this framework, friendship, excitement, and hedonistic enjoyment of the moment are praised, and so are lack of concern for the future and reckless spending without concern for the welfare of the family (Fleisher, 1995; Shover & Honaker, 1992). Women and sexual conquest are stressed, whereas marriage is viewed as getting into trouble and limiting autonomy (Jacobs & Wright, 1999; Miller, 1958).

The last evaluative context, much neglected in the field of criminology, on the basis of which offenders' behavior and identity may be condemned and deviant labels resisted, is that of human strengths. Among such strengths are included courage, honesty, hope, perseverance, resourcefulness, planning for the future, work ethic, and responsibility (Seligman, 2002). These strengths are valued by most of the cultures and religions of the world because they are all-purpose qualities that allow the successful performance of tasks necessary for human survival (Dahlsgaard, Peterson, & Seligman, 2001; Seligman, 1998a, 1998b). As a result, the possession of such strengths gives rise to a sense of confidence and self-efficacy perception (Bandura, 1993).

Findings

Given the context of prison or the hostel for released prisoners, male and female offenders interviewed were immediately cast into pejorative roles and identities that needed to be negotiated. To account for the imputed labels of criminal, drug addict, drug dealer, or prostitute, offenders were faced with two possible alternatives. The first was to accept the deviant role or action, while refusing to endorse responsibility by providing excuses. The second was to provide justifications. Justifications enabled the offenders either to accept responsibility for their actions while rejecting the deviant labels, or to minimize the pejorative meaning of such labels and denounce them as meaningless lies.

When looking at themselves through the lenses of the past, male and female offenders alike often chose the first option. They accounted for their engagement in illegal activities by providing biographical information related to a dismal childhood and terrible and unfortunate circumstances over which they had no control. Offenders' biographies were filled with instances of harsh physical punishment and extreme emotional abuse, uncaring parents unable to love their children, and domestic violence. These autobiographical data combined to create the nightmare that excused a life of crime, prostitution, and/or drugs. Lisa tells us about the physical abuse she had been subjected to. "I was regularly beaten up. I thought I deserved it!" Danny also remembered:

> One time when I was 12, I did not answer right to my father. My father came to beat me up. He would beat me with a stick and a cord attached to the stick like a whip. I caught the cord to stop him. My father was amazed, then he beat me up to death.

Iris's father did not beat her up, yet she had witnessed so much violence. She recounts, "He [my father] would beat my mother up. He knifed her. I saw a lot of blood. Then he put the house on fire. The police was always coming to our home. There was so much violence."

Offenders pointed a finger at significant figures in their life who had corrupted their way of thinking. Usually, it was one of the parents who had sanctioned their engagement in crime and prostitution as a legitimate money-making opportunity. Moshe told about his father's consenting attitude toward theft:

> When I was 15 years old I had a great amount of money as a result of breaking in. My father offered me to open a savings account so that I could have money when I grow up. Today, when I think about it, my father legitimized the fact that I was a criminal. He knew that I had stolen this money. But he looked at it as if I had earned this money.

Beni also explained, "My father observed the Sabbath and other commandments, but that did not keep him from stealing and beating me for every little thing." Similarly, Carol told about her mother who had pushed her into the streets and forced her into prostitution to support her addiction. "When I was 15 years old my mother wanted me to bring money. She suggested, and, then, ordered that I bring money through prostitution and regularly called me a whore."

Esti also attributed her engagement in prostitution to her mother's emotionally abusive and neglectful behavior:

> I became a prostitute because of my mom, because of this man, because of everything at home. No one related to me or gave a damn about me. No one respected me. I didn't know what was warmth, love. No one ever caressed me. No one ever gave me a hug. She would only yell and curse "whore." All the time she ridiculed and humiliated me. I never knew why.

Constantly called prostitute, Esti decided to fulfill her mother's prophecy by incorporating this label into her own identity. Challenging her mother, she recounts how she started to enact this role:

> I want to tell you something. My mother never called me by my name. She all the time called me *Sharmouta* [whore in Arabic]. Whenever she saw me, even in the streets, she would yell at me *Sharmouta*. Sol said "I am a *Sharmouta*, so be it. I am a *Sharmouta*, and there is nothing you can do!"

Drugs for both genders were a way to forget a terrifying childhood. Blaming his father for becoming a drug addict, Itzik said, "The person who brought me to drugs was my father, who always was beating me up. I felt that at home they did not love me." Esti also took drugs to repress her feelings:

> In those days it was not like today, it was opium. You could inject it or get it under your tongue. My cousin was using it. I told her, "I want to try. I see you sit there and not worry about anything; I want to be like you, to freeze the feelings in me, not to feel, not to hear, not to listen."

Such external attributions allowed offenders of both genders to reject all blame and culpability for the deviant roles they had been forced to assume. In so doing, offenders implicitly claimed that there was nothing wrong with them (Warner, 1986; Wong & Weiner, 1981). They were not accountable for their criminal actions. To the contrary, they were the ones who had been wronged and victimized.

Resisting Labels

The second strategy offenders used to account for a pejorative role or identity was the provision of justifications. Male offenders were more adept than female offenders in utilizing techniques of neutralization (Sykes & Matza, 1957) and/or after-the-fact rationalizations (Hirschi, 1969) to deny the victims or the injury caused to them, condemn the condemner, and appeal to higher loyalties.

Moshe accounted for his marijuana-dealing behavior by minimizing the injury that resulted from his drug transactions. He, in fact, argued that his involvement in selling drugs did not hurt anyone:

> I sold only grass. Those who smoke grass are not drug addicts. I believe that in the future the law will allow smoking grass. Light drugs are okay, even if they are not legal. The law is not important, what is important is that you keep control of yourself. Light drugs do not hurt you.

Moti and Danny denied their victims or the harm they had caused to them as a consequence of their theft and robbery. In reality, it was the rich from whom they had stolen who had victimized them by letting them live in poverty! In general, the person who steals does not have any means, but the ones he steals from does. If he takes some of the wealth, he won't get hurt:

> I did not want to steal from people's houses or pickpocket. My conscience would not let me. So I decided to go to the bank, it is the money of the government, and also of the people, but they do not have to worry about their money. If their money is stolen, the government will guarantee it (Moti).

By denying the injury or harm, male offenders could accept responsibilities for actions while implicitly claiming that the gravity of such actions had been exaggerated. Thus, the stigmatizing labels were unbecoming to them. Similarly, by denouncing the dishonesty of all those who wanted to condemn them, offenders implicitly contended that all they had done by committing crime was nothing more than restore social justice. Furthermore, the so-called agents of the criminal justice system who had so often condemned were often more corrupt than they themselves were. Danny explained,

> These maniacs, the police, the son-of-a-bitch judge, he thinks he is God. This is a judge? They should put the police in jail, not me. What did we do after all? We did not even have a good hit!

Female offenders had difficulty utilizing similar rationalization techniques to justify their criminal behavior. Unlike their male counterparts, as we shall see in a later section, female offenders perceived their children to be the primary victims of their crimes. To their children, they were unable to provide justifications that could minimize the injury or deny the harm they had caused by abandoning them. Nevertheless, female offenders were condemning their condemners for their dishonesty. Dina condemned the whole criminal justice system for separating her from her child: "I felt I had been cheated, and they had stolen my daughter. I was very bitter and felt that the whole world was destroyed. There was nothing left to do but cry."

Similarly, Adi explained how helpless and destitute she had been when the court had condemned her as an unfit mother and removed her son from her custody to place him for adoption. Adi recounts:

> I was sentenced to five years in prison, and I was addicted. I did not have a home. I did not have anything. I did not have a guardian for the child. The Child Protection Agency called the treatment wing and told me that the judge had decided to take the child away. They decided that I was not capable of being a mother. I appealed twice, but they said I was not capable. Until today I am bitter that I did not have my baby with me.

Esti condemned her mother who had lived off the money she had earned from prostitution. Esti recounted how after pronouncing her dead, her own mother had brainwashed her grandchild to hate her:

> She has so much hatred toward me; my mother has put it in her heart. She would tell her [Esti's daughter] when she was four or five, and understood a little, she would say, "Do you know who is you father? Is he Jewish or Arab?" She would tell her, "Your mother is a whore. Your mother is dead."

Appeal to higher loyalties was another rationalization technique used by offenders of both genders to preserve their integrity. Offenders justified drug deals, fraud, and theft as permissible because they served the interest of conventional others, to whom they were obligated. Thus, by appeal to the filial duty of helping one's elderly parent in need, Beni could neutralize the label of thief. In his own words,

> With some of the money [I stole] I opened a savings account and with the rest I decided to open a kiosk [mini-market or newspaper and coffee stand] for my parents. I wanted to help them. It hurt me to see my mother so sick who worked so hard to earn a living.

Similarly, Bonnie appealed to her children's welfare to justify her involvement in drug dealing. Selling drugs to rescue her children from misery and to prevent them from enduring poverty was a necessary course of action any mother would opt for in the same situation. Bonnie recalls:

> It seemed so easy to make money through drugs. Within two years I bought a car, a video for my son, and had become an independent drug dealer. In 1986, I was arrested with 50 grams of cocaine.

Negating and Switching Labels

Another strategy adopted to construct a favorable self-concept was the outright rejection of stigmatizing labels. Female offenders were often ready to endorse the labels of prostitutes and "druggies." Yet they vehemently resisted the psychiatrist and prison social worker's label of insane. Angered by the social worker, who refused to let her make a phone call to her daughter, Dina punched the glass door of the social worker's office. With a torn arm, leaking with blood, she was transported to the hospital where she received 300 stitches. She had to submit to psychiatric treatment as a condition to maintain contact with her daughter. Nevertheless, Dina refused to endorse the prison psychiatrist's label of psy-

chotic. She exclaimed, "Maybe I did psychotic things, but I do not agree that I am psychotic!" Similarly, Iris poured gasoline onto herself and threatened to light a match in protest when the social worker refused to tell her where her daughter was. Iris told us about her struggles to escape an institution that would have indefinitely stigmatized her as insane:

> The psychiatrist was giving me shots. He was destroying me. I wanted out! I preferred not to deal with them. If you are insane it follows you all your life! The difference between prison and psychiatry is that in prison you have a date when you come out. In psychiatry you never know when you come out. God forbid! They give you electric shocks!

These testimonies denounce the ease with which the "insane" label was applied to discredit female offenders any time their behavior was judged as going beyond the limits of the socially tolerable (Schur, 1984; Yarrow, Green-Schwartz, Murphy, & Calhoun-Deasy, 1955). Similarly feminists have pointed out how easily deviance becomes medicalized and psychologized when applied to women who do not fit into the "proper" gender roles (Belknap, 2001; Foucault, 1977; Geiger, 2002). In contrast, male offenders never mentioned the label "insane" to have been imputed onto them.

Reconciling Deviant Status With Prized Conventional Values

To negotiate a more favorable identity, offenders could also deny stigmatizing labels by reconciling them with prized values in the conventional world. For instance, appeal to the desirability of financial success allowed the offender to save face and maintain self-respect. Just like Merton's (1957) innovators, theft, drug dealing, and prostitution were avenues for those deprived of conventional means to achieve the much-prized cultural goal of financial success. Working the streets while using cocaine, Esti was able to afford anything money could buy. In her own words,

> In brief, cocaine fitted me good, *Sababa* [Arabic expression meaning great]. I had obtained a driving license and a car. I had a house. I took driving lessons from the money I made from prostitution and bought myself an Audi 100 from a car dealer in Tel-Aviv.

Danny and Moti told how the aspiration of being financially successful had led them to crime:

> The person who follows the law may also succeed, but with a great deal of effort. Also,

it is not for sure. At my age, I think that I have enough experience to deal with delinquency in clever ways so that they do not catch me. So, if I get the opportunity for a big score without the chance of getting caught, I would do it (Danny).

If I do not succeed when I get out of prison and someone offers me a tempting proposition, I do not know if I will not fall for it! (Moti)

Thus, inclusion of financial success into the offenders' self-definition allowed for the rejection of societal condemnation.

Appeal to Human Strengths and Virtues

Appeal to human strengths and virtues, such as skill, loyalty, and honesty, was another potent strategy to reject the deviant labels by challenging the boundaries between conventional and delinquent worlds. By calling themselves honest thieves and/or reliable drug dealers, male offenders stressed self-confidence and personal worth in both worlds. Moti expressed his pride for being a skillful and talented delinquent:

I used to break in houses. I was very good at it. Everyone wanted to break in with me. I felt good with this image. It gave me self-confidence. I felt I was belonging, wanted. When you steal cleverly, elegantly, you make a big hit and you live forever like a king.

Itzik recounts how much respect he had gained during his drug-dealing career because he had always been reliable and trustworthy:

For a while I was the most respected grass dealer. Everyone knew that I was reliable, and I was selling quality stuff. Drug dealing was my job. It was a hard work, a 24-hour-a-day job. Anyone who wanted grass knew where to find me.

Similarly, even though Danny had been convicted for his offenses, he remained proud of his talent. In his own words, "I got caught and I got punished. But I have all the talent to succeed. Today I am calmer. Age has something to do with it."

Offenders oftentimes perceived themselves as honest. They might have temporarily been blinded by money, yet their conscience and sense of justice allowed them to maintain a sense of personal integrity. In the words of some of the offenders:

I know how to differentiate between right from wrong. Money blinded me and I stopped thinking. I never thought that I was doing okay. I just stopped thinking (Danny).

I will not play with my conscience any more. I always had a strong conscience. And because of that, I felt bad about many things I did (David).

All in all, I am a good guy. I can differentiate between right from wrong (Itzak).

Appeal to human strengths and virtues that transcended both conventional and street norms allowed for the outright denial of deviant labels and/or for an identity split into a good and a bad self. Thus, Moshe appealed to the "good me" to claim that the "bad me" was not real:

But from outside I played it like a man, as if it does not bother me. I did not look at myself as a criminal. It was a mask. It was not me. Today I do not need a mask.

Similarly, Miki stated, "A criminal like me is not really a criminal. I am just a law violator."

In contrast and by comparison to male offenders, attribution of self-competence was conspicuously missing from female offenders' accounts. Female offenders' narratives reflect their low self-esteem, lack of self-confidence, and self-efficacy perception. Success was usually attributed to external factors such as drugs, not to the self-efficacy evaluation. For instance, for Esti it was the cocaine she had used that had given her power to become one of the greatest prostitutes while working in the streets downtown. In her own words,

The woman told me "Try yourself [cocaine], you will see how much strength you will have. You'll make double money." And me, like *habblah* [idiot in Arabic], I said, "Okay!" I became like a *Ninja* [turtle]. No one could compete with me. I was a real monster. I would curse at work and fight with everyone. In the harbor no other woman could mess with me. I did not care about the men; I cared about the money. Then there were American ships and sailors. It was a good time then.

Accounting for the Role of Incompetent Mother

Female offenders' inability to provide accounts and positive self-definitions reached a peak when having to negotiate for the imputed label of incompetent mother. Their life in crime, prostitution, drugs, and subsequent incarceration had, all too often, led female offenders to abandon their children. Yet despite excuses and contempt for the whole world, female offenders' continued commitment and attachment to the master status of motherhood prevented them from casting off the label of incompetent mother. They had failed to provide their children with the love, affection, and care any competent mother was expected to give. Unable to put a roof over the head of their children, or even maintain custody of them, no alternative life goal could bolster a positive sense of self. No technique of neutralization or after-the-fact rationalization was powerful enough to minimize the harm they had caused to the very children they had so much wanted to mother. Iris told us,

> I do not only feel that I am not a mother! I know I have not been a mother! I have two girls that I do not know. I did not give them anything that a mother gives. That they have a mother on their birth certificate is not enough! I had also a mother on my ID card. What counts is who takes care of you, who runs around for you, not who brought you into the world.

Internal attributions, self-blame, shame, and guilt were the inescapable consequences of the ultimate offense of abandoning one's children. Self-condemnation often resulted. Contrary to male offenders, appeal to human strengths or virtues was no longer possible once the labels of incompetent and irresponsible mother had been incorporated in female offenders' own identity. Iris, therefore, admitted, "I know I am not a mother. I do not have the ability to be a mother."

Neutralizing the Label of Incompetent Husband and Father

By contrast, and contrary to female offenders, male offenders had no problem accounting for their failure as father and breadwinner. The normative contexts, that of conventional society and that of the street culture and the wide variety of roles and obligations men could assume in both contexts, afforded offenders with plenty of excuses and justifications to reject the labels of incompetent fathers and husbands. For instance, they could shake off the obligations of fatherhood by reminding us that in both the conventional and street worlds it was the role of females and not of males to take care of the children. Nissim, who had so much wanted to kill his wife because she had cheated on him, knew that to harm his spouse would be to hurt his children.

> I even thought of hurting her physically so that she stops hurting me this way. I have many friends outside who know exactly with whom she hangs around, and where.

They could help me punish her. But this is only a thought, because I know that any hit will hurt the children and me badly. No one will be able to take care of the children.

Offenders' unfaithfulness to their spouse was accounted for by appeal to the double standards concerning males and females' sexual behavior in both conventional and nonconventional normative contexts. In the words of some of the offenders,

> I am not a chauvinist, but when a man cheats on his wife she can forgive him. But when a woman cheats on a man, it is a real humiliation. It is a hit to the ego, and for this I am not ready to forgive (Nissim).

> A man with many women is a Don Juan. A woman with many men is a whore. That's how it is in our society (Morris).

In the street culture, exploitation of women and sexual conquest were additional norms legitimizing unfaithfulness. In the words of Itzik, "In the circle I grew up in, there was a lot of cheating on your wife. This is how our society was. There were no permanent wives."

Appeal to males' biological nature and uncontrollable sexual appetite provided the ultimate excuse to reject as unreasonable the normative expectation of faithfulness. It was simply unnatural for a man to remain faithful to his spouse. Moshe, thus, explained, "A man is like dog. When you give him meat he takes it. There are a lot of women who stick to you and seduce you. You cannot get rid of them."

Finally, even though by conventional norms male offenders had neglected their roles of breadwinner and family provider, they could justify such transgressions by appeal to the street culture's code of honor. Adherence to such a code required sacrificing one's welfare and that of one's family in the name of higher loyalty for one's male friends. In the words of Nissim, "You stay loyal to your friends, you sacrifice yourself. This is our code."

Conclusion

In conclusion, the naming of oneself or being named by others as criminal, prostitute, drug addict, and/or incompetent parent, emerges as a powerful tool in understanding gender differences in offenders' accounts and autobiographical construction in the process of negotiating a favorable identity.

Content analysis of in-depth interviews and narratives indicates that offenders of both genders had no trouble excusing their behavior by appeal to a dismal childhood filled with incidents of physical, emotional, and sexual abuse and negative role models. Offenders of both genders explained their life in crime and drugs by the abuse to which they had been subjected in their childhood. These narratives concur with other quantitative and qualitative studies indicating high correlations for both genders between childhood victimization and involvement in drugs and later criminality (Ben-David, Alek, & Silfan, 2002; Geiger & Fischer, 2003; Geiger & Timor, 2002; Ireland & Widom, 1992; Widom, 1992).

The findings of the present study also show that male offenders are the most talented actors in the drama of accounts. They were much more adept than female offenders were at providing justifications, external attributions, and alternative labels to reconstruct their autobiography and resist the stigmatizing labels imposed on them by conventional others. They did so by appeal to both conventional and street norms. Furthermore, possession of character strengths valued in all social groups, such as loyalty, know-how, self-efficacy, and courage played a determinant role in challenging the boundaries between delinquent and non-delinquent worlds. Equipped with those strengths, male offenders were able to cope with adversity and feel confident in their ability to do something worthwhile, no matter the normative framework within which they were evaluated.

In contrast, the distinctive characteristic of female offenders was their inability to negotiate a favorable identity once the label of incompetent mother had been imputed to them. Their lack of opposition and resistance to such labels reflects the impact of differential gender socialization on male and female offenders. Motherhood is for female offenders the only realm within which they could gain or show a sense of competence. Separation from children destined female offenders to become anomic, without a center or future direction (Shils, 1975). When asked what would give her back her self-confidence, Amira replied, "Bring back my kid. Nothing else. I want to be with him, and listen to him call me 'Mom.'"

Paradoxically, for female offenders adherence to the master status of motherhood compromised gaining any positive sense of self. The only way they were expected to gain a sense of worth and personal strength in both the conventional and street world was to fulfill the essential duties of motherhood successfully. These normative contexts constrained female offenders to attribute to self rather than to others the blame for neglecting their maternal duties (Lee & Seligman, 1997). The findings of this study, thus, show a pronounced gender difference in attribution and explanatory style. Female offenders interviewed attributed their failure to an unchangeable, permanent, and internal cause—their own incompetence. In contrast, the variety of roles male offenders played in both the conventional and street culture allowed for much flexibility in self-attribution (Seligman, 1992). Furthermore, competence, know-how, and skillfulness, which were prized in both normative contexts, reinforced male offenders' self-efficacy perception and evaluation (Bandura, 1993). As a result, male offenders often exhibited a pronounced self-serving bias in their explanatory style (Greenberg, Pyszczynski, & Solomon, 1982). They often were able to attribute their successes to internal causes—their own competence, skill, and know-how—and their failure to external causes, such as dishonest judges and delinquent friends. Consequently, male offenders' explanatory style was optimistic, whereas that of female offenders was pessimistic and self-defeating, leading to self-alienation and despair.

Given gender differences in identity negotiation, accounts, self-serving bias, and explanatory style, rehabilitation endeavors must follow different paths for female and male offenders. Male offenders often succeeded at exhibiting a sense of mastery from criminogenic enterprises. They were proud of the personal strengths they had acquired, such as courage, honesty, autonomy, and loyalty. These strengths have in the past been viewed as rationalizations, illusions, and manipulations (McCarthy & Steward, 1998; Miller, 1958; Toch, 1986). A substantial part of offenders' rehabilitation included undergoing cognitive restructuring to confront their rationalizations and break their ego-defenses. A more innovative approach suggested by our data would be to build on male offenders' ingenuity and sense of mastery, while redirecting their personal strengths into conventional endeavors. Rather than destroy male offenders' rationalizations, the real challenge of rehabilitation would be to find conventional enterprises through which offenders could exhibit the same know-how, skill, and competence that they exhibited in the delinquent world.

Learning from male offenders, building female offenders' personal strengths becomes a primary goal of rehabilitation. Female offenders have come to see themselves as helpless and hopeless victims, passively responding to oppressive circumstances. They must be empowered to perceive themselves as decision-makers making choices despite malignant circumstances. Competence acquisition in areas other than motherhood through education, on-the-job training, and gainful employment are some enabling conditions that would help these women acquire confidence in their ability to do something worthwhile (Corey, 1996).

As female offenders acquire a sense of competence and autonomy, they could learn to retell their stories and explore alternative self-definitions in order to change their attribution style and reconstruct a positive identity. There is no need to add that to transcend their histories of trauma, depression, and substance abuse, female offenders' relationships with their children must be renegotiated and reinstated.

In summary, male and female offenders may not be able to repair all the damage they have caused to themselves, their children, and society. Nevertheless, by creating enabling conditions, female offenders could gain courage and resourcefulness to fight adversity, and male offenders could learn to rechannel their personal strengths into normative endeavors so that offenders of both genders could function as competent parents and productive citizens.

Discussion Questions

1. Why is it that some deviant women who do not fit their stereotyped gender role are labeled "crazy" or as having psychological problems? How does this label overlap with criminal behavior?

2. How might a person resist or cast off a criminal or deviant label once applied? Give examples from the chapter.

3. How did the mothers and fathers differ in their accounts of their failure as parents? Why did their interpretations differ?

4. Were men or women better able to justify their behavior and resist the stigmatization of a label? Why?

5. Given what we know about women, labeling, and identity definitions, what elements of rehabilitation or treatment should be included in a program to better serve female offenders?

References

Bandura, A. (1993). Perceived self-efficacy in cognitive development and functioning. *Educational Psychologist, 28,* 117–148.

Becker, H. (1963). *Outsiders: Studies in the sociology of deviance.* New York: Free Press.

——. (1973). Labeling theory considered. In *The outsiders* (Rev. ed.). New York: Free Press.

Belknap, Joanne. 2001. *The invisible woman: Gender, crime, and justice.* 2d ed. Belmont, CA: Wadsworth.

Ben-David, S., Alek, M., & Silfan, P. (2002). Female prisoners in Israel: Trauma and crime. In M. Haddad & I. Wolf (Eds.), *Delinquency, social deviance theory and practice* (pp. 107–124). Ramat Gan, Israel: Bar Ilan University Press.

Bruner, J. (1990). *Acts of meaning.* Cambridge, MA: Harvard University Press.

Corey, F. (1996). Personal narratives and young men in prison: Labeling the outside inside. *Western Journal of Communication, 60* (1), 57–75.

Dahlsgaard, K. A., Peterson, C., & Seligman, M. E. (2001). *Toward a classification of strengths and virtues: Lessons from history.* Unpublished manuscript, University of Pennsylvania.

Denzin, N. K. (1989). *Interpretive interactionism.* Newbury Park, CA: Sage.

Fleisher, M. S. (1995). *Beggars and thieves: Lives of urban street criminals.* Madison: University of Wisconsin Press.

Foucault, M. (1977). *Discipline and punishment* (A. Sheridan, Trans.). New York: Pantheon.

Garfinkel, H. (1962). Common sense knowledge of social structures. In J. M. Scher (Ed.), *Theories of the mind* (pp. 689–712). Glencoe, Ill: Free Press.

Geiger, B. (2002). From deviance to creation: Women's answer to subjugation. *Humanity and Society, 26* (3), 214–227.

Geiger, B., & Fischer, M. (2003, October). Female repeat offenders negotiating identity. *International Journal of Offender Therapy and Comparative Criminology, 47* (5), 496–515.

Geiger, B., & Timor, U. (2002). An inside look at prisoners' world of values. *Journal of Offender Rehabilitation, 34* (2), 64–83.

Gergen, K. (1980). Toward intellectual audacity in the social sciences. In R. Gilmour & S. W. Duck (Eds.), *The development of social psychology* (pp. 239–270). New York: Academic Press.

Glaser, B. G., & Strauss, A. L. (1967). *The discovery of grounded theory: Strategies for qualitative research.* New York: Aldine.

Greenberg, J., Pyszczynski, T., & Solomon, S. (1982). The self-serving attributional bias: Beyond self-presentation. *Journal of Experimental Social Psychology, 18,* 56–57.

Henley, N., & Freeman, J. (1979) The sexual politics of interpersonal behavior. In J. Freeman (Ed.), *Women: A feminist perspective* (2nd ed.). Palo Alto, CA: Mayfield Pub. Co.

Hirschi, T. (1969). *Causes of delinquency.* Berkeley: University of California Press.

Holsti, O. (1969). *Content analysis for social science and humanistics.* Reading, MA: Addison Wesley.

Ireland, T., & Widom, C. (1992). *Childhood victimization and risk for alcohol and drug arrests.* Washington, DC: National Institute of Justice.

Jacobs, B., & Wright, R. (1999). Stick-up, street culture, and offender motivation. *Criminology, 37* (1), 149–173.

Ker-Conway, J. (1994). *True north: A memoir.* New York: Random House.

Lee, Y., & Seligman, M. E. P. (1997). Are Americans more optimistic than the Chinese? *Personality and Social Psychology Bulletin, 23,* 32–40.

Lemert, E. (1972). *Human deviance, social problems and social control* (2nd ed.). Englewood Cliffs, NJ: Prentice Hall.

McCarthy, J. G., & Steward, A. L. (1998). Neutralization as a process of graduated desensitization: Moral values of offenders. *International Journal of Offender Therapy and Comparative Criminology,* 42 (4), 278–290.

Merton, R. (1957). *Social theory and social structure.* Glencoe, IL: Free Press.

Miller, W. B. (1958). Lower class culture as a generating milieu of gang delinquency. *Journal of Social Issues, 14,* 5–19.

Nagel, I., & Hagen, J. (1983). Gender and crime: Offense patterns and criminal court sanctions. In M. Tonry & N. Morris (Eds.), *Crime and Justice: An annual review of research* (pp. 91–144). Chicago: University of Chicago Press.

Patton, M. Q. (2002). *Qualitative research and evaluation methods* (3rd ed.). Thousand Oaks, CA: Sage Publications.

Schur, E. M. (1984). *Labeling women deviant: Gender, stigma and social control.* New York: McGraw-Hill.

Scott, M. B., & Lyman, S. M. (1968). Accounts. *American Sociological Review, 33,* 46–62.

Seligman, M. E. P. (1992). *Learned optimism.* New York: Pocket Books.

——. (1998a). President's column: Building human strength: Psychology's forgotten mission. *APA Monitor,* 29 (1). Retrieved May 5, 2004, from *www.apa.org/monitor/jan98/pres.html.*

——. (1998b). President's column: Positive social science. *APA Monitor,* 29 (4). Retrieved May 5, 2004 from *www.apa.org/monitor/apr98/pres.html.*

——. (2002). *Knowing the nature of the beast.* Correspondence with S. Pinker, MIT: Mass.

Shils, E. (1975). *Center and periphery.* Chicago: University of Chicago Press.

Shover, N., & Honaker, D. (1992). The socially bounded decision making of persistent property offenders. *Howard Journal of Criminal Justice,* 31, 276–293.

Stiles, W. B. (1993). Quality control in qualitative research. *Clinical Psychological Review,* 13, 593–618.

Sykes, G., & Matza, D. (1957). Techniques of neutralization: A theory of delinquency. *American Sociological Review,* 22, 664–670.

Toch, H. (1986). *Psychology of crime and criminal justice.* Prospect Heights, Ill: Waveland Press.

Warner, C. T. (1986). Anger and similar delusions. In R. Harre (Ed.), *Social construction of emotions* (pp. 135–166). New York: Blackwell.

Weber, A. L. (1992). Account-making process: A phenomenological approach. In T. L. Orbuch (Ed.), *Close relationship loss: Theoretical approaches* (pp. 174–191). New York: Springer-Verlag.

Widom, C. (1992). *The cycles of violence.* Washington, DC: National Institute of Justice.

Wong, W. P. T., & Weiner, B. (1981). When people ask "why" questions and the heuristics of attributional search. *Journal of Personality and Social Psychology,* 40, 650–663.

Yarrow, M. R., Green-Schwartz, C., Murphy, H., & Calhoun-Deasy, L. (1995). The psychological meaning of mental illness in the family. *Journal of Social Issues,* 11, 12–24.

Section II

The Nexus Between Criminal Behavior and Family

We acknowledged in the first section that socialization determines how women define themselves and their relationships with others. In this second section, we delve more deeply into families of origin and how they intersect with criminal behavior. Families establish individual identity and initial communication with others as social beings. The family is the first exposure to intimate relations to which all other relationships are compared. What happens when members of the family of origin are involved in criminality?

Early family experiences based on socioeconomic status, family structure, parental styles of control, and stability have a significant effect on later behavior, including criminality. In her book *Street Woman*, Miller (1986) found that poverty limited the influence and exercise of parental control over children. While familial networks served as a safety net in cases of economic hardship, they also prohibited individuals within the network from achieving meaningful upward mobility. This further exacerbated economic inequality and made it more difficult to eradicate the cycle of poverty (Heimer 2000).

Nonabusive nuclear family units insulated children the most from recruitment into crime. Extended households with definite boundaries insulated youths to a lesser extent. Domestic networks linked by kinship, particularly those that were abusive or dysfunctional in nature, were the least likely to protect youths and may, in fact, help initiate them into crime (Miller 1986). About 70 percent of incarcerated women in California had one or more family members with arrest histories (Owen 1998).

The first two readings in this section explore the intersection between lawbreaking behavior and family ties. **First, Geoffrey Hunt and colleagues** discuss the premise that despite hardships, abuse, and family violence, Latina gang girls maintain familial relationships, and their closest relationships are with either their mother or sister. The girls had higher expectations and standards for female family members and homegirls than for male family members and boyfriends. **The second article, by Karen Joe-Laidler,** examines how extended Asian-Pacific American family networks overlap with young women's initiation into drug use.

The Role of Being a Parent

Whereas the previous discussion has been on how members of the family of origin contribute to women's criminality, it is also important to mention how dependent children overlap with a mother's criminal behavior. Children play a central role in many women's lives, as many women are the primary caretakers of these children. Female-headed households accounted for 18 percent of all households in 1997 (Heimer 2000), and evidence indicates that the current rate is even higher. Research shows that mothers who lack employment skills and education may commit crimes to provide for their children (Miller 1986). Women with employment skills who were convicted of white-collar crimes, such as fraud and embezzlement, provided the same rationalization of committing crime because of financial needs of their family (Daly 1989).

Being a mother contributes to how a woman defines herself and is frequently a source of increased self-esteem. At the same time, being a mother while incarcerated can also be a source of oppression and punishment (Thornburg and Trunk 1992, 208). Being separated from children is a source of grief in itself, but incarcerated moms or mothers who have lost custody because of crime experience a tremendous source of guilt for not being present in the everyday lives of their children. As we will see from the **third selection, by Kathleen Ferraro and Angela Moe,** the responsibilities of children influence a mother's decision to commit crime just as much as children are a motivator for women to desist from crime.

Violence Against Children

Tied to themes of one's family of origin, childhood experiences, and feelings of self-worth are the quality of relationships women maintain as adults and the way they treat their children. It is thought that women who did not grow up with nurturing parents have trouble developing their own positive self-worth. Daly (1992, 27) termed this kind of woman as "harmed and harming" because she was abused or neglected as a child. For example, she may have some psychological problems that contribute to her acting out violently when she is unable to handle her situation. Further, women with low self-esteem to begin with find it difficult to leave an abusive relationship.

Although there is research about battered women who kill their spouses, less is known about the reasons women abuse or harm their children. Unlike an abusive spouse, children do not pose the same threat. Scholars have most recently hypothesized that women harm children for different reasons than do men. One view suggests that women abuse their power as parents, and death results when discipline goes too far. An alternative view argues that within a patriarchal context of oppression, women's feelings of powerlessness and despair become rage, which is turned inward to a woman's only extension of herself—her children (Dougherty 1993).

Many suspected cases of sudden infant death syndrome (SIDS) remain unsubstantiated, and the link between abuse and the numbers of missing children is questionable, which creates a largely unknown number of cases where parental violence against children may have occurred. **The final reading in this section, by Susan Crimmins and colleagues,** explores reasons why women kill children as one example of a crime by a "harmed and harming woman."

References

Daly, K. 1989. "Gender and Varieties of White-Collar Crime." *Criminology* 27: 769–794.

——. 1992. "Women's Pathways to Felony Court: Feminist Theories of Lawbreaking and Problems of Representation." *Southern California Review of Law and Women's Studies* 2 (1): 11–52.

Dougherty, J. 1993. "Women's Violence Against Their Children: A Feminist Perspective." *Women and Criminal Justice* 4 (2): 91–114.

Heimer, K. 2000. "Changes in the Gender Gap in Crime and Women's Economic Marginalization." *Criminal Justice 2000: The Nature of Crime: Continuity and Change.* Washington, DC: National Institute of Justice, Office of Justice Programs.

Miller, E. M. 1986. *Street Woman.* Philadelphia: Temple University Press.

Owen, B. 1998. *In the Mix: Struggle and Survival in a Women's Prison.* Albany: State University of New York Press.

Thornburg, T., and D. Trunk. 1992. "A Collage of Voices: A Dialogue With Women in Prison." *Southern California Review of Law and Women's Studies* 2 (1): 155–217. ✦

5

'I'm Calling My Mom'

The Meaning of Family and Kinship Among Latina Homegirls

Geoffrey P. Hunt
Kathleen MacKenzie
Karen A. Joe-Laidler

This chapter explores the relationships and experiences of a group of young Latina women. The material is drawn from an ongoing comparative qualitative study of ethnic youth gangs in the San Francisco Bay area. The authors conducted face-to-face interviews with 47 Latina gang members who belonged to 23 different groups. The interviews were conducted by a Latina social scientist who previously had been a gang member and was generally familiar with the gang scene. Although the interviewer did not know the girls personally before the interviews, given her background and knowledge, she had few difficulties in establishing rapport and trust. She conducted the interviews in a variety of settings, such as the respondent's or a peer's residence, parks, church youth centers, and coffee shops. The information collected highlights the female gang members' complex relationships with their families, with one another, and with male counterparts. Unlike many researchers studying gang members, the authors take the family as their starting point. They do not seek to blame the family for society's social problems, nor for the increase in female adolescents' involvement in gangs; instead, they illuminate the complexities, paradoxes, and ambiguities of day-to-day relations between adolescent women, their parents, other family members, and gang members. By focusing on the elaborate networks of support and strong attachments that women form, the authors suggest a reexamination of the relationships between family and gang in the gang members' lives.

Public concern about crime has centered increasingly on the rise of female participation in crime, especially by young women. Some of the increasing concern about female crime focuses on girls' participation and role in youth gangs. Some researchers argue that girl gang membership is increasing; others are more cautious, believing that participation has remained relatively stable over time. Researchers traditionally have minimized females' roles in street gangs as well as the social processes and consequences of their involvement in gangs. Male gang researchers typically have characterized female members as maladjusted tomboys or sexual deviants who, in either case, were no more than appendages to male gang members (Joe and Chesney-Lind 1995). This traditional view contrasts sharply with recent public discussions about female gang members, which indicate that these females are no longer simply male gang members' "molls" but are establishing their own ground, taking an active, independent role in crime and violence (Joe and Chesney-Lind 1995).

This most recent image of gang girls has created much public alarm because it highlights more than the problems of adolescent maladjustment or teenage rebellion. For male gang members, being on the streets is a natural, legitimized social activity governed by rules of masculinity (Campbell 1986; Kennedy and Baron 1993). Girls on the street, however, are less typical (McRobbie and Garber 1976; Moore 1990) and are somewhat less of a problem than boys, because they are more likely to be regulated within the home. As Nava (1984) points out, "[O]n the whole parental policing over behavior, time, labor and sexuality of girls has not only been more efficient than over boys, it has been different. For girls, unlike for boys, the principal site and source for the operation of control has been the family" (p. 11). The family thus plays a central role in the structure and process of "gender as social control" (Bottcher 1995).

Consequently, young women's involvement in gangs is disquieting precisely because females in gangs are perceived to be outside the traditional arena of family control. More specifically, female gang participation generates alarm because it signifies, yet again, fears about the decline of the "traditional family." We emphasize again because the family has been the target of both praise and condemnation in America since early colonial days, and has been defined clearly in class and culturally biased terms.

In this paper, then, we begin to look more critically at female gang members' relationships and experiences with their families and with their peers. Unlike many researchers studying gang members, we take the family as our starting point. We do not seek to blame the family for society's social problems, nor for the increase in female adolescents' involvement in gangs; instead we want to illuminate the complexities, paradoxes, and ambiguities of day-to-day relations between adolescent women, their parents, other family members, and gang members.

Many studies of gang members, whether male or female, have focused primarily on gang members' behavior and activities, partly divorced from their relationships with their families. Here, following the lead of such writers as Campbell (1984), Decker and Van Winkle (1996), and Moore (1991), we attempt to construct a perspective that joins family and gang, in which these two arenas are viewed as interrelated rather than as distinct social realms. We try to illustrate the continuity that exists for these homegirls between the two most important social groups in their lives: family and gang. In doing so, we examine the following questions: What types of relationships exist between female gang members and their families? Is gang involvement associated with a detachment from family relations? In what ways are family and gang interconnected, and what really is the meaning of family in these young women's lives?

In addressing these questions, we try to illuminate two important points about the relationship between family and girl gang members. First, our data suggest that gang girls maintain relatively strong ties to particular family members, predominantly their mothers and also (to a lesser extent) their sisters, aunts, and other female kin. Second, gang and family for many young women intersect; this intersection raises questions about the influence and control of the family versus that of peers in delinquency.

In the following sections, we attempt to show that although joining a gang may create tension within the family, especially when parents disapprove, gang members do not necessarily sever all ties with the family. In many cases, the gang members and their parents, or other significant adults, maintain their relationships in spite of these tensions and conflicts. Furthermore, although a significant number of gang members express negative feelings toward particular family members, they often call on those persons when they need help. Female gang members, at least in our sample, exhibit complex ongoing and changing relationships with their parents, especially their mothers, as well as with other female relatives, with nonrelated women in the gangs, and (in many cases) with family members in the gangs. We present findings that explore a broader understanding of family, which extends beyond kinship and into the streets.

Family Relations

Latina gang members' relationships with their parents and other family members are varied and complex. Some reported strong family ties; others described violent confrontations, and sexual and physical abuse; still others expressed extreme hatred (Moore and Hagedorn 1996). Three significant relationships emerged from the homegirls' discussions of family: relations with their mothers, relations with fathers and stepfathers, and relations with other significant family members.

Mothers

For the majority of the young women, the most significant relationship was with their mothers. Most described generally positive ties, seeing their mothers in "traditional terms" as well as accommodating to changes in the mother's role and position in the family. One respondent, for example, stated that her mother "is a very nice woman, family oriented. . . . When she divorced my dad, she took care of us kids and always worked and was a good role model."

As the respondents grew older, many began to consider their relationships with their mothers in a new light. A change was noted by one-quarter of those respondents who classified their relationships as good. Some of the respondents assessed their mothers and their own relationships with them more even-handedly. One respondent emphasized how her mother had "put up with all my things." Another suggested that although her relationship with her mother was still not perfect, it was improving. In some cases, a more realistic and more practical perspective on their mothers emerged, occasionally furthered by their own experiences as they began to raise children of their own.

Even among the more positive accounts, we heard many references to disruptive features in the family. One 15-year-old respondent, who described her relationship with her mother as good, remarked, as though in passing, that she currently lived with her sister. When asked why, she replied "'Cause my mom got locked up. . . . 'Cause of drugs. Shooting up." Many respondents described intense conflict between their mothers and their fathers, and found themselves siding with their mothers. One 16-year-old respondent remarked that her parents fought a lot and that "my sister doesn't talk to my dad. I talk to my sister. I talk to my mom."

In contrast to these more positive relationships, many homegirls described conflictual relationships with their mothers, often with the same intensity of expression. Nearly three-quarters blamed the poor relationship on their mothers. Over half of these attributed it to their mothers' drinking or drug use. Even so, some of the girls accepted their mothers' problems and assumed the parental role over the mother as well as over younger siblings. One 20-year-old married respondent described her mother's drinking in this way:

> My mom drank every chance she got, but she was always at home doing it. And . . . we always used to take care of her, and put her to sleep when she had too much . . . she would get real emotional, she cried about everybody and how she couldn't help us when we had our problems. . . . After a while, I got used to it. . . . I'd have to be there to watch her.

Two respondents' criticisms of their mothers stemmed from their mothers' failure to take their side when they were raped or sexually molested by their stepfathers. The respondents reported that their trust in their mothers had been undermined and that a "lot of hatred" now existed in the home, which made living there impossible. In almost all cases, however, even when the women reported hostile and negative relations with their mothers, some interaction still occurred. Contact was completely severed in only two cases.

In all these negative accounts, only one respondent admitted that her own behavior had contributed to the quality of the relationship with her mother:

> My mom . . . she's done a lot for me so it's time for me to . . . show her what I can do. That I can do a lot for myself and I just don't want to disappoint her anymore . . . I've been in too many problems. And the way she sees it, I have no reason to be in these problems. So . . . I guess she just wants me to straighten out and I just can't seem to do it . . . I know she won't kick me out but I guess it's really gotten to her 'cause it's like she tells me . . . I ain't no little girl no more. I should know what I'm doing.

In spite of these respondents' negative feelings towards their mothers, they felt and maintained ties, partly out of familial loyalty and love, but also for instrumental reasons. They relied on their mothers when they needed assistance. Although a few respondents expressed strong animosity toward their mothers for past behaviors, they called on them for help in looking after their children, providing shelter, and even supplying protection. This seemingly contradictory behavior was highlighted strikingly in one case: The respondent, who had described her mother in the early part of the interview as "a fuckin' bitch" and "a fuckin' drunk," later described proudly how, having been in a fight with an older woman, she telephoned her mother to come and defend her. Her mother "hunted down" the older woman and "kick(ed) her ass":

> I went and called my mom. I said the bitch wants to fuck with me. I said "Mom, drop off my son and come and look at my face 'cause she got two hits on me. . . ." and I said "Mom, get over here. I just fought this bitch and she's as old as you." . . . She came . . . and said "Where's this bitch at?" . . . Everybody . . . thought I was going to go snitch . . . and call the cops. I said "Nah, I'm calling someone better. I'm calling my mom."

The intricacy of these relations and the intensity of these young women's feelings towards their mothers was also evident when the respondents recounted situations in which they had physically defended their mothers. One 22-year-old respondent, in detailing her attitude towards anyone who attempted to hurt anyone in her family, described one such incident:

> A woman beat up my mom really bad, and I went back and I beat that lady to the point of death. I beat her, I took her out of the bar—well, she came out of the bar—and I took her and I grabbed her and I set her up at the back, and I beat her for like 20 minutes nonstop . . . and my mom was standing right there just watching me do it, . . . and that was 'cause [that woman] hurt something of mine, and you don't hurt what's mine.

The young women's defense of their mothers, and their sense of loyalty, also were clear in their home lives, as they often witnessed conflict between their parents or between the mother and the mother's boyfriend or spouse. Forty percent of the women reported such incidents of violence in the home; most of the time they sided with their mothers.

Fathers and Stepfathers

Just as the respondents' relationships with their mothers were varied, so were their relationships with their fathers, although these were less intense and less complex. We found one significant difference, however, in comparing respondents' relationships with their mothers and with their fathers: Respondents had much less to say about their fathers. Nearly one-fourth provided little or no information about these relationships. In some cases they mentioned their fathers only in passing; in others, their fathers appeared to be nonexistent. This feature is not surprising when we consider the small proportion of respondents (32%) who had lived with their fathers for most of the time before their sixteenth birthday. Other respondents complained that their fathers suddenly reappeared after a period of absence, stayed for a short time, and then disappeared again:

> My dad came back when I was nine—my ninth birthday. That fucked me up. 'Cause before that I seen him when I was five, going on six. And then he popped up . . . out of nowhere . . . came for a surprise, and that fucked me up. You know, "What the fuck are you doing here?" Then I figured he was staying. . . . And then he left without even saying goodbye. So one morning I wake up and he's gone.

Only two of the women who lived with both parents described the relationships with their fathers as normal or unproblematic. One of these, a recent immigrant from Mexico, stated "We don't have any problems in our family . . . I don't think anybody has parents like me . . . Cuz I have my love in my dad, and they are always there for us even if we're doing bad." In addition, both of the respondents who lived only with their fathers described the relationships as strong and positive. One recalled how her father helped look after her daughter. She had a high regard for her father, whom she considered "funny and smart." This young woman had little or no contact with her mother, saying "I don't really talk to her." Although she allowed her daughter to see her, she herself didn't visit.

A few respondents described growing up as "just normal" and reported good relationships with their fathers, but many recounted situations of tension and disruption in the family. One 20-year-old woman, while describing her father as the most important person in her life, went on to explain how her father began using cocaine, which ultimately led to her parents' divorce: "We really didn't have problems, till my dad . . . had a drug problem, so my mom left my dad and they just divorced." After the divorce she, her mother, and her brothers and sisters moved in with her grandmother and aunt. Unfortunately her mother, unlike her father, was unable to control her: "My dad was real strict with rules. . . . Whatever he said . . . that's what we did." Consequently, in the respondent's view, her father's cocaine use had catastrophic effects on her and her family. Her father ended up

in prison (he was currently serving a 10-year sentence), her sister was "locked up . . . [because] she was under the influence of some drug," and her brother had been locked up since October. Tragically, the respondent blamed herself for the situation, especially her father's imprisonment, commenting that if "I would have talked to my dad better, um . . . more, he wouldn't be locked up now."

Alcohol and drug consumption and alcohol-related violence also played a much more significant role in the respondents' accounts of their relationships with their fathers than with their mothers, a characteristic also evident in the discussions of their stepfathers. Accounts of the latter were generally more negative than those of their fathers. Of the 12 respondents who had grown up with stepfathers, only three described the relationships in positive terms. Like the fathers, the majority of the stepfathers were described either in passing or in harsh terms such as "He disgusts me" and "I hate him a lot." Sometimes tension resulted in violence, especially between the respondents' mothers and their fathers/stepfathers or between their mothers and the mothers' boyfriends. The matter-of-fact way in which these violent incidents were described suggests that often they were regular occurrences in the family.

When the respondent was the victim of family violence, it usually involved fathers or stepfathers. The most extreme form of violence described by the young women was rape or sexual molestation: In two of the three cases where this had occurred, stepfathers were the perpetrators; and the father's best friend was the offender in the third case.

In the case involving the father's best friend, the young woman described how she hated her father not only because she blamed him for his best friend's raping her, but also because of his violence towards her: He often pointed a gun at her head. Finally, she observed that these events explain why she is violent today:

> I would get . . . hate for my dad 'cause he didn't take care, he left me alone when he was supposed to take care of me and his best friend raped me when I was seven . . . that's why I got so violent, . . . where I could just kill somebody . . . 'cause that anger that was inside of me . . . I feel a lot of that frustration . . . those people hurt me, man, they hurt me when they do that to me, and that's why I guess I got to a point where I said nothing's gonna hurt me no more, nobody's gonna see me shed a tear for nothing that they did to me. I remember when my dad used to put a gun to my head, it took all fear away from me from dying . . . everything was always

stripped from me, I didn't have nothing no more . . . something in me was already taken away as a little girl.

Other young women remembered violent events with their mothers' boyfriends. In the following example, the respondent describes her attempts to protect her mother, whom she says was beaten up regularly:

> He would always beat up on my mom, and I was the one that would call the police because my sister would get scared and go and run and put herself in a corner. They were usually at night. We are trying to go to sleep and we always wake up to my mom screaming. I would wake up and my sister would be all scared and I would be like, "It is okay. I will call the police." Every single time I would try and help my mom. Try to beat him with something. I would always grab some shit and . . . throw it at him or something, and try to get him off her. That motherfucker was strong.

Despite the ups and downs in the young women's relationships with their mothers, they maintained emotional and instrumental ties. In many cases, the relationship was reciprocal in the sense that sometimes the mothers provided the nurturing and protective role for their daughters, while at other times the daughters assumed the motherly role of caregiver and protector. This intimacy and reciprocal caregiving was largely absent from the young women's relationships with their fathers, where interaction was characterized most accurately as distant, periodic, and strained. That relationship was essentially nonrelational. Only a few of the female gang members described feelings of affection and warmth toward their fathers.

Other Significant Family Members

Although relationships with parents, stepfathers, and mothers' boyfriends dominated many of our respondents' accounts of their family experiences, they were not the only prominent family relationships in their lives. When both parents were absent from the family home, for whatever reason, parental responsibility fell to the grandparents, specifically to the grandmothers. In three cases, respondents referred to their grandmothers as significant people in their lives. In one of these, although the mother was alive and living with the respondent, the grandmother nevertheless was the primary mother figure. Her death, when the respondent was 14, was particularly difficult for the respondent because as she said, "I didn't really like my mom. My grandmother was like my mom." In the other two cases, because their mothers were absent from the family home,

the grandmothers acted as the real mothers. The grandmother's role as mother had such a lasting effect on one young woman that even when her mother returned home, that event hardly changed the respondent's feelings towards her mother and her grandmother: "With my grandma, it's more mother and daughter . . . but (with) my mom, it's just like sisters."

Significantly, in these three accounts, references to grandfathers are different from references to grandmothers. As in the descriptions of their fathers, the respondents' grandfathers are largely absent from these accounts, with the exception of one homegirl's description of her grandfather's drinking and violence:

> My grandpa had an alcoholic problem while we were young. He used to spank us a lot when he used to get drunk. He'd come home angry, right after drinking at bars. I never remember him hitting [my grandmother], but my aunt told me that he used to hit her when they were young. But when all three of us were there, then he'd come home and get mad at every little thing, and just go off.

Relationships with siblings are also a significant feature in the homegirls' lives. Ninety-five percent of the respondents had grown up with other siblings. Only two respondents were the only children in the family. The young women described their sisters, particularly older ones, as supportive, both in the past and at present. Caregiving featured prominently in sister relationships; like homegirls' relationships with their mothers, it was often reciprocal. Support extended not only from siblings to respondents, but also from respondents to siblings. One respondent, for example, who had a child, had set up a home on her own, and looked after her daughter and her younger sister and brothers. Parenting was not unusual for the homegirls: One respondent described how she had stayed away from school for two years in order to look after her four younger brothers, while her father was working in Washington state and her mother worked in a restaurant.

Homegirls' relationships with brothers seemed much less significant than those with sisters. Brothers, however, were important to the respondents when they described their relationships within the gangs. Other than those instances in which the homegirl acted as surrogate mother, the brothers played a significant role in only two accounts of family relationships, one positive and one negative. In the former case, the respondent described a caring relationship: "[H]e was always there for me and everything. I always looked up to him. Like whenever I needed money or like whenever I needed . . . somebody to talk to, he was always there." In the latter case, the respondent described how she had been sexually abused by her elder brother. The homegirl agreed to his request to remove her clothes because even though she knew it was wrong, she was "used to doing what he said." Fortunately the grandmother discovered them before anything else occurred.

Family disruption was a major reason for running away. The homegirls cited problems with their mothers or stepfathers, or parental drug use. Sixty-three percent had run away from home at least once, some for only a day; others left home for as long as two years, and some left as often as 20 times. Yet the desire to escape family conflict was not the only reason for leaving the family, for whatever length of time. Other reasons included a desire to be independent, the attraction of life outside the family, and (in one case) simply the desire to attend a rave.

A few respondents were adamant that far from running away, they had been "kicked out." As one respondent said wryly,

> My mom tried to report me as a runaway. But I said "No, the bitch kicked me out." So it was like her word against mine. But they had her on file as child-abusing me, 'cause one time she beat me up so badly that I had welts on my legs and I wore shorts to school and the teacher said: "Where'd you get them bruises?" I was like: "Oh! I didn't know I had those." . . . She said "Does your mom hit you?" and I [said] "Yeah, so what?" You know, it was normal.

Even those women who were physically separated from their families described ongoing and caring interaction with them. One 17-year-old respondent, who had left home to live with her homeboys and homegirls, and in spite of feeling estranged from her mother, still telephoned her mother regularly to let her know that she was okay: "I always like to let my mom know where I am at. At least I let her know if I'm doing good and everything, that I'm safe."

The homegirls exhibited a wide range of relationships and feelings towards their parents and other significant family members. The diversity of their accounts underscores the ongoing interaction with family members and the crucial role of family in their lives, even when they lived outside the family unit. At no time in the accounts did we find a sense of separation from ties with the family. Thus, in spite of these periods of conflict and tension, and in some cases even physical separation, the female gang members' relationships with their families continued both inside and outside the gang.

From Family to Gang: Expanding the Family Circle

Despite homegirls' problems with various family members at different times in their lives, they generally viewed their mothers, sisters, and extended kin as a support system. They also found a strong, stable source of emotional and practical support in other gang members. Initially we had assumed that the girls' families and their gang were two distinct and separate associations, but we found that these two seemingly disconnected groups were intimately linked. Far from choosing a sharply different alternative to the family, the homegirls in effect were joining an extension of their families. Homegirls did not relinquish one for the other; they were not thrust into gang membership because of family dysfunction, nor were they necessarily looking for a youth gang to join as a rebellion against their families. Doing so was unwarranted because the gang already was part of their daily lives. Gangs were present in their schools, next door, in the park, on the bus, and, most important, in their families. Many of the homegirls did not formally join a gang; they were already hanging out with their siblings, extended-family members, and other gang members. As one respondent explained, when asked how she came to choose a particular gang,

> Well, I had my cousins that used to live around here, and I used to go over there, and then from there . . . I started meeting all the guys around there. I always wanted to be going over there, and that's how I got into it.

Nearly all (96%) of the respondents had family members who had been in gangs or currently were involved in gangs. For many, growing up in the family was the same as growing up in the gang. Nearly 40 percent of our respondents admitted current or previous gang involvement by either their fathers or their mothers. A similar percentage (nearly 40%) had brothers in a gang, more than one-third had sisters in a gang, and 11 percent had both. Extended-family members were also active in gang activities: 22 of the 47 women had cousins who were involved, as well as 11 with uncles and seven with aunts who were gang members. Moreover, family involvement did not include only single members of the family: 66 percent of our respondents had more than one family member in gangs, and nearly one-fifth of our sample had three or more.

The extension of family into the gang was also evident in our respondents' reasons for belonging to a gang. Eighty percent stated that the primary reason for being a gang member was the sense of "family feeling" that membership gave them. Overall this complex interweaving of family and gang may support the idea, recently suggested by Kandel (1996), that the family/peer dichotomy may be too simplistic for examining accurately the countervailing influences of family and of peers on future adolescent behavior. This is not to suggest that friends were not also important in encouraging our respondents to join a gang. In fact, equal numbers of respondents noted that friends as well as family had influenced their involvement.

Nevertheless, whether family or friends provided the most encouragement, one feature was absolutely clear: Other girls and women were by far the most direct influence when these young women became involved in the gangs. Almost one-third were influenced by girlfriends, either a best friend or a group of friends that they hung out with. Only seven respondents were influenced by male friends; three of these were boyfriends. Three of the young women had sisters and two had brothers who introduced them to the gang. Seven said they had learned about the gangs through their cousins, mostly female cousins. Thus, although friends may have exerted a more immediate effect or influence when these girls began to hang out with other gang members, a web of family influences also operated both inside the family and in their peer groups.

Gang Relations

Many of the characteristics of family life continued in the young women's associations within their gangs. Notions of family, including attachment, pride, loyalty, protection, solidarity, safety, and familiarity, as well as conflict, were replicated in relationships with homeboys and boyfriends, and with other homegirls. Sometimes these relations involved real family members; in other cases, family-like relationships or "fictive kin" relations developed in addition to the family bonds already in place.

Relations With Homeboys/Boyfriends

Whether their homeboys were actual relatives or fictive kin, the girls valued the respect and protection embedded in their relationships with the males; these features sometimes were absent from their relationships with their parents. Respect in the male dominated gang included characteristics such as not letting a fellow gang member down, loyalty, the ability to fight, the ability to protect oneself and others, "backing up your shit," and being prepared to follow through with what you say you will do.

Of these features, a homeboy's street prowess and fighting ability are key attributes. We heard the most glowing accounts in some of the homegirls' descriptions of their older brothers and uncles.

Earlier we noted the predominance of negative accounts of male family members, particularly fathers who were absent or exploitative, or who failed to assume the protective paternal role. By comparison, the respondents' discussions of male family members in the gang were predominantly positive. In these accounts we witness, for the first time, homegirls' consistent expression of admiration for their brothers and uncles, and for their reputations as impressive gang fighters:

> My brother Ernesto is crazy. Ernesto is what I call a warrior 'cause that homeboy has seventeen, eighteen, nineteen stab wounds, and two bullet shots. He's got two facial disfigurements. They shot at his cheekbone . . . and they busted the bridge to his nose all the way down to the jawbone. They had to reconstruct his face.

Later in the interview the respondent described how both of her brothers saved her and her homegirls from being caught in the middle of a major gang fight:

> Me and my girlfriends were walking up on Story Road, it was like a hot August night. We were on foot. . . . Anyway my brother Ernesto, he had seen me and he was yelling from across the street for me to turn around. My brother starts running across the street, and then I remember looking . . . and then my brother Carlos came from behind and he jumped and tackled us to the ground, [saying] "Stay down." Anyway, shit broke down quick, right. . . . Ernesto came up on the ground like a grunt, and he . . . crawls to the back of that building . . . "Don't look back. Don't look back." He said it like that. . . . So we did it. Four of us just stuck together like dogs. We were running through the streets, right, crawling like Ernesto said.

In other cases, brothers and homeboys were admired because they had come to the rescue when the respondents were drunk and could not fend for themselves, or when they were involved in one-sided fights. Some of the respect and admiration given to older male family members in the gang reflects the extent to which age and experience in the gang also provided status, even though the gangs generally had no explicit organizational structure.

Although almost half of the women (45%) claimed that everyone was equal, the protective nature of their relationships with their brothers and homeboys often resulted in too much protection and too many restrictions:

> Some of the older guys try to keep us from doing things, like with the younger guys. 'Cause the younger guys . . . they're like . . . who gives a shit . . . get high or whatever. But the older guys say "Hey, why you giving her that shit, you know, she's gonna get all fucked up." They . . . give us their little lectures and then we're like "Okay, yeah, now go away so I can do what I want to do."

The homeboys' "brotherly" protection, support, and respect were often interspersed with control, especially from older, more protective homeboys. Although none of the respondents acknowledged that the older homeboys were in charge, they regularly described circumstances in which the men told them what to do, ordered them around, or restricted them from participating in certain activities.

Relations With Homegirls

In choosing an existence on the street, homegirls found themselves under the control of homeboys and boyfriends. They used a variety of strategies to avoid being regulated by homeboys, such as disagreeing, agreeing but then ignoring the control, or (as in the following case) waiting until the homeboys were absent before engaging in a taboo activity: "[I]f I were to do any other drug besides weed, I wouldn't do it in front of the guys." They also formed alliances with each other as a way of countering this control and potential regulation. To a large extent, these relationships both reflected and extended the important relations in their families. As we discussed earlier, many of the respondents had cousins and sisters in their gangs. All of these relations, whether created by blood, family or by friendship, were amalgamated into sisterhood. In this process the homegirls created a new family and a new kin group: fictive kin, or kin-in-gang.

Twenty-one of the women claimed that they got together with their homegirls every day. Another 19 said that they met on weekends. When queried about the amount of time they spent with their group, almost one-quarter of the women used the term *twenty-four/seven* (24 hours a day, seven days a week) to describe the extent and strength of their connection. The majority of the respondents said that some contact with their homegirls occurred regularly, and the activities were similar to those among the males: hanging out, going to the mall, walking around, talking, partying, and fighting.

In spite of their attempts to counter homeboys' controls by forming their own connections with their homegirls, the respondents found themselves under another system of control, one imposed and enforced by their own homegirls and implicitly by themselves. A key part of a homegirl's behavior on the street, especially in her relationships with other homegirls, was the notion of *respect*. The image of the tough, independent homegirl on the streets, portrayed increasingly in the media and in popular culture, is one to which many working-class Latinas can relate. In aspiring to live up to this image, these women sought an alternative to their role within the family. In the context of gang membership, the image provided homegirls with an opportunity to achieve respect, a feature they perceived to be relatively rare in their home lives. Forty-two of the 47 respondents had particular ideas about what constituted respect. Within the gang, respect and disrespect are ideological expectations and often are the pivotal base for gang relationships, both positive and negative (Bourgois 1996). Although all the respondents were familiar with the notion, and all knew that they aspired to gain respect, some had difficulty in specifying its components. This is not surprising because respect and the construction of respect within the gang were frequently contradictory and changing.

A number of elements constituted respect. More than one-quarter of the young women said that restraint, especially from excessive drug and alcohol use, was a feature of gaining and maintaining respect. Overindulgence was not respectable behavior. The women were directly responsible for the respect they received. Respect had to be earned and maintained; many women believed that this began with self-respect. As one homegirl remarked,

> Well, it's not how the homeboy is going to treat the homegirl. The homegirls gotta put in their two cents [if] . . . they wanna be respected. They got to respect themselves first. . . . You know, don't be fucked up . . . 'cause that's real bad and shit, 'cause you know girls have different feelings than what guys do. You know, guys can take it. But girls don't take shit like that, they become drug addicts, hoes, and shit, 'cause that brings them down . . . they got to learn how to respect themselves.

To ensure that homegirls maintained respect, the women used a number of different strategies to regulate and control behavior. Gossip, "talking shit," and exclusion were all tools for punishing other women who they felt had stepped out of line. More than one-third of the respondents discussed the power of "talking shit," which one respondent succinctly defined as "putting down my reputation."

Even though these young women spent time on the streets in the pursuit of respect, especially in their relations with their homegirls, they were often disappointed in these relations. As in their real families, where they had high expectations of their mothers and looked up to their sisters, grandmothers, and female cousins, so in their fictive families the respondents expected much more from their homegirls than from their homeboys and boyfriends. They held other homegirls to higher standards than men, and when important women in their lives failed to live up to their expectations, they reacted with surprise, a sense of betrayal, and sometimes even violence. One young woman was placed in juvenile detention for assault and battery on a homegirl who disrespected her by becoming involved with her man:

> It is like I found out she was a banging on my boyfriend. She was supposed to be my friend. And I was like, well, she is my friend. Why is she doing this? . . . And I would be talking to her on the phone, and it is like . . . "What are you doing?" "Oh nothing." And his sister told me . . . "Yeah, the night you were talking on the phone she be kissing on him and everything." She told me everything. And after I found out, I was like to mad. . . . I just started beating on her. And she had like three kids. . . . And my friend put her kids in the other room so they wouldn't see anything. . . . And you know I just started beating on her.

Conclusion

In our analysis we have tried to illuminate the relationships and meaning of family among homegirls. In doing so, we have tried to dispel popular conceptions about the disintegration of contemporary inner-city families of color, and about the pushing of young minority youths onto the streets. Family relationships, particularly homegirls' ties to mothers, sisters, grandmothers, and other extended kin, are based on reciprocal and mutual forms of emotional and practical support. Not surprisingly, we have found, like Decker and Van Winkle (1996), that although homegirls make a heavy investment of time in gang friendships, related activities, and loyalty to the gang, almost all of the women named family members as the most important people or role models in their lives. Of the 33 young women who spoke about the most important people in their lives, 13 mentioned their mothers along with other family members, 12 mentioned their sisters, nine spoke of their fathers, seven mentioned their brothers, and nine made reference to other relatives. Only three referred to either their homegirls or homeboys, and two mentioned their boyfriends.

When they spoke of their mothers and sisters, our respondents often stated that "they're the ones I can count on" and "those are the people who are there for me." As one respondent said forcefully, " . . . Those are the ones that are there for me right now, and if I didn't have them, I wouldn't have nothing." Even those who described the most turbulent and most contentious relations with their mothers mentioned (sometimes very surprisingly) moments of pride and respect. As we saw above, as much as some of the respondents were critical toward their mothers and expressed these criticisms in harsh and derogatory ways, they felt it was legitimate to call on their mothers when they were in need. For the majority of the homegirls, she was there, she could be relied on when necessary, and she would remain "there" during this transitional period in their lives and beyond. As the young women began to mature, they increasingly valued and prized their relationships with their mothers for the quality of caring. This finding is consistent with feminist studies of girls (Taylor et al. 1995).

Many of these women had a fairly elaborate and strong extended-family structure. Many of the other women whom the homegirls admired were to be found in their immediate and extended families and among their homegirls. In their accounts, these two groups were frequently intertwined: Blood sisters, female cousins, and aunts doubled as homegirls and "gang sisters." Such loyalties and bonds call into question the standard and traditional notions about what constitutes family. In the homegirls' formation of their domestic and family units, we may be witnessing a pragmatic process encouraging survival in what may be less than ideal environments and situations.

In looking up to these women, homegirls respected independence over all other characteristics. This is not surprising, given their attempts to seek some life outside the family. In one case, a cousin who was also a homegirl was admired because she was successful at being independent and raising her child on her own despite the lack of support from her father, who had kicked her out of the family home. In another case, a homegirl admired her aunt, also an ex-homegirl, who had become an independent, famous, successful interior designer.

These young women may choose to look up to female family members because of their childhood dependence and reliance on the female support networks in their families. Most of the important relationships in their lives are those with the women in their families and extended kin networks, whether their mothers, sisters, aunts, grandmothers, or cousins. These homegirls' relationships with their mothers were by the far the most significant.

Our respondents discussed these relationships with intensity, and far more intensely than their relations with their fathers. This suggests that they expected much more from their mothers, and consequently from other women, than from their fathers and other males. Although they discussed their relationships with male family members, these men played a much less prominent role in our respondents' accounts. The women expressed much less confidence in the men, who had not been consistently present in their lives. Only six respondents designated their fathers as among the most important people in their lives; six cited their boyfriends. Some observers may interpret these findings as an argument favoring the prevailing view that the dysfunctional family or absentee fathers are key factors in encouraging young women to join gangs. To the homegirls, however, as revealed in their narratives, the gaps are less relevant than the relations that operated.

Although these networks were modified during the respondents' lives, they continued to operate even within the gang. It appears that no sharp disjuncture occurred when these young women began to spend less time in the family home and more time on the streets with the gang. The strong family ties continued when the women became involved in gang activities. The absence of any disjuncture may be due to the abundance of family/gang ties in their lives. If gang ties already existed within the family, whether in the past (for mothers, fathers, uncles, and aunts) or in the present (for brothers, sisters, and cousins), then the movement to joining the gang, whether officially or unofficially, should be viewed as a natural progression for a teenager growing up in a working-class minority neighborhood.

This analysis calls into question current policy discussions about the demise of the "traditional family" and its negative effects on young people. Many of today's policy debates are based on idealistic notions about parenthood, particularly motherhood. As Taylor et al. point out, "the idealization of motherhood finds expression in a sentimental political rhetoric about mothers and children and families that goes hand in hand with a denigration of mothers and motherhood and an economic squeeze on families . . .

mothers in general are held responsible for many of society's ills" (1995: 73–74).

As we and other observers try to emphasize, many of today's popular assumptions about gangs, working-class youths, their families, and their home lives oversimplify and underestimate the salience and the positive dimensions of immediate and extended kinship. Among our respondents, for instance, the domestic unit cannot be equated with the family. Nor can working-class culture continue to be viewed as a male-dominated arena in which women are peripheral members. Women as heads of household and primary providers are a growing trend; many of the homegirls work, as do most of their mothers. Also, although the home may be considered to be a locus of negative forces and stresses for these women, it also has positive qualities and offers support. The same can be said of the streets; this may tell us a great deal about the ease with which these women navigate between these two environments. Moreover, their experiences highlight the extent to which the gang may be an extension of the family rather than a distinct or even an opposing influence. We should not underestimate the salience and flexibility of family relationships, particularly those involving women.

It may be, however, that the prominence of family relations in the accounts of these Latina gang members reflects the importance of family ties in women's lives more generally. Until we examine the importance of family, both for male gang members and for other ethnic groups, we cannot be sure how fully the findings discussed above are applicable to other gang members. In any case, the data from this research call into question the conservatism in public policy attacks on contemporary families, as well as assumptions about the dichotomous nature of the peer-versus-family debate. Certainly our findings highlight several new avenues for contemplating gang issues from a more contemporary perspective, in consideration of the complexity of the environments in which these young women are growing up.

Discussion Questions

1. Compared with the influence of delinquent peers, in what ways does the family affect gang girls?

2. Why do gang girls maintain stronger ties to mothers and other females (e.g., sisters, aunts) than to male family members?

3. Why isn't Latina female gang involvement associated with detachment from family

relations as previous research has documented for some male gang members?

4. What theory would best explain the meaning of family for Latina gang girls?

5. Given strong familial ties among Latina homegirls, why isn't the family playing a greater role in decreasing female gang involvement?

References

Apter, T. 1993. "Altered Views: Fathers' Closeness to Teenage Daughters." Pp. 163–90 in *The Narrative Study of Lives*, vol. 1, edited by R. Josselson and A. Lieblich. London: Sage.

Bean, F. D., L. Russell, and J. P. Marcum. 1977. "Familism and Marital Satisfaction among Mexican Americans: The Effects of Family Size, Wife's Labor Force Participation, and Conjugal Power." *Journal of Marriage and the Family* 39: 759–67.

Biernacki, P. and D. Waldorf. 1981. "Snowball Sampling." *Sociological Methods Research* 10: 141–63.

Bottcher, J. 1995. "Gender as Social Control: A Qualitative Study of Incarcerated Youths and Their Siblings." *Justice Quarterly* 12: 33–57.

Bourgois, P. 1996. *In Search of Respect: Selling Crack in El Barrio*. Cambridge, UK: Cambridge University Press.

Bowker, L. R. and M. W. Klein. 1983. "The Etiology of Female Juvenile Delinquency and Gang Membership: A Test of Psychological and Social Structural Explanations." *Adolescence* 18: 739–51.

Brotherton, D. C. 1996. "'Smartness,' 'Toughness,' and 'Autonomy': Drug Use in the Context of Gang Female Delinquency." *Journal of Drug Issues* 26 (1): 61–77.

Brown, W. K. 1977. "Black Female Gangs in Philadelphia." *International Journal of Offender Therapy and Comparative Criminology* 21 (3): 221–28.

Burbank, V. K. 1994. *Fighting Women: Anger and Aggression in Aboriginal Australia*. Berkeley: University of California Press.

Campbell, A. 1984. *The Girls in the Gang*. New Brunswick: Rutgers University Press.

——. 1986. "Self-Report of Fighting by Females." *British Journal of Criminology* 26: 28–46.

——. 1991. *The Girls in the Gang*. 2nd ed. Cambridge, MA: Basil Blackwell.

Cauce, A. M., Y. Hiraga, D. Graves, N. Gonzales, K. R. Finn, and K. Grove. 1996. "African American Mothers and Their Adolescent Daughters: Closeness, Conflict and Control." Pp. 100–16 in *Urban Girls: Resisting Stereotypes, Creating Identities*, edited by B. Leadbeater and N. Way. New York: New York University Press.

Chesney-Lind, M. 1993. "Girls, Gangs and Violence: Anatomy of a Backlash." *Humanity and Society* 17: 321–44.

——. 1997. *The Female Offender: Girls, Women, and Crime*. Thousand Oaks, CA: Sage.

Chodorow, N. 1978. *The Reproduction of Mothering*. Berkeley: University of California Press.

Curry, G. D., R. A. Ball, and R. J. Fox. 1994. *Gang Crime and Law Enforcement Record Keeping*. Washington, DC: National Institute of Justice.

Decker, S. H. and B. Van Winkle. 1996. *Life in the Gang: Family Friends and Violence*. Cambridge, UK: Cambridge University Press.

Dunlap, E. 1992. "Impact of Drugs on Family Life and Kin Networks in the Inner City African American Single Mother Household." Pp. 181–207 in *Drugs, Crime, and Social Isolation*, edited by A. Harrell and G. Peterson. Washington, DC: Urban Institute Press.

Esbensen, F. A. and D. Huizinga. 1993. "Gangs, Drugs, and Delinquency in a Survey of Urban Youth." *Criminology* 31: 565–89.

Fagan, J. 1990. "Social Processes of Delinquency and Drug Use among Urban Gangs." Pp. 183–222 in *Gangs in America*, edited by C. R Huff. London: Sage.

Federal Bureau of Investigation (FBI). 1995. *Crime in the United States—1994*. Washington, DC: U.S. Department of Justice.

——. 1996. *Crime in the United States—1995*. Washington, DC: U.S. Department of Justice.

Fishman, L. 1988. *The Vice Queens: An Ethnographic Study of Black Female Gang Behavior*. Burlington, VT: University of Vermont.

Fleisher, M. S. 1998. *Dead End Kids: Gang Girls and the Boys They Know*. Madison: University of Wisconsin Press.

Harris, M. 1988. *Cholas: Latino Girls and Gangs*. New York: AMS Press.

Herrnstein, R. J. and C. Murray. 1994. *The Bell Curve*. New York: Free Press.

Hirschi, T. 1969. *Causes of Delinquency*. Berkeley: University of California Press.

Horowitz, R. 1983. *Honor and the American Dream: Culture and Identity in a Chicano Community*. New Brunswick: Rutgers University Press.

Joe, K. 1991. "Milk Carton Madness: The Heart of the Missing Children's Crisis." Doctoral dissertation, University of California, Davis.

Joe, K. and M. Chesney-Lind. 1995. "Just Every Mother's Angel: An Analysis of Gender and Ethnic Variations in Youth Gang Membership." *Gender and Society* 9: 408–31.

Joe-Laidler, K. 1997. "The Life and Times of Asian American Women Drug Users: An Ethnographic Study." *Journal of Drug Issues* 26 (1): 199–218.

Joe-Laidler, K. and G. Hunt. 1997. "Violence and Social Organization in Female Gangs." *Social Justice* 24 (4): 148–69.

Kandel, D. B. 1996. "The Parental and Peer Contexts of Adolescent Deviance: An Algebra of Interpersonal Influences." *Journal of Drug Issues* 26: 289–315.

Kennedy, L. W. and S. Baron. 1993. "Routine Activities and a Subculture of Violence: A Study of Violence on the Street." *Journal of Research in Crime and Delinquency* 30: 88–112.

Klein, M. W. 1995. *The American Street Gang: Its Nature, Prevalence, and Control.* New York: Oxford University Press.

Martin, E. and J. Martin. 1978. *The Black Extended Family.* Chicago: University of Chicago Press.

McRobbie, A. and J. Garber. 1976. "Girls and Subcultures: An Exploration." Pp. 209–22 in *Resistance through Rituals,* edited by S. Hall and T. Jefferson. London: Hutchinson.

Messerschmidt, J. W. 1997. *Crime as Structured Action: Gender, Race, Class, and Crime in the Making.* Thousand Oaks, CA: Sage.

Moore, J. 1990. "Gangs, Drugs, and Violence." Pp. 160–76 in *Drugs and Violence: Causes, Correlates, and Consequences,* edited by M. D. L. Rosa, E. Lambert, and B. Gropper. Washington, DC: U.S. Government Printing Office.

——. 1991. *Going Down to the Barrio: Homeboys and Homegirls in Change.* Philadelphia: Temple University Press.

Moore, J. and J. Hagedorn. 1996. "What Happens to Girls in the Gang?" Pp. 205–18 in *Gangs in America,* edited by C. R. Huff. Thousand Oaks, CA: Sage.

Murray, C. 1984. *Losing Ground: American Social Policy 1950–1980.* New York: Basic Books.

Nava, M. 1984. "Youth Service Provision, Social Order and the Question of Girls." Pp. 1–30 in *Gender and Generation,* edited by A. McRobbie and M. Nava. London: Macmillan.

Padilla, F. M. 1992. *The Gang as an American Enterprise.* New Brunswick, NJ: Rutgers University Press.

Platt, A. 1969. *The Child Savers.* Chicago: University of Chicago Press.

Quicker, J. C. 1983. *Homegirls: Characterizing Chicana Gangs.* Los Angeles: International University Press.

Stack, C. 1974. *All Our Kin: Strategies for Survival in a Black Community.* New York: Harper and Row.

Sutton, J. 1988. *Stubborn Children: Controlling Delinquency in the U.S., 1640–1981.* Berkeley: University of California Press.

Taylor, J. M. 1996. "Cultural Stories: Latina and Portuguese Daughters and Mothers." Pp. 117–31 in *Urban Girls: Resisting Stereotypes, Creating Identities,* edited by B. Leadbeater and N. Way. New York: New York University Press.

Taylor, J. M., C. Gilligan, and A. Sullivan. 1995. *Between Voice and Silence: Women, Girls, Race, and Relationship.* Cambridge, MA: Harvard University Press.

Vigil, J. D. 1988. *Barrio Gangs: Street Life and Identity in Southern California.* Austin: University of Texas Press.

Way, N. and H. Stauber. 1996. "Are 'Absent Fathers' Really Absent? Urban Adolescent Girls Speak Out about Their Fathers." Pp. 132–48 in *Urban Girls: Resisting Stereotypes, Creating Identities,* edited by B. Leadbeater and N. Way. New York: New York University Press.

Wilson, M. 1989. "Child Development in the Context of the Black Extended Family." *American Psychologist* 44: 380–85.

Yanagisako, S. J. 1977. "Women-Centered Kin Networks in Urban Bilateral Kinship." *American Ethnologist* 4: 207–26.

Youniss, J. and J. Smollar. 1985. *Adolescent Relations with Mothers, Fathers, and Friends.* Chicago: University of Chicago Press.

Zavella, P. 1987. *Women's Work and Chicano Families: Cannery Workers of the Santa Clara Valley.* Ithaca: Cornell University Press.

6

The Lives and Times of Asian-Pacific American Women Methamphetamine Users

Karen A. Joe-Laidler

Although Asian-Pacific Americans have a long history in American society and represent the fastest growing minority group, they remain a relatively "unknown" and "obscure" population. In particular, while ethnic myths about Asian women continue to persist, ranging from the erotic Oriental beauty to the evil dragon lady to the obedient wife and mother, the complexities of the lives of Asian-Pacific American women remain a mystery. Such myths create a number of barriers to understanding the problems of their everyday life, including coping and stress, financial worries, family conflict, and drug use. This article is the first ethnographic account of Asian-Pacific American women drug users, and it specifically explores their onset and patterns of drug use and coping strategies in relation to the competing cultural claims on their lives.

The data are drawn from a cross-cultural community-based study of moderate-to-heavy methamphetamine users in Honolulu, San Francisco, and San Diego. These three sites were selected because each one was associated with the highest usage and problems in the United States. Also, the predominant mode of use differed in each of the sites. Whereas San Francisco had a significant rate of intravenous use, San Diego had a high rate of nasal methamphetamine use. By contrast, Honolulu users primarily smoked ice. Interviews were conducted with 150 active users in each site. This analysis is based only on data from the Honolulu interviews with 37 women of Asian-Pacific American ethnicity.

During the latter part of the 1800s, Asians represented a small proportion of the nation's immigrant population. Chinese, Japanese, Filipinos, and Asian Indians were the primary Asian ethnic groups moving to the United States (Chen 1991). A common misconception of the times, fueled by racism, was that "the Orientals" (in particular, the Chinese) presented a threat to Americans because of their cultural differences and their alleged addiction to opium. Ethnic myths emerged with Asian men being portrayed as the "inscrutable Fu Manchu" and the "opium loving Oriental" (Sante 1991). The "Oriental woman" brought other dangers as well; she was the promiscuous and erotic creature who could turn into the evil Dragon Lady or the submissive China Doll (Tong 1994).

Since the passage of the 1965 United States immigration law reforms, Asian-Pacific Americans have become the most diverse minority population in the United States. At least 32 different Asian-Pacific American ethnic groups now reside in the United States. Asians are also the fastest growing group with an increase of 5 million during the last 20 years (Chen 1991). In 1990, the Asian population climbed to 7.3 million, and by 2020, is expected to reach 20 million (*Honolulu Advertiser* 1993). With the complexity and diversity of Asian-Pacific Americans across ethnic origins, cultures, languages, regional dialects, socioeconomic levels, and historical waves of immigration—they have been cast in a number of contradictory roles. While many of the historical depictions of the "mysterious Oriental gangster" and the "erotic Asian femme fatale" continue to persist, contemporary portrayals of Asians, paradoxically, also cast them as the diligent, hardworking and obedient "role model minority." In this latter scenario, they are typically described as a population with few social problems, especially crime and illicit drug use.

As a result of such stereotypes, Asian-Pacific Americans' drug-use problems are often neglected in research studies (Joe 1993; Kuramoto 1994; Austin et al. 1989). As recently noted by Zane and Sasao (1992), there is a critical need for empirical information on the substance use issues of this diverse minority group. A number of studies (Chi et al. 1989; Kitano and Chi 1985, 1986; Johnson et al. 1987) on drinking patterns among Asian-Pacific Americans have made important inroads into alcohol research, discrediting popular stereotypes about the nondrinking Asian-Pacific American and underscoring the variations in the cultural values toward alcohol consumption among different Asian ethnic groups. Drug research on

Asian-Pacific users, however, has not made similar progress. The paucity of information on drug use among this "hidden population," especially Asian-Pacific American women, has created barriers to moving beyond existing stereotypes and has hampered the formulation of a theoretical foundation (Zane n.d.; Sue 1987) and the development of culturally relevant and effective treatment programs.

This paper challenges the persistent stereotype of the passive yet exotic Asian-Pacific American woman, and is concerned with uncovering the complexities of the lives of a group of women drug users and their strategies for coping with and managing their problems. I first consider existing drug-use studies on Asian-Pacific American populations and offer a path to building a theoretical foundation for understanding their use patterns and problems. Essentially, the combined use of ethnographic data and the grounded theory approach provide an important methodological and theoretical vehicle for uncovering the hidden dimensions of use among hard-to-reach populations such as Asian-Pacific Americans. I then turn to examine the ways in which the cultural claims in their lives interact with and shape their initiation into and continued use of illicit substances based on an ethnography of female methamphetamine users in Hawaii.

Research on Drug Use Among Asian-Pacific Americans

The small number of studies on drug use among Asian-Pacific Americans have primarily involved survey research with household and student populations (Sue et al. 1979; Newcomb et al. 1987; Trimble et al. 1987; Skager et al. 1989). According to these studies, Asian-Pacific Americans report less drug use than non Asian-Pacific Americans, however, a number of methodological problems make it difficult to access the prevalence and the factors associated with use among different Asian ethnic groups. As Zane and Sasao (1992) point out, these studies typically have had relatively small sample sizes, represent student-age populations, and more acculturated groups like Chinese and Japanese. Absent from most of these studies are those who are at high risk such as immigrants, refugees, and the economically marginalized. Treatment-based studies have not clarified prevalence issues as they also tend to have relatively small samples, lump different Asian ethnic groups together, and reflect the experience of those who have been able to access services (Zane and Sasao 1992; Kuramoto

1994). Treatment staff indicate that language differences, lack of awareness of services and social resources, and cultural beliefs (e.g., shame, guilt) account for low utilization rates (Joe 1990).

In addition to problems of estimating prevalence rates among Asian-Pacific American populations, very little is known about the social-cultural factors associated with their use patterns. In this regard, alcohol research and mental health studies on Asian-Pacific Americans indicate that stressful life events such as competing cultural demands and obligations, economic marginality, and family and kinship networks are critical factors to consider in understanding drug use patterns.

The family and extended kinship networks among Asian-Pacific Americans are particularly important to investigate as two diametrically opposing patterns have been identified as being related to health and social problems. On the one hand, the family—its ties, loyalties, cultural expectations, and beliefs—can serve as a significant source of stress as the individual tries to develop a sense of autonomy, often in an extended multigenerational household, and, in turn, contribute to deviance and health-related problems (Hunt et al. 1995; Loo 1991). On the other hand, the demands, values, and structure of Asian-Pacific American families can have a preventive effect (Zane and Sasao 1992).

Clearly, the few existing survey research studies on Asian-Pacific Americans are an important first step to ascertaining drug use patterns and problems. However the "close-ended" nature of the social survey approach limits the depth of our understanding of how the family may foster or hamper drug use. In this approach, assumptions must be made about how the family is structured and operates, and respondents' experiences are neatly fitted into preconstructed categories. As Zane and Sasao (1992) note, many substance abuse studies on Asian-Pacific Americans have not taken into account cultural and generational differences.

By contrast, a qualitative approach offers an invaluable method for uncovering and fully exploring the distinct experiences and problems associated with drug use among hidden populations like Asian-Pacific Americans. The multiple methodologies of qualitative research are intended to provide an in-depth understanding of social phenomen[a] guided by a commitment to the naturalistic, interpretive perspective (Denzin and Lincoln 1994). As such, theory building begins by describing the world from the individual's viewpoint and examining the constraints of everyday life (Denzin and Lincoln 1994.) In this way, the analyst navigates through culture from the individual's place of reference rather than prematurely demarcate "what is relevant" from "what is not" as is required in close-ended survey questionnaires.

The ethnographic approach and its dialectical process of data gathering and analysis (Agar 1993) have been instrumental in moving beyond the stereotypical views of the "double deviance status" of women substance abusers and in "unpacking" the ways in which cultural norms of gender affect the everyday life of women and their drug use. Rosenbaum's (1981) landmark ethnography of women heroin users revealed the gendered constraints and the "narrowing of options" they experience with prolonged use. Recent ethnographies of the sex-for-crack exchange have dispelled the demonized portrayals of women crack users and uncovered the patriarchally driven subordination of women into the "secondary 'secondary labor market'" of the informal drug economy (Maher and Curtis 1992: 225; see also Bourgois and Dunlap 1993).

As demonstrated below, the ethnographic approach is crucial to dispelling the passive and erotic stereotypes of Asian-Pacific American women and to breaking away from preconceived notions of the Asian-Pacific American family structure. Through in-depth interviewing and field observations, it was possible to uncover the complex ways in which different Asian ethnic family systems foster or hamper initial and continued use of drugs among women.

The Ice and Other Methamphetamine[s] Study

Health and law enforcement authorities grew increasingly concerned in the mid-to-late 1980s over the emergence of ice and other forms of methamphetamine. Many believed that ice, a smokable form of methamphetamine, had already reached "epidemic" proportions in Hawaii, and would become the drug of the 1990s (*San Francisco Chronicle* 1989; *Newsweek* 1989; Miller and Tomas 1989). Hospital and emergency room reports indicated that this central nervous system stimulant had a highly addictive quality within a short period of use, and was also connected with several physical and psychological problems, including insomnia, hypertension, emaciation, irritability, and depression. Aside from the limited information available from clinical and treatment populations, little was known about the demographic, social, and cultural attributes of methamphetamine users. Clinical staff in Hawaii reported that the state's diverse ethnic population, including its

Asian-Pacific American populations were using ice. Moreover, they observed growing numbers of young women and housewives using ice as a diet suppressant (Miller 1991).

Asian-Pacific American Women Ice Users and Their Family Ties

Who Are They?

Our female respondents represent the ethnic diversity of Hawaii. The majority of the sample, however, identified as Hawaiian (54%) and Filipina (30%). The Hawaiian, the Portuguese, and to a slightly lesser extent, the Filipino women were of mixed ethnicity; this reflects the complexity of ethnicity in the state. Nearly all of the women were born in the United States, usually Hawaii, and only two of the Filipinas immigrated to the United States during early childhood. The Samoan and a few of the Filipinas report that their parents were immigrants.

Overall, the women's median age was 27 years. Over one-half of the women (57%) had never been married, but had at least one child (60%). Among those women with children, 68% of them were living with their offspring.

Overall, 40% had obtained a high-school diploma and another 30 had dropped out prior to completing the 12th grade. Because the state's major industry is tourism, the most readily accessible job opportunities are in the service sector, particularly in the hotel, restaurant, retail, and construction businesses. Overall, 38% of the women supported themselves during the last year through a job, and most of them worked in retail or clerical positions (19%). Others principally supported themselves through government assistance (30%), their family (22%), or illegal activities (11%). The majority of the women (54%) were living in poverty, with a yearly income of $10,000 or less.

Growing Up in Chaos

Several themes emerged from the qualitative interviews which underscore the strained interplay between economic marginality, and the cultural traditions and norms of Asian-Pacific American families. Many of our female respondents grew up, in various degrees, in an extended family network, known locally as the ohana system (Joe 1995). Ohana derives from Hawaiian culture, and historically referred to the family clan and its strong sense of solidarity, shared involvement, and interdependence. This kinship system has changed over the decades as Hawaii's culture has come to reflect the blending of its various Asian and Pacific Islander populations and their cultures. In contemporary Hawaii, ohana has retained the traits of cooperation and unity, but extends to persons who are not necessarily blood-related, but closely connected to the family and considered part of the social support system (Handy et al. 1972; Pukui et al. 1972).

In Hawaii, today, where the cost of living is among the highest in the United States, this extended family arrangement acquires new meaning in the Western economic context. The extended family system offers financially strapped families a readily accessible and stable source of help and relief. Over 70% of all the women in this study came from working and lower working-class families where their fathers, when employed, worked principally in skilled and unskilled labor intensive jobs. Seventy percent of their mothers worked in similar occupations. Overall, 18% of the women reported that they had lived principally with other relatives—grandparents, aunties, uncles, cousins—until adulthood. One-fourth of the Hawaiian women indicated that they had grown up primarily with relatives. Our respondents' life histories, however, suggest a more complex pattern whereby many lived between households, shifting constantly from various relatives to their parents.

The ohana system acts not only as a resource for economically strained families, but also as a source of relief for heated conflicts within the family. With only a few exceptions, women described growing up in tension-filled households. While the ohana system provides relief, it can also introduce intergenerational gaps.

Mary is a 23-year-old Chinese-Hawaiian woman who is the fourth child of six. Her mother has been married three times, and her children are from different marriages. Mary never knew her father. Mary's older sister was sent to stay with their rich aunt, and as Mary angrily reflects, "the spoiled brat grew up in another lifestyle." By comparison, Mary and her younger brothers lived with their grandmother in the early childhood years. While Mary contends that she was sent to live with her grandmother to "take care of her and to help her with the house and cook," in light of her young age, it is more probable that her mother relied on her own mother to help care for two of her children while she worked and tried to look after the other children and a physically abusive husband who suffered from severe diabetes. Mary returned to her mother's home in her teen years to help her mother take care of her diabetic stepfather. She describes her childhood as "difficult" and adds, "when I was growing up, I never had

anybody to talk to. Just grandma, and you know how that goes." [446]

Part of the tension in the family was due to financial worries, but also to the presence of alcohol and other drug use by one or both parents.

Several studies report a high incidence of family problems among female substance users including parental alcohol and drug abuse and domestic violence (see Inciardi et al. 1993; Ettorre 1992). Overall, 84% of the women indicate that at least one of their parents drank alcohol. Nearly half of the parents used marijuana, and over one-third of them used cocaine. Alcohol appeared to be the most problematic. Forty percent of the women report that their parents had problems with alcohol. The proportion very likely is higher as many more attempted to normalize their parents' level of alcohol use and problems when describing their life histories.

Joanne, a 44-year-old homeless Hawaiian Filipina, states that her father consumed several cases of beer on the weekends, but was only a "recreational drinker" because he "never missed work due to his drinking" and, most importantly, provided for his family. She had her first drink at 22 years of age when her father became seriously ill and died, and, "for the next ten years stayed in an unconscious drunken state by noontime everyday." [551]

Lani is an 18-year-old Filipina, and lives with her parents and siblings. Her parents and her older sister immigrated to the United States, and she and her younger brother were born in Hawaii. She hints that her father drinks too much, but has been a very "good provider" for the family. She attributes the constant fighting between her parents as well as with her to herself rather than to any problems the father might be having with alcohol. She believes that the strain at home is due to her parents' perceptions of her as being "too Americanized," "uncontrollable." When the conflict flares at home, she seeks refuge at her aunt's house, where, she says, "they understand me." [463]

Parental alcohol or drug use was typically connected with violence. More than 40% of the females describe their home life as violent. In some cases, the intensity of the violence was extreme as Susan, a 19-year-old Hawaiian woman, recalls her "unhappy" childhood.

From about five years old, Susan remembers that her father would routinely beat up her mother to the point where she would be unable to walk. Subsequently her father would come looking for her or her mother would take out her own anger and hostility by beating on Susan and her siblings. Both parents were heavily involved in drugs, and her father was a dealer. She describes having a loose family structure as her father had several children by other women.

While growing up, she was exposed to many "adult" situations including drug deals and hanging out in bars. Her father was sent to prison for hanging a man on a fence and beating him to death while drunk. At 14, an unknown teenage male raped her at a family function. She tried to isolate herself, but when her mother learned of the incident, punished her for "promiscuity" by repeatedly hitting her on the head and sending her to a group home for troublesome teenagers. [462]

In some cases, the violence was expressed through sexual assault.

Jacky is 20 years old, and of Hawaiian, Korean, and Filipino ancestry. She has one older brother who she has not seen since she was six when they were both placed in foster care. Her mother died when she was five. She and her brother lived with the step-father who was an "abusive drinker" and sexually molested them repeatedly. This went on for one year at which point, six-year-old Jacky stabbed her stepfather for sexually abusing them. Although she does not have a clear recollection of the stabbing incident, she does remember having her arm broken by her step-father while he was trying to sexually assault her. [537]

Another important dimension of the family centers around the cultural expectations of Asian-Pacific American women. This was clearly felt by women who were living in chaotic family situations as well as those few who described their family life as "normal." In traditional Samoan families, gender relations are organized around Polynesian traditions of male dominance, separation, and obligation (Joe and Chesney Lind 1995). While Hawaiian customs were similar to the Polynesian model of separation, this was severely altered with the death of Kamehamehakunuiakea in 1819, and subsequent arrival of the missionaries (Nunes and Whitney 1994). Although the Hawaiian system retains some male domination features, it is the women who have "learned the ways of the malihini (strangers). Women adjusted to and became clever at cultural and economic transactions with the new world" (Nunes and Whitney 1994: 60). At the same time, however, Hawaiians, who are the most marginalized group in the state, have accommodated to poverty through normalizing early motherhood, high dropout rates, and welfare dependency for girls (Joe and Chesney Lind 1995). In modern Filipino families, girls and women have been socialized according to colonial cultural and religious, usually Catholic, norms that emphasize the secondary status of women, girl's responsibility to their families, and the control of female sexual experimentation (Aquino 1994).

Cultural expectations about "being a good girl" combined with economic marginality and heavy parental alcohol consumption erupts into violence. Helen, a 38-year-old Filipino, Hawaiian, Portuguese woman, recalls her childhood years:

> I come from a family of six children and I'm the fourth. We are all scattered. One brother is in prison and one passed away. When we was growing up we lived with both my parents. They stayed married until my dad passed away. Home was very strict. My dad was an alcoholic so he couldn't hold a job. He always had a strict hand on us. Discipline kind. He was either drunk or coming down from a hangover when he hit us. My mom was the one that went to work. Beatings were all the time from my dad. Severe kind with belt buckles.
>
> The last time my dad hit me was when I was 17 years old. He found out that I was smoking cigarettes. I was almost 18. My youngest brother was able to drink with him, smoke cigarettes, and pot with him! But not me. The boys could do what they wanted. My mom wasn't the one to discipline us. She really had no say in it. [449]

Coping Strategies in Managing Family Chaos

The women's first response is to endure the turmoil in their families. Given the extended kinship network, some women stayed with relatives when the situation at home became unbearable. As Whitney (1986) points out, local cultural norms stress that "outsiders" not be brought into family problems, and children's respect for their elders should be shown through deference. In his clinical work with young adult Asian-Pacific American male alcoholics, those who were physically abused tended to retreat temporarily to a relative's house and were unable to negatively evaluate their parents' abusive behavior (Whitney 1986).

The majority of women, however, eventually, could no longer endure the chaos and family violence and sought refuge in one of two ways. Approximately one-half of them believed that the best strategy for dealing with the violence in their own home was by starting their own family and became pregnant in their teen years.

Marty, a 34-year-old Hawaiian-Chinese woman, describes the process:

> . . . my father got sick, mom had to go on welfare. Things started not working out for the family. My parents was fighting, my father used to give my mother lickings every time and put us down. They were strict. We pretty much rely on each other [the siblings].
>
> I never did get along with my dad. I don't know why. I've always tried, cleaning up, never had to be told what to do, I took care of my sisters and brothers. Cleaned the house, cook, did all kinds of house chores, but my father couldn't stand me. . . . I couldn't take it anymore, so I got about to the seventh grade, that's when I met my husband. I wanted to get married but I couldn't. So I got pregnant, my first daughter, about a year after that, I quit school already. I came home, I told my mom I wanted to get married. So she gave me consent. My father, never. So I forged his name . . . I was 15 years old. Stayed with my husband and never went back home. Only went back home once in awhile to give my mom money and see how she doing. [411]

Other women took a different path and escaped the violence by running away, living periodically with friends, relatives, or on the streets, and sometimes turning to prostitution for survival.

> Linda is 28 years old and of Hawaiian Caucasian ancestry. Her parents divorced after her birth, and she has never known her mother. She and her sister were raised principally by her grandmother. Her father raped her and her sister, in addition to constantly beating them. The sexual abuse started when she was nine and continued until she ran at 12 years of age by "hopping on a bus to Waikiki" and getting lost. She had been in and out of foster homes and on the streets, but this break was permanent. She hooked up with a girl in her 20s. "I watched her, she was a prostitute. I asked her how to do that cause she had a lot of money. She taught me the ropes and I went for it. I made my money and stayed away from home. I lived out of hotel rooms." [510]

The problems these women confronted, usually from an early age—poverty, gendered expectations and obligations, parental alcohol and illicit drug use, violence, living on the streets—underscore the complexities of Asian-Pacific American families, and raise questions about their initiation into drug use, especially ice.

Initiation Into Drug Use

The majority of women have used alcohol, tobacco, marijuana, cocaine, and crack. Over one-half of them reported regular use of tobacco, alcohol and marijuana. Many of them report experimentation with psychedelics (46%) and speed pills (54%), but few used these substances regularly. [Fewer] than 30% of them have tried PCP, quaaludes, or tranquilizers, and even fewer women have used ecstasy, opiates, heroin, and inhalants.

According to their life histories, the most common pattern in their initiation started with alcohol, tobacco, marijuana, cocaine, and then went into ice. Initial use of crack varied, with some women moving back and forth from ice to crack depending on availability. Their peer groups from school and the neighborhood, and/or family members usually introduced them to alcohol, tobacco, and marijuana during their early teen years. In some cases, the family member was a parent, usually the father, or an uncle. Evie, a 27-year-old Chinese woman, remembers the setting when she began smoking marijuana:

> When I was 11. Yeah, my first hit. My first joint. He [father] rolled a joint. Back then, they used to have those little rolling machines and my dad would have ounces of weed in his freezer. So we'd sit there eating ice cream and rolling joints and making bags. Then the boys would come over, hang out. My dad was, he was hanging out, was involved in underground entertainment so he knew all of the entertainers, all the promoters, artists, drug dealers, he always had hip parties. [401]

Women continue to use alcohol, tobacco, and marijuana with their peers and family members. Eventually they are introduced to cocaine, but by this point, the family member is usually a sibling, cousin, or other relative. As indicated earlier, many have tried to leave home for short- and long-term relief from the family chaos. One 32-year-old Hawaiian-Chinese woman recalls her route into alcohol and illicit drugs, which paralleled the accounts described by other female respondents:

> Our next door neighbor was this mother who had seven kids. My two brothers were going with their two sisters. I was 13 at the time I started drinking. . . . Pakololo [marijuana] I don't remember. . . . My girlfriend asked me if I ever tried acid before. I said no. My sister was already taking it. . . .
>
> I was 16 when I graduated. That's because I graduated a year early. When I was 17, I moved with my uncle because he was run-

ning this condominiums so I was like a maid. I was making $7 an hour! My cousin was a mason there. He was like maintenance on the grounds. That's when I first, I didn't know to, what to feel. We went into this place where my aunt and uncle would let us kick back in. He asked me if I wanted to try it [cocaine] . . . I had a lot of friends that had coke or I'd be in the house and they'd be weighing their coke and I didn't want to do it. . . . He gave me a line and told me to stick the straw in the nose and he showed me. He did one first and told me to just do that. I did it and we went back into my uncle's place . . . I panicked and said I'll never do this shit again. And I didn't not until later. Later I was doing a lot, lines, mega lines. [405]

The majority of women (62%) were first introduced to ice from 1988 to 1992. While nearly all of the Filipinas started during this period (82%), 45% of the Hawaiian women tried ice earlier, between 1984 and 1987. Given the broadening of their social networks from the use of other drugs, there were several sources by which women first encountered ice. Approximately 46% of the women first tried ice with a small group of their girlfriends. Another 16% were introduced to ice by a relative, typically a cousin or sister-in-law. The combination of curiosity and camaraderie with and trust of a relative or their girlfriends were often the reason for trying ice.

As other studies have shown, male dealers and partners are also a significant group in introducing women to various illicit drugs (Morningstar and Chitwood 1987; Anglin et al. 1987; File 1976). Several of the younger women indicated that male dealers mediated their first encounter with ice. Like this 23-year-old Hawaiian Cacausian woman states, our female respondents were well aware that dealers usually had other motives than just increased sales.

My girlfriend was using and she introduced me to a man who introduced her to ice. My first experience with it was good. The guy was attracted to me and the more he gave me, the more he thought I'd be nice to him. We were at his house. The year was about 1987. [516]

Thirty-eight percent of the Asian-Pacific American women first tried ice with their partner or spouse, and the experience often was associated with enhancing sex.

That was my 23rd birthday. I wanted to go out and drink and come home and make love. I didn't want to stay home. He went to the store, bought drinks, came home and we had some drinks before we went out to a

show. I got drunk, I was so ripped. . . . We came home and he said, "Here's the pipe, just inhale!" I had five big hits. . . . I was wide-eyed and ready. We smoked some more . . . we watched t.v. and hung for a while. Then we fucked for hours! [laughs] [446]

With continued use, however, our respondents' relationships to their partners, families, and friends begin to change.

Continuing Use and Family Ties

After the introduction to ice, most of the women began using regularly. Overall, the median number of grams used per month was 3.5. Filipinas tended to use slightly more ice than Hawaiian women, reporting a median of 4 grams per month. The median number days of using ice in an average month was 15.6. Their longest period of use without sleeping was a median of 6 days. Filipinas reported a slightly longer binging episode compared to the other women, with a median of 6.9 days.

Women first rationalize their regular use of ice in very gendered ways (Joe 1995). The appetite suppressant quality of the drug allows them to keep thin, and in turn, provides them with self-confidence. Also, the long-lasting speedy energy associated with ice allows them to clean up after their children and partners, and to transcend and enjoy the mundane tasks of domestic chores.

There were a number of ways in which they would obtain their supply, and this would vary depending on their existing financial situation. While approximately one-third principally bought their supplies, 46% received it free by "hanging around the dealers" or by running an array of errands for their supplier who was sometimes a relative:

I started buying from one of my cousins. I used to always burn myself cause I was trying to learn how the hell to do this thing without wasting 'em. My cousin used to see me do that so she taught me. . . . I caught on that night! That's when I really felt good! I was up all night long till the next day. . . . I stayed with her for three months. They were big time dealers. They was selling big quantities. I help her clean up the house, a big big house. My auntie's house because I would help her clean and cook, she always used to give me free stash. . . . Right now, the only one supply me is my husband [who does not use]. Then check in one hotel. . . . [411]

With prolonged use, however, they become increasingly isolated from others—their children, partners, friends, and families. When this occurs, ice becomes medicinal.

Their isolation, sometimes periodic, stems from several sources. First, they are growing increasingly irritable with long episodes of limited or no sleep and food. Over half of them have experienced anxiety, depression, hallucinations, and paranoia. Many respondents spoke of periods of paranoia. The paranoia usually involved their being watched and followed by the police and by other users wanting to steal their stash, and consequently, they tried to limit their interaction with others. Second, nearly all of them report weight loss (89%). Some have grown emaciated and exhibit facial sores from tweaking and dehydration.

As such, they try to limit contact with their family and friends, hoping that they will not see their deterioration. Third, if the partner is also using ice, they are both becoming more irritable as a result of lack of sleep and food, and money problems. The partner's irritability often is expressed through domestic violence (Joe 1995).

Although many of these women have become isolated and have a strained relationship with their family, because of the ohana family system and its traditions, they rely on various relatives—immediate family members as well as extended kin—to manage their everyday life. This includes financial support, temporary shelter for themselves, but especially the shelter and care of their own children. While this extended kinship system provides them with a stable resource, it has the paradoxical consequence of enabling their use, intensifying dependency and further aggravating family tensions.

> Stephanie is a 35-year-old Hawaiian Irish woman. While growing up, she recalls that her parents, both alcoholics, began physically beating her at five years of age with "extension cord wires, water hoses, punches, everything." She ran away, and after high school, married and became pregnant. Her husband died shortly after the son's birth in a work-related accident. She has been homeless for seven years, and sometimes stays with friends. Periodically she visits her mother and son, but adds that her ice use has "interfered" with her relationship with her mother. Her mother has been caring for her son since she has "no place for me and my boy." She regularly gives half of her welfare monies to her mother for her son's food and clothing. [475]

Like other women in this study, Stephanie takes refuge in ice as she finds her options narrowing. As she states, "I can't get no help finding me and my boy a place. So because I'm homeless, that's why I do the drug, I get so depressed cause I don't have no roof over my head

for me and my boy." Ironically, her family, which caused her to run away, is one of her few remaining resources.

Conclusion

This paper underscores the importance of using a qualitative approach to studying drug use among hidden populations like Asian-Pacific Americans. An ethnographic strategy is crucial to dispelling popular stereotypes of Asian-Pacific Americans' passivity and women's "submissiveness," and in laying the groundwork for theory building and program planning.

Unlike mental health studies on Asian-Pacific Americans, this analysis suggests that stress from the family is not restricted to cultural and generational conflict. Social problems like drug use among Asian-Pacific American women are quite complex. From their early childhood, these women lived in the midst of heated, sometimes violent, conflict, which was connected to economic marginality, parental problems with alcohol, and distinctive cultural norms of femininity. Neighborhood and school peers, and male relatives initially introduced them to alcohol and marijuana. Over time, their user networks widen and their introduction into cocaine and ice is through friends, extended kin (e.g., cousins), and partners. Despite the long-standing tension in their family and their more recent isolation from others from using ice, the cultural traditions embedded in the extended kinship system allow many to "return home."

Discussion Questions

1. How has the "ohana" extended family system of Pacific Americans affected women's initiation into drug use, if at all?

2. How do women in this study respond to family turmoil?

3. Compare and contrast Latina family networks (as discussed in Chapter 5) with Asian-American family networks (discussed in Joe-Laidler's study).

4. Describe how continued methamphetamine use changed these women's lives and how they interacted with their family after such use.

5. Would power-control theory be a viable explanation for the role of the families in Asian-American women's criminality? If so, describe how.

References

Agar, M. 1993. Ethnography: An aerial view. In *Proceedings* of the National Institute on Drug Abuse: Community Epidemiology Work Group, Vol. II, December, San Francisco.

Anglin, M., Y. I. Hser, and W. H. McGlothlin. 1987. Sex differences in addict careers: Becoming addicted. *American Journal of Drug and Alcohol Abuse* 13: 59–71.

Aquino, B. 1994. Filipino women and political engagement. The Office for Women's Research, Working Paper Series. Vol. 2. Honolulu: University of Hawaii.

Asian Women United of California. 1989. *Making waves: An anthology of writings by and about Asian American women.* Boston: Beacon Press.

Austin, G., M. Pendergast, and H. Lee. 1989. Substance abuse among Asian American youth. *Prevention Research Update* No. 5. Winter. Portland, Ore.: Western Regional Center, Drug Free Schools and Communities.

Bourgois, P., and E. Dunlap. 1993. Exorcising sex for crack: An ethnographic perspective from Harlem. In *Crack as pimp: An ethnographic investigation of sex for crack exchanges*, ed. M. Ratner, 97–132. New York: Lexington Books.

Chen, S. 1991. *Entry denied: Exclusion and the Chinese community in America 1882–1943.* Philadelphia: Temple University Press.

Chi, I., J. Lubben, and H. Kitano. 1989. Differences in drinking behavior among three Asian American groups. *Journal of Studies on Alcohol* 50: 15–23.

Denzin, N., and Y. Lincoln. 1994. Introduction: Entering the field of qualitative research. In *Handbook of qualitative research*, ed. N. Denzin and Y. Lincoln, 1–17. Thousand Oaks, Calif.: Sage.

Ettorre, E. 1992. *Women and substance use.* New Brunswick, N.J.: Rutgers University.

File, K. 1976. Sex roles and street roles. *International Journal of the Addictions* 11: 263–268.

Froner, G. 1989. *Digging for diamonds: A lexicon of street slang for drugs and sex.* San Francisco: ALL-TEC.

Handy, E., S. Craighill, and M. Kawena Pukui. 1972. *The Polynesian family system.* Rutland, Vt.: Charles Tuttle.

Honolulu Advertiser. 1993. Asian-Pacific Americans. Focus, B4. May 9.

Hunt, G., K. Joe, and D. Waldorf. 1995. Born to kill? Culture and ethnic identity among southeast Asian gang members. Paper presented at the annual meeting of the Pacific Sociological Association, San Francisco, Calif.

Inciardi, J., D. Lockwood, and A. Pottieger. 1993. *Women and crack cocaine.* New York: MacMillan.

Joe, K. 1990. Final evaluation report on the Asian Youth Substance Abuse Project to the Office of Substance Abuse Prevention. Asian American Residential Services: San Francisco, Calif.

———. 1993. Getting into the gang: Methodological issues in studying ethnic gangs. In *Drug abuse among minority youth: Methodological issues and recent research advances*, eds. M. De La Rosa and J. Adrados. National Institute on Drug Abuse Research Monograph #130: 234-257. Rockville, Md.: NIDA.

———. 1995. Ice is strong enough for a man but made for a woman. *Crime, Law and Social Change* 22: 269–289.

Joe, K., and M. Chesney Lind. 1995. Just every mother's angel: An analysis of gender and ethnic variations in youth gang membership. *Gender and Society* 9: 408–431.

Johnson, R., C. Nagoshi, F. Ahern, J. Wilson, and S. Yuen. 1987. Cultural factors as explanations for ethnic group differences in alcohol use in Hawaii. *Journal of Psychoactive Drugs* 19: 67–75.

Kitano, H., and I. Chi. 1985. Asian Americans and alcohol: The Chinese, Japanese, Koreans and Filipinos in Los Angeles. In *Alcohol use among United States ethnic minorities*, ed. D. Spiegler et al., 373–382. Rockville, Md.: National Institute on Alcohol Abuse and Alcoholism.

———. 1986. Asian Americans and alcohol use: Exploring cultural differences in Los Angeles. *Alcohol, Health and Research World*, Winter: 42–47.

Kuramoto, F. 1994. Drug abuse prevention research concerns in Asian and Pacific Islander populations. In *Scientific methods for prevention intervention research*, ed. A. Cazares and L. Beatty, 249–271. Research Monograph 139. Rockville, Md.: United States Department of Health.

Loo, C. 1991. *Chinatown: Most time, hard time.* New York: Praeger.

Maher, L., and R. Curtis. 1992. Women on the edge of crime: Crack cocaine and the changing contexts of street level sex work in New York City. *Crime, Law, and Social Change* 18: 221–258.

Miller, M. 1991. Trends and patterns of methamphetamine smoking in Hawaii. In *Methamphetamine abuse: Epidemiologic issues and implications*, eds. M. Miller and N. Kozel. National Institute on Drug Abuse Research Monograph 115: 72–83. Rockville, Md.: United States Department of Health.

Miller, M., and J. Tomas. 1989. Past and current methamphetamine epidemics. *Proceedings* from the Community Epidemiology Workgroup. December National Institute on Drug Abuse Monograph. Rockville, Md.: United States Department of Health.

Morgan, P., D. McDonnell, J. Beck, K. Joe, and R. Gutierrez. n.d. Uncharted communities: Preliminary findings from a study of methamphetamine users. In *Methamphetamines: An illicit drug with high abuse potential*, eds. B. Sowder and G. Beschner. Forthcoming.

Morningstar, P., and D. Chitwood. 1987. How women and men get cocaine: Sex role stereotypes and acquisition patterns. *Journal of Psychoactive Drugs* 19: 135–142.

Newcomb, M., E. Maddahian, R. Skager, and P. Bentler. 1987. Substance abuse and psychological risk factors among teenagers: Associations with sex, age, ethnicity and type of school. *American Journal of Alcohol and Drug Abuse* 13: 413–433.

Newsweek. 1989. The fire of "Ice." 37: 7–9, November 27.

Nunes, K., and S. Whitney. 1994. The destruction of the Hawaiian male. *Honolulu Magazine* July: 58–61.

Pukui, M. L., E. W. Haertig, and C. Lee. 1972. *Nana I Ke Kumu.* Vol. 1. Honolulu, HI: Hui Hanai.

Rosenbaum, M. 1981. *Women on heroin.* New Brunswick, NJ: Rutgers.

San Francisco Chronicle. 1989. New drug "Ice" called worse peril than crack. August 31.

Sante, L. 1991. *Low life.* New York: Vintage.

Skager, R., S. Frith, and E. Maddahian. 1989. *Biennial survey of drug and alcohol use among California students in grades 7, 9, and 11.* Winter 1987–1988. Sacramento: Office of the Attorney General, Crime Prevention Center.

Sue, D. 1987. Use and abuse of alcohol by Asian Americans. *Journal of Psychoactive Drugs* 19: 57–66.

Sue, S., N. Zane, and J. Ito. 1979. Alcohol drinking patterns among Asian and Caucasian Americans. *Journal of Cross Culture Psychology* 10: 41–56.

Tong, B. 1994. *Unsubmissive women: Chinese prostitutes in 19th century San Francisco.* Norman, Okla.: University of Oklahoma Press.

Trimble, J., A. Padilla, and C. Bell. 1987. *Drug abuse among ethnic minorities.* Rockville, Md.: National Institute on Drug Abuse.

Whitney, S. 1986. Getting sober local style: Strategies for alcoholism counseling in Hawaii. *Alcoholism Treatment Quarterly* 3: 87–107.

Zane, N., and T. Sasao. 1992. Research on drug abuse among Asian-Pacific Americans. In *Ethnic and multicultural drug abuse: Perspectives on current research,* eds. J. E. Trimble, C. S. Bolek, and S. J. Niemcryk, 181–209. New York: Haworth.

Zane, N. n.d. Research on drug abuse among Asian-Pacific Americans. *Drugs and Society.* Forthcoming.

7

The Impact of Mothering on Criminal Offending

Kathleen J. Ferraro
Angela M. Moe

This chapter examines the relationships [among] mothering, crime, and incarceration through the narratives of 30 women incarcerated in Pima County (Arizona) adult detention facility. The racial and ethnic distributions within the sample represent those found at the facility. Interviews were semistructured, and the authors used a grounded theory approach to data analysis. The topics that emerged included the relationship between crime and economic needs, addictions and child protective services, and the ways in which race and class intersect with ideas about mothering. The responsibilities of child care, combined with the burdens of economic marginality and domestic violence, led some women to choose economic crimes or drug dealing as an alternative to hunger and homelessness. Other women, arrested for drug- or alcohol-related crimes, related their offenses to the psychological pain and despair resulting from loss of custody of their children. Many women were incarcerated for minor probation violations that often related to the conflict [among] work, child care, and probation requirements. For all women with children, mothering represented both the burdens of an unequal sexual division of labor and opportunities for resistance to marginalization and hopelessness.

This chapter focuses on women's experiences with mothering, crime, and incarceration. Each of these socially constructed categories reflects and reinforces gendered expectations for women's performance, as well as race and class hierarchies. Some research has suggested that the legal system tends to de-emphasize, excuse, justify, and downplay women's crimes, even those that are targeted at or incidentally harm their children (Allen 1987; Daly 1994). According to such reports, women are portrayed within the legal system in ways that are consistent with paternalistic hegemonic standards of passivity and weakness and, as such, are unable to be held fully accountable for their criminal activities. Such research, supportive of the chivalry thesis in criminology (see Pollak 1950), contrasts with other studies that find that women are processed through the criminal justice system in misogynist ways, demonized and vilified for countering hegemonic womanhood and motherhood vis-à-vis their criminal offenses (Chesney-Lind 1997; Gilbert 1999; Nagel and Hagan 1983; Young 1986). The women most likely to benefit from hegemonic notions of womanhood and motherhood within the criminal justice system are those that fit the ideal image within society at large, namely white, middle to upper class, heterosexual women (Belknap 2001). Much current research suggests that the disproportionate rate of incarceration of women of color is a reflection of racist perceptions, policing, and sentencing policies (Belknap 2001; Gilbert 1999; Richie 2001).

While women are capable of and certainly do commit many forms of crime, including interpersonal violent crimes that in some cases harm their children, they also commit their crimes from gendered, as well as raced and classed, positions that are politically, economically, and historically rooted (Allen 1987; Humphries 1999). Despite instances in which the contexts of women's crimes resemble those of men's (see as examples Miller 1998; Sommers, Baskin, and Fagan 2000), overall, women are more likely to commit minor property offenses than serious or violent offenses as compared to men and are less likely to recidivate than men (Smart 1995). The crimes for which they are most often arrested and incarcerated are suggestive of their gendered and raced social positioning (Richie 2001; Ross 1998). Such crimes include nonviolent and minor property crimes such as prostitution, larceny, shoplifting, check or credit card fraud, forgery/counterfeiting, and drug possession. The growth in the number of incarcerated women between 1990 and 2000 is composed largely of drug offenders (Harrison and Beck 2002).

Despite the relative infrequency and nonviolent nature of female offending, the numbers of women under control of the "correctional" system in the United States have been growing over the past twenty years at a faster pace than the numbers of men (Chesney-Lind 1997; Greenfield and Snell 1999; U.S. General Accounting

Office 1999). Between 1990 and 2000, the rate of female incarceration increased by 108 percent (Beck and Harrison 2001). Yet the proportion of women composing the total correctional population remains small. Only about 6.7 percent of the total prison population and about 11 percent of the local jail population are women (Greenfield and Snell 1999; Stephan 2001). The research, facilities, and programs for criminal offenders in the United States focus primarily on adult male offenders. Knowledge of incarcerated women's experiences and responsiveness of prisons and jails to women's circumstances have both been retarded by neglect of the gendered dimensions of incarceration.

The vast majority of prisons and jails have not developed the most rudimentary resources for women inmates (Morash 1998; U.S. General Accounting Office 1999). Women are assessed and classified using instruments designed for males, and programming is designed without consideration of the differing needs of women. Although at least 70 percent of women in jail have minor children, few jails have programs that foster parenting skills or contact between mothers and children, and there are virtually no programs designed to assist children with problems related to the incarceration of their mothers (Greenfield and Snell 1999).

There have been several studies of mothering from inside prisons and jails over the past twenty-five years, including Bloom (1992), Bloom and Steinhart (1993), Watterson (1996), Henriques (1982), Snell (1994), Enos (2001), Baunach (1985), Stanton (1980), Zalba (1964), and Glick and Neto (1977). The existing literature indicates that mothering is a central concern of incarcerated women and that correctional facilities have failed to respond adequately to this concern. Studies on incarceration and mothering report that many women commit minor property crimes to provide for their children, although there is no systematic data on the prevalence of this influence on women's crimes (Henriques 1982; Watterson 1996). Previous research has documented that women's concerns about their children's well-being, as well as their distress at separation, are the most salient features of incarceration for women with children (Boudin 1998; Enos 2001; Henriques 1982; Watterson 1996). Comparison of incarcerated mothers and fathers indicates that women are more likely to have custody of children prior to incarceration and that men are much more likely to have female partners to care for children during their incarceration (Mumola 2000; Schafer and Dellinger 1999). Women most commonly use female relatives rather than male partners to care for children in their absence. This suggests that women's incarceration creates unique concerns about the welfare of their children from which most men are protected by the presence of a female partner who attends to their children.

Social Constructions of Good Mothers

Mothering is simultaneously a positive source of pleasure and identity formation and a vector for the social control of women. For women with children, mothering is a central component of identity, daily activity, and life plans. At the same time, the burdens and social expectations of mothering reinforce oppressive notions of femininity including self sacrifice and subordination of personal goals to the needs of "the family." Naturalized assumptions regarding masculinity and femininity and raced and classed standards of gender performance saturate and reinforce constructions of mothering (Smart 1998). The ability to mother one's children according to social expectations and personal desires depends ultimately on one's access to the resources of time, money, health, and social support. A significant proportion of mothers negotiates their child rearing through obstacles that undermine their efforts to be "good mothers," both on their own terms and in the eyes of the state.

Kline (1995) described the dominant ideology of motherhood as "the constellation of ideas and images in Western capitalist societies that constitute the dominant ideals of motherhood against which women's lives are judged" (p. 119). The ideology is composed of historically constituted conceptions of maternal fitness that reflect race and class biases, as well as heterosexist and patriarchal notions of the family (Fineman 1995; Hill Collins 2000; Kline 1995). Women who are deemed "bad" or "unfit" mothers are often those who deviate from this ideology. Ikemoto (1997) outlined the stereotypes that are applied to women classified as "bad" or "unfit" mothers:

> She has little education. . . . She is unsophisticated, easily influenced by simple religious dogma. She is pregnant because of promiscuity and irresponsibility. She is hostile to authority even though the state has good intentions. She is unreliable. She is ignorant and foreign. She does not know what is best. . . . These assumed characteristics are particular to stereotypes of poor women of

color. So . . . she is Black; she is Hispanic; she is Asian; and she is poor. (p. 140)

The dominant ideology of motherhood reflects essentialist conceptions of women as inherently caring and self-sacrificing and simultaneously enforces distinctions among women based on race and class prejudices. While the dominant ideology of motherhood may distort the experiences and aspirations of all women, white, heterosexual, married, middle-class women continue to represent the most desired mothers in popular culture and social policy in the United States (Roberts 1995). Women who are identified as inadequate mothers are especially susceptible to social and legal regulation of their maternal rights (Kline 1995). Thus, motherhood resembles more of a privilege for some women rather than a right for all women (Molloy 1992). As such, it may be withheld from women who are not members of dominant social groups and women deemed unfit by social and legal standards (Kline 1995).

Despite rhetoric of a robust economy and envious standard of living, approximately 40 percent of all single mothers in the United States in 2000 lived at or below poverty level (Caiazza 2000). Women at the lower end of the economic spectrum work tedious, unstable jobs; negotiate the rough terrain of "dating" or maintaining intimate relationships; transport children to less than optimal "child care" arrangements; cook; clean; shop; wash; attend whatever classes may lead to better jobs or are required by caseworkers or probation officers; and provide the hugs, stories, conflict resolution, and moral guidance that help their children grow. Their identities and choices may revolve around their children, but the conditions in which they labor to nurture, protect, and educate their children are determined by others in increasingly miserly ways.

Impact of the Role of Mothering on Criminal Offending

Some of the mothers interviewed correlated this economic situation directly with their participation in criminal activity. Women with children in their custody conceptualized crime as an alternative to hunger and homelessness. Women without dependent children did not discuss the relationship between economic survival and economic crimes and most often referenced drugs and alcohol as the basis for their offenses. Several women linked their financial difficulties, and the crimes they committed to obtain money, to efforts to escape from or cope with violent men while providing for their children. These women articulated the structural barriers to successful mothering and viewed nonviolent crime as a rational, responsible action taken to meet their children's needs. This interpretation of the reasonableness of crimes contrasted with individualistic and self-blaming views expressed by most women incarcerated for drug and prostitution crimes committed to support addictions. In this way, the role of mothering served as catalyst and a rationale for crime that was not available to women without children in their custody.

Racial differences were apparent in the accounts of women, as African American women were more fully cognizant of the ways in which race, gender, and poverty were intertwined through institutionalized patterns of exclusion. All the African American women in our sample had been battered, and they were the most realistic about economic exclusions and their sole responsibility for meeting the economic needs of their children. American Indian women also discussed their experiences with racism but linked them more to addictions than to poverty. Latina women most often described their offending in terms of individual deficiencies and/or victimizations rather than structural economic constraints.

Alicia, a twenty-one-year-old biracial (African American/white) woman with two children, ages three and five, reported that she had been on her own since she was seventeen, having left the abusive father of her children. She completed a training program as a nursing assistant and had been working as well as selling crack. She was in jail for possession of crack, powder cocaine, and paraphernalia. The "paraphernalia" was the cigarette case she used to transport the drugs for sale. Although she thought that selling was wrong "because crack destroys people's lives," she felt her actions were "right at the time" because they allowed her to support her children:

I don't regret it because without the extra income, my kids wouldn't be fed every day. Even though I do have a good job when I work and stuff like that, it's hard raising two kids by yourself. . . . You get used to having money every day and you don't have to worry about the electric being off or the rent being paid. Your check is like your hard earned money; you're not going to spend it ridiculously like, "Oh, let's go buy a hundred-dollar pair of shoes with it." You know what I'm saying? You budget it because it's the only thing you look forward to for paying your bills. . . . But with that other money [paycheck] it goes so fast. As soon as you get it, the kids need new clothes or spend twenty dollars at the Circle K for candy. . . . We may not have chosen the right paths to go along in life, but I'm not a dummy. They get mad at you if you can't get a job in two weeks. Who in the hell is going to employ you? I'm not going to McDonald's. McDonald's is not going to pay my rent. That's what they want you to do, lower your self-esteem to where you will take anything. I'm sorry, I have never worked for a five dollar an hour job, not since I was a teenager. I'm not going to now. I have two kids to support. Where am I going to live with them? In a shelter, making five dollars an hour. I'm not going to subject my kids to something like that. I'd rather just do my prison time if I have to do it and get rid of all of this.

Although she was one of the youngest women in the sample, Alicia rejected total, individual responsibility for her crime. Her explanation for selling crack reflects some of the aspects of individual worth in the African American community described by Gilbert (1999, 239): self-help, competence, confidence, and consciousness. She understood that the options available to her as a single mother were limited and that she was "a grain of sand" in the underground economy that would grind on with or without her participation. Her "good job" as a nursing assistant was sporadic and unreliable and paid about ten dollars an hour. She made a decision to sell crack to support her family and preferred going to jail to working at a minimum wage, dead-end job and living in a shelter with her children. She had a boyfriend who was also in jail, but she had no expectation that he would support her or her children.

Angel also committed crimes to support her seven children. A forty-one-year-old African American woman who grew up in an extremely abusive and violent environment, Angel disclosed that her father was a pimp and that she grew up in a house full of people who "used drugs twenty-four/seven." She moved out and lived on her own at age seventeen and put herself through two and a half years of college. She had been working at a well-paying sales job when her violent husband tracked her down and began to harass her. She quit her job and moved her family to Phoenix but was unable to find a job that would pay her bills. She began writing bad checks as a way of making ends meet. When asked if she was receiving any benefits while she was writing checks, she responded,

Sometimes yes, as the check writing went off and on for a period, for a number of years, so yes. Sometimes I was getting benefits; sometimes I wasn't. I would have to supplement my income writing the checks, buying the groceries, stealing money from the bank to pay for rent or to pay for a car repair. You know, it was always something. [Question: How much is your restitution?] Six thousand dollars, which isn't that bad, because most of it I was buying was just stuff for the kids: groceries, and clothing for the children, toys for the kids, just basic stuff, and my rent. There were a couple of times I went to the bank and wrote checks for cash and made it out for one thousand dollars cash that was for covering things, bills, stuff like that. There's a lot of girls in here that have restitution much greater than mine.

Restitution was one of the burdens women faced as they left jail, which added to their already precarious economic situations. The other significant burden was the terms of probation. Eight women (27 percent) had been incarcerated because of minor probation violations, such as failing to inform a probation officer of one's whereabouts or missing an appointment because of work, sickness, or lack of transportation. Complying with probation requirements, or drug court requirements, places tremendous demands on the resources of single mothers, which are already strained. Alicia explained the difficulties of parenting and following the guidelines of intensive probation services (IPS):

This is my probation's terms. Three to four times a week, counseling, but you have to pay for it. One girl said she was paying like sixty dollars a week just for three counseling sessions. Every time it was twenty bucks, bang. . . . They expect us to have a full-time job, which is fine, counseling four times a week, on top of community service two hours a day; so that's ten hours a week, so where is the time for your kids? And they know some people have kids, but they don't care. You mess up any step of the law and they're violating you and putting you in prison. That's a lot of things to look forward to. That's a lot of stuff. And if you don't go to counseling when they say to go, you're violated even if you drop clean every day. If you mess up in any of those areas. Say the traffic is bad, or say my daughter is asthmatic. She goes into an asthma attack in the middle of the night, I have to make sure I page my IPS worker and make sure he calls me back in time before I go to the doctor. My daughter could be suffocating in this time while he's taking his time calling me back and they don't care. You leave without them knowing, you're violated. They don't care if you're dying or your kids are dying. Good thing my daughter hasn't been in the hospital. She has a heart murmur. Anything can happen to her, and I don't feel like that's right for them to violate if I am at the hospital with my child. Even if I get there right away and I page them, they say, "Well, too bad. You're prison bound." That's what IPS stands for: in prison soon. A lot of people say that.

One other African American woman's original crime, welfare fraud, was obviously related to providing for her three children. She was not incarcerated for welfare fraud, however, but for violating the probation she received for that original offense by smoking marijuana. Her "dirty" urine analysis prompted the judge to revoke her probation and give her a felony conviction plus 120 days in jail. She felt this was unfair, created additional problems for her children, and limited her opportunities for employment. Patrice explained that at the time she "signed the welfare check," her baby's father was in prison, and she had no source of funds:

I wanted my baby a baby bed and wanted her this and I wanted her that, and he wasn't there. I didn't know where he was. Just one day he disappeared and I didn't know where he was. When I went for my sentencing, I thought he was going to let me go because I paid for all of my restitution for the welfare check and everything. My lawyer's like, "We think she should be released." And the judge goes, "No, I'm going to give her about 121 days." I said, "Why?" He goes, "'Cause you shouldn't have smoked that joint."

Patrice had recently obtained work release status and was trying to find a job. She wanted to get her three children back from her sister and move into a house but was worried about finances. Her story reflects the spiraling effects of getting caught up in the criminal justice system while trying to make ends meet:

Is there anything preventing me from getting a job? Yes, the felony that he gave me because of a little joint. I don't think he was very fair at all. I think that a felony is for somebody who did something really actually bad or something like that. I ain't sayin' what I did wasn't a crime. I know it was a crime. I just can't imagine why he would give me a felony because I broke probation and smoked a joint. I write down "felony" on my applications and everybody goes, "Oh no, we can't hire you." . . . A lot of us are in here for probation violations. The judge didn't care that we had kids or care that we lost our house or anything.

Lonna, a thirty-one-year-old biracial (Latina/white) woman with three children, was also in jail for violating probation after arrest for welfare fraud. She blamed her abusive husband for taking her money and creating an economic situation in which she felt compelled to commit welfare fraud:

I don't want to make it sound like it was all his fault, but it is. I've been married since 1986. There came a time, about 1995, when there was sometimes no water in the house, no electric, no food. So while I was working I collected welfare. Not only that, sometimes he would take my money anyway no matter if he was working or not. It didn't matter. Sometimes he'd just take my money anyway, so I would go and get extra checks.

Lonna was sentenced to probation and was able to maintain a good job. After she was switched to a new probation officer, however, she had trouble maintaining contact, was arrested, and was jailed for four months.

While these women's initial crimes were motivated by a desire to provide for their children, it was minor violations of probation terms that caused the greatest problems for them. Women attempted to manage the demands of motherhood, interlaced with traditional prescriptions for femininity, while providing income and dealing with prior and ongoing victimization. Scripted notions of successful mothering and of femininity made compliance with elaborate probation terms difficult as the women's lives were filled with expectations of caring for others while under the gaze of the state.

Jail as a Retreat

For many women, life was so arduous and precarious that incarceration was actually perceived as an improvement. This was particularly true for women who had lived in extreme battering situations, who felt protected from their abusers while in jail (although some women continued to be terrorized through prison and jail networks and threats to their children). Jail and prison are also dangerous for women, as abuse by correctional staff, neglect of health, and overuse of medications are common (see Human Rights Watch Women's Rights Project 1996; Amnesty International 1999, 2001; Moe and Ferraro 2002). The women in PCAD described many problems with the care and level of safety they experienced, but some also commented on the jail as a break from the demands of mothering, street life, and male violence. Angel, for example, was passionate about literature and was using her time to read and write. She said she had read more than fifty books since she had been in jail and was writing a novel called *My Sister's Wedding* in longhand. She also had plans for another book designed to help women find jobs after getting out of prison. She planned to write at least three books if she received the longest prison term possible. With six young children at home and her oldest son in prison, she viewed her time in jail as a "vacation":

> Yeah, this has really been like a vacation for me in a way, 'cause I get a chance to, when I was at home with the kids, I never got a chance to sit down and read books. It's impossible to find the time to write when you have to work and you have to get the kids off to school or you have to do all of the things. I want to try to take this time and use it the best that I can to prepare myself for a career as a writer. If I'm paid to write and that's all I have to do, well then I can do that at home when my kids are at school. I don't have to get up and go to work.

Angel had a positive outlook on life. "You have to try to find the goodness in all the bad things that happen to us in life, and there's plenty if you look." She placed all six of her little girls with her mother in Florida when she was arrested. Although she was in a good relationship with a man at the time of her arrest, "he wasn't able to handle all six of the girls 'cause they're all girls." She discussed working with this man as photographers in a restaurant, but she had no expectation that he would share in parenting activities. The children's biological fathers were abusive or had abandoned them, and thus Angel took full responsibility for their care and delayed her personal goals. This was true for all women, none of whom had male partners on whom they could rely for child care.

Other women viewed the minimal health and nutrition services as a respite from street life. Boo was pregnant with her fourth child, and she felt the care she received in jail was positive. She had been incarcerated so many times that she knew the guards like family:

> To me this is my home away from home 'cuz I don't have nobody on the outside. So it's kind of hard for me but then at the same time I like it in here 'cuz I get that special attention that I crave. . . . I know all of the COs [correctional officers] here. They're like my uncles and aunts in my way, you know what I'm saying. They're real good people to me. I like them. . . . I get taken care of in here very well. They give us three pregnancy bags a day which contain two cartons of milk, two orange juices, and two fruits, and you get three pills three times a day during breakfast, lunch, and dinner, so you have your little snack bag.

Although most women complained about the food and health care available in the jail, for Boo, who lived on the streets, the jail provided a relatively healthy environment for her pregnancy.

Other women viewed their incarceration as a way to get away from an abusive husband. Lonna, quoted earlier, who was jailed for violating her probation for welfare fraud, explained that her jail time allowed her to break from her husband and that she would not return home. Her children were having problems while she was in jail, but she felt a divorce would benefit them eventually:

> They don't have a mom or a dad. My mother-in-law asked my son, "Why are you acting this way?" He says, "Why do I have to come home? I don't have a family." I hear in the background my older daughter says, "It's true. My mom's in jail and my dad's out partying." Damn. Anyway, I think it's a good thing that I came to jail. . . . I'm not going back home. I'm getting a divorce when I leave here. I'm just going to take the kids and leave. That's my plan when I leave here. . . . It's a good thing I'm here I guess. Not for the kids but it will be better in the long run.

Lonna had tried for fifteen years to make her marriage work, keep her family together, and have their bills paid. She assumed all the responsibility for her three children while her husband used her paycheck to buy drugs and liquor. She was attending classes in jail, which she believed were helping her to break free of that relationship and to help her children.

Similar to the women in Bosworth's (1999) study of women prisoners in England, femininity established the burdens and constraints women at PCAD faced as well as provided a grounds for resistance. The socially structured mandate for maternal responsibility for children's well-being and the failure of fathers and other men to provide support for parenting create a situation in which low-income women must struggle for money while providing care and denying their own dreams and interests. The state's intervention creates additional burdens through incarceration and terms of probation that further complicate the already overwhelming demands on mothers. Jobs and wages are lost due to violent husbands, women are arrested for crimes of economic survival, and criminal records make it more difficult to find good jobs. At the same time, the care of children provided grounds on which women could focus on future goals and improvements: a career in writing, a healthy pregnancy, and divorcing an abusive husband. While some women could embrace the role of mothering as an opportunity for personal growth and social acceptance, for others, that opportunity had already been lost through state intervention in custody.

Addictions and Child Protective Services

The majority (80 percent) of women interviewed were addicted to illegal drugs or alcohol. Crack cocaine was the most common drug, followed by heroin and crystal methamphetamine. Both crack and crystal were cheap and easily available in southern Arizona. A small "rock" of crack could be purchased for five dollars on the street. Heroin from Mexico was also quite easy to obtain. Thirteen women (43 percent) indicated that they were addicted to crack, with several of these women also using heroin, powder cocaine, or alcohol. Three women were alcoholics, and two women used crystal methamphetamine. Three of the six women who were not addicted to any substance were in jail because of their sale of crack or crystal. As Chesney-Lind (1997) and others have noted, the war on drugs clearly translates into a war on women.

Many women had lost custody of their children because of their addictions. Twelve women had children removed by CPS because of their alcohol or drug use. Ten had their parental rights severed and could not see their children until they turned eighteen, and two were still actively trying to have their children returned. The other twelve women with addictions had placed their children with relatives prior to incarceration. Several women indicated that the final severance decision was what pushed them into resumption of drug or alcohol use or into more serious addiction.

Theresa, a thirty-nine-year-old white woman with four children younger than sixteen and a twenty-two-year-old son, had much difficulty during her interview because of her extreme sadness and pain over the loss of her children. She showed no expression and spoke in a monotone. She was not pressed to elaborate on answers as it was obviously hard for her to remember and talk about her life. She was in jail because of a second driving under the influence charge that occurred when she resumed drinking after being sober for three and a half years. Her parental rights were severed because she reunited, briefly, with her abusive husband:

I quit for three years, three and a half years, since 1995, and then when they said severance and adoption, I slightly fell off the wagon. [Question: You actually quit for three years and they still?] Yeah, they just brought up so many different things. They said we caused problems for the kids because of our arguments and our fighting and this and that. They bring up so many different things. [Question: Don't they have a plan, though, that you follow? And if you follow the plan then you get your kids back?] Yeah, I followed the plan. But then I got back with their dad, and he messed up and so then CPS said because it was my choice to get back with him that it ruined both of our chances of getting the kids back. And I told them, "I don't see how." That's when I lost it. The hardest I've ever drank in my life was last year. They were doing random drug testing and I was dropping clean. And I was doing all of their parenting classes and all their going to their psychiatrists plus going to my own psychiatrist plus doing my groups and doing AAs [Alcoholics Anonymous] and still, it didn't matter.

According to Theresa, her husband had received a two-and-a-half-year prison sentence for "trying to kill us." As she explained, "He beat me up severely so where one eye, this whole side of my face was just black and blue and swollen shut for like a whole month, and he cut me, stabbed me, three times." Although her husband was out of the situation because of his incarceration, CPS severed Theresa's rights and placed her children up for adoption. As Theresa phrased it, "Until they're eighteen they've been sentenced to adoption." Her plans focused on the day of their reunification: "What are my plans? To stay sober. I want to finish my education, get on with my life. Hopefully it will go a little faster so I can see my kids when they're eighteen."

Theresa's case illustrates the importance of children to women's recovery from alcohol and drugs and the despair that emerges when rights are severed. Her case also reflects the ways in which CPS agencies fail to respond appropriately to domestic violence by removing children from women who are abused. The district court ruling in *Nicholson v. Scoppetta* found that New York City's Administration for Children's Services had demonstrated "benign indifference, bureaucratic inefficiency and outmoded institutional biases" in removing children from the custody of women who had been beaten by their abusers (Friedlin 2002).

Marie's situation was similar, only she turned to crack and powder cocaine, heroin, and methadone when her children were removed. Marie, a twenty-seven-year-old white women with two young children (three and five years old), had also lost her children due to her husband's conduct. They were removed after he had gotten high on drugs and pushed them in a stroller onto a busy highway. Marie was home sick when the incident occurred. Because her family was living in a motel room at the time, the environment was considered unfit and CPS removed the children. Marie started using drugs after this but stopped, filed for divorce, rented an apartment, and followed all of the demands of CPS when she thought she had a chance of reunification:

> Everything was goin' good. Got an apartment of my own to get my kids back up on the north side of town where it's really expensive so they could live in a good place. The psychological evaluator was there and he suspected that I was doing this just to fool CPS, but he never voiced his suspicions to me. He voiced them to my CPS worker and he just changed it. The night before we went to court, he changed the whole plan from givin' them back to me to severance and adoption. I called up the psychological evaluator and asked, "How come you didn't ask me about this?" He said, "I told them there wasn't any furniture." I said, "Well, that's because I had just moved in. I have lots of furniture now." "Oh, well, I didn't think about that." And then he said, "Well, you don't have no food in your house." I said, "That's because I live by myself and I work in a restaurant and I eat there all the time. I don't need food." "Well, yeah, I guess I didn't think about that." And I said, "Well, why didn't you ask me before you told my CPS worker?" It was too late then because they were changin' things. They told me again that they were going to take my kids away, so I started doin' drugs again. And then, prostitution came in.

Marie had been sentenced to six months in jail for prostitution, plus a $1,000 fine and two years on supervised probation. Although her children were in an adoptive home and CPS was moving to sever her rights, she believed she still had a chance of getting them back, and that was her motivation for staying clean:

> I know I'll get them back. They have no reason to keep them from me. I know I'll get them back. Plus, I pray. I know I will have them. [Question: Do you see any barriers to getting your kids back? Staying out of the drugs?] No. I think getting them back is a real strong drive for me to stay out of drugs. It gives me something to concentrate on. I know if I touch those drugs, the kids are gone. I'll never even have a fighting chance. So, I know I can't. The only barriers I see is just the last court date. I didn't go because I

was high. I knew they were takin' them and I couldn't bear to hear a severance and adoption as they planned, so I just didn't go. That didn't help. I just hope it ain't the same judge.

Gillian, a thirty-six-year-old white woman, also began using crack after CPS severed her rights to her daughter. Her only child was removed from the home after reporting to her grandmother that her father had sexually molested her. Gillian and her daughter moved in with Gillian's mother after her husband assaulted and threatened to kill her. Her daughter was nine at the time and intellectually gifted, while Gillian had a learning disability and had not graduated from high school. Although she was following all the guidelines set by CPS, her rights were severed and she felt as if she had lost everything:

> She [her daughter] had been sexually molested when she was younger than that. I didn't know it. I had been going through the courts doing everything they asked me to, and they lied to me. [Question: Child protective services?] Yeah, CPS lied to me. [Question: What did they lie to you about?] Saying that if I did everything they told me to I would get her back. They lied to her too saying that she was going to be moving back in with me. They lied to both of us. We went to court. I didn't have a GED [general equivalency diploma]. I have dyslexia. I have a learning disability. They said her intelligence would be wasted if they gave her back to me because I couldn't afford her education and I couldn't teach her how to read as she got older. I have dyslexia and I see words backward sometimes if I'm not careful. They used her IQ. It was 121 at the age of seven. She could not read. They figured her being with me would be a waste of time because I couldn't give her the education she needed. I didn't know that education was more important than love. I guess it is in their eyes. . . . I was like, "They've been lying to me all this time." Finally we went to court and they tried to say I had a drug and alcohol problem. I didn't even do drugs back then. I smoked pot, but since I've been in Tucson, I haven't smoked no weed. I did drink. They said I had a drug problem, and I don't even know where they got that. I wasn't even doing drugs. I did start drugs after I lost her. About two to three months later, I did it. I was like, "Hell, they said I did it." I didn't have nothing to lose then. I had already lost her, so that's when I started doing drugs.

Certainly, there is a possibility that women misunderstood or misrepresented the severance process that resulted in the loss of their children. The important point that can be drawn from these narratives, however, is that women's use of drugs or alcohol was often related in their own minds to the loss of their children. With "nothing to lose," and easy access to crack and alcohol, these women were drawn into usage that eventually resulted in their incarceration.

For some addicted women, use of crack cocaine preceded state intervention; however, they felt it was impossible to stop using. The threat of losing their children, or even damaging their children, could not overcome their dependence on crack. All the women indicated their sincere desire to stop using crack and their belief that crack had "taken everything." Many were awaiting limited bed space in residential treatment centers. All were attending Narcotics Anonymous and AA groups, and most felt that God was helping them get off drugs by sending them to jail. Women addicted to crack indicated that it was not possible for them to stop using while they lived in the neighborhoods where crack was easily available and all their acquaintances were using.

Two women had used crack while they were pregnant and felt enormous grief and guilt about endangering their babies. Peaches, a thirty-two-year-old African American woman, gave birth to a stillborn baby because of her use of crack. In jail for prostitution, she described a horrendous history of childhood sexual abuse. Peaches was the youngest of thirteen children, and her mother forced her to have sex with all of her siblings, as well as herself and her boyfriend. Her father took her away from this situation when she was six, but he also sexually abused her. She had a seventeen-year-old daughter and fourteen-, thirteen-, twelve-, and nine-year-old sons and had lost custody of all of them. Of all of the traumas she had experienced, however, she described the death of her baby as the worst:

> I have six kids. I have four boys, and I have a daughter, and then I have a little boy who passed away. [Question: Oh, I'm sorry. When did that happen?] In 1990. He was a crack baby. He was stillborn. I carried him for the whole nine months. I felt his last kick. That was the hardest thing I had to go through in my life. I don't think all the molestation and everything that I've been through has been worse than having a stillborn. I carried that baby for nine months. I don't think none of that that I've been through can top that day. I think that's the biggest problem that I'm having. I can't forgive myself for that. That's my biggest problem. [Question: You think the drugs did it?] Oh yes. There's no doubt in my mind that the drugs did it. I was doin' drugs as I was in

labor. [Question: Did the doctors actually say that it was because of the drugs?] No, they didn't exactly say it was because of the drugs, but deep down inside, I know that was what it was. They wanted to go before a judge and get court orders to do autopsies. At that time, they had just passed a law that if a woman has a baby that's dead or something's wrong with the baby . . . like, my baby was dead so they could have charged me for murder on that child because I had been smokin' drugs. I didn't want that to happen so I did not give them permission to do an autopsy on my baby. The judge wouldn't give them permission because at the time that I was going for prenatal care, they were tellin' me that the baby was fine.

Peaches could not forgive herself and had little hope of ever seeing her children again. She had decided, however, that she was at the end of the line with crack and had to give it up or die:

> When I leave, I'm leaving here with nothing. No probation. When I do go to rehab, it's because I want to. . . . Matter of fact, I think it is the only option for me because there's only two lives. If we choose drugs, that's death. That's the way I feel. If you choose to not do drugs, that's life. I don't want to die doin' drugs. I don't want to die and have to be put in a cardboard box and buried in a cemetery because nobody claims me. That's the only option for me.

Tina's baby did not die, and she had not yet lost custody of her two children who were living with her parents. A twenty-seven-year-old Latina, Tina had been taken directly to jail after giving birth. She was arrested for violating probation, which she had received for drug trafficking and racketeering. During her interview, she lifted her T-shirt to show forty to fifty small, round burn scars on her stomach that had been caused by hiding her hot crack pipe in the waistband of her maternity pants. Tina had also been molested as a child, raped at age twelve, and stabbed and beaten by a group of girls who attacked her for her jewelry. At the time of the interview, her baby was a month old and Tina had been in jail for three weeks and four days. She had stopped using crack for six months during her pregnancy and was living far from town with a friend. There was no public transportation available, and she did not have a car, so her probation officer issued a violation for missed appointments. Tina knew she was facing IPS anyway, so she decided to attend a party with her friend and succumbed to the offer of crack. She cried heavily as she explained:

I did it; and I was laughing; and I remember hitting it and then feeling her move inside of me, like right after I hit the crack; and I still didn't stop; and then the fourth time I hit it, my plug broke and then my water broke. They wanted to go get more drugs and I was there by myself, and I called my dad and I told him. I was scared, you know? What if she died? They could at least treat her for the cocaine. They didn't violate me for probation for it or anything. I figured I couldn't stop; I mean, I stopped because I was away from it. But I couldn't stop when I was around it. So that's why I needed the help. And after seeing her go through the IV, you know, they were testing her, making sure. . . . It threw her complete blood count off. It was real bad; it was real off. But she's healthy now, but to see her hooked up to all them things and bruised up from them. She's just a little baby. It's awful, just seeing her. . . . She's a little angel from God. For me to just imagine one hit . . . what it does to me. Imagine what it did to her little brain. . . . Looking at her little eyes, her little smiles, thinking every little thing, "Is that because I did crack?" You know? "Is that because I had smoked when she had first developed?" I was scared, 'cuz I didn't know I was pregnant. But every little thing that I saw, I was just paranoid. Excuse me [crying hard], I'm like, just like for me to hurt her, just horrible. . . . CPS got involved; I mean, I don't blame them, the hospital called them, and you know, they treated me like a monster, and I felt like a monster; I knew I was a monster. But the remorse I feel, the hurt. . . . My dad gets mad when I tell him I love my kids and I'm gonna change. He says, "Don't tell me you love them; every time you tell me, that makes me sick after what you did."

Tina and Peaches expressed a desire to stop using crack and bore tremendous sadness and guilt about the harm caused to their babies and their families. They shared the hegemonic public view of crack mothers as evil baby killers who deserve nothing but contempt, and they felt self-contempt as "monsters." They desperately wanted help and had long histories of abuse in addition to their addictions. The intensive assistance required to help them recover from their addictions and return to a mothering role was not available to them. Instead, the only motivation for recovery, their children, had been taken away, and they have nothing to look forward to except guilt and regret. These data suggest that decisions about child custody play a central role in women's resistance to the psychological anesthesia offered by drugs and alcohol. Balancing the need to protect children and promote women's health and well-being re-

quires programs that are attuned to both mothers and children and flexible in their ability to provide support to both.

Mothering and Identity From Inside

The majority of women in jail had identities that reflected some of the social approbation that their incarceration signified. Like Tina and Patrice, cited earlier, the linkage of their drug usage with harm to their children contributed to self-images as "monsters," and they were unable to forgive themselves. Women who had prostituted for drugs or lost custody because of drugs also had negative judgments about those aspects of their identities. Other women resisted stigmatization by contextualizing their offenses within the realities of economic marginalization and violent victimization. As Alicia pointed out, "We're not all bad people."

In struggling to develop positive identities, mothering was critical in sustaining perceptions of value and goodness. In the abstract, motherhood is a highly valued status, and women viewed the facts of their motherhood as a potential source of social acceptance. At a deeper level, however, many women indicated that their links to their children were central to their selfhood. Children were extensions of their own identities, separate yet constitutive of women's subjectivity. In one case in which it was physically possible, a woman returned to one of us with pictures of her children after her own interview ended. Other women indicated regret that they did not have photographs available to show us and spoke of how beautiful and cute their children were.

India, a thirty-one-year-old American Indian woman with six children, illustrated the importance of children to women's identities most graphically. She had tattoos for each child's name on various parts of her body. A heart with flowers around a blank space on her right breast was reserved for her youngest child whose name she had not yet had tattooed. She had lost her children to CPS at one point but regained custody after following their requirements. Her children were with their father's sister, and she planned to reunite with them after completing her sentence.

Even women whose rights had been terminated and who were prohibited from interacting with their children believed that they would be reunited one day. Julianna had lost custody of her four children but believed that some day they would be together again:

I believe in my heart of hearts, once you birth a child, they can take your child from you for so long, but that child will come back. Listen to a lot of these talk shows on how families are starting to reunite. Just look at the awesome power of God to bring families back together that haven't been together for fourteen, twenty, thirty years. I have a dream that one day my two children that is within the state, I will see them. We will reunite and be together. With my other children in Nebraska, I have no doubt that I will see them. They'll be family. God will show me the way for us to reunite and be together again. That's my strong belief.

The likelihood of Julianna reuniting her family was small, but focusing on this dream gave her the hope and strength to go on living. Like many jailed women, she believed that God was guiding her life and would ultimately return her children to her. She described what she believed to be direct communication with God:

That's when He spoke to me, sternly this time. "I'm gonna pick you up, and I will turn your life around, and I will make you want success and great things. Most of all, I will make you a great woman of God and you will be a great woman. I'm gonna bring you back to your children again." That, right there, is enough for me to hold on, to walk through the storm and the rain, and move on with my life.

Linda, who lost custody of three children because of her crack and heroin addictions, also believed that God would return her children to her:

I ask God to give me my life back, give me my children back. And so now, this is a start. I'm okay with where I'm at because I know when I leave here it won't be long before I can reunite with my children. Not right away, but eventually it's goin' to come together. I know God is gonna give them back to me. I know I'm goin' to see them real soon. Without them, I'm nothin'. I just thank God.

Even women whose children had died carried their memories and the grief over their loss as a central aspect of their identities. Buckwheat's son had been killed in a drive-by shooting five years before we met her. She said that she went into a "blackout" for eight days and was finally awakened by the boy's father. He told her, "You didn't do nothin'. I had to go up to you and put the mirror to your face to see if you were alive." She described how a recent Valentine's Day visit at the jail had confirmed her son's eternal life and continued relationship to her:

This past Valentine's, they had these Christian women come out here for a Valentine's

thing in here. They gave out these little heart-shaped doilies and they had a little prayer on them, and they said to all of us, "These are special gifts that we're goin' to give you and hopefully the right one is goin' to reach you." Well, it surprised me about the one that they gave me because it said, "I gave my son to the Lord and for. . . ." I can't think of all of it but that he would live forever. I said, "Oh my God." And He told me to let it go. To let him go.

The continued importance of children to women's identities, despite severance or even death, was clear in all the women's narratives. This connection helped women to survive and look forward to the future with hope. It also made incarceration and separation from children more painful and worrisome due to the impact on children and the difficulties of mothering from inside the detention facility.

Conclusion

Mothering in an environment of scarce resources places women in a web of demands and constraints that may lead to incarceration. Selling drugs or cashing bad checks to meet bills and turning to drugs and alcohol as a way of coping with the psychological pain of childhood sexual abuse or the ongoing pain of domestic violence are the primary pathways that lead women to jail (Daly 1994; Henriques and Manatu 2001; Katz 2000). Incarceration then creates greater burdens for maintaining positive relationships with children and for managing the demands of probation once released. Women interviewed at the PCAD had survived horrendous abuse and poverty yet maintained hope for a positive future and eventual reunion with their children.

Mothering simultaneously reproduces the unequal sexual division of labor and provides possibilities for resistance to marginalization and despair. The assumption that women will be primary caretakers and will provide resources and love for children when men do not demands that women obtain money and dispense care without much assistance. The possibility that women will become involved in crime as a result of trying to meet these demands is exacerbated by race and class hierarchies that restrict access to incomes adequate to support children.

The chaotic and demanding community contexts that lead women to view jail as a "vacation" suggest that there are complex problems facing low-income mothers that cannot be resolved either through programs for the children of incarcerated mothers or through revisions in sentencing policies. Reversing the trend of incarceration of minor drug and property offenders would ameliorate some of the harsh circumstances for both mothers and children created by incarceration. However, the violence, poverty, drug abuse, and mental health problems that women face outside of jail can only be addressed through systematic attention to the sources of these problems for women. Recent social policy trends exacerbate the obstacles facing many women. Exclusion of convicted drug offenders from social welfare programs, zero-tolerance housing policies that evict battered women from public housing, punitive and restrictive Temporary Assistan[ce] to Needy Families guidelines, and programs that encourage women to marry as a solution to poverty make it more difficult for low-income single mothers to survive in the United States than at any time since the Great Depression. The narratives of jailed women reflect this difficulty and the failure of social policies to remedy the cumulative effects of violent victimization, poverty, racism, drug addictions, and mental health problems on women's abilities to mother their children.

While mothering complicates women's abilities to negotiate marginalized existence, it also provides a resource for hope and positive identity. The dominant ideology of motherhood is reflected in women's accounts of their inadequacies and failures but also in their insistence on fighting against addictions, male violence, and poverty. Although the desire to be a "good mother," and the dimensions of that construct, may be a vector of the social control of women, it is simultaneously a ground from which women challenge structured and individual sources of oppression.

Discussion Questions

1. Discuss the importance of mothering as a primary form of identity formation as well as a method of social control for women.

2. How are criminal behaviors linked to women trying to meet parental demands in the face of restrictions that deny them incomes adequate to support children?

3. How is a "good mother" defined? Which of the women interviewed in this study are "good mothers"? Defend your answer.

4. Discuss the issue of motherhood as a right versus a privilege for mother deemed "unfit" by social or legal standards.

5. Why did some women view jail as a retreat or a vacation from their lives?

6. What can be done to assist single, head-of-household mothers to meet the demands of parenting without resorting to crime?

References

Administration for Children and Families. 2002. *Information Memorandum on Promoting Safe and Stable Families Amendments of 2001.* Available from *http://www.acf.hhs.gov/programs/cb/laws/imJim0201.pdf.*

Allen, Hilary. 1987. Rendering them harmless: The professional portrayal of women charged with serious violent crimes. In *Gender, crime and justice,* edited by Pat Carlen and Anne Worrall, 81–94. Philadelphia: Open University Press.

Amnesty International. 1999. *"Not part of my sentence": Violations of the human rights of women in custody.* Available from *http://web.amnesty.org.*

———. 2001. *New reports of children and women abused in correctional institutions. Findings from Amnesty International research trip.* Available from *http://web.amnesty.org.*

Arnold, Regina. 1990. Processes of victimization and criminalization of black women. *Social Justice* 17: 153–66.

Baunach, Phyllis Jo. 1985. *Mothers in prison.* New Brunswick, NJ: Transaction Publishing.

Beck, Allen J., and Paige M. Harrison. 2001. *Prisoners in 2000.* Washington, DC: U.S. Department of Justice.

Belknap, Joanne. 2001. *The invisible woman: Gender, crime, and justice.* 2d ed. Belmont, CA: Wadsworth.

Bloom, Barbara. 1992. Incarcerated mothers and their children: Maintaining family ties. In *Female offenders: Meeting the needs of a neglected population.* Laurel, MD: American Correctional Association.

Bloom, Barbara, Meda Chesney-Lind, and Barbara Owen. 1994. *Women in California prisons: Hidden victims of the war on drugs.* San Francisco: Center on Juvenile and Criminal Justice.

Bloom, Barbara, and David Steinhart. 1993. *Why punish the children? A reappraisal of the children of incarcerated mothers in America.* San Francisco: National Council on Crime and Delinquency.

Bosworth, Mary. 1999. *Engendering resistance: Agency and power in women's prisons.* Aldershot, UK: Ashgate.

Boudin, Kathy. 1998. Lessons from a mother's program in prison: A psychosocial approach supports women and their children. In *Breaking the rules: Women in prison and feminist therapy,* edited by Judy Harden and Marcia Hill, 103–125. New York: Haworth.

Caddle, Diane. 1998. *Age limits for babies in prison: Some lessons from abroad.* London: Home Office Research, Development and Statistics Directorate.

Caiazza, Amy B. 2000. *The status of women in Arizona.* Washington, DC: Institute for Women's Policy Research.

Chesney-Lind, Meda. 1997. *The female offender: Girls, women, and crime.* Thousand Oaks, CA: Sage.

Chesney-Lind, Meda, Mary Kay Harris, and Gabrielle deGroot. 1998. Female offenders. *Corrections Today* 60 (7): 66–144.

Daly, Kathleen. 1994. *Gender, crime and punishment.* New Haven, CT: Yale University Press.

DeVault, Marjorie L. 1999. *Liberating method: Feminism and social research.* Philadelphia: Temple University Press.

Dobash, Russell P., R. Emerson Dobash, and Sue Gutteridge. 1986. *The imprisonment of women.* London: Basil Blackwell.

Elliott, Terri. 1994. Making strange what had appeared familiar. *Monist* 77: 424–33.

Enos, Sandra. 2001. *Mothering from the inside: Parenting in a women's prison.* New York: State University of New York Press.

Fineman, Martha A. 1995. Images of mothers in poverty discourse. In *Mothers-in-law: Feminist theory and the legal regulation of motherhood,* edited by Martha A. Fineman and Isabel Karpin, 205–23. New York: Columbia University Press.

Friedlin, Jennifer. 2002. Judge exposes agency harm to battered mothers, kids. *Women's E News,* April 28.

Gilbert, Evelyn. 1999. Crime, sex, and justice: African American women in U.S. prisons. In *Harsh punishment: International experiences of women's imprisonment,* edited by Sandy Cook and Suzanne Davies, 230–49. Boston: Northeastern University Press.

Gilfus, Mary E. 1992. From victims to survivors to offenders: Women's routes of entry and immersion into street crime. *Women and Criminal Justice* 4: 63–90.

Glaser, Barney G., and Anselm L. Strauss. 1967. *The discovery of grounded theory: Strategies for qualitative research.* Chicago: Aldine.

Glick, Ruth M., and Virginia V. Neto. 1977. *National study of women's correctional programs.* Washington, DC: U.S. Department of Justice.

Greenfield, Lawrence A., and Tracy L. Snell. 1999. *Bureau of Justice Statistics special report: Women offenders* (NCJ 175688). Washington, DC: U.S. Department of Justice.

Harrison, Paige M., and Allen J. Beck. 2002. *Bureau of Justice Statistics Bulletin: Prisoners in 2001* (NCJ 195189). Washington, DC: U.S. Department of Justice.

Hartsock, Nancy. 1987. The feminist standpoint: Developing a ground for a specifically feminist historical materialism. In *Feminism and methodology,* edited by Sandra Harding, 157–76. Milton Keynes, UK: Open University Press.

Henriques, Zelma W. 1982. *Imprisoned mothers and their children.* Lanham, MD: University Press of America.

Henriques, Zelma W., and Rupert N. Manatu. 2001. Living on the outside: African American women before, during, and after imprisonment. *The Prison Journal* 81 (1): 6–19.

Hill Collins, Patricia. 1989. The social construction of black feminist thought. *Signs* 14: 745–73.

——. 2000. *Black feminist thought: Knowledge, consciousness, and the politics of empowerment.* New York: Routledge.

Human Rights Watch Women's Rights Project. 1996. *All too familiar: Sexual abuse of women in U.S. state prisons.* New York: Human Rights Watch.

Humphries, Drew. 1999. *Crack mothers.* Columbus: Ohio State University Press.

Ikemoto, L. C. 1997. Furthering the inquiry: Race, class, and culture in the forced medical treatment of pregnant women. In *Critical race feminism: A reader,* edited by Adrien K. Wing, 136–143. New York: New York University Press.

Immarigeon, Russ, and Meda Chesney-Lind. 1992. *Women's prisons: Overcrowded and overused.* San Francisco: National Council on Crime and Delinquency.

Karush, Sarah. 2002. Kremlin pardons imprisoned mothers. *The Globe and Mail,* March 20, p. A16.

Katz, Rebecca S. 2000. Explaining girls' and women's crime and desistance in the context of their victimization experiences: A developmental test of revised strain. *Violence Against Women* 6 (6): 633–60.

Kline, Marlee. 1995. Complicating the ideology of motherhood: Child welfare law and First Nation women. In *Mothers-in-law: Feminist theory and the legal regulation of motherhood,* edited by Martha A. Fineman and Isabel Karpin, 118–41. New York: Columbia University Press.

Kvale, Steiner. 1996. *Interviews: An introduction to qualitative research interviewing.* Thousand Oaks, CA: Sage.

Lofland, John, and Lynn H. Lofland. 1995. *Analyzing social settings: A guide to qualitative observation and analysis.* 3rd ed. Belmont, CA: Wadsworth.

McGowan, Brenda G., and Karen L. Blumenthal. 1978. *Why punish the children?* Hackensack, NJ: National Council on Crime and Delinquency.

Miller, Jody. 1998. Up it up: Gender and the accomplishment of street robbery. *Criminology* 36: 37–65.

Moe, Angela M., and Kathleen J. Ferraro. 2002. Malign neglect or benign respect: Women's health care in a carceral setting. Paper presented at the annual meetings of the Academy of Criminal Justice Sciences, March 5–9, Anaheim, CA.

Molloy, Maureen. 1992. Citizenship, property, and bodies: Discourses on gender and the inter-war labor government in New Zealand. *Gender and History* 4: 293–304.

Morash, Merry. 1998. *Women offenders: Programming needs and promising approaches.* Washington, DC: U.S. Department of Justice.

Mumola, Cristopher J. 2000. *Incarcerated parents and their children.* Bureau of Justice Statistics special report. Washington, DC: U.S. Department of Justice.

Nagel, Irene H., and John Hagan. 1983. Gender and crime: Offense patterns and criminal court sanctions. In *Crime and justice*, vol. 4, edited by Michael Tonry and Norval Morris, 91–144. Chicago: University of Chicago Press.

Narayan, Uma. 1988. Working together across difference: Some considerations on emotions and political practice. *Hypatia* 3 (2): 31–47.

National Institute of Corrections. 2002. Services for families of prison inmates. Longmont, CO: National Institute of Corrections Information Center.

Orbuch, Terri L. 1997. People's accounts count: The sociology of accounts. *Annual Review of Sociology* 23: 455–78.

Pollak, Otto. 1950. *The criminality of women.* Westport, CT: Greenwood.

Richie, Beth E. 1996. *Compelled to crime: The gender entrapment of battered black women.* New York: Routledge.

——. 2001. Challenges incarcerated women face as they return to their communities: Findings from life history interviews. *Crime & Delinquency* 47: 368–89.

Roberts, Dorothy E. 1995. Racism and patriarchy in the meaning of motherhood. In *Mothers in law: Feminist theory and the legal regulation of motherhood,* edited by Martha A. Fineman and Isabel Karpin, 224–49. New York: Columbia University Press.

Ross, Luana. 1998. *Inventing the savage.* Austin: University of Texas Press.

Sandoval, Chela. 2000. *Methodology of the oppressed.* Minneapolis: University of Minnesota Press.

Schafer, N. E., and A. B. Dellinger. 1999. Jailed parents: An assessment. *Women and Criminal Justice* 10 (4): 73–118.

Smart, Carol. 1995. Criminological theory: Its ideology and implications concerning women. In *Law, crime and sexuality: Essays in feminism,* edited by Carol Smart, 16–31. London: Sage.

——. 1998. The woman of legal discourse. In *Criminology at the crossroads: Feminist readings in crime and justice,* edited by Kathleen Daly and Lisa Maher, 21–36. New York: Oxford University Press.

Smith, Dorothy. 1987. *The everyday world as problematic: A feminist sociology.* Toronto, Canada: University of Toronto Press.

Snell, Tracy L. 1994. *Women in prison: Survey of state prison inmates, 1991.* Washington, DC: U.S. Department of Justice.

Sommers, Ira B., Deborah Baskin, and Jeffrey Fagan. 2000. *Workin' hard for the money: The social and economic lives of women drug sellers.* Huntington, NY: Nova Science Publishers.

Stanton, Ann M. 1980. *When mothers go to jail.* Lexington, MA: D. C. Health.

Stephan, J. J. 2001. *Census of jails 1999.* Washington, DC: U.S. Department of Justice.

U.S. General Accounting Office. 1999. *Women in prison: Issues and challenges confronting U.S. correctional systems.* Washington, DC: U.S. General Accounting Office.

Watterson, Kathryn. 1996. *Women in prison: Inside the concrete womb.* Rev. ed. Boston: Northeastern University Press.

Young, Vernetta D. 1986. Gender expectations and their impact on black female offenders and victims. *Justice Quarterly* 3: 305–27.

Zalba, Serapio R. 1964. *Women prisoners and their families.* Albany, NY: Delmar.

8

Women Who Have Killed Their Children

Susan M. Crimmins
Sandra C. Langley
Henry H. Brownstein
Barry J. Spunt

How do we understand homicides involving women who have killed their own children? Official records in the state of New York indicated that 86 out of a total of 443 women convicted for murder or manslaughter were incarcerated for the death of a child. Of those, 42 women (49 percent) participated in an interview. Findings from these 42 interviews are the focus of this chapter. The interview included life history questions concerning family, drug involvement and drug treatment, participation in illegal activities, and issues of violence in subjects' lives as both victims and perpetrators while growing up and as adults. In addition, subjects were asked detailed questions about the homicide for which they were convicted. Repeated experiences of damage to the self, including physical and sexual victimization, suicide attempts, and substance abuse, were evident throughout the lives of these women. This chapter discusses the extent to which these self-damage indicators interfered with the offender's ability to parent children.

The innocence and vulnerability of children, particularly of infants, typically arouse instincts of nurturance and protectiveness on a universal level. In addition, sociocultural expectations dictate that women are primary caretakers for the young. What then, would prompt a woman to kill an infant or child who is helpless and dependent upon her for survival?

Research shows that about two thirds of the victims of women who commit homicide are family members, with the most common event being the killing of a spouse or partner (Daly & Wilson, 1988; Jones, 1980). Research concerning women killing children is narrow in scope and often anecdotal in presentation due to small numbers. The paucity of reports on this topic may be related to truly low incidence of the crime, the underreporting or mistaken reporting of these crimes, or a combination of both. Crib deaths or Sudden Infant Death Syndrome (SIDS) overlap many times with the less socially acceptable report of infanticide (Asch, 1968; Nowak, 1993). Another complicating factor is the number of missing children reported each year, which may mask a more accurate count of child deaths by mothers. However, we do know that homicide remains one of the top five leading causes of death during early childhood in the United States (Abel, 1986).

Despite the relative infrequency of reports of child killing by mothers, as compared to the overall homicide rate, its seriousness and moral implications render it worthy of further examination to identify contributing factors as well as to reflect upon society's handling of such violence. Data derived from interviews with women convicted of killing children are presented in an attempt to understand the factors that contribute to committing such an exceptional crime.

Literature Review

Child killing has occurred throughout the ages, although the reasons given for its existence have varied. Malformation of the infant, economic distress, and social disgrace were all prevalent motives in dispensing with children, and killing was the most efficient method of ensuring that the burden was eliminated permanently (Friedman, 1993; Hoffer & Hull, 1981; Lyon, 1985; Piers, 1978; Weir, 1984). Additional literature has suggested that infant and child killing has also been influenced by complicating factors of jealousy and revenge, psychiatric conditions, and violence within families (Resnick, 1969; Scott, 1973a; Silverman & Kennedy, 1988).

The 1922 Infanticide Act and later, the Not Guilty by Reason of Insanity (NGRI) plea allowed the first opportunity to peer into the mind and intent of the mother who kills her child (see, e.g., Parker & Good, 1981; Pasewark, Pantle, & Steadman, 1979). These legal concepts also set the stage for controversy and labeling in attempting to decipher if these mothers were "mad or bad" in their killings. "Mad" mothers were believed to be psychiatrically unstable and killed as a result of their mental illness, whereas "bad" mothers were considered intrinsically evil and killed because of this predisposition (Warren, 1989; Wilczynski, 1991).

Contemporary motives for killing children involve more psychological reasoning than having enough food to provide or being a victim of social disgrace. Revenge, sometimes referred to as the Medea Syndrome, involves the killing of children in an attempt to punish the husband or partner. Greek tragedy portrays Medea as the jealous, vengeful wife who gets back at her husband, Jason, by murdering their two children (Arboleda-Florez & Power, 1983). Although this drama may be sensationally appealing, it leaves us with the question of why angry wives choose this pathological means of revenge toward their husbands when there are many other options available to them.

In recent literature, additional motives or reasons for these killings fall under the rubric of: acute psychosis or gross mental pathology (Resnick, 1969; Scott, 1973a); unwanted child (Resnick, 1969; Scott, 1973a); mercy killing (d'Orban, 1979; Lomis, 1986; Resnick, 1969; Scott, 1973a); victim-precipitated (Daniel & Kashani, 1983; Scott, 1973a, 1973b); childhood maltreatment of women ("learned violence") (Korbin, 1986); and poverty, stress, "social disorganization" (Kaplun & Reich, 1976; Totman, 1978). Silverman and Kennedy (1988) distinguish between two different types of female child killers. The Type 1 mother commits infanticide due to severe psychological stress and is usually young, single, and immature. The Type 2 mother kills her child because she goes "too far" in physical abuse of the child, which may be the result of displaced anger, either conscious or unconscious. More often than not, she is married. The "goes too far" or Type 2 hypothesis is also proposed by Scott (1973a) who theorizes that killing is the result of learning or frustration for these women. Perhaps Daniel and Kashani (1983) advance this thinking by linking the theory of intergenerational violence within families as the basis for the killing. They suggest that a mother with a history of physical abuse and serious psychopathology is a strong candidate for murdering a child.

Child Killing: A Self-Psychology Theoretical Consideration

Consistent with examining the characteristics of women who have killed children and combining, as well as enhancing, some of the above-mentioned reasons for child killing is the self-psychological perspective, which suggests the woman's sense of self is too damaged for her to care about another human being. Self becomes damaged not simply because trauma occurs but also because an absence of social sup-

ports and an inability to rely upon others in times of need lays the foundation for the message that self is unimportant (Crimmins, 1995).

With this perspective in mind, when a woman kills a child, it may be that the child is not the literal object that she intends to destroy (similar to the Medea Syndrome), but rather that the child is representative of some other object worthy of destruction. Often the impulse to destroy emanates from a feeling of rage. "Rage is associated with imagery of attacking whatever forces one can identify and hold responsible for the death and for one's own survivor pain" (Lifton, 1979, p. 148). The death may be real or imagined, physical or psychological. To clarify and simplify in the instances of women killing children, death may be perceived as synonymous with the terms *loss* and *threat* to the woman who is experiencing the rage.

Violence often emanates from the need to protect or preserve the self from an impending threat (Crimmins & Foley, 1989). The death threat loss is so powerful to the person who has a very fragile, damaged sense of self that the only possible means of gaining a balance of power is through physical force. Clearly an infant or small child does not pose a physical threat to a mother but may indeed represent a real threat to a shaky identity in a woman with little or no self-esteem. Horner (1989) wrote,

> Children, unbeknownst to them, often wield parental power over their own parents because of the kinds of conscious and unconscious attributions made by the parents to what the child does or says. Rejection by a son or daughter can have exactly the same emotional impact on the parent as did rejection by his or her mother or father in the past, evoking the same anxiety, rage, or depression. (pp. 20–21)

The threat, which may be manifested as rejection, is then introjected as an annihilation of self (death), a loss of self, and a wipe-out of power and identity due to the woman's unsuccessful separation from her own parents. As the result of poor object relations, object and self are fused together, so that the killing of the child may be viewed as a symbolic suicide. Because the message in the threat is "I am nothing," which is too painful for the mother to acknowledge, killing the child becomes an act of self-preservation. By killing the object of threat (the bad self), the true or core self is allowed to survive and the balance of power is restored.

Consistent with the thought that child killing is a result of going too far, Shengold (1989) takes the disturbed mother's thinking one step further by introducing the concept of soul murder. This is

> a dramatic term for circumstances that eventuate in crime—the deliberate attempt to eradicate or compromise the separate identity of another person . . . a crime most often committed by psychotic or psychopathic parents who treat the child as an extension of themselves or as an object with which to satisfy their desires. (pp. 2–3)

Because the mother identifies with the aggressors (her own parents), she unconsciously becomes intent upon carrying out punishment whenever the child exhibits willful statements or behaviors in an attempt to separate from her. Again, this may be manifested as the child merely behaving like his or her father would, and this would be sufficient for the mother to witness it as betrayal or defiance of her power.

Katz (1988) has suggested that a sense of "righteous slaughter" has been perceived by the woman who has determined that the child has, either realistically or symbolically, teased, dared, or defied the killer. In the killer's perception, she is acting in an attempt to "defend the Good." This subtle, slowly emerging phenomenon is often elusive to the general public, and it may escape others, who view the killing of a child as senseless or insane. However, the perpetrator's emotional and moral logic has developed to the extent that this path of action, killing, is the only possible way to defend and to preserve the integrity of self.

Katz outlines three essential components that characterize a righteously enraged slaughter: First, the killer interprets the victim (child) and his/her behaviors in a very particular way that is threatening to the value/livelihood of self and that "requires a last stand in defense of his (her) basic worth" (pp. 18–19). Second, an emotional process that is intense, all-consuming, and overwhelming has been initiated within the killer. Feelings of eternal humiliation, shame, and degradation are transformed into rage as the first step toward self-preservation. In a rage, the future can be discounted with an emphasis being placed on preserving the moral good. Finally, the perspective and posture outlined above must be maintained throughout the implementation of the entire situation. The punishment inflicted gives credence to the pain/anguish that the killer has withstood, and death of the child is then viewed as a sacrificial slaughter.

Given the perceptions and processes that the child killer embraces, it is emotionally logical to suppose that following the killing, the mother would feel a sense of relief, accomplishment, and peacefulness that self has been preserved. However, this is not an inevitable outcome. Post killing reality sets in and tampers with the trauma-based mind-set of the killer. Most mothers are remorseful about the killings but are unable to do more than acknowledge that it happened due to feelings of frustration or despair. It would appear that after the rage has been satiated, feelings return to or transform back into their homeostatic form of insecurity, self-doubt, and humiliation, so that a full cycle of victimization has been enacted with the only accomplishment being a greater entrenchment into feelings of despair. This dynamic may be reflective of the depression that overcomes mothers who kill their children and then become suicidal. If the killing was, indeed, supposed to remedy and preserve a true sense of self and this did not occur, the only available alternative is suicide (Katz, 1988).

One may ask how it is that there exists a need to defend the "righteous good" from threats to begin with. Why is it that everyone does not move toward violence when threatened? The answer is not monolithic in nature and may only be categorized as being a response to cumulative exposure of traumatic and unpredictable experiences that have injured one's sense of self. The formation of identity, or sense of self, is affected strongly by experiences that occur during our earliest years of life (Bowlby, 1973, 1988; Mahler, 1979; Zulueta, 1993). Feelings about self, also known as self-esteem or self-worth, are derived largely from a succession of interactions and experiences between significant others in the social environment and self. Mastery of social experiences builds positive self-worth, whereas a series of experiential failures contributes to frustration and a fragmented sense of self.

How you feel about yourself is largely influenced by how others conveyed they felt about you during your youngest years. During early childhood, a mother is usually the person upon whom you can rely for security, warmth, and feelings of comfort. An absence of nurturance by a primary caretaker will interfere with the ability to develop positive feelings about yourself or the ability to build positive social experiences, unless alternative social and emotional supports are in place. Without having a "secure base" from which to operate, one is unable to develop positive or healthy attachments with others (Bowlby, 1988). In situations where the mother may be emotionally unavailable to her child (e.g., mental illness, neglect) and other supports are absent, the child grows up with an impoverished emotional repertoire from which to gauge interpersonal relationships and an adequate sense of self-worth. When this child grows up and becomes a mother, she is then unable to give her own child a sense of warmth or security, for as a "motherless mother," she cannot give what she has not been given (Edelman, 1994; Zulueta, 1993).

There are several other areas of trauma that we know have deleterious effects upon the formation of personality or self in children who have early and prolonged exposure to them without the ameliorating benefits of social supports. Specifically, growing up in a family where alcohol and/or drugs are used on a regular basis or growing up where serious physical harm and sexual harm compromise a child's sense of safety and trust (Herman, 1992; Levin, 1987; Terr, 1990; Wood, 1987). Both of these scenarios are likely to result in the child developing a history of substance abuse to ward off feelings of psychic pain, as well as a plethora of mental health problems, including depression and suicidal behavior.

The influence of alcohol and drugs upon the formation of self have been well documented in the literature (e.g., Levin, 1987; Wood, 1987). From a self psychology perspective, people often ingest substances to replace or substitute an object or an object's love that they have lost or never had. Characteristically, there is a lack of predictability in the lives of families who abuse substances. All children need to be surrounded by caretakers who are predictable in their responses so that trust may be established and to ensure that a sense of safety may be developed. Substance abuse may be interpreted as an expression of yearning for a substitute to soothe or numb feelings of anxiety and/or pain and to block out unpleasant realities.

As part of a dissociative process, the child then learns to separate emotions from actions or events that are too painful. This coping mechanism is used frequently by trauma victims (Herman, 1992; Terr, 1990; Zulueta, 1993) and has characteristically been documented during times of war. The trauma victim often reports a "numbing" that occurs following the killing of another (Lifton, 1973). In situations of physical or sexual trauma by a parent or otherwise "trustworthy adult," this "disavow" of painful or distressing stimuli, also known as numbing, permits the child to collude with the parental perception that all is fine. The payoff for this distortion is the fantasy of parental love and security, which is guaranteed if the emotions are squelched. Disavowal becomes the developed defense against the meaning of an external perception. Reality is intact, but its meaning is not accepted (Basch, 1982). "For as long as you are not allowed to see something, you have no choice but to overlook it, to misunderstand it, to protect yourself against it in one way or another" (Miller, 1984, pp. 9–10).

What, then, are the experiences and sense of self held by women who kill children? Are they too damaged to care adequately for children? If so, what are the primary, damaging factors that so influenced their lives and development to the extent that they were rendered unable to care for and protect their children? Why did they resort to committing an act of lethal violence? These issues were examined via interviews with women who have been convicted of killing children.

Findings and Discussion

Sociodemographic variables of race/ethnicity, age, education, and income status were examined for these 42 women with the following results: Race/ethnicity: 20 women of the 42 (48%) were Black, whereas 16 (38%) were White, 3 (7%) were Hispanic, and 3 (7%) were from other racial/ethnic backgrounds. Age of the subjects at the time of the homicide ranged from 16 years to 42 years. The median age was 25.5 years. Education was measured as the highest grade completed. The median level of education was eleventh grade (range third grade to 2 years of college). An examination of income sources revealed that some subjects had more than one source of income at the time of the homicide, with the most frequently reported being welfare/public assistance for 13 women (31%), legitimate employment for 12 women (29%), and spouse/partner support for 12 women (29%). No more than three women reported each of the following sources of income: family, illegal means, unemployment, and social security benefits. One woman reported no income, and data for another woman was missing.

As mentioned before, the following variables are prominent self-damage indicators that are influential in personality development and thus in the shaping of a person's responses toward society: characteristics of "motherless mothering," drug/alcohol abuse in family of origin, self-drug history, serious childhood harm and serious adult harm (including physical and sexual harm by others), and self-harm. Examination of relevant interview data clearly indicates that many of these women were exposed to multiple experiences of damage that influenced their lives and their ability to parent children.

Twenty-seven of the women (64%) were categorized as being motherless mothers based upon their reports of early experiences with their own mothers. Several types of behaviors resulted in the subjects' mothers being unavailable to them: serious and prolonged verbal abuse, serious physical abuse, alcoholism, mental health problems, and absence due to neglect/death. More than a third of the women (38%) had alcoholic mothers, 19% experienced serious physical abuse by their mothers, and the mothers of 17% were absent. Almost a quarter of the women (24%) had mothers who had more than one characteristic that made them unavailable to these subjects during childhood.

Alma spoke about the immediate effects that being abused had upon her:

> I didn't have a family life. My mother used to sit on my head to make me still so she could beat me with a cord, belt, or anything she could get her hands on, and things got worse when she burned me with an iron, and she allowed certain relatives to have sex with me and get away with it. She sexually abused me too. . . . [All the abuse] made me feel less important and didn't care about myself too much.

Later in the interview, Alma also spoke about how her childhood abuse affected her parenting skills with her 4-year-old son.

> I was very scared cause I was pregnant and I was scared. I didn't know what to do because my daughter's father left me alone 'cause he got me pregnant and I was ready to move. I was packing up my stuff and my son was acting up and I didn't know what to do 'cause I don't understand nothing about disciplining a child cause I was raised by my own family, how they abused me and I didn't know what to do, so I took it out on my son and sent him to his room and I made him go to bed and he went to bed. I went near and he wasn't breathing, he stopped breathing, wouldn't breathe. I know he was sleeping and he didn't wake up. I hit him, I only hit him twice in the head with my hand. I don't know, with my shoe, my flat shoe in the head twice and that was it, and I sent him to his room cause I didn't want to hit him no more. . . . It was very hard for me 'cause I didn't know what to do. The only thing I knew was to take him to the doctor when he needed to go to the doctor and feed him and keep him clean, that was it. I didn't know how to love him, 'cause I didn't have, didn't love myself, I didn't know how to love him.

Abusive Partners and Motherless Mothers

Table 8.1 shows that slightly more than half (52%) of the women who killed children were motherless mothers who also had been involved with an abusive partner. A likely reason these women became involved with abusive partners

Table 8.1
Comparison of Having an Abusive Partner and Being a Motherless Mother (N = 42)

| | Abusive Partner | | |
	Yes	No	Total
Motherless Mother			
Yes	22 (52%)	5 (12%)	27 (64%)
No	11 (26%)	4 (9%)	15 (36%)
Total	33 (79%)	9 (21%)	42 (100%)

was because their self-perceptions were damaged to the extent that they believed abuse was all they deserved. Only 12% of the women who were motherless mothers did not become involved with an abusive mate. An additional 26% were not characterized as motherless mothers but still became involved with an abusive partner. Although this group of women did not fit the description of being a motherless mother, they did have mothers who may be considered codependent in their behaviors. The possible impact this may have had upon the subjects' becoming involved with an abusive partner requires further research.

Substance Use in Family of Origin

Twenty-five of the 42 women (60%) reported that drugs/alcohol were used in their families of origin on a daily basis. Alcohol was overwhelmingly the most commonly used drug, as it was used on a daily basis in 24 of the families (57%). As previously mentioned, more than half of the 25 women were in families where the mother used alcohol on a regular basis. For these women, one can assume that their mothers were unavailable to them emotionally and were unable to provide them with the safety and comfort a child requires. Thus emotional abandonment was a common experience for these women, who, in turn, could not provide for their own children the safety and nurturance that they never had (Zulueta, 1993).

Subject Use of Alcohol and Drugs

In terms of their own usage, 27 women or 64% of the group described using drugs or alcohol on at least a regular basis. Regular basis was defined as using 3 or more days per week for a month or more. The most common drugs that were used regularly by the 27 women were marijuana (11 or 26%), alcohol (8 or 19%), and tranquilizers (7 or 17%). Eighteen respondents, or 43%, who reported growing up in families where alcohol or drugs were used on a regular basis also reported regular alcohol or drug usage in their own lives.

Serious Harm Witnessed by Subjects During Childhood

Serious physical harm, another self-damage indicator, was measured with a modified version of the Conflict Tactics Scales (Straus, Gelles, & Steinmetz, 1981). Behaviors such as kick, punch or bite, beat up, threaten with a weapon, and use of a weapon are included in the definition of serious physical harm. Sexual harm was added to the assessment of harm and was measured by two items: inappropriate sexual touching and forced sexual penetration. Subjects were asked about the incidence of these behaviors in their childhood (up to age 16) and in their adult years.

Three fourths (74%) of the women said they witnessed or experienced serious physical and/or sexual harm during childhood. Two thirds of the women witnessed or experienced serious physical harm, and half witnessed or experienced sexual harm. Most of the serious childhood physical harm was witnessed or experienced by the subjects equally with their mothers and with siblings (10 or 24%). On the other hand, most of the serious sexual harm during childhood was witnessed or experienced by the women with their father, stepfather or mother's boyfriend (9 or 21%), other relatives (i.e., male cousins, grandfathers), 8 or 19%, and then male siblings (6 or 14%). Thus an overwhelming majority of the harm witnessed or experienced by these women as children occurred in their own families among people they were supposed to trust or with whom they should have felt safe.

Serious Harm Experienced as an Adult

The prevalence of serious harm during adulthood were experienced by 30 of 42 (71%) women. All 13 of the women who experienced sexual harm were also victims of serious physical harm. Two thirds of the women (67%) were physically harmed by husbands or boyfriends. Another 11 women, or slightly more than one quarter of the sample (26%), reported that sexual harm toward them was committed by partners. Again, in relationships where a certain degree of intimacy and trust is expected, we see that these relationships are characterized by behavior that has rendered the woman unsafe. Lisa explained how the effects of being abused affected her self-esteem:

> When I was home from school one day and my mother had to go out for awhile, my older brother came in my room and forced me to have sex with him. I didn't want to, so

he beat me up a little first and said he'd kill me if I told anyone. I can see now that I had very low self-esteem and would do anything for someone to love me.

Later in the interview, Lisa described how she ended up killing her own child to maintain the love of another and to preserve her own safety.

> I had gotten up, taken a shower and gotten dressed. Then I was walking down the street to catch the bus, and I missed the bus by 2 seconds. I walked back home and got my mother up and asked her to take me to work. She got up, got dressed, and had a cup of coffee and drove me to work. We hardly ever even speak. She didn't speak to anybody that day. When I got to work I went to the bathroom, got my things out of my locker, then went up and counted out my drawer. It was early in the morning that day so it was difficult. It was back and forth to the bathroom. [You were pregnant?] Yes. I was basically a robot that day just going through the motions and not really feeling anything. I was having pains and I wanted to go home, but I couldn't tell anyone I was pregnant. I just couldn't. [What month were you?] Ninth. [You weren't showing?] I guess to some people I was, but I basically wear big shirts to begin with so nobody knew. They may have suspected, but they didn't really know. I wasn't allowed to tell anybody that I was pregnant because the child's father threatened to kill me and that person I told it to. I took his threat very seriously. . . . I went out to lunch and the pains got worse. Came back to work. I wanted to leave so bad but I couldn't 'cause I wouldn't get relieved till 5 o'clock. I kept on checking out the customers and the pain got worse and worse and worse. I just wanted to go home and tell my mother to take me to the doctor but I couldn't. I went back into the bathroom and as I was sitting on the toilet, something came out. I don't really know what happened from there. It's still a blur, but all I remember is that I took a box cutter and cut his throat. Then I stuffed some toilet paper in his mouth so he wouldn't make no noise. [What did you do with the body?] I put it in the trash.

Self-Inflicted Harm

In addition to experiencing harm at the hands of others with whom there should have been trust, 17 of the 42 women (41%) reported that they also inflicted harm upon themselves. It is striking that of the 17 women who reported that they tried to kill themselves, most of them (14) tried to kill themselves more than once. These figures were not significantly different from the rest of the sample. Of the women convicted of killing a child, 59% reported a history of emotional or mental health problems, compared to 37% of the other women in our sample. This difference was statistically significant ($\chi^2 = 6.42, p > .05$). The most common method of self-harm was overdose with various legal drugs (13 or 31%), followed by cutting wrists (6 or 14%).

Seven of the 17 women who had attempted suicide made their first attempt before age 13. Another 7 women (17%) first tried to kill themselves during adolescence (13 to 19 years). Women were asked if their attempts to hurt themselves were related to others trying to hurt them. About 71% (12) stated that their self-harm attempts were related to others trying to hurt them. This sample of women who killed children had experienced severe damage to self during their formative years to the extent that life, at times, was perceived as no longer worth living. In fact, all of the 42 women experienced more than one self-damage indicator prior to killing a child. Given this shaky sense of self, it is not hard to imagine that for most of the women giving birth and raising a child under life conditions already considered stressful and harsh would be a most difficult feat to accomplish.

The Victims

Table 8.2 shows the ages of 45 victims who were killed by the 42 convicted women identified for this sample (one woman killed two children, another woman killed three). Slightly more than one third of the children (38%) were killed before age 1, and thus these cases can be considered cases of infanticide. Only about one quarter (22%) were older than 3 years at the time of their deaths. Thus these results support other findings that younger children and infants are considerably more at risk for being killed than older children.

Table 8.2
Age of Homicide Victims (N = 45)

	n	Percentage
Birth to 6 months	12	27
7 to 12 months	5	11
1 to 3 years	17	38
4 to 8 years	10	22
Missing	1	2

Most of the women (75%) were the natural mothers of the children whom they killed. The remaining quarter killed their foster child or adopted child, a neighbor's child, or other relatives. Victims were slightly more likely to be male (*n* = 24), 55%, than female (*n* = 20), 45%. About 38% (16) of the 42 women reported that they had killed the child, whereas a slightly higher proportion, 41% (17 of 42), denied any involvement in the killing. Of the 17 women who denied killing children, 59%, or 10 of the women, reported that the child was killed by a partner/intimate, usually as a result of physical force. All of the women involved in neglect cases described a failure to protect their child, whereas the remaining 4 women either could not remember the incident or declined to discuss their role in it. Almost half of the victims (47%) were killed by physical force. This included shakings and beatings with hands or weapons (i.e., a shoe, a belt), as well as throwing out a window and shooting. The next most common method, asphyxiation, was used to kill almost a fifth of the victims. This was typically done by sticking materials in the child's mouth to block his/her air passage. Child neglect occurred in 13% of victims, manifested by children being starved or dehydrated, as well as medical conditions being ignored. Another 11% were burned in fires purposely set, whereas 7% were drowned or scalded. For two children, method was unknown as these women declined to discuss the incident.

Motives for Killings

Although only 8 of the women (19%) had motives attributed to some type of psychological distress (e.g., depression, schizophrenia, "snapped"), almost twice as many women (14 or 33%) reported elsewhere in the interview that they were depressed at the time of the homicide. Similarly, an additional 4 women indicated mental health problems by stating that they were stressed, unable to cope with problems and had flashbacks at the time of the homicide. In fact, 59% of the women reported a history of emotional or mental health problems, compared to 37% of the other women in our sample. The paucity of internal resources that affected the women's ability to cope was overwhelming. Opportunities to engage external social supports were noticeably absent as these women admittedly felt isolated in their situations. Long ago, as children, they learned to "suffer in silence" with their pain, as no one was available then to provide them with comfort. It is of little surprise then that discipline of a child was also a common motive (19%) for killing. Circumstances of child killings were most commonly abuse (67%); neglect of children (21%) was the second most prevalent circumstance. In situations of child abuse, the parent often resorts to projective identification in the raising of children. This means that the disowned aspects of the parent's self are put onto the child, who is then expected to fulfill them or be "wiped out." The child then becomes the hated aspect of the parent, which then has to be corrected or disciplined (Zulueta, 1993, p. 118).

In addition to motive and circumstance, it is important to acknowledge that the women reported 13 of the child killings (31%) were drug-related. In 11 of these situations, the homicide was related to the mother using alcohol or other drugs, whereas in the other two situations, partners were using alcohol or other drugs. These women all indicated that the alcohol and drug usage seriously impaired their or their partner's judgment at the time of the homicide.

The Link to Lethal Violence

For the sample of women discussed herein, there was no single factor that led them into actions of lethal violence. Rather, their early years were characterized by various kinds of losses that were followed immediately by gross insensitivity to their emotional needs. This was typically the result of inadequate parenting and a paucity of social supports. Thus losses evolved into traumas that eroded their sense of self, and when self no longer exists, the roots of violence are born (Zulueta, 1993). Blatant disregard of these women's childhood needs was so profound that their voices were silenced and their spirits broken at very early ages. These women, too, were betrayed by those who should have protected them. Their voices, even when exercised, were to no avail. The learned, maladaptive methods of coping with harm and trauma (e.g., drug and alcohol abuse), in turn, exacerbated the women's difficulties and left them vulnerable to becoming involved in additional situations of harm. Pervasive social isolation, coupled with their learned silence, only serve to reinforce the cycle of poor self-esteem that had been initiated in their families of origin. Self was sacrificed in an attempt to remain connected to a larger social community called humanity. Factors that resulted in their resorting to lethal violence was built upon years of frustration, prior experiences of using violence as a means to "settle" disputes, and a desperate wish to alter their life situations, either immediately or long term.

Periodic expressions of rage became assertions of vitality in an attempt to keep self alive.

Deprivation, loss, and abuse so depleted the self that defending itself becomes of paramount importance, whatever the cost to the Other (Zulueta, 1993, p. xii). As Miller (1984) stated, "If their psyche is killed, they will learn how to kill—the only question is who will be killed: oneself, others, or both" (p. 98). Kohut (1985) said that empathy involves others making an effort to understand self. Parents who are themselves deficient because of their own emotional deprivation are unable to offer empathy to their children's developing sense of self. When emotional needs are consistently unmet, attachments to others are disrupted and self-esteem does not develop in a healthy way. If empathy is an extension of self, then the child who has a poor sense of self is unable to feel compassion for others. When "self-objects," such as parents, lack empathy, the child often develops an insecure sense of self as a result of feeling low self-worth, isolation, and rejection. Such feelings often generate additional feelings of rage and despair that later erupt into violent, aggressive behaviors (Zulueta, 1993).

Conclusion and Recommendations

Women who kill children are still somewhat of an enigma in the latter part of the 20th century. Whereas reasons and motives are complex, the literature still tends to focus upon these women as mad or bad. In an attempt to skirt further examination of this dichotomized thinking, attention has been diverted from the perpetrator and shifted onto the victims. Thus little is still known about those women who commit this crime.

The theoretical considerations raised here indicate that the mad or bad reductionistic thinking needs to be put aside in an attempt to understand better the intricacies of the process involved in child killing. There is a need for further research about women who kill children with an emphasis on exploring their own dilemmas as well as their reasoning. Findings presented here indicate they, too, are victims who have been unable to extricate themselves from this vicious cycle of self-damaging experiences, including suicide attempts, drug use, and physical and sexual victimization.

At the end of the interview, each woman was asked what type of advice or recommendations for programming she would give to women who found themselves in situations similar to her own. The emphasis of the women's suggestions points to rectifying those life situations and circumstances that have been outlined as self-damage indicators. Almost half (45%) of the women suggested that programs where their self-esteem could be developed were critical to their successful functioning. Low self-esteem, reliance upon a dysfunctional partner, and feelings of worthlessness characterized these women to the extent that their judgment about safety for themselves and their children was impaired. Due to the tremendous guilt feelings about their crime and to being ostracized within the prison system, as well as in society at large, these women hoped for a program that would help them deal with the loss of their children (Kaplan, 1988). Currently, there are no programs in prison for those who lost or killed a child. Women also wanted more parenting programs available to teach them about how to care for their children and identify their children's needs. Programs addressing domestic violence were also important to these women, who stated that they must first learn to care for themselves before they could adequately care for their children.

Acknowledging and identifying women who are perpetual victims is possible via day care centers, school programs, and child health care systems. However, outreach and subsequent education to prevent violence is a major effort that requires interest, skill, empathy, and resources. The findings here support the aggressive use of prevention and intervention services regarding the identification of parental needs and fulfillment of those needs. Self-esteem builders and self-care programs for new mothers should also be offered in communities while providing nursery care for newborns. If we can correct the deficits of living in those who give life, we stand a chance of breaking the cycle of abuse and offer a future to children who otherwise may have been robbed of one.

Discussion Questions

1. What factors figured most prominently in the womens' inability to parent children that led to the children's deaths?

2. What does it mean to be a "motherless mother"?

3. Which circumstances (if any) can be viewed as mitigating in a woman's situation that may result in less punishment or a lighter sentence? Why?

4. What criminological theories would best explain why women kill their children?

5. If child abuse is a cycle that continues through the generations, what kinds of policies might prevent child abuse from occurring?

References

Abel, E. L. (1986). Childhood homicide in Erie County, New York. *Pediatrics, 77* (5) 709–713.

Arboleda-Florez, J., & Power, A. (1983). The Medea syndrome: Multiple infanticide, a Canadian case. *The American Journal of Forensic Psychiatry, 4* (2), 61–66.

Asch, S. S. (1968). Crib deaths: Their possible relationship to postpartum depressions and infanticide. *Journal of Mount Sinai Hospital, 35,* 214–220.

Basch, M. F. (1982). *The perception of reality and the disavowal of meaning.* New York: International Universities Press. (Reprinted from the Annual of Psychoanalysis, 11)

Bowlby, J. (1973). *Attachment and loss: Volumes 2 & 3.* New York: Basic Books.

——. (1988). *A secure base.* New York: Basic Books.

Crimmins, S. (1995). Early childhood loss as a predisposing factor in female-perpetrated homicides. *Dissertation Abstracts International, 56* (10), 4155A. (University Microfilms No. AA19605583)

Crimmins, S., & Foley, M. (1989, November). *The threshold of violence in urban adolescents.* Paper presented at the 41st Annual Meeting of the American Society of Criminology, Reno, NV.

Daly, M., & Wilson, M. (1988). *Homicide.* New York: Aldine.

Daniel, A. E., & Kashani, J. H. (1983). Women who commit crimes of violence. *Psychiatric Annals, 13* (9), 697–713.

d' Orban, P. T. (1979). Women who kill their children. *British Journal of Psychiatry, 134,* 560–571.

Edelman, H. (1994). *Motherless daughters: The legacy of loss.* Reading, MA: Addison-Wesley.

Friedman, L. M. (1993). *Crime and punishment in American history.* New York: Basic Books.

Herman, J. L. (1992). *Trauma and recovery.* New York: Basic Books.

Hoffer, P., & Hull, N. E. H. (1981). *Murdering mothers: Infanticide in England and New England 1558–1803.* New York: New York University Press.

Horner, A. (1989). *The wish for power and the fear of having it.* Northvale, NJ: Jason Aronson.

Jones, A. (1980). *Women who kill.* New York: Fawcett Crest.

Kaplan, M. F. (1988). A peer support group for women in prison for the death of a child. *Journal of Offender Counseling, Services, and Rehabilitation, 13* (1), 5–13.

Kaplun, D., & Reich, R. (1976). The murdered child and his killers. *American Journal of Psychiatry, 133* (7), 809–813.

Katz, J. (1988). *Seductions of crime.* New York: Basic Books.

Kohut, H. (1985). *Self psychology and the humanities: Reflections on a new psychoanalytic approach* (C. B. Stozier, co-editor). New York: Norton.

Korbin, J. E. (1986). Childhood histories of women imprisoned for fatal child maltreatment. *Child Abuse and Neglect,* 10, 331–338.

Levin, J. (1987). *Treatment of alcoholism and other addictions: A self-psychology approach.* Northvale, NJ: Jason Aronson.

Lifton, R. J. (1973). *Home from the war.* New York: Basic Books.

——. (1979). *The broken connection.* New York: Basic Books.

Lomis, M. (1986). Maternal filicide: A preliminary examination of culture and victim sex. *International Journal of Law and Psychiatry,* 9, 503–506.

Lyon, J. (1985). *Playing God in the nursery.* New York: Norton.

Mahler, M. (1979). *The selected papers of Margaret S. Mahler: Volume 2. Separation-individuation.* Northvale, NJ: Jason Aronson.

Mann, C. R. (1993). Maternal filicide of preschoolers. In A. Wilson (Ed.), *Homicide: The victim-offender connection.* Cincinnati, OH: Anderson.

Miller, A. (1984). *For your own good: Hidden cruelty in child-rearing and the roots of violence.* New York: Farrar, Straus, Giroux.

Nowak, R. (1993). Investigating infant deaths: An ill-equipped system struggles to cope. *The Journal of NIH Research,* 10 (5), 29–31.

Parker, E., & Good, F. (1981). Infanticide. *Law and Human Behavior,* 5, 2–3.

Pasewark, R. A., Pantle, R. L., & Steadman, H. J. (1979). Characteristics and disposition of persons found not guilty by reason of insanity in New York State, 1971–1976. *American Journal of Psychiatry,* 136, 655–660.

Piers, M. W. (1978). *Infanticide: Past and present.* New York: Norton.

Resnick, P. J. (1969). Child murder by parents: A psychiatric review of filicide. *American Journal of Psychiatry,* 26, 325–334.

Schloesser, P., Pierpont, J., & Poertner, L. (1992). Active surveillance of child abuse fatalities. *Child Abuse and Neglect,* 16, 3–10.

Scott, P. D. (1973a). Fatal battered baby cases. *Medicine, Science, and the Law,* 13, 197–206.

——. (1973b). Parents who kill their children. *Medicine, Science, and the Law,* 13, 120–126.

Shengold, L. (1989). *Soul murder.* New Haven, CT: Yale University Press.

Silverman, R. A., & Kennedy, L. W. (1988). Women who kill their children. *Violence and Victims,* 3 (2), 113–127.

Straus, M. A., Gelles, R. J., & Steinmetz, S. K. (1981). *Behind closed doors: Violence in the American family.* Beverly Hills, CA: Sage.

Terr, L. (1990). *Too scared to cry: Psychic trauma in childhood.* New York: Harper & Row.

Totman, J. (1978). *The murderess: A psychosocial study of criminal homicide.* San Francisco: R & E Research Associates.

Warren, J. (1989). *Women who murder (Violence in America).* Paper presented at FBI Academy, 158th session, Quantico, VA.

Weir, R. F. (1984). *Selective nontreatment of handicapped newborns: Moral dilemmas in neonatal medicine.* New York: Oxford University Press.

Wilczynski, A. (1991). Images of women who kill their infants: The mad and the bad. *Women and Criminal Justice,* 2 (2), 71–88.

Wood, B. L. (1987). *Children of alcoholism: The struggle for self and intimacy in adult life.* New York: New York University Press.

Zulueta, F. De (1993). *From pain to violence: The traumatic roots of destructiveness.* Northvale, NJ: Jason Aronson.

Section III

Crime Partnerships, Networks, and Gangs

The law does not serve her [criminalized and victimized women]; it only serves us [the middle and upper classes] by keeping her away from us. Because she knows that the law does not address her, she has little respect for its rules. (Thornburg and Trunk 1992, 181)

As we discussed in the first section, many women enter deviant networks through running away, childhood abuse, and addiction to drugs and alcohol. In the second section, we talked about how familial networks affected multigenerational involvement in criminal behavior. In this section, we take the peer path of crime partnerships, gangs, and deviant networks a step further to examine actual roles in crime and how involvement in group behavior such as gangs increases the propensity for victimization.

Women who commit crimes tend not to specialize in any one type of crime. Rather, they are involved in a wide variety of offending behaviors based on accessibility and convenient opportunity. Most criminal acts are committed with accomplices and are less likely to be committed alone. When crimes are committed without accomplices, they tend to be reactionary behaviors to the situation at hand, such as an assault in an abusive relationship or a theft of property from an unlocked vehicle. Women who commit crimes with accomplices vary in the degree to which they play a primary or secondary role in crime, according to **the first reading in this section, by Leanne Alarid and her colleagues.** The authors also examine how these roles differ by race and ethnicity and whether women are taking a more assertive role in criminal networks. **The second selection, by Scott Decker and colleagues,** takes a look at the crime of burglary, which is often committed with two or more persons. The researchers compare female burglars who worked as partners compared with women who acted as accomplices.

Some researchers have argued that the drug economy has expanded or increased women's status in crime (Fagan 1994) or contributed to an increase in women's violent crimes. Previous studies show that women have replaced men in the drug economy in inner-city neighborhoods when men have been arrested, incarcerated, or otherwise killed over drugs (Baskin, Sommers, and Fagan 1993). Others have criticized this view, saying that women drug users remain confined in secondary crime roles and are more often victimized by violence rather than creating it (Maher 1997). For example, out of their sample of 24 women who used crack, only one woman had a legitimate job, four women sold crack through their boyfriends or managed a crack house, and the rest were involved in prostitution or were supported by someone else. The women who sold crack inevitably lost their positions if they broke up with their boyfriend or if he became incarcerated (Koester and Schwartz 1993).

Group Dynamics of Networks and Gangs

Mixed-gender criminal networks were intended to be a social support system that provided food, shelter, drugs, and support if needed. These networks relegated women to marginal drug-selling roles, while reserving more lucrative distribution roles to men (Maher 1997). Within these networks, social class influences women's participation in the drug economy, but few researchers have distinguished among women of various racial or ethnic groups. In Maher's (1997) work with white, Latina, and black women drug users in Brooklyn, she found success and position in drug and sex-for-crack exchanges were largely dependent on gender and race. Each of the three racial/ethnic groups seemed to sustain separate criminal networks for support, with African-American women having the strongest networks. While Latina women were viewed as "price cutters and sexual barterers" who took less money for sex, they entered the market without having been "turned out" by male pimps. White women were the most highly desired in the sex market, but were also viewed as potential victims or easily intimidated, and were less likely to fit into selling or distributing within the drug economy because they did not "look the part" and would be more likely to attract law enforcement attention. Overall, racial discrimination and sexism were pervasive within criminal partnerships and group networks, in that race and gender determined earnings, location, and times that lawbreaking behavior occurred (Maher 1997).

Youth gangs are another type of criminal network. It is estimated that between 8 percent and 38 percent of young women surveyed in urban areas are self-identified gang members (Moore and Hagedorn 2001). Joining a gang can initially provide emotional support or protection from childhood abuse or a poor family life. However, some female gang members are sexually exploited or sexually abused by male gang members, which further contributes to their plight (Moore and Hagedorn 2001). We present two readings in this section about female gang members. **The article by David Brotherton (Chapter 11)** examines the pathways that young women of various ethnicities take to gang involvement, and the roles the female gang members play within the gang. Drug dealing is common among female gang members. **In the final selection, Jody Miller and Scott Decker** study the involvement of young women in gang violence in St. Louis, along with the role that violence plays in membership status. In conjunction with one of the overriding themes of this text, both of these readings explore the incidence of victimization of female gang members.

References

Baskin, D., I. Sommers, and J. A. Fagan. 1993. "The Political Economy of Violent Female Street Crime." *Fordham Urban Law Journal* 20: 401–417.

Fagan, J. A. 1994. "Women and Drugs Revisited: Female Participation in the Cocaine Economy." *Journal of Drug Issues* 24 (2): 179–225.

Koester, S., and J. Schwartz. 1993. "Crack, Gangs, Sex, and Powerlessness: A View From Denver." Pp. 187–203 in *Crack Pipe as Pimp: An Ethnographic Investigation of Sex-for-Crack Exchanges* (edited by Mitchell S. Ratner). New York: Lexington.

Maher, L. 1997. *Sexed Work: Gender, Race, and Resistance in a Brooklyn Drug Market*. New York: Oxford.

Moore, J., and J. Hagedorn. 2001. *Female Gangs: A Focus on Research*. Washington, DC: Office of Juvenile Justice and Delinquency Prevention, U.S. Department of Justice.

Thornburg, T., and D. Trunk. 1992. "A Collage of Voices: A Dialogue With Women in Prison." *Southern California Review of Women's Studies* 2 (1): 155–217. ✦

9

Do Women Play a Primary or a Secondary Role in Felony Offenses?

A Comparison by Race/Ethnicity

Leanne Fiftal Alarid
James W. Marquart
Velmer S. Burton Jr.
Francis T. Cullen
Steven J. Cuvelier

In this chapter, the authors present findings from a study of 104 adult female felons. They gathered data for this study from felons sentenced to a residential community facility (a court-ordered boot camp program) in a large southern metropolitan area. About half of the women had been sentenced directly to the camp as an alternative to prison. The other half (51 percent) had violated their conditions of probation, most often with a "technical violation," such as drug use, failure to obtain employment, or failure to attend treatment/education classes. Some of the women, however, violated probation with a new conviction. The sample consisted of first-time felony offenders between 17 and 28, who averaged 20 years of age. The racial/ethnic breakdown was split between Anglo (45 percent) and African-American women (44 percent), with Latinas composing the smallest group (11 percent). Most of the women had been convicted of drug offenses (43 percent) or property crimes (38 percent), and nearly one-fifth (19 percent) had been sent to boot camp for either robbery or assault. The women were interviewed regarding their roles during their criminal offense. The researchers examined the women offenders' perceptions of their involvement with accomplices and the degree to which men influenced their general involvement in criminal behavior. They sought to determine the extent to which women play either dominant leadership roles or secondary follower roles during crimi-

nal events. They found that a larger proportion of African-American women played primary and equal crime roles than did Anglo and Hispanic women. However, crimes such as robbery, burglary, and drug dealing were more likely to be committed with male accomplices who provided women an opening into deviant networks.

Despite women's recent economic, political, legal, and social gains, substantial sex segregation remains in legitimate opportunity structures (Bielby and Baron 1986; England 1981; Reskin 1984; Rosenfeld 1983). Research also indicates the presence of this situation in illegitimate opportunity structures. Recent studies on the role of gender relations in organized profit-seeking criminal organizations (Steffensmeier 1983) and in street-level hustling (Maher and Curtis 1992; Miller 1986; Pettiway 1987) have found that sex segregation increases as criminal organizations become more rational, more complex, and more professional, and as they require more physical strength (P. Adler 1993; Steffensmeier 1983). The majority of male and female offenders, however, do not commit organized criminal acts. Instead, most offenders engage in a wide range of "normal crimes" based on convenience and accessibility (Osgood et al. 1988; Steffensmeier 1983).

Some criminologists posit that crime is socially structured and can be understood most clearly through the idea of illegitimate opportunity structures (Cloward 1959; Cullen 1984). This concept assumes that crime, like noncriminal behavior in the legitimate sector, is structured by factors such as age, social class, and gender. Therefore access to learned deviant skills, values, and roles is differentially available and is not distributed uniformly across criminal populations. Extending this logic to gender, one should expect women, regardless of ethnic and racial background, to play secondary or nonleadership roles in crime networks. Further, the differential opportunity tradition assumes that most crimes committed by women will be unorganized, unskilled, and low in pecuniary rewards (Cloward and Piven 1979; Maher and Curtis 1992; Steffensmeier 1983). The concept of differential opportunity structures would also predict that in robbery, burglary, and drug dealing, crimes in which men dominate as offenders, men will take leadership roles in relationships with women. Furthermore, men's leadership may be less or absent during female-dominated offenses such as shoplifting, petty theft, or credit card abuse. Finally, differential opportunity theory recognizes that women's motives for committing crime will be an extension of their roles in the wider society. Thus women's roles in society overall will be influenced by what Cloward (1959:169) called "socially structured differentials . . . limiting the fulfillment of illegitimate [and legitimate] roles."

We draw from differential opportunity theory and develop it further by focusing on the relationships between offense type and women's crime roles. Thus, to determine whether female criminals play primary or secondary roles in criminal events, researchers must examine the crime event itself and how female offenders perceive their role in the actual crime. In studying female crime roles, the key issue is whether and to what extent female offenders view themselves as leaders or as followers. To address this issue, we interviewed adult women offenders who committed felony street crimes in a large southern metropolitan area.

Defining Women's Crime Roles

One dilemma facing scholars who assess the nature of female crime is operationally defining roles played by women offenders. Ward, Jackson and Ward (1979) contended that female felons played one of four criminal roles in violent offenses:

> The *conspirator*, who instigates or who has knowledge of the crime but who does not participate in committing the criminal act itself; the *accessory*, who plays a secondary role in committing the crime—acting as a lookout, driving a getaway car, carrying weapons, tools, or the proceeds [of the crime]; the *partner*, who participates equally in all aspects of the crime; and finally, the woman who acts as the *sole perpetrator* of the crime (p. 116).

The current study employs the four crime roles defined by Ward et al. (1979). Our sample of female offenders closely resembled those described in their research. In addition, we reduced their four role categories into a primary/secondary dichotomy because of our small sample size. Thus the conspirator and the accessory are defined as occupying secondary crime roles; the partner and the sole perpetrator are classified as playing primary crime roles. Our definition of a "leadership" crime role is assertive participation in a criminal act, along with accomplices, and planning the essential or critical elements. Moreover, leaders direct their accomplices in the criminal event. A sole perpetrator is considered primary because she is involved in all components of the act, from beginning to completion.

Findings

Recall that according to Cloward's (1959) theory of differential opportunity, access to deviant networks is differentially available in the underworld, depending on gender, social class, race, or age. Thus we expected that women who committed crimes alone would more likely be involved in typical female offenses (e.g., larceny and forgery), whereas women who committed crimes with men would be involved in nontraditional criminal acts (e.g., robbery, assault, driving while intoxicated, and burglary). We also expected that most crimes committed by women would generally be unorganized and unprofitable.

In this section we report findings on five questions: (1) In what types of crime were women acting alone or in concert with others? (2) Who initiated the idea for the current criminal act? (3) In accomplice crimes, did women play a primary or a secondary role? (4) Over the past year, what proportion of women committed crimes with accomplices? (5) Over the past year, how did men influence the women's deviant behaviors, if at all?

Current Crime Type: Women as 'Sole Perpetrators'

To differentiate women who acted alone from those who acted in a group, we asked a series of open-ended questions such as "Tell me what you remember about your crime" and "Were you alone or with others during your offense?" Sixteen women (15 percent) said they committed the crime alone. The crimes most often committed by sole perpetrators were assault, theft, forgery, and driving while intoxicated (DWI).

We listed assault in this category because in most of these cases, the women directed the assaults, first, at their children, and second, at spouses. Women convicted of theft and forgery gave numerous reasons for their deviant acts, including stealing clothes, money, jewelry, or cosmetics for personal consumption, for their children's needs, or to support a drug habit. Women convicted of DWI reported that they had been arrested as they drove home from a nightclub or party.

Our data support the contention that crimes committed by women when alone were less prevalent than crimes in the other categories. The position based on differential opportunity theory, that women who commit crimes alone are more likely to be involved in female-oriented criminal behaviors, was not entirely supported by our data. Forgery and theft are typical of women criminals, but assault and DWI are considered "nontraditional" for women.

Women as Accomplices

Crimes with accomplices occurred in 9 cases out of 10. Most of the women were involved in drug offenses, notably selling crack and cocaine. Most women convicted of possession or sale of illegal drugs admitted using and abusing a variety of substances. We found, like Miller (1986) in her research with female street hustlers, that women who used drugs more frequently were less active in deviant networks than occasional users.

Women frequently committed larceny, burglary, and robbery in the presence of others. In the following sections we provide further analysis of criminal involvement through excerpts of interviews with the women themselves.

Access to All-Female Deviant Networks

To specify who initiated the criminal act that led to conviction, we asked the women "Whose idea was it to become involved in the current offense?" Thirty-four women (33 percent) who committed an accomplice crime stated that the current offense was their idea; either they told someone else about the idea or asked others to participate with them as codefendants. On the other hand, 14 women said that another woman involved them in criminal activity. Alyssa described the following situation:

I had been using marijuana since I was 10 years old, and I got tired of buying it. . . . I didn't need to sell it; I was raised upper class. A female friend taught me how to sell weed. . . . She helped me to establish customers. My first arrest was when I was 17, when I was caught selling weed with . . . a friend, who was my bodyguard. I got better at avoiding arrest, and I'd only sell in large amounts, no less than 25 pounds to any one person . . . and the most was 400 pounds at a time. For the big deals, it would be a problem for some customers that they were buying from a female, so I direct my bodyguard (my lover), she looked like a guy, to cut the deal while I pretended to be an onlooker.

Unlike those women who "knew what they were getting into when it came to selling drugs and shoplifting," two women reported that their female accomplices were less candid during robbery and burglary situations:

My friend had done more than I had; she was more devious and she would lie to me to get me to do what she wanted. (Maria)

My one friend has a way of conning people. I trusted her at first, but she lied a lot. It was her idea to do the robbery . . . she had a way of talking. She has a long criminal record,

and went to prison for awhile. . . . Me, well, I've never been to jail before. (Kimberly)

One Anglo woman said she initiated a series of residential burglaries, encouraged another female to assist her, and then divided the profits.

In a comparison of all-female crime groups by race and ethnicity, we found that African-American women were more often members of female deviant networks than were Anglo or Hispanic women. We did not discover any previous study to support or refute this contention. Pettiway (1987) examined all-female groups by offense type and found that all-female deviant networks most typically involved prostitution and did not carry weapons or use opiate based drugs. Our study supports Pettiway's conclusions concerning opiate use and weapons. We found, however, that most all-female groups were not involved in prostitution but committed a variety of other crimes such as selling drugs or burglary.

Access to Male-Female Deviant Networks

[Forty] women said that a boyfriend ("my old man") or close male friend had given them access to what we viewed as nontraditional criminal activities. We also found that 28 of the 40 male-female partnerships were composed of Caucasians and Hispanics, while 12 African-American women were associated with a man who initiated the idea for the current crime. When asked about their initial introduction to deviance, their responses ranged from "I didn't know anything" to statements that they were attracted to men who lived the "fast life."

Many women in the sample knew that "friends" were manipulating them, but cooperated with the group for the sake of acceptance. Monique recalled:

It was all my [male] friends' idea . . . but I took the rap for all six of them.

Chantelle, convicted for robbery, said:

All four of em were male. Those motherfuckers used me because I had a car. . . . I feel they already planned the robbery before they asked me. Then they just asked me to take them somewhere.

Approximately half of the women who reported that a man initiated the crime also stated that that man was not prosecuted, while she received a "bad rap." Others informed us either that they had no idea of what had happened to their accomplices, or that their boyfriend or husband was currently incarcerated. When asked if they would return to their boyfriends or to the same group of friends, most women claimed they were "staying away from the bad crowd." Yet a few women insisted that their feelings were too strong to leave their boyfriends, despite a court order to stay apart or risk a probation violation.

The women who were prone to return to male friendship groups were also admitted gang members. Elizabeth, an Anglo member of a predominantly African-American male gang, stated:

> I'll still be around the same crowd.... I like to get into trouble, it's excitement . . . robberies of dope fiends and C [convenience] stores.... My friends give me lots of respect and mostly never look down on me. If I needed money, clothes, food, they give it to me. If I'm in trouble, they would always help. I'd do the same [for them]. It's better than my mother.

Most boot camp graduates were transferred to an intensive aftercare probation program. After graduation, 85 of the 104 women reported that they would return to the previous social situation, even to an abusive relationship or to parents who had had no interest in them as children. This appeared to the women to be the only alternative until they could obtain employment, finish school, and secure custody of their children. Ten women, however, wished to lead more independent lives by living alone and supporting themselves.

In sum, initiation into either all-female or male-female deviant networks was differentiated by offense type and race/ethnicity. First, we found that all-female crime groups varied as to their involvement in behaviors typical of women criminals, such as larceny and drug crimes, as well as nontraditional offenses such as burglary and robbery. Women initiated into male-female partnerships were more often involved in such crimes as larger-scale drug dealing, robbery, and burglary.

Second, deviant networks differed by race. African-American women were more often members of all-female deviant groups than were Anglo or Hispanic women. At the same time, African-American women were less likely to be involved in a partnership with a man who initiated criminal activities. Our study supports Pettiway's (1987) conclusion that Anglo or Hispanic women were more likely to form crime partnerships with other men, and that male-female deviant networks committed "male-typed" crimes.

Differential opportunity theory assumes that women who commit crimes as accomplices, notably with men, will be led into male-oriented criminal acts. Our data show that the presence of accomplices was associated with drug offenses, larceny, burglary, and robbery.

Thus our findings support the proposition that "access to illegitimate learning environments" (Cloward 1959:169), measured in part by the accomplice variable, would allow women to participate in crimes they probably would not perform by themselves. We would suspect that the same holds true for men.

Crime Role in the Current Offense

We asked each woman "What actually happened, and what part did you play in the crime?"

Leadership roles. A total of 44 women, most notably African-Americans, participated in either a primary role ($n = 14$) or an equal role ($n = 30$) in a crime group or partnership. A primary role was defined as not only initiating the crime but also participating as a central figure in planning and committing crimes with others. Drug offenses were the most frequent crimes for Anglo and African-American women who acted in a primary role. Ten women reported that other people were working for them; two women initiated and participated in burglaries with others; one led other women into a series of felony thefts; and one operated a crack house and prostitution ring. The following quotes from two of these women illustrate the primary crime role:

> I have never worked for anyone. My friend showed me how he makes his money, and then he wanted me to sell crack for him. I didn't want to work that way; I wanted my own. I even got some of his customers. Before I got arrested, I had 12 people working for me. (Crystal)

> I started stealin' alone. My [theft] habit became worse. . . . Me and my two friends [female] could get more between the three of us . . . [about $350 worth of merchandise]. The theft I'm in for was my idea; my friends just went along. (Suzanne)

Equal crime partnerships. Equal roles in crime partnerships, considered to be assertive, categorized 30 out of 44 women. These women typically felt that they were "one of the guys" and were equally capable at "the job." The women who played an equal role in drug offenses said they received "equal pay for equal work." Many of these women either sold drugs alongside accomplices or took turns selling so that their partners could sleep for a few hours. As Monique described it,

> We sold dope 24/7 [24 hours a day, 7 days a week], and we gotta stop at some time so we could get our fix.

Among the violent offenders, an Anglo woman described her role in an aggravated robbery. Wynona said that she and two male friends robbed a convenience store: she demanded the money from the clerk after pretending to buy cigarettes, one male partner held the gun, and the second male drove the getaway car. Other women, such as Jennifer, reported dissatisfaction at being treated as less than equal in terms of profits, when they felt they had participated equally in the crime:

> I didn't get equal pay for an equal part . . . I was tired of fighting and being beaten up by my codefendants. . . . Recently I started committing burglaries of houses alone . . . about 30 or 40 . . . I brought along this female the time we got caught.

Secondary crime roles. Forty-two percent of our female offenders ($n = 44$) participated in secondary roles during their current offense. Women drug offenders typically reported that while drug deals occurred, they held drug money or illegal weapons, or waited in the car. Our examination of secondary roles revealed activities similar to those observed in Campbell's (1990) research on gang girls. The women who dealt drugs usually split the profits with a man, who protected her from being "ripped off" and provided her with drugs. Although one female boasted that she was a leader of an all-female auxiliary gang, she immediately stated that she was treated badly by male gang members, like "a pawn to be pushed around." Still, some women explained that they did not "work" (participate in any criminal activities); they just went along to obtain drugs and for excitement.

In summary, a larger proportion of African-American women played primary and equal crime roles than did Anglo and Hispanic women. Of the 16 African-American women who played a secondary role, 12 were involved in a male-female partnership, while 4 participated in a crime partnership with at least one other female. When we compare these differences among women, differential opportunity would propose that women in lower-class environments would have more criminal opportunities than their middle- or upper-class counterparts, and thus would be more likely to perform primary crime roles. Miller (1986) and Cohen (1980) suggested that African-American women had more highly developed deviant street networks than Hispanic or Anglo women. Our data suggests that this may be true for drug offenses, but not for property or violent offenses. According to our data, Anglo women were more likely than African-American women to take secondary roles in drug offenses. We found no role differences among ethnic and racial groups for property offenses. Except for Pettiway's (1987) study of drug users, no other studies assess racial differences in female crime roles.

Roles in Previous Crimes

We questioned the women about their deviant activities and crime roles over the past 12 months. Questions focused on three areas: (1) crimes committed alone or with other accomplices; (2) the degree of negative influence by men in crime and deviance; and (3) women as leaders or followers when associating with others.

Participation with accomplices over the past year. In the past year, most of the women (80 percent) had been involved with accomplices when committing crimes such as burglary, robbery, motor vehicle theft, and selling drugs. The other 20 percent acted alone when committing deviant behaviors such as prostitution, drug use, and larceny. Approximately one-third of these solo actors were influenced by someone else in their current offense. Our findings support Pettiway (1987:747), who found that women offenders were more likely to be involved in "vice-related" crimes by themselves.

Influence of men in crime and deviance. The women were asked three questions: (1) "Have men influenced you to do something against the law?" (2) "Have men gotten you into trouble?" and (3) "What was your relationship with male accomplices?" (assuming that such accomplices existed). Sixty-three percent of the women stated that men were not influential in their deviance, despite their apparent preference for male to female friends. When separated by race and ethnicity, Anglo and Hispanic women were divided in half between those who said that men had negatively influenced their criminal activities and those who said they had not. On the other hand, 37 out of the 46 African-American women (80 percent) said that men had not negatively influenced their criminal activities.

At the same time, approximately 12 women admitted being victimized by parents or boyfriends either physically, sexually, or psychologically. Male accomplices were usually lovers or husbands. The potential for abuse was recognized by Miller (1986), who noted that deviant street networks were necessary for survival but were a source of victimization of women. The women who were victimized by men appeared to us to be reluctant to admit a possible connection between intimate relationships with men and the consequences of a felony conviction. Before she met Ricardo, for example, Violet described herself as easygoing, with dreams of attending college. Ricardo, a cocaine dealer, introduced her to the street life. She began to ex-

periment with drugs and became addicted to cocaine. Violet admitted that she was not aware of
Ricardo's assaultive tendencies until after he assaulted her sexually. Her dreams of college were
soon replaced by thoughts of getting money for
drugs through burglary and shoplifting.

On the other hand, ten women were not
abused but were introduced to deviance through
acquaintances or boyfriends. Brandi said:

> Initially, a female friend introduced me to
> some Colombian guys. . . . I sold for them for
> eight months. Then I sold for myself for 3
> years. . . . I didn't make as much money sell-
> ing alone.

Criminal deviance was unknown to some
women before they met their current boyfriends. These women now preferred deviance
to a straight life. Janine stated that she would
not be in boot camp, had she not met her current boyfriend:

> Before I moved in with my boyfriend 9
> months ago, I would have never thought of
> breaking the law. My boyfriend's friends
> wanted me to do burglaries, but I didn't know
> how to do the things they did. My boyfriend
> taught me how to get into houses without
> being seen and not to leave fingerprints.

Veronica, however, made it clear that many
women, including herself, were drawn to the
"bad boy" image of their boyfriends, who
shared their sense of excitement:

> I have a deviant side of me. . . . My boyfriend
> was already heavily involved in the drug
> business when I met him at [a topless bar]
> where I danced. I'm attracted to these kinds
> of men. . . . He taught me how to "recon"
> [reconstitute] cocaine, cutting and
> repacking a brick from 91 proof to 50 proof,
> just like a business. He treats me like an
> equal partner, and any of the friends are
> business associates. I am a catalyst. . . . I
> even get other guys turned on to drugs.

Many drug-using women admitted that the excitement and good times ended when the drug
supply ran out. When this happened, some
women reported leaving their current man to
seek another "sucker" (a term used by some
women to describe men) to provide them with
shelter, protection, money, and drugs. The
younger women in our sample (ages 18–20)
more often reported that they did not want to
be "tied down" to one particular male. A
smaller number of women sought stability or
cited the need to "settle down" or to "stop moving around from the law."

Women as leaders or followers. The women
were asked "In general, over the past year, were
you a leader or a follower when you were with
your friends?" Most women (57 percent) perceived themselves as leaders rather than followers (34 percent) of other friends; we found no distinct variations by race and ethnicity. They
provided various reasons for their views; Sylvia,
for example, "tried to talk them out of drive-bys"
(drive-by shootings). Another example of a leader
is Tricia, who commented:

> I am a leader because I don't follow nobody.
> I'm just doing my own thing, no matter
> what my friends do.

Other female offenders perceived themselves
as followers because they were so easily per-
suaded:

> People that use cocaine in front of me
> caused me to use. (Violet)

> My friends saw me as a cool person when I
> broke laws. I thought I should do what they
> did. (Jessica)

> It depends on who I'm with. I can be easily
> influenced either way. (Linda)

One of the distinguishing features of leaders
was their assertiveness and their stronger
self-concept. Leaders were sure of themselves
and made their own decisions. The followers
"went with the flow" and drifted into the criminal
lifestyle (Matza 1964). Furthermore, followers
generally believed that external forces governed
their lives and choices. Women followers claimed
that fate ruled their lives, a characteristic common among unorganized, lower-class criminals
(Irwin 1985). On the other hand, women who defined themselves as leaders admitted that some
of the life choices they had made were not always
the best in terms of deviant and criminal acts.

Summary and Conclusion

Cloward (1959) recognized that crime was differentially available in legitimate and illegitimate
environments. In this paper we have applied his
framework to examine the roles played by 104
adult female felons during criminal acts. Differential opportunity theory presupposes several
lines of inquiry. First, women offenders would
commit traditional female-oriented crimes
alone. Second, women who committed crimes
with men would act as accomplices and would
play secondary roles. Finally, women's criminal
behavior represents an extension of their roles in
the legitimate environment.

In our research, a small proportion of the
total sample (15 percent) committed the following crimes alone: assault, driving while intoxicated, forgery, and theft. Our findings for

assault were similar to those obtained by Ward et al. (1979), who found that most women convicted of assault acted independently. Our results, however, did not entirely support the first assertion of differential opportunity theory: forgery and theft represented female-oriented criminal behaviors, but assault and driving while intoxicated were not considered typical convictions for women.

Differential opportunity theory indicates that women will more often commit crimes alone. We found that more than 80 percent of our subjects committed crimes with accomplices in offenses such as drug dealing, robbery, larceny, and burglary. Thus, nontraditional criminal behaviors were more likely to be committed with male accomplices, who provided women with the opening into deviant networks. Our data also underscored the complexity of the accomplice issue: 14 women whom we interviewed revealed that they had committed their most recent criminal act with at least one other woman, a pattern supported in other studies of vice-related activities (Pettiway 1987) and robbery (Sommers and Baskin 1993).

We found that 14 percent of the sample played primary roles, while almost 30 percent characterized themselves as performing an equal role when committing felonious behavior with others. When we examined these data by race/ethnicity, we found that African-American women more often played primary or equal crime roles, whereas Anglo and Hispanic women tended to describe themselves as secondary role players.

Women who played a primary role felt that men had little influence in initiating or leading them into crime. Most women also stated that they had made a conscious decision to become involved in deviant and criminal behaviors. Furthermore, in many cases, the women revealed that they influenced other men and women to commit crime. This finding supports recent studies of serious female criminal behavior, which report that women are taking more assertive roles in deviance (Decker et al. 1993; Inciardi et al. 1993; Sommers and Baskin 1993). Our findings here are at odds with Cloward's model as well as with the bulk of past literature, which depicts women as playing only secondary roles or no role at all in crime and deviance (Campbell 1990; Hoffman-Bustamante 1973; Quicker 1983).

Nevertheless, 40 women in our research (38 percent) did not aspire to primary deviant roles. Many others (e.g., Covington 1985; Morash 1986; Pettiway 1987) have observed the stereotypical male female-criminal event in which men planned and committed the crime while women played a minor role. In our research, males were regarded as more trustworthy than women. These 40 women, however, admitted to being physically and sexually abused by these men (Gilfus 1992; Miller 1986). Clearly, more research is needed on the influence of men as crime partners and victimizers of women.

Finally, a few of the women (12) believed that men were generally opposed to women's participating equally in crime. This study suggests that sexual stereotyping occurs within the criminal world, making it difficult for women to free themselves from stereotypical roles and behaviors. Such a view of sex roles reflects support in the literature for the existence of differential opportunities, stratified by gender and race/ethnicity in both legitimate and criminal worlds (Cloward and Piven 1979; Daly and Chesney-Lind 1988; Kollock, Blumstein, and Schwartz 1985; Legerman and Wallace 1985; Maher and Curtis 1992; Steffensmeier 1983). Steffensmeier (1983) noted sex segregation in organized, lucrative, professional criminal enterprises, as did Patricia Adler (1993). We contend that sex segregation persists in the unorganized, street-level realm of the criminal world, as in the larger society. This condition more often typified Anglo and Hispanic women offenders. This recent turn of events has numerous social structural explanations that are beyond the scope of this paper (e.g., high mortality and incarceration rates among African-American men) but represent critical areas for future research.

In sum, a substantial proportion of women in our study initiated criminal behavior, led others into crime, and took primary roles in committing numerous criminal offenses. These conclusions, however, do not discount Steffensmeier's (1980) caution that general patterns of female crime have shown more stability than change over the past two decades. We found it difficult to assess how much our findings deviate from that of past years, but our work suggests two possibilities: (1) scholars in the past neglected to clearly differentiate between women's crime roles, and (2) structural changes at the street level allowed women more independence and active role taking in criminal events (Fagan and Chin 1991; Maher and Curtis 1992). Scholars recently have been paying more attention to women's roles both in the larger society and in the criminal world. Future research must be sensitive to the intersection of race/ethnicity, gender, and crime roles on street-level felony offenses.

Discussion Questions

1. What criminological theories support the social construction of mixed-gender criminal networks?

2. How do women's roles in crime represent an extension of gender roles in everyday life?

3. How do women's crime roles vary by type of crime?

4. What accounts for the difference by race/ethnicity in crime roles played by young women?

5. In this study, no women acted alone or took a leadership role in robbery. Why do women who commit robbery play a secondary role in mixed gender company, while women who assault someone else act alone?

References

Adler, F. 1975. *Sisters in Crime: The Rise of the New Female Offender.* New York: McGraw-Hill.

Adler, P. A. 1993. *Wheeling and Dealing: An Ethnography of an Upper-Level Dealing and Smuggling Community,* 2nd ed. New York: Columbia University Press.

Berger, R. J. and S. Balkan. 1983. "The Violent Female Delinquent: Myth or Reality?" Presented at the meetings of the Academy of Criminal Justice Sciences, San Antonio.

Bielby, W. T. and J. N. Baron. 1986. "Men and Women at Work: Sex Segregation and Statistical Discrimination." *American Journal of Sociology* 4: 759–99.

Blom, M. and T. van den Berg. 1989. "A Typology of the Life and Work Styles of 'Heroin-Prostitutes.'" Pp. 55–69 in *Growing Up Good: Policing the Behavior of Girls in Europe,* edited by M. Cain. London: Sage.

Bowker, L. R. 1978. *Women, Crime and the Criminal Justice System.* Lexington, MA: Heath.

Bowker, L. R. and M. W. Klein. 1983. "The Etiology of Female Juvenile Delinquency and Gang Membership: A Test of Psychological and Social Structural Explanations." *Adolescence* 18: 740–51.

Browne, A. 1987. *When Battered Women Kill.* New York: Free Press.

Burton, V. S., J. W. Marquart, S. J. Cuvelier, R. J. Hunter, and L. E. Fiftal. 1993. "The Harris County CRIPP Program: An Outline for Evaluation, Part 1." *Texas Probation* 8 (1): 1–8.

Campbell, A. 1990. *The Girls in the Gang.* 2nd ed. New York: Basil Blackwell.

Carlen, P. 1985. *Criminal Women: Autobiographical Accounts.* Cambridge, UK: Polity.

Chesney-Lind, M. and R. G. Shelden. 1992. *Girls, Delinquency, and Juvenile Justice.* Pacific Grove, CA: Brooks/Cole.

Cloward, R. A. 1959. "Illegitimate Means, Anomie, and Deviant Behavior." *American Sociological Review* 24: 164–76.

Cloward, R. A. and F. F. Piven. 1979. "Hidden Protest: The Channeling of Female Innovation and Resistance." *Signs* 4: 651–69.

Cohen, B. 1980. *Deviant Street Networks: Prostitution in New York.* Lexington, MA: Lexington Books.

Covington, J. 1985. "Gender Differences in Criminality among Heroin Users." *Journal of Research in Crime and Delinquency* 22: 329–54.

Cromwell, P., J. Olson, and D. Avary. 1991. *Breaking and Entering: An Ethnographic Analysis of Burglary.* Newbury Park, CA: Sage.

Cullen, F. T. 1984. *Rethinking Crime and Deviance Theory: The Emergence of a Structuring Tradition,* Totowa, NJ: Rowman and Allenheld.

Daly, K. 1989. "Gender and Varieties of White-Collar Crime." *Criminology* 27: 769–94.

———. 1994. *Gender, Crime, and Punishment.* New Haven: Yale University Press.

Daly, K. and M. Chesney-Lind. 1988. "Feminism and Criminology." *Justice Quarterly* 5: 497–538.

David, P. R. 1974. *The World of the Burglar: Five Criminal Lives.* Albuquerque: University of New Mexico Press.

Decker, S., R. Wright, A. Redfern, and D. Smith. 1993. "A Woman's Place Is in the Home: Females and Residential Burglary." *Justice Quarterly* 10: 143–62.

Del Olmo, R. 1986. "Female Criminality and Drug Trafficking in Latin America: Preliminary Findings." *Studies in Third World Societies* 37: 163–78.

England, P. 1981. "Assessing Trends in Occupational Sex Segregation, 1900–1976." Pp. 273–95 in *Sociological Perspectives on Labor Markets,* edited by I. Berg. New York: Academic Press.

Fagan, J. and K. Chin. 1991. "Social Processes of Initiation into Crack." *Journal of Drug Issues* 21: 313–43.

Fehrenbach, P. A. and C. Monastersky. 1988. "Characteristics of Female Adolescent Sexual Offenders." *American Journal of Orthopsychiatry* 58: 148–51.

Fenster, C. 1981. "Societal Reaction to Male-Female Co-Defendants: Sex as an Independent Variable." *California Sociologist* 4: 219–32.

Finkelhor, D. and D. Russell. 1984. "Women as Perpetrators." Pp. 171–87 in *Child Sexual Abuse: New Theory and Research,* edited by D. Finkelhor. New York: Free Press.

Gilfus, M. E. 1992. "From Victims to Survivors to Offenders: Women's Routes of Entry into Street Crime." *Women and Criminal Justice* 4 (1): 63–90.

Giordano, P. C. and S. A. Cernkovich. 1979. "On Complicating the Relationship between Liberation and Delinquency." *Social Problems* 26: 467–81.

Gribble, L. 1965. *Such Women Are Deadly.* New York: Arco.

Hagedorn, J. M. 1990. "Back in the Field Again: Gang Research in the Nineties." Pp. 240–59 in

Gangs in America: Diffusion, Diversity and Public Policy, edited by C. R Huff. Newbury Park, CA: Sage.

Hoffman-Bustamante, D. 1973. "The Nature of Female Criminality." *Issues in Criminology* 8 (2): 117–36.

Inciardi, J. A., D. Lockwood, and A. E. Pottieger. 1993. *Women and Crack Cocaine.* New York: Macmillan.

Irwin, J. 1985. *The Jail: Managing the Underclass in American Society.* Berkeley: University of California Press.

Jackson, B. 1969. *A Thief's Primer.* New York: Macmillan.

Jones, A. 1980. *Women Who Kill.* New York: Fawcett.

King, H., as told to Bill Chambliss. 1972. *Box Man: A Professional Thief's Journey.* New York: Harper and Row.

Kollock, P., P. Blumstein, and P. Schwartz. 1985. "Sex and Power in Interaction: Conversational Privileges and Duties." *American Sociological Review* 50: 34–46.

Legerman, P. and R. Wallace. 1985. *Gender in America.* Englewood Cliffs, NJ: Prentice-Hall.

Maher, L. and R. Curtis. 1992. "Women on the Edge of Crime: Crack Cocaine and the Changing Contexts of Street-Level Sex Work in New York City." *Crime, Law, and Social Change* 18: 221–58.

Matza, D. 1964. *Delinquency and Drift.* New York: Wiley.

Maurer, D. 1955. *Whiz Mob.* New Haven: College and University Press.

Miller, E. M. 1986. *Street Woman.* Philadelphia: Temple University Press.

Moore, J. W. 1978. *Homeboys.* Philadelphia: Temple University Press.

Morash, M. 1986. "Gender, Peer Group Experiences, and Seriousness of Delinquency." *Journal of Research in Crime and Delinquency* 23: 43–67.

Osgood, D. W., L. Johnston, P. O'Malley, and J. Bachman. 1988. "The Generality of Deviance in Late Adolescence and Early Adulthood." *American Sociological Review* 53: 81–93.

Parker, T. 1965. *Five Women.* London: Hutchinson.

Pettiway, L. 1987. "Participation in Crime Partnerships by Female Drug Users: The Effects of Domestic Arrangements, Drug Use, and Criminal Involvement." *Criminology* 25: 741–66.

Quicker, J. 1983. *Homegirls: Characterizing Chicana Gangs.* San Pedro, CA: International Universities Press.

Reskin, B. F. 1984. *Sex Segregation in the Workplace: Trends, Explanations, and Remedies.* Washington, DC: National Academy Press.

Rosenbaum, M. 1981. *Women on Heroin.* New Brunswick, NJ: Rutgers University Press.

Rosenfeld, R. 1983. "Sex Segregation and Sectors: An Analysis of Gender Differences in Returns from Employer Changes." *American Sociological Review* 48: 637–55.

Russell, D. H. 1985. "Girls Who Kill." *International Journal of Offender Therapy and Comparative Criminology* 29: 171–76.

Sommers, I. and D. E. Baskin. 1993. "The Situational Context of Violent Female Offending." *Journal of Research in Crime and Delinquency* 30: 136–62.

Steffensmeier, D. J. 1978. "Crime and the Contemporary Woman: An Analysis of Changing Levels of Female Property Crime, 1960–75." *Social Forces* 57: 566–84.

——. 1980. "Sex Differences in Patterns of Adult Crime: 1965–77: A Review and Assessment." *Social Forces* 58: 1080–1108.

——. 1983. "Organization Properties and Sex-Segregation in the Underworld: Building a Sociological Theory of Sex Differences in Crime." *Social Forces* 61: 1010–32.

Steffensmeier, D. J. and R. M. Terry. 1986. "Institutional Sexism in the Underworld: A View from the Inside." *Sociological Inquiry* 56: 304–23.

Sutherland, E. 1937. *The Professional Thief.* Chicago: University of Chicago Press.

Sutter, A. 1970. "A Hierarchy of Drug Users." Pp. 666–76 in *The Sociology of Crime and Delinquency,* 2nd ed., edited by M. Wolfgang. New York: Wiley.

Varna, A. 1957. *World Underworld.* London: Museum Press Limited.

Ward, D. A., J. Jackson, and R. E. Ward. 1979. "Crimes of Violence by Women." Pp. 116–17 in *Criminology of Deviant Women,* edited by F. Adler & R. J. Simon. Boston: Houghton-Mifflin.

Wright, R., S. H. Decker, A. K. Redfern, and D. L. Smith. 1992. "A Snowball's Chance in Hell: Doing Fieldwork with Active Residential Burglars." *Journal of Research in Crime and Delinquency* 29: 148–61.

Zietz, D. 1981. *Women Who Embezzle or Defraud: A Study of Convicted Felons.* New York: Praeger.

Excerpted from: Leanne Fiftal Alarid, James W. Marquart, Velmer S. Burton, Francis T. Cullen, and Steven J. Cuvelier, "Women's Roles in Serious Offenses: A Study of Adult Felons." In *Justice Quarterly* 13 (3): 431–454. Copyright © 1996 by Academy of Criminal Justice Sciences. ✦

10

A Woman's Place Is in the Home

Females and Residential Burglary

Scott H. Decker
Richard Wright
Allison Redfern
Dietrich Smith

We know little about the nature of women's participation in residential burglary, an offense statistically dominated by males. The present study is the only extant research directed specifically toward an understanding of residential burglary by females. The authors conducted extensive interviews and ride-alongs with 18 female and 87 male residential burglars in St. Louis. This chapter examines women's involvement in burglary by comparing the characteristics of female burglars with those of male burglars, and by developing a typology of female burglars that emphasizes their roles during offenses. The authors suggest that, in many ways, female burglars do not differ significantly from their male counterparts. For example, both groups display long criminal histories that span a variety of property, violent, and public-order offense categories. Both groups tend to have long, diverse substance abuse histories that overlap with and contribute to their involvements in burglary. However, the study did reveal several differences. Female burglars begin offending at a later age, are more likely to co-offend, and have less contact with authorities. The authors argue that women's involvement in residential burglary is marked by diversity of crime roles.

Despite growing interest in female criminality, little is known about the nature of women's participation in crimes statistically dominated by males. Certainly that is the case for residential burglary, an offense labeled by Shover (1991) as an overwhelmingly male enterprise. For example, we hardly know how females become involved in such offenses or what roles they play. Are they tempted into these crimes, for instance, by the influence of delinquent peers or by the use of drugs? Because we lack detailed knowledge, we cannot assess the extent to which the processes underlying burglaries committed by females differ from those underlying burglaries by males. This lack also restricts our capacity to detect important differences among female burglars. An assessment of these differences, however, is crucial in formulating effective policy responses to female criminality and to developing theories of lawbreaking by women (Simpson, 1991).

Short of observing burglaries, perhaps the best way to acquire this information is to go to the offenders themselves. As Feeney (1986) noted, the first-hand perspective possessed by offenders is unique and must be taken into account in attempting to explain and prevent crime. In setting a research agenda for feminist criminology, Daly and Chesney-Lind make a similar point: "The most pressing need today is . . . to get our hands dirty [through observation and interviewing], and to plunge more deeply into the social worlds of girls and women" (1988: 518–19). Such a strategy, they observe, will allow researchers "to comprehend women's crime on its own terms."

This article, based on field interviews with currently active offenders, examines women's involvement in residential burglary by (1) comparing their characteristics to those of their male counterparts and (2) outlining a typology of female burglars which emphasizes the roles they play during offenses.

Findings: Comparison of Male and Female Burglars

We compared the male and female offenders in regard to their participation in crimes other than residential burglary, their offending "styles" (i.e., tendency to specialize, to co-offend, to use alcohol and drugs), their histories of offending, and their contact with the criminal justice system. Before reporting these comparisons, we must emphasize that any observed differences may be sampling artifacts. In addition, the small number of female burglars may introduce some instability into the comparisons.

Self-Reported Crimes

Often it is claimed that offenders are versatile and commit a wide range of offenses (see, for example, Gottfredson and Hirschi, 1990). This observation, however, is derived largely from studies of males conducted in criminal justice settings rather than on the street. During our interviews we asked the subjects whether they ever had committed other sorts of crimes beside residential burglary. We did so because we were concerned primarily with prevalence—that is, whether the subject ever had engaged in other kinds of offenses. The eleven crimes mentioned most often by our interviewees are presented in Table 10.1.

Stealing (which includes shoplifting and corresponds to the legal definition of this activity), auto theft, and assault were the offenses most commonly reported by the males. Stealing and assault were mentioned most frequently by the females; these offenses were comparable in rank of frequency to those reported by the males. Beyond these two offenses, however, little other criminality was reported by the females. The only meaningful difference between the men and the women for this measure was found in regard to auto theft. This crime was fairly common among the males, but unknown among the females. The explanation for this difference might reside in a strong cultural tradition linking masculinity to driving and car ownership. Alternatively, males may have "cornered the market" in auto theft; to be profitable, such a crime requires sophisticated connections with garage owners, junkyard employees, and car dealerships.

Styles of Offending

One important aspect of offending style concerns the degree of crime specialization—that is, the extent to which offenders concentrate on one particular type of offense. The results reported in Table 10.1 revealed considerable diversity among our respondents over time. A somewhat different picture emerged, however, when we asked the offenders whether they had been involved in crimes other than residential burglary during their most recent period of offending.

Thirty-four percent of the males and 42 percent of the females claimed that they had committed only residential burglaries during this period (roughly the last six months). This finding is consistent with a substantial body of previous research showing that offenders display considerable diversity over the course of their criminal careers, but may specialize in a particular "line" for short periods. Maguire and Bennett (1982: 80) labeled this phenomenon "short-term specialization" (also see Shover, 1991).

Another element of offending style concerns the inclinations to work with others in carrying out crimes. Previous research demonstrated that "more often than not, [burglary] is committed by two or more persons acting in concert"

(Shover, 1991: 89).The results of our study bear this out: 79 percent of the males and all of the females reported that they had worked with others in the past. The males showed considerable variation in frequency of working with others: 39 percent said they "seldom" worked with others, while another 39 percent reported that they "always" did so. For the women, however, the picture was much clearer: an overwhelming 83 percent reported that they "always" worked with others, and the remaining 17 percent stated that they "usually" did so.

Table 10.1
Percentages of Respondents Engaging in Criminal Acts

	Males (n = 87)	Females (n = 18)
Stealing (includes shoplifting)	27	33
Auto theft	26	0
Commercial burglary	6	0
Drug sales	5	0
Robbery	15	6
Weapons offenses	14	6
Assault	26	17
Prostitution	0	6
Public order offenses	14	6
Forgery	2	0
Murder, manslaughter	1	0

The final aspect of offending style that we examined here relates to drug and alcohol use among our respondents, as well as to their perceptions of the role played by intoxicants in leading them to commit such crimes. We found little difference between the males and the females in self-reported drug use.

When the drug users were asked whether addiction had anything to do with their burglaries, 71 percent of the males and 82 percent of the females answered affirmatively. A majority of those in both groups said they committed burglaries to obtain the money they needed to buy more drugs. In addition, slightly more than three-quarters of the users in each group—76 percent of the males and 79 percent of the females—claimed that they used drugs *before* committing their burglaries. A higher percentage of females than of males stated that they "always" or "usually" used drugs beforehand.

One explanation seems to be that many female burglaries arise from crack "runs." This point, however, is difficult to determine conclusively because (as noted above) use of the drug is heavily stigmatized.

History of Burglary Offending

We explored male-female difference on three dimensions designed to measure burglary offending histories: age at first burglary, total number of lifetime burglaries, and *lambda,* the mean number of annual burglaries.

The ages at which males and females committed their first residential burglary differed significantly: the males generally started much earlier in life. None of the female burglars had committed their first offense before age 12, but 22 percent of the males had done so. The modal category for males was the 13–16 age bracket, which accounted for 53 percent of the cases. Sixty-one per cent of the females, on the other hand, were over 16 years old when they carried out their first burglary.

Given that the females started to commit burglaries later, on average, than their male counterparts, we are not surprised that a greater proportion of females had been involved in fewer than 20 residential burglaries in their lifetime. Perhaps more interesting, 39 percent of the females had committed more than 70 lifetime residential burglaries, a proportion roughly comparable to the males' figure of 41 percent. The bimodal distribution of the females' responses suggests that women are likely to engage in burglary at two very distinct levels, and perhaps to employ two different styles.

Contact With the Criminal Justice System

The males were more likely than the females to have had contact with the system for offenses of all types. This difference was most notable at the stage of the criminal justice process that resulted in incarceration. Over 90 percent of the respondents in each group had been arrested previously, but only one woman (6 percent) had been convicted and sentenced to a term of imprisonment. In contrast, 26 percent of the males had served time in the past. This difference may exist in part because the females began offending later and consequently had fewer "years at risk." Other factors, however, are probably at work as well, including (1) an assumption by the police that most burglars are male, which allows females to remain above suspicion (Horowitz and Pottieger, 1991), and (2) a tendency for those females who are arrested to receive preferential treatment in the courtroom (Simon, 1975). Certainly the women in our sample believe that their sex conferred a degree of protection from the law. Several expressed the belief that authorities would not take action against them simply because they were female.

Findings: Types of Female Burglars

The data reported above suggest some of the ways in which female residential burglars may differ from their male counterparts. This information, however, tells us little about the nature of female participation in these crimes. Do female burglars, for example, tend to play "secondary roles" (Ward et al., 1979: 122) during offenses? To answer questions such as this, we constructed a typology of female residential burglars, using detailed descriptions of offenses provided by the women themselves.

In constructing our typology, we used the categories of *accomplice* and *partner* identified by Ward et al. (1979). Our sample contained no *sole perpetrators.* By definition, *conspirators* were not included in the research because they did not participate directly in committing the offence. We categorized six of the females in our study as *accomplices* because of their subservience to others—usually men—during their burglaries. (Not only females act as accomplices; a few of the males whom we interviewed also assumed this role. In no case, however, did a male respondent admit to being subservient to a woman during offenses.) We classified the 12 remaining females as *partners* because they participated as equals in their burglaries. Although some of these females co-offended with males, they did not take orders from them.

Partners could be distinguished from accomplices in a number of important ways, including (1) their motivation for committing the crimes, (2) their participation in target selection and planning, and (3) the work roles they adopted while committing the burglaries.

Motivation

The factors that the female burglars regarded as leading them to commit their crimes differentiated the partners clearly from the accomplices. Those who worked as partners, whether with other women, with men, or both, reported making an independent decision to commit their burglaries. They did not see themselves as drawn into offending against their will by other offenders or by the irresistible pressure of circumstances. The independence of such offenders is illustrated in the following quote:

> My partners ain't got to influence me. I just want to do it. I'm so used to doing it.

Women who carried out burglaries as partners often were motivated by material or instrumental concerns. Their responses reflected an affirmative commitment to burglary. Some, for example, saw the offense simply as an easy way of obtaining money. As one of them said,

> [Burglary's] a damn good way of getting over. It's like a white-collar crime. Hell, it's just fast money.

The women who worked as partners displayed considerable diversity in motives. Some reported engaging in burglary because they found it fun or enjoyable. These women derived a psychic reward from such offenses. One of the women said she committed burglaries for "the thrill," adding

> I get off on it. I do it for the enjoyment, 'cause I do truly enjoy it. It's a hobby; it's recreation to me.

The women who worked only as accomplices had a far different perspective. These offenders felt that they were caught up in circumstances beyond their control, which compelled them to commit burglaries. Often these circumstances arose in the context of an unequal relationship in which the females were reduced to carrying out the will of other, more dominant people. The dominant parties in such cases typically were males, though occasionally they were females. The woman quoted in the following passage expresses the belief that she was trapped by her companions' activities:

> [The burglaries] got worse when we moved and I started hanging with a different crowd. It wasn't too bad where I first did it. It's getting worse now, though, 'cause I'm with older guys and they go for bigger things, and when they go, they got things planned—if somebody walks in before they are done, they would rather hurt them first.

Another entanglement for accomplices involved the lack of employment:

> Sometimes I have to wonder myself why I [commit burglaries]. And I always come to the conclusion that my kids need things. I always go and fill out applications and everything like that, but they don't never seem to call back. Every time I want to go and finish school, something is always in my way.

Drugs also played a prominent role:

> I got into this thing with cocaine with my friend, and she don't work or anything, and it ain't cheap. So I pretty much go out with the boys to get what we want. It is getting pretty deep.

Alcohol also was [a] contributory factor. One woman explained that she and a male friend were enticed into burglaries by a third offender while they were intoxicated:

> [Another offender would] always get us both either drinking alcohol, or [my friend] smoked marijuana a lot. I only smoked it two times in my life and I didn't like it and I don't do it, but he would get me drunk and say we need some more money. Then they would go to a house.

Target Selection and Planning

Females' participation in burglary can be examined with reference to their role in finding targets and planning offenses. The extent to which offenders participate in these tasks distinguishes partners clearly from accomplices. A number of the women with partner status played an important role in finding targets and planning offenses, as illustrated by the following quote:

> Last time I took him. It was a real good, decent neighborhood, you know, like in the county. I mean, we just sit up and . . . spot them up, and I find what I find and he get what he get and we just go. It's like a sharing thing with us. He come to me and ask me what's up. I tell him nothing, but I know where we can get some money. We just come to each other. "I ain't doing nothing, what's happening?" "Well, I ain't got no money either, but I know where we can get some." He asked me if I been watching a house. "Yeah, I've been watching a house. There's some old people and they go to church every Sunday. Every Sunday they go. They be gone from like about four to five hours. They go to church in the morning, Sunday school then, you know, all of that. I had watched that one. They be old people. They be having good stuff."

Planning was crucial for many of the females who worked as partners in committing burglaries:

> That's one reason why we got so many youngsters in jail today. I see this, so let's make a hit. No, no, no. If they see this and it looks good, then it's going to be there for a while. So the point is, you have to case it and make sure you know everything. I want to know what time you go to work, the time the children go to school. I know there's no one coming home for lunch. So plan it with somebody else. We'll take the new dishwasher, washing machine, and this other stuff. We just put it in the truck. Do you know when people rent a truck, nobody ever pays that any attention? They think you're moving [but] only if you rent a truck. Now if

you bring it out of there and put it in the car, that's a horse of another color.

A few of the females classified as partners occasionally engaged in more spontaneous burglaries. The women who worked in this way, however, did not do so exclusively. These "spur-of-the-moment" burglaries emerged in the course of their day-to-day activities.

Women involved in burglaries as accomplices exercised much less control over the selection of targets and the planning of crimes. (In fact, some were unaware that a burglary was going to take place until they arrived at the site.) Other people invariably set up the burglaries:

He'll call me, you know. And he'll say "I don't think we're going out today." I'll say "OK." It's nothing really specific why he do it that way. He just stop for a little while and start back . . . [H]e'll pick them out. You can tell if it's a nice neighborhood or bad neighborhood. What areas we go in, he picks them out.

Work Roles

For the females who worked as partners, burglaries could involve a variety of tasks. Many of these tasks were indistinguishable from those traditionally associated with men, such as gaining entry, searching the house, carrying goods outside, and disposing of them. The following interview segment describes some of the tasks performed by a female acting as a partner. Although this was her first offense, she helped to find the transportation to reach the target (by stealing a truck) and took part in the actual break-in:

Well, it wasn't up on me, somebody else who was in there different, not state, in a different county. He just came up and told me he knew about it, a rich guy that was gonna be gone for the weekend. He knew this person, knew who it was, and he knew about it. When he left that night about two or three in the morning, we went down there. We had stolen a truck, we had stolen my ex-boyfriend's father's truck, went down there. We tried to get in, but we couldn't get in. Everything was locked. Right. . . . We couldn't get in for nothing, so what we does was, we had some shit in back of the truck and we took some tape. Then we put it over the window real tight, then we busted it, and then we took the tape down and the window was shattered. It had no window in it. So—everybody used gloves of course—so we went in there, you know, and we knew, when we went, we knew nobody was gonna be home. There wasn't a house around for two blocks, each way you went. So . . . my first one was basically the easiest one.

As noted earlier, the target often was located by a female partner, who also took the lead in planning the offense. In these cases the woman had a substantial say in determining how the proceeds of the crime were divided:

. . . whatever you chose to give to the other person. We tried to split everything equally. We were all good friends, you know, so I got the best deal out of it because of the *fact* that I needed the money more than everybody else. Me and my sister needed the money more than everybody did and . . . we were the ones that said hey, we pointed it out, we found a way to get in, we knew where everything was, we told them how, we had everything planned out down to the TV. This is where this is at and this is where that is at.

The roles played by female burglars are dynamic and can change over time. Many of the women who currently participate in offenses as partners started out as accomplices. The woman quoted below clearly has an equal relationship with her co-offenders, but this was not always the case:

The first burglary I ever committed, I was in the house and I was smoking weed at the time. A friend came in and said "I want to go in this house." I said "Okay, it was around the corner . . . what part am I going to play?" He says "All you got to do is watch the doors for me. The bags I bring down, take them out, and you also drive the car for me."

As should be obvious from the above, women who work as accomplices in burglary play much more limited roles. They seldom participate in planning the crime, and often do not even enter the dwelling. Some claimed to prefer working with others because they lacked the skills needed to be a successful burglar: "I can't do it all by myself . . . I haven't mastered that yet."

Others simply felt more comfortable when relying on a colleague's expertise; they were uncertain about their ability to work alone. In the following case, a woman reports that she deferred to her boyfriend's judgment in determining the suitability of a given target:

He can look at them and tell. He's better at it than me. Sometimes I give him tips to go on, but he checks them out. I feel safer for him to check them out.

A common work assignment for accomplices was acting as a lookout or driver. Several of the women stated that driving was their primary job in burglaries:

Well, see, me and my boyfriend had been together for a year, and he done them all the time. Well, not all the time, but it was no big deal, and all I had to do, all I ever do, is drive. I just go like he'll go, him and his friend. He don't do 'em every week or anything like that. Like it's not really 'cause we need the money or anything either. Like he'll go during the day and he'll look at a house and he'll find one, and then he'll tell me about where the house is . . . all I have to do is drive to the place and wait for them to start bringing out the stuff, and then drive off.

Others said that they typically kept a lookout for their colleagues:

They came and picked me up with a stolen automobile. I didn't know that it was stolen. We went out there to this house and they got out. I just assumed—I didn't know what was going on at first. We got out and they went in first, and then they came back out. One of the men came back out and told me to come in and to keep an eye out to see if anybody was there or anybody comes down the sidewalk or if anybody drives down the street or anything.

In both of these cases the women, as accomplices, did not choose to perform these secondary tasks. Instead the tasks were assigned to them by a dominant co-offender.

Conclusion

What light does this quantitative and qualitative information shed on the nature of female criminality? Our sample was not generated randomly; with this fact in mind, the quantitative findings suggest that women involved in residential burglary do not differ significantly from their male counterparts on a number of relevant dimensions (e.g., drug and alcohol use, degree of offense specialization). Nevertheless, the results show that some important differences may exist as well. Compared to the males, for example, the females (1) more often committed burglaries with others, (2) began offending at a later age, and (3) had less contact with the criminal justice system. Further examination of these apparent differences is warranted.

The qualitative data demonstrate that women's involvement in residential burglary is marked by diversity and that the debate about whether women play a primary or a secondary role in the offense is probably a red herring. In fact, as among males, some assume primary roles exclusively, some adopt secondary roles exclusively, and other[s] move from one type of role to another as they become more experienced. This observation has important implications for research into women's involvement in crimes committed more often by males. To be

sure, a much lower percentage of women than of men participate in residential burglary (Shover, 1991). Even so, our qualitative data reveal substantial similarities between males and females. This fact suggests that the activities of women who do engage in such offenses may be explained by some of the same factors that explain men's participation.

Discussion Questions

1. Why did women involved in burglary tend to specialize in this type of crime rather than commit a wide variety of crime?

2. How did female burglars compare with male burglars in terms of crime roles and gender stratification? Did the partner differ substantially from the accomplice?

3. What criminological theory would best describe women's involvement in burglary, and why?

4. How did the women's crime roles in burglary differ from the women depicted in the Alarid et al. study (Chapter 9) who committed crimes with other men?

5. From a male offender point of view, what advantages might there be to involving women in burglary as opposed to having only other males? What might be the disadvantages?

References

Bennett, T. and R. Wright (1984) *Burglars on Burglary: Prevention and the Offender.* Aldershot, UK: Gower.

Cromwell, P., J. Olson, and D. Avary (1991) *Breaking and Entering: An Ethnographic Analysis of Burglary.* Newbury Park, CA: Sage.

Daly, K. and M. Chesney-Lind (1988) "Feminism and Criminology." *Justice Quarterly* 5: 497–538.

Feeney, F. (1986) "Robbers as Decision Makers." In D. B. Cornish and R. V. Clarke (eds.), *The Reasoning Criminal*, pp. 57–71. New York: Springer-Verlag.

Glassner, B. and C. Carpenter (1985) "The Feasibility of an Ethnographic Study of Adult Property Offenders." Unpublished report prepared for the National Institute of Justice.

Gottfredson, M. and T. Hirschi (1990) *A General Theory of Crime.* Stanford: Stanford University Press.

Horowitz, R. and A. Pottieger (1991) "Gender Bias in Justice Handling of Seriously Crime-Involved Youths." *Journal of Research in Crime and Delinquency* 28: 75–100.

Ianni, F. (1972) *A Family Business: Kinship and Control in Organized Crime.* New York: Russell Sage.

Maguire, M. and T. Bennett (1982) *Burglary in a Dwelling*. London: Heinemann.

McCall, G. (1978) *Observing the Law*. New York: Free Press.

Parisi, N. (1982) "Are Females Treated Differently? A Review of the Theories and Evidence on Sentencing and Parole Decisions." In N. H. Rafter and E. A. Stanko (eds.), *Judge, Lawyer, Victim, Thief*, pp. 205–20. Boston: Northeastern University Press.

Rengert, G. and J. Wasilchick (1985) *Suburban Burglary: A Time and Place for Everything*. Springfield, IL: Thomas.

Reppetto, T. (1974) *Residential Crime*. Cambridge, MA: Ballinger.

Shover, N. (1973) "The Social Organization of Burglary." *Social Problems* 31: 208–19.

——. (1991) "Burglary." In M. Tonry and N. Morris (eds.), *Crime and Justice: A Review of Research*, Vol. 14, pp. 73–113. Chicago: University of Chicago Press.

Simon, R. (1975) *Women and Crime*. Lexington, MA: Lexington Books.

Simon, R. and N. Sharma (1979) *The Female Defendant in Washington, D.C.—1974 and 1975*. Washington, DC: INSLAW.

Simpson, S. (1991) "Caste, Class and Violent Crime: Explaining Differences in Female Offending." *Criminology* 29: 115–35.

Ward, D., M. Jackson, and R. Ward (1979) "Crimes of Violence by Women." In F. Adler and R. Simon (eds.), *The Criminology of Deviant Women*, pp. 114–38. Boston: Houghton Mifflin.

Weppner, R. (1977) *Street Ethnography*. Beverly Hills, CA: Sage.

West, D. and D. Farrington (1977) *The Delinquent Way of Life*. London: Heinemann.

Wright, R., S. Decker, A. Rooney, and D. Smith (1992) "A Snowball's Chance in Hell: Doing Fieldwork with Active Residential Burglars." *Journal of Research in Crime and Delinquency* 29: 148–61.

11

Comparing Female Gangs of Various Ethnicities

Young Women of African-American, El Salvadoran, and Mexican Descent

David C. Brotherton

This study analyzes the historical background and social context in which the actions, choices, and behaviors of self-defined gang females are carried out. The research is based on interviews with 46 female gang members ranging in age from 15 to 22. These women were recruited from three gangs in San Francisco, and each gang's membership was characterized by a single dominant ethnicity. Within the sample, 10 of the women agreed to complete life history interviews that included information about family background and school and work history. The study included the Portrero Hill Posse (PHP), an all-female African-American gang; the El Salvadoran Posse (ESP), a mixed-gender gang; and Las Locas (LL), a mixed-gender Mexican gang. The respondents were recruited using the "snowball sampling" method (Biernacki and Waldorf 1981), which is particularly appropriate for the study of "hidden populations." The author asked questions about the pathways by which the woman had joined the gang, the gang's organizational structure, the status and roles of females within the gang, involvement of drug dealing and criminal activities, and the incidence of victimization. This research refocuses attention on the importance of female gang members, showing how the degree of autonomy obtained [by these females] is shaped by the entrepreneurial success of their delinquent activities, especially in the field of drug sales.

Introduction

I ran away from home because of all the things I was seeing at home. I was like only in the sixth grade and that is when I met the ESP [El Salvadoran Posse] gang and I started hanging out with them. There was times which I didn't have nowhere to go or nowhere to sleep. I would stay on like door steps, somebody's door step, sitting down all night, or ride up to X and Y street on the bus to the top of the hill and back to where it stops all night. So that is when I met ESP. I felt like it was like a family thing. I found something, I didn't have a home. I had friends and they helped me out. They would steal to get food for me. And you know we had no money. I became real close to them. That is how it started. I joined the gang by 12. (La Muneca, ESP)

La Muneca, above, describes her pathway into an adolescent street gang. She makes references to the variety of functions that the gang as performed in her struggle to survive and the stage she chose for the gang to enter her life. Whether in the form of a surrogate family, a refuge, a source of income, or a circle of close friends, the gang necessarily filled a social void. Later in La Muneca's story, the gang's influence on her takes on a less benign tone. Acting as the social milieu in which she was introduced to hard drugs, the gang is partly blamed by La Muneca for her finding herself in a crack house at the age of 15, then telephoning an outreach worker to come and get her, and finally entering a city "rehab" program as an addicted user of crack cocaine.

Taking a cue from La Muneca, this paper is an effort to provide an analysis of the historical background and social context in which the actions, choices, and behaviors of self-defined gang females are carried out.

The Gang as a Focal Group and Social Context

In the early work of Walter Miller (1958), he suggests that lower-class adolescents, particularly gang boys, have a different set of values than their middle-class counterparts. These values grow out of the lower-class cultural milieu which surrounds adolescents, effectively socializing them through a number of focal concerns that could be empirically observed in their street behavior and street guises.

In contrast to his contemporary, Albert Cohen (1955), Miller argued that lower-class adolescent deviance could not be understood by comparing it to the mainstream's middle-class value system, as if it were a mere inversion. Rather, Miller insisted that the lower-class culture system had its own history and traditions which were "many centuries old with an integrity of its own."

Conceptually, Miller saw the youths' behavior break down into six thematic "dimensions": trouble, toughness, fate, smartness, autonomy, and excitement. In Miller's eyes, the behavior associated with these concerns could yield either positive or negative outcomes for the gangs and their members, depending upon the social situation in which their actions were played out in street and neighborhood settings. The relationship between the mode of individual or group behavior, the admixture of socioeconomic conditions and the specific form that the gang's cultural system takes is therefore the crux of his analysis.

The Hidden Influences of Gender and Race

While Miller's (1958) conceptualization of the lower-class gang youth is overly one-dimensional, smacking too often of voluntarism, he makes a convincing argument that the adolescent street gang constitutes a self-created and meaningful subcultural focal group. In practical day-to-day situations, this notion is understood not only by the gang's members and other youth peripherally associated with it, but also by the many who have to formally and informally negotiate with the gang's presence, i.e., parents, relatives, neighbors, police, teachers, and youth peers. Nevertheless, there are two further shortcomings with Miller's early work that need to be addressed.

As Campbell (1991) has forcefully stated, 1950's social science was dominated by a white male world view that ignored questions of gender and race (see also Chesney-Lind 1989). One oft-repeated critique of Miller (1958) is that he dismisses the active and self-directed role of females in gangs, preferring to assign them subordinate statuses such as auxiliaries or "molls."

The second major shortcoming is again indicative of the "situated knowledge" (Haraway 1991) that determined the era's social scientific parameters, and relates to the narrow realm within which the dynamics of race were considered.[1] For example, a study by Miller (1958) which compared the incidence of violence in black male gangs to their white male counterparts, while questioning the violent black gang stereotype, avoided any mention of race structuring or the resultant social pathologies (Anderson 1990) that are prevalent in ghetto communities (Brown 1965; Wilson 1987; Sampson 1987).

Such a limited race discourse not only obscures the differences between one gang and another but also limits a discussion of the specific social ecology (Suttles 1968; Sullivan 1989) within which white and nonwhite gangs emerge and the contrasting subcultural practices and traditions that inform their development.

This latter point has especial relevance for an understanding of the hidden social contexts in which alcohol and drugs are used, sold, and distributed. For, failure to consider holistically the actions or patterned behaviors of "deviant" individuals or groups, makes it difficult to (1) develop meaningful intervention or prevention strategies that embrace the individual as part of the community, and (2) avoid the charge that social science further pathologizes, isolates, and decontextualizes the lives of already stigmatized groups and individuals (see Liazos 1972).

Taking these critiques into fuller consideration while continuing to draw on Miller's (1958) concepts of "focal group" and "focal concerns," the gang is defined for the purposes of this study as:

1. A neighborhood-based, multifunctional, adolescent and adult grouping whose subcultural practices are embedded in the sociocultural history, values, and experiences of the community.

2. An alternative space constructed for self-directed cultural and subcultural practices.

3. A structured and relatively stable friendship arena where criteria for membership is often predicated on some combination of residentiality, race/ethnicity, and potential for group loyalty.

4. A street-level organization within which opportunities for financial rewards, pleasure, excitement, status, respect, and refuge are all possible.

Three Groups of Gang Females: Comparative Characteristics

Not all gangs are the same. There are broad variations among their memberships based on race/ethnic backgrounds, subcultural traditions, and types of delinquent/criminal behaviors, particularly those involving the use and sales of licit and illicit drugs.

[The] Portrero Hill Posse (PHP) was an all-female, African-American gang that restricted its operations to the housing projects in which most of the members lived and had grown up. The respondents, ranging in age from 15 to 25 years, reported the patterned use of alcohol, mainly beer, and the restricted use of crack. The criminal activities of PHP's members were primarily the buying and selling of crack cocaine, organized shoplifting, and crack-related pimping.

[The] El Salvadoran Posse (ESP) was a predominantly male gang with a small but stable female contingent. Most of its members were from El Salvador, but the gang also included a smaller number of males and females from other Central American nations such as Nicaragua and Guatemala. Some, though not all, respondents reported the use of alcohol, mainly beer and fortified wine, and the frequent use of marijuana. As for their participation in the illicit economy, all the respondents stated that it was not drug-related, [a]lthough several respondents referred to a consistent pattern of shoplifting (for which two had served jail sentences) and occasionally acting as a "look-out" for male gang members who broke into lock-up shops in the local area.

Las Locas (LL) [was] also a group of females belonging to a gang consisting mainly of Mexican and Chicano males. The respondents reported a broader range of drug use than the other two groups, including alcohol (mainly beer and Mexican brandy), PCP, LSD, marijuana, and powdered cocaine. The criminal activities of the respondents were largely restricted to the selling of powdered cocaine. It was revealed during interviews at the end of the study that more of the group's females were turning to the selling of crack based on powdered cocaine's lessening demand and crack's higher profit margins.

The remainder of this paper comprises a descriptive analysis of the interview data conceptually organized around three of the six focal concerns originally outlined by Miller (1958): "smartness," "toughness," and "autonomy."

'Smartness'

"In its essence, smartness involves the capacity to achieve a valued entity—material goods, personal status—through a maximum use of mental agility and a minimum use of personal effort." This is how Miller (1958: 9) describes gang members' ability and penchant for outwitting the normative system of production and exchange. This orientation and focal concern that Miller found to be a characteristic trait of male gang members can be particularly observed in the activities of female members from the PHP gang.

The Case of Portrero Hill Posse (PHP)

The PHP gang is based in one of the predominantly African-American public housing projects of San Francisco. Its members stated that they grew up together, living in the same public housing (see Lauderbeck et al. 1992), and in the same conditions of relative poverty. They decided to form a gang after their male gang boyfriends had consistently refused to let them participate in the trading of crack cocaine, a street enterprise that African-Americans had dominated in the city since the drug's inception during the late 1980s (Waldorf 1993). In fact, PHP members considered entering the drugs business almost like entering an old-fashioned legitimate "ethnic enterprise" (Bonacich and Modell 1981).

In the interview data, the kind of "smartness" that emerged from PHP's members was a direct contrast to that of the two other gangs in that they practiced a business value system that became an operating trait of the group rather than that of the individual. Thematic examples of this entrepreneurial consciousness and its attendant set of practices are outlined below.

(1) Learning to keep risks to a minimum. Originally, PHP members started selling their drug wares to buyers on streets adjacent to the public housing projects where they lived. In time, they changed this "marketing strategy" after one of their members was "busted" for selling to an undercover narcotics agent from a car. Marsha, a 17-year-old, described the new strategy:

> Well we have customers come up to us and we will sell it to them or, you know, sometimes they will drive by, but we wait for them to get out of the car. We don't go up to the car and sell it because it might be an undercover cop.

After this encounter with the criminal justice system, for which the youth received a probation sentence, the gang moved their operations to the safer confines of a member's house. Periodically, they would change the location to avoid detection. This pragmatic response to surveillance reduced the risks of selling considerably and resulted in few, if any members, thereafter being busted for the drugs sales.

(2) Internal order is good for business. According to classical sociological theory (Durkheim 1933), for a group or a society to maintain a heightened level of internal cohesion and solidarity, members have to maintain a shared value system. What Durkheim termed a "collective conscience" was particularly apparent in interviews with PHP's members. This took the form of a distinctly entrepreneurial "worldview" that translated into the street practice of drug selling. Group cohesion was maintained, therefore, through the gang's merchandising "traditions" of buying and selling in the

drug market and a policy of abstinence when doing business.

At the same time, group cohesion was practically reinforced by a strictly sanctioned and selective system of in-group membership. This partly bore out Miller's (1958) observation that since "the corner group supports and enforces a rigorous set of standards which demand a high degree of fitness and personal competence, it tends to recruit from the most 'able' members of the community."

Thus, while physical "fitness" may not have been a priority of the PHP gang, a quick mind and a flair for this risk-taking world was a definite qualification of membership. For example, all sellers had to be members of the gang, and on this issue there was little compromise. Further, there was no consorting with outsiders about business operations that originated within the group. When new members wanted to join—they did not recruit—the "wannabes" had to pass a risk-taking initiation process which usually meant taking part in the group's regularly organized shoplifting expeditions.

The successful completion of their initiation cemented a wannabe's affiliation to the group, i.e., they were now "in" or "down," a term that indicates a process that is somewhat similar to the bonding initiation of Latino gang females who have to fight their way in by "doing the line."[2]

Once in the group, PHP members distributed the drug profits equitably among those who participated in the specific business operation that led to the profits. This norm ensured the continued presence of a collective group consciousness, since there was little evidence of any formal hierarchy of individual statuses. In other words, the everyday business practices of "the gang" kept members thinking of the whole rather than the individual, which helped to guard against overly ambitious, opportunistic, and potentially divisive members. This is important when considering the impact that $1,000 or more in cash might have on an impoverished 15- or 16-year-old novice gang member.

(3) Preventing predators from invading the marketplace. The entrepreneurial "smartness" of PHP had led it to successfully claim for itself a small slice of the drug turf in a competitive arena. In other words, not only had the members symbolically claimed their turf but they had substantively outcompeted other male gangs in the area who, over time, gave in to their market expertise.

'Toughness'

Like any enterprise mindful of its position in the marketplace, PHP did not want other drug-based gangs to encroach. Consequently, PHP members would occasionally engage in actions to ward off rivals—sometimes through the force of firearms in which case they exhibited another focal dimension of gang life that Miller (1958) refers to as "toughness." The difference between Miller's conception of "toughness" and that of these gang females is that their demonstration of physical prowess is highly instrumental. For Miller and his street-corner males, "toughness" was interpreted as a case of exaggerated masculinity, largely resulting from the "lack of a consistently present male figure with whom to identify and from whom to learn essential components of a 'male' role." This is how one PHP member described "fighting":

(I): You said you had fights. Tell me about some of the fights that you guys had. Would you use any weapons or anything?

(R): Whatever we got—knives or whatever. Basically we just try to strip them down.

(I): What do you mean strip them down?

(R): Rip off all their clothes. They won't have nothing to wear. Then they won't mess with us no more. They won't come back and fuck with us no more. (PHP member)

The "toughness," therefore, that PHP members exuded and practiced was a function of their business, much like in other studies of street dealing in the drugs economy (Goldstein et al. 1989; Sullivan 1989). But unlike most typical notions of "turf" (Taylor 1989), in which gang males are said to unequivocally defend their territories, the members of PHP stated that their drug turf was negotiable. Their "toughness" was therefore contingent on their "smartness" and its use depended on the demands of the economic situation and social context.

For example, if a rival black female "crew" (i.e., a group that is ephemerally organized for the purpose of carrying out an action versus a gang that is consistently organized over time) were to come selling its drugs, it could do so providing they agreed to share some of their profits, in the form of rent for entering the marketplace.[3]

(4) Adapting to consumer trends. Noting that male customers of crack liked to be sexually entertained and that there were a number of female crack addicts willing to trade sex for drugs (known as "toss ups"), the PHP gang entered the sex industry in a small but lucrative way. Essentially, PHP members helped to run the crack

houses by not only supplying the crack but also the crack prostitutes.

(I): What happens? [in the crack houses] (author)

(R): Well, there would be some guys in there smoking crack and there would be some girls in there smoking crack, and [w]hen the girls have no more crack to smoke they will do anything to get their next hit.

(I): So you guys provide women for some of these guys?

(R): Yes, they just want to get high. The broads just want to get high, if she want to do it, then. . . .

(I): What do you think of the crack prostitutes?

(R): They just toss ups. You know, somebody going to spend a lot of money or something and they want a little female. I will go find one for them, someone that I know will entertain them.

(I): How are the women who exchange sex for crack treated by the men?

(R): Treat them like they present themselves, like bitches, like tramps. They don't get no respect because they are not respecting themselves. But, hey, you know it is like their bitch or toss up.

(5) Diversifying operations. In addition to the drug and sex trades, PHP engaged in highly organized boosting, which involved "casing" department stores, setting up distractions, systematically removing the detection devices from clothes and shoplifting thousands of dollars of goods from major stores to fulfill orders from families and friends in the neighborhood. Again, PHP had a market strategy which kept the business operation low key, in-house, and away from "fences" and middlemen who could prove to be an additional risk to the operations.[4]

Entrepreneurial Comparisons [Among] Portrero Hill Posse (PHP), El Salvadoran Posse (ESP), and Las Locas (LL)

El Salvadoran Posse

In contrast to PHP and LL, ESP did not have supply links to the drug trade. Their lack of connections was mostly due to two factors: (1) their more recent entry into United States society, with most of ESP's members coming from war-torn zones of El Salvador and Nicaragua, and (2) the location of their gang turf next to a public housing project where the drugs trade was already dominated by a black male gang specializing in crack cocaine sales.

Like PHP and LL, ESP's members were severely economically marginalized, with many members barely able to survive on Aid to Families with Dependent Children (AFDC) payments in attempting to support several children. Their economic conditions were made that much worse by the tendency of many of the males to be unwilling or unable (especially if they were consistently imprisoned) to accept any responsibility for their offspring.

What Miller (1957) described as "serial-monogamy" in his descriptions of lower-class, urban black sexual practices, is a term that could be applied to the kind of male-female relationships engaged in by ESP females. These relationships saw female gang members frequently bear children from gang-involved fathers, who, strangely enough, might not necessarily be from the same gang. In such cases, the group places sanctions against females who consort with rival gang members, and these usually prove too much pressure for the relationship to stay intact. Such internal group pressures, when added to the tendency of some gang males to be "players" (i.e., engage in multiple-partner sexual relationships), leads many relationships to end before the child is born.

The prospect of raising a child (or children) alone forced many of the ESP females to "double-up," i.e., raise their children semi-collectively, especially if they were from the same family. Their social and economically disadvantaged position in both the formal and informal market sectors was a major reason they resorted to boosting as their primary practice of entrepreneurial "smartness."

(I): Was shoplifting the thing to do to get money?

(R): No, I did it because when I felt my kids didn't have no shoes or anything I would go steal. I got three [years]. If they didn't have nothing to eat I would go, if she didn't have nothing to eat for her house I would go with her. That is mainly the reason why we steal. It was not a habit. It is for a reason. I mean you know I have a probation officer and I tell him you know you guys might think we steal because we want to or because we have a drug habit but I don't need drugs. And I just steal because I need something for my kids. (Gloria, ESP).[5]

Las Locas

Las Locas members were strongly tied to a network of cocaine traffickers on both sides of the United States-Mexican border. This trading relationship was based on an historical connection that cocaine importers had developed in the barrio dating back to the early 1970s.[6]

Many LL males exploited their domestic Mexican connections, especially those members who came from the state of Jalisco and who had connections in the major drug-trafficking city of Guadalajara. Eventually, a significant proportion of the females were also attracted to the relatively "easy money" (Miller 1958).

(I): Are there many home girls involved in selling drugs?

(R): Basically all of them do it. You know, some of them use it and some of them just sell it because they need money. It is fast money. Who doesn't like making $200.00, $300.00 a day? I mean, that is what somebody makes in a week. Yeah, some of them have a real job. They make $200.00 or $300.00 a week but that is just to cover up like if they get caught with crack or anything like that. They can say, well look I work for it, here is my pay check. (La Muneca, Las Locas)

In time, certain females in the gang developed a reputation for themselves as proficient street entrepreneurs, and were looked upon by other gang members as people who can "take care of business." It was noticeable how self-confident and stridently independent many of the LL gang females appeared in the interviews. The respondent below, a 4-year veteran, is a good example.

I sell drugs, I sell chiva, coca and marijuana. I been selling since I was 13 and now I can make $200 a day. That's what people make in a week. I don't do any, you know, I don't get into that side of it. I just get into it for the money. You know what it's like, you have to do what you do to survive. It's always the same for Latins and Blacks, we're always at the bottom trying to survive, I know that. But I'd like to get a normal job if I could. I'd like to get out of this business especially now I'm pregnant and have a kid on the way, cos' anything can happen out there. If I get shot then it's not just me is it? (Loony, Las Locas)

Autonomy

In female gang studies the struggle for autonomy and independence (Campbell 1991; Quicker 1983) was found to be a powerful theme of female participation in the gang subculture. Nonetheless, the class, race, and gendered position of the subjects always placed severe limitations on their ability to achieve their aspirations and goals.

For Miller (1958), the quest for independence among lower-class youths was also riddled with contradictions. On the one hand, they outwardly bristled with "resentment of the idea of external controls, restrictions on behavior, and unjust or coercive authority," but covertly they valued restrictions and superordinate authority as a form of being "cared for." In the cases of the females in this study, the contradictions between their overt and covert thinking and behavior make little sense outside of considering their gendered positions in society as a whole.

Although African-American and Latino lower-class women have traditionally been socially and economically subordinate to males from their respective communities as well as from the dominant society, they have still held powerful roles within the family. One such role, for example, as developers of strong extended kinship and familial support networks to combat structured conditions of poverty and marginalization (Stack 1974; Baca Zinn 1989) is particularly important in considering the issue of autonomy among gang females.

An important finding of this study is that the female members of the three gangs all achieved different levels of autonomy from the males. As stated earlier, PHP were the only independent female gang, while the other two groups of females were both affiliated to a male-dominated gang organization. The importance of this fact is that PHP members were the least likely to be dominated by males in or out of the gang. As a result, they were rarely ambivalent about the relative importance of males to their lives:

(I): How important is the girl group to you?

(R): It is important.

(I): Which one do you consider more important [boys or girls]?

(R): The group [girls].

(I): Why?

(R): Because you can always get a man. But the group is like a family.

In contrast, although some level of autonomy from males for both LL and ESP females was present, it was sharply correlated to the characteristics of their economic activities. Thus, LL females were able to achieve more social distance from their male counterparts and seemed to have more control over individual and group decision-making than ESP females due both to their entrepreneurial success and to the self-organization they had learned in the selling of powdered and crack cocaine.

Nonetheless, it was only PHP as a group that had complete control over their social and economic lives as far as drug selling was concerned, while LL females had a relatively high degree of independence with respect to their drug sales as individuals. In contrast, ESP females, who only had boosting to provide them with extra income were able to achieve less autonomy both as a group and as individuals than the others.

One indication of this heightened level of subordination was reflected in the acts of victimization suffered by ESP female members at the hands of male members. While it can be easily argued that respondents were unlikely to be very candid about this discussion, the data suggest that incidents of victimization among LL's females (consisting of rape and other forms of physical abuse) came more frequently from parents than from gang males. In contrast, ESP's females reported many more actual or potential rape situations at the hands of gang males. In contrast, PHP members failed to report one single victimization that they had suffered during the time in which they had been members of the gang.

(R): None of the Home Girls have ever been jumped by men. But because of what happened in the barrio [a female gang member was accused of betraying the gang], she got raped at the park on X and Y street. She got raped there by them. So that was very traumatizing for her. She went through a lot of head trips and she became this real heavy drug user for awhile. (ESP member)

Finally, a further indication of the lessened autonomy among ESP's female members was revealed in their contrasting responses to the question, "What do you think of players?" (i.e., gang males who have multiple sex partners). Among ESP's female members it was more likely that they would accept this behavior of gang males, albeit grudgingly, whereas LL members were almost universally opposed to such behavior, even though they admitted that it happened. In fact, a number of LL's female members spoke of beating their male partners when they heard about their philanderings. ESP females were more likely to state that since they also "played around" then they could not really expect their male partners not to do the same.

Conclusion

Gang Females Are Not Separate From Society

All the groups' members, alongside their gang roles have "mainstream" roles and identities as daughters, workers, students, and parents. As such, they learn to live and articulate much of their existence through a kind of dual consciousness. Part of this consciousness embraces the rituals, customs, obligations, and practices that come with gang membership and part of it draws on the norms and values of the dominant society. Thus, the gang, while exhibiting a number of "focal concerns" and while constituting a "focal group," as similarly observed in the early work of Miller (1958), is not as some have suggested a "total institution" (Harris 1988).

As such, gang females should not be viewed as purely deviant phenomena cordoned off from the normative daily workings of the political economy and the community, and it is to the specific nature of the social context that we should look to understand gang females' evolution and development. Since this context is constituted by and within families, schools, communities, and the manifold cultural practices of "the street," it should not surprise us that the gang female reflects all the contradictions of these different social spheres.

As stated, all the females were in need of extra finances for themselves, their children, and their parents—with only one reporting a full-time job from which she was laid off. This paper argues that the subjects react to their marginalization from the legitimate and illegitimate labor markets by developing different aspects of their gang "smartness," eventually forming their own individual and group economic operations. The type and character of their economic activities depends both on the particular "tradition" of their gang and on the position their gang holds within the racial/ethnic hierarchical composition of the illegal economy. The degree to which the gang females developed a viable economic self-organization, in turn, influenced the different levels of "autonomy" they were able to achieve.

In time, the PHP group of females became economically self-sufficient, with their operations achieving more rationality as members started to sell up to an ounce of crack on a daily basis. ESP females, by contrast, never really established a group "tradition" of boosting and it was largely carried out in an ad hoc fashion by several individual "big timers." This form of "smartness" was much more risky than the drug sales and eventually the members spent several years in county jail. Meanwhile, LL females engaged in the crack cocaine trade but as individual salespersons rather than as a centrally organized gang endeavor. For them, the gang's connection to a supply market was not a major reason for being a member but it was decidedly a perk of membership.[7]

These findings suggest that what gang females reflect is the peculiar intersection of class, race, and gender among the inner-city poor. While they are all purposive social actors, refusing to settle for their lot in any passively fatalistic manner, the consequences of their actions might be self-destructive, life-threatening, and potentially negative for themselves and the community. Nonetheless, like millions of poor women before them, they are resourceful and resilient as they actively seek alternative meanings and opportunities within the structured void created by the currently ordered society.

Endnotes

1. The consideration of gender and race was never seriously paid attention to by researchers of the fifties and sixties. One result is that street gangs have tended to be seen as homogenous collections of lower-class youth that together constitute an adolescent "hard core." As such, they became, and continue to become in different renditions, either constellations of aberrant social behaviors or social caricatures.

2. This is a form of gauntlet, or "going one on one" (or two or three), i.e., the incoming member has to fight other member(s) up to a minute. Often, the fight is supposed to last for a certain number of seconds, usually the same number that is part of the gang's name if the name is a numbered form.

3. This entrepreneurial reasoning was unlike the concern for "toughness" exhibited by members of either of the two Latina groups. This was because "toughness" for the Latina gangs is connected to the defense of a symbolic order rather than an entrepreneurial zone. "Turf" for the Latinas is connected to self-identity, i.e., "mi barrio," and its defense is much more personal and symbolic of gang membership itself. In short, the Latina gang females rarely, if ever, would allow any other group, especially of the same race or ethnicity, to come into its territory for any reason.

> We were kicking back on X street and then she comes. I come up to hella girls. I say, "What you girls claming?" Nobody said nothing. I said, "Fuck X, it is all about Las Locas." And then I came back to the same girl that I came at first and I said, "What you claim?" She said nothing. And then I went around and saying to the different girls and then I came back to her and I said, "Well fuck X, it is all about Las Locas." (Brenda, Las Locas)

4. Few of the respondents reported arrests for their drug or boosting activities, which, since they had been involved in the practice for at least 3 years, suggests that they were both cautious and proficient in their assignments.

5. It is important to note that ESP females were the ones who did the boosting, the males hardly ever became involved in this activity.

6. The males of LL had controlled much of the cocaine dealing in the area for some years and were starting to encroach on a turf that bordered other neighborhoods, leading to frequent turf disputes.

7. It is worth noting that of all the Latino gang subcultures in the area, LL's members were seen as better off, if a little more ostentatious than other rivals, which perhaps explains LL's consistent popularity for the area's young Latinas.

Discussion Questions

1. Is there a link between "doing gender" and crime? Do you think women choose to be gang members in order to be feminine or masculine?

2. Describe the gender stratification of the women who occupy various roles in the PHP (the all-female group) compared with the women in the mixed-gender gangs.

3. Which of the three gangs seem to have the most organized gang structure and why?

4. What theoretical explanations might there be for a young female gang member's increased probability of crime victimization as well as her propensity to commit crime?

5. Why do young girls join gangs?

6. How do gang activities depend on racial/ethnic group position in the illegal economy and in the larger society?

References

Anderson, Elijah. 1990. *Streetwise: Race, class and change in an urban community.* Chicago: University of Chicago Press.

Baca Zinn, Maxine. 1989. Family, race and poverty in the eighties. *Signs: Journal of Women in Culture and Society* 14 (4): 856–874.

Becker, Howard. 1963. *Outsiders: Studies in the sociology of deviance.* New York: The Free Press.

Biernacki, Pat, and D. Waldorf. 1981. Snowball sampling: Problems and techniques of chain referral sampling. *Sociological Methods and Research* 10 (2): 141–163.

Bonacich, Edna, and J. Modell. 1981. *The economic basis of ethnic solidarity.* Berkeley: University of California Press.

Brown, Claude. 1965. *Manchild in the promised land.* New York: Signet Books.

Buroway, Michael. 1991. *The extended case study method in ethnography unbound.* Berkeley: University of California Press.

Campbell, Anne. 1991. *Girls in the gang.* 2d ed. London: Blackwell.

Chesney-Lind, Meda. 1989. Toward a feminist model of female delinquency. *Crime and Delinquency* 35 (1): 5–29.

Cohen, Albert. 1955. *Delinquent boys: The culture of the gang.* Glencoe: The Free Press.

Crichter, Chas. 1976. Structures, cultures and biographies. In *Rituals and resistance*, eds. S. Hall, C. Critcher, T. Jefferson, J. Clarke, B. Roberts. London: Hutchison and Co.

Denzin, Norman K. 1989. *Interpretive interactionism.* Newbury Park, Calif.: Sage Publications.

Douglas, Mary. 1982. *In the active voice.* London: Routledge and Kegan Paul.

Durkheim, Emile. 1933. *The division of labor in society.* New York: The Free Press.

Fagan, Jeffrey. 1992. Set and setting revisited: Influences of alcohol and illicit drugs on the social context of violent events. Paper presented at the Working Group on Alcohol-Related Violence, National Institute on Alcohol Abuse and Alcoholism, Washington, D.C.

Fine, Michelle. 1994. Working the hyphens: Reinventing self and other in qualitative research. In *Handbook of qualititative research*, eds. N. K. Denzin and Y. S. Lincoln. New York: Sage Publications.

Fontana, Andrew, and J. Frey. 1994. Interviewing the art of science. In *Handbook of qualtitative research*, eds. N. K. Denzin and Y. S. Lincoln. New York: Sage Publications.

Goldstein, Paul, H. H. Brownstein, and P.A. Bellucci. 1989. Crime and homicide in New York City, 1988: A conceptually based event analysis. *Contemporary Drug Problems* 16: 651–687.

Haraway, Donna. 1991. *Simians, cyborgs and women: The reinvention of nature.* New York: Routledge.

Harris, Mary. 1988. *Cholas: Latino girls and gangs.* New York: AMS Press.

Lauderbeck, David, J. Hansen, and D. Waldorf. 1992. Sisters are doin' it for themselves': A black female gang in San Francisco. *The Gang Journal* (1): 57–70.

Liazos, Alexander. 1972. The sociology of deviances: Nuts, sluts and perverts. *Social Problems*, vol. 20, Summer: 103–120.

Matza, David. 1969. *Becoming deviant.* Englewood Cliffs, NJ: Prentice-Hall.

Miller, Walter. 1957. Cultural features of an urban lower-class community. Report to the U.S. Public Health Service. Washington, D.C.

———. 1958. Lower-class culture as a generating milieu of gang delinquency. *Journal of Social Issues* XIV, No. 3.

Quicker, John. 1983. *Homegirls: Characterizing Chicana gangs.* San Pedro, Calif.: International Universities Press.

Sampson, R. J. 1987. Urban black violence: The effect of male joblessness and family disruption. *American Journal of Sociology* 93 (2): 348–382.

Smith, Dorothy. 1987. *The everyday world as problematic.* Boston: Northeastern University Press.

Stack, Carol. 1974. *All our kin.* New York: Harper and Row.

Sullivan, Mercer. 1989. *Getting paid: Youth crime and work in the inner city.* Ithaca, New York: Cornell University Press.

Suttles, Gerald. 1968. *The social order of the slum: Ethnicity and territory in the inner city.* Chicago: University of Chicago Press.

Taylor, Carl. 1989. *Dangerous society.* East Lansing, Mich.: Michigan State University.

Thompson, Edward. 1963. *The making of the English working class.* New York: Random House.

Waldorf, Dan. 1993. Final Report of the Crack Sales, Gangs and Violence Study. Alameda, Calif.: Institute for Scientific Analysis.

Wilson, William J. 1987. *The truly disadvantaged.* Chicago: University of Chicago Press.

Excerpted from: David C. Brotherton, "Smartness, Toughness, and Autonomy: Drug Use in the Context of Gang Female Delinquency." In *Journal of Drug Issues* 26 (1): 261–278. Copyright © 1996 by Journal of Drug Issues, Inc. Used with permission. ✦

12
Young Women and Gang Violence

Gender, Street Offending, and Violent Victimization in Gangs

Scott H. Decker
Jody Miller

This chapter examines how gendered situational dynamics shape gang violence, including participation in violent offending and experiences of violent victimization. Data from this study were taken from two sources: in-depth interviews with 27 female gang members in St. Louis, and reports from the Homicide Division of the St. Louis Metropolitan Police Department as part of the St. Louis Homicide Project. The interviews were drawn from a larger comparative study that included both gang and nongang girls in two cities. Respondents ranged in age from 12 to 20, with a mean age of 15.6. Young women were recruited for the study with the cooperation of several organizations working with at-risk youths, including a street outreach program, agencies providing drop-in programs, a local public high school serving youths suspended or expelled from other settings, and the local detention center. Interviews were voluntary and confidential, and youths were paid a nominal sum for their participation. To extend the analyses, the authors used data from the St. Louis Homicide Project. Here they examined case records of homicides in the city from 1990 to 1996. Combining an analysis of in-depth interviews with young women in St. Louis gangs and an examination of homicide reports from the same city, they found that young women, even regular offenders, highlight the significance of gender in shaping and limiting their involvement in serious violence. They use gender both to accomplish their criminal activities and to temper their involvement in gang crime. Consequently, their risk for serious physical victimization in gangs is considerably less than young men's. St. Louis homicide data corroborate these qualitative findings. Not only are young women much less likely to be the victims of gang homicide, but the vast majority of female gang homicide victims are not the intended targets of the attack. In contrast, ho-micide reports suggest that the majority of male gang homicide victims are the intended targets. The authors suggest that gendered group processes and stratification within gangs are key factors explaining both violent offending and victimization risk in gangs.

Much contemporary gang research has been spurred by recognition that a strong relationship exists between gang membership and participation in crime and delinquency. Gang members account for a disproportionate amount of crime, particularly serious and violent acts, and gang membership itself increases both the frequency and the severity of offending (Battin et al. 1998; Esbensen and Huizinga 1993; Thornberry 1998; Thornberry et al. 1993). More recently, researchers also have focused on the victimization risks associated with gang involvement. Gang youths are more likely to participate in violence; in addition, there is growing evidence they are at high risk for violent victimization (Decker 1999; Huff 1996, 1998; Miller and Brunson 2000). Given that the primary targets of gang violence—particularly gang homicides—are other gang members, this is a particularly important line of inquiry (Block and Block 1993; Decker and Van Winkle 1996; Maxson and Klein 1996; Rosenfeld, Bray, and Egley 1999).

These findings, based primarily on studies of male gang involvement, raise additional questions about young women in gangs. Evidence suggests that female gang members' crime patterns are complex. Like their male counterparts, gang girls are disproportionately involved in delinquency. Young men in gangs, however, still are involved more extensively in the most serious forms of gang crime (Bjerregaard and Smith 1993; Esbensen and Winfree 1998; Fagan 1990; Miller and Brunson 2000). Several recent studies have examined gender-specific victimization risks for young women in gangs (Fleisher 1998; Miller 1998a), but less attention has been given to victimization associated with gang-related offending, or to victimization resulting from gang-motivated offenses. In particular, little attempt has been made to examine gang homicides involving females, both as victims and as offenders.

To investigate these issues, we draw from several sets of data in St. Louis, Missouri, including survey and in-depth interviews with female gang members, and quantitative and narrative data from the St. Louis Homicide Project (Rosenfeld, Decker, and Kohfeld 1990). We are concerned with the gendered situational dynamics shaping gang violence—what Hagan and McCarthy (1997: 81; also see Short 1998) call "foreground causal factors" of crime. We address the following questions: What situational factors help account for gender differences in gang youths' patterns of offending, particularly serious offending? Given the well-documented relationship between offending and victimization risk (Lauritsen, Sampson, and Laub 1991), how does gender shape the relationship between gang membership, participation in gang-related offending, and victimization risk? Finally, what of homicide, the most serious and perhaps quintessential gang crime? Given the distinct character of (male) gang homicides (Block and Block 1993; Maxson and Klein 1996; Rosenfeld et al. 1999), how do gang homicides involving females fit into these patterns of violence?

Gangs, Gender, and Street Offending

In view of what the literature suggests, we are not surprised that the gang girls interviewed reported considerable involvement in delinquency. The majority of gang girls interviewed in St. Louis have engaged in an array of violent acts; for instance, 85 percent have hit someone with the idea of hurting them, and fully 74 percent have attacked someone with a weapon or with the intention of hurting them seriously. In addition, most of these young women have sold marijuana or crack cocaine. Moreover, except for robbery and other drug sales, a sizeable majority of gang girls committed all these offenses within six months preceding their interviews.

Gang-Motivated Violence

These findings are clarified by an examination of the context of gang crime. Scholars who discuss gangs' facilitation of delinquency emphasize the strength of gang members' associations with peers who are also involved in delinquency, as well as gang norms and group processes that encourage youths to engage in these activities (Battin et al. 1998; Short and Strodtbeck 1965; Thornberry et al. 1993). In fact, Klein and Crawford (1967) suggest that delinquency is more than an outcome of gang membership; instead it provides group cohesion for its members. Challenging and fighting with rival gangs is an important element of gang life. Youths often stake out the identity of their gang at the level of these antagonisms: the presence of common enemies facilitates members' perceptions of themselves as a unified group (see Decker and Van Winkle 1996; Klein and Crawford 1967). In St. Louis in particular,

strongly territorial gangs are based on long-standing neighborhood boundaries. Thus gang youths' group identity is intensified by claiming and protecting neighborhood turf; these activities often result in violence (Decker and Van Winkle 1996; Miller 2001).

In view of the ample evidence supporting these arguments, what accounts for young women's reports of limited involvement in serious violent confrontations, including gang fights? As noted above, one explanation may be reflected in the recent decline in gang-motivated homicides in St. Louis, reported by Rosenfeld and his colleagues (1999). If homicide trends represent gang conflicts in general, St. Louis witnessed shifts in the kinds of gang conflict occurring in the mid- to late 1990s. In fact, these scholars suggest that the continuing increase in gang member homicides may be linked to gang members' participation in drug markets (Rosenfeld et al. 1999). Young women's relatively high rates of self-reported drug sales add credence to these scholars' suggestion about possible shifts in the nature of gang activities. These rates in themselves, however, cannot explain young women's limited involvement in serious violence, particularly in light of the high risks generally associated with drug sales.

Young women's accounts of gang-related conflict help to explain this seeming contradiction. Although girls are involved in altercations with rival gangs, they rarely escalate to violence, and even more rarely to serious violence involving weapons. Opposition to rival gangs is a central theme in gang youths' cultural imagery and symbolism. Often confrontations with rivals are a consequence of these displays, particularly in conjunction with the defense of neighborhood boundaries. For instance, Crystal explained, "If a Blood come on our set and we Crips, as long as they come on our set saying, 'What's up Blood,' they . . . just gonna start a fight. 'Cause they diss [disrespect] us by coming on our set and saying 'What's up Blood.' There ain't nobody no Blood over there." Vashelle agreed: "A dude come over [to our neighborhood from a rival gang], he know what kind of 'hood it is to begin with. Any dude that come over there from a gang and know that's a Blood 'hood, you try to come over there Cripped out [wearing Crips colors or symbols], you know you gonna eventually have it some way."

The great majority of the girls' confrontations involved fists; occasionally they involved knives, but not guns. Most young women, however, said that when they encountered rivals, as long as they weren't met with a direct challenge, they were willing to tolerate their presence rather than escalate into a fight. Pam explained:

> We going to the show or skating, to the mall. We be seeing some of our enemies too when we do those things, clubs and stuff, we be seeing a lot of our enemies. [If] they don't say nothing to us, we don't say nothing to them. They say something to us, we say something to them. So that way everybody just go they own little way if they don't want nothing to happen.

Many young women echoed Pam's account. Although violence and confrontations with rivals were normative features of their gangs, on which gang girls placed value, young women typically did not choose to engage in these activities themselves. Instead they were often content to leave them to young men. The normative quality of these activities is reflected in the girls' discussions of status hierarchies in their groups, and in their descriptions of individuals they admired in their gangs. These included persons who "did dirt" for the gang by committing gang-motivated assaults and by confronting rivals. Status was gained in part from proving oneself in these ways. The young women's admiration of such gang members indicates their acceptance of these gang norms.

Nonetheless, most girls viewed males as the group members most likely to carry through these activities at their extreme. As Tonya exclaimed, "We ain't no supercommando girls!" Young women held males and females to different standards based on their perceptions of what "femaleness" or "maleness" brought to their interactions and behaviors. They used this difference as a basis for limiting their participation in serious gang violence, particularly gun violence. As Crystal noted, "Girls don't be up there shooting unless they really have to." Pam stated that girls don't use guns because "We ladies, we not dudes for real . . . we don't got to be rowdy, all we do is fight."

As Pam's comments suggest, gang girls did not avoid nor participate in certain crimes simply as a means of enacting femininity. They also used gender norms to modify their involvement in serious and dangerous gang violence. Moreover, they played on beliefs about gender in other circumstances, using their presence to divert suspicion from their gang's actions. Tonya described this function:

> Like when we in a car, if a girl and a dude in a car, the police tend not to trip off of it. When they look to see if a car been stolen, police just don't trip off of it. But if they see three or four niggers in that car, the police stop you automatically, boom. . . . [Girls have] little ways that we got to get them out of stuff sometimes. We can get them out of stuff that dudes couldn't do.

Thus young women often drew on gender—and on gender stereotypes—both to negotiate and to limit their involvement in gang violence, and to facilitate the success of gang members' crimes.

Drug Sales

As stated earlier, just under two-thirds of the young women interviewed in St. Louis had sold crack and marijuana, and seven of these young women (26 percent) sold drugs regularly. Success in the drug trade also was described routinely as a quality that young women admired in gang members. Brittany, in describing a fellow member she looked up to, commented, "She's a smart gang member. She don't go out fighting and starting stuff, she just chill out and make her money." In fact, young women who reported selling drugs routinely emphasized that it was a key element of their gang activities. Tonya said, "Mostly dudes was . . . selling guns and jacking cars and stuff like that. But everybody was selling drugs." Older girls in particular emphasized the economic benefits of the gang. Latisha explained, "We don't just be standing outside, 'What's up Blood' and all that, throwing up little signs or whatever. Cars come by, they know what we claim or whatever, but we all making our money."

These comments were themes in many interviews with older girls; again, they offer support for the suggestions of Rosenfeld et al. (1999) about shifts in gang homicides in St. Louis during the mid- and late 1990s, away from gang-motivated events. Yet in light of the violence often associated with street-level crack dealing, it is notable that young women were often able to avoid participation in such violence.

Several factors appear relevant. Though young women viewed drug sales as a viable means of making money, most described their involvement as sporadic rather than an everyday activity; in this way they indicated some difference between their activities and those of young men. Shandra said, "The times when I sold, I only did it for a short while. I only did it to make a little money to do something big. I ain't never really made it a career." Similarly, Pam explained:

> Some girls just sell some drugs and then they'll quit. They just sell it just to get them some money 'cause they need some. Whatever they need, they'll make they money and then probably won't sell drugs no more until

they need something else. And then they'll go buy them some drugs and sell it, and that's it. The dudes, they keep on, keep on, keep on. They like to sell it and stash they money, cards and all that.

Moreover, young women typically described their suppliers as older members of the gang. Probably as a consequence of both these factors, young women were not viewed as serious competition for male drug sellers; thus they faced less risk of involvement in violent altercations in the drug marketplace.

Nonetheless, young women sometimes reported that potential predators saw female drug sellers as particularly easy marks for robbery. They described two methods of dealing with such problems. First, some young women sold with young men, and relied on these male peers to protect them. Mia said that the young men in her gang assisted in her drug sales by watching her back to "make sure don't nobody do nothing to take nothing from me when I'm on the streets." Similarly, Pam said that girls sometimes would "have somebody standing by, one of your boys or something." When young women were not involved in ongoing drug sales, young men appeared willing to assist them on those occasions when they sold.

Second, young women involved more routinely in drug sales sometimes employed more discreet methods of selling, which not only decreased their risk of violent altercations but also drew less police attention. Vashelle explained, "the police, they don't be on the girls for real, . . . but if they see a whole crowd of niggers sitting out, they gonna get down on them. But I'm saying if there are niggers out there and I'm with them too, they gonna shake me too. If I'm walking up the street by myself they ain't gonna trip off me 'cause I'm a gal." She said she avoided such scrutiny by not "sit[ting] out with a crowd. I sit out by myself . . . on the back porch." Vashelle sold drugs so as to avoid calling attention to herself, and also used beliefs about gender to conceal her activities and to avoid being caught. This approach probably reduces exposure to violence as well (also see Jacobs and Miller 1998).

Gang-Related Risk

As documented above, gang girls interviewed in St. Louis moderated their involvement in serious gang violence. When involved in drug sales, they used methods to avoid exposure to violence related to drug markets. As a corollary question, how did gender shape their exposure to gang-related victimization risk? As noted earlier, strong evidence suggests that "adolescent involvement in delinquent lifestyles strongly increases the risk of both personal and property victimization" (Lauritsen et al. 1991: 265). In fact, Lauritsen and her colleagues found that gender, as a predictor of victimization risk, becomes less significant with controls for participation in delinquent lifestyles. That is, much of young men's greater victimization risk can be explained by their greater involvement in offending behaviors.

To be sure, young women in gangs witnessed a great deal of violence, and some were victims of serious violence themselves. A sizable majority of gang girls had witnessed serious violence, including shootings and homicides. In addition, nearly half had been the victims of serious violent assaults; 41 percent had been stabbed. Only one girl had been shot; this was an accidental shooting that occurred when she was a child. As evidence of the violence endemic in these young women's neighborhoods (the site of most of the violence they reported), about half of the girls who reported having seen an attack, guns shot, shootings, and drive-bys had first witnessed these events before their gang involvement.

On the other hand, nearly all of the girls who had been threatened with a weapon or stabbed reported that this first occurred after they became involved in a gang, and 75 percent had first witnessed a homicide after joining their gangs. Not surprisingly, of the 11 girls who reported having been stabbed, eight were among the 10 girls most involved in serious offending (see above); Rhonda and Debra had been stabbed in multiple incidents. Half of the girls threatened with a weapon were among these ten, including Rhonda and Toni; both reported having been threatened multiple times. These young women were living in volatile neighborhoods, as witnessed by the amount of violence they witnessed as children. Nonetheless, gang involvement itself appeared to increase their exposure to violence, specifically witnessing lethal violence and being victims of weapons threats and knife assaults. This was further exacerbated for girls involved in offending.

Because intergang rivalries and delinquency are important elements of gang activities, some risk of victimization is an expected part of gang life. Young women recognized that they might be the targets of rival gang members and were expected to "be down" for their gang at those times, even when physical harm was involved. On the other hand, many young women not only spoke of the empowerment they gained from gang involvement, but also described how the gang could offer protection, backup, and re-taliation for its members, both in their day-to-day lives and when they were involved in gang-related activities or drug sales. As Tonya explained, "Shoot, you ever need to fool with anybody, you can call your homies up and they'll just be there." Moreover, as stated earlier, young women could use gender within gangs to shield and control their exposure to gang vio-lence, at least to a certain extent. Because status hierarchies in most of their gangs were male-dominated, the young women actually seemed to enjoy greater flexibility in their gang activities than the young men (also see Miller 2001; Miller and Brunson 2000). Fewer expec-tations were placed on them with regard to in-volvement in criminal activities such as gun use, drug sales, and other serious crimes; this situation apparently limited their exposure to risk of gang-related victimization.

In addition, girls reported that young men's perceptions of females as peripheral members of gangs typically functioned to keep girls from being targets of serious physical violence at the hands of rival young men, who were concerned mainly with rival gang males. As Sheila re-marked, "The dudes think they run it all." Conse-quently, in describing male-on-female gang con-frontations, Pam explained, "Some dudes, they be tripping with you 'cause they know you from the other side and they be trying to slap you or something. . . . You don't want to say nothing to no dudes 'cause you know you can't beat them or nothing. So you be like, 'yeah, wait 'til my boys come, they gonna get you.'" Shawanda re-marked, "A nigger and another nigger, it ain't gonna be no talk thing, you know what I'm say-ing, it's just some static [a confrontation] or something. But a nigger and a girl, no."

Moreover, girls' routine confrontations with rivals were typically female-on-female rather than female-on-male. [Because] young women were not likely to resort to serious violence (par-ticularly gun violence), their risk of serious vic-timization was reduced even further. As Vashelle explained, "Most girls, they ain't gonna do noth-ing for real but try to stab you, cut you, or some-thing like that. As far as coming shooting and stuff like a dude would do, no." Being stabbed, although serious, is much less likely to be lethal than being shot.

The young women agreed despite their decla-rations of the protections offered by the gang or their attempts to avoid risky behaviors, that be-longing to a gang endangered their well-being. Because of the gendered nature of gang activities, girls generally did not believe that they faced the same threats as young men. Even so, they recog-nized that being with other gang members increased their chances of being present when vi-olence broke out. For instance, Crystal said that when "you got one gang member that got a prob-lem with another person, they'll shoot at the whole set or whatever. . . . A whole bunch of them will start shooting at people that got nothing to do with it." As her comment suggests, young women did not fear being the specific target of rival gang members who were shooting. Instead they were concerned about being shot while in a group where someone opened fire. Because young women believed that gunfire was the purview of male-on-male violence, they didn't feel that be-longing to the gang was life threatening as it was for young men, who were more likely to be tar-gets of a rival gang. As a consequence, when young women talked about gang homicides and shootings, they spoke mostly about the worry and sorrow of seeing young men they cared about killed in gang violence.

Gender and Gang Homicide

The homicide reports offer further support for these young women's accounts. Of the 229 gang homicides that occurred in St. Louis be-tween 1990 and 1996, 19 (8 percent) involved female victims. Moreover, despite speculation that women's participation in street violence is increasing, and in keeping with young women's reports in interviews, only one of the gang ho-micides (less than 1 percent) committed during this period involved a female perpetrator. Nota-bly, this woman did not act alone, and was not herself a gang member. The homicide was clas-sified as gang-related because the young man she shot was a gang member. In the remaining analysis we focus on victims of gang homicide: 210 males and 19 females. The relatively small number of female homicides makes us cau-tious about generalizing the results of our anal-ysis, but it is consistent with the reports by fe-male gang members interviewed in St. Louis.

In many ways, gang homicides involving fe-male victims were similar to those involving male victims in regard to participant and event characteristics. Because of the primarily Afri-can-American composition of St. Louis gangs, and their location in extremely racially segre-gated communities, it is not surprising that the great majority of gang homicide victims were African-American. Victims of both sexes also were young on average and were killed primar-ily by gunfire at the hands of young black men. Each of these findings is consistent with the broader literature (see Maxson and Klein 1990, 1996). Women were slightly more likely to be killed indoors rather than out (21 percent versus 14 percent for males), though this is probably an artifact of the low base rate of female victims.

Nearly all victims of gang homicide, both male and female, were killed by strangers or acquaintances rather than by their primary relations. Men, however, were much more likely to be killed by acquaintances, while women were more likely to be killed by strangers. Moreover, for the majority of male gang homicide victims (57 percent) only one suspect was identified, but the reverse was true for female victims: 74 percent involved the identification of multiple suspects. As we turn to the narrative analysis of police incident reports, these differences become more meaningful as features that seem to distinguish female gang homicides from their male counterparts. In comparison with female gang homicides, women killed in nongang events were older on average (with a mean age of 34), were less likely to be African-American (74 percent), and were killed by older suspects who were also less likely to be African-American and who were more likely to have committed the homicide alone (81 percent). Women killed in nongang homicides were significantly more likely to be killed by someone in a primary relationship (35 percent versus none of the female gang homicides), and much less likely to be killed by strangers (15 percent versus 46 percent). In addition, they were significantly less likely to be killed by a firearm (54 percent versus all of the female gang homicides) and were much more likely to be killed in a dwelling (59 percent versus 21 percent) rather than on the streets. These differences, coupled with the similarities in gang homicides involving male and female victims, suggest that gang homicides involving women follow the distinctive pattern of gang homicides in general.

The most striking finding from police narratives is that the great majority of women killed in gang homicides were not the intended targets. Fourteen of the 19 homicides (74 percent) were drive-by or walk-by shootings in which the suspect or suspects opened fire into a group of people. In 13 of these cases, the victim was not the intended target in the group; the fourteenth case was ambiguous, though the young woman was clearly not the only target. In fact, in 10 of these 14 cases at least one additional individual was injured, including one homicide victim. In several cases, the intended target was identified among the injured; in others, no specific target was identified or the intended target escaped injury. The following examples were typical:

Case 1: The victim was a 14-year-old African-American girl, who was on the front porch of a multifamily residence when she was shot in the chest. She was with five other youths age 15 to 19 when the shooting occurred: her boyfriend, two cousins, and two friends. At this time five suspects drove up, got out of the car, fired on the group, and then fled. According to the police report, the shooting was part of an ongoing feud between two rival gangs, and the groups had engaged in numerous shootings throughout the previous few days. Other shootings had taken place over the previous few months. The victim was not the intended target.

Case 2: The victim was a 30-year-old African-American female, shot in the front yard of the multifamily residence where she lived. Her son reportedly was a gang member. At the time of the shooting, the victim was standing in the yard talking to two acquaintances: a 29-year-old male who was shot in the chest and buttocks, and a 17-year-old male who was uninjured. Four suspects fired approximately 10 shots. The report notes that the victim was not the intended target; it was unclear whether the 17-year-old witness was the target, the victim's son, or someone else. The victim's son and his friends retaliated several times over the next day, injuring one of the suspects.

Case 3: The victim was an 18-year-old African-American female, shot in the backyard of a single-family residence where she was attending a party. The victim's cousin was a 25-year-old gang member and the apparent target. The police report states that the victim's shooting was a "mistake." According to the report, "The victim's cousin and his gang had been feuding with the suspect's gang for a year. There had been shootings. The victim's cousin had recently been released from jail after shooting someone in the suspect's gang. At the time in question there had been a party. The victim had been standing near her cousin when the suspect opened fire."

In contrast to these patterns reported for female gang homicides, male gang homicide victims were the intended target in 68 percent of the incidents. The circumstances varied: they included confrontations (gang-motivated and otherwise) that escalated into gun violence, retaliatory shootings targeting the individual killed, and (less often) robberies and drug disputes. An additional 23 percent of the male gang homicides occurred when the suspect or suspects fired into a group. In these cases, the victim was not singled out as a specific target but was one of a group of targets, typically identified by the suspects as rival gang members. Finally, 9 percent of the male gang homicides resulted in the killing of an individual who was not the intended target. All told, then, male victims were the intended targets in over two-thirds of the gang homicides in which they were victims. In contrast, at most, women were the intended targets in five gang homicides (26 percent), and four of these occurred during robberies. In the modal and by far predominant pattern for female gang homicides, the victim was killed when suspects opened fire into a group.

Two features distinguish female gang homicides from their male counterparts. Women are more likely to be killed by strangers, men by acquaintances; and gang homicides involving female victims are more likely to involve multiple suspects. Evidence from homicide narratives offers an explanation for these differences. Women are likely to be killed in gang homicide events because they are in the wrong place at the wrong time, and with the wrong people, rather than because they are the specific targets of gang retaliation or other violent confrontations. Women probably are more likely to be killed by multiple strangers because of a large proportion of female homicide victims who were not the intended targets when rival gang members opened fire into groups. The converse—that males are more likely to be killed by single perpetrators who are known to them—appears to result from the greater likelihood that they are the intended targets of rival gang violence.

Discussion

We opened this chapter by asking how gendered situational dynamics shape gang violence, including violent offending and violent victimization. By combining interviews with young women in St. Louis gangs with homicide reports from the same city, we could examine these questions in depth. Much of the previous work on female gang violence either focused on young men's perspectives, highlighting their structural exclusion of young women, or explained young women's limited participation in violence in terms of gender differences in normative beliefs. Although both approaches contain some truth, neither can account fully for the complex role of gender in shaping the foreground of gang violence.

In our approach we highlight the significance of group processes in gangs, observing how gender shapes participation in risky activities as well as perceptions and experiences of threat. Moreover, by drawing on interviews with female gang members, we can address their participation in negotiating their roles and activities within these groups. Our research shows that young women in gangs in fact involve themselves in some gang-related violence as well as activities such as drug sales, which are linked to violence on the streets. Fully 74 percent of our sample had attacked someone with a weapon or with the intention of injuring them seriously, and 63 percent reported having sold crack cocaine. The majority of the young women, however, engaged regularly in neither violence nor drug sales; just over one-third of the sample committed by far most of the regular serious offenses.

Regardless of whether the young women were regular offenders, they highlighted the significance of gender in shaping and limiting their involvement in serious violence. In keeping with evidence of gender stratification in offender networks and the structural exclusion of females from gang crime, the young women observed that young men "think they run it all." In addition, they themselves held young women and young men to different standards of conduct based on their beliefs about gender. Most important, the young women used gender as a resource, both to accomplish gang crime and drug sales, and to temper their involvement in gang violence. Rather than simply using gang activities to enact normative femininity (Messerschmidt 1995), they used normative femininity to negotiate their activities in gangs. This reciprocity between gender and gang practices provides important insights into the situational dynamics that shape gang violence for young women.

Because young women choose not to be "supercommando girls" and because young men believe they "run it all," young women's risks of serious physical victimization within gangs—including shootings—are considerably less than young men's risks (also see Hagedorn 1998). According to the young women we interviewed, male gang members do not perceive females as viable targets of gang retaliation; thus the threat of serious physical danger posed by rival gangs is much greater for young men. This is not to suggest that young women in gangs are not exposed to considerable amounts of violence. Gender inequality in youth gangs, however, appears to protect young women in regard to the victimization risk associated with much gang violence.

Our investigation of homicides further corroborates the girls' accounts. Our evidence suggests that women not only are less likely to be homicide victims, but also, when these homicides occur, are very rarely the intended targets of lethal gang violence. Instead, young women's greatest risk of gang homicide is due to being in the wrong place at the wrong time. Thus the associational features of membership, more than the specific activities involved, place gang girls in harm's way. In contrast, young men are most often the intended targets of gang homicide.

Women's lower levels of involvement in gang homicide, as both victims and offenders, may reflect their lower rates of participation in gang life. Apparently, however, it is the nature of young women's gang involvement that is at issue. At the situational level, gendered group processes and stratification within gangs are key factors that help explain both violent offending and victimization risk in gangs.

Discussion Questions

1. How is participation in risky and delinquent activities shaped by gender?

2. Why do young women in this study hold males and females to different standards? How are women able to limit participation in gang violence?

3. Why are female gang members victimized less by gun violence than male members?

4. How does gender shape the relationship between gang membership and victimization risk?

5. How do the women gang members in this study compare with Brotherton's study of three gangs in Chapter 11?

References

Battin, S. R., K. G. Hill, R. D. Abbott, R. F. Catalano, and J. D. Hawkins. 1998. "The Contribution of Gang Membership to Delinquency Beyond Delinquent Friends." *Criminology* 36: 93–115.

Bjerregaard, B. and C. Smith. 1993. "Gender Differences in Gang Participation, Delinquency, and Substance Use." *Journal of Quantitative Criminology* 4: 329–55.

Block, C. R. and R. Block. 1993. "Street Gang Crime in Chicago." *Research in Brief*. Washington, DC: National Institute of Justice.

Bowker, L. H., H. S. Gross, and M. W. Klein. 1980. "Female Participation in Delinquent Gang Activities." *Adolescence* 15: 509–19.

Campbell, A. 1993. *Men, Women and Aggression*. New York: Basic Books.

Chesney-Lind, M. 1993. "Girls, Gangs and Violence: Anatomy of a Backlash." *Humanity and Society* 17: 321–44.

Curry, G. D. 1997. "Selected Statistics on Female Gang Involvement." Paper presented at the Fifth Joint National Conference on Gangs, Schools, and Communities, September, Orlando.

——. 1998. Personal correspondence, August 13.

Curry, G. D., R. A. Ball, and R. J. Fox. 1994. "Gang Crime and Law Enforcement Recordkeeping." *Research in Brief*. Washington, DC: National Institute of Justice.

Decker, S. H. 1993. "Exploring Victim Offender Relationships in Homicide: The Role of Individual and Event Characteristics." *Justice Quarterly* 10: 585–612.

——. 1996. "Collective and Normative Features of Gang Violence." *Justice Quarterly* 13: 243–64.

——. 1999. Short presentation on Future Directions of Gang Research. Gang Research Cluster Meeting, Office of Juvenile Justice and Delinquency Prevention and National Institute of Justice, October, Washington, D.C.

Decker, S. H. and K. Kempf. 1991. "Constructing Gangs: The Social Construction of Youth Activities." *Criminal Justice Policy Review* 5 (4): 271–91.

Decker, S. H., S. Pennell, and A. Caldwell. 1996. Arrestees and Guns: Monitoring the Illegal Firearms Market. Final Report submitted to the National Institute of Justice. Washington, D.C.

Decker, S. H. and B. Van Winkle. 1996. *Life in the Gang*. Cambridge: Cambridge University Press.

Deschenes, E. P. and F. Esbensen. 1999. "Violence Among Girls: Does Gang Membership Make a Difference?" Pp. 277–94 in *Female Gangs in America*, edited by M. Chesney-Lind and J. M. Hagedorn. Chicago, IL: Lake View Press.

Esbensen, F. and D. Huizinga. 1993. "Gangs, Drugs, and Delinquency in a Survey of Urban Youth." *Criminology* 31: 565–89.

Esbensen, F., D. Huizinga, and A. W. Weiher. 1993. "Gang and Non-Gang Youth: Differences in Explanatory Factors." *Journal of Contemporary Criminal Justice* 9: 94–116.

Esbensen, F. and L.T. Winfree, Jr. 1998. "Race and Gender Differences Between Gang and Non-Gang Youth: Results from a Multi-Site Survey." *Justice Quarterly* 15: 505–25.

Fagan, J. 1989. "The Social Organization of Drug Use and Drug Dealing Among Urban Gangs." *Criminology* 27: 633–67.

——. 1990. "Social Processes of Delinquency and Drug Use Among Urban Gangs." Pp. 183–219 in *Gangs in America*, edited by C. R. Huff. Newbury Park, CA: Sage Publications.

Fleisher, M. 1998. *Dead End Kids: Gang Girls and the Boys They Know*. Madison, WI: University of Wisconsin Press.

Glassner, B. and J. Loughlin. 1987. *Drugs in Adolescent Worlds: Burnouts to Straights*. New York: St. Martin's Press.

Hagan, J. and B. McCarthy. 1997. *Mean Streets: Youth Crime and Homelessness*. Cambridge: Cambridge University Press.

Hagedorn, J. M. 1998. *People and Folks: Gangs, Crime and the Underclass in a Rustbelt City*, 2nd Edition. Chicago, IL: Lake View Press.

Hagedorn, J. M. and M. L. Devitt. 1999. "Fighting Female: The Social Construction of Female Gangs." Pp. 256–76 in *Female Gangs in America*, edited by M. Chesney-Lind and J. M. Hagedorn. Chicago, IL: Lake View Press.

Huff, C. R. 1996. "The Criminal Behavior of Gang Members and Nongang At-Risk Youths." Pp. 75–102 in *Gangs in America*, 2nd Edition, edited by C. R. Huff. Thousand Oaks, CA: Sage Publications.

——. 1998. "Comparing the Criminal Behavior of Youth Gangs and At-Risk Youths." *Research in Brief*. Washington, DC: National Institute of Justice.

Jacobs, B. A. and J. Miller. 1998. "Crack Dealing, Gender, and Arrest Avoidance." *Social Problems* 45: 550–69.

Joe, K. A. and M. Chesney-Lind. 1995. "'Just Every Mother's Angel': An Analysis of Gender and Ethnic Variations in Youth Gang Membership." *Gender and Society* 9: 408–30.

Klein, M. W. 1995. *The American Street Gang: Its Nature, Prevalence and Control*. New York: Oxford University Press.

Klein, M. W. and L. Y. Crawford. 1967. "Groups, Gangs and Cohesiveness." *Journal of Research in Crime and Delinquency* 4: 63–75.

Lauritsen, J. L., R. J. Sampson, and J. H. Laub. 1991. "The Link between Offending and Victimization among Adolescents." *Criminology* 29: 265–92.

Maher, L. 1997. *Sexed Work: Gender, Race and Resistance in a Brooklyn Drug Economy*. Oxford: Clarendon Press.

Maxson, C. L. and M. W. Klein. 1990. "Street Gang Violence: Twice as Great, or Half as Great?" Pp. 71–100 in *Gangs in America*, edited by C. R. Huff. Newbury Park, CA: Sage Publications.

——. 1996. "Defining Gang Homicide: An Updated Look at Member and Motive Approaches." Pp. 3–20 in *Gangs in America*, 2nd Edition, edited by C. R. Huff. Newbury Park, CA: Sage Publications.

Messerschmidt, J. W. 1995. "From Patriarchy to Gender: Feminist Theory, Criminology and the Challenge of Diversity." Pp. 167–88 in *International Feminist Perspectives in Criminology: Engendering a Discipline*, edited by N. H. Rafter and F. Heidensohn. Philadelphia, PA: Open University Press.

Miller, J. 1998a. "Gender and Victimization Risk Among Young Women in Gangs." *Journal of Research in Crime and Delinquency* 35: 429–53.

——. 1998b. "Up It Up: Gender and the Accomplishment of Street Robbery." *Criminology* 36: 37–66.

——. 2001. *One of the Guys: Girls, Gangs and Gender*. New York: Oxford University Press.

Miller, J. and R. K. Brunson. 2000. "Gender Dynamics in Youth Gangs: A Comparison of Male and Female Accounts." *Justice Quarterly* 17: 801–30.

Nurge, D. 1998. "Female Gangs and Cliques in Boston: What's the Difference?" Paper presented at the annual meeting of the American Society of Criminology, November, Washington, DC.

Rosenfeld, R., S. H. Decker, and C. W. Kohfeld. 1990. "The St. Louis Homicide Project." Unpublished document. St. Louis, MO.

Rosenfeld, R., T. Bray, and A. Egley. 1999. "Facilitating Violence: A Comparison of Gang-Motivated, Gang-Affiliated, and Non-Gang Youth Homicides." *Journal of Quantitative Criminology* 15: 495–516.

Sanders, W. 1994. *Gangbangs and Drive-Bys: Grounded Culture and Juvenile Gang Violence*. New York: Aldine de Gruyer.

Short, J. F. 1998. "The Level of Explanation Problem Revisited—The American Society of Criminology 1997 Presidential Address." *Criminology* 36: 3–36.

Short, J. F. and F. L. Strodtbeck. 1965. *Group Process and Gang Delinquency*. Chicago, IL: University of Chicago Press.

Simpson, S. 1991. "Caste, Class and Violent Crime: Explaining Differences in Female Offending." *Criminology* 29: 115–35.

Simpson, S. and L. Elis. 1995. "Doing Gender: Sorting Out the Caste and Crime Conundrum." *Criminology* 33: 47–81.

Spergel, I. and G. D. Curry. 1993. "The National Youth Gang Survey: A Research and Development Process." Pp. 359–400 in *The Gang Intervention Handbook*, edited by A. Goldstein and C. R. Huff. Champaign-Urbana, IL: Research Press.

Steffensmeier, D. J. 1983. "Organizational Properties and Sex-Segregation in the Underworld: Building a Sociological Theory of Sex Differences in Crime." *Social Forces* 61: 1010–32.

Thornberry, T. P. 1998. "Membership in Youth Gangs and Involvement in Serious and Violent Offending." Pp. 147–66 in *Serious and Violent Juvenile Offenders: Risk Factors and Successful Interventions*, edited by R. Loeber and D.P. Farrington. Thousand Oaks, CA: Sage Publications.

Thornberry, T. P. and J. H. Burch, II. 1997. "Gang Members and Delinquent Behavior." *Juvenile Justice Bulletin*. Washington, DC: Office of Juvenile Justice and Delinquency Prevention.

Thornberry, T. P., M. D. Krohn, A. J. Lizotte, and D. Chard-Wierschem. 1993. "The Role of Juvenile Gangs in Facilitating Delinquent Behavior." *Journal of Research in Crime and Delinquency* 30: 75–85.

West, C. and S. Fenstermaker. 1995. "Doing Difference." *Gender and Society* 9: 8–37.

West, C. and D. H. Zimmerman. 1987. "Doing Gender." *Gender and Society* 1: 125–51.

Wilson, W. J. 1996. *When Work Disappears: The World of the New Urban Poor*. New York: Alfred A Knopf.

Winfree, L. T., Jr., K. Fuller, T. Vigil, and G. L. Mays. 1992. "The Definition and Measurement of 'Gang Status': Policy Implications for Juvenile Justice." *Juvenile and Family Court Journal* 43: 29–37.

Section IV

Economic Marginality and Survival Crimes

By interpreting these resistances solely as lawbreaking and responding to them solely within the confines of the criminal justice system, we neglect the conditions of their existence and criminalize what are, in effect, women's survival strategies. (Maher 1997, 200)

Different hypotheses have surfaced over the last 30 years in relation to explaining women's crime trends. One explanation is the emancipation hypothesis and another is the economic marginalization hypothesis. The emancipation hypothesis assumes that women's crime rates will increase as women achieve social and economic *independence* from men (Adler 1975). To date, not much empirical support for this hypothesis exists. There is more support for female crime increases due to women becoming more economically marginalized relative to men. The economic marginalization hypothesis bases its argument on two measures: offending rates between women and men and a gender comparison of economic and financial well-being. This hypothesis maintains that in comparison to men, as women become more economically *disadvantaged*, women's rates of crime will increase (Heimer 2000).

In Owen's (1998) study of California prisoners, about half of all incarcerated women had no employment record whatsoever, with an even larger number having not worked in the 12 months prior to arrest. These women relied on public support, hustling and drug dealing, or support from a family member. Almost 30 percent of women did not complete high school and did not have a GED, while 12 percent completed a GED, and 15 percent completed high school. Only about one-fourth had any post-high school training or secondary college education. Being that most women offenders lack education and occupational and vocational skills, they view themselves as having limited options in the legitimate work world. Some view crime as a way to unburden themselves from economic hardship. However, even in criminal markets, women's opportunities are restricted by gender (Alarid et al. 1996).

Survival Crimes

The first article, by Nikki Levine, is a personal view that best explains survival crimes. Survival crimes are lawbreaking behaviors that are committed disproportionately by marginalized women who have few if any marketable job skills. Survival crimes are typically committed to live on a daily basis, to support dependent children, or to maintain a drug or alcohol addiction. Some survival crimes occur when women try to prolong or escape intimate violent relationships (Richie 2000). Sex work through street-level prostitution is linked to the drug economy and remains a source of survival for marginalized women who have no other way of supporting their habit. Sex workers are therefore vulnerable to victimization, as our next two readings attest. The **second selection, by Steven Kurtz and his colleagues,** examines the disproportionate number of sex workers who are violently victimized by their "johns" or "dates." An earlier study of 130 prostitutes found that most had suffered one or more types of victimization by customers: 88 percent had been physically threatened, 83 percent had been threatened with a weapon, and 82 percent had been physically assaulted (Farley and Barkan 1998).

While the law deters the vast majority of the general population from committing crime, the law may also criminalize impoverished or otherwise powerless people (Thornburg and Trunk 1992). The response of law enforcement to the will of the community in the arrest of prostitutes is what is known as "agency" in the criminalization of women who commit certain types of survival crimes. **The reading by Lisa Sanchez (Chapter 15)** clearly distinguishes the paradox between the way police enforce prostitution ordinances and the ill-treatment that this group of marginalized women endures.

Survival crimes to support oneself or one's children typically take the form of property offenses (theft, shoplifting), whereas sustaining an addiction given limited opportunities is made possible through prostitution or small-time drug sales. Sexual bartering or nonsexual companionship is used in exchange for money, drugs, protection, or even a place to stay for women in the inner-city crack culture, as you will read about in **the article by Lisa Maher and colleagues**. These women attempt to procure short-term places to stay over hotels and homeless shelters because more public forms of assistance reportedly increase the women's level of alcohol and drug use and involvement in illegal activities. Women crack users have been sexualized in some of the literature as desperate individuals who would do anything for a hit of crack (Inciardi, Lockwood, and Pottiger 1993). In other research, women drug users were extremely averse to having sex, but reluctantly did so because of their marginalized position in an unstable economy where crack cocaine decreased earnings from street-level sex work (Maher 1997).

Drug-addicted women generally seemed to have fewer options to earn money than drug-addicted men. Even with limited education and language barriers, impoverished drug-addicted men had more freedom to find manual labor or temporary jobs as a way to earn money, while women reluctantly resorted to sex for money or sex for drugs (Koester and Schwartz 1993).

Addiction

Heavy or persistent drug users who began at an early age tend to be involved in more serious crime. As Owen (1998, 45) remarked, "Substance abuse paves the pathway to imprisonment." Drug users and alcoholics were also more prone to incidences of victimization than non-drug users, such as the link between substance abuse and intimate violence. When a sample of married alcoholic women was compared with a random sample of the general population of married women, spouses of alcoholic women were more abusive than spouses of women from the general population (Miller, Downs, and Gondoli 1989). The researchers were unable to determine whether victimization led to alcoholism or if being an alcoholic led to victimization by one's spouse.

References

Adler, F. 1975. *Sisters in Crime.* New York: McGraw Hill.

Alarid, L. F., J. W. Marquart, V. S. Burton, F. T. Cullen, and S. J. Cuvelier. 1996. "Women's Roles in Serious Offenses: A Study of Adult Felons." *Justice Quarterly* 13 (3): 431–454.

Farley, M., and H. Barkan. 1998. "Prostitution, Violence Against Women, and Posttraumatic Stress Disorder." *Women and Health* 27 (3): 37–49.

Heimer, K. 2000. "Changes in the Gender Gap in Crime and Women's Economic Marginalization." *Criminal Justice 2000: The Nature of Crime: Continuity and Change.* Washington, DC: National Institute of Justice, Office of Justice Programs.

Inciardi, J. A., D. Lockwood, and A. E. Pottigier. 1993. *Women and Crack Cocaine.* New York: Macmillan.

Koester, S., and J. Schwartz. 1993. "Crack, Gangs, Sex, and Powerlessness: A View From Denver." Pp. 187–203 in *Crack Pipe as Pimp: An Ethnographic Investigation of Sex-for-Crack Exchanges* (edited by Mitchell S. Ratner). New York: Lexington.

Maher, L. 1997. *Sexed Work: Gender, Race, and Resistance in a Brooklyn Drug Market.* New York: Oxford.

Miller, B. A., W. R. Downs, and D. M. Gondoli. 1989. "Spousal Violence Among Alcoholic Women as Compared to a Random Household Sample of Women." *Journal of Studies on Alcohol* 50 (6): 533–540.

Owen, B. 1998. *In the Mix: Struggle and Survival in a Women's Prison.* Albany: State University of New York Press.

Richie, B. E. 2000. "Exploring the Link Between Violence Against Women and Women's Involvement in Illegal Activity." *Research on Women and Girls in the Justice System: Plenary Papers of the 1999 Conference on Criminal Justice Research and Evaluation—Enhancing Policy and Practice Through Research, Volume 3* (NCJ 180973). Washington, DC: National Institute of Justice, Office of Justice Programs.

Thornburg, T., and D. Trunk. 1992. "A Collage of Voices: A Dialogue With Women in Prison." *Southern California Review of Law and Women's Studies* 2 (1): 155–217. ✦

13
One Woman's Voice

My Mother Was a Whore

Nikki Levine

In this reading, the author describes her life growing up with a heroin-addicted, drug-dealing, prostitute mother and an abusive, drug-addicted stepfather. She views her past life as a prostitute as the inevitable outcome of her early experiences living in an impoverished home.

It's something I've known for much of my life, though I couldn't even begin to say it out loud until I sucked my first dick for money. It's never been a big conversation piece, not something I bring up to people, because it always seemed like any other job to me. Not a lot of people actually had jobs in Jersey City when I was growing up, at least not legal ones, and definitely none of the people around me. I didn't have a home for years, unless you count other people's cars, motel-room floors, and pitched tents in Lincoln Park behind the projects we were kicked out of after a drug bust occurred in our tiny apartment.

"We were dealt a shitty hand," my grandma once told me after I interrupted her watching *Wheel of Fortune,* her weekday 7:30 scream-along session, to complain about what the kids around town had been making fun of me for that day (I'd worn the same shirt two days in a row). "SOLVE THE PUZZLE, YOU FUCKIN' SCHMUCK!" she'd be yelling at the polished people on the black-and-white screen who'd stare blankly at obvious phrases, or at least phrases that were obvious to Grandma. As the oldest and the first-generation American, as well as the loudest in the family, Grandma was regarded by everyone as the genius, the one who knew everything. It still blows my mind that she never figured out my mother was a whore—or maybe she was so smart that she knew the whole time but kept her knowledge a secret from my mother and me.

Grandma kicked us out of the family's average-sized Ocean County house in 1986. We had lived there for almost a year, along with my aunt, her husband, Grandma, Grandpa, and Grandma's parents. I was in first grade, and all I knew is we were "moving to the city." Mom had met a guy named Tony, who I hated from the start because of his creepy voice and the fact that he wore ribbed tank tops over thermal underwear shirts in the summertime. He wore a gold chain with someone's head hanging from it like a museum exhibit. I later learned this was Jesus, someone that the Catholics worshipped. I knew nothing about that in my sheltered Reform-Jew world. Reform, mostly because we couldn't afford to join a temple. Grandma said we had to leave because she didn't want my mother to be with Tony—who I later found out wore those thermal shirts to hide the track marks that stained his arm like paint on a canvas. "MY WAY OR THE HIGHWAY!" Grandma screamed at my mother one day as she opened the broken front door, pointing to the proverbial "highway." My mother chose the highway, a.k.a. drugs and the chance to be a Mafia wife, and we moved to Jersey City.

My mother walked the streets for years in her late twenties and early thirties. She was a genius and could have been the doctor that her grandma always told her she'd better be. But by the time she was twenty-eight, it wasn't an option for her. My mother was a heroin addict. Her addiction was like having another child to keep alive with the easy money she made with her body, with her hands, her mouth, her pussy.

My mother became a whore because she had a daughter and a dead-beat ex-husband. She was a single mother in a dead, brick city in northern New Jersey, dividing her time between finding places for me to sleep and having sex with strangers. Tony was living with his parents, who hated my mother because she wasn't Italian. Regardless, we were allowed to eat Sunday dinner at their house. Tony slept in their garage and always had needles hanging out of his arm when we'd show up. He said he loved me and wanted me to call him "Daddy."

My mother's addiction was serious, it controlled almost everything, but she never forgot that she had a daughter to take care of. She'd cry us both to sleep at night on motel-room floors, the floors of her Johns who were kind enough to let their homeless whore and her daughter sleep in their $20-per-night first-floor unit. They'd wake up early in the morning and shoo us out in time for me to get to school. My mother would walk me to school in her stiletto heels and black cat suit. The other kids thought she was a goddess just like I did. We didn't know she was a whore, or that a whore could be a goddess.

My mother was a whore. The black sheep of the family. Divorced from my father and now dating Italian men exclusively. She wanted to be Italian, not Jewish. My mother dated Mafia bottom-feeders and changed my last name in my school registration so I wouldn't have to be a "Levine" anymore. I was now an Italian girl, a DiFeo, just like her and her Tony. I was sworn to secrecy.

She sold cocaine on the job. She didn't have a real pimp, just Tony, who she was selling co-caine for—to make money to support his habit. I knew she was out in the streets for me, though, her daughter that she didn't mean to have but loved more than anything in the world. She was a dealer, but the money she made from whoring was different from the drug money. When I was thirteen or fourteen she told me the story of what she was really doing. How she never spent drug money on me, that's what the fuck money was for. My dad disappeared and didn't pay child support; she had to get money for me somehow.

My mother always told me that I should respect the sex industry, though not in those words. We were inner-city to the core; she didn't know that it was an "industry." I look at all of the hype about sex work now, how it's the new cool feminist occupation and how young whores are spreading the gospel of prostitution to the Third Wave, the no wave, the whatever-the-fuck wave of feminists now. Unfortunately, most of this is on the Internet or in fanzines. In most cases, inner-city whores and their children do not have access to this kind of information. I've come across a multitude of fanzines and Internet websites geared toward The Sex Worker—resources that are intended to provide safety tips to, and instill the feeling of community among, sex workers. My mother was an older woman (relatively) from the streets of Jersey City; if someone had handed her a modern fanzine about sex work, she most likely wouldn't have understood what was presented to her. Phrases like "sex work" would have been alien to her. A loner in the industry, my mother would have shunned the idea of a "safety call"; she was too proud to have anyone else know what she was doing when she left our roach-infested apartment in her cat suit and cheap, broken stilettos. Though I think it's important that sex-worker harm-reduction information be brought into the inner cities for people like my mother, I'm unsure as to who would be capable of translating information origi-

nally intended for college-oriented young people into something that an older inner-city prostitute with not much formal education could process.

Before she was a whore, my mother was a stripper. I would try on her costumes when she wasn't looking; they always made me feel so glamorous. I'd use duct tape to keep the thongs up high on my little thighs; pasties covered my tiny five-year-old tits. I'd dance around our tiny bedroom to her collection of 45s, singing along in my shrill baby voice while slowly removing my sequined panties. *"I wanna rock with you . . ."* I'd sing along with Michael Jackson. When Mom would catch me, she'd move the needle off the record and tell me it was O.K. to wear the outfits, but not O.K. to remove them while dancing. She told me that she never got fully unclothed for any job. She said she hoped I would never have to do what she does.

After a year of fruitless efforts to find a way to escape Tony (who had been beating both of us and taking my mother's money), she finally called the police on him. I'll never forget that day—I sat on the counter of the apartment we were sharing with another family for the month and watched Tony as he carefully loaded his syringe and got down to business and suddenly the front door was broken down and in pieces on the floor. Police filled the room, my mother grabbed me, and we hid in the corner behind an undercover agent who we had been getting to know. Her name was Michelle and she helped my mother set the trap. We were free.

We entered the world of the mysterious witness-protection program. We were put up in a hotel on Staten Island and told to wait. We waited, and during this time my mother detoxed. I had no idea what was wrong with her. While she lay in bed curled into the fetal position, screaming about the demons she saw, I would roam the streets of Staten Island looking for a cure. I described my mother's symptoms to random street runners, dealers, thugs, whores, you name it. Finally, I met a guy named Gooch who told me he had what my mother needed. He handed me a clear bag with whitish brown powder in it. A heart decorated the bag. I brought it home to my mother, excited that I had the antidote to her sickness. She looked at the bag and threw up, commanding me to flush it down the toilet quickly. She told me that bag contained the demon. I did as she told me and lay next to her in the bed she'd soaked with her sweat, and she held me tight and told me she'd never be this sick again.

About a week later, my mother was feeling a lot better. We watched *Good Day New York* every morning, and my mother told me that if I saw myself on the show I shouldn't be scared, because we were moving. She didn't know where, but she said we'd have new names, new hairstyles, and new stories to tell people. Stories we'd need to maintain in order to keep us from Tony. Right as *Good Day New York* was ending and *I Love Lucy's* beginning credits rolled, the hotel phone rang. It was Michelle. She said we were not allowed to be a part of the program because my mother's drug test came out positive. At least, that's what my mom told me. The next day, we checked out of the hotel and moved to the shore for *A Better Life*, with the fear of Tony's return constantly lingering in the backs of our minds.

My mother became an agent at a "fantasy entertainment" company run by an old family friend named Lee. She was essentially a pimp—finding dancers for private parties and making sure she got Lee's cut. She made $5 an hour, which wasn't enough to pay for my lunch at school. It paid the rent, though, keeping us alive in our one-bedroom apartment in Brick, New Jersey. And it was off the books, so my mother was now able to collect welfare and get food stamps. The food stamps were embarrassing to me; I refused to go shopping with my mother when she used them. The town itself was mostly filled with families, "whole families," families with bay views and their own attics and basements that nobody lived in. Maybe they kept their toys there, or had a "family room." I don't even think there was a welfare office in town.

One day, Tony showed up on our doorstep, crying and begging to be let in. "I'm clean, I'm clean," he said over and over again. I wondered what his hygiene had to do with letting him into our tiny roach-infested apartment. He'd just get dirty again. And she let him in. He detoxed in my bedroom, and I wondered why they were both so sick all the time. Soon they were both feeling great. They had gone back to heroin, and Tony returned to dealing out of our apartment. I was once again to call him "Daddy," and I had to start walking differently. Apparently I didn't walk "heel-toe, heel-toe." This infuriated him, and he'd spend hours watching me walk around the house. On one particularly memorable occasion, he followed me around with a .357 Magnum and told me that I'd "better get it right." My mother screamed and cried, begging him not to hurt me. He used the gun to hit my mother in the face and she fell to the ground, bleeding and sobbing. I started to run to my mother but I also caught a pistol whip to the face and was knocked out immediately. I don't really remember what happened after that.

My mama was a whore but it didn't upset me. When money got tough after she died, I never thought of whoring. I figured I was too fat, too this, too that. I didn't want to be called a Whore. It seemed so dirty. But my mother taught me that if I needed to, I could be a whore and it wouldn't be terrible. It would be a job.

What am I now? My mother taught me how to take care of myself in the presence of older men. Older men were the ones who would fuck us over all the time. We were both deathly afraid of men in their forties. Mustaches, beards, white skin, little purple dicks. She taught me not to fear; she taught me how to take charge and make them fear me, which was a totally new concept. Mama taught me that if I had to be a whore, I wouldn't be scared or ashamed.

So when my hands clutch unfamiliar balls, my mouth on unfamiliar dicks, unfamiliar hands on my tits and grabbing for my pussy, I don't get frightened. My knife gives me power. My mother carried a gun. She also walked the streets, and did it alone. I work with my girlfriend and we do it sober, watching out for each other and keeping ourselves out of danger.

When they thrust green bills into my hands I remember my mother sucking dick for food stamps. I remember going hungry because there was a blizzard in Jersey City and she couldn't walk around in stilettos in the snow. Borrowing cranberry sauce from our next-door neighbors Dennis and Cathy, coke customers of Tony and my mom. They were adamant about us buying them another can once the sidewalks were plowed.

In 1999, AIDS claimed the life of my mother, thanks to Tony. She never shot anything into her veins—she snorted her dope. Tony, on the other hand. . . .

My mother watches over me like an angel. It wasn't her time to go, but she did leave. She must have had a plan. She always had a plan.

I never thought I'd be here, a sex worker, a pro-domme, but I am and I'm not afraid. Because where I go, there's my mother, hovering to make sure I don't get hurt. And when their prying hands find their way to my pussy she intervenes, drawing everyone's attention to something across the street or across the room.

I walk into every call knowing my mother is there and that it's going to be O.K. I walk out of every call with a smile on my face because we're that much richer. I get my money, and I learned how from my mother, who was a genius, a goddess, and a whore.

Discussion Questions

1. Do you think that living the life the author lived caused her to inevitably follow in her mother's footsteps? How might she have done otherwise?

2. Can you, as the reader, conceive of living a life such as that lived by the author? How might you have dealt emotionally and socially with that environment?

3. Who is to blame for Nikki's present life? Her mother? Grandmother? Tony? Nikki herself? On what factors do you base that opinion?

14
Violent Victimization of Street Sex Workers

Steven P. Kurtz
Hilary L. Surratt
James A. Inciardi
Marion C. Kiley

Prostitution is a risky business and due to the nature of this work, women are frequently victims of a wide range of violent assaults. They are victimized by their customers as well as by pimps, drug dealers, and other predators. This study employed survey and focus group methods to examine the characteristics and sex work-related behaviors of 294 female street-based sex workers in Miami that make them more likely to be victimized by their clients, or "dates." More than half the respondents had experienced date violence in the prior year. Economic desperation, using crack or heroin while working, not controlling the date location, and having sex in the car were strong predictors of victimization. This study was conducted as a part of an HIV/AIDS intervention and prevention study at the University of Miami School of Medicine. Most of the sex workers interviewed and the 21 women who participated in the focus groups worked the "Boulevard," an 80-block stretch of road in Miami with a reputation for prostitution, drug dealing, and fencing operations and widespread availability of cheap, "no-tell" hotels. Six focus group sessions were conducted, and they each lasted one hour. Participants were compensated $25 for their participation. The article concludes with recommendations for a harm-reduction approach to outreach and education, and it calls for increased legal protections for victimized sex workers.

Female sex workers who "stroll" the boulevards and back streets of urban centers are typically at high risk for assault, rape, and other forms of physical violence from a variety of individuals, including muggers, serial predators, drug dealers, pimps, and even police and passersby. However, most of the violence experienced by female sex workers comes from their own customers, or "dates," as they typically refer to them (Church, Henderson, Barnard, & Hart, 2001; Coston & Ross, 1998; Davis, 2000; Farley & Barkan, 1998; Hoigard & Finstad, 1986; Inciardi, Lockwood, & Pottieger, 1993; Silbert & Pines, 1983; Sterk & Elifson, 1990). In fact, the majority of street-based sex workers are embedded in a complex of social situations other than prostitution that are independently associated with adult violent victimization, including homelessness and drug abuse (Baseman, Ross, & Williams, 1999; Davis, 2000; Falck, Wang, Carlson, & Siegal, 2001; Gilbert, El-Bassel, Rajah, Foleno, & Frye, 2001; Inciardi, 1993; Inciardi & Surratt, 2001; Teets, 1997; Wenzel, Leake, & Gelberg, 2001). Moreover, significant numbers also have histories of childhood sexual and physical abuse (El-Bassel, Witte, Wada, Gilbert, & Wallace, 2001; Farley & Barkan, 1998; Gidycz, Coble, Latham, & Layman, 1993; Maher, 1997; Sterk & Elifson, 1990). Indeed, these problems often become cyclical insofar as (a) childhood sexual and physical abuse beget drug addiction, homelessness, and associated street survival strategies, including sex work; and (b) the trauma from living on the street results in attempts at self-medication and escape, increasing the need for drugs and the activities necessary to pay for them (El-Bassel et al., 1997; Erickson, Butters, McGillicuddy, & Hallgren, 2000; Gilbert et al., 2001; Maxwell & Maxwell, 2000; McKegany & Bernard, 1992; Miller, 1986; Phoenix, 2000; Young, Boyd, & Hubbell, 2000).

It is well documented that street sex workers are perceived by themselves and by their victimizers to be largely outside of the protections of the legal system (Boyle, 1994; Hoigard & Finstad, 1986; Karen, 1998; Lowman, 2000; Miller & Schwartz, 1995). It has also been reported that much of the violence directed toward female sex workers is often, in the minds of the perpetrators, morally justified (Bourgois & Dunlap, 1993; Miller & Schwartz, 1995; Monto & Hotaling, 2001). At the same time, there is a lack of evidence suggesting that men who purchase services from sex workers differ significantly from men in the general population in their attitudes and beliefs (Boyle, 1994; Monto & Hotaling, 2001) or that violent dates are of a type that may be readily identified (Maher, 1997; Phoenix, 2000). And going further, studies suggesting correlates of violence or mechanisms for reducing the levels of victimization experienced by sex workers are virtually absent from the literature. Only one study, an ethnography of 13 street sex workers, attempted to identify risk factors for date violence (Williamson & Folaron, 2001). This work suggested that (a) having "young strangers" as customers, (b) being high on crack cocaine while working, and (c) going with a date to an unfamiliar place increased the likelihood of violence. Similarly, successful strategies women can use to protect themselves have been addressed by just a few studies (Carole, 1998; Hoigard & Finstad, 1986; O'Neill & Barberet, 2000).

Within this context, this study is intended to increase and contextualize our understanding of the nature and extent of violence perpetrated against street sex workers, specifically by their dates, with the ultimate aim of integrating effective techniques for violence prevention into social service and public health interventions targeted at female sex workers. In a sample of 294 street-based sex workers in Miami, we examine the demographic and drug use characteristics and sex work-related behaviors that increase women's risks for victimization by dates. This is supplemented by in-depth focus group interviews. We also report on their strategies for reducing violence once they become aware that they are in danger. Based on the findings of this study, some suggestions are offered for assisting sex workers in further reducing their levels of risk.

Before going further, however, a brief comment seems warranted on two of the terms used throughout this manuscript—namely, *sex workers* and *dates*. Our research approach is grounded by the perspective that the women's voices are of primary importance to our inquiry and that they must comprise the focus of the analysis if we are to understand the phenomenon of violent victimization as they experience it. For this reason, we have chosen to use their language throughout this article to maintain the integrity of their accounts. Although we are aware that *women in prostitution* and *prostituted women* are more frequently used in the violence literature, the term *sex worker* is commonly used in both the substance abuse and infectious disease literatures. Furthermore, virtually all of our clients emphasized in the focus groups and the in-depth interviews that they prefer the terms *sex worker* and *working woman* and refer to themselves as such. Many felt that the terms *prostitute* and *prostitution* were insulting and heavily value-laden. At the same time, all of the women in this study refer to their customers as *dates* rather than *tricks* or *Johns*.

Findings

Research and popular culture indicate that sex workers are of many types, ranging from highly paid "call girls" who work independently with a "book" of steady "monied" customers accumulated through clients' word of mouth (Delacoste & Alexander, 1998) to the down-and-out "crack whores" and "skeezers" who populate inner city streets and crack houses "turning tricks" sometimes for as little as a few "hits" on a crack pipe (Ratner, 1993). The great majority of the women encountered in this study are situated close to the latter end of this continuum, with almost all reporting that they were physically and mentally exhausted as a result of their attempts at surviving on the streets for many years. Eighty-six percent of the participants were over 30 years of age, and almost half were homeless at the time of recruitment. Only 39.8% were receiving any legal income, which largely consisted of some type of government assistance (21.4%) and/or family support (19.7%). Few respondents (10.9%) received income from legal employment. A slight majority had less than a high school education, and for reasons noted earlier, the sample is largely African American and non-Hispanic White. Finally, the vast majority reported having been exposed to physical (85.7%) and/or sexual (70.4%) abuse during childhood.

Drug Use

Because crack cocaine has been the primary drug of abuse in the Miami area since the mid-1980s (Inciardi & Surratt, 2001), it is not surprising that crack was used by even more respondents than alcohol was. Few of the women were current injection drug users, and only 20.1% reported the use of any form of heroin in the past 30 days.

Sex Work

Coincident with the fact that this is an older population, the median length of time in the sex trade was 17 years. But as Miami has always been somewhat of a transient city (Allman, 1987; Fortes & Stepick, 1993; Reiff, 1987), it is not surprising that the median time working the sex trade in the area was only 5 years. Very few of the women in the sample (6.8%) worked with pimps or paid protectors, primarily because, historically, the low prices for sexual services on the Boulevard never provided an incentive for the emergence of the culture of "living off the earnings of a prostitute" (i.e., pimping). Competition is high and prices have remained low because drug addiction and homelessness raise desperation levels, and local dates are reportedly aware of this. One Latina put it this way:

> Since crack came out, crack is the pimp, drugs are the pimp. I haven't seen pimping since '85. Prostitutes just do anything for a little bit of money because they want to get high, so they messed it up. Now, it's like when you ask a date home [and give them a price of] $50, they'll be like, "$50? What are you thinking?" It's like they get aggressive because they think you're not worth it.

Another focus group member added,

> They will come up [and say], "I can get it for $10, I can get it for this dollar." I mean, I have actually had a guy telling me that he had sex with a girl for $2 because she was $2 or $3 short of getting a rock, you know? And it messes it up for us. I don't like to go out and get $20 or $30 and go back. I like to stay out and get all the money I need so I can just chill and relax. I see some girls that go out, get $10, go back, $10, back, $50, and it don't make no sense. They are being called chicken heads—the ones that just doodle doodle doodle do . . . they run back and forth.

These comments reflect similar observations made about the Miami sex-for-crack scene a decade ago (see Inciardi et al., 1993).

The median rate charged by respondents was $35 for vaginal sex and $25 for oral sex, generating very limited incomes for all but the most sexually active women. Overall, median weekly income from sex work was only $200. Prices were somewhat higher for more exotic sexual services—anal and sadomasochistic sex, golden and brown showers (sex involving urination and defecation), baby dressing (dressing as a very young girl, or dressing the date as a baby), and other fetishes as well as orgies. Less than a third (32.3%) of the sample was willing to provide such services, however.

Almost all of the participants (87.1%) used drugs while engaged in sex work during the previous 30 days. Many of the focus group members said that getting high was the only way they could bear sex work. A young Latina explained:

> It's easier, it's like more comfortable to do it. When you're not high, you think about doing it twice, three times. You're like, "I don't want to do it." But then when you're high, you don't want to deliver, but you like it more. You take the risk because you know you got to do it.

Another respondent who recently stopped using drugs said,

> I found that even though I don't have to have a fix, I am often greedy and need money for errands, so I'll still be out there, and since I'm not getting high I can't stand it. They just make me [vomit]. Anyway, I'm gay, and now that I'm off drugs, it really, really, really messes with me. I mean I get to the point where I try to rob them 'cause I just get so sick of it.

Victimization by Dates

Attesting to the generally violent world of street prostitution, 222 (75.5%) women had been victimized by someone during the previous 90 days (data not shown). More than half (51.7%) of the respondents had experienced physical violence from dates in the past year, and almost one third (31.6%) of the women had been victimized in the prior 30 days. Being cornered (put in a position where escape was impossible) or ripped off (robbed of valuables or of the payment for sex) were the most common types of victimization, although more that one quarter (25.5%) had been beaten and others raped (13.9%) or threatened with a weapon (14.6%) in the past year.

Because almost half of the respondents had not experienced violence from dates in the past year, analyses were undertaken to assess the demographic and drug use characteristics as well as sex work behaviors that put women at higher risk for victimization. White non-Hispanic women were much more likely to experience violence from dates than were African Americans. Focus group participants suggested that White women are perceived by dates to be both physically weaker and less street smart than Black women, and therefore, they are less risky for the date to attack. African American women said that they were less likely to give dates even the smallest opening to rip them off or put them in a vulnerable position. As one put it,

> They [the dates] do think White girls are pussies. A White woman will take more shit off a Black man than a Black woman off a Black man. Because Black men talk to women, and Black women get nasty. They don't give them respect. A White woman, she going to take that shit. If he say lick my ass, [she says], "Okay, baby, where you want me to start?"

A White participant expressed similar sentiments:

> In my opinion, a White girl will get beat up more. Caucasian women, they seem to be more, like, weaker, more vulnerable, more susceptible. The Black girl, you know, I mean she will turn around and beat up the guy. And Black women, they always have [a weapon].

Black women have something, and men know that.

It was also found that White women were more likely to engage in certain behaviors that were highly correlated with victimization, independent of ethnicity—namely, using heroin while working, offering nontraditional sex services, and working the main stroll. These factors are discussed later in this article.

Two additional risk factors appear to be related to relative economic desperation, thus leading to less selectivity in providing sexual services to men—namely, homelessness and crack and/or heroin addiction. Homeless women charged about 15% less, on average, than other sex workers for oral sex and about 20% less for vaginal sex. These observations were borne out by the focus group discussions. A number of women observed that their relative financial health at any given time drives their decision making as to whether to trust a particular date. If lacking a safe space in which to live is an obviously desperate situation, the need to satisfy a drug habit is often the more immediate one. Many women in the focus groups acknowledged poor control over their sex trades when they were "jonesing" (suffering drug withdrawal symptoms). At such times, they would do just about anything with anyone for enough money to buy another rock of crack or bag of heroin.

Finally, women who admitted to committing violence in the last 90 days were more likely to be victimized by dates. One cannot be certain of the reasons for this finding, because data were not collected on the targets of the women's violence, only the numbers and types of violent acts they committed. Focus groups were quite informative on this issue, however, and highlighted several kinds of situations in which the violence was directed toward dates. Some women had become violent toward customers in response to violence they received. A White heroin injector described her reaction to being raped by a date:

> I didn't used to be like that until I got raped a couple of times and beaten a couple of times. Then I started carrying a box cutter. I cut some guy from his ear to the corner of his lip and his whole face just popped open. He was a pretty boy, you know, and I looked at him and said, "Now, pretty boy, you'll remember me for the rest of your life. You're not so pretty any more." I was shaking from the adrenaline rush but I didn't regret it, and I didn't lose any sleep over it. I was shocked that some nice girl. . . . I never dreamed that I would be in a situation like this, never. I was as normal, upper middle-class as you

can get, you know, and [now] I can get just as down and dirty. . . .

A second type of violent scenario was sometimes precipitated by the women themselves and usually involved their own drug use. An African American woman described how smoking crack before or during a date made her more prone to receive violence from dates because the drug made her more aggressive and more difficult to get along with:

> See, once I start getting high, I don't want to do shit. I don't want you to touch me. I don't want you to put your hands on me. You're gonna have problems, problems, problems. I will smoke his stuff up, get his money, and will not do nuthin'. A crack smoker is the best con artist there is. We start getting high, and our head is already calculating, "Alright, where's my next one coming from?" We get in a situation where we're in process, okay? And we are on this date, and they start getting stupid. I don't talk when I'm on a trip. "Now, alright, you know what, you'd better stop, leave me alone now, I've got to get out of here." And they're going to put me out because I start being loud.

In such cases, dates often responded with threats of violence to obtain the services for which they had paid or for revenge. One experienced sex worker elaborated:

> You got these females that want to be slick and smoke all his shit up and try to walk away. That brings a lot of violence, too. They smoke first and don't ask no questions, . . . then they try to get missing [sneak away]. It's not good to smoke a man's crack and not ask no questions. I don't care how nice he seems to you, . . . it's about finding out how many strings are attached to that piece of crack that you're going to put into your lungs. I learned that the hard way. I seen a female been put over a meat hook over a $5 crack rock, 'cause she didn't want to give up no pussy.

Overall length of experience in the sex trade was unrelated to experiencing date violence, but women who were victimized had, on average, a few years less experience working in Miami. Victimized women had about 60% more paying partners, but earned about the same money from sex work as others, again suggesting that relative economic desperation is an important factor in making poor judgments about which dates are "safe."

Victimization by dates was far more common among women who worked on or very near to the main stroll. This observation from the interview data was fed back into the focus group discussions to determine why working the Boulevard proper—a wide, well-lighted, and busy street—would entail more risk of violence from dates than quieter streets. Part of the explanation lies in interaction effects. Boulevard workers were more likely to be White, to have more paying partners, and to be homeless. In addition, Boulevard workers had less experience working in Miami than other women; respondents attributed this to the notoriety of the strip, the proximity of the bus terminal, and the availability of cheap temporary housing and homeless service agencies.

But focus group members who work the main stroll also said that the Boulevard "is infamous for girls, and most of the girls out here are on drugs, and most will go into a car and pretty much do whatever [the dates] want." Boulevard workers agreed that the strip's reputation brought out dates who are "mostly wackos—psycho kinds where you wonder if they are the ones who leave bodies in the dumpster." One woman described a recent experience with a date she saw on a regular basis:

It was like five in the morning, and we could not find a place to date, so we went by the railroad tracks. Out of nowhere he just flipped on me. I mean he gave me a beating that I never would wish on anyone. And we are talking about a big guy. He just focused on one side of my head . . . just boom, boom, boom. I figured if I just would have closed my eyes I would have died, but you know you never know that inner strength that you have in you. You know, "You are not going to take me out." By the time I got away from him, my head was like a mountain, it was all lumpy. I couldn't eat for a month.

Not all of the women who work at some distance from the Boulevard agreed, however; they said that danger for sex workers was everywhere. A respondent who works traditionally poor neighborhoods west of the Boulevard said:

Those guys don't really expect to pay much money. And a lot of them, are not expecting to pay any money at all. So you've got a good chance of getting raped in those areas. They pay the money up front and take it away from you later. They'll put their hands around your neck and say, "Give me my money back!" Or they'll pull a gun or a knife. And they get their money back. Of course you're going to give the money back and get out of the car and hopefully not die.

The analyses also suggest that women who engage in nontraditional sex acts are more likely to experience violence. Although this might indicate that dates who ask for unconventional sex are also violent men, all focus group participants maintained that such dates are actually safer, overall, than other customers. As one Latina put it,

Actually, they are nice. Less violent. I have this guy that likes for me to hit him in the balls, okay? And he's the sweetest man in the whole world. I don't see him anymore because the last time he wanted me to cut him. I don't do that, but [I said] I'd get him somebody who would. But I know these guys are actually nicer.

Such dates—that is, men who most of the respondents said were the safest kind—are reportedly older, White, and wealthier. Two possible explanations may be relevant here. First, willingness of the sex worker to participate in unconventional sex may be yet another sign of relative desperation and lack of selectivity over date choice rather than an indication that violence is perpetrated by these particular dates. Second, African American women were less willing than White women to engage in exotic sexual practices, but their reservations were on grounds of aesthetic or moral disgust rather than danger. By this latter interpretation, willingness to perform unconventional sex may be a proxy for ethnicity and bear a spurious relationship to victimization; Black women's greater street smarts and their reputation on the street for fighting back if attacked may mark the real difference from White women in their relative safety from date violence.

Several other sex work practices were strongly associated with being physically attacked by dates; these include picking up dates in the street or in bars or clubs, having sex with dates in cars, getting in a car with a date, and not knowing the destination where the sex services would be provided. The focus groups were quite helpful in illuminating why these practices were so dangerous. All of them reduced the sex worker's level of control over the interaction with the date. Picking up dates in the street, getting in the car with the date, and having sex in the car all diminish the safety otherwise provided by more visible public environments. Street pickups require rapid decision making by both parties; too much time negotiating the transaction risks police action and/or the date being spotted by an acquaintance or a relative. Women who work the Boulevard said that the strip is subject to more regular stings by the police than other sites, forcing them to rush their negotiations and decisions.

Both getting in the date's car and performing the sexual services there—this is associated with many street pickups—gives almost total control to the customer. Twenty-four (8.2%) of the women found themselves locked in a date's car with no safe means of escape during the prior 30 days. One woman described the experience:

> I got in the car with him because I knew him. He wanted to go somewhere I didn't want to go, and I tried to get out of the car. He had no doorknob, the window couldn't let down. I done give him some free hand [job] and some free cookies [vaginal sex] . . . "just don't hurt me." And then his two friends ran out of the bushes. One of them had a wrench in his hand this long [gestures about 2 feet]. They wanted some money. I had no money; I hadn't enough for myself. One of them made me suck his thing, and the other one was gonna have sex with me. I couldn't even suck the man's thing right because I was so scared, lifting my head up. Then next thing I look, the man must have hit me and knocked me out.

One of the more frightening signs of a date going bad is when he drives to an unknown location.

> This good-looking guy pulled up in this nice car, but when he started driving I didn't like know . . . you know, familiarity, where I got my little get out and safety. I didn't know where I'm going to be . . . there's nothing worse. He just pulled the car down a dark alley and turned that car off and then—BOOM!—put that little 38 police special or whatever it was . . . and [he said], "do this, and do that." He got what he wanted.

The risks associated with picking up dates in bars, although they are more public places in which decisions must not be rushed, was attributed by the focus group participants to the effects of alcohol on a date's sexual performance and aggression. Often the violence women experienced emerged from the intoxicated date's frustration at being unable to achieve an erection or to ejaculate:

> A guy that's been smoking [crack], he will say, after a while, he can't cum. He's like, "okay, alright, thank you." But then I got into a car with a drunk, and he was like, "I'm going to cum, I'm going to cum," and you know, he refuses. . . . You end up with black jaw (bruises on the mouth). Drunks are more likely to get nasty; they are very violent. It's not about the money, they are just more violent.

Alternatively, women who pick up dates in public places such as bus stops, convenience stores, laundromats, and gas stations tended to be less likely to experience violence, although not all such findings were statistically significant. It is important to note here that most women who did not exclusively pick up dates in the street identified multiple types of places to work, making these data somewhat difficult to interpret. Nevertheless, focus group participants verified the increased danger associated with working the street or in bars, as well as the increased safety provided by well-lighted sites frequented by the general public.

It was also found that working while high on crack or heroin significantly increased women's risk for victimization by dates, even when they did not become aggressive or "rush the date"—that is, giving him little time to get an erection and ejaculate. Although a few focus group members argued that their judgment of dates was actually enhanced by a crack high, most said that being high impaired their ability to be selective, to negotiate properly, and to maintain control over the sex trade. One experienced crack user explained, "If I'm all high on crack, I feel like they can take advantage of me. I can't talk right, and I'm not thinking straight. I'm worried about the police." A second echoed the thought:

> I can't go out there like that exactly. I'm nervous. I feel like everyone else is high. I slip, or find that I will get real bold; I will take a chance. Just to get the money, I will jump into a car knowing that it might be a cop. I don't care.

As for cues that women believe are key to recognizing potentially violent dates, focus group participants said that younger men and those high on crack or alcohol were not to be trusted. Not only do younger dates have a reputation for being cheap, they are reportedly more emotionally volatile and more likely to become violent. Men who are overly aggressive or vulgar are also to be avoided. Participants were particularly fond of "regulars," usually older men who would sometimes stop by to give the women money without expecting anything in return.

When confronted with a potentially violent situation while dating, focus group participants had several strategies for escape. When riding in the car, red traffic lights could be used strategically as spots for jumping out or, if locked in, attracting the attention of neighboring cars. On the street, one woman suggested that screaming for help usually caused passersby to hurry away from the scene; alternatively, screaming a person's name—she suggested the name John—will not only get passersby to pay attention, thinking that an acquaintance has spotted them, but will also often make the date calm down and perhaps hurry away, fearing that the sex worker may have a protector nearby.

A White heroin user reported using an insanity pretense, telling the date, "I have tried to kill myself four times already, do me a fuckin' favor." Another talked about her children and how much they needed her. Others had successfully escaped by threatening to vomit in the date's car, wielding a weapon, or getting the date so high on drugs that he passed out. Finally, one African American woman offered a strategy that many others agreed had the greatest likelihood of success:

> If they get violent with me (because they can't get an erection or ejaculate), I always blame it on myself. "I'm sorry, I did something wrong. It's not you, okay? You're not the one to blame. But you've got to understand that I got to go out and make more money." So I always blame myself because the men, with that macho stuff inside of them, . . . he's going to say, "Hey, wait a minute! This is not my fault, I can cum with other girls." I blame it on myself first, and you know, [then they say], "You're so nice," and like that.

As a final point here, focus group participants indicated that in the event of a physical assault or rape, regular county and city police were rarely helpful, sometimes even arresting the sex worker for solicitation rather than the date for assaulting her. The women reported, however, that the sex crimes units of police departments were more responsive to sex workers' physical and emotional needs and more likely to help them press charges.

Discussion

Many of the findings of this study are either entirely new to the literature or confirm aspects of the very few existing ethnographic works on this topic. It should be noted that the eligibility criteria for this study include both sex work and heavy drug use, so that the strength of associations between these two variables cannot be examined using our data. This aspect and the social geographies specific to Miami and to Biscayne Boulevard limit our ability to generalize our findings to other sex worker populations. In addition, Miami's subtropical climate provides an environment for sex work that includes numerous opportunities for year-round performance of sexual services in outdoor public locales. Nevertheless, we believe that the behavioral predictors of date violence found here are very likely to apply to other women who perform street-based sex work.

With a sample size larger than those seen in most studies of street-based sex workers, the data presented here confirm the intimate association of street prostitution with childhood abuse, homelessness, drug use, and violence. Given these strong relationships, as well as the lack of power women have in transacting sexual services and obtaining protection from the legal authorities, our data present a strong case for finding ways to empower, rather than blame, women sex workers. We dispute any suggestion that sex workers are at fault for the violence they receive and suggest that educating women about active techniques that may reduce their exposure to violence is a useful approach. Clearly, effective violence intervention and prevention must also be focused on the perpetrators; however, this was beyond the scope of this women-focused study.

The proportion of our sample who reported incidents of date violence in the prior year (50.7%) is in line with the few other studies that have examined this particular source of victimization. A study of 113 street-based sex workers in New York found that 32.1% had suffered physical or sexual abuse in the prior year (El-Bassel et al., 2001), and a British study of 115 similar women found that 50% had been victimized by a commercial customer in the prior 6 months (Church et al., 2001).

We were surprised to find that White women in our study were at greater risk for date violence than African American women. This finding is supported by related research, however. Although within the general population African American women are more likely to be victimized than White women (Bureau of Justice Statistics, National Crime Victimization Survey, 1998), a recent study of 974 homeless women (of which there is a large overlap with the population in this study) found that African Americans and Latinas were less likely to be victimized than Whites (Wenzel et al., 2001). Similarly, in a study of 171 female crack cocaine users, a smaller percentage of African American than White women had been physically attacked or raped in that past year, although that difference did not reach the .05 level of significance (Falck et al., 2001). As noted earlier, our clients attributed this finding to African American women's less timid relationships with men, as well as their relatively greater street smarts. Clearly, however, all women enmeshed in the context of chronic drug addiction, sex work, and homelessness are extremely vulnerable to violent victimization, regardless of race or ethnicity.

Another surprising finding was that despite their lengthy average time living on the street, few of the women had ever been contacted by an outreach worker from a public health, research, HIV/AIDS, or other human-service agency. Furthermore, the women in this study are largely cut off from the rest of the community, and few are knowledgeable about sources of help. In fact, many of the women who had been raped prior to participating in this intervention research were unaware of the availability of rape crisis centers in the community. What exacerbates their isolation, furthermore, is that sex workers, in general, are not members of a community. Rather, they represent a collection of loosely connected, desperate women with similar circumstances and problems.

Within this context, an important aspect of this research has been to develop harm-reduction approaches for helping street sex workers to identify probable perpetrators of violence and to aid them in reducing their risks of violence. Harm-reduction measures are the foundation of our study design because the majority of our clients lack the financial resources to immediately stop working the streets. Most face substantial barriers to leaving the streets, including a lack of treatment beds, limited social and economic support, and childcare responsibilities.

In this regard, several important correlates of victimization of sex workers by their dates have been identified that may be used in educational outreach efforts. The research suggests that the most important step a sex worker can take to avoid violence is to delay her drug use—to delay it until she is off the street and finished working for the night. This is important for three critical reasons: judgment, control over the date, and self-control. It was found that being high while working reduced women's awareness, frequently resulting in poor date selection and poor negotiation. Being high while working further reduced a sex worker's ability to control the process—as one phrased it, to "watch her four walls." For controlling where the sex services are delivered, what activities are included, and what is going on around her at all times, sobriety is critical. Finally, women who were high while working, especially on crack cocaine, acknowledged that they were more likely to precipitate violent situations because their state of intoxication or their need for more drugs caused them to rush the date. As such, delaying drug use until after the sex worker has earned enough money for the night appears to be a critically important strategy for reducing date violence.

Unfortunately, this may be one of the most difficult strategies to implement because many women report being unable to engage in sex work without using drugs. Nevertheless, women in our focus groups and other clients who have left sex work confirm that delaying drug use is the most important step toward both physical safety and life off the street. Crack users expressed greater self-efficacy in accomplishing this than heroin users, as their physical need for drugs was more manageable. However, a number of heroin users reported being able to time their working hours to coincide with their most coherent and vigilant hours of the day.

A second factor in reducing the likelihood for victimization is choosing the most public location possible for having sex with the date. The data in this study suggest that having sex in the date's car is highly associated with victimization, because of the kinds of dates who choose to have sex there and the relatively high level of privacy afforded. Respondents suggested that getting out of the car to perform sex services—for example, in between parked cars, in public parking lots, or among bushes or trees—is preferable because they can be heard by passersby if something goes wrong.

A third line of approach to reducing sex worker victimization involves increasing their defenses. The sharing of street knowledge among sex workers is an important aspect of self-defense. Although many of the respondents were reluctant to carry weapons because of fear of complications on arrest, whistles and other attack prevention devices can be helpful in times of crisis. Some focus group participants also suggested that self-defense courses would be helpful to them. Finally, the women in this study said that it is best never to carry money or drugs on the street while working, because possession of these increases the likelihood of being ripped off or assaulted. The findings from these preliminary analyses have been fed back into the intervention program, and future follow-ups should provide some idea of their potential effectiveness.

In terms of a research agenda, this study suggests, as others also have, that research on customers of sex workers would be quite helpful in better understanding the problem of date violence. Although such research may not help to specify a "violent date" profile, ethnographic accounts of dates' violent interactions with sex workers would aid in understanding the circumstances that precede such events. Unfortunately, the lack of prosecution of dates makes them even harder to reach than sex workers themselves. Local advertisements with cash incentives for interviews with such men may be one avenue for targeting this population.

Finally, from a public policy perspective, it is imperative that basic legal protections for sex workers be implemented. As women without resources of any sort, sex workers, such as those studied here, have no recourse for redressing victimization as long as law enforcement authorities are reluctant to address the problem of date violence. In addition to being unable to press charges against dates and others who physically or sexually assault them, sex workers are harmed by the failure of law enforcement agencies to even collect reliable reports of violence against them. As reported here, significant differences were found in victimization in different working locations, but there was no way that these findings could be buttressed with police reports. A recent study (Lowman, 2000) that documented differences in murder rates across strolls in Vancouver noted that lesser crimes against sex workers went unreported even in a city in which prostitution is legal. Such knowledge would be invaluable to social service agencies interested in helping this population avoid violence.

Discussion Questions

1. The women in the study prefer the terms "sex worker" to "prostitute" and "dates" to "johns." What is the basis for this preference? What do labels mean in terms of self-image?

2. What factors have resulted in fewer pimps in the sex work industry in Miami? Why?

3. What sex work practices increase women's chances of being victimized? How might women avoid these circumstances?

4. What is the relationship between "getting high" and performing as a sex worker? Is it more than simply obtaining enough money to buy drugs?

5. How do black and white women differ with respect to sex worker victimization?

References

Allman, T. D. (1987). *Miami: City of the future*. New York: Atlantic Monthly Press.

Baseman, J., Ross, M., & Williams, M. (1999). Sale of sex for drugs and drugs for sex: An economic context of sexual risk behaviors for STDs. *Sexually Transmitted Diseases, 26*, 444–449.

Bourgois, P., & Dunlap, E. (1993). Exorcising sex-for-crack: An ethnographic perspective from Harlem. In M. S. Ratner (Ed.), *Crack pipe as pimp; An ethnographic investigation of sex-for-crack exchanges* (pp. 97–132). New York: Lexington.

Boyle, S. (1994). *Working girls and their men*. London: Smith Gryphon.

Bureau of Justice Statistics, National Crime Victimization Survey. (1998). *Criminal victimization 1997: Changes 1996–1997 with trends 1993–1997* (NJC 173385). Washington, DC: U.S. Department of Justice.

Carole. (1998), Interview with Debra. In E. Delacoste & P. Alexander (Eds.), *Sex work: Writings by women in the sex industry* (2nd ed., pp. 91–95). San Francisco: Cleis.

Church, S., Henderson, M., Barnard, M., & Hart, G. (2001). Violence by clients towards female prostitutes in different work settings: Questionnaire survey. *British Medical Journal, 322*, 524–525.

Coston, C. T. M., & Ross, L. E. (1998). Criminal victimization of prostitutes: Empirical support for the lifestyle/exposure model. *Journal of Crime and Justice, 21*, 53–70.

Davis, N. J. (2000). From victims to survivors: Working with recovering street prostitutes. In R. Weitzer (Ed.), *Sex for sale: Prostitution, pornography, and the sex industry* (pp. 139–158). New York: Routledge.

Delacoste, E., & Alexander, P. (Eds.). (1998). *Sex work: Writings by women in the sex industry* (2nd ed.). San Francisco: Cleis.

El-Bassel, N., Schilling, R. F., Irwin, K. L., Faruque, S., Gilbert, L., Von Bargen, J., et al. (1997). Sex trading and psychological distress among women recruited from the streets of Harlem. *American Journal of Public Health, 87*, 66–70.

El-Bassel, N., Witte, S. S., Wada, T., Gilbert, L., & Wallace, J. (2001). Correlates of partner violence among female street-based sex workers: Substance abuse, history of childhood abuse, and HTV risks. *AIDS Patient Care and STDs, 15*, 41–51.

Erickson, P. G., Butters, J., McGillicuddy, P., & Hallgren, A. (2000). Crack and prostitution: Gender, myths, and experiences. *Journal of Drug Issues, 30*, 767–788.

Falck, R. S., Wang, J., Carlson, R. G., & Siegal, H. A. (2001). The epidemiology of physical attack and rape among crack-using women. *Violence and Victims, 16*, 79–89.

Farley, M., & Barkan, H. (1998). Prostitution, violence and posttraumatic stress disorder. *Women and Health, 27*, 37–49.

Fortes, A., & Stepick, A. (1993). *City on the edge: The transformation of Miami*. Berkeley: University of California Press.

Gidycz, C. A., Coble, C. N., Latham, L., & Layman, M. J. (1993). Sexual assault experience in adulthood and prior victimization experiences: A prospective analysis. *Psychology of Women Quarterly, 17*, 151–168.

Gilbert, L., El-Bassel, N., Rajah, V., Foleno, A., & Frye, V. (2001). Linking drug-related activities with experiences of partner violence: A focus group study of women in methadone treatment. *Violence and Victims, 16*, 517–536.

Hoigard, C., & Finstad, L. (1986). *Backstreets: Prostitution, money and love*. University Park: Pennsylvania State University Press.

Inciardi, J. A. (1986). *The war on drugs: Heroin, cocaine, crime, and public policy.* Palo Alto, CA: Mayfleld.

——. (1993). Kingrats, chicken heads, slow necks, freaks, and blood suckers: A glimpse at the Miami sex-for-crack market. In M. Ratner (Ed.), *Crack pipe as pimp: An ethnographic investigation of sex-far-crack exchanges* (pp. 37–68). New York: Lexington Books.

Inciardi, J. A., Lockwood, D., & Pottieger, A. E. (1993). *Women and crack cocaine.* New York: Macmillan.

Inciardi, J. A., & Surratt, H. L. (2001). Drug use, street crime, and sex-trading among cocaine-dependent women: Implications for public health and criminal justice policy. *Journal of Psychoactive Drugs, 33*, 379–389.

Karen. (1998). Police as pimps. In F. Delacoste & P. Alexander (Eds.), *Sex work: Writings by women in the sex industry* (2nd ed., p. 58). San Francisco: Cleis.

Lowman, J. (2000). Violence and the outlaw status of (street) prostitution in Canada. *Violence Against Women, 6*, 987–1011.

Maher, L. (1997). *Sexed work: Gender, race and resistance in a Brooklyn drug market.* Oxford: Clarendon.

Maxwell, S. R., & Maxwell, C. D. (2000). Examining the "criminal careers" of prostitutes within the nexus of drug use, drug selling, and other illicit activities. *Criminology, 38*, 787–809.

McCoy, H. V., McCoy, C. B., & Lai, S. (1998). Effectiveness of HIV interventions among women drug users. *Women and Health, 27*, 49–66.

McCoy, H. V., McKay, C. Y., Hermanns, L., & Lai, S. (1990). Sexual behavior and the risk of HIV infection. *American Behavioral Scientist, 33*, 432–450.

McCoy, C. B., Miles, C., & Metsch, L. R. (1999). The medicalization of discourse within an AIDS research setting. In W. N. Elwood (Ed.), *Power in the blood* (pp. 39–50). Mahwah, NJ: Lawrence Erlbaum.

McCoy, C. B., Rivers, J. E., & Khoury, E. L. (1993). An emerging public health model for reducing AIDS-related risk behavior among injecting drug users and their sexual partners. *Drugs and Society, 7*, 143–159.

McKegany, N., & Bernard, M. (1992). *AIDS, drugs and sexual risk: Lives in the balance.* Buckingham, UK: Open University Press.

Miller, E. M. (1986). *Street woman.* Philadelphia: Temple University Press.

Miller, J., & Schwartz, M. D. (1995). Rape myths and violence against street prostitutes. *Deviant Behavior, 16*, 1–23.

Monto, M. A., & Hotaling, N. (2001). Predictors of rape myth acceptance among male clients of female street prostitutes. *Violence Against Women, 7*, 275–293.

O'Neill, M., & Barberet, R. (2000). Victimization and the social organization of prostitution in England and Spain. In R. Weitzer (Ed.), *Sex for sale: Prostitution, pornography, and the sex industry* (pp. 123–138). New York: Routledge.

Phoenix, J. (2000). Prostitute identities: Men, money and violence. *British Journal of Criminology, 40*, 37–55.

Ratner, M. (Ed.). (1993). *Crack pipe as pimp: An ethnographic investigation of sex-for-crack exchanges.* New York: Lexington.

Reiff, D. (1987). *Going to Miami: Exiles, tourists, and refugees in the new America.* Boston: Little, Brown.

Silbert, M. H., & Pines, A. M. (1983). Early sexual exploitation as an influence in prostitution. *Social Work, 28*, 285–289.

Sterk, C. E., & Elifson, K. W. (1990). Drug-related violence and street prostitution. In M. De La Rosa, E. Y. Lambert, & B. Cropper (Eds.), *NIDA Research Monograph Series #103* (pp. 208–221). Rockville, MD: National Institutes on Drug Abuse.

Teets, J. M. (1997). The incidence and experience of rape among chemically dependent women. *Journal of Psychoactive Drugs, 29*, 331–336.

U.S. Department of Labor, Bureau of the Census. (1999). *County and city data book.* Washington, DC: U.S. Government Printing Office.

Wenzel, S. L., Leake, B. D., & Gelberg, L. (2001). Risk factors for major violence among homeless women. *Journal of Interpersonal Violence, 16*, 739–752.

Williamson, C., & Folaron, G. (2001). Violence, risk, and survival strategies of street prostitution. *Western Journal of Nursing Research, 23*, 463–475.

Young, A. M., Boyd, C., & Hubbell, A. (2000). Prostitution, drug use, and coping with psychological distress. *Journal of Drug Issues, 30*, 789–800.

Adapted from: Steven P. Kurtz, Hilary L. Surratt, James A. Inciardi, and Marion C. Kiley, "Sex Work and 'Date' Violence." In *Violence Against Women*, 10 (4): 357–385. Copyright © 2004 by Sage Publications. Used with permission. ✦

15
The Entanglement of Agency, Violence, and Law in the Lives of Women in Prostitution

Lisa E. Sanchez

Women in prostitution remain among the most marginalized of all women. Operating in the shadows of the law and social life, they are both active participants in illicit sexual activities and frequent victims of physical and sexual assault. Yet the complex entanglement of agency and victimization in the everyday lives of women in prostitution remains widely unacknowledged in law and culture. "Agency" refers to the response of law enforcement to the will of the community, in this case, in the arrest of prostitutes. Feminist scholars have proposed that a more contextualized and gender-specific theory of women's crime and punishment must start from the position of those women who are most marginalized in society. It is within the spirit of recent feminist studies that contest these forms of marginalization and seek to complicate rather than reinforce the dichotomy between victimization and offending that this chapter resides. The author's analysis of the intersection of agency and victimization in the lives of five women involved in prostitution is drawn from a broader ethnographic study conducted with prostitutes, their customers, and police officers in one American city over a five-year period.

This chapter explores the relationship between agency and victimization among women involved in prostitution through an interpretation of the everyday life narratives of five women in "Evergreen." Although the sample of participants is limited, the ethnographic method I use places participants' stories within the dynamics of the geographic and social contexts in which their activities take place. As such, it paints a more complex picture of everyday life experiences and provides a more solid interpretational framework for reconceptualizing women's law-breaking experiences.

All five of the women whose testimonies I will discuss were involved in street prostitution. They ranged in age from 18 to 34 at the time of these interviews. With the exception of one woman, who began prostitution in her mid-20s, all turned their first "date"[1] while they were still teenagers. One of them was initially compelled into prostitution by a boyfriend, who she eventually identified as a pimp. Another began working for an escort service but later turned to street prostitution. The most consistent factors influencing these women's initial involvement in prostitution include age, socioeconomic position, strained interpersonal and family relationships, drug use, exposure to the sex trade via informal social networks and geographic location, and basic needs, such as housing, food, and clothing. Only one of the women in this study had stable housing at the time of her initial involvement in prostitution, one stayed with her grandparents on occasion, and the remaining three frequented motels and "flop houses," searching daily for a place to stay. The unemployment rate in Evergreen is 16 percent for young women age 16 to 20, as compared to 7 percent on the average for all Evergreen residents who can be counted by the Census Bureau. Each of those women had struggled to support herself for an extended period of time, and some had worked jobs in the mainstream economy, but these "straight jobs" did not pay well enough for the women to support themselves on that income alone.

Drug use was also a significant factor shaping women's involvement in prostitution. Three of these young women were addicted to heroin and sometimes used cocaine and methamphetamine as well. One other participant used cocaine on occasion and one was drug-free. Each of these women used alcohol, though none of them appeared or claimed to be addicted to alcohol. For some of these women, drug use came at a significant financial and personal cost, drawing much of their time, energy, and money into supporting their drug habit, procuring and using drugs, and recovering from their drug use. For these women, however, drug use and prostitution did not take shape as a simple cause-and-effect relationship. Only one of these women claimed that she began prostitution to support her drug habit. Others began using drugs to cope with the risks and insults of prostitution, and others stayed away from drugs completely or kept their drug use to a minimum. However, all women claimed that using drugs or finding some other way to alter their consciousness, at least temporarily, made the experience of prostitution more manageable.

A remarkable illustration of the contradictions between women's agency and their victimization was expressed in one of the first interviews I conducted in the field. "Cory's" road to involvement in prostitution began at age 14, when she left home. Describing a physically and sexually abusive relationship with her stepfather, Cory said, "I was just old enough that I had some options. Just old enough to go out and make a choice." Shortly thereafter, Cory met and moved in with "Mike," whom she described as a "speed cook."[2] With Mike's "help," Cory became addicted to speed and later began using heroin to help her come down from her speed high (regular users of speed report staying awake for one to two weeks at a time).

At age 17, addicted to speed and heroin, Cory began walking the streets of Evergreen after her boyfriend kicked her out of the house. As she put it,

I first got involved in prostitution by myself. I couldn't take care of the habit I had any more . . . but I didn't know how much they charged or where to go. So . . . I went down to this one area and just walked and walked before I got brave enough to realize who was stopping and who wasn't stopping.

She explained that even though she got "screwed over" a lot at first, she always met a few people who were "concerned" for her: "They were mostly the guys I dated, told me how to do it."

Cory's explanation that she got involved in prostitution both by herself *and* with the assistance of the guys she met who "told [her] how to do it" highlights the copresent quality of these paid sexual exchanges. *Copresent* interactions refer to face-to-face or bodily interactions in which two or more people interact in the same physical space and time. The copresent interactions of prostitution differ from constructions of such activities as *rational actions* or *individual choices* because the presence of two active bodies requires negotiation of the desires and intentions of each interacting party and because power differentials between the two interacting parties influence outcomes in a way that favors the more powerful party (see, for example, Boden and Molotch 1994; Giddens 1979; Goffman 1969; and Sanchez 1997, 1999). While Cory did not and could not

have engaged in prostitution in social isolation, she refrained from characterizing her involvement as a form of forced sexual abuse or "sexual slavery,"[3] stating that she "did what [she] had to do."

Cory: You just kinda keep going and make yourself do it because when you got 50 dollars in your hand, all of the sudden, now you know tomorrow you're not gonna be sick [from heroin withdrawal]. So, it makes it pretty easy to go back out. Until you get hurt. Then the first time you get hurt, you get scared when you go back out.

LS.: Have you been hurt before?

Cory: Yeah. Raped, getting beat up and stuff.

LS.: How often would you say that happened?

Cory: Probably a hundred times. The hurt just kinda goes along with it. Getting stranded, having your clothes stolen, having your money stolen, robbed at gunpoint, whatever, all of that. Just hurt.

In Cory's experience, agency and victimization are inseparably linked. Agency surfaces in her narrative as an expression of "practical consciousness." By practical consciousness I mean talk that focuses on "making do" or "doing what has to be done" (de Certeau 1984; Garfinkel 1967; Giddens 1979). The language of practical consciousness is a way of expressing what one does under conditions she would not otherwise "choose," while violence is represented as that part of experience that is unexpected and out of her locus of control. Having become involved in prostitution, Cory's everyday practices involved not only active and copresent participation in illicit sexual activities but also an understanding of how to resist violence. But it is important to remember that basic necessities and physical addictions motivated Cory's participation in prostitution. She understood her activities not as a "free choice" but as a way to get by or make do. This does not mean, however, that she voluntarily consented to everything that happened, as many customers, police officers, and community members assume.

Cory's description of an assault and attempted rape shows how the spatial context of prostitution as framed by conditions of illegality and gender inequality can benefit customers. As Cory explained, a man picked her up in his car and wanted to have sex with her, but she refused because, in her words, "the guy was sketchy." When she asked the man to drop her off where he had picked her up, he pulled a knife on her and attempted to rape her:

> He had the knife right up against my neck. The guy got pissed off at me because I wouldn't shut the fuck up, you know, which was probably stupid, but I was just pushin' as hard as I could push, and I just wanted to get out of there. He was goin' "No, no, no, give it up, give it up," and I was saying, "Get away from me" . . . and I had like maybe a dozen little poke holes that I wasn't aware of at that time, but I could feel it. Finally he just got so pissed off that I grabbed the door handle, and he shoved me out on the ground. I was just thinking I wanted to get out of there as fast as I could. I just wanted to get out alive.

Cory's narrative punctuates the felt experience and volatility of these embodied interactions. Her expressed knowledge of how to resist these sorts of attacks further highlights the role of space and the element of time in these interactions:

> You gotta watch 'em close, and if they move or anything or they turn around and face you in the car, you gotta watch out. You know, if they got one hand on the wheel, if they slow down and look at you like this, that's not good—I'm like back against the door handle . . . and you never wanta close your eyes when you're with 'em, never, never, never, because it's just that fast and they've got a knife out and you don't really have too many options too quick.

As Cory put it, "Out here you got a 50–50 chance every time you get in a car. Now you know what *time* that is."

Close attention to the microeffects of practice reveal these paid sexual interactions not as arm's-length contractual arrangements or as forced sexual slavery but as dynamic, copresent, and embodied interactions that are structured by gender inequality and marked with conflict. Cory's narrative emphasizes these points: The potential for violence was always linked to her efforts to "do what [she] had to do."

Similar contradictions between agency and violence emerged in the stories of two teenage girls, "Helen" and "Mary," who had each participated in street prostitution and heroin use for over a year at the time of these interviews. At ages 17 and 18, Helen and Mary had met each other in a psychiatric inpatient clinic and had subsequently run away together both from the clinic and from their families. In one conversation, Helen and Mary began to discuss their vulnerability to violence within their life con-

text. The two girls agreed that Helen was "picked on" more often than Mary because Mary "tells it like it is":

> Mary: I tell 'em if I don't want to do something. I tell them.
>
> Helen: Yeah, I tell them too. But you're more assertive than me.
>
> Mary: I'm very, you know, like they push your head down when you start a blowjob or something, I say, "No." I can't handle it being forced or manhandled.

It was clearly important for Helen and Mary to represent themselves as the authors of their own life experience. But the fact that their actions formed in relation to being "manhandled" or forced to perform sexual acts in ways that they did not expect highlights the centrality of violence and coercion in shaping the girls' understandings of what it means to participate actively in prostitution. A conversation between the girls about a situation in which Mary was raped illustrates the degree to which routine subjection to violence shaped daily life and contributed to the girls' desensitization to their own victimization.

> Mary: There was this one time I was raped. It's been quite a while actually.
>
> Helen: Yeah, but he didn't really, I mean he just barely got in you.
>
> Mary: Helen woke up and helped me out. I was sleeping.
>
> Helen: Then she woke up and he was in her. Then we just left. He crashed, passed out, and we stole twenty bucks from him. We just did it 'cuz of what he did. We didn't really need the money.
>
> Mary: Well, he deserved it.
>
> Helen: In a way he paid for it too.
>
> LS: Was he one of your dates or just some guy you were hanging out with?
>
> Mary: No, he was just drunk . . . or he was . . .
>
> Helen: No, he was not. I thought he was a date.

Helen and Mary debated over whether this man had been a "date" or just some guy who "wanted to party." Then Helen decided that he was "just drunk." Turning her attention to Mary, Helen said, "He picked us up and took us to a Holiday Inn. He seemed nice, too. Then he just turned on you. He wasn't being violent. He was just really horny and he took advantage of you." Casually, Mary replied, "He ordered some pizza."

What is most striking about Helen and Mary's matter-of-fact representation of these events is that in the space of a few hours, a number of extraordinary events (represented as ordinary) had taken place. The girls had been picked up by an older man with the means to rent a hotel room, and they had "partied" with this man and fallen asleep, at which time Mary was raped. They then stole $20 and left the room only to return to the city streets in the middle of the night. Yet there was some confusion between the girls about their role in these exchanges and about whether Mary had "really" been raped. But the girls' concurrence that stealing $20 from this man was justified indicates that they had a sense that this man had mistreated them, and both of them took comfort in what *they did* to rectify the situation. Although the men that Helen and Mary dated probably perceived their sexual involvement with these two young girls as an expression of sexual desire, the girls experienced these interactions as violent and coercive. In spite of their mutually undisputed understanding of their overall role as active agents in prostitution, they described their activities as, in a word, "survival."

The kinds of experiences Helen and Mary described were not uncommon among the women who participated in this study: for every negotiation that went smoothly, the possibility that the next one would end in violence or conflict was great. The examples of active participation in prostitution represented here cannot be interpreted as freely chosen "sex work," nor can they be interpreted as the blanket enforcement of sexual slavery. Rather, these young women's articulation of their experiences suggests that acts of prostitution take shape as practically oriented sexual interactions and as tactics of resistance within the violent and unpredictable spaces of the Evergreen sex trade.

Some of the young women were initially compelled into prostitution by a pimp. At age 12, "Meagan" was "hanging out downtown" when she met a guy who later became her boyfriend: "Here was this older guy telling me he loved me, and that made me feel secure. I finally realized he was a pimp after about one month. People told me." Meagan then went on to detail how her "boyfriend" eventually convinced her to start turning dates:

Meagan: [Darryl] needed some money and asked if I would work, and I said no. Finally I said I'd try once, so his brother's girlfriend took me out. I didn't know how much to charge, so I came back with too little money, and he beat me up severely.

LS: How much did you get?

Meagan: Ninety dollars. I didn't want to leave him and the security I had. But he changed. He became highly controlling. I couldn't talk to anyone. . . . The beatings still occurred; he would get mad for no reason. I had to go in the hospital twice. I was 14 by that time.

Meagan's discussion of a rape that she was subjected to underlines some of the same kinds of conflicts that surfaced in the other girls' lives. Describing two different occasions in which she was raped, Meagan stated that the first man was "nice" and "didn't intend to hurt [her]," but she described the second experience as a "violent rape":

This other man who raped me, he raped me violently. He had a gun, and then afterwards he told me he was sorry. "I'm so sorry." He dropped me off and I went to the hospital and I was all beat up.

Unlike what Cory described, Meagan thought she would be better off just to "get it over with." She did, however, attempt to deal with the situation after the fact by reporting it to the police. But, according to Meagan, the police officer told her that it was her own fault and refused to take a report. Having had her claim ignored, Meagan turned to extralegal channels to deal with the problem:

The tables got turned around on him though at the end, because I did get his license plate number [even though] no one [referring to the police] listened to me. I had a guy [customer] that worked at the DMV and I had this man's license plate number and I found out where he was at and, you know, beat him up. That made me feel better.

The legal construction of women in prostitution as "offenders" who are unrapable by virtue of their involvement in prostitution had serious consequences for Meagan. Paralleling the testimonies of the other women who participated in this study, Meagan emphasized what she did to handle the situation. She foregrounded what was within her control, while the violent and coercive context of prostitution and the legal practices that facilitated her abuse remained in the background, framing her every action.

As a final illustration of the entanglement of agency and violence in these women's everyday lives, I turn to a story provided by "Amanda," who was the oldest, most experienced, and probably least marginalized individual who participated in this study. Amanda was working as a secretary when the owner of an escort service asked whether she would be interested in taking some clients. Amanda expressed her opinion of prostitution using a language of sexual liberation and free choice: "If two consenting people want to do that and it's comfortable for both of them, so be it." However, as our conversation progressed, Amanda's articulation of her own reasons for becoming involved in prostitution unfolded as deeply rooted in violence:

> When I was raped at gunpoint, this was a way for me to get men to give me their money for me having the control. [So you thought of it that way?] That's right, revenge. It's like, you want it, you pay for it, I'll tell you when, I'll tell you how, I'll tell you why.

For Amanda, active participation in prostitution was a kind of payback or "revenge" against men who had previously abused her.

The practices described in the foregoing narrative analysis involve bodily contact and cannot be reduced to a single moment of choice. They are better understood as a series of copresent, embodied interactions negotiated and renegotiated for the duration of each interaction. Although women frequently use a language of choice to describe their actions, their narratives are shaped by their social and economic situation, by the context of practice, by legal/regulatory practices, and by the desires and demands of their customers. Although the women in this study each represented themselves as active participants in prostitution, they do not "choose" many of the interactions that took place, nor do they "choose" the conditions under which the actions occurred. Under these conditions, the women who participated in this study at best negotiated an interaction that satisfied their instrumental needs and the emotional and physical desires of their customers. Often, however, agency in these interactions played out as active resistance and survival tactics.

Policing Identities, Policing Space

In this section, I look at the legal construction and imposition of the prostitute identity and question the separation of agency and violence into mutually exclusive categories by analyzing the everyday practices of Evergreen police officers. The Evergreen Metropolitan Police Bureau distributes specific prostitution enforcement duties to patrol, prostitution detail, and vice. Each neighborhood is patrolled by a different precinct within the bureau, and individual precincts occasionally conduct "prostitution missions" in their area. Prostitution detail officers and street patrol officers in each precinct handle the day-to-day enforcement of prostitution and prostitution procure-

ment, and the vice division investigates cases of promoting and compelling prostitution. Detail and patrol officers can arrest women for prostitution procurement if the women have taken significant action toward procuring prostitution, meaning they have been spotted flagging down cars, hitchhiking, lingering at phone booths and street corners, or walking the street alone in a "high vice" area. If a woman makes an explicit offer to exchange sex acts for money, she can be charged with prostitution (city ordinance, police interview, 4/97).

I have intentionally chosen to use the feminine subject to describe the target of police officers' enforcement practices. In my conversations and ride-alongs with police officers, many described their enforcement of the law prohibiting *prostitution procurement* in explicitly gendered terms, but they did not seem to understand their practices as unfair and even unlawful gender discrimination. In everyday conversation, police officers rationalized their enforcement practices, claiming that "women *walking* the street" were more visible and more likely to be the subject of a "citizen complaint" (field conversations, 3/97, 8/97). One officer even stated that "prostitution procurement applies just to the girls, whereas the guy gets a prostitution charge" (police interview, 3/97). Though the procurement ordinance is worded in gender neutral terms, most officers refrain from enforcing the law against male customers because men's solicitation practices—*driving* up and down the same street in a privately owned car—are seen as more elusive than women's solicitation practices.

The officers viewed these unevenly gendered enforcement practices as innocuous because, after all, the men get a prostitution charge. But procurement is the more frequently used charge, since prostitution is presumably harder to prove. By police officers' own accounts of their practices, procurement is thought to be an easy charge but only if the subject of the charge is a woman. In addition to treating women's habits of conduct as disproportionately actionable, officers often rely on a woman's prior record of prostitution as testimony to her guilt in the event that she attempts to contest the charge in court. The Evergreen Police Bureau claims gender neutrality in the enforcement of prostitution laws and supports its claim by publicizing arrest statistics gathered in *prostitution missions*, which target female solicitors and male buyers primarily. However, the majority of prostitution arrests come from the *day-to-day enforcement* of prostitution procurement. The same women are often arrested repeatedly for violating the prostitution procurement law, while a vastly larger number of individual men who engage in prostitution never get arrested. Predictably, the bureau rarely publishes statistics on daily arrests for prostitution procurement in the local news media.

From these enforcement practices, we can locate the construction of "suspicious activities" at the intersection of discourses of gender, sexuality, public space, and socioeconomic status. While male customers *driving* the boulevards are arguably just as "visible" as women *walking* the streets, police officers implicitly locate men's activities within the normal range of masculine conduct; such practices are perceived as natural expressions of masculinity and sexual desire. As one officer stated, "It's a quick, easy deal [for men who have a] high sex drive." Continuing, he explained that these men often have "personal problems and dysfunctional sexual relationships with their wives; 85 percent want blowjobs and their wife won't do it." Male customers are further privileged by the mobility and privacy that property ownership—in this case, ownership of a car—signifies. While the officers believe they have to catch a man "in the act" or have tight evidence of an explicit offer to enforce the law, their practices more realistically reflect the power differential between these marginalized women and male customers, who have the status and resources to contest questionable police practices.

The language police officers use to describe their enforcement practices makes explicit their unself-consciously gendered construction of prostitution. Male customers are viewed as nameless, faceless bodies while the bodies of the women are inscribed with the prostitute identity. This is not just a matter of semantics. Police practices operate quite concretely as surveillance and record keeping practices directed specifically at the women. For example, prostitution detail officers keep a book with them during their patrol that contains the names, addresses, telephone numbers, birth dates, and partial information on the criminal record of women with prior prostitution convictions. During a ride-along, a detail officer proudly claimed that he was the best person for the job because he was the "most knowledgeable" officer on the force—he had a "great memory for names, faces, and birth dates" (field conversation, 8/97). When asked whether he used the same techniques to monitor male customers, the officer said he didn't keep records on the customers because "to do Johns, you have to have decoys." In other words, customers can only be arrested during prostitution missions. Continuing, the officer added, "If I stop a man just because he has a prostitute in his car, he would deny it and say that he was only giving the girl a ride" (8/97). By contrast, the officer claimed that the woman could not deny it: "Even if they deny it, they know I know what they're doing."

Additionally, the precincts and the vice division keep a book of mug shots of women who have been convicted of procurement or prostitution within the previous few years. Although the police encourage citizens to take photographs of men thought to be engaging in prostitution, these photographic records are not maintained on file in the bureau. Rather, the act of taking a man's photograph is thought to deter him from further involvement in prostitution (police interviews, 3/97, 8/97, neighborhood association meeting, 8/97). Presumably, male customers are not considered a threat to the community but rather are seen as behaving in mischievous but predictably understandable masculine ways. Mirroring the unevenly gendered enforcement of late-nineteenth-century statutes prohibiting vagrancy, nightwalking, and disorderly conduct, the contemporary enforcement of legal prohibitions against prostitution is designed to regulate the activities of prostitutes and would-be prostitutes. In essence, these laws are like *status offenses*, making it illegal to be *identified* as a prostitute and to occupy visible public spaces. They are effective visibility-management tools that make nomads out of women in prostitution by requiring them to "keep moving."

Perhaps even more troubling are the discrepancies engendered in the process of taking rape and assault reports. Evergreen police officers sometimes file reports of rape and assault against women who are actively engaged in prostitution when the initial call comes from a hospital or social service agency, or when the crime can be linked to pimping or organized crime (police interviews, 8/97). However, by the officers' own admissions and women's testimonies, the police are far less likely to take a report when the complaint comes directly from the victim. As one women explained,

> I flagged [an officer] down after I had been raped, and he didn't even give me the time of day. He said, "It's your fault you're out here. I've got other things to do than worry about that." I think it's wrong. It's a crime that was committed, and every crime should be looked at the same—just because he was an *honorable* citizen doesn't give him the right to hurt me.

Negative experiences of this sort compound women's problems and make them more reluctant to report physical and sexual assault to the police. The men who pick them up are aware of that fact and frequently take advantage of it. One male customer summarized the situation this way:

> I feel sorry for [these girls] because I have so much and I see that they have nothing. I mean they carry their clothes in a paper sack, and many times they even lose those. One of the girls I know got raped and then thrown out into the road without her clothes, and the only reason [these guys] can get away with it is because no workin' girl is gonna call the cops. So they're preying upon them is what they're doing.

Conclusion

This chapter has focused on the entanglement of agency and victimization in women's illicit lives and livelihoods, and it has critiqued the artificial separation of these two interrelated dimensions of experience into mutually exclusive domains through the imposition of legal identity categories and spatial forms of sex and gender regulation. Legal discourses on prostitution, like those illustrated in field interviews with police officers, oversimplify women's agency and misunderstand the negotiated quality of paid sexual exchanges. My analysis of women's testimonies illustrates that the necessary preconditions for making choices—knowledge, alternatives, power, and safe space—are absent in women's sphere of activity. First, women's material needs act in concert with the demands of customers to draw women into the sex trade and shape their ongoing participation. Second, women's initial involvement and daily practices are not individual, but copresent, embodied interactions. Finally, violence is used routinely as a definitive trump card on women's agency, drawing their energy into avoiding and resisting victimization.

Understanding the copresent quality of sex trade participation sheds light on the conflicted narratives of these women, particularly the tension between their agency and their victimization. While it is clear that women consent to, and in fact initiate, many of their activities, they also face unsolicited pressures and violations on a regular basis. Irrespective of the fact that women acknowledge the routine violence and marginalization in their lives, none of these women represented themselves as passive victims. They are active participants in the process of negotiating sexual interactions and resisting physical and sexual abuse. The fact that women's activities can neither be interpreted as those of a free agent—[n]or as those of a helpless victim is testimony not to women's confusion, but to contradictions that are structured into the practice of prostitution.

The details of these negotiated interactions constitute a particular microstructure of practice whose continuities have to do with power relations and whose disjunctures have to do with the multiple positionings of those involved and the various tactics women use to cope with their situation. Domination of women's personal (bodily) space and the physical space in which prostitution takes place is one of the primary strategies of power used by customers and perpetrators. Importantly, this kind of spatial territoriality is also used by police officers who target women in their enforcement practices. Together, these spatial strategies of sexual regulation reproduce a long history of gender confinement and exclusion that is deeply rooted in American law. A woman can only respond to this kind of power by engaging in tactics of resistance and moving into spaces of secrecy. Paradoxically, the very tactics that women use to resist violence and police surveillance increase their chances of being victimized.

Can a more just strategy be conceived to regulate prostitution? The problem presented by the displaced woman of prostitution is that she faces multiple forms of oppression. She is not simply an offender to be punished or a victim to be recovered. She has no place in the community and no voice in law, politics, or society. To be sure, more just legal practices must recognize the multiple displacements and oppressions she faces. Opening space for women to speak in the public forum provides a good first step toward empowering women in prostitution. A second role for advocates is to provide these women with the tools for subverting the law's power to construct their identity and to limit their access to fundamental legal rights. The criminal justice system has been complicit with the sexual exploitation of these young women, while treating customers with relative impunity. Prostitution laws that criminalize women's status and speech should be challenged on the basis of their constitutionality, and law enforcement practices that facilitate exploitation and abuse should be challenged on the basis of their legitimacy.

Supporting these women's right to bodily integrity does not equate to legitimating broad-scale sexual commodification in legal and deregulated commercial sex markets. Other research has shown that women operating in loosely regulated, ostensibly legal, sex businesses, such as exotic dancing and escort services, are also subject to exploitation and are not necessarily any less victimized (Sanchez 1997). As part of the process of capital accumulation and market specialization, "open markets" of commercial sex lead to accelerated processes of commoditization and sexual exploitation (Sanchez 1997). Under favorable market conditions, the number of sex clubs also tends to increase rapidly; necessitating an increased supply of expendable and marginalized workers (Sanchez 1997). Perhaps a preferable alternative strategy would be to decriminalize or remove the penalties for those who engage in prostitution. Reducing enforcement efforts against women in prostitution would free up resources that could be used to enforce laws prohibiting third-party profiteers from promoting and compelling prostitution. Given these women's stories, some of the men who are considered "customers" are in violation of the laws prohibiting promotion and compelling and would also be subject to arrest. At the same time, police departments and other regulatory agencies need to concentrate on limiting the expansion of legal sex businesses and on controlling the exploitation and abuse of women working in legal sex businesses by regulating employer, *not employee*, practices.

Ideally, these strategies stand to benefit women, but an overly narrow focus on the big legal questions of prohibition, legalization, and decriminalization leaves as unacknowledged, unrepresented, and effectively sacrificed the many women who continue to engage in prostitution under conditions of illegality. As we continue to debate and wait for the big legal question to be resolved, laws prohibiting serious violent crimes are already in place. Knife-point rape, kidnapping, and assault to the point of medical emergency would not be so readily tolerated under any other circumstances, save perhaps the position of prisoners and undocumented workers. When the victim is a "known prostitute," people all too often shrug their shoulders and feel safe in the knowledge that her victimization can be explained by her failure to obey the code of proper feminine sexuality. Thus, perhaps even more immediately, a campaign is needed to pressure law enforcement to engage in more serious efforts to enforce existing laws prohibiting crimes of sexual violence, *even when the victim is a "prostitute" and even when the violence occurs during an act of prostitution.*

Perhaps the hardest question is how to effect movement in the political economy so that women would have more humane and lucrative opportunities to support themselves. Given the continued history of gender and economic subordination, it is unclear what it would take for young, working-class women to participate more fully in the mainstream economy. Economic change has come slowly for older, middle-class women, but young women are already in a position of limited economic citizenship. While it is expected that all girls will be protected and financially supported by their families at least until the age of majority, many poor and working-class girls, like the ones who participated in this study, do not study such reasonable benefits.

In this chapter, I attempted an alternative representation of women's experiences by paying attention to the relationship between agency and violence in the everyday lives of a small group of women. My interpretation should be considered contingent and locally specific, but it may provide a theoretical framework for developing a more contextualized and participatory knowledge of sex trade practices. Identifying sites of resistance to sexual exploitation and discriminatory legal practices can provide a small ray of hope in a generally dark domain. Thus, as researchers and advocates, we can whittle away at small pieces of the larger techniques of power operating in commercial sex markets and their regulatory bodies.

I end this chapter by highlighting women's voices. To quote Amanda:

> There's a really big price to be paid [for some of these offers]. There's a certain level of confidentiality that's necessary, and in those circles, all they do is pass you around. . . . Obviously, the price to be paid is that you have no freedom . . . and they pay you big bucks because you're being paid for your silence.

By far, our most important role is to listen to what this silence tells us.

Endnotes

1. The women in this study use the term "dating" to refer to exchanges of sex acts for money, which is more commonly known as prostitution.

2. A "speed cook" is someone who prepares methamphetamine, also known as speed, crank, or crystal meth, for sale.

3. See, for example, Kathleen Barry's (1979) discussion of prostitution as female sexual slavery. While her book, *Female Sexual Slavery*, represents a groundbreaking study of sexual trafficking and abuse, many of the women involved in prostitution, particularly those operating in Western democratic countries and those operating in their own neighborhoods without a pimp or other third-party profiteer, have re-

jected the characterization of their activities as a form of sexual slavery.

Discussion Questions

1. What are the differences (if any) between the sex workers in the previous reading by Kurtz et al. and the prostitutes that Sanchez studied?

2. What is the connection between drugs and prostitution? How could this connection be interrupted?

3. According to the author, why do many police officers not admit or understand that arrest of prostitutes is not a viable solution?

4. Is arresting sex workers an example of gender discrimination? Defend your answer.

5. What policies or procedures would you suggest to help economically marginalized sex workers avoid detention by the criminal justice system?

References

Adler, F. 1975. *Sisters in Crime*. New York: McGraw-Hill.

Barry, K. 1979. *Female Sexual Slavery*. New York: Basic Books.

Boden, D. and Molotch, H. L. 1994. "The Compulsion of Proximity." In Roger Friedland and Dierdre Boden, eds., *Now Here: Space, Time and Modernity*. Berkeley: University of California Press.

Bumiller, K. 1990. "Fallen Angels: The Representation of Violence Against Women in Legal Culture." *International Journal of the Sociology of Law* 32: 125–42.

Chesney-Lind, M. 1997. *The Female Offender: Girls, Women, and Crime*. Thousand Oaks, CA: Sage.

Collier, J. F., Maurer, B., and Suarez-Navaz, L. 1995. "Sanctioned Identities: Legal Constructions of Modern Personhood." *Identities* 2 (12): 1–27.

Crenshaw, K. 1994. "Mapping the Margins: Intersectionality, Identity Politics, and Violence Against Women of Color." In Martha Albertson Fineman and Roxanne Mykitiuk, eds., *The Public Nature of Private Violence*. New York: Routledge.

Daly, K. 1994. *Gender, Crime and Punishment*. New Haven, CT: Yale University Press.

Daly, K. and Chesney-Lind, M. 1988. "Feminism and Criminology." *Justice Quarterly* 5: 497–538.

Danielson, D. and Engle, K. (eds.) 1995. *After Identity: A Reader in Law and Culture*. New York: Routledge.

de Certeau, M. 1984. *The Practice of Everyday Life*. Los Angeles: University of California Press.

Estrich, S. 1987. *Real Rape*. Cambridge, MA: Harvard University Press.

Fineman, M. A. and Mykitiuk, R. (eds.) 1994. *The Public Nature of Private Violence*. New York: Routledge.

Frohmann, L. 1997. "Convictability and Discordant Locales: Reproducing Race, Class, and Gender Ideologies in Prosecutorial Decision Making." *Law and Society Review* 31: 533–55.

Garfinkel, H. 1967. *Studies in Ethnomethodology*. Englewood Cliffs, NJ: Prentice Hall.

Giddens, A. 1979. *Central Problems in Social Theory: Action, Structure, and Contradictions in Social Analysis*. Berkeley: University of California Press.

Gilfoyle, T. J. 1992. *City of Eros: New York City, Prostitution and the Commercialization of Sex, 1820–1920*. New York: Norton.

Goffman, E. 1969. *Strategic Interaction*. Philadelphia: University of Pennsylvania Press.

Gora, J. 1982. *The New Female Criminal: Empirical Reality or Social Myth*. New York: Praeger.

Hartog, H. 1993. "Abigail Bailey's Coverture: Law in a Married Woman's Consciousness." In Sarat and Kearns, eds., *Law in Everyday Life*. Ann Arbor: The University of Michigan Press.

Hobson, B. M. 1987. *Uneasy Virtue: The Politics of Prostitution in the American Reform Tradition*. New York: Basic Books.

Hooks, b. 1981. *Ain't I a Woman: Black Women and Feminism*. Boston: South End Press.

Kandel, M. 1992. "Whores in Court: Judicial Processing of Prostitutes in the Boston Municipal Court in 1990." *Yale Journal of Law and Feminism* 4: 329–52.

Locke, J. 1689. *Second Treatise of Government*. (C. B. MacPherson, trans.) Indianapolis: Hackett Publishing Company, 1980.

Lucas, A. M. 1995. "Race, Class, Gender and Deviancy: The Criminalization of Prostitution." *Berkeley Women's Law Journal* 10: 47–60.

MacPherson, C. B. 1962. *The Political Theory of Possessive Individualism: Hobbes to Locke*. Oxford, UK: Oxford University Press.

Maher, L. and Curtis, R. 1991. "Women on the Edge of Crime: Crack Cocaine and the Changing Contexts of Street-level Sex Work in New York City." *Crime, Law, and Social Change* 18: 221–58.

Mahoney, M. R. 1994. "Victimization or Oppression? Women's Lives, Violence, and Agency." In Martha Albertson Fineman and Roxanne Mykitiuk, eds., *The Public Nature of Private Violence*. New York: Routledge.

Merry, S. E. 1995. "Narrating Domestic Violence: Producing the 'Truth' of Violence in 19th- and 20th-Century Hawaiian Courts." *Law and Social Inquiry* 19: 967–93.

Messerschmidt, J. W. 1993. *Masculinities and Crime: Critique and Reconceptualization of Theory*. Lanham, MD: Rowman and Littlefield.

Miller, J. 1993. "Your Life Is on the Line Every Time You're on the Streets." *Humanity and Society* 17 (4): 422–442.

Musheno, M. 1995. "Legal Consciousness on the Margins of Society: Struggles Against Stigmatization in the AIDS Crisis." *Identities* 2 (1–2): 101–122.

Pateman, C. 1988. *The Sexual Contract.* Stanford, CA: Stanford University Press.

Perry, R. and Sanchez, L. 1997. "Transactions in the Flesh: Toward an Ethnography of Embodied Sexual Reason." *Studies in Law, Politics and Society* 18: 29–76.

Radin, M. J. 1996. *Contested Commodities.* Cambridge, MA: Harvard University Press.

Rosen, R. 1982. *The Lost Sisterhood: Prostitution in America, 1900–1918.* Baltimore: Johns Hopkins University Press.

Rubin, G. 1984. "Thinking Sex: Notes for a Radical Theory of the Politics of Sexuality." In Carol Vance, ed., *Pleasure and Danger.* New York: Basic Books.

Sanchez, L. E. 1997. "Boundaries of Legitimacy: Sex, Violence, Citizenship, and Community in a Local Sexual Economy." *Law and Social Inquiry* 22 (3): 543–580.

——. 1999. "Sex, Law and the Paradox of Agency in the Everyday Lives of Women in the 'Evergreen' Sex Trade." In Stuart Henry and Dragan Milovanovic, eds., *Constitutive Criminology at Work: Agency and Resistance in the Constitution of Crime and Punishment.* New York: SUNY Press.

Schneider, E. M. 1994. "The Violence of Privacy." In Martha Albertson Fineman and Roxanne Mykitiuk, eds., *The Public Nature of Private Violence.* New York: Routledge.

Steffensmeier, D. J. 1980. "Sex Differences in Patterns of Adult Crime, 1965–1977." *Social Forces* 58: 1080–1108.

Thomas, K. 1995. "Beyond the Privacy Principle." In Dan Danielson and Karen Engle, eds., *After Identity: A Reader in Law and Culture.* New York: Routledge.

Tushnet, M. 1981. *The American Law of Slavery: 1810–1860, Considerations of Humanity and Interest.* Princeton, NJ: Princeton University Press.

Walkowitz, J. R. 1980. *Prostitution and Victorian Society: Women, Class, and the State.* New York: Cambridge University Press.

Williams, P. 1991. *The Alchemy of Race and Rights: Diary of a Law Professor.* Cambridge, MA: Harvard University Press.

16

Homelessness and Temporary Living Arrangements in the Inner-City Crack Culture

Lisa Maher
Eloise Dunlap
Bruce D. Johnson
Ansley Hamid

Impoverished crack-abusing women are usually without a regular place to live, sleep, relax, bathe, eliminate, eat, and store possessions. They therefore go to great lengths to find alternative and temporary living arrangements. This [chapter] draws from a rich descriptive repository of field notes, field diaries, and transcribed tape-recorded data from two ethnographic projects conducted in New York City. These projects spanned seven low-income neighborhoods and included data from a broad sample of women crack users of different ages and racial-ethnic backgrounds who exhibited considerable diversity in terms of their drug use. One study, the Natural History of Crack Distribution/Abuse, is an ethnographic study of 23 African-American women, nine Latinas, and one white woman involving the structure and economics of cocaine and crack distribution in low-income, minority communities. Although these women were active sellers and distributors of crack (and often other drugs), the vast majority were rarely able to afford housing and were usually without a regular conventional place to live.

The second study (Maher 1995) consists of a multisite ethnographic study focusing on the economic lives of women crack users in three Brooklyn neighborhoods. In the course of this a three-year project, field observations and interviews were conducted with more than 200 women crack users. Although the majority of subjects were African-American women (36 percent) and Latinas (44 percent), a significant

minority (20 percent) were European-American women. A majority were polydrug users and nearly all were homeless or involved in lifestyles that exhibited a high degree of residential instability. These women were both perpetrators and victims of violence, and all were engaged in lawbreaking activity—principally street-level sex work—at the time of the study.

The advent of crack cocaine has had a profound effect on the economic and social life of many low-income inner-city communities (Johnson, Williams, Dei, and Sanabria 1990). The crack economy has also extracted a much higher price from its participants than [in] previous drug eras, taking an excessive toll on users' lives (Hamid 1990). Within this context, shelter has become a crucial and sought-after commodity. This article will document processes by which impoverished crack-abusing women resolve their human needs for shelter and personal safety and describe the strategies they pursue in constructing little-known alternative living arrangements for themselves. The core question addressed is this: Among inner-city women without legal income (for instance, who have no legal employment or welfare payments), who are excluded from assistance by their family and kin networks, and who expend most of their monetary and labor resources to procure and use crack, how and where do they find shelter with some semblance of personal security?

Recent scholarship on homelessness (Barak 1991; Hopper and Hamburg 1984; Jencks and Peterson 1991; Ropers 1988; Rossi 1989; Vanderstaay 1992) has documented many forces associated with the increased numbers of homeless persons in America but has neglected two themes. Although the homeless literature occasionally mentions the importance of crack abuse (Jencks and Peterson 1991), few studies have sought to specify the mechanisms by which crack abusers become homeless. Moreover, homeless women living without children are rarely mentioned or studied; such women appear to constitute less than 10% of persons living in shelters or other institutions where homeless persons are found. The relative absence of homeless crack-using females in the homeless literature may be largely due to their success in obtaining alternative living arrangements, which keep them out of shelters and institutional settings.

The literature on crack use and sex-for-crack reveals many factors that contribute to women becoming crack abusers and having no conventional place to live. First and foremost has been the influence of social and economic forces in limiting options for low-income women. Since 1965, inner-city minority neighborhoods have been marked by persistent poverty, structural unemployment, and urban dispossession. In many neighborhoods, the drug economy has become a way of life and a means of survival for a significant segment of the local population (Bourgois 1989, 1995; Dunlap and Johnson 1992; Hamid 1992a; Johnson et al. 1990; Kasarda 1992; Moore 1991; Sullivan 1989). Few of the women studied here had held employment in legal jobs during the preceding decade, and at the time of interview most failed to comply with welfare regulations; thus they were not in receipt of any legitimate income.

These crack-abusing women typically grew up in family and kin systems severely affected by these structural forces. Little prepared these women for licit jobs or conventional marriages. Few women had even one parent who held steady employment, and welfare support was often intermittent and never enough. Mothers or other caregivers (typically a grandmother or aunt) supplemented income by informal sector activity (e.g., serving alcohol at afterhours clubs, working for a numbers runner, etc.—see Dunlap 1992; Maher, Dunlap, and Johnson unpublished). For many women, both community and family-level involvement facilitated access to informal sector labor markets. Within some families, alcohol, heroin, marijuana, and cocaine use and abuse, as well as the illicit sale of such substances, had been a primary economic activity across several generations (Dunlap and Johnson 1994; Dunlap, Johnson, and Maher forthcoming).

The majority of women respondents here (see following) initiated illicit drug use prior to 1985–1986, when crack use became widespread in New York City. Many were former heroin and cocaine powder users with a history of intravenous drug use. A significant minority also used alcohol and marijuana on a near-daily basis (Golub and Johnson 1994; Johnson et al. 1985). However, despite the fact that most were not drug neophytes, these women's lives were severely disrupted by crack use. The demands of crack use and the crack lifestyle forced many of them to develop new and innovative ways of meeting their instrumental needs. In particular, the advent of crack had a dramatic effect on the nature, frequency, and dollar value of sexual acts in street-level sex markets (Maher 1996; Maher and Curtis 1992).

The cumulative effect of these influences was a large number of crack abusing women who had no legal income, expended all their illegal income on crack, had no relatives or friends who allowed them in their households, and were excluded by male crack sellers who dominated them sexually or as employers. One of the most pressing problems confronted by the crack-using women encountered in this research—in addition to their constant mission (the search for crack and the illegal activities this typically entailed)—was the search for shelter and respite from the street. Although they vacillated between homelessness and periods of temporary residence with family, kin, friends and associates, most of the women in this study could be classified as homeless and certainly almost all had experienced homelessness at some point. Day after day, month after month, these women had no conventional place to go to sleep, eliminate, bath[e], eat, rest, relax, and restore themselves. Using ethnographic data based on observations and interviews with active women crack users, this article documents the existence of a set of gendered "solutions" to the problems of homelessness and residential instability encountered by women crack users.

A major theme emerged: The majority of these women did not have a conventional place (a home or apartment where someone [rarely the subject] paid the rent and maintained the household) to sleep, rest, eat, eliminate, bathe, and store possessions. Instead, these woman crack users, regardless of whether primarily active in sexwork or drug distribution and sales, demonstrated considerable effort and skill in finding places to stay for relatively limited time periods. These alternative living arrangements reflected their persistence and extensive experience in continuously locating a place day-by-day and week-by-week to restore themselves. This rich descriptive repository of field notes, field diaries, and transcribed tape-recorded interviews documented both similarities and variations in local social and economic conditions as well as how the larger context of drug use, income generation, and gender relations affected these women. (It should be noted that many male crack users exhibited similar difficulties in finding places to live and often resorted to nonconventional living arrangements, but the focus of this article is upon female crack users and the gendered nature of their arrangements.)

As the following sections demonstrate, for many of the women in this study, homelessness served both to cement and intensify their involvement in and commitment to the street-level drug economy. However, the nature, form, and physical location of accommodations utilized by these women exhibited wide variation, as did the relationships to which such coresidencies gave rise. Although in this context the considerable evidence of exchange and support patterns gives lie to the stereotype of the predatory thirsty crackhead, it needs to be borne in mind that such relationships are also responses to the exigencies of life on the margins. The variability of these alternative living arrangements and the social relations they reflected and spawned are discussed below.

Starting Out: A Little Help From Your Friends

The more I looked into homelessness, the more it appeared to be misstated as merely a problem of being without shelter: homelessness is more properly viewed as the most aggravated state of a more prevalent problem, **extreme poverty** (Rossi 1989, p. 8).

For many poor people, homelessness is the end result of a gradual and piecemeal shift from a tenuous existence that encompasses economic and social marginality, substandard housing, and family breakdown. Among the socially and economically isolated, and the precariously housed to begin with, the experiences of most of the women in this study appear to fit this model of homelessness as "the last stage in the downward spiral of poverty and abandonment" (Vanderstaay 1992, p. 60). Even though drug use clearly accelerates this process, a majority of women maintained precarious accommodations prior to problematic drug use. For some women, involvement in drug sales led to arrest or eviction, serving to expedite official homelessness, as reported by Carol, a 41-year-old African American woman.

I had my own apartment, myself and my daughter. I started selling crack. From my house. [For who?] Some Jamaican. [Yeah, how did you get hooked up with that?] Through my boyfriend. They wanted to sell from my apartment. They were supposed to pay me something like $150 a week rent, and then something off the profits. They used to, you know, fuck up the money, like not give me the money. Eventually I went through a whole lot of different dealers. Eventually I stopped payin' my rent because I wanted to get a transfer out of there to get away from everything 'cause soon as one group of crack dealers would get out, another group would come along. [So how long did that go on for?] About four years. Then I lost my apartment, and I sat out in the street.

Whereas the majority of women in this study had not sold drugs from their apartments, the experiences of those who had done so suggest that such arrangements only rarely represent a form of female entrepreneurship and are typically short-lived.

Initially, whether they were evicted, pushed out, or left of their own accord, many of the women in this study avoided formal acknowledgment of their homeless status by becoming "couch people"—alternating between households among extended kin networks (see Dunlap and Johnson 1992) or roaming from friend to (so-called) friend in search of short-term accommodations. As is evident in the following quotation from Jonelle, a 32-year-old African American woman, such offers are usually limited to a shower or brief rest or perhaps an overnight stay, usually in exchange for drugs.

[So where do you stay mostly now?] Walk the street. [You don't have one particular place where you go?] Oh, we got a girlfriend named Jeanette that lives on J——, you know. She let us go up there and wash up or sometimes I might fall asleep up there, but I'm not—I don't consider myself stayin' with her though. [Does she charge you anything to go there?] Not really. . . . With her, she's just lookin' to get high. You come with some "get high" which most likely we'll do, and you turn her on and you know it's cool.

Occasionally, women were able to negotiate short-term living arrangements with other women drug users. More often than not, however, such hospitality was contingent on the approval of coresident males. As Sugar, a 36-year-old Latina, reported:

I found me a new room. [Yeah, how did that happen?] So you know, uh, Angel, she lives right here on I—— and T—— okay, she's one of my co-workers. And her old man said, "Hey let her stay here," you know. And I appreciate that. [You have to pay them?] She never said nothing like that, but of course I've gotta give them something. Yeah, you know. [Throw them something anyway.] Of course, definitely. But I mean they didn't make any kind of formal arrangement? [They just kind of expect you to, when you have, to, you know?] Um-huh.

Contingent on the strength and nature of the relationship, a few women were able to negotiate longer term arrangements when various forms of payment were provided, as did Shorty, a 22-year-old Latina.

I was living with a friend of mine and her husband, and then this guy came along and started living there too, and they were into getting high and stuff; and at that time, I was getting high too. [On what?] On crack. You know, and I was having a very hard time there, and I didn't have no financial help, as far as my husband working, he wasn't working, I wasn't on welfare or nothing like that. So, finally these guys weren't satisfied with the money we were giving them. They wanted me to support their habit, buy food and pay rent money. You know? [How much were you giving them?] I was giving them $75 a week for both of us, which wasn't bad. I could deal with that, but then they wanted, you know, crack. I had to buy them crack too, plus feed her, her husband, and this guy that started living there.

However, such arrangements rarely last when the household is immersed in drug use. Even long-standing relationships between women are rapidly depleted by one or both party's use of drugs, as happened between Dee Dee, a 29-year-old African American woman, and her "homegirl," Rita.

She lives in the projects on Marcy. She used to live right around the corner from me. She's one of the first people that we lived with when we came in this neighborhood. But then they abandoned her building. [Is she somebody that you could stay at her house?] Yeah, but everybody, you know, to get in the door it's like you got to have something for them. And I don't really feel like they're such a friend, you know. I told her when I first came there, I said, "Look I got a bag of dope. I'll give you some, all right." I'm like, "Just give me a washcloth and a towel. That's all I want to do. I want to take a shower and clean up and then I'll talk to you," you know. So of course I was taking my time. I wanted to relax and really get clean, you know. So when I come out it's like a big thing now. It's like, "Well you just walk in my house, and just walk into my shower," and all this is 'cause all the time I'm in the bathroom she's thinking I'm gettin' high. She think I don't have no more dope. So I played it off like I didn't. I said, "You know what the bag was so small, I did the whole thing." And honey she must have caught on fire, right; and when I seen her attitude, and I felt like—and I really had the bag of dope. I just wanted to see how she was gonna act. And she acted just like I thought. "And you ain't got nothin' for me, you're not welcome here." So when I seen it was like that I said, "Yeah well I'll just go, and I won't come again."

These accounts illustrate that although the need for reciprocity was clearly understood, the terms were often vague, suggesting that among this population, conflict over the precise nature of reciprocal obligations would be frequent and perhaps inevitable. For the most part, however, the women crack users in this study were rarely in a position to extend shelter to each other. Most of them were homeless, a majority were estranged from both their families of orientation and procreation and all could be characterized as possessing severely limited economic and social resources. For a majority of women, this meant that they had three choices—either resort to the city shelter system, go it alone on the streets, or rely on men.

Engaging the System: Welfare Hotels and Shelter Accommodation

Without exception, the women in this study identified Single Room Occupancy (SRO) or welfare hotels, as criminogenic, dangerous, and conducive to drug use. Although Jenny, a 25-year-old European American, had experimented with drug use in the context of her relationship with a violent and abusive husband, it was not until after they split up that she began to use heroin, cocaine powder, and crack. Evicted from her apartment in Queens because she could no longer afford to pay the rent, Jenny and her two children were made homeless and wandered the streets before eventually being relocated to an SRO hotel in mid-town Manhattan. Her story clearly illustrates the way in which social and economic factors converge with situational factors, such as the availability of drugs and the proximity of experienced (usually male) users/sellers to render homeless women even more vulnerable.

After I split up with him [husband] I couldn't pay the rent, and he wouldn't give me no money unless I let him stay with me. So I had to take him to court. But in the meantime, I still couldn't pay my rent. So I went down to Welfare, and Welfare wouldn't pay that amount. So they got me in the welfare hotel in the Holland. . . . So I had to go to the Holland Hotel on 42nd Street between Eighth and Ninth Avenues. And it was like pimps, crack, dope, you know, drug hotel—pimp hotel. And I was, like, I never knew anything about this stuff you know 'cause I came from Queens, in a quiet area. . . . He [drug seller and pimp] conned me into staying with him, and I did, you know. I was vulnerable, hungry, you know. I lost my welfare, and they were kicking me out of the hotel; and he had a room in the same hotel; the Holland, which he paid the security guards to have it. It wasn't like welfare benefits. He just paid to keep that room and I was staying there because I had no other place to stay, and then he turned me out to the streets. I was sniffing dope, coke, and smoking a lot of crack. [Yeah, and he turned you onto all those drugs.] Yeah and that's how I became like really hooked because I had a habit and I didn't know [it].

Boy, a 29-year-old African American woman, was one of the few women who from time to time made use of this system. Her views of the shelter system were reinforced by many other women, most of whom refused to even contemplate shelter accommodation.

I was scared the first time I ever went to a shelter. [When was this?] It was about eighteen months ago. An' I was scared. They took me to a single shelter, I only stayed two days an' I went to 116 Street. Is called [Women's Shelter], the wors'es shelter ya can ever go to 'cos deres dikes and every thin' there. An' dat taught me a lot. Thassa woman shelter. I wouldn' put ma dog in it. But I havta stay. There's two accommodations dere, dykes and crack. There's nine a y'all inna room. If you look at one person—"You looked at ma woman, I'm gon' kick your ass." Y'know dykes are the worsest things there ever is. I don' like it, but I havta deal wid it, so you can' really—in nis place you don' get ta lay down. You gotta get up eight a' clock inna morning. An' you don' get ta go back upstairs till, like, six a'clock in afternoon. [What do most of the women do during the day?] I sit ou'side. I sit right ou'side. But I don' 'cumulate wid none o' dem nere because once you start ta be frens wid dem, dey're wrapped up in nat system. [So do some women do crack?] Crack it up inside the place, they be crackin' it up ou'side the place. Shootin' up. Sellin'. I mean I was like marked. Is like an animal house.

Although the women in this study were critical of the conditions of shelter life in general, they reserved greatest hostility for those [who] worked in the system. In particular, women received little comfort or indeed protection from the security guards employed to police behavior and maintain order in the shelter system (see Rossi 1989, p. 199; Waterston 1993). Guards were widely perceived as being involved in drug use, and, in particular, female guards were frequently cited as being implicated in lesbian relationships with shelter residents.

Is bad when dere own guards do it. How can da guards protect you when they do the same thing? You got guards dat go tagether. You got guards dat smoke. How can you protect me if you're smokin' an' you a dyke? So you're 'cumulated wid daresta them. If you have a fight with a dyke, okay, the guard's gonna be onna dyke's side, not yours, so you fucked.

The violence and criminality endemic to shelter life also promote the use of instrumental aggression (Campbell 1993) by women in an effort to ward off potential aggressors. As Boy explained in response to a question about how she protected herself:

Myself. Okay, when I went there Tuesday I laid ma law straight, I hadda argument, but dey know me from before, alrigh'. I jus' let you know. Okay, iss a certain way you can look at a person, y'know. An' nas wa' I did, y'know. An' by me bein' there before, people know, don' mess wid me, I'm not one adem suckers. See if you go in nere wimpy, they're gonna kick your ass. But if ya go in nere lay ya law down, an' don' fuck wid no one. Thas all—you don' fuck wid dem, dey won' fuck wid you.

Although women appeared more likely to reside in shelters during pregnancy, shelters specifically for pregnant women were similarly perceived by Boy.

Dey placed me inta [S-Shelter.] I don' wanna be dere, y'understan'. I don' like ta be wid a groupa people. Now dey got me inna room like eleven o' clock, I'm ready ta doze off, y'know. Dere playin' cards an' playin' music, an' lights on. Iss like you never can sleep when ya wanna sleep. Ya can't watch TV when ya wanna watch TV. Y' gotta sign fa soap, ya gotta sign fa toilet tissue. Iss jus' like bein' inna detention home. [Do the women fight with each other?] Dey argue like cats 'n' dogs okay, ya got it inside an' ya got it outside. Right around the corner on the side of the building is a crack area. On number one crack dealers. [What do they sell, mix?] Yeah. Crack, dope, heroin, um wass dat stuff, dat orange stuff? [Methadone?] Methadone. Anythin' you want they got, okay? It makes it bad on us. Because at night you hear, "You took ma money bitch" an' "ba, ba, ba."

These accounts suggest that for many women, current system responses to female homelessness were perceived in a negative light. At best, hotels and shelters "constitute a subculture that makes any attempt toward sobriety extremely difficult" (Zimmer and Schretzman 1991, p. 174). At worst, they provided an environment that served to amplify drug and alcohol use, fostered involvement in illegal activities, and encouraged the neglect or abuse of children. Most of the women interviewed in this research preferred to take their chances elsewhere. Thus the recent proliferation of alternative living arrangements can also be seen, in part, as a response to the city's failure to meet these women's needs.

Going to the Curb: Squatting and Sleeping on the Street

For most women, city accommodations failed to provide a viable alternative even when the only other option was to sleep on the street or in an abandoned building (see also Boyle and Anglin 1993). Queen Bee, a 25-year-old African American user/seller, was squatting in an abandoned apartment building. She held the keys to two apartments on the fourth floor of this building. Cable wire attached to a city outlet brought electricity into both apartments. Water was acquired from the fire hydrant outside. As the following field note excerpt suggests, the conditions of life were both unsafe and unsanitary.

> The first apartment can only be explained as a garbage can. It is extremely disorganized and reeks of garbage and decay. The floors are littered with old clothing and rags and each room is adorned with broken pieces of discarded furniture and piles of refuse. Queen Bee took me into this apartment to retrieve a lamp, consisting of a bulb screwed into a broken base, before quickly proceeding to the other apartment. This apartment is also filthy and smells terrible but is in slightly better condition than its neighbor. There is a long hallway and several rooms open off it but it is too dark to see into these rooms. The only source of light emanates from the lamp Queen Bee is holding. We enter a room off to the right of the hallway containing an old beat up dresser with a mirror, two chairs in decayed condition, a stool, various boxes, a tray table with a hot plate on it, and assorted other junk. The dresser is covered with empty vials, about eight empty lighters, and a lot of debris. Queen Bee uses a sweep of her arm to clear the contents of the dresser top and create a space for the lamp.

This abandoned building was an active drug dealing spot. Several other individuals besides Queen Bee dealt drugs from this spot. Booby traps were set for police and strangers. The steps on the third landing had been rigged. Everyone lived above this landing and anyone that did not know his or her way around this particular step would fall through to the first floor.

Similarly, Princess, a 32-year-old African American woman also chose to create her own living arrangements. Unlike Queen Bee, however, Princess did not have access to an abandoned building and her accommodations were strictly curbside. As she related:

> [Where did you go when you moved out?] Well I started staying here, there. Mainly I break night a lot so, mainly in the streets. Not that I have to be in the streets. Just that I don' choose to take these drug vices into my family's home.

Princess rationalized her choice by saying that she preferred to stay on the street rather than in someone's house because, in her opinion, either way people were out to rip you off. As she saw it, in some ways sleeping rough may even reduce the risk of victimization insofar as she believed that there was less chance of others thinking that you had anything to steal.

> I'll stay here [in the lot], y'know I paid anywhere I went, but besides gettin' robbed, y'know 'cos when you stay in somebody's house all they do is rip you off. I've gotten by better in the streets, y'know. That's right. You sleep, fall asleep in the streets nobody think you got nothin'. So they're not gonna search you for anything. You know you wake up with any dime—you go to somebody's house and you have nothing, not even a wake up.

Sleeping on the street, or sleeping rough, typically entailed the construction of a makeshift shelter, usually in the form of a cardboard box shanty or lean-to against a wall or fence. Ironically, these structures were referred to in one study neighborhood as "condos." For most women, however, the high likelihood both of victimization and of police harassment meant that condos were not a viable option unless they were in partnership with a male. Following the eviction of Dream from her apartment, three African American couples who had been staying there were forced to relocate to a vacant lot where they set up a large communal condo. Below, Dee Dee, a 29-year-old African American woman described this arrangement.

> In the backa da lot, dere a couch back dere. Wen I'm finally pooped, I can' take it no more, I step back dere and fall asleep. An' iss gota Johnny pump das open. [But it's not too good when it rains.] No, but we done made it like a canopy or whatever wid de pallets on each side o' da couch. [How many people are staying over there?] Iss really six of us there, but we be in there at different times. An' if there's not room for the nex' one we lay a pallet out. We got enough blankets and stuff. We put a blanket on the pallet an' layout there. [But anyone can go in there?] They can yeah, there's nothin' stoppin' 'em, but dey don'. Iss not as popular as dat lot dere. Guess a lot o' people know about it but never think to go in there. Jus' an empty lot, a parkin' lot. An' iss got trees ona sides dat block us out, iss cool for now.

Although most males who were part of street-level drug-using networks were neither inclined nor particularly well placed to provide for women's needs, some relationships endured. Latisha, a 32-year-old African American woman and her mate, Tre, resided in an abandoned truck situated on an empty lot hidden from the roadside by undergrowth and adjoining a large warehouse. Even though it was located a 30-min walk away from the drug market area, Latisha and Tre made this journey at least once a day. Latisha and Tre managed to successfully hide the fact that they lived in this truck from other drug users (and for a time, from the ethnographer) by claiming that they lived in an apartment in an adjacent neighborhood. Following the ethnographer's visit to the site, Latisha discussed their accommodation.

It's very hot in the summer. You have to keep the doors open when you're sleepin' and God forbid if you try to put a cover on you, and mosquitoes, my God. [What about rats?] Well, you see the bag hangin' up over the ceiling. Thas where we put the food. If we didn't eat it all we have to hang it up in the ceiling because the rats would smell it and come in. You gotta remember you're on the outside and those are big rats. [What about other people in the neighborhood?] They know that we're around and we don't bother them or steal or nothing. . . . I keep myself pretty much clean, I mean I can't take a bath every day, but we have access to hot water. The guy across the street give us hot water. [So you take a bath over there?] No, we fill up buckets, we got a big barrel, you fill the barrel, get in and wash. Outside. Last winter was three feet of snow and I still went outside.

Although involved in a physically abusive relationship, Latisha saw herself as fortunate in that she at least had a "roof over her head." Moreover, sleeping rough was not an option for women who depended on street-level sexwork because of the undesirable message it sends out to customers.

I refuse to just sleep right over here [in the drug market area]. I don't want people to see me lyin' out here on the sidewalk. Dates come through these areas too and they see a girl laying out here and then they see her back on the street. You know, it's gonna be hard for you, they figure out you ain't shit.

Within the street-level drug economy, sexwork, as a primary means of economic sustenance necessitated a basic level of attention to looks, physical hygiene, and, ironically, moral propriety (see Maher 1995).

Older Males

By far the most common alternative living arrangement for the women in this study was as part of the household of an older male for a period of time. Most of the women in this sample patronized older men to secure and satisfy their needs for shelter. However, as Hamid (1992b) has argued, these relationships cannot be considered in isolation from the economic position of young minority women generally.

While the real income and other benefits of elderly men or senior citizens have improved appreciably in the past two decades . . . young women have seen their income decline steeply over the same period of time. (p. 344)

By middle-class standards, these older men do not control significant resources, but in the inner-city context, the resources of a steady income and maintenance of an apartment enabled them to obtain a sense of mastery or control over women. These older males usually had some form of dependable or steady income, such as a low-wage job, pension, social security, or retirement benefits. They owned or had a long-established lease on a house or apartment and were well positioned to provide women crack smokers (and sometimes their children, as well) with shelter and a place to wash and rest up, and sometimes food.

Although individual arrangements exhibited considerable variation, these accommodations always came at a price. Women typically paid in either sex or drugs or less often, cash, and sometimes all three. In addition to sexual availability and drugs, these older men received the companionship of younger women and, in some instances, were able to exert considerable control over them. Some also extracted further benefits in the form of unpaid domestic labor, such as cleaning, cooking, and laundry.

Cash for shelter. Although few of the women were able to negotiate these relationships with older males on strictly economic terms by paying in either cash or crack, Connie, a 24-year-old gay Latina, maintained that she was able to keep the transaction at a purely financial level.

[Where do you stay now?] At my [male] friend's house on W——. [The friend smokes crack too?] Yes. [You have to—] Pay him. Pay him cash, right, in order for me to sleep and take a bath. [What, he doesn't ask for sex or anything like that?] No, he's an old, old man. Well, I tell him I don't like mens. I tell him, and I don't like mens. [You like women?] Exactly. [You pay him by the night or by the week?] Oh, I give him ten, fifteen dollars a day.

Crack for shelter. Similarly, Jo-Beth, a 23-year-old and Candy, a 41-year-old [both European American] were part of a group of women who stayed at the apartment of an elderly Latino on a regular basis and claimed they always paid in crack.

> I'm in this old man's house. He's a crack-head. A lot of the girls go there. You give him crack. [Do you find that there's a lot of old guys that smoke?] I don't know. I don't hang out with old guys. I pay my way. (Jo-Beth)

> I bought a nickel crack for this old man right here so I can come in here. It cost me a nickel or two to get here. And he's still not happy. If you go out ten times a day, if it be ten times, you got to bring him a bottle [of crack]. It took me so long to make that damn money and the bastard, me so sick. At least I had that nickel to get in here, you know. (Candy)

Sex for shelter. More often than not, however, sex was part of the deal. Shorty, a 22-year-old Latina, recalled a typical former relationship.

> Well, he's the type of guy that used to help all the girls from the Avenue. And they would go up there and take a shower and sleep, you know. He was like very perverted, and to get a place to sleep, you had to do something with him, you know? "For a couple of weeks, I'll help you out," so we started staying there, but he had a drinking problem and was perverted. [Did he use crack also?] No, he used to drink. Just drink. And when my husband wasn't there, he would try to get fresh with me, 'cause you know, he's a pervert. So that didn't go over too tough, either.

Whole networks of women crack users informed one another of possible sites of shelter with older males, as Jackie, a 29-year-old Afro-Caribbean woman, explained.

> Mo used to live right upstairs in a bad apartment. And he invite the same Joclyn up to, you know—fuck around. . . . After a while it was like everybody get—ya know, the word pass around, and people see how people live here, a lot of girls used to live there, and guys use to be lookin' for girls, too. . . . Everybody tell you all about him and ya know, everybody start livin' there . . . gettin' high, gettin' high, gettin' high.

Frequently, the older males who offered their space to be entertained by these women were retired and many were alcoholics. How-

ever, some older men were initiated or "turned on" to smoking crack through their associations with these younger women. In many places, a typical scene involved a group of old men who were playing cards and drinking beer while women smoked crack. Later, the old men might take their pick of the females and some would also smoke crack. In addition to older retired males, middle-aged working men may also offer various forms of hospitality to women crack users. For example, George, an electrical engineer, worked everyday—often with a charge from "Scottie" for the road. According to women, George treated them to a less exploitative time: they showered, cooked, listened to music, and beamed up together.

Companionship/affection for shelter. In several instances, these older men were dates or former dates who claimed affections for individual women. For example, Tameka, a 41-year-old African American woman, met her common law husband as a date in a local bar and remained in this union throughout the study period.

> He told me he said, "Look I'm not worth the fuck all I want is companionship," he said, "Look I'll give you $50 you go home with me." So I said, "Cool, no problem." We never did anything together or anything like that other than lay in the bed and sleep, and that was it. . . . [W]hoever he bought with him they would take his money. Because I knew that it was somebody that I wanted to see again who would be there for me. . . . So I knew if I rolled [stole from] him he wouldn't have wanted me. So I didn't roll him and thank God I didn't, and the man's been there ever since.

Similarly, Peggy, a 34-year-old European American woman, lived with an older Italian man who worked as a numbers runner. Although not a drug user, Peggy's boyfriend gave her money to purchase drugs in an effort to keep her from prostitution. The relationship, however, was not without its problems.

> The man that I live with, I met on the stroll up here. We would see each other once a week, then he would come twice a week, then he would come three, four times a week, take me to lunch, take me to dinner, take me to the house . . . And then, I never moved out. . . . Well, it's my home. I'm living there eight months already. I mean, he knew what he was getting. But, I cook, I clean the house, I wait on him hand and foot. He never was married, so I'm like his baby. I was never home when he got home from work and that's all he asks, that I'm home. He don't care if there's no food, if the house

is burning; as long as I'm there when he gets home. He says, "I'm going to chain you," and he did one day. I swear to God! He put shackles on my feet. I freaked out.

Domestic duties for shelter. Chef, a 27-year-old African-American woman, lived with Clyde (70 years old), who had his own apartment for many years. Clyde did not use crack nor allow Chef to bring others into his apartment. She was required to keep the apartment and his clothes clean, cook the food, and to complete a number of other well-defined domestic duties in return for staying there. Sex was not involved.

Similarly, Linda, a 31-year-old European American woman, negotiated a deal with an older man whereby she was given food, shelter, and a few dollars in return for her services as a sitter for his elderly invalid mother, an arrangement she later described as "too good to be true."

> I've been babysittin' the old lady. I'm still over there but, you know, he's got a lot of problems—he drinks. Yeah, her son. [How much do they pay you for watchin' over her?] You know whatever. I don't have a set thing, you know. I'm just happy with the roof over my head. [How old is this guy?] Fifty-five. [You don't have to take care of him?] No, only when he gets drunk, real, real drunk. He just wants me to cuddle up next to him. I don't do anything, but I get mad 'cause he wakes me up. You know, he drinks all night until two, there, four o'clock in the morning, and he has the radio blastin', and then he comes and wakes me up. He goes on and on.

However, despite variations in the nature of the commodity exchanged, living arrangements with older males typically took the form of short-term instrumental associations. Over a 2-month period during fieldwork observations, Linda had had four such associations.

> Remember I told you I was living on J——? You know that guy died? [Since then where have you been staying?] Well I was staying with this other guy on the Southside, on B——, you know. How do I know him? Well I used to go out with him. You know I give him a blow job to stay there, you know. But then he threw me out, 'cause, he says, "I don't want no more injections in the house." He don't get high. He drinks, you know, when he got the money. [Since then where have you been staying?] I found this other guy, right. But he got on a program, and he was doing good, you know. So then I left there. So now I'm staying with this other guy, this old man, he don't get high or nothing. [How'd you hook up with him?] I used

to date him. But now, he just lets me stay up there. He's a little bit off. So I told [him], "Hey easy with the sex" (laughing).

Most women, by virtue of their crack use and depleted economic and social resources, were forced to rely on short-lived associations with older males during which they exchanged drugs, sex, cash, or services (or some combination thereof) for shelter. Although most of these men used alcohol and some also used crack, these males were peripheral to street-level drug using or selling networks. They were simply older neighborhood males, who, by virtue of their apartments and somewhat better economic status, were able to offer these younger women shelter—in exchange they received a number of benefits, including sexual favors, drugs, money, and domestic labor. But there was a fine line between these households and their commodified forms as "freakhouses" and other commercial settings for crack consumption.

Freakhouses and Other Commercial Settings

In many impoverished inner-city neighborhoods, crack has become the "de facto currency of the realm"—a liquid asset with cash value that can be exchanged for shelter, sex, food, and other durables (Inciardi et al. 1991). The rise of the freakhouse, which specialized in sex-for-crack exchanges between chronic crack-using women and men who were less heavy consumers (or were nonusing males), exemplified crack's capacity for the commodification of human relationships. In New York City, freakhouses generally took the following form.

> The elderly man receives sexual services and gifts of crack from a core group of five or six crack-abusing women. In exchange they gain a sanctuary in highly transient lifestyles where they can wash, prepare meals or feel at home. They promptly attract several other crack-abusing women, and the combined "harem" lures male users and working men of all ages. The latter come to "freak" (use any and all of the women sexually—a favorite pastime is "flipping," with the male going from one to as many women that are present in continuous succession), and some use crack (but many do not). The visitors pay the old man or one of his appointees cash or crack for any activity: going out to buy crack, beer, or cigarettes; use of private space (by the half hour); or access to the women. (Hamid 1992b, p. 344)

Joe, a 31-year-old Afro-Caribbean male, inherited a beautiful frame house when his mother died. A regular crack user, Joe was not employed at the time of the study and used the house to accommodate a core of six female crack users and a shifting number of crack-using transients. Although he was unable to pay the monthly mortgage, his female house guests kept Joe in drugs. The presence of women willing to provide sexual services in exchange for crack quickly turned Joe's place into a freakhouse. However, freakhouses are sustained by male sexual desires that extend beyond the inner-city crack culture. The freakhouse created and maintained a setting for sexual commodities neither readily accessible nor cheaply available in the commercial marketplace of street-level sexwork.

The social and economic organization of such households ranges from anarchic to authoritarian (see also Ouellet, Wiebel, Jiminez, and Johnson 1993). Isolated from other sources of social and economic support, many women initially entertained freakhouse accommodation and the accompanying sexual demands as a response to scarcity and deprivation. However, whereas the freakhouse was by definition a commercial setting for sexual transactions and crack/drug use, often the relationships among individual residents suggest that it functioned along the lines of a household unit, however unstable and exploitative. According to both owners and other residents, many freakhouses exhibited social obligations of affection and limited trust developed among household members. Residents exchanged food, money, goods, services—and drugs—and sometimes considered each other as family. Members looked out for each other and provided protection against serious violence. For the most part, then, freakhouses provided a more congenial setting than other commercial locations.

In contrast to the freakhouse, this research also identified a number of commercial settings variously described as crack houses or shooting galleries, which often catered to both intravenous drug users and crack smokers (but rarely present were nonusing males interested only in sex). These settings tended to operate along the lines of the traditional heroin shooting gallery (e.g., see Murphy and Waldorf 1991) insofar as they created a relatively secure environment where street-level drug users gathered primarily to consume drugs. Although some establishments provided rooms for rent on a half-hourly basis for sexual transactions, payment was typically extracted in exchange for entry and a range of drug-related services including equipment hire and the purchase of drugs. Within such establishments, the margin

of profit, or house take, depended on how long people stayed and how much they consumed—encouraging excessive use and a high incidence of theft and violence (Inciardi et al. 1993; Ouellet et al. 1993; Ratner, 1993b).

Women known to the owners were permitted to spend the night in these establishments in return for either drugs or cash. Commercial sexual transactions were generally not permitted in these settings, although a minority facilitated sex-for-drugs exchanges and some provided private rooms for rental on a half-hourly basis. Unlike freakhouses, however, these commercial settings were drug focused, rather than sex focused. Women made important distinctions between the two types of settings—freakhouses and crack house/shooting gallery operations—on the basis of perceived safety. Personal and material safety emerged as primary considerations in the search for shelter, and these women were extremely reluctant to stay in locations identified as commercial consumption settings.

> Pappy's I don't trust. I have walked passed it and I don't trust it because if dey see somebody with you and it looks like somebody das got a lot of money dey rob them. Dey set them up. Pappy's, dey [potential dates] look at his place and say, "Oh, all these guys out here, no I don' want to go," and dey would drive off. (Keisha)

> Uh, well you know it's so busy over there at Pap's house. And man, I swear to God, I can't hold nothin'. I can't have nothin' there. They took my wick [tampon] from out my underwear while I was sleepin'. (Sugar)

> [You ever stay at Kizzy's place?] No I don't like it there, she robs you when you're there. She robs your stuff while you're there and then say she doesn't know what happened to it. [Have you been robbed there?] Yeah. I bought a sweat suit for $75 and when I woke up the top of my sweatsuit was gone. She said she didn't know what happened to it. (Rachel)

Within the inner-city crack culture studied here, settings for drug use and sexual transactions can be located along a continuum of alternative living arrangements that attest to crack's capacity for commodification. Whereas the more commercially oriented settings are more strictly drug focused and the less commercial tend to exploit the potent combination of sex and crack, strictly commercial settings are further differentiated by the absence of exchanges rooted in domestic labor, companionship, and affection. The reality for many crack-using women was a choice between a rock and a hard place—between submitting to the exploitation and potential sexual degradation offered within the relative safety of the freakhouse or retaining sexual autonomy but at the increased risk of physical and material victimization in other commercial settings. For many women, the relative insulation from the exigencies of street life provided by being a sexual partner/drug conduit to elderly males or freakhouse owners (and their clientele) appeared to render such arrangements the least undesirable option.

Discussion

Recent research has drawn attention to the existence of new opportunities for female participation in street-level drug markets and the influence of structural changes on the gender composition of street networks (e.g., Baskin, Sommers, and Fagan 1993; Mieczkowski 1994). As Fagan has suggested:

Some women have constructed careers in illegal work that have insulated them from the exploitation and destructive behaviors that characterize heavy cocaine and crack use.... Signs of the changing status of women in drug markets are evident in the relatively high incomes some achieve, and the relatively insignificant role of prostitution in generating income. (Fagan 1994, p. 210)

However, the findings of this research suggest that many crack-using women are seriously impoverished and unable to maintain stable living arrangements. This was true both of women who engaged in street-level drug distribution and sales activities (Bourgois and Dunlap 1993) and those who relied primarily on the street-level sex economy (Maher 1995; Maher and Curtis 1992). The women in this study clearly lacked the necessary resources for maintaining physical security and economic independence and for assuring sexual autonomy. Many expended their incomes exclusively on crack consumption with little or nothing left over to pay rent or meet other basic needs.

The failure of the city system to meet these women's needs meant that for most, shelters and welfare hotels were regarded as the least desirable accommodation option. The alternatives, however, were loaded with risk and uncertainty and skewed by the gendered distribution of power within the inner-city crack culture. In particular, the costs of sleeping rough and in commercial establishments were high and included the risks of theft and violent victimization. On the other hand, older males provided an elastic source of accommodation. Many of them lived alone and welcomed crack-using women as companions or house guests. Within the context of this particular form of alternative living arrangement, women remained vulnerable to exploitation by virtue of their relative powerlessness vis-à-vis older men with apartments and economic resources. It is ironic then, that these households—some of which spawned new depths of sexual degradation and new forms of indentured labor—were seen by women to minimize the risk of victimization. However, when viewed in the context of other options for accommodation, such arrangements reflected women's search for what they clearly regarded as the least vulnerable situations.

Conclusion

Rather than seek to isolate the sexual and economic practices of women crack users, this article has sought to identify and describe some of the changing contexts in which these practices are situated. Bolstered by widespread sex-segmentation in the street-level drug economy, the relative powerlessness and economic marginality of women crack users undergirded an array of alternative living arrangements that fueled female participation in both prostitution and sex-for-drug exchanges. Although important distinctions clearly existed between the sex trade on the streets and sexual activities in the context of crack use behind closed doors, these women's accounts suggest that women crack users continue to experience significant levels of exploitation and degradation (see also Bourgois and Dunlap 1993). Within this context, the advent of crack cocaine has served to reproduce, rather than rupture, existing gender divisions.

This study indicates that however freed from the confines of family life, the lives of these women remained firmly anchored within the confines of a gender regime that served to disadvantage them both as social actors and economic agents. Although women crack users have ostensibly been liberated from the confines of oppressive pimping structures that characterized previous eras of street-level sexwork (Maher and Curtis 1992), reliance on males for drugs, shelter, and other commodities prompted new forms of female dependence (see also Goldstein et al. 1992, p. 360; Inciardi et al. 1993, p. 85). Moreover, the data presented here indicate that drug dealers, lookouts, and participants in the street-level drug economy were not the only males to whom women crack users relinquished their meager incomes and their bodies.

The proliferation of alternative living arrangements devised by female crack users in the inner city has clearly prompted shifts in gender relations. Women crack users, in developing creative responses to homelessness, have redefined the boundaries of household forms and the nature of domestic economies. Within these contexts, gender relations have been reconstituted. However, underlying imbalances of power continue to structure the positioning of women in the street-level drug economy and the cultural meanings that attach to female drug use and homelessness. Even though the crack culture serves to amplify existing gender inequalities, it does not create them (Maher 1995). The privileged access of males, and older males in particular, to social, cultural, and economic resources, works to ensure that they remain the principal beneficiaries of these reconstituted gender relations.

Discussion Questions

1. How can we measure the economic marginalization of women to ensure a valid hypothesis? What are the drawbacks of the economic marginalization theory?

2. What are the available housing options open to drug-addicted women? In which housing arrangements do women feel most safe?

3. How do homelessness and alternative living arrangements reflect women's powerlessness and degradation in the inner city? Why can't these women break out of this cycle?

4. What realistic options are available, or what must be done differently in response to addressing homelessness and drug use?

5. Are there any crimes of survival that you think should be decriminalized?

References

Barak, G. 1991. *Gimme Shelter: A Social History of Homelessness in Contemporary America*. New York: Praeger.

Baskin, D., I. Sommers, and J. A. Fagan. 1993. "The Political Economy of Violent Female Street Crime." *Fordham Urban Law Journal* 20: 401–7.

Bourgois, P. 1989. "In Search of Horatio Alger: Culture and Ideology in the Crack Economy." *Contemporary Drug Problems* 16: 619–49.

——. 1995. *In Search of Respect: Selling Crack in El Barrio*. New York: Cambridge University Press.

Bourgois, P. and E. Dunlap. 1993. "Exorcising Sex-for-Crack: An Ethnographic Perspective From Harlem." Pp. 97–132 in *Crack Pipe as Pimp: An Ethnographic Investigation of Sex-for-Crack Exchanges*, edited by M. S. Ratner. New York: Lexington Books.

Boyle, K. and M. D. Anglin. 1993. "To the Curb: Sex Bartering and Drug Use Among Homeless Crack Users in Los Angeles." Pp. 159–86 in *Crack Pipe as Pimp: An Ethnographic Investigation of Sex-for-Crack Exchanges*, edited by M. S. Ratner. New York: Lexington Books.

Campbell, A. 1993. *Out of Control: Men, Women and Aggression*. London: Pandora.

Carlson, R. G. and H. A. Siegel. 1991. "The Crack Life: An Ethnographic Overview of Crack Use and Sexual Behavior Among African-Americans in a Midwest Metropolitan City." *Journal of Psychoactive Drugs* 23: 11–20.

Dunlap, E. 1992. "Impact of Drugs on Family Life and Kin Networks in the Inner-City African-American Single-Parent Household." Pp. 181–207 in *Drugs, Crime and Social Isolation: Barriers to Urban Opportunity*, edited by A. Harrell and G. Peterson. Washington, DC: Urban Institute Press.

Dunlap, E. and B. D. Johnson. 1992. "The Setting for the Crack Era: Macro Forces, Micro Consequences 1960–1992." *Journal of Psychoactive Drugs* 24: 307–21.

——. 1994. Gaining Access and Conducting Ethnographic Research Among Drug Dealers. Presented at the meeting of the Society for Applied Anthropology, Cancun, Mexico, April.

——. 1996. "Family Resources in the Development of a Female Crack Seller Career: Case Study of a Hidden Population." *Journal of Drug Issues* 26: 177–200.

Dunlap, E., B. D. Johnson, and L. Maher. Forthcoming. "Female Crack Dealers in New York City: Who They Are and What They Do." *Women and Criminal Justice*.

Dunlap, E., B. D. Johnson, and A. Manwar. 1994. "A Successful Female Crack Dealer: Case Study of a Deviant Career." *Deviant Behavior* 15: 1–25.

Dunlap, E., B. D. Johnson, H. Sanabria, E. Holliday, V. Lipsey, M. Barnett, W. Hopkins, I. Sobel, D. Randolph, and K. Chin. 1990. "Studying Crack Users and Their Criminal Careers: Scientific and Artistic Aspects of Locating Hard-to-Reach Subjects and Interviewing Them About Sensitive Topics." *Contemporary Drug Problems* 17: 121–44.

Edlin, B. R., K. L. Irwin, D. D. Ludwig, H. V. McCoy, Y. Serrano, C. Word, B. P. Bowser, S. Faruque, C. B. McCoy, R. F. Schilling, and S. D. Holmberg. 1992. "High-Risk Sex Behavior Among Young Street-Recruited Crack Cocaine Smokers in Three American Cities: An Interim Report." *Journal of Psychoactive Drugs* 24: 363–71.

Fagan, J. A. 1994. "Women and Drugs Revisited: Female Participation in the Cocaine Economy." *Journal of Drug Issues* 24: 179–225.

Fullilove, M. T. and R. E. Fullilove. 1989. "Intersecting Epidemics: Black Teen Crack Use and Sexually Transmitted Diseases." *Journal of the American Medical Association* 44: 146–53.

Goldstein, P. J., L. J. Ouellet, and M. Fendrich. 1992. "From Bag Brides to Skeezers: A Historical Perspective on Sex-for-Drugs Behavior." *Journal of Psychoactive Drugs* 24: 349–61.

Golub, A. and B. D. Johnson. 1994. "The Shifting Importance of Alcohol and Marijuana as Gateway Substances Among Serious Drug Abusers." *Journal of Alcohol Studies* 55: 607–14.

Hamid, A. 1990. "The Political Economy of Crack-Related Violence." *Contemporary Drug Problems* 17: 31–78.

——. 1992a. "The Developmental Cycle of a Drug Epidemic: The Cocaine Smoking Epidemic of 1981–1991." *Journal of Psychoactive Drugs* 24: 337–48.

——. 1992b. "Drugs and Patterns of Opportunity in the Inner-City: The Case of Middle Aged, Middle Income Cocaine Smokers." Pp. 209–39 in *Drugs, Crime, and Social Isolation: Barriers to Urban Opportunity*, edited by Adele Harrell and George Peterson. Washington, DC: Urban Institute Press.

Hopper, K. and J. Hamburg. 1984. *The Making of America's Homeless: From Skid Row to New Poor, 1945–1984.* New York: Community Service Society.

Inciardi, J. A., D. Lockwood, and A. E. Pottieger. 1993. *Women and Crack Cocaine.* New York: Macmillan.

Inciardi, J. A., A. E. Pottieger, M. A. Forney, D. D. Chitwood, and D. C. McBride. 1991. "Prostitution, IV Drug Use, and Sex-for-Crack Exchanges Among Serious Delinquents: Risks for HIV Infection." *Criminology* 29: 221–35.

Jencks, C. and P. E. Peterson. 1991. *The Urban Underclass.* Washington, DC: Brookings Institution.

Johnson, B. D., P. J. Goldstein, E. Preble, J. Schmeidler, D. S. Lipton, B. Spunt, and T. Miller. 1985. *Taking Care of Business: The Economics of Crime by Heroin Abusers.* Lexington, MA: Lexington Books.

Johnson, B. D., T. Williams, K. Dei, and H. Sanabria. 1990. "Drug Abuse and the Inner City: Impact on Hard Drug Users and the Community." Pp. 9–67 in *Drugs and Crime*, Vol. 13, *Crime and Justice Series*, edited by Michael Tonry and James Q. Wilson. Chicago: University of Chicago Press.

Kasarda, J. D. 1992. "The Severely Distressed in Economically Transforming Cities." Pp. 45–98 in *Drugs, Crime, and Social Isolation: Barriers to Urban Opportunity*, edited by Adele Harrell and George Peterson. Washington, DC: Urban Institute Press.

Maher, L. 1995. "Dope Girls: Gender, Race and Class in the Drug Economy." Ph.D. Dissertation, Rutgers University, Newark, New Jersey.

——. 1996. "Hidden in the Light: Occupational Norms Among Crack-using Street-level Sex Workers." *Journal of Drug Issues* 26: 145–175.

Maher, L. and R. Curtis. 1992. "Women on the Edge of Crime: Crack Cocaine and the Changing Contexts of Street-level Sex Work in New York City." *Crime, Law and Social Change* 18: 221–58.

——. 1994. "In Search of the Female Urban Gangsta: Change, Culture and Crack Cocaine." Pp. 147–66 in *The Criminal Justice System and Women*, edited by B. Raffel-Price and N. J. Sokoloff. 2nd ed. New York: McGraw-Hill.

Maher, L., E. Dunlap, and B. D. Johnson. "Black Women's Pathways to Involvement in Illicit Drug Distribution and Sales: An Ethnographic Analysis." In review.

Mieczkowski, T. 1994. "The Experiences of Women Who Sell Crack: Some Descriptive Data From the Detroit Crack Ethnography Project." *Journal of Drug Issues* 24: 227–48.

Moore, J. W. 1991. *Going Down to the Barrio: Homeboys and Homegirls in Change.* Philadelphia: Temple University Press.

Murphy, S. and D. Waldorf. 1991. "Kickin' Down to the Street Doc: Shooting Galleries in the San Francisco Bay Area." *Contemporary Drug Problems* 18: 9–29.

Ouellet, L. J., W. W. Wiebel, A. D. Jiminez, and W. A. Johnson. 1993. "Crack Cocaine and the Transformation of Prostitution in Three Chicago Neighborhoods." Pp. 69–96 in *Crack Pipe as Pimp: An Ethnographic Investigation of Sex-for-Crack Exchanges*, edited by M. S. Ratner. New York: Lexington Books.

Ratner, M. S., ed. 1993a. *Crack Pipe as Pimp: An Ethnographic Investigation of Sex-for-Crack Exchanges.* New York: Lexington Books.

——. 1993b. "Sex, Drugs and Public Policy: Studying and Understanding the Sex-for-Crack Phenomenon." Pp. 1–36 in *Crack Pipe as Pimp: An Ethnographic Investigation of Sex-for Crack Exchanges*, edited by M. S. Ratner. New York: Lexington Books.

Ropers, R. H. 1988. *The Invisible Homeless: A New Urban Ecology.* New York: Insight Books.

Rossi, P. H. 1989. *Down and Out in America: The Origins of Homelessness.* Chicago: University of Chicago Press.

Sullivan, M. L. 1989. *Getting Paid: Youth Crime and Work in the Inner City.* Ithaca, NY: Cornell University Press.

Vanderstaay, S. 1992. *Street Lives: An Oral History of Homeless Americans.* Philadelphia: New Society.

Waterston, A. 1993. *Street Addicts in the Political Economy.* Philadelphia: Temple University Press.

Weatherby, N. L., J. M. Schultz, D. D. Chitwood, H. V. McCoy, C. B. McCoy, D. D. Ludwig, and B. R. Edlin. 1992. "Crack Cocaine Use and Sexual Activity in Miami, Florida." *Journal of Psychoactive Drugs* 24: 373–80.

Williams, T., E. Dunlap, B. D. Johnson, and A. Hamid. 1992. "Personal Safety in Dangerous Places." *Journal of Contemporary Ethnography* 21: 343–74.

Zimmer, R. and M. Schretzman. 1991. "Issues for Homeless Women and Their Children." Pp. 173–77 in *Alcohol and Drugs Are Womens' Issues*, Vol. 1, *A Review of the Issues*, edited by P. Roth. Metuchen, NJ: Women's Action Alliance and Scarecrow Press.

Excerpted from: Lisa Maher, Eloise Dunlap, Bruce D. Johnson, and Ansley Hamid, "Alternative Living Arrangements in the Inner-City Crack Culture." In *Journal of Research in Crime and Delinquency* 33 (2): 181–205. Copyright © 1996 Sage Publications, Inc. Used with permission. ✦

Section V

Women's Crime as Rational Choice

We've discussed throughout this text how most women's lawbreaking behavior is linked to an outcome of previous or persistent victimization. However, evidence indicates that some women commit crimes as a result of free will, planning, and rational choice. This means that some types of women's crimes are less deterministic and more a product of selection and preference based on what seems reasonable to the woman *from her perspective*. Most women prisoners reportedly take responsibility for their actions that ultimately led to their incarceration and see committing crimes as a product of conscious decision making (Owen 1998). This section examines a variety of crimes that include some aspect of rational choice. For example, **the first reading, by Dorothy Allison,** captures motivations for theft while the author is an indigent undergraduate college student. This chapter illustrates that planned criminal activity can occur in a wide range of circumstances and, like most theft, often remains undetected or unreported. Next, **the article by Deborah Baskin and Ira Sommers** examines how women employed in low-wage jobs with limited access to satisfying long-term careers instead chose careers in crime. **The third selection, by Barbara Denton and Pat O'Malley,** describes how women involved in drug networks generate more money to finance their position by becoming involved in property crimes, such as bank fraud, burglary, shoplifting, and theft.

Rational choice theory is frequently attached to violent crimes such as robbery. Miller (2002) advocates the position that there is no such typology as "male-oriented" or "female-oriented" crime, but that both women and men strategically draw on and use their gender to an advantage when committing a crime. For example, some women act "distraught," approach men for directions or help, and then proceed to rob their victim. Another role for women may be that of identifying or trying to emulate a masculine identity for acceptance or respect of other males, which is termed "gender crossing" (Miller 2002, 442). **Jody Miller's research (in Chapter 20 in this section)** on active female robbers details how women use their gender to target victims and complete the robbery event. Women are motivated to commit robbery to get money for material goods or to party. These reasons are identical to motivations that male robbers convey.

Recall that previously we focused on women who kill in a domestic setting because they are being vehemently abused, they are acting in self-defense, or they are triggered by underlying problems caused by low self-esteem, powerlessness, and oppression. Most women who kill do so as a form of escaping dominance of a male partner and are not acting based on rational choice. **The selection by Henry Brownstein and his colleagues** takes a look at 19 women who murdered strangers during a drug deal. This situation is an uncommon motive and represents only 8.8 percent of all murders committed by women. The purpose of the research was to determine whether it is possible that women commit murder to protect their economic interests and profits, which would signify an element of rational choice, or if they commit murder out of fear or on behalf of a male partner, which may suggest something different.

Criminal Careers

The prevailing literature suggests that most female offenders age out of crime, which means that as they age, they decrease their criminal involvement and become more law-abiding. Suggested reasons for the aging-out phenomenon include marriage, pregnancy, childcare responsibilities, and employment, which serve to increase conventional bonds and ties to legitimate opportunities and relationships (Moore and Hagedorn 2001; Sampson and Laub 1993). With increased responsibility at work or for dependent children, women simply do not have the time to engage in crime. Few researchers have been able to find evidence for chronic female career criminals who persist on a criminal path. In a longitudinal study of abused and neglected girls and women, Widom (2000) challenged the traditional view. She found that about 8 percent of abused and neglected females in their sample were persistent and frequent offenders well through the age of 35. Peak offending rates for these women occured around age 26 or 27, older than the age of other offenders' peak rates, which lie between 16 and 18 years of age. **The final reading in this section, by Sommers, Baskin, and Fagan,** examines the pathways and thinking processes that persistent offenders take when they decide to discontinue criminal behavior.

In conclusion, it is important to note that women commit significantly less crime overall than men. National arrest data in 2002 indicate that women accounted for only 10 percent of robberies, 11 percent of murders, 13 percent of burglaries, and 20 percent of those arrested for aggravated assault. Crimes involving nearly as many women offenders as men include embezzlement (50 percent), fraud (45 percent), and forgery (40 percent) (Federal Bureau of Investigation, 2003). The numbers over time also show that since 1960, women have contributed to a growing percentage of arrests for most felony crimes (Heimer 2000). We have attempted to contribute to an understanding of the complex reasons why women commit crime.

An underlying theme of this text is how gender definitions and cultural definitions control and penalize various groups of girls and women, some more so than others. However, the manner in which some people think about women's involvement in crime has more to do with their personal beliefs about what girls or women "should" or "should not" be doing. When we begin to better understand why some women commit crime, we can redefine our response accordingly and intervene to decrease and prevent behaviors that lead to criminalization and victimization.

References

Federal Bureau of Investigation. 2003. *Uniform Crime Reports, 2002.* Accessed on September 1, 2004, at: *http://www.fbi.gov/ucr.*

Heimer, K. 2000. "Changes in the Gender Gap in Crime and Women's Economic Marginalization." *Change.* Washington, DC: National Institute of Justice, Office of Justice Programs.

Miller, J. 2002. "The Strengths and Limits of 'Doing Gender' for Understanding Street Crime." *Theoretical Criminology* 6 (4): 433–460.

Moore, J., and J. Hagedorn. 2001. *Female Gangs: A Focus on Research.* Washington, DC: Office of Juvenile Justice and Delinquency Prevention, U.S. Department of Justice.

Owen, B. 1998. *In the Mix: Struggle and Survival in a Women's Prison.* Albany: State University of New York Press.

Sampson, R. J., and J. H. Laub. 1993. *Crime in the Making: Pathways and Turning Points Through Life.* Cambridge, MA: Harvard University Press.

Widom, C. S. 2000. "Childhood Victimization and the Derailment of Girls and Women to the Criminal Justice System." *Research on Women and Girls in the Justice System: Plenary Papers of the 1999 Conference on Criminal Justice Research and Evaluation—Enhancing Policy and Practice Through Research, Volume 3* (NCJ 180973). Washington, DC: National Institute of Justice, Office of Justice Programs. ✦

17

One Woman's Voice

Stealing in College

Dorothy Allison

In this brief selection, Dorothy Allison details her experiences as a thief while she attends college during her undergraduate years. Her motives ranged from need, to greed, to revenge. Many of the items she took were thrown away, taken only for excitement or as a reaction to some real or imagined slight. This selection illustrates that criminal behavior can be found anywhere, even on a college campus.

My hands shake when I am hungry, and I have always been hungry. Not for food—I have always had enough biscuit fat to last me. In college I got breakfast, lunch, and dinner with my dormitory fees, but my restless hunger didn't abate. It was having only four dollars till the end of the month and not enough coming in then. I sat at a lunch table with the girls who planned to go to the movies for the afternoon, and counting three dollars in worn bills the rest in coins over and over in my pocket. I couldn't go see any movies.

I went, instead, downtown to steal. I became what had always been expected of me—a thief. Dangerous, but careful. Wanting everything, I tamed my anger, smiling wide and innocently. With the help of that smile I stole toilet paper from the Burger King rest room, magazines from the lower shelves at 7-Eleven, and sardines from the deli—sliding those little cans down my jeans to where I had drawn the cuffs tight with rubber bands. I lined my pockets with plastic bags for a trip to the local Winn Dixie, where I could collect smoked oysters from the gourmet section and fresh grapes from the open bins of produce. From the hobby shop in the same shopping center I pocketed metal snaps to replace the rubber bands on my pantleg cuffs and metal guitar picks I could use to pry loose and switch price tags on items too big to carry away. Anything small enough to fit

a palm walked out with me, anything round enough to fit an armpit, anything thin enough to carry between my belly and belt. The smallest, sharpest, most expensive items rested behind my teeth, behind that smile that remained my ultimate shield.

On the day that I was turned away from registration because my scholarship check was late, I dressed myself in my Sunday best and went downtown to the Hilton Hotel. There was a Methodist Outreach Convention with meetings in all the ballrooms, and a hospitality suite. I walked from room to room filling a JCPenney shopping bag with cut-glass ashtrays showing the Hilton logo and faceted wineglasses marked only with the dregs of grape juice. I dragged the bag out to St. Pete beach and sailed those ashtrays off the pier like frisbees. Then I waited for sunset to toss the wineglasses high enough to see the red and purple reflections as they flipped end over end. Each piece shattered ecstatically on the tar-black rocks under the pier, throwing up glass fragments into the spray. Sight and sound, it was better than a movie.

The president of the college invited all of the scholarship students over for tea or wine. He served cheese that had to be cut from a great block with delicate little knives. I sipped wine, toothed cheese, talked politely, and used my smile. The president's wife nodded at me and put her pink fleshy hand on my shoulder. I put my own hand on hers and gave one short squeeze. She started but didn't back away, and I found myself giggling at her attempts to tell us all a funny story. She flushed and told us how happy she was to have us in her home. I smiled and told her how happy I was to have come, my jacket draped loosely over the wineglasses I had hooked in my belt. Walking back to the dorm, I slipped one hand into my pocket, carefully fingering two delicate little knives.

Junior year my scholarship was cut yet again, and I became nervous that working in the mailroom wouldn't pay for all I needed, St. Vincent de Paul offered me a ransom, paying a dime apiece for plates and trays carted off from the cafeteria. Glasses were only good for three cents and hard to carry down on the bus without breaking, but sheets from the alumni guest-room provided the necessary padding. My roommate complained that I made her nervous, always carrying boxes in and out. She moved out shortly after Christmas, and I chewed my nails trying to figure out how to carry her mattress down to St. Vincent de Paul. I finally decided it was hopeless, and spent the rest of the holidays reading Jean Genet and walking through the art department hallways.

They had hardwood stools in the studios, and stacking file boxes no one had opened in years. I wore a cloth cap when I took them, and my no-nonsense expression. I was so calm that one of the professors helped me clear paper off the third one. He was distracted, discussing Jackson Pollock with a very pale woman whose hands were marked with tusche. "Glad they finally decided to get these out of here," was all he said to me, never once looking up into my face. My anger came up from my stomach with an acid taste. I went back for his clipboard and papers, but his desk was locked and my file broke on the rim. In compensation I took the silk lining out of the pockets of the corduroy coat he'd left thrown over a stool. The silk made a lemongrass sachet I gave my mother for her birthday, and every time I saw him in that jacket I smiled.

My sociology professor had red hair, forty shelves of books, four children, and an entirely cordial relationship with her ex-husband. When she invited me to dinner, I did not understand what she wanted with me. I watched her closely and kept my hands in my pockets. She talked about her divorce and the politics in the department, how she had worked for John F. Kennedy in 1960 and demonstrated for civil rights in Little Rock in '65. There were lots of books she could lend me, she insisted, but didn't say exactly which ones. She poured me Harvey's Bristol Cream, trailing her fingers across my wrist when I took the glass. Then she shook her head nervously and tried to persuade me to talk about myself, interrupting only to get me to switch topics as she moved restlessly from her rocking chair to her bolster to the couch beside me. She did not want to hear about my summers working in the mop factory, but she loved my lies about hitchhiking cross-country.

"Meet me for lunch on Monday," she insisted, while her eyes behind her glasses kept glancing at me, turning away and turning back. My palms were sweaty, but I nodded yes. At the door she stopped me, and put her hand out to touch my face.

"Your family is very poor, aren't they?"

My face froze and burned at the same time. "Not really," I told her, "not anymore." She nodded and smiled, and the heat in my face went down my body in waves.

I didn't want to go on Monday but made myself. Her secretary was confused when I asked about lunch. "I don't have anything written down about it," she said, without looking up at her calendar.

After class that afternoon the sociology professor explained her absence with a story about one of her children who had been bitten by a dog, but not seriously. "Come on Thursday," she insisted, but on Thursday neither she nor her secretary were there. I stood in the doorway to her office and tilted my head back to take in her shelves of books. I wanted to pocket them all, but at the same time I didn't want anything of hers. Trembling, I reached and pulled out the fattest book on the closet shelf. It was a hardbound edition of *Sadism at the Movies,* with a third of the pages underlined in red. It fit easily in my backpack, and I stopped in the Student Union bookstore on the way back to the dorm to buy a Hershey bar and steal a bright blue pen.

On the next Monday, she apologized again, and again invited me to go to lunch the next day. I skipped lunch but slipped in that afternoon to return her book, now full of my bright blue comments. In its spot on the shelf there was now a collection of the essays of Georges Bataille, still unmarked. By the time I returned it on Friday, heavy blue ink stains showed on the binding itself.

Eventually we did have lunch. She talked to me about how hard it was to be a woman alone in a college town, about how all the male professors treated her like a fool, and yet how hard she worked. I nodded.

"You read so much," I whispered.

"I keep up," she agreed with me.

"So do I," I smiled.

She looked nervous and changed the subject but let me walk her back to her office. On her desk, there was a new edition of Malinowski's *The Sexual Life of Savages.* I laid my notebook down on top of it, and took them both when I left. Malinowski was a fast read. I had that one back a day later. She was going through her date book looking for a free evening we could have dinner. But exams were coming up so soon. I smiled and nodded and backed out the door. The secretary, used to seeing me come and go, didn't even look up.

I took no other meals with professors, didn't trust myself in their houses. But I studied their words, gestures, jokes, and quarrels to see just how they were different from me. I limited my outrage to their office shelves, working my way through their books one at a time, carefully underlining my favorite passages in dark blue ink—occasionally covering over their own faded marks. I continued to take the sociology professor's classes but refused to stay after to talk, and when she called my name in the halls, I would just smile and keep walking. Once she sat beside me in a seminar and put her hand on the back of my neck where I was leaning back in my chair. I turned and saw she was biting her lips. I remembered her saying, "Your family is very poor, aren't they?" I kept my face expressionless and looked forward again. That was the afternoon I made myself a pair of harem pants out of the gauze curtains from the infirmary.

My parents came for graduation, Mama taking the day off from the diner, my father walking slow in his back brace. They both were bored at the lunch, uncomfortable and impatient to have the ceremony be over so we could pack my boxes in the car and leave. Mama kept pulling at the collar of my robe while waiting for the call for me to join my class. She was so nervous she kept rocking back on her heels and poked my statistics professor with her elbow as he tried to pass.

"Quite something, your daughter," he grinned as he shook my mama's hand. Mama and I could both tell he was uncomfortable, so she just nodded, not knowing what to say. "We're expecting great things of her," he added, and quickly joined the other professors on the platform, their eyes roaming over the parents headed for the elevated rows at the sides and back of the hall. I saw my sociology professor sharing a quick sip from the dean's pocket flask. She caught me watching, and her face flushed a dull reddish gray. I smiled widely as ever I had, and held that smile through the long slow ceremony that followed, the walk up to get my diploma, and the confused milling around that followed the moment when we were all supposed to throw our tassels over to the other side. Some of the students threw their mortarboards drunkenly into the air, but I tucked mine under my arm and found my parents before they had finished shaking the cramps out of their legs.

"Sure went on forever," Mama whispered, as we walked toward the exit.

The statistics professor was standing near the door telling a tall black woman, "Quite something, your son. We're expecting great things of him."

I laughed and tucked my diploma in Mama's bag for the walk back to the dormitory. People were packing station wagons, U-Haul trailers, and bulging little sedans. Our Pontiac was almost full and my face was starting to ache from smiling, but I made a quick trip down into the dormitory basement anyway. There was a vac-uum cleaner and two wooden picture frames I'd stashed behind the laundry-room doors that I knew would fit perfectly in the Pontiac's trunk. Mama watched me carry them up but said nothing. Daddy only laughed and revved the engine while we swung past the auditorium. At the entrance to the campus I got them to pull over and look back at the scattered buildings. It was a rare moment, and for a change my hunger wasn't bothering me at all. But while my parents waited, I climbed out and pulled the commemorative roses off the welcome sign. I got back in the car and piled them into my mama's lap.

"Quite something, my daughter," she laughed, and hugged the flowers to her breast. She rocked in her seat as my stepfather gunned the engine and spun the tires pulling out. I grinned while she laughed.

"Quite something."

It was the best moment I'd had in four years.

Discussion Questions

1. What were the primary motives behind Dorothy's thefts? How did she justify her offenses?

2. What was Dorothy's reaction to the overtures by her sociology professor? Why do you think she took the books and then returned them?

3. Do rational choice crimes apply to women who have limited economic opportunities or who have been abused as children? Why or why not?

4. Is this a crime of rational choice? Why or why not? Would your opinion of Allison's crime change if she had been less educated, or been abused as a child?

5. Why isn't there more research on crimes committed by educated women or women of middle or upper socioeconomic levels?

Reprinted from: Dorothy Allison, "Steal Away." In *Without a Net: The Female Experience of Growing Up Working Class* (Live Girl Series), Michelle Tea (ed.), pp. 15–20. Copyright © 2004 by Seal Press. Used with author's permission. ✦

18
Women, Work, and Crime

Deborah R. Baskin
Ira Sommers

The purpose of this study is to explore the impact of women's life experiences on their involvement in legal and illegal work. The authors consider issues such as how job opportunities, skills, and aspirations affect the work-crime relationship and how certain illegal activities attract women away from jobs in the licit economy and even from involvement in other, gender-stereotypical crimes (e.g., prostitution). The authors describe how a sample of women involved in violent street crime make a living, and they follow the women's involvement in the legal and illegal economies.

The research is based on in-depth life history interviews with 170 women who committed nondomestic violent felony crimes (e.g., robbery, assault, homicide) in New York City. The women were recruited from various segments of society and included (1) those arrested and arraigned for violent crimes (n = 49); (2) those in state prison for violent crimes (n = 48); and (3) women actively involved in violent criminal offending (n = 73).

Interviews were open-ended, in-depth, and, when possible, audiotaped. The open-ended technique created a context in which respondents were able to speak freely and in their own words. Furthermore, it facilitated the pursuit of issues that were raised by the women during the interview but had not been recognized beforehand by the researchers. The in-depth interview approach enabled the authors to pursue information about specific events as well as provide an opportunity for respondents to reflect on those events. As a result, the researchers were able to gain insight into the women's attitudes, feelings, and other subjective orientations to their experiences.

A typical member of the sample was a black woman who was 27 years old and a high school dropout with two children, possessing limited legal work experience. The youngest was 16 years old and the oldest, 43. The median age of the respondents was 30 years. Seventy-five percent of the subjects were high school dropouts,

having typically left school by Grade 11. Although most of the women had worked in a legitimate job (80 percent), the median number of months employed was only 16 and the average was 35.9. Most of the women worked in unskilled and semiskilled working-class occupations (e.g., clerical and factory jobs).

The relationship between crime and work has become the focus of much criminological research (Bourgois 1995; Crutchfield 1997; Fagan 1996; Fagan and Freeman 1994; Grogger 1994; Reuter, MacCoun, and Murphy 1990; Sommers, Baskin, and Fagan 1996; Sullivan 1989; Wilson 1996). This is due, in part, to major shifts over the past two decades in inner-city legal and illegal labor markets as well as to important changes in the social, cultural, and political dynamics within urban communities. Thus far, research in this area has concentrated almost exclusively on males with only passing reference to and/or conjecture regarding women.

Nonetheless, the macro transformations in urban communities that have been identified as affecting males' decisions concerning criminal involvement have also had an impact on women's choices as they relate to work and crime. Therefore, the purpose of the present research is to explore key issues concerning the interaction between legal and illegal work in terms of the impact that the study of women's life experiences had on that relationship. Here, we will explore how such human capital issues as job opportunities, skills and aspirations mediated the work-crime relationship; how illegal work, especially drug distribution and robbery, drew women away from their positions in the licit economy, as well as from their involvement in gender stereotypical crimes such as prostitution; and how an increasing and eventual full-time commitment to street life and drug abuse ended their relationship to careers in both the legal and illegal labor markets altogether.

The Literature on Crime and Work

The sharp rise in violent crime and drug trafficking that characterized many inner cities during the 1980s and early 1990s has often been associated with a precipitous decline in formal employment opportunities. This "disappearance of work" (Wilson 1996) has been seen as altering the basic calculus used by young people to influence their choice of economic activities. By and large, the outcome of such decision-making, in the context of dwindling wages and satisfactory job opportunities in the legal world of work, has been increased participation in illegal income-generating activities (Fagan 1992; Freeman 1983; Hagedorn 1994; Witte and Tauchen 1994).

In recent years, research based on this model of decision-making has flourished. Elements of the economic calculus have been dissected and results supporting the choice of crime *over* legal work have been reported. Increasing unemployment and underemployment have been identified as significantly related to crime participation (Chiricos 1987; Blackburn, Bloom, and Freeman 1990; Corcoran and Parrott 1992; Fagan and Freeman 1994); income from crime, especially from drug dealing, has been found to be higher than income from other, legal sources (Vicusi 1986; Reuter et al. 1990; Fagan 1992, 1994a; Freeman 1992); and the social and psychic payoffs from illegal work seem to outweigh the concern over, if not the risks of legal sanctions (Fagan 1996). Thus, the choice of illegal work is understandable, at least, intellectually.

Once the decision to enter the world of illegal enterprise has been made, another body of research has sought to explain the persistence of illicit income-generation activities. Here, ethnographic studies have documented a renouncement of the secondary labor market by inner-city males. Young males who have turned to the illegal economy now rely on street networks for status (Anderson 1990, 1994; Fagan 1994a, 1994b; Hagedorn 1994; Hagedorn and Macron 1988; Padilla 1992; Taylor 1990; Moore, 1991, 1992). And, they use the discourse of work, like "getting paid," or "going to work" (Sullivan 1989) to describe their criminal careers. Thus, for these young males, money from crime and reputation from criminal success form the bases for commodity consumption and status that would be unavailable to them from the legal workaday world.

The persistence of criminal careers from adolescence to adulthood is also understood in terms of the structural changes in legal employment patterns in urban centers. Where once manufacturing jobs and other semiskilled labor market positions provided egresses from criminal careers as young males moved from adolescence to adulthood, the disappearance of such opportunities has resulted in cross-generational joblessness with attendant cultural, social, and legal disadvantages (Wilson 1996; Tienda 1989; Sullivan 1989). Thus, young males in the transition to adulthood who suffer from social capital deficits (Bourgois 1995), the stigma of legal sanctions (Anderson 1990;

Sullivan 1989), and exaggerated tastes and preferences (Anderson 1990; Bourgois 1995) further narrow their options for economic and social success in the world of licit work (Hagan and Pallioni 1990; Bourgois 1995; Anderson 1990; Sampson and Laub 1993).

Over time, the perception that entry into the world of legal work is possible dwindles. At this stage of criminal career development, research points to the rise of a rigid bifurcation between licit and illicit economic activities (Anderson 1990, 1994; Hagedorn 1994; Hagedorn and Macron 1988; Taylor 1990; Moore 1992). Thus, young males eventually choose to *either* abandon their involvement in illegal work and accept the economic and social parameters of the conventional workaday world, or they commit themselves to illegal work and its concomitant social and legal implication. However, once the decision to commit to the illicit economy is made, the option to return to the licit world is narrowed, if not eliminated altogether (Hagan 1993). This bifurcation has become, if not an empirical reality, one that at least characterizes much thinking in this area.

Recent research, however, suggests that participation in the *worlds* of work may not be exclusive. In fact, several studies show a much more dynamic and flexible interaction between legal and illegal work. Some qualitative studies have documented regular career "shifts" from illegal to legal sources of income and even simultaneous participation in both economies over the course of an individual's work history (Shover 1985; Biernacki 1986; Sullivan 1989; Padilla 1992; Adler 1992; Baskin and Sommers 1998).

Despite the talk of "young people," "individuals," and "inner-city residents," much of what we know about the interaction between legal and illegal work is based on information obtained from male respondents. This is unfortunate. Recent research on female offenders has documented dramatic changes in women's participation in income-generating criminal activities. From robbery to drug dealing, women in inner cities have increased their involvement as well as other aspects of their participation in crime, such as roles and statuses. Thus, we find more women acting as principals in criminal events, as crew bosses and owners of drug distribution enterprises, and as recruiters of other women into the illicit world of work (Baskin and Sommers 1998; Fagan 1994b; Inciardi, Lockwood, and Pottieger 1993; Mieczkowski 1994; Miller 1998; Taylor 1993). Further, we find more women entering crime apart from domestic partnerships, more within single-sex peer groups, and more ready to employ violence as part of doing business (Baskin and Sommers 1998; Curry, Ball, and Fox 1994). And, we find that for some women, their involvement in other forms of street crime, such as robbery, burglary, and drug dealing, has led to a decrease in their participation in prostitution (Sommers et al. 1996).

Nonetheless, these changes do not *erase* the fact that gender does indeed make a difference in daily life experiences and in decision-making patterns (Brown and Gilligan 1992; Pipher 1994), albeit in different ways for different groups of women. Therefore, research needs to focus on women within specific contexts if we are to understand how the dynamics of gender impact on particular criminal career decisions.

The research reported within is a step in that direction. Here, we describe how a sample of women involved in violent street crime tried to make a living. We explore their progression from early involvement in the legal and formal economy, their joint involvement in these two spheres and their ultimate embeddedness in the informal and illicit economy. Through a description of their experiences in these various "work" sectors, the women provide us with an understanding of the bases for and types of decisions they made when choosing their "vocations."

It is clear from their accounts that even from the outset, a tension always existed between their involvement in legal and illegal work and between the asocial world of formal labor and the seemingly social atmosphere promised by criminal involvement. Further, we find that the "economic" calculus so often reported in the literature is only partially the basis for their decision making; and that their maintenance in these criminal activities comes to resemble less the workaday world described in relation to male criminal careers and more the world of drug addicts that the traditional literature on females and crime suggests (Bourgois and Dunlap 1993; Maher and Daly 1996; Hunt 1990).

Participation in the Secondary Labor Market

For the women we interviewed, legal employment was viewed as important, at least initially. By the time they were sixteen, the majority had left school. Therefore, securing a job took on great significance. And, at least at first, they were successful. Unlike their male counterparts, most of whom experienced high rates of joblessness from the start (Wilson 1996), 80 percent of the women we interviewed were able to secure employment in the formal economy. These jobs were exclusively in the secondary labor market.

Research on the effects of labor distribution on criminal involvement has suggested that relegation to the secondary labor market, that is, working at jobs that are low-paying, have few, if any benefits, and offer little in terms of advancement, will result in greater participation in violent crime (Crutchfield 1989).[1] Further, it is hypothesized that the mechanism through which this relationship is fostered is that of social bonding. In other words, the "weaker bonds . . . associated with employment in secondary occupations, will lead to higher crime rates" (Crutchfield 1989). Those who work in the secondary labor market, therefore, are less likely both to develop attachments and commitments to their jobs as well as stakes in conformity as compared to their peers in the primary labor market. Thus, the "qualities" of a job, rather than the presence or absence of employment, seem to affect criminal involvement (Rosenfeld and Messner 1989; Sampson and Laub 1993; Uggen, Piliavin, and Matsueda 1992), at least among males.

Of the women in our study who worked, the vast majority were employed in entry level, unskilled positions as office clerks (32 percent), factory laborers (28 percent), and salespeople (25 percent). Fifteen percent of the women were able to obtain "aide" positions in home health care or education. These positions were acquired either through temporary employment agencies or public programs, never through personal networks. They lasted no more than a few months and were characteristically low paying and offered little long term security and no chances for advancement.

The women in our study entered the labor force with an acute awareness that their employment, even in the future, would, in all probability, be sporadic or remain in the lowest echelons of the secondary market. For the few women who hoped for more lucrative futures in the licit job sector, training in cosmetology and having their own "station" at the local beauty salon was their loftiest goal. But, even at the outset, these women did not think that the jobs available to them would bring the "prestige, pride, and self-respect" (Liebow 1967, 60) found in white-collar occupations. Thus, like the men Liebow described in *Tally's Corner* (1967), these women ascribed "no lower value on the job than does the larger society" (57). In other words, these women were keenly aware of the social value of the types of jobs available to them.

The work descriptions offered by the women we interviewed confirmed this perspective. Furthermore, like the men Liebow described and those studied by Bourgois (1995), the women eventually came to view these jobs with an active disinterest. They were routinely fired due to excessive absenteeism or were absent frequently as a way of quitting. They would often show up for work high on drugs, or coming down from a night of heavy drinking and partying. Often, especially towards the end of their involvement in the formal economy, they used their work environments as settings for their increasingly prevalent criminal activities.

Descriptions of Initial Experiences in the Legal Economy

Herminia told us about her first job:

I worked for like minimum wage at Duane Read Pharmacy. I enjoyed it cause, you know, I felt, like independent. I was bringing a little money home. But, fast I stopped liking it. I never liked a job that would be just standing like in one place, you know, like doing the same thing over and over. I got tired of it—the monotony, the routine everyday, so I stopped showing up. I lasted there about four months. Then, I worked in Mac-Donald's for maybe four weeks. I hated MacDonald's. It was boring. I was there for about four weeks. So, I went through a few other jobs. These were the only ones I could get. I had to lie about my age just to get these. I was only 15 and 16 and who was going to hire me?

Herminia's description was typical of the women in this study. For that matter and without exception, regardless of the actual position, and like the men who Liebow spoke with in *Tally's Corner*, the women did not display an "overt interest in job specifics . . . in a large part perhaps because the specifics are not especially relevant" (Liebow 1967, 57). This was due to the fact that the secondary job market was comprised of "a narrow range of nondescript chores calling for nondescript, undifferentiated, unskilled labor" (Liebow 1967, 57).

Janelle, too, described her dissatisfaction with the types of jobs available to her. Furthermore, given her early involvement in violent street crime and drug use, it was especially difficult for her to accept the drudgery and routine of employment in the secondary market. Clearly, these types of jobs did not compete with the excitement she had and enjoyment she received from hanging out and partying with her friends.

I used to work at—this was when I was 16—I used to work at Wendy's. Yeah, at Roy Rogers too. I worked like, for six months at the first job and two months for the second. I quit because I couldn't function every day, gettin' up and goin' to work and then partyin' the night before. I didn't feel too great about these jobs. Wearing a stupid uniform and flipping burgers. That's lame.

Yeah, I was trying to do something for myself by working these jobs. But it wasn't working. I rather go home and get high and hang out with my people. So, it wasn't workin' and neither was I.

Interestingly, even among those who worked in the human service sector, principally as home attendants, work was viewed similarly as demeaning, boring, and no different from clerical or sales work:

I started out as a home health aide. It was O.K. for a little while. But then I got sick of it. You know what I'm saying—they like, they were driving me crazy. I felt like a housekeeper. It was nothing special, no different than working burgers or cleaning tables. There's not much else to say about it. (Denise)

Thus, the women in our study came to view their involvement in the licit job world with the same emptiness as the countless ghetto, barrio, and streetcorner males studied by other researchers. The difference for the women in our study, though, was that they were at least initially drawn to the legal economy and remained there for almost three years.

The Intermingling of Licit and Illicit Work

At the beginning of their employment careers, the women attempted to make a living, primarily through legitimate employment. Over time, however, they decided that the low economic and cultural returns from their marginal employment were not satisfactory. They then turned to crime and illegal hustles for supplementation. For many women, the workplace itself came to serve as a setting for these activities. And, it was these activities that provided them with important sources of income, identity, and excitement.

Here Denise, a former home attendant, describes how she combined licit and illicit work to augment her desires for more money, more excitement, and the respect of her peers on the street:

Yeah, so I hated doing things for these rich people, so after a while me and my friends developed a gimmick. I would go into the house, and I would case it out and get all the necessary information. When they would be out, my friends would come in and like vandalize it. Then we'd all go out and party and celebrate our success. I was really a key connection for them. And, funny thing is, I would go back to work the next day like nothing ever happened and act shocked.

I did that for about six months. But I really couldn't stand cleaning up after these rich people and so I went to work at _____ Hospital in their dietary department. Then I got the key to the supplies and I had my girlfriends come up with a truck and unload the block. This was fun and made us lots of money too. But, I got arrested and had to give them my paycheck. I worked there for about six months too.

Monica, too, used her place of employment for her illegal enterprises. In this case, she dealt drugs from her office.

I started as a summer youth worker for a City agency. But then they kept me permanently as a floater, which means like I worked diversified duties. I made, like, $9,000 a year. At this point I was already indulging in cocaine and I started selling drugs. So, uh, I started going to work and showing people my material—people that I knew that got high. And they started buying from me. So then they started buying weight which would mean that I would have to get more material—and give it to them. And, uh, it's like I used the messenger companies from the office. I used to call the messenger companies, and they used to pick everything up. And they would come pick it up at the agency and drop it off at someone else not knowing what was really inside. I made like $4000 to $5200 a week. But then I just started using all the money for getting high and I stopped going to the office.

"Doubling up" in crime and work (Fagan 1994a), as these women had done, is not unusual among active offenders, regardless of gender, especially among those involved in drug distribution. Research has indicated that between 25 percent and 57 percent of active offenders report participating in income producing crime, thereby optimizing extant opportunities (Grogger 1994; Hagedorn 1994; Fagan 1992; Reuter et al. 1990). Nonetheless, research in this area, again using predominately male respondents, has explained such behavior solely in economic terms. It has been argued that young males will "double up" for the purpose of optimizing income generation opportunities, plain and simple. What was different for the women in our study was the fact that "doubling up" provided these women with opportunities for optimizing *both* the economic and the social facets of their lives; one no less important

than the other. Thus, "doubling up" permitted the intermingling of fun, excitement, and adventure with occasions for both legal and illegal income generation—all within the same work setting.

Crime on the Side

For some of the women with whom we spoke, "doubling up" took a different form. These women recounted for us incredible work schedules in which, for the majority of the time that they were employed in the legal sector, they would also hold down "second jobs" during their *off* hours. Many, but not all, of these women had an overarching addiction to drugs that pushed them to secure money by any means possible—legal and otherwise. April was one such woman:

I was makin' like $7 an hour at this Sears job. That was actually pretty good money, but I was gettin' high. I was stealin', robbin'. I used to forge checks to get more money. I worked there for maybe six months. I guess I was into fast money, a fast life. I needed money to support my habit. So I went out, and, uh, the person that I was buying from, I asked him, you know, how can I get into it.

So, after I was done with my day at Sears, I was selling on the street. I turned out to be one of the carriers—the person that, uh, pick up the drugs and distribute it to people on the street to sell. I bring in about $2000 to $3000 a week. Sometimes I, I would be up two or three days in a row because the money would be coming so fast that I'd be, I wouldn't want to go to sleep because I knew if I would go to sleep, I would miss money—the Sears money and the other—I wanted both.

For the drug addicted women, losing sleep, being absent from legal work, partying, and hustling formed their day-to-day experiences.

For other women, crime on the side was a continuation of their long-term involvement in offending. Initially, it counterbalanced the asocial and boring nature of their jobs in the legal sector. It provided these women with the excitement, adventure, and camaraderie absent from jobs in the secondary labor market. Further, and not unimportantly, crime on the side supplemented the meager incomes they received from their marginal jobs.

As L.G. recounts:

When I was like 15—when I dropped out of school after, you know, a lot of places weren't taking people that didn't have a high school diploma and stuff like that—I went to a temporary agency, you know, which allowed me

to work for different companies. I did clerical work for the Department of Probation. I
did clerical work for AT&T and Citibank. I
worked six or seven months in each of these
places. Usually the job itself had ended and
I'd go back to the agency and they place me
again. But they were all boring—no one to
talk to, to hang out with, but I kept going.
But even though I was workin' and still
doin', you know, the right thing, I always
was drawed to doin' the wrong thing somewhere down the line.

When I'd get home from work, I'd go hang
out with my friends. We got hooked up with
some people who were, uh, transportin'
drugs from New York to New Jersey to
Washington, and I started doin' that for a
while after work, on weekends, or between
jobs. I would get paid large sums of money
and I, you know, I clung to that for a while.
But I was really into for the fun and for
things to do with my friends. I did like the
real money, though.

I did other stuff during this time, like stealin'
in stores and rippin' people off. Me and
friends would go to parks and 34th and
42nd streets and stick people up. We got
money, real money for clothes, jewelry, and
fun. But really soon getting the real money
became the important thing.

L.G. was socialized initially into illegal behavior and violence for principally nonpecuniary
reasons. The money she received at the early
stages of her criminal career was secondary to
the excitement and adventure she received from
her participation. However, as L.G. and her counterparts entered their late teens and experienced
a desire for a more sustained source of income,
they applied the criminal "skills" learned earlier
to economically motivated activities. But, even
within this context, noneconomic motives were
still important. For these women, committing
crime with friends and enjoying the fruits together were still meaningful.

We should say that at this point in their lives,
and unlike their male counterparts, these women
were relatively successful in avoiding serious
legal sanctions for their already lengthy involvement in criminal activity. On the average, first arrests occurred when these women were in their
early (for robberies) to mid-twenties (assault and
drugs), later than for males (Fagan 1996; Fagan
and Freeman 1994; Grogger 1994; Sampson and
Laub 1993; Good, Pirog-Good, and Sickles 1986).
Therefore, commitment to the illegal economy
was viewed by these women as a relatively
low-risk endeavor and the length of time that
they were able to "double up" far exceeded that of
their male counterparts.

Furthermore, the deterrent influences of social sanctions, such as family, peer, and community disapproval, also did not seem to affect the
decisions of these women in the same way as for
men (Fagan 1989). For that matter, by the time
these women were in their very early twenties,
they were emotionally, if not physically, estranged
from their foster families or families of origin. By
and large, as the women's commitment to their
criminal careers increased, they became increasingly estranged from their families. This estrangement followed several patterns: the
women would initially maintain legal residence
with their families but come to spend more of
their time in and out of apartments with friends,
lovers, or other strangers; or these women eventually would be kicked out of their families'
households or their own project apartments due
to their increasing involvement in criminal and
drug careers, most often permanently leaving
their children behind with family or friends, or in
the custody of child welfare; or, when they experienced a downturn in their criminal careers they
would wander the streets, living in abandoned
buildings, welfare hotels, or shelters, avoiding
contact with their significant others, including
children.

There were a few women with children who
left their "always nagging and interfering" families when welfare found them and their children
an apartment in the projects. And, for those fortunate and very few who were lucky enough to
have a steady income from drug dealing, they
moved into public housing or low-income apartments. However, the continued involvement of
the majority of these women in drug dealing and
other street crimes led eventually to eviction and
often pushed them into the street.

One thing was clear though: when speaking
about families, especially their children, these
women considered all such relationships as fetters—fetters, initially on their criminal careers
and social lives and later on, in their missions to
obtain drugs and stay high. Accounts of children getting in the way abounded. As Wanda
told us:

Yeah, I have a son. I have been away from
him for five years while I've been runnin' the
streets. I was never with my son. He lives
with his grandmother. BCW took him away
from me. My mother called them because I
was neglectin' him. I was always out leaving
him alone in the house. Never thought anything about how my mom and him felt.

Another woman recounted:

Oh yeah, my kids. I have three of them. But
they never stayed with me. They always

lived with my mom or my sister. I started dropping them off when I would be out doing stuff. But then I finally stopped bringin' them back to my place. They were always gettin' in the way. What with my hours, I couldn't be there and then, all that cryin'. It used to bother my friends when we'd come back to the apartment to party.

The estrangement of these women from their families reduced the salience of both formal and informal social networks and therefore did not influence their "calculus" on the risks and benefits of participation in the illegal economy. As Danelle explained:

Who's going to care? My ma gets money from me and doesn't ask where it's from. She just takes care of my kid for me and doesn't complain. Sometimes she tells me to be careful. I got my friends to run with me and we're doin' just fine. No one bothers us, not even the cops. Yeah, my brother's in prison, but he just got stupid. He'll be out and back into it. It's the way things are here. So, I don't get the question. Why should I think about the problems of doing business? They're not my problems. Who cares, anyway?

Here, Danelle expresses a very common theme in the narratives offered by most of the women. Not only did the women not perceive arrest or incarceration as a risk, but when commenting on others' criminal justice involvements, they dismissed them as endurable, temporary, and not the least bit unusual. Furthermore, most perceived their families and communities as highly tolerant or just plain indifferent to their behavior, whether the behavior was "decent" or "street" (Anderson 1994). For some of the women, the fact that their families were receiving "benefits," i.e. money [or] commodities, as a result of their involvement in criminal enterprises, seemed to reduce, further, any perception of familial rejection. Thus, for these women, commitment to the illegal economy did not produce any particularly strong strains between them and their families and communities.

Commitment to the Illegal Economy

Patterns of illegal work varied among the women. As we have heard, some abandoned work after periods of licit employment, others drifted in and out of legal work while firmly committed to the illegal economy. Herminia's account was typical of this latter group of women:

I had lots of little jobs, but selling cocaine was always how I really made my living. My last job was, I was 18, I was a receptionist at a showroom. I was there maybe one year. It was okay. But I was already into selling cocaine. I started that much earlier when my father went to jail. I felt that as my duty as taking care of my family I started selling coke. My father didn't know anything about it at first. But there came a time when we were doin' it together. We were selling together.

Now, I'd be selling for about seven years. I went up and down. I could make $500. I could make $3000 a week. I never stood on the corner and sold bags or anything like that. It would always be quantity. I had a few customers, four or five customers. I was selling ounces with some Colombians. They became like my suppliers and stuff. I started like with myself, when my father came out I started like working with him. Then I stopped working in offices altogether.

Alicia, too, considered her criminal activities as more important and more regular than her sporadic experiences within the legal economy:

I had two jobs. I used to do factory work. I didn't like it [because] it was too much labor, you know. You had to do everything. I did home attendant for a little while. It was okay. But, my main commitment was to doing robberies. After awhile doing both things, the home attendant thing and the robbery thing, I tried to slow down a bit. So, I had to devote myself to one thing. I went full time to robbing people.

Other women from the outset considered the illegal economy as their primary job commitment. They chose *exclusive* "careers" in crime and never participated in the secondary labor market. For these women, given the alternatives of low-wage payoffs from legal work and the expectation of relatively high returns from income-generating criminal activities, they viewed illegal work as a rational choice not unlike choices made among legitimate occupational pursuits and not unlike their male counterparts (Fagan 1994a).

Jocorn and Rose both had a rich history of pre- and early adolescent involvement in violence and crime. For them, by the time they reached their mid-teens, hustling was a way of life. As Rose recalls:

Like I said, I use to live in a neighborhood full of hustlers. And um, they use to watch me go to school, giving me $5 or $10 [to] buy clothes off the street for all the kids in the neighborhood. And then just, we started hanging down there by them. Then we started holding drugs for them. And paying us, $100 a day, and we would hold a 100 quarters, now if I would have gotten caught with that, lord knows how much time, but I was too naive and young to know what was going on. The money was good to me. I thought I was rich, you know what I am saying. And I liked to buy. So, by the time I left school, I was already into my job on the streets. I knew how to do the job and I had no problem protecting myself while I was doing it.

Jocorn, too, was deeply entrenched in her "career" by the time she left school. And, she stayed in this one "job," advancing through the ranks until she had her own organization.

I was about 11 or 12 when I started selling drugs. It was fast money. I guess that's what attracted me to it, the fast money and the fun. I was makin' about $500 a week. Much later on, when I was about 17, I started like putting people to work for me. I was pulling in $10,000 a day.

I sold it all. Crack too. I've been dealing for 19 years. The more I had, you know, the more money I wanted. I had people in Brooklyn, Manhattan, the Bronx, Boston, in upstate. All I was basically doing was gettin' the drugs and receiving the money.

The "career" trajectories of the women in the above accounts reflect the influences of structure and context in shaping their choices and options. With limited access to satisfying legal work, and in segregated neighborhoods with high concentrations of joblessness, alienated views of legal work and diminished expectations for conventional employment became normative. For some of the women, the criminal involvement of family, friends, and neighbors were more likely to integrate them into the criminal world than into referral networks for legal and stable employment. For others, immersion in crime during childhood and early adolescence marginalized them early on from interest in or access to job contacts in the licit workaday world.

But, for those women who had some experience in the secondary labor market, commitment to criminal careers eventually ended their involvement in legal work. Denise, who earlier described her job experiences, told us about her break with marginal labor:

Well, I still went from job to job pulling new scams. Worked for some lawyers and ran a prostitution thing out of their office. I quit working for the lawyers and with my two babies of my own and I got on welfare. Once I had that system figured out, I took the bus over to another town, and, uh, I got on welfare out there. I used a wig and glasses, somebody else's baby, and I had a birth cer-

tificate printed up with my name, and I go on welfare out there too. I tried this from town to town. I was collecting numerous checks. It was good money.

But there was more money to be made. About when I was 20, I started to sell drugs with my father and uncle. I made about $1500 a day! I dealt heroin for about two years. Then I went into business for myself. I sold heroin and coke. I was clearing $4500 to $5500 a week.

For other women, drug use exerted a strong influence on their ultimate commitment to the illegal economy over employment in the secondary labor market. Even at the outset, commitment to licit work was weak. But, with the onset of cocaine smoking, such investments diminished and quickly disappeared. Further, once addicted to harder drugs, i.e., crack cocaine, most of the women in this study experienced the ultimate rupture in ties to the licit workaday world and a decline in the importance of excitement, adventure, and peer participation in criminal activities. Thus, drug addiction and not peers came to organize most of daily life's activities.

Barbara's involvement in legitimate work ended with her abuse of crack:

I worked for the Board of Education as a teacher's aide from like '84 to '86. When I was working I didn't need to be involved in crime at that time because I had my own income. But I was smoking crack. I was fired from the Board of Ed because of my lateness and absenteeism.

I got so involved in getting high that I was kind of glad that I didn't have to get up in the morning anymore. I didn't care about that job or those people on that job, or even the kids like I was supposed to. That's when I started gettin' into crime.

For some, cocaine smoking intensified the illicit activities in which they already were active. Evelyn recalls:

What happen was I didn't have any money, I didn't have any way of getting a job, I was already addicted into crack. Like I said, my parents threw me out of the house, there was no way of getting any money from them or anything like that, I had bumped into people who were selling, and I got connected with them Two Spots selling drugs with their bosses. I said [I] can help you out, be your lookout or whatever, and from there I started working and I met the bosses and I started working like that.

From Some Involvement in the Legal Economy to Immersion in the Cocaine Economy and Ultimate Withdrawal From Crime as Work

While the women's stories show that illicit behaviors were continuous over time, their intensification suggests some important transitions. These transitions were structured by economic changes and social opportunities as well as key developments within drug markets. For instance, the development of the cocaine economy created opportunities for drug selling that did not exist in prior, especially heroin, markets. The changing economic structure of inner-city neighborhoods also created the possibility of changes in gender roles that in the past determined options for status and income within street drug networks.

At one time, women were excluded from selling by rigid gender roles and male hegemony in deviant street networks. The expanding cocaine economy and the increasing presence of women in the public domain may have neutralized the social processes that in the past consigned them to secondary roles in street networks. As a result, the women were able to form new organizations for drug selling, or pursue independent careers in drug selling.

For Gayle, making money through drug selling was her career ambition:

> I sold all kinds of drugs. I knew from the start that I wanted to be big in this. From weed I went to selling heroin and to coke. I started dealing weed at 15. I used to steal weed from my father and deal it. Somebody approached me to deal crank [speed]. I was making $200 a week. I sold in this parking lot where kids hung out. I made $800 to $900 a week from speed.
>
> Then I sold heroin. I already had the knowledge of dealing. I went straight to somebody who sold heroin. The idea was strictly to make money. At first I sold it myself. Then I would cut ounces and bag it and let my female friends sell it for me off the street. I was making $2500 a week. I dealt heroin for years and I started dealing coke. At this point I really learned how to make lots of money selling drugs.

Viewing women's involvement in drug markets in economic and career terms suggests an active role in decision-making. Earlier deterministic conceptions of women and drugs described a passive drift into the secondary roles of hustling and prostitution in a street world dominated by men. However, the accounts provided by the women in this [chapter] indicate that within contemporary drug markets, women often made decisions to enter based on a logical evaluation of career options. Here, the women considered both economic (wages) and nonpecuniary (status) returns from work in the secondary labor market. Furthermore, they realistically assessed their chances of obtaining economic and social support from domestic arrangements. Recognizing their constrained options, these women opted for illicit work which to them seemed to represent a rational choice.

Stephanie's account reflects this weighing of options:

> Well, I've been working off and on in different cashiers and stuff like since I'm 15 years old. I always knew that a woman couldn't depend on a man to take care of her. I grew up on Public Assistance. I saw how it affected my mom when we on PA. People always coming to check up on your home.
>
> So, I knew I would have to get a career or something. But work was just menial jobs to me, and they really didn't matter.
>
> But then I saw that dealing drugs was a way to make real money. I started freelancing. I purchased coke from a guy that I used to cop for myself. So I began to bring people to him. But since I still had a job, in the hair business there's a lot of drugs flowing. So I used to just buy in large quantities and sell to people at work. I sold to people I knew, who I knew were into drugs. When I got off from work, I usually went to a friend's house that I know got high. I sat and got high with them, and I usually sold to whoever was in their home.

For Stephanie and many of the other women, criminal career choices provided them with higher incomes than were reachable by their peers in conventional careers. Furthermore, their involvement and success in these career trajectories placed them in contexts offering status (Williams 1989; Padilla 1992), excitement (Adler 1985; Anderson 1990), and commodities.

Dealing also helped many women avoid or exit from the types of street hustling, including prostitution, that characterized women's illicit income-generating strategies (Goldstein, Ouellet, and Fendrich 1992; Ouellet, Weibel, Jimenez, and Johnson 1993; Ratner 1993). Stephanie's preference for dealing was typical among the women we studied:

> You see, as a prostitute or hooker, you know, I don't know. For me it's like, uh, you would rather sell drugs or even rob somebody than to perform a service. The last thing I wanted

to do is lay down for somebody. I'd rather deal or rip people off.

Further, dealing provided new ways to expand their traditionally limited roles, statuses and incomes within the street economy.

For many of the women in our study, however, their involvement in the workaday world of criminal enterprise was shortlived. The same drug—crack—that opened new career opportunities for a lot of them, also brought many of them down. Crack *abuse* resulted in their immersion in a social world where options became narrower and exploitation more likely (Rosenbaum 1981). The narrowing options reflected both the social contexts where crack was used and the effects of the drug itself.

Similar to heroin use in past eras, heavy crack use closed off social exits from drug use or hustling (Fagan 1994b; Rosenbaum 1981). One woman said that the intense pleasure from smoking crack, and the reinforcement when it was repeated, made it impossible "to make any space between [herself] and the world where [she] smoked it."

Reinarman, Waldorf, and Murphy (1989) described the isolation that accompanies obsessive crack use, the suspicions toward friends and family members, the withdrawal from social interactions, the rejection of activities that do not lead to refilling the pipe, and the cashing of limited economic and social assets in pursuit of an elusive but mythically powerful high. Thus, it is not surprising that with an increase in crack use, prostitution returned as an important income source for the women who used crack.

Prolonged crack use eventually led to deeper immersion in the social scenes and behaviors that limited their participation in both the licit and illicit work and social worlds. Although some walked away from crack after experimentation or maintained limits on their use of crack, others immersed themselves in crack use and reconstructed their social and economic lives to accommodate their frequent crack use.

The point of immersion into the world of crack was an important turning point for the women in our study. Their *economic* lives, for instance, became increasingly intertwined with their *social* worlds. They organized their lives around drugs and immersed themselves in those activities and with those people with whom they shared economic and social behaviors. Their roles and identities, as well as their primary sources of status and income, became defined, exclusively, within these street networks. Their options for transition to legal work, marriage, or educational settings were limited. And, their en-gulfment in street networks reinforced their pathway into an abyss. Any notion of a "calculus" disappeared as "chasing the pipe" became the one and only goal of daily life.

For the majority of women, then, the problem of maintaining an addiction came to take precedence over other interests and participation in both the legal and illegal work worlds. The women also came to define themselves in relationship to their drug problems. They were "junkies," "crackheads," or "cokebitches." Few women came to see themselves as criminals, workers, or in any way other than as addicts. Whatever deviant behaviors they engaged in came to be justified by their "drug compulsion."

The increased salience or primacy of their drug habits led to their "role engulfment." Schur pointed out that one major consequence of the processes through which deviant identity is ascribed is the tendency "of the deviator to become 'caught up in' a deviant role . . . that his behavior is increasingly organized 'around' the role . . . and that cultural expectations attached to the role come to have precedence in the organization of his general way of life" (Schur 1971, 69). As a result, the women progressively became totally immersed in the networks of the drug markets. They became committed to the drug world's norms, values, and lifestyle, and they limited their involvement with nondeviant individuals and groups.

As the circumstances of the women's lives changed, and they became more engulfed in the drug world, it became less and less likely that they actively considered working, even at crime. Thus, for the majority of the women in our study, the short period between adolescence and adulthood took them through various positions vis-à-vis the workaday worlds. For many there was, indeed, an early engagement in the legal economy; all went on to embrace the social and pecuniary benefits of criminal participation; and most disengaged totally from both economies, immersed instead in an all-consuming search for the next hit of crack.

Conclusion

There remains little doubt that women's experiences within the worlds of licit and illicit work remain gendered. This is the case, especially, as one reaches through the upper echelons of both the primary and illegal labor markets. In the primary market, women's gains during the 1970s and 80s were tempered by their placement in lower status specialties, less desirable work settings, lower paying industries and professions, and part-time rather than full-time work (Baca

Zinn and Eitzen 1998; Jacobs 1989; Reskin and Roos 1990; Herz and Wootten 1996).

In terms of the upper levels of criminal networks, women continued to confront sex discrimination. In part, the ethnic and family segmentation of drug labor markets made it difficult for women to achieve higher ranks. The retail drug trades, particularly in immigrant communities, reproduced traditional perceptions of women's limited capabilities. Thus, women involved in the drug trade in Hispanic communities were often refused access to upper level roles that required the routine use of violence or involved the handling of large sums of money or drugs (Williams 1989; Waterston 1993).

However, such a pattern seems somewhat moderated in both the legal secondary labor and the lower levels of illicit, street markets. In both these venues, the 1980s opened doors for inner-city women. In terms of the secondary labor market, transformations in the economy resulted in poor women having greater success than their male counterparts in claiming service sector and clerical jobs (Baca Zinn and Eitzen 1998; Wilson 1987). At the same time, inner-city women were faced with new opportunities that were brought about by demographic, social, and particularly, drug market changes. These opportunities resulted in increased participation in street crime (Sommers and Baskin 1992) as well as greater diversification in roles and statuses and types of crimes. For instance, most of the women crack dealers were involved in direct sales either in curbside or indoor locations, a relatively rare role in earlier drug markets (Baskin and Sommers 1998; Johnson et al. 1985).

Nonetheless, the "success" of women in street crimes such as robbery and drug distribution was temporary. And, it is perhaps the transitory nature of their fortuity that is most the result of gendered life experiences. Despite evidence that women enter into street crime for many of the same reasons as their male counterparts (Baskin and Sommers 1998; Miller 1998) and are more successful at avoiding legal sanctions, they are less successful than men at avoiding the pitfalls of addiction. Furthermore, despite the doors opened to these women as a result of changes associated with crack cocaine, it was also this drug that made their downfall so dramatic and their return to gendered crimes, such as prostitution, almost unavoidable.

Again, the role that crack-cocaine played in the lives of inner-city women during the 1980s cannot be minimized. It was far-reaching and profound. Unlike the underrepresentation of females in street heroin scenes (Rosenbaum 1981), several studies have documented that women accounted for almost 50 percent of crack customers (Bourgois and Dunlap 1993; Deschenes 1988; Greenleaf 1989). Furthermore, whereas males who worked in crack distribution during this time period were less likely to use crack (Ratner 1993), this was not the case for women. In addition, the effects of crack use on females were far more serious than for males (Ouellet et al. 1993), resulting in greater depravation, devastation, and return to prostitution (Bourgois and Dunlap 1993).

In conclusion, the women we interviewed were members of distinct communities that mediated between them and the larger society. It was within these local communities that the women interacted and made decisions regarding school, family, and work. Additionally, it was within these local communities that they devised ways of handling the exigencies that were imposed by the larger economic and political structures. Community levels of family dysfunction, economic and social dislocation, and changing demographics as well as the presence of illegitimate opportunities all contributed to a landscape in which decisions were made concerning key aspects of everyday life, including work.

These landscapes, though, exist within specific time frames. As such, they are dynamic. Therefore, changes both in legal and illegal labor markets as well as in gender socialization should be considered in future research. In this way, we will be able to understand better the complex processes that influence local criminal and drug career decisions. Certainly, it will be interesting to see whether the decline in crack cocaine markets in inner-city neighborhoods have had any impact on women's roles on the street.

Endnote

1. Similar to the primary labor sector, in the secondary sector there is a white-collar upper level (which includes sales and clerical workers), where working conditions, pay, and benefits are better than in the blue-collar lower level (private household, laborer, and most service jobs). Turnover is high in both levels of this sector because these workers have relatively few marketable skills and are easily replaced (Kelly 1991).

Discussion Questions

1. Explain the gradual process of how crime draws women away from legal occupations.

2. Is there such a thing as a *criminal career*? Support your view.

3. Do you see committing crime for *supplemental* income to a legal job the same or different than committing crime to *fully* support oneself (i.e., where the person does not also have a legal job)? Why or why not?

4. How do the women in this study differ from women in other chapters?

5. What theories might explain "drifting" between legal and illegal forms of work and employment?

References

Adler, Patricia. 1992. "The Post Phase of Deviant Careers: Reintegrating Drug Traffickers." *Deviant Behavior* 13: 103–126.

——. 1985. *Wheeling and Dealing: An Ethnography of an Upper-Level Dealing and Smuggling Community.* New York: Columbia University Press.

American Correctional Association. 1990. *The Female Offender: What Does the Future Hold?* Arlington, VA: Kirby Lithographic Company.

Anderson, Elijah. 1994. "The Code of the Streets." *The Atlantic Monthly* May: 81–94.

——. 1990. *Streetwise.* Chicago: University of Chicago Press.

Baca Zinn, Maxine and Stanley D. Eitzen. 1998. "Economic Restructuring and Systems of Inequality." In Margaret L. Andersen and Patricia Hill Collins (eds.) *Race, Class and Gender: An Anthology.* Belmont, CA: Wadsworth Publishing Co.

Baskin, Deborah and Ira Sommers. 1998. *Casualties of Community Disorder: Women's Careers in Violent Crime.* Boulder, CO: Westview Press.

Baunach, Phyllis Jo. 1992. "Critical Problems of Women in Prison." In I. L. Moyer (ed.) *The Changing Roles of Women in the Criminal Justice System.* Prospect Heights, IL: Waveland Press.

——. 1982. "You Can't Be a Mother and in Prison . . . Can You? Impact of the Mother-Child Separation." In Barbara Raffel Price and Natalie J. Sokoloff (eds.) *The Criminal Justice System and Women: Women Offenders/Victims/Workers.* New York: Clark, Boardman Company, Ltd.

Bertram, J. 1982. "My Real Prison Is Being Separated From My Children." *Prison Watch.* San Francisco: National Council on Crime and Delinquency.

Biernacki, P. 1986. *Pathways From Heroin Addiction: Recovery Without Treatment.* Philadelphia: Temple University Press.

Blackburn, M., D. Bloom, and R. Freeman. 1990. "The Declining Economic Position of Less Skilled American Men." In Gary Burtless (ed.) *A Future of Lousy Jobs? The Changing Structure of U.S. Wages.* Washington, DC: The Brookings Institution.

Bourgois, Phillipe. 1995. *In Search of Respect: Selling Crack in El Barrio.* New York: Cambridge University Press.

——. 1989. "In Search of Horatio Alger: Culture and Ideology in the Crack Economy." *Contemporary Drug Problems* 16: 619–649.

Bourgois, Phillipe and Eloise Dunlap. 1993. "Exorcising Sex for Crack: An Ethnographic Perspective From Harlem." In Mitchell S. Ratner (ed.) *Crack Pipe as Pimp: An Ethnographic Investigation of Sex-for-Crack Exchanges.* New York: Lexington Books.

Brown, Lyn Mikel and Carol Gilligan. 1992. *Meeting at the Crossroads: Women's Psychology and Girls' Development.* New York: Ballantine Books.

Campbell, Anne. 1991. *The Girls in the Gang.* Cambridge, MA: Basil Blackwell.

Carlen, Pat. 1988. *Women, Crime and Poverty.* Milton Keynes: Open University Press.

Chesney-Lind, Meda, Marilyn Brown, and Dae-Gyung Kwack. 1996. "Gender, Gangs and Violence in a Multiethnic Community." Presented at the annual meeting of the American Society of Criminology, November 21, Chicago, IL.

Chiricos, Ted. 1987. "Rates of Crime and Unemployment: An Analysis of Aggregate Research." *Social Problems* 334: 187–212.

Church, George. 1990. "The View From Behind Bars." *Time* Magazine (Fall) 135: 20–22.

Corcoran, Mary and Susan Parrott. 1992. "Black Women's Economic Progress." Paper presented at the Research Conference on the Urban Underclass: Perspectives from the Social Sciences. Ann Arbor, MI: June.

Crutchfield, Robert. 1997. "Labor Markets, Employment, and Crime." National Institute of Justice Research Preview. Washington, DC: U.S. Department of Justice.

——. 1989. "Labor Stratification and Violent Crime." *Social Forces* 68 (2): 513–530.

Curry, David, Richard Ball, and Robert J. Fox. 1994. "Gang Crime and Law Enforcement Record Keeping." Research in Brief. Washington, DC: National Institute of Justice.

Daly, Kathleen and Meda Chesney-Lind. 1988. "Feminism and Criminology." *Justice Quarterly* 5: 497–538.

Datesman, Susan and G. Cales. 1983. "I'm Still the Same Mommy." *The Prison Journal* 63 (2): 142–154.

Deschenes, Elizabeth. 1988. "Cocaine Use and Pregnancy." Drug Abuse Series Paper of the Drug Abuse Information and Monitoring Project, California Department of Alcohol and Drug Programs, Health and Welfare Agency.

Deschenes, Elizabeth, Fran Bernat, Finn Esbensen, and D. Wayne Osgood. 1996. "Gangs and School Violence: Gender Differences in Perceptions and Experiences." Presented at the annual meeting of the American Society of Criminology, November 20, Chicago, IL.

Fagan, Jeffrey. 1996. "Legal and Illegal Work: Crime, Work and Unemployment." In Burton Weisbrod and James Worthy (eds.) *Dealing With Urban Crisis: Linking Research to Action.* Evanston, IL: Northwestern University Press.

——. 1994a. "Legal and Illegal Work: Crime, Work and Unemployment." Paper presented at Metropolitan Assembly on Urban Problems: Linking Research to Action. Northwestern University, Center for Urban Affairs and Policy Research.

——. 1994b. "Women and Drugs Revisited: Female Participation in the Cocaine Economy." *Journal of Drug Issues* 24: 179–226.

——. 1992. "Drug Selling and Licit Income in Distressed Neighborhoods: The Economic Lives of Drug Users and Drug Sellers." In Adele Harrell and George Peterson (eds.) *Drugs, Crime and Social Isolation: Barriers to Urban Opportunity.* Washington, DC: The Urban Institute Press.

——. 1989. "Cessation of Family Violence: Deterrence and Dissuasion." In Lloyd Ohlin and Michael Tonry (eds.) *Family Violence,* Volume 11 of *Crime and Justice: An Annual Review of Research.* Chicago: University of Chicago Press.

Fagan, Jeffrey and Richard Freeman. 1994. "Crime and Work." Unpublished. Newark, NJ: Rutgers University, School of Criminal Justice.

Freeman, Richard. 1992. "Crime and the Employment of Disadvantaged Youths." In George Peterson and Wayne Vroman (eds.) *Urban Labor Markets and Job Opportunities.* Washington, DC: Urban Institute Press.

——. 1983. "Crime and Unemployment." In James Q. Wilson (ed.) *Crime and Public Policy.* San Francisco: Institute for Contemporary Studies Press.

Goldstein, Paul. 1979. *Prostitution and Drugs.* Lexington, MA: Lexington Books.

Goldstein, Paul, Laurence Ouellet, and Michael Fendrich. 1992. "From Bag Brides to Skeezers: An Historical Perspective on Sex-for-Drugs Behavior." *Journal of Psychoactive Drugs* 24: 349–361.

Good, David H., Maureen Pirog-Good, and Robin Sickles. 1986. "An Analysis of Youth Crime and Employment Patterns." *Journal of Quantitative Criminology* 2: 219–236.

Greenleaf, V. D. 1989. *Women and Cocaine: Personal Stories of Addiction and Recovery.* Los Angeles: Lowell House.

Grogger, Jeffrey. 1994. "Criminal Opportunities, Youth Crime, and Young Men's Labor Supply." Unpublished. Department of Economics, University of California, Santa Barbara.

Hagan, John. 1993. "The Social Embeddedness of Crime and Unemployment." *Criminology* 31: 465–492.

Hagan, John and Alberto Pallioni. 1990. "The Social Reproduction of a Criminal Class in Working Class London, Circa 1950–1980." *American Journal of Sociology* 96: 265–299.

Hagedorn, John. 1994. "Neighborhoods, Markets and Gang Drug Organization." *Journal of Research in Crime and Delinquency* 31: 264–294.

Hagedorn, John and Parry Macron. 1988. *People and Folks: Gangs, Crime and the Underclass in a Rustbelt City.* Chicago: Lake View Press.

Herz, Diane and Barbara Wooten. 1996. "Women in the Workforce: An Overview." In Cynthia Costello and Barbara Kivimae Krimgold (eds.) *The American Woman, 1996–1997.* New York: W. W. Norton.

Hossfield, Karen J. 1997. "'Their Logic Against Them': Contradictions in Sex, Race, and Class in Silicon Valley." In Maxine Baca Zinn, Pierette Hondagneu-Sotelo, and Michael A. Messner (eds.) *Through the Prism of Difference.* Boston: Allyn and Bacon.

Hunt, Dana. 1990. "Drugs and Consensual Crimes: Drug Dealing and Prostitution." In Michael Tonry and James Q. Wilson (eds.) *Drugs and Crime. Crime and Justice, Volume 13.* Chicago: University of Chicago Press.

Inciardi, James A., Dorothy Lockwood, and Anne Pottieger. 1993. *Women and Crack Cocaine.* New York: Macmillan.

Jacobs, Jerry. 1989. "Long-Term Trends in Occupational Sex Segregation." *American Journal of Sociology* 95: 160–173.

Joe, Karen and Meda Chesney-Lind. 1995. "Just Every Mother's Angel: An Analysis of Gender and Ethnic Variations in Youth Gang Membership." *Gender and Society* 9: 408–430.

Johnson, Bruce, Paul Goldstein, Edward Preble, James Schmeidler, Douglas Lipton, Barry Spunt, and Thomas Miller. 1985. *Taking Care of Business: The Economics of Crime by Heroin Abusers.* Lexington, MA: Lexington Books.

Kelly, Rita Mae. 1991. *The Gendered Economy: Work, Careers, and Success.* Newbury Park, CA: Sage Publications.

Koban, Linda A. 1983. "Parent in Prison: A Comparative Analysis of the Effects of Incarceration on the Families of Men and Women." *Research in Law, Deviance and Social Control* 5: 171–183.

Laub, John and R. Sampson. 1993. "Turning Points in the Life Course: Why Change Matters to the Study of Crime." *Criminology* 31: 301–326.

Liebow, Elliot. 1967. *Tally's Corner: A Study of Negro Streetcorner Men.* Boston: Little, Brown and Company.

Maher, Lisa and Ric Curtis. 1992. "Women on the Edge of Crime: Crack Cocaine and the Changing Contexts of Street-Level Sex Work in New York City." *Crime, Law, and Social Change* 18: 221–258.

Maher, Lisa and Kathleen Daly. 1996. "Women in the Street-Level Drug Economy: Continuity or Change?" *Criminology* 34: 465–492.

Mieczkowski, Thomas. 1994. "The Experiences of Women Who Sell Crack: Some Descriptive Data From the Detroit Crack Ethnography Project." *Journal of Drug Issues* 24: 227–248.

Miller, Eleanor. 1986. *Street Woman.* Philadelphia: Temple University Press.

Miller, Jody. 1998. "Up It Up: Gender and the Accomplishment of Street Robbery." *Criminology* 36: 37–66.

Moore, Joan. 1990. "Mexican-American Women Addicts: The Influence of Family Background." In Ronald Glick and Joan Moore (eds.) *Drugs in Hispanic Communities.* New Brunswick, NJ: Rutgers University Press.

——. 1991. *Going Down to the Barrio: Homeboys and Homegirls in Change*. Philadelphia: Temple University Press.

——. 1992. "Institutionalized Youth Gangs: Why White Fence and El Hoyo Maravilla Change So Slowly." In J. Fagan (ed.) *The Ecology of Crime and Drug Use in Inner Cities*. New York: Social Science Research Council.

National Advisory Commission on Criminal Justice Standards and Goals. 1973. Task Force on Corrections. Washington, DC: U.S. Government Printing Office.

Ouellet, Lawrence, W. Wayne Weibel, A. D. Jimenez, and W. A. Johnson. 1993. "Crack Cocaine and the Transformation of Prostitution in Three Chicago Neighborhoods." In Mitchell Ratner (ed.) *Crack Pipe as Pimp: An Ethnographic Investigation in Sex-for-Crack Exchanges*. New York: Lexington Books.

Padilla, Felix. 1992. *The Gang as an American Enterprise*. Boston: Northeastern University Press.

Pettiway, Leon. 1987. "Participation in Crime Partnerships by Female Drug Users: The Effects of Domestic Arrangements, Drug Use, and Criminal Involvement." *Criminology* 25: 741–766.

Pipher, Mary. 1994. *Reviving Ophelia: Saving the Selves of Adolescent Girls*. New York: Ballantine Books.

Rafter, Nicole. 1985. *Partial Justice: Women in State Prisons, 1800–1935*. Boston: Northeastern University Press.

Ratner, Mitchell. 1993. "Sex, Drugs and Public Policy: Studying and Understanding the Sex-for-Crack Phenomenon." In Mitchell Ratner (ed.) *Crack Pipe as Pimp: An Ethnographic Investigation of Sex-for-Crack Exchanges*. New York: Lexington Books.

Reinarman, Craig, Dan Waldorf, and Sheila Murphy. 1989. "The Call of the Pipe: Freebasing and Crack Use as Norm-Bound Episodic Compulsion." Paper presented at the Annual Meeting of the American Society of Criminology, Reno, Nevada, November.

Reskin, Barbara and Patricia Roos. 1990. *Job Queues, Gender Cues: Explaining Women's Inroads Into Male Occupations*. Philadelphia: Temple University Press.

Reuter, Peter, Robert MacCoun, and Patrick Murphy. 1990. *Money From Crime*. Report R3894. Santa Monica, CA: The Rand Corporation.

Rosenbaum, Marsha. 1981. *Women and Heroin*. New Brunswick, NJ: Rutgers University Press.

Rosenfeld, Richard and Steven Messner. 1989. *Crime and the American Dream*. Albany: SUNY Press.

Sampson, Robert J. and John H. Laub. 1993. *Crime in the Making*. Cambridge, MA: Harvard University Press.

Sarri, Rosemary. 1987. "Unequal Protection Under the Law." In J. Figuera-McDonough and R. Sarri (eds.) *The Trapped Woman*. Newbury Park, CA: Sage.

Schur, E. 1971. *Labeling Deviant Behavior: Its Sociological Implications*. New York: Harper and Row.

Shover, Neil. 1985. *Aging Criminals*. Newbury Park, CA: Sage.

Sommers, I. and D. R. Baskin. 1992. "Sex, Race, Age, and Violent Offending." *Violence and Victims* 7: 191–201.

Sommers, I., D. Baskin, and J. Fagan. 1996. "The Structural Relationship Between Drug Use, Drug Dealing and Other Income Support Activities Among Women Drug Dealers." *Journal of Drug Issues* 26: 975–1006.

Sullivan, Mercer. 1989. *Getting Paid*. Ithaca, NY: Cornell University Press.

Taylor, Avril. 1993. *Women Drug Users: An Ethnography of a Female Injecting Community*. Oxford: Clarendon Press.

Taylor, Carl. 1993. *Girls, Gangs, Women and Drugs*. East Lansing: Michigan State University Press.

——. 1990. "Gang Imperialism." In R. Huff (ed.) *Gangs in America*. Newbury Park, CA: Sage Publications.

Tienda, Marta. 1989. "Neighborhood Effects and the Formation of the Underclass." Paper presented at the Annual Meeting of the American Sociological Association, San Francisco, August.

Uggen, Christopher, Irving Piliavin, and Ross Matsueda. 1992. *Job Programs and Criminal Desistance*. Washington, DC: The Urban Institute.

Vicusi, W. Kip. 1986. "The Risks and Rewards of Criminal Activity: A Comprehensive Test of Criminal Deterrence." *Journal of Labor Economics* 4: 317–340.

Waterston, Alisse. 1993. *Street Addicts in the Political Economy*. Philadelphia: Temple University Press.

Williams, Terry. 1989. *The Cocaine Kids*. New York: Addison-Wesley.

Wilson, William J. 1996. *When Work Disappears: The World of the New Urban Poor*. New York: Alfred Knopf.

——. 1987. *The Truly Disadvantaged*. Chicago: University of Chicago Press.

Witte, Ann and Helen Tauchen. 1994. "Work and Crime: An Exploration Using Panel Data." Unpublished paper.

Wolf, Naomi. 1997. *Promiscuities: The Secret Struggle for Womanhood*. New York: Random House.

19
Property Crime as It Relates to Women Drug Dealers

Barbara Denton
Pat O'Malley

Commission of property crimes by drug users is often regarded as driven by the need to support a habit, or as merely an aside to involvement in the drug "industry," or both. However, this study comes to additional surprising conclusions, based on direct observation, informal and formal discussions, and in-depth interviews carried out over more than four years with a group of women and their friends, families, and associates. Research began by interviewing more than 60 women in a Melbourne prison, 16 of whom went on to form a core group of key informants. These 16 women were selected because they were all actively involved in networks or businesses that distributed illicit drugs. The women dealt in a variety of drugs. At the time of the research, heroin was the primary drug marketed by nine of the women, cannabis by five, and amphetamines by two. All 16 were user/dealers in the sense that they used illicit drugs from time to time, although only 11 administered such drugs intravenously. The authors conclude that property offenses are tightly integrated with the women's drug businesses. Success in property offending is a characteristic of successful drug dealers, and stolen property and money play a key part in the trade—providing a lucrative source of income, gifts, payments, and rewards. Most important, property crime also provides excitement and other, valued, nonmonetary satisfactions, including status and self-esteem.

Introduction

One of the most familiar arguments raised in the early literature focusing on drug-related crime is that illicit drug users are compelled into property offending in order to support their drug use. With regard to women, this was perhaps especially thought to be the case, although the portrayal was focused far less on property offenses and far more on women's necessary resort to prostitution to support drug consumption. As Inciardi and his colleagues note, "[o]ne of the most prevalent images of the female criminal generally, and more specifically of the female heroin addict, is the image of the hooker exploiting her only means of revenue for her next 'fix'" (Inciardi et al., 1982, pp. 244–245).

These negative images of women drug users have partly been formed from research among captive populations, either in treatment or in custodial settings. In the treatment milieus, the high incidence of sex workers among drug users quite probably led to an overemphasis on this connection, with the result that other forms of criminal activity among women drug users were overlooked (Taylor, 1993, pp. 3–4). This neglect was reinforced by assumptions that women offenders do not have the resources to enter or survive as entrepreneurs in the illicit economy. Thus, for example, Covington (1985) reports that "females passively acquiesce and follow males into crime rather than launching their careers independently in female-dominated peer groups . . . there is no female subculture that supports and reinforces crime among women in a manner parallel to male cultures" (p. 348).

More recent research, however, affirms that many women, rather than being "driven" into crime, make pragmatic, intelligent, and rational choices about how to generate money to finance their participation in the drug economy (e.g., Pettiway, 1987; Taylor, 1993; Fagan, 1994). Such work has found that women participate in a wide variety of crimes and that prostitution plays a considerably less important role in supporting drug use than was previously thought (Hser, Anglin, & McGlothlin, 1987; Pettiway, 1987). Thus Fagan found that while women drug users in the cocaine economy who were not active in drug selling turned to prostitution to generate income, women drug user/sellers tended to become involved in property and other crimes. Fagan (1995) concluded that "incomes from drug selling were sufficiently high to discourage or 'protect' some women from the dependence on prostitution that dominated the lives of non-sellers" (p. 179). This paper seeks to contribute to this growing line of theory and investigation.

An obvious point to be made here is that, despite the stereotypes, there is no one variety of female drug user. But perhaps more important is the implication that we should consider more closely the ways in which illicit drug use and "drug-related crime" among women are linked. Leaving aside the now generally disputed assumption that prostitution is the 'natural' or default option for women, the assumption that still recurs in much of the literature is that all drug using women's other criminal activities are drug-driven. The clear implication is that such offending would not occur but for the need to pay for their drugs (and as such, is therefore simply a substitute for, or safety net against, prostitution). Thus property crime is not thought to be practiced—let alone be valued as an activity in its own right—by those women who can support the financial demands of illicit drug consumption. Perhaps most of all, this implies that women who are successful drug user/dealers would have no need to engage in property offending.

An alternative model and certainly one that has currency among studies of male drug users (e.g., Elliot, Huizinga, & Menard, 1989) is that drug use is not necessarily an all-absorbing activity among illicit drug users. Drug users and dealers are seen to be engaged in other illicit activities by choice and preference. In such cases, both drug taking and property crime could be seen to provide attractions, to be mutually supporting, intertwining and more or less continuous activities. Applying such a model to women, "drug-related crime" would not appear just as an economic safety net, nor need it be the case that dealers who engage in property crime are those 'unsuccessful' women whose businesses will not provide for all their personal drug needs. Indeed, it could be argued that failures are the last people we are likely to confront where careers in property offending are concerned. To sustain a career in property crime would appear to imply ability, skill, and resourcefulness. It might also imply the possession of social respect and of attributes to provide access to a social network that can provide markets, information, labor, specialist skills, security, and so on. The possession of such resources would suggest that the women concerned are not likely to be failures or victims in the drug market and that systematic engagement in property crime might be the sign of a social category comparatively rarely explored in the literature—that of successful women in the drug scene. We are not, of course, proposing that all women who engage in property offenses are successful operators, whether as users or dealers. This would be to fall into a reverse and misleading stereotype. Rather the study seeks to examine some alternative connections between property crime as revealed by close, long-term qualitative

research among successful women drug dealers who are also drug users.

Women User/Dealers and Drug-Related Crime

Two observations supported throughout the field research form a framework for much that follows. First, the women included in the study generated money not only by the sale of drugs, but also by committing a wide variety of property offenses: crimes of fraud, forgery, theft, burglary, shoplifting, and handling of stolen goods. The majority of these women were involved in the drug scene prior to entering into frequent or serious criminal activity. Most, however, had participated in some form of crime, such as shoplifting, receiving stolen goods, and credit card fraud, *prior* to entering the drug economy. No across-the-board assumptions should thus be made in their careers about crime leading to drug use or vice versa. Rather we saw more complex and variable patterns of the nexus between property and drug offending. Second—an important observation reported by virtually all participants—the women *escalated* their income-producing crimes as they became more established and successful in the drug business. Involvement in careers of property offending among these women, as emerges in detail throughout this paper, was the mark of the successful drug user/dealer, whatever role such crimes might have played in the lives of other users. But as this suggests, what also emerges is that "involvement" in property crime is a weak term if used as a single index, for it fails to distinguish between the nature of the engagement. Early in the women's careers, when most were users rather than user/dealers, such property-focused criminal activity was sporadic or otherwise limited. They largely acted in supportive roles: handling stolen merchandise, functioning as a go-between or a lookout, hiding criminals on the run, or acting as gun carriers. One such case was Kim, who worked for a street-level dealer and drug wholesaler. This dealer, early in her career, was a member of a family of criminals whose activities included armed burglary, bank hold-ups, car theft and drug dealing. Kim acted as a go-between; she would be given large amounts of money to deliver to drug and criminal associates. Another of her tasks was to visit the family's members and their associates in prison, a task for which she was deemed suitable as she had no criminal record.

Each of the women had a parallel story to tell, but as the following sections illustrate, by the time the research took place Kim and all the women in the study had become active in their own right in a wide variety of areas of crime. One of these activities, albeit the central one for all participants, was drug dealing. While some elected to act alone, most operated in leadership roles in property offenses involving "employees" and other drug users, a fact that reflected and drew upon their skills, status, and resources in the drug sector.

We suggest that just as users' forms of involvement in the drug industry may range from subordinate and vulnerable users to superordinate and capable user/dealers, so too their drug-related participation in property offending is likely to vary in related ways. Success in the field of the illicit drug industry is likely to be related to success in relation to property offending because of the parallel needs for accumulation of skills and resources such as those required for evading or managing criminal justice intervention, developing the experience and knowledge of leadership and business practice, and accumulating contacts and opportunities—often across a very blurred divide between drug dealing and property offending. For these reasons, this association is likely to be reflected temporally in the women's career paths. Such broad observations, which we will now explore in more detail, accord well with those emerging from Taylor's (1993) ethnographic work among women drug users and dealers in Glasgow.

Shoplifting

Shoplifting has been recognized as an important means of generating revenue for both women and men in the illicit drug economy (Culliver, 1993); this appeared to be the case in Melbourne. Kim was a professional shoplifter before diversifying her activities to include drug dealing. Like most "shoppers," she established a routine and schedule to work by, usually operating late mornings and lunch times, saving the late afternoons to fence stolen goods. "I work the busy times; that way there's not that many [shop assistants] watching for you." She preferred to work alone: "I like to go on my own and do it, just me. I have no one to worry about except myself, and if it goes wrong it's just me." She wanted her independence, free from encumbrances, shying away from any responsibility that working with a partner may bring.

Certain technical skills are critical for the shoplifter, for example, the knack of rolling up clothes tightly with one hand, while the other hand sorts through items on the rack, creating the impression that the shoplifter is a genuine customer who belongs in the setting (see also Faupel, 1991). The women agreed that shoplift-

ing had altered over the years, creating new demands for skillful work. In particular, technical innovations and security tags made the work more complex: "The game's changed so much; it's harder with the electronic and surveillance stuff they have now. You have to know what you're doing." Several women overcame this obstacle by carrying bags especially insulated to prevent electronic detection. Another demand was the market consideration. One shoplifter, Sonya, carefully planned and structured her shoplifting expeditions in relation to what her buyers, associates and friends wanted. She had a ready market for her merchandise and took orders for her customers' needs.

> I would ask them what they wanted, some would put their order in, size and all, "Sonya, can you get that coat I saw?" Mostly I'd get it back to them the same day. Better for me not to have the stuff hanging around.

At times Sonya would target up to four shopping centers a day. "I'd dress properly, tidy up and that, and I'd go to different places, wouldn't hang around the one place for long." When she returned from her "work," her customers would be waiting for her. "There was always some of them waiting for me when I got back, I'd kind of lay them [the goods] all out so they could decide what they wanted." As well as "shopping" for friends, Sonya knew a legitimate shop owner who took all the goods she obtained. She claimed that she would sell them for "two-thirds the retail price."

> I've got this Asian sheila [woman] who runs this boutique who'll take anything I get. If the others aren't around she takes it all. She's always after the stuff I get, can't get enough for her, because I get top quality gear that's hard to come by, not rubbish.

The money Sonya earned from shoplifting was channeled into her family, "lovely furniture, antiques, expensive clothes and lots of jewelry." She had a reputation for being prodigal: "I was generous with people, threw my money around." Money was also channeled into her drug business: "It was used to set me up to buy and sell the stuff." Crime, drugs, and lifestyle coexisted, a mixture of work and play. Of course, not all the women followed this model, and for some drugs were much more central. Larissa, a heroin user, relied more on shoplifting to fund her drug use. She had several outlets for her goods; her drug dealer would swap her heroin for the goods, and her friends and other associates would pay Larissa cash. But this was not the norm. Other women shoplifted intermittently depending on their specific needs. Christmas was a special occasion, as one woman stated, "Shopping helps us get by, and gets things for the kids." Shoplifting, in short, was used by these women for a variety of purposes. The fact that they were all drug users did not mean that crime was merely a reflex of their drug needs.

In other ways, drugs did sometimes play a key role through interfering with successful property offending. One of the main risks associated with shoplifting was operating while in drug withdrawal. Kim recounted that,when she was "hanging out" badly, she deviated from her usual safe routine.

> What brings me undone is doing it when I'm sick, real sick, that's the dangerous time, I'm hanging out for that first hit, that's the only time I've been caught in all the years I've done it. Waiting for the shops to open, strung out, that's when I'm done. Once I've had a hit I'm fine. I have my hit, then I go back and do it real relaxed like.

Even so, in 15 years of shoplifting Kim received only two short sentences: "I did four months, ah, about ten years ago, and this last one where I did six months . . . I have never been done for drugs. That never gets a mention in court."

Coming through in the accounts provided by these women was their initiative, planning, and business acumen. Despite occasional lapses, shoplifting was not done in a random or indiscriminate way. They did not appear simply as "driven," although as Kim's case suggests, there were times when she behaved in such a fashion. As Koester and Schwartz have argued,

> Stealing requires a degree of planning and skill, and there is a delay between the time the act is committed and the time the desired end is achieved. Experienced shoplifters often take orders from customers or spend time selling their merchandise . . . it is possible for them (heroin users) to "work" for long periods between ingestion (1993, p. 194).

When considering the length of time Kim had been involved in crime, the small amount of time spent in prison indicates how well she planned her activity around the high risk conditions. In cost-benefit terms, two short periods "inside" did not appear to her to be an excessive time to serve.

Theft and Burglary

A further observation linked with the careers of these women is that many pursue specialties in crime that were commenced before they began using drugs. Living in social contexts where crime was part of a lifestyle, it often appears a matter of chance whether in any woman's biography drug use preceded prop-

erty offending or vice versa. Indeed it was often hard to sort out which came first. When Sherrie became the girlfriend of a very successful criminal, she found herself propelled into a lifestyle beyond her dreams. Surround[ed] by huge amounts of money, she was able to have anything she wanted: clothes, jewelry, an up-market apartment, and expensive furniture. This abundant lifestyle brought her into contact with drugs and drug use. This pleasant but dependent arrangement came to an abrupt end when the relationship turned sour and was terminated after some years.

> I was completely under his control being with him so young, I did everything he said, but then after a while I started to think for myself and speak out and do what I wanted to do. He didn't like it, he took everything back, the jewelry, the presents, the lot, and kicked me out with nothing.

It was a shock for Sherrie to find herself out on her own and with a drug habit. "I was in a pretty bad way. I'd got used to having everything done for me and suddenly it all ended." She returned to live with her parents, who sought the services and skills of a counselor who helped her reestablish herself. But Sherrie was left yearning for her former life and companions. Having been around criminals, listening to their gossip and exploits, she concluded that crime was simple. "I thought it sounds pretty easy walking into somewhere and taking what you want . . . and that's how I got started. I had the contacts to get rid of any stuff I got." Other women also enjoyed being around the illicit economy, like Chris: "I found it fun listening to what the crooks got up to." Yet such social enjoyment was also linked to learning the trade and finding opportunities for gain. Knowing the right people and being one of the crowd were useful for picking up information about when, where, and what to steal. With all of the women, as with Sherrie and Chris, involvement in drug-using networks was not something divorced from property crime, in the sense that they had to be brought together by the impetus of drug needs. If there was a norm, it was that they were intertwined, with drug use supplying a social network and access to skills, opportunities, and markets, as well as one among a number of stimuli to offend.

Sonya made a point of noting the movements of prospective victims. She also familiarized herself with their location and the surrounding streets. She constantly pored over her street map before setting out on a job and developed a knowledge of alarms and surveillance systems—knowledge she had gained through her male associates. "Owen's always playing about with alarms, taking them to pieces and putting them back again, so I get to have a gig too," she explained. (See also Faupel, 1991.) Rita too was an experienced operator when it came to planning and carrying out a burglary. She left nothing to chance and thought carefully about every last detail. One specialty was to identify the premises of organizations that had sufficient numbers of employees to warrant the provision of staff locker room facilities. After checking out a building, Rita presented herself: well-groomed, smartly dressed, and carrying a large brief case. She walked in a business-like manner into the premises. Being challenged on the job did not faze her; she would pose as either a business associate, a prospective customer, or whatever was fitting at the time. "I'm dressed up, and I make out I'm legit and visiting someone. I say anything that comes into my head at the time. I say I'm a debt collector, anything I can think of that fits in at the time." She would make her way to the locker room and steal as many handbags as possible, quickly placing them in her own case and then exiting the building and making her getaway. Depending on the location, she would use a car, or, if the job were located in the inner city, she would have a taxi waiting.

On one occasion, while drinking coffee in a cafe, Rita told her two companions that she was going to get a cab and visit a friend in a private hospital and invited them to "[c]ome along and wait in the taxi while I drop in for a quick visit." She carried an overnight bag and had a basket of fruit and a bunch of flowers to give to her friend, and she left her companions in the taxi. In a short time she reappeared, jumped into the taxi, and said, "Let's go." As the taxi drove along, Rita produced a number of handbags and wallets from her overnight bag. She had snatched the bags while the patients were occupied in the television lounge. Swiftly and efficiently she went through the bags, putting aside any money, bankbooks, and credit cards On leaving the taxi she dumped the bags and wallets in a nearby garbage bin and then proceeded to a bank outlet to use the bankcards. "You'd be surprised how many people have their pin number next to their card," she said. Rita explained to her companions that she did not tell them beforehand what she was up to for she wanted the scam "to look legit and natural enough."

Chris had a long-time association with criminals dating from her time as a sex worker. She had lived with two burglars, Gary and Ron, and she thought it sounded pretty simple, robbing a factory or a house. When Ron was arrested and imprisoned, she decided to try her hand at house burglary: "Ron was doing robberies and then he went to prison. Yeah, and I just thought how easy it was. So I teed up with his sister and we started doing it together. We did alright, we got TVs, videos, money, and heaps of jewelry." Being one of the crowd, mixing with criminals and their families, Chris readily found an accomplice who was willing to try her hand at house burglary. Like Chris, Ron's sister shared the view that "knocking off a house was dead easy" and working together they carried out a series of house burglaries. "We did well for a time, we got a lot of gold, all Italian gold, and then I'd give it to my drug dealer to flog." The women would randomly select a street of houses, looking in letter boxes and garages to see which of these were most likely to be unoccupied. Chris would knock on the door of a targeted house. If the occupant answered the door she would pose as a real estate agent, or a friend, who had the wrong address. If the house were unoccupied she would gain entry by either prising open the door or window with one of the small tools she carried or through an unlocked door or window. "I climb in through an unlocked door or open window. You'd be surprised how many people leave their doors open or a window. I make sure no one is home, well as much as I can." Once inside she would quickly and methodically search the premises.

> I'm looking for money, wallets, credit cards, watches, jewelry, any gold I can get, stuff that's easy to get rid of. . . . When I do a car I'm looking for bags and wallets. It's the credit cards I want. The money comes in handy too. Before I go, I check outside to see if there are any witnesses and when the coast is clear I clear off.

The women belonged to networks and social contexts in which drugs and crime are linked socially and culturally. Certainly, drug consumption sets up a need for income, and in these contexts crime is seen as one way of generating it. Indeed, as the women say, it is a very "smart," "efficient," and "convenient" way of generating money. But it was not the rule that the need for drugs "drove" the women to crime (e.g., Stewart, 1987). Sometimes this was the case, but among the women in this study the need to resort to burglary to generate money specifically for drugs was usually a short-term issue, a way of dealing with a temporary shortage of funds. More often, drugs themselves are a source of income, drug dealing being one among many opportunities available. For these successful women, drug dealing, drug use, and property crime coexist within a range of related behavior under diverse circumstances.

The women who were burglars agreed that the secret of being a successful thief was to have as much "front"—nerve and audacity—as possible. "To be any good you have to have dash, and lots of it," Sherrie explained. Successful women criminals were fearless. Sherrie, Sonya, and Rita demonstrated their "have a go at anything" manner. They would enter domestic or commercial premises in the hope of finding money or "making a score." What also emerged here was that these women were attracted by what Katz (1988) refers to as the *seductions* of crime. In particular, they emphasized the thrill of committing crime. For Michelle "there's nothing like pulling off a job, it beats sex any time," and for Robyn, "the excitement of it keeps you going, trying for the next one." Thus for some women at least, property offending and drug use are integrated by another means: they relished the "rush" that went with drugs and with crime. Indeed, Sherrie thought she was more addicted to crime than to drugs.

> It's [crime] the best buzz you can get. I'm addicted to that, it beats the "slow" [heroin] every time. . . . For me, it's when I stand at the counter and pass over the cheque, and I'm not who I'm supposed to be. She looks at me and I look her in the face, and I'm putting one over, conning her. That's the greatest thrill at that moment. Walking out with money is nothing compared to that.

For Marcia, being a cat burglar was all risk, excitement and fun. "I get my money in certain ways, like doing cat burgles and things like that . . . I dress in a dark tracksuit and wear sneakers. It's something I'm good at, getting into peoples' houses." Marcia was particularly agile and athletic, and could scale fences and walls and enter premises without much effort. "That's my thing to do it in the night, I get around in the middle of the night and burgle houses." When speaking about being a cat burglar, her face lit up and a sense of pride crept into her voice. "That's my crime, and I'm good at it. I get a kick out of it." This woman obviously liked having "fun"; for her the good life was a mixture of crime and drugs.

Michelle, Marcia, and Sherrie, among others, negotiated the criminal economy as a site of pleasure by actively seeking excitement through their participation in illicit activity. On one occasion, one of Michelle's arresting police officers gave her some friendly advice. "The last pinch, one of the coppers I knew pulled me aside and told me, 'Why don't you keep yourself to just selling dope, it's this stuff [passing cheques] that keeps getting you into trouble?'" Sound advice from the police.

In Michelle's lengthy criminal record, drug trafficking had never been mentioned, but the mixture of crime and drugs, putting herself on the edge, was a highly satisfying pastime. This contrasts with the views reported in Katz' study on the motivations and seductions of crime, which largely excludes women from the role of thrill seekers and in which men are presented as having "balls" and "heart," and women are viewed by their male counterparts as "pathetic" and fearful of "losing self control" (Katz, 1988, p. 243). Perhaps such views, common currency among men in the drug field, have also influenced researchers (Miller, 1991).

While the women emphasized that success in crime was exciting and boosted their self-esteem, making money was not underestimated. "Where else can you earn five grand in half an hour's work . . . life on the pension gets you shit." But these women robbed, not because they were poor or because their children had insufficient food to eat (Denton, 1994). Or at least if this idea of poverty has any bearing at all, it is mostly that orthodox sources could not support the lifestyle they wanted and enjoyed. Likewise, the plea that women are driven to crime to pay for their drugs, commonly put forward to clinicians and legal bodies (Fitzroy Legal Service, 1988; D'Arcy, 1995) appeared to be only one rationale among many. A more precise reading of why women enter into supposedly male territories might begin by looking at an alternative possibility: that at least some of them, like some men, achieve success in social networks where drug use and dealing, crime, illicit commodities, stolen money, etc. are linked together in ways that are often a source of excitement, pride, and self-esteem.

Distributing Stolen Goods

It was common for the women to have a range of stolen goods for disposal, and knowing how to offload goods was an essential part of the business. The Melbourne drug dealers were constantly trading in such commodities, which were clearly a reliable and relied upon source for generating cash. Gold and jewelry would quickly be sold to a fence or traded to a drug supplier (and the drugs might then be used or resold, for cash or further stolen goods). Sonya had two regular fences who would take any goods she wanted to dispose of; one was a pawnbroker who would "do business" with her "after hours," and the other worked around the drug scene, looking for "bargains."

It also was common for the women to offload received stolen goods upon their relatives. Robyn and Chris channeled them through the networks that their respective families had built up over the years. "There's plenty in my family that would want any of this," Robyn explained as she inspected a bundle of soft furnishing and bedding that had been traded as part of a drug deal. Chris's sister, Kay, had been married to a well-established member of the illicit economy: in their time together she had built up many contacts. One of her specialities was moving stolen goods, and any goods that Chris wanted to sell were easily put through her sister's network. Kay had an established network of contacts at the local hotel through which to channel her goods. The goods sold off quickly; a rationale for direct sales was that these brought higher prices than those paid by a fence because a middleman was not in the position to pay as highly as someone who was going to use the goods themselves (see also Akerstrom, 1985). A member of Robyn's family who worked at the docks was also involved in a network that pilfered a variety of consumer goods. Robyn, at times, would purchase certain goods from this source. "My supplier puts out the word when he wants something, and I pass it on to Jeff." Pam and her family followed the horses; members of her family frequented the Totalisator Agency Board (TAB) betting outlet at their local hotel. Here was another network through which to barter and channel goods. According to Pam's sister, "down the TAB you can get anything you want, you only have to put out the word, and the same way you can get rid of things too."

There is little in this that differentiates women in the drug industry from illicit dealers in many other areas. Family networks have long been recognized as important channels for illicit goods. Many communities in the United States, Britain and elsewhere have a long history of obtaining household goods and services from family members who inhabit the informal economy sector. In such areas, "shady economic transactions" are often tolerated, and such tolerance is relied upon by illicit traders whether or not they are in the drug trade (Preble & Casey, 1969; Johnson et al., 1985; Leonard, 1990, p. 186). In such communities and networks, the women in this study learned their crime and drug skills via men or friends or through family members. Such networks are also conduits through which to channel a variety of commodities and services to their members, of which drugs were never the sole commodity—only the most important.

Bank Fraud

A major source of revenue generated by women was bank fraud. The women who operated bank scams operated either alone or with a single accomplice usually recruited for a specific task or operation. Rita preferred to work alone, but due to the nature of the work, she often needed to recruit a partner from her "gang" as she referred to her accomplices: "there's plenty that want to get into my rorts [illicit schemes]," she laughed. Her accomplices were attracted by the quick money that bank fraud could bring; they were frequently drug users, ex-prisoners, or people on the move from interstate. Non-drug accomplices were given a cut of the takings, and drug users were paid with drugs. In one instance, Rita and Sarah had made the rounds, trading drugs for stolen credit cards and bank books. Rita "bought a cheque book from a junkie for $200 and made $5000 out of it." It was arranged that Sarah was to be the "front" at the bank the following day: it was her job to present the forged cheques, running the risk of detection if a forged cheque was challenged. This risk factor was instrumental in the high rate of accomplices passing through Rita's scams, and even she was cautious: "I don't do it too often. The camera's got my face a few times, so I've eased back." As there was a large network of contacts available, and invariably more than one among these who needed quick money, the illicit economy provided no shortage of "one-off" workers.

Rosie's speciality also was bank fraud; part of her skill was her knowledge of many aspects of banking and her familiarity with the checks and balances the banks put in place to guard against fraud. She had a working knowledge of the bank's computer system, and the various codes put in place to process banking accounts. Before presenting a cheque, Rosie, masquerading as a bank employee, would investigate the financial state of the victim's account. This involved phoning around local or interstate banks.

> I ring up the bank and say I'm from another bank, I know the bank code. The bank has a special code to say which books have been found. I rang up Queensland and found out which cheques had been cancelled, and which numbers were alright to use. I gave them the right codes and computer numbers and they gave me the information.

Having established the amount of funds in the accounts of the stolen bankbooks and credit cards, on the night before a job Rosie would set about learning the appropriate signatures. From an overnight bag, she would produce inks, pens, pencils, paper, adhesive tape, scissors, razor blades, and a "special" desk lamp. After setting up the lamp, she would examine each bankbook under a blue lamp and the previously invisible signature would be easily distinguished. "Some of them I have only to see once and I can copy them. I seem to have a flair for it, copying the signatures comes easy to me." Specific banks and times of the day would be chosen for the transactions. Bank subagencies lacking sophisticated computer systems were popular, as were large busy banks at peak periods—early Monday mornings and near to closing time on Fridays were most often chosen, as at these times bank employees were busy and preoccupied. Like Rita, Rosie often worked with an accomplice who would pass the forged cheque at the bank. In Rosie's words:

> I do what I'm good at, rorts. I work it all out. I put all the work in getting the stuff [credit cards, bank books]. Once I work the rort out I have to find someone to front for me. My face is never seen. I'm completely out of it. It's fool-proof. I wait outside the bank, take the money straight out of their hand and then give them their cop [share].

From prior experience Rosie had learned to be in the vicinity when her "fronts" were working. Entrusting them with large sums of money led them into temptation to abscond with the lot.

> I've been caught out by Sam and Ann who skipped out on me without giving me any money. So now I'm always waiting outside the bank and catch them when they come out. I need Ann's face in this rort to get my $15,000 back, then I'm dropping her.

Rosie's plan was to use Ann for the next job, partly to get back the money she owed. But in any case Rosie had no time to find another partner, as the job had to be done before the stolen bankbook was cancelled. She put in place a strategy which minimized the risk of being ripped off again. "As she walks out I take the money straight off her." Through the use of technical, organizational, and manipulative skills, Rosie's scams gained her various amounts of money, depending on how much cash was in the stolen bank books. When a book of company pay cheques fell into her hands, she was able to put herself on the payroll, and withdrew fortnightly pay cheques worth $2,000 for three months. "I did a pay cheque for $2,000. I knew this chick from Perth. I got her to pass the cheque. I gave her $500 for her trouble."

Networks in the informal economy were held together by forming and bolstering relationships that center on committing crime as well as consuming and selling drugs. All these activities overlap in variable degrees and ways. This reading of such activities raises the question of how sustainable the illicit economy would be if networks were driven by drugs alone. Or if they depended upon the one dimensional drug users and dealers, especially women, that abound in some parts of the literature. In this sense, the difficulty with such simplistic typifications of women in the drug industry is not simply that they represent a misunderstanding with respect to gender. It is part of a broader failure to understand the nature of the social world of the informal economy.

Shopping on the Card

It has been suggested that the growth of a credit-based economy in Western society has enabled more women to take part in fraudulent crimes (Biernacki, 1979), the increased opportunities for credit card fraud being noted as one major example (Steffensmeier, 1983). While this probably applies also for men, there is no doubt that many women in the Melbourne drug economy specialized in credit card fraud. Stolen credit cards were relatively easy to obtain, through either trading or bartering with associates or directly stealing from their holder. Credit card shopping was a favorite occupation of Rita's. When she set out on a "shopping excursion," she would be immaculately dressed, with no hint of her being a heavy drug user. She would shop at large department stores, boutiques, and markets. She would make conversation with the sales assistants, asking for their advice and help. In this manner, she would build up rapport with the shop assistants creating an image of credibility and trust. When a shop assistant showed any sign of hesitation or uncertainty, Rita would cancel the sale. "I pull the plug if I think there's any danger."

Rita was calm under pressure, never looking flushed or hassled. She would shop in a carefree and casual way, inventing any number of stories along the way to suit the prevailing circumstances. She also had a selection of shopkeepers to visit who were not concerned if her purchases were made with stolen credit cards. "There's plenty of them [shopkeepers] in it too, rorting the system. They don't give jack shit. It's not them that's losing out." When visiting a corrupt jeweler, Rita purchased an amount of gold that was over the credit card limit, she was instructed to come back the next day, when the daily credit limit was automatically renewed, to complete the transaction.

> I've been dealing with him [jeweler] for three years. He knows the credit cards are stolen. He told me to come in tomorrow, after six, before he closed up when things were quiet. He put through $480's worth and told me to come back tomorrow, and he'll put the rest through.

Rita had what Sutherland (1937) calls "larceny sense," similar to "business sense" when applied to a legitimate entrepreneur: an understanding whether to desist or persist with a job. Rita felt she was "very rarely wrong . . . you get to know if it's going to be alright."

Conclusions

We have argued in this paper that the relationship between women's involvement in drug dealing and drug use and their involvement in property crime needs to be looked at in ways that take into account both the women's own views of their activities and that recognize property offending and drug dealing as skillful accomplishments. In part, this also involves recognizing that simply because it is committed by drug dealing women, property crime is not to be seen as simply a reflex of involvement in the drug economy. Rather, drug dealing and property crime are interrelated—almost symbiotic—sources of income and satisfaction. Each of these forms of illicit "enterprise" provides opportunities, skills, knowledge, contacts, and other resources that assist with the success of the other. In this sense, they are braided together in particular lifestyles, career paths, and forms of economic activity. For the Melbourne women crime was work, and, as with the legitimate sector, such work was a source of many satisfactions other than monetary—from self-esteem and a sense of accomplishment to emotional returns including thrills and excitement. Drugs and the drug experience were central to this; they could not meaningfully be separated from—or straightforwardly given causal priority in relation to—the rest of the women's involvement and activities in the illicit economy.

None of this is meant to imply that other studies have been mistaken when they identify so many women drug users as prostitutes and/or victims, although as indicated above recent research clearly indicates that this pattern has been overstated. We stress that we are focusing on a particular and underresearched type of women drug user/dealers. Nevertheless, we wish to reassert two final points that are of more general relevance to our understanding of women's participation in drug culture and in "drug-related" offending.

First, many women are capable operators in the illicit market, and those who deal in drugs are likely to be competent property offenders. For the successful Melbourne women, at least, property offending is thus not a sign of a failing drug selling practice. If anything, the more successful the drug business, the better connected and better skilled the women as illicit entrepreneurs and the more likely it will be they have lucrative scams in their repertory. As well, the better their drug business, the more they will have illicit goods passing through their hands, both provided in payment for drugs delivered or received and to be used as payments, gifts, or rewards to their workers. Much of this is a corollary of our observation that we need to distinguish between types of involvement in property offending, for as the women became more successful in the drug business, so too they moved from marginal to substantial participants in such crime. Consequently, to understand property offending among women drug users, we should pay attention not just to how "successful" they are in each activity, but at what points they might be in their illicit careers. Thus women in this study began as drug users, and others as partners and apprentices of men, but moved "up" into successful drug dealing and property offending.

Second, like others in illicit business, they sought to satisfy a wide range of needs and desires from their property offending: providing friends, family, and themselves with gifts; generating an effective source of income; bartering for all manner of other services, and so on. Only sometimes, and rarely solely, is property offending geared to paying for their own drug consumption. For the successful user/dealers, property crime, drug use, and drug dealing are closely bound together and are part of a pattern that changes through the course of their careers. Sometimes one leads in terms of priorities of need or opportunity, sometimes another. The changes may be related to different points in their careers, but they may also relate to changing justice environments and markets—to the variable phases in the intermittent business activity that characterizes a "drug dealership."

In all of this, this [chapter] seeks to contribute to the developing line of theory and research that challenges more traditional views of women drug users and dealers as in some sense victims or failures. It stresses that property offending and drug dealing are closely and functionally related. As well, and most generally, the observations made in this research directly challenge assertions, such as those made by Rosenbaum (1981), that regard the careers of female drug users as involving "narrowing options," in which legitimate and thus implicitly preferred lifestyles are closed off and in which women find themselves trapped in a world of addiction. With Taylor (1993, p. 158) we would agree that "rather than a career of narrowing options, the career of these working class female drug users is one which highlights the capabilities of such women."

Discussion Questions

1. Support or refute the author's assertion that women rationally choose to finance their participation in the drug economy by committing other crimes.

2. How does this study compare with Baskin and Sommers' study of violent women offenders?

3. This study found that women are generalists in the area of property crime and drug dealing. Why didn't the authors find a relationship with violent crime?

4. How large a problem are crimes such as bank fraud and credit card fraud? Are the punishments severe enough?

5. How generalizable is this study?

References

Akerstrom, M. 1985. *Crooks and squares*. New Brunswick: Transaction Books.

Anglin, M., & Hser, Y. 1987. Addicted women and crime. *Criminology*, 25, 359–397.

Biernacki, P. 1979. Junkie work, "hustles," and social status among heroin addicts. *Journal of Drug Issues*, 9, 535–549.

Covington, J. 1985. Gender differences in criminality among heroin users. *Journal of Research in Crime and Delinquents*, 22, 329–354.

Culliver, C. 1993. Women and crime: An overview. In C. Culliver (Ed.) *Female criminality: The state of the art*. New York: Garland Publishing.

D'Arcy, M. 1995. Women in prison: Women's explanations of offending behaviour and implication for policy. Unpublished Masters Thesis, School of Law and Legal Studies, La Trobe University, Melbourne.

Denton. B. 1994. *Prison, drugs and women: Voices from below* (National Drug Strategy, Research Report Series, Report No. 5). Canberra: Commonwealth Department of Health and Family Services.

Denton, B., & O'Malley, P. 1999. Gender, trust, and business. Women drug dealers in the illicit economy. *British Journal of Criminology*, 39, 513–530.

Denton, B. 2001. *Dealing: Women in the Drug Economy*. Sydney: University of New South Wales Press.

Elliot, D., Huizinga, D., & Menard, S. 1989. *Multiple problem youth: Delinquency, substance use, and mental health problems*. New York: Springer-Verlag.

Fagan, J. 1994. Woman and drugs revisited: Female participation in the cocaine economy. *Journal of Drug Issues*, 24, 179–225.

——. 1995. Women's careers in drug use and drug selling. *Current Perspectives on Aging and the Life Cycle*, 4, 155–190.

Faupel, C. 1991. *Shooting dope: Career patterns of hard-core heroin users*. Gainesville, FL: University of Florida Press.

Fitzroy Legal Service. 1988. *Women and imprisonment in Victoria*. Submission to the Social Development Committee into Community Violence, Fitzroy Legal Service, Melbourne.

Hser, Y., Anglin, M., & McGlothlin, W. 1987. Sex differences in addict careers: Initiation of use. *American Journal of Drug and Alcohol Abuse*, 13, 33–57.

Hunt, D. 1990. Drugs and consensual crimes: Drug dealing and prostitution. In M. Tonry & J. Wilson (Eds.), *Drugs and crime*. Chicago: University of Chicago Press.

Inciardi, J., Pottieger, A., & Faupel, C. 1982. Black women, heroin and crime: Some empirical notes. *Journal of Drug Issues*, 12, 241–251.

Koester, S., & J. Schwartz. 1993. Crack, gangs, sex, and powerlessness: A view from Denver." In M. S. Ratner (Ed.) *Crack pipe as pimp: An ethnographic investigation of sex-for-crack exchanges, 187–203*. New York: Lexington.

Johnson, B., Goldstein, P., Preble, E., Schmeidler, J., Lipton, D., Spunt, B., & Miller, T. 1985. *Taking care of business: The economics of crime by heroin abusers*. Lanham, MD: Lexington Books.

Katz, J. 1988. *Seductions of crime*. Chicago: Aldine.

Leonard, M. 1994. *Informal economic activity in Belfast*. London: Athenaeum Press.

Miller, E. 1994. Assessing the risk of inattention to class, race, ethnicity and gender: Comment on Lyng. *American Journal of Sociology*, 96, 1530–45.

Nurco, D., Shafter, J., Ball, J., & Kinlock, T. 1984. Trends in the commission of crime among narcotic addicts over successive periods of addiction and nonaddiction. *American Journal of Drug and Alcohol Abuse*, 10, 481–489.

Pettiway, L. 1987. Participation in Crime Partnerships by Female Drug Users. *Criminology*, 25, 741–766.

Preble, E., & Casey, J. 1969. Taking care of business: The heroin user's life on the street. *International Journal of the Addictions*, 4, 1–24.

Rosenbaum, M. 1981. *Women on heroin*. New Brunswick, NJ: Rutgers University Press.

Sargent, M. 1992. *Women, drugs and policy in Sydney, London and Amsterdam*. Dartmouth: Ashgate Publishing Company.

Steffensmeier, D. 1983. Organization properties and sex-segregation in the underworld: Building a sociological theory of sex differences in crime. *Social Forces*, 61, 1010–1032.

Stewart, T. 1987. *The heroin users*. London: Pandora Press.

Sutherland, E. 1937. *The professional thief*. Chicago: University of Chicago Press.

Taylor, A. 1993. *Woman Drug Users: An Ethnography of a Female Injecting Community*. Oxford, UK: Clarendon Press.

Excerpted from: Barbara Denton and Pat O'Malley. "Property Crime and Women Drug Dealers in Australia." In *Journal of Drug Issues* 31 (2): 465–486. Copyright © 2001 by Journal of Drug Issues, Inc. Used with permission. ✦

20

Up It Up
Gender and the Accomplishment of Street Robbery

Jody Miller

Attempts to understand women's participation in violence have been plagued by a tendency either to overemphasize gender differences or to downplay the significance of gender. The goal of this research is to reconcile these approaches through an examination of the experiences of 14 female street robbers in an urban setting. Based on in-depth interviews, the respondents were recruited through snowball sampling in impoverished neighborhoods in St. Louis, Missouri. To be included in the study, the person had to be an active criminal who has recently committed a robbery. The street ethnographer used to obtain the sample was African-American, so the sample is not necessarily representative of persons who engage in robbery. The sample group ranged in age from 16 to 46, the majority of respondents being in their late teens to mid-20s. Twelve of the women were African-American, and two were white. The research suggests that while women and men articulate similar motives for robbery, their enactment of the crime is strikingly different—a reflection, in part, of practical choices women make in the context of a gender-stratified street setting.

With the exception of forcible rape, robbery is perhaps the most gender differentiated serious crime in the United States. According to the Federal Bureau of Investigation's Uniform Crime Report for 1995, women accounted for 9.3% of robbery arrestees, while they were 9.5%, 17.7%, and 11.1% of arrestees for murder/manslaughter, aggravated assault, and burglary, respectively (Federal Bureau of Investigation, 1996). And while recently there has been considerable attention among feminist scholars to the question of why males are more violent than females, there have been few attempts to examine women's participation in these "male" crimes. Though their numbers are small, women who engage in violent street crime have something significant to teach us about women's place in the landscape of the urban street world.

Simpson (1989: 618) recently noted that feminist scholars' "reticence [to address issues concerning women's criminality] leaves the interpretive door open to less critical perspectives." Nowhere is this more the case than with the issue of women's participation in violent street crime. Sensational accounts of the "new violent female offender" (e.g., Sikes, 1997; see Chesney-Lind, 1993), which draw heavily on racial imagery of young women of color, must be countered with accurate, nuanced accounts of women's use of violence in the contexts of racial and economic inequalities. This research compares the experiences of male and female robbers active in an urban underclass environment with the goal of expanding understanding of women's use of violence in nondomestic street settings.

Masculinities and Crime: Robbery as Gender Accomplishment

In the late 1980s, feminist sociologists began theorizing about gender as situated accomplishment (West and Fenstermaker, 1995; West and Zimmerman, 1987). According to these authors, gender is "much more than a role or an individual characteristic: it is a mechanism whereby situated social action contributes to the reproduction of social structure" (West and Fenstermaker, 1995: 21). Women and men "do gender" in response to normative beliefs about femininity and masculinity. These actions are "the interactional scaffolding of social structure" (West and Zimmerman, 1987: 147) such that the performance of gender is both an indication and a reproduction of gendered social hierarchies.

This approach has been incorporated into feminist accounts of crime as a means of explaining differences in women's and men's offending (Messerschmidt, 1993, 1995; Newburn and Stanko, 1994; Simpson and Elis, 1995). Here, violence is described as "a 'resource' for accomplishing gender—for demonstrating masculinity within a given context or situation" (Simpson and Elis, 1995: 50). Further, it is suggested that although some women may engage in violent behavior, because their actions transgress normative conceptions of femininity, they will "derive little support for expressions of masculine violence from even the most marginal of subcultures" (Braithwaite and Daly, 1994: 190).

Several authors suggest that robbery epitomizes the use of crime to construct masculine identity (Katz, 1988; Messerschmidt, 1993). Messerschmidt argues as follows:

> The robbery setting provides the ideal opportunity to construct an "essential" toughness and "maleness"; it provides a means with which to construct that certain type of masculinity—hardman. Within the social context that ghetto and barrio boys find themselves, then, robbery is a rational practice for "doing gender" and for getting money (Messerschmidt, 1993: 107).

Moreover, given the disproportionate use of robbery by African-American versus white men (Federal Bureau of Investigation, 1996), the masculinity that robbery constructs may be one that fits particularly well in urban underclass settings, which are unique from areas in which poor whites live (see Sampson and Wilson, 1995). Katz, in fact, suggests that "for some urban, black ghetto-located young men, the stickup is particularly attractive as a distinctive way of being black" as well as male (1988: 239).

Examining violence as masculine accomplishment can help account for women's lack of involvement in these crimes, just as this approach offers explanation for women's involvement in crime in ways scripted by femininity (e.g., prostitution). However, it leaves unexplained women's participation in violent street crime, except as an anomaly. Perhaps this is because femininity in this approach is conceived narrowly—specifically "within the parameters of the white middle class (i.e., domesticity, dependence, selflessness, and motherhood)" (Simpson and Elis, 1995: 51). Given urban African-American women's historical patterns of economic self-sufficiency and independence, this passive feminine ideal is unlikely to have considerable influence and is "much more relevant (and restrictive) for white females" (Simpson and Elis, 1995: 71).

Messerschmidt himself has recently recognized this oversight. Given that urban African-American females are involved in violent street crime at higher rates than other females, he suggests that "theory must not universalize female crime" (1995: 171) and must consider significant women's involvement in presumably "male" crime. Simpson (1991: 129; see also White and Kowalski, 1994) concludes: "The simplistic assertion that males are violent and females are not contains a grain of truth, but it misses the complexity and texture of women's lives."

Women's Violence as Resistance to Male Oppression

Feminist scholars who address the use of street violence by women often suggest that women's violence differs from that of men's—women use violence in response to their vulnerability to or actual victimization in the family and/or at the hands of men (Campbell, 1993; Joe and Chesney-Lind, 1995; Maher, 1997; Maher and Curtis, 1992; Maher and Daly, 1996). In her ethnography of a Brooklyn drug market, Maher notes that women adopt violent presentations of self as a strategy of protection. She explains, "'Acting bad' and 'being bad' are not the same. Although many of the women presented themselves as 'bad' or 'crazy,' this projection was a street persona and a necessary survival strategy" (1997: 95; see also Maher and Daly, 1996). These women were infrequently involved in violent crime and most often resorted to violence in response to threats or harms against them. She concludes that "unlike their male counterparts, for women, reputation was about 'preventing victimization'" (Maher, 1997: 95–96; see also Campbell, 1993). In this account, even when women's aggression is offensive, it can still be understood as a defensive act, because it emerges as resistance to victimization.

Maher's research uncovered a particular form of robbery—"viccing"—in which women involved in the sex trade rob their clients. Although the phenomenon of prostitutes robbing tricks is not new, Maher's work documents the proliferation of viccing as a form of resistance against their greater vulnerability to victimization and against cheapened sex markets within the drug economy. Comparing viccing with traditional forms of robbery, Maher and Curtis conclude, "The fact that the act [of viccing] itself is little different to any other instrumental robbery belies the reality that the motivations undergirding it are more complex and, indeed, are intimately linked with women's collective sense of the devaluation of their bodies and their work" (1992: 246). However, it is likely that not all of women's street violence can be viewed as resistance to male oppression; instead, some women may be motivated to commit violent crimes for many of the same reasons some men are. In certain contexts, norms favorable to women's use of violence may exist, and they are not simply about avoiding victimization, but also result in status and recognition.

Race, Class, and Gender: Women's Violence as Situated Action

It is necessary to consider that some of women's participation in violent street crime may stem from "the frustration, alienation, and anger that are associated with racial and class oppression" (Simpson, 1989: 618). The foregrounding of gender is important; however, there are structural and cultural underpinnings related to racial and economic inequalities that must simultaneously be addressed when one considers women's involvement in violent street crime (Simpson, 1991).

Research suggests that urban African-American females are more likely to engage in serious and violent crime than their counterparts in other racial groups and/or settings (Ageton, 1983; Hill and Crawford, 1990; Laub and McDermott, 1985; Mann, 1993). Ageton's analysis of the National Youth Survey found little difference across race or class in girls' incidence of crimes against persons, but she reports that "lower class females report . . . the greatest involvement in assaultive crime . . . [and] a consistently higher proportion of black females are involved in crimes against persons for all five years surveyed" (1983: 565). This is not to suggest that African-American women's participation in these offenses parallel or converge with that of urban African-American males (see Chesney-Lind and Shelden, 1992: 21–24; Laub and McDermott, 1985). Rather, my point is to highlight the contexts in which these women negotiate their daily lives. Violence is extensive in the lives and communities of African-American women living in the urban underclass. As a result, some women in these circumstances may be more likely than women who are situated differently to view violence as an appropriate or useful means of dealing with their environment. As Simpson (1991: 129) notes,

> Living daily with the fact of violence leads to an incorporation of it into one's experiential self. Men, women, and children have to come to terms with, make sense of, and respond to violence as it penetrates their lives. As violence is added to the realm of appropriate and sanctioned responses to oppressive material conditions, it gains a sort of cultural legitimacy. But not for all.

Evidence of the significance of the link between underclass conditions and African-American women's disproportionate involvement in violence may be found in recent research that examines factors predicting women's criminal involvement. Hill and Crawford (1990) report that structural indicators appear to be most significant in predicting the criminal involvement of African-American women, while social-psychological indicators are more predictive for white women. They conclude that "the unique position of black women in the structure of power relations in society has profound effects not shared by their white counterparts" (Hill and Crawford, 1990: 621). In fact, Baskin et al. (1993: 413) suggest that "women in inner city neighborhoods are being pulled toward violent street crime by the same forces that have been found to affect their male counterparts. As with males, neighborhood, peer and addiction factors have been found to contribute to female initiation into violence."

This is not to suggest, however, that gender does not matter. Gender remains a salient aspect of women's experiences in the urban street milieu, and must remain—along with race and class—at the forefront of attempts to understand their involvement in violent crime. Some research that stresses race and economic oppression as factors in women's criminality overlooks the significance of gender oppression in these contexts. For instance, Baskin et al. (1993: 415) argue that "women's roles and prominence have changed in transformed neighborhoods" such that there exist "new dynamics of crime where gender is a far less salient factor" (p. 417).

However, there is overwhelming evidence that gender inequality remains a salient feature of the urban street scene (Anderson, 1994; Maher, 1997; Maher and Curtis, 1992; Maher and Daly, 1996; Oliver, 1994; Steffensmeier, 1983; Steffensmeier and Terry, 1986; Wilson, 1996). As Maher notes, for scholars who suggest that gender has lost its relevance, women's "activity is confused with [their] equality" (1997: 18). Research that examines women's participation in violent street crime without paying sufficient attention to the gendered nature of this participation or the ways in which "gendered status structures this participation" (Maher, 1997: 13) cannot adequately describe or explain these phenomena.

The strength of the current study is its comparative analysis of women's *and* men's accounts of the accomplishment of one type of violent crime—street robbery. In comparing both the question of *why* women and men report engaging in robbery, and *how* gender organizes the commission of robbery, this research provides insight into the ways in which gender shapes women's involvement in what is perhaps the typification of "masculine" street crime. As such, it speaks to broader debates about women's place in the contemporary urban street world.

Motivations to Commit Robbery

In this study, active robbers' articulation of the reasons they commit robbery is more a case of gender similarities than differences. What they get out of robbery, why they choose robbery instead of some other crime, why particular targets are appealing—the themes of these discussions are overlapping in women's and men's accounts. For both, the primary motivation is to get money or material goods. As Libbie Jones notes, "You can get good things from a robbery." For some, the need for money comes with a strong sense of urgency, such as when the individual is robbing to support a drug addiction—a situation more prevalent among older respondents than younger ones. But for the majority of women and men in this sample, robberies are committed to get status-conferring goods such as gold jewelry, spending money, and/or for excitement. For instance, T-Bone says he decides to commit robberies when he's "tired of not having money." When the idea comes about, he is typically with friends from the neighborhood, and he explains, "we all bored, broke, mad." Likewise, CMW says she commits robberies "out of the blue, just something to do. Bored at the time and just want to find some action." She explains, "I be sitting on the porch and we'll get to talking and stuff. See people going around and they be flashing in they fancy cars, walking down the street with that jewelry on, thinking they all bad, and we just go get 'em." For both males and females, robberies are typically a means of achieving conspicuous consumption.

If anything, imperatives to gain money and material goods through robbery appear to be stronger for males than females, so that young men explain that they sometimes commit robberies because they feel some economic pressure, whereas young women typically do not. Masculine street identity is tied to the ability to have and spend money, and included in this is the appearance of economic self-sufficiency. Research has documented women's support networks in urban communities, including among criminally involved women (see Maher, 1997; Stack, 1974). This may help explain why the imperative for young men is stronger than for young women: Community norms may give women wider latitude for obtaining material goods and economic support from a variety of sources, including other females, family members, and boyfriends; whereas the pressure of society's view of men as breadwinners differentially affects men's emotional experience of relying on others economically. This may explain why several young men specifically describe that they do not like relying on their parents in order to meet their consumer needs. As Mike J. notes, "My mother, she gives me money sometimes but I can't get the stuff like I want, clothes and stuff . . . so I try to get it by robbery." Though both males and females articulate economic motives for robbery, young men, more than young women, describe feeling compelled to commit robberies because they feel "broke."

Asked to explain why they commit robberies instead of other crimes with similar economic rewards, both women and men say that they choose robberies, as Cooper explains, because "it's the easiest." Libbie Jones reports that robbery provides her with the things she wants in one quick and easy step:

> I like robbery. I like robbery 'cause I don't have to buy nothing. You have a herringbone, I'm gonna take your herringbone and then I have me a herringbone. I don't have to worry about going to the store, getting me some money. If you got some little earrings on I'm gonna get 'em.

The ease with which respondents view the act of robbery is also reflected in their choice of victims—most frequently other street-involved individuals, who are perceived as unlikely to be able to go to the police, given their own criminal involvement. In addition, these targets are perceived as likely to have a lot of money, as well as jewelry and other desirable items. Less frequently, respondents report targeting individuals who are perceived as particularly easy marks, such as older citizens. However, most robberies, whether committed by females or males, occur in the larger contexts of street life, and their victims reflect this—most are also involved in street contexts, either as adolescents or young adults who hang out on the streets and go to clubs, or as individuals involved (as dealers and/or users) in the street-level drug economy. Because of this, it is not uncommon for robbers to know or at least know of their victims.

In addition to the economic incentives that draw the respondents toward robbery, many also derive a psychological or emotional thrill from committing robberies. Little Bill says, "when my first robbery started, my second, the third one, it got more fun . . . if I keep on doing it I think that I will really get addicted to it." Likewise, Ne-Ne's comment illustrates the complex dynamics shaping many respondents' decisions to commit robberies, particularly the younger ones: "I don't know if it's the money, the power or just the feeling that I know that I can just go up and just take somebody's stuff. It's just a whole bunch of mixture type thing."

Others describe a similar mixture of economic and emotional rewards. Buby notes, "you get like a rush, it be fun at the time."

When individuals on the street are perceived as "high-catting" or showing off, they are viewed by both male and female robbers as deserving targets. Ne-Ne describes the following dialogue between herself and a young woman she robbed: "[The girl] said 'if you take my money then I'm gonna get in trouble because this is my man's money.' He told you to keep it, not showboat. You talking 'nigger I got $800 in my pocket,' pulling it out. Yeah, you wanted us to know." Likewise, describing a woman he robbed at a gas station, Treason Taylor says, "really I didn't like the way she came out. She was like pulling out all her money like she think she hot shit." A few respondents even specifically target people they don't like, or people who have insulted or hurt them in the past.

For both women and men, then, motivations to commit robbery are primarily economic—to get money, jewelry, and other status-conferring goods, but they also include elements of thrill seeking, attempting to overcome boredom, and revenge. Most striking is the continuity across women's and men's accounts of their motives for committing robbery, which vary only by the greater pressure reported by some young men to have their own money to obtain material goods. There are clear differences in the accomplishment of robbery by gender; however, these differences are apparently not driven by differences in motivation.

Male robbers clearly view the act of robbery as a masculine accomplishment in which men compete with other men for money and status. While some rob women, those robberies are deviations from the norm of "badass" against "badass" that dominates much of men's discussions of street robbery (see Katz, 1988). The routine use of guns, physical contact, and violence in male-on-male robberies is a reflection of the masculine ideologies shaping men's robberies. Women's enactment of robbery is much more varied than that of men's and provides a telling contrast about the nature of gender on the streets.

Women's Enactments of Street Robbery

The women in the sample describe three predominant ways in which they commit robberies: targeting female victims in physically confrontational robberies, targeting male victims by appearing sexually available, and participating with males during street robberies of men. Ten

women (71%) describe targeting female victims, usually on the streets but occasionally at dance clubs or in cars. Seven (50%) describe setting up men through promises of sexual favors, including two women who do so in the context of prostitution. Seven (50%) describe working with male friends, relatives, or boyfriends in street robberies; three (21%) report this as their exclusive form of robbery.

Robbing Females

The most common form of robbery reported by women in the study is robbing other females in a physically confrontational manner. Ten of the 14 female respondents report committing these types of offenses. Of those who do not, three only commit robberies by assisting men, whose targets are other males (see below), and one only robs men in the context of prostitution. Typically, women's robberies of other females occur on the streets, though a few young women also report robbing females in the bathrooms or parking lots of clubs, and one robs women in cars. These robberies are sometimes committed alone, but usually in conjunction with one or several additional women, but not in conjunction with men. In fact, Ne-Ne says even when she's out with male friends and sees a female target, they don't get involved: "They'll say 'well you go on and do her.'"

Most robberies of females either involve no weapon or they involve a knife. Four women report having used a gun to rob women, only one of whom does so on a regular basis. Women are the victims of choice because they are perceived as less likely to be armed themselves and less likely to resist or fight back. CMW explains, "See women, they won't really do nothing. They say, 'oh, oh, ok, here take this.' A dude, he might try to put up a fight." Yolanda Smith reports that she only robs women because "they more easier for me to handle." Likewise, Libbie Jones says, "I wouldn't do no men by myself," but she says women victims "ain't gonna do nothing because they be so scared." The use of weapons in these assaults is often not deemed necessary. Quick explains that she sometimes uses a knife, "but sometimes I don't need anything. Most of the time it be girls, you know, just snatching they chains or jewelry. You don't need nothing for that." Quick has also used a gun to rob another female. She and a friend were driving around when they spotted a young woman walking down the street with an expensive purse they liked. "We jumped out of the car. My friend put a gun up to her head and we just took all of her stuff." However, this approach was atypical.

On occasion, female victims belie the stereotype of them and fight back. Both Janet Outlaw and Ne-Ne describe stabbing young women who resisted them. Janet Outlaw describes one such encounter:

> This was at a little basketball game. Coming from the basketball game. It was over and we were checking her out and everything and she was walking to her car. I was, shit fuck that, let's get her motherfucking purse. Said let's get that purse. So I walked up to her and I pulled out the knife. I said "up that purse." And she looked at me. I said "shit, do you think I'm playing? Up that purse." She was like "shit, you ain't getting my purse. Do what you got to do." I was like "shit, you must be thinking I'm playing." So I took the knife, stabbed her a couple of times on the shoulder, stabbed her on the arm and snatched the purse. Cut her arm and snatched the purse. She just ran, "help, help." We were gone.

Ne-Ne describes a similar incident that occurred after an altercation between two groups of young women. When one young woman continued to badmouth her, she followed the girl to her car, pulled out a knife, "headed to her side and showed the bitch [the knife]." The girl responded, "I ain't giving you shit," and Ne-Ne said, "please don't make me stick you." Then, "She went to turn around and I just stuck it in her side. . . . She was holding her side, just bleeding. And so when she fell on the ground one of my partners just started taking her stuff off of her. We left her right there."

As with pulling guns on women, stabbing female victims is a rare occurrence. Nonetheless, women's robbery of other women routinely involves physical confrontation such as hitting, shoving, or beating up the victim. Describing a recent robbery, Nicole Simpson says, "I have bricks in my purse and I went up to her and hit her in the head and took her money." Kim Brown says that she will "just whop you and take a purse but not really put a gun to anybody's face." Libbie Jones says she has her victims throw their possessions on the ground, "then you push 'em, kick 'em or whatever, you pick it up and you just burn out." Likewise, CMW describes a recent robbery:

> I was like with three other girls and we was like all walking around . . . walking around the block trying to find something to do on a Saturday night with really nothing to do and so we started coming up the street, we didn't have no weapons on us at the time. All we did was just start jumping on her and beating her up and took her purse.

According to Janet Outlaw, "We push 'em and tell them to up their shit, pushing 'em in the head. Couple of times we had to knock the girls down and took the stuff off of them." She explains the reason this type of physical force is necessary: "It's just a woman-to-woman thing and we just like, just don't, just letting them know like it is, we let them know we ain't playing." As discussed below, this approach is vastly different from women's approaches when they rob men, or when they commit robberies with males. It appears to be, as Janet Outlaw says, "a woman-to-woman thing."

As noted above, sometimes female-on-female robberies occur in or around night clubs, in addition to on the streets. Libbie Jones explains, "you just chill in the club, just dance or whatever, just peep out people that got what you want. And then they come out of the club and you just get them." Likewise, Janet Outlaw says, "we get a couple of drinks, be on the blow, party, come sit down. Then be like, damn, check that bitch out with all this shit on." Libbie Jones came to her interview wearing a ring she had gotten in a robbery at a club the night before, telling the interviewer, "I like this on my hand, it looks lovely." She describes the incident as follows:

> This girl was in the bathroom. I seen the rings on her hands. Everybody was in there talking and putting their makeup on, doing their hair. So I went and got my godsister. She came back with her drink. She spilled it on her and she was like, "oh, my fault, my fault." She was wiping it off her. I pulled out my knife and said "give it up." The girl was taking the rings off her hand so when we got the rings we bounced up out of the club.

Though most of the women who rob females are teenagers or young adults and rob other young women, two women in the sample—Lisa Wood and Kim Brown—also describe targeting middle-aged or older citizens. It is notable that both are older (in their late 30s) and that both describe robbing in order to support drug habits, which make them more desperate. As with the younger women who choose to rob other young women because they believe them unlikely to resist, both of these women choose older targets because they won't fight back. Lisa Wood says sometimes they accomplish these robberies of non-street-involved citizens by getting victims to drop their guard when they are coming out of stores. She describes approaching the person, "say 'hi, how you doing,' or 'do you need any help?' A lot of times they will say yeah. They might have groceries to take to they car and get it like that." She says once they drop their guard she will "snatch they purse and take off running."

To summarize, notable elements of women's robberies of other women are that they most frequently occur within street-oriented settings, do not include male accomplices, and typically involve physical force such as hitting, shoving and kicking, rather than the use of a weapon. When weapons are used, they are most likely to be knives. In these contexts, women choose to rob other females rather than males because they believe females are less likely to fight back; they typically do not use weapons such as guns because they perceive female targets as unlikely to be armed.

Setting Up Males by Appearing Sexually Available

Women's robberies of men nearly always involve guns. They also do not involve physical contact. Janet Outlaw, who describes a great deal of physical contact in her robberies of other women (see above), describes her robberies of men in much different terms: "If we waste time touching men there is a possibility that they can get the gun off of us, while we wasting time touching them they could do anything. So we just keep the gun straight on them. No touching, no moving, just straight gun at you." The circumstances surrounding the enactment of female-on-male robberies differ as well. The key, in each case, is that women pretend to be sexually interested in their male victims, whose guard drops, providing a safe opportunity for the crime to occur. Two women—Jayzo and Nicole Simpson—rob men in the context of prostitution. The other five typically choose a victim at a club or on the streets, flirt and appear sexually interested, then suggest they go to a hotel, where the robbery takes place. These robberies may involve male or female accomplices, but they are just as likely to be conducted alone.

Nicole Simpson prostitutes to support her drug habit, but sometimes she "just don't be feeling like doing it," and will rob her trick rather than complete the sexual transaction. Sometimes she does this alone, and other times has a female accomplice. She chooses tricks she feels will make safe victims. She explains, "like I meet a lot of white guys and they be so paranoid they just want to get away." When Nicole Simpson is working alone, she waits until the man is in a vulnerable position before pulling out her knife. As she explains, "if you are sucking a man's dick and you pull a knife on them, they not gonna too much argue with you." When she works with a female partner, Nicole Simpson has the woman wait at a desig-

nated place, then takes the trick "to the spot where I know she at." She begins to perform oral sex, then her partner jumps in the car and pulls a knife. She explains, "once she get in the car I'll watch her back, they know we together. I don't even let them think that she is by herself. If they know it's two of us maybe they won't try it. Because if they think she by herself they might say fuck this, it ain't nothing but one person." Jayzo's techniques parallel those of Nicole Simpson, though she uses a gun instead of a knife and sometimes takes prospective tricks to hotels in addition to car dating.

Young women who target men outside the context of prostitution play upon the men's beliefs about women in order to accomplish these robberies—including the assumptions that women won't be armed, won't attempt to rob them, and can be taken advantage of sexually. Quick explains, "they don't suspect that a girl gonna try to get 'em. You know what I'm saying? So it's kind of easier 'cause they like, she looks innocent, she ain't gonna do this, but that's how I get 'em. They put they guard down to a woman." She says when she sets up men, she parties with them first, but makes sure she doesn't consume as much as them. "Most of the time, when girls get high they think they can take advantage of us so they always, let's go to a hotel or my crib or something." Janet Outlaw says, "they easy to get, we know what they after—sex." Likewise, CMW and a girlfriend often flirt with their victims: "We get in the car then ride with them. They thinking we little freaks . . . whores or something." These men's assumptions that they can take advantage of women lead them to place themselves at risk for robbery. CMW continues: "So they try to take us to the motel or whatever, we going for it. Then it's like they getting out of the car and then all my friend has to do is just put the gun up to his head, give me your keys. He really can't do nothing, his gun is probably in the car. All you do is drive on with the car."

Several young women report targeting men at clubs, particularly dope dealers or other men who appear to have a lot of money. Describing one such victim, Janet Outlaw says she was drawn to him because of his "jewelry, the way he was dressed, little snakeskin boots and all. . . . I was like, yeah, there is some money." She recounts the incident as follows:

> I walked up to him, got to conversating with him. He was like, "what's up with you after the club?" I said "I'm down with you, whatever you want to do." I said "we can go to a hotel or something." He was like "for real?" I was like, "yeah, for real." He was like, "shit,

cool then." So after the club we went to the hotel. I had the gun in my purse. I followed him, I was in my own car, he was in his car. So I put the gun in my purse and went up to the hotel, he was all ready. He was posted, he was a lot drunk. He was like, "you smoke weed?" I was like, "yeah shit, what's up." So we got to smoking a little bud, he got to taking off his little shirt laying it on a little table. He was like, "shit, what's up, ain't you gonna get undressed?" I was like "shit, yeah, hold up" and I went in my purse and I pulled out the gun. He was like "damn, what's up with you gal?" I was like, "shit, I want your jewelry and all the money you got." He was like, "shit, bitch you crazy. I ain't giving you my shit." I said, "do you think I'm playing nigger? You don't think I'll shoot your motherfucking ass?" He was like, "shit, you crazy, fuck that, you ain't gonna shoot me." So then I had fired the thing but I didn't fire it at him, shot the gun. He was like "fuck no." I snatched his shit. He didn't have on no clothes. I snatched the shit and ran out the door. Hopped in my car.

Though she did this particular robbery alone, Janet Outlaw says she often has male accomplices, who follow her to the hotel or meet her there. While she's in the room, "my boys be standing out in the hallway," then she lets them in when she's ready to rob the man. Having male backup is useful because men often resist being robbed by females, believing that women don't have the heart to go through with what's necessary if the victim resists. Janet Outlaw describes one such incident. Having flirted with a man and agreed to meet him, she got in his car then pulled her gun on him:

I said "give me your stuff." He wasn't gonna give it to me. This was at nighttime. My boys was on the other side of the car but he didn't know it. He said "I ain't gonna give you shit." I was like, "you, gonna give me your stuff." He was like "I'll take that gun off of your ass." I was like, "shit, you ain't gonna take this gun." My boy just pulled up and said, "give her your shit." I got the shit.

In the majority of these robberies, the victim knows that the woman has set him up—she actively participates in the robbery. Ne-Ne also describes setting up men and then pretending to be a victim herself. Her friends even get physical with her to make it appear that she's not involved. She explains:

I'll scam you out and get to know you a little bit first, go out and eat and let you tell me where we going, what time and everything. I'll go in the restroom and go beep them [accomplices] just to let them know what time we leaving from wherever we at so they

can come out and do their little robbery type thing, push me or whatever. I ain't gonna leave with them 'cause then he'll know so I still chill with him for a little while.

Only Ne-Ne reports having ever engaged in a robbery the opposite of this—that is, one in which her male partners flirted with a girl and she came up and robbed her. She explains:

I got some [male friends] that will instigate it. If I see some girl and I'm in the car with a whole bunch of dudes, they be like "look at that bitch she have on a leather coat." "Yeah, I want that." They'll say "well why don't you go get it?" Then you got somebody in the back seat [saying] "she's scared, she's scared." Then you got somebody just like "she ain't scared, up on the piece" or whatever and then you got some of them that will say well, "we gonna do this together." It could be like two dudes they might get out like "what's up baby," try to holler at her, get a mack on and they don't see the car. We watching and as soon as they pulling out they little pen to write they number, then I'll get out of the car and just up on them and tell them, the dudes be looking like, damn, what's going on? But they ain't gonna help 'cause they my partners or whatever.

Street Robberies With Male Robbers

As the previous two sections illustrate, women's accomplishment of robbery varies according to the gender of their victims. As a rule, women and men do not rob females together, but do sometimes work together to set up and rob males. In addition, half of the women interviewed describe committing street robberies—almost always against males—with male accomplices. In these robberies, women's involvement either involves equal participation in the crime or assisting males but defining their role as secondary. Three women in the sample—Buby, Tish, and Lisa Jones—describe working with males on the streets as their only form of robbery, and each sees her participation as secondary. The rest engage in a combination of robbery types, including those described in the previous two sections, and do not distinguish their roles from the roles of male participants in these street robberies.

Lisa Jones and Tish each assist their boyfriends in the commission of robberies; Buby goes along with her brother and cousins. Lisa Jones says "most of the time we'll just be driving around and he'll say 'let's go to this neighborhood and rob somebody.'" Usually she stays in the car while he approaches the victim, but she is armed and will get out and assist when necessary. Describing one such incident, she says, "One time there was two guys and one guy was in the car and the other guy was out of the car and I seen that one guy getting out of the car I guess to help his friend. That's when I got out and I held the gun and I told him to stay where he was." Likewise Buby frequently goes on robberies with her brother and cousins but usually chooses to stay in the car "because I be thinking that I'm gonna get caught so I rather stay in the back." She has never done a robbery on her own and explains, "I know what to do but I don't know if I could do it on my own. I don't know if I could because I'm used to doing them with my brother and my cousins." Though her role is not an active one, she gets a cut of the profits from these robberies.

Tish and Lisa Jones are the only white respondents in the study. Each robs with an African-American boyfriend, and—though they commit armed robberies—both reject the view of themselves as criminals. Lisa Jones, for instance, downplays her role in robberies, as the following dialogue illustrates:

> Interviewer: How many armed robberies have you done in your life?
>
> Lisa Jones: I go with my boyfriend and I've held the gun, I've never actually shot it.
>
> Interviewer: But you participate in his robberies?
>
> Lisa Jones: Yeah.
>
> Interviewer: How many would you say in your whole life?
>
> Lisa Jones: About fifteen.
>
> Interviewer: What about in the last month?
>
> Lisa Jones: Maybe five or six.
>
> Interviewer: What other crimes have you done in your life, or participated with others?
>
> Lisa Jones: No, I'm not a criminal.

It is striking that this young woman routinely engages in robberies in which she wields a weapon, yet she defines herself as "not a criminal." Later in the interview, she explains that she would stop participating in armed robberies "if I was to stop seeing him." She and Tish are the only respondents who minimize the implications of their involvement in armed robbery, and it is probably not coincidental that they are young white women—their race and gender allow them to view themselves in this way.

Both also describe their boyfriends as the decision makers in the robberies—deciding when, where, and whom to rob. This is evident in Tish's interview, as her boyfriend, who is present in the room, frequently interjects to answer the interviewer's questions. The following dialogue is revealing:

> Interviewer: How do you approach the person?
>
> Tish: Just go up to them.
>
> Interviewer: You walk up to them, you drive up to them?
>
> Boyfriend: Most of the time it's me and my partner that do it. Our gals, they got the guns and stuff but we doing most of the evaluating. We might hit somebody in the head with a gun, go up to them and say whatever. Come up off your shit or something to get the money. The girls, they doing the dirty work really, that's the part they like doing, they'll hold the gun and if something goes wrong they'll shoot. We approach them. I ain't gonna send my gal up to no dude to tell him she want to rob him, you know. She might walk up to him with me and she might hit him a couple of times but basically I'm going up to them.

These respondents reveal the far end of the continuum of women's involvement in robbery, clearly taking subordinate roles in the crime and defining themselves as less culpable as a result. Tish's boyfriend also reveals his perception of women as secondary actors in the accomplishment of robbery. For the most part, other women who participate in street robberies with male accomplices describe themselves as equal participants. Older women who rob citizens to support their drug habits at times do so with male accomplices. For instance, Lisa Woods sometimes commits her robberies with a male and female accomplice and targets people "like when they get they checks. Catch them coming out of the store, maybe trip 'em, go in they pocket and take they money and take off running." Among the younger women, robberies with male accomplices involve guns and typically come about when a group of people are driving around and spot a potential victim. Janet Outlaw describes a car jacking that occurred as she and some friends were driving around:

> Stop at a red light, we was looking around, didn't see no police, we was right behind them [the victims]. . . . So one of my boys got out and I got out. Then the other boy got up in the driver's seat that was with them. My boy went on one side and I went on the other side and said "nigger get out of the car before we shoot you." Then the dudes got out. It was like, shit, what's up, we down with you all. No you ain't down with us, take

222 Section V ✦ *Women's Crime as Rational Choice*

they jewelry and shit off. It was like, damn, why you all tripping? Then my boy cocked the little gun and said take it off now or I'm gonna start spraying you all ass. So they took off the little jewelry, I hopped in, put it in drive and pulled on off.

Likewise, Ne-Ne prefers committing street robberies with males rather than females. She explains:

I can't be bothered with too many girls. That's why I try to be with dudes or whatever. They gonna be down. If you get out of the car and if you rob a dude or jack somebody and you with some dudes then you know if they see he tryin' to resist, they gonna give me some help. Whereas a girl, you might get somebody that's scared and might drive off. That's the way it is.

It is not surprising, then, that Ne-Ne is the only woman interviewed to report having ever committed this type of street robbery of a male victim on her own. Her actions parallel those of male-on-male robbers described above. Ne-Ne explicitly indicates that this robbery was possible because the victim did not know she was a woman. Describing herself physically, she says, "I'm big, you know." In addition, her dress and manner masked her gender. "I had a baseball cap in my car and I seen him. . . . I just turned around the corner, came back down the street, he was out by hisself and I got out of the car, had the cap pulled down over my face and I just went to the back and upped him. Put the gun up to his head." Being large, wearing a ballcap, and enacting the robbery in a masculine style (e.g., putting a gun to his head) allowed her to disguise the fact that she was a woman and thus decrease the victim's likelihood of resisting. She says, "He don't know right now to this day if it was a girl or a dude."

Discussion

Feminist scholars have been hesitant to grapple with the issue of women's violence, both because a focus on women's violence draws attention away from the fact that violence is a predominantly male phenomenon and because studying women's violence can play into sensationalized accounts of female offenders. Nonetheless, as this and other studies have shown, "gender alone does not account for variation in criminal violence" (Simpson, 1991: 118). A small number of women are involved in violent street crime in ways that go beyond "preventing victimization," and appear to find support among their male and female peers for these activities. To draw this conclusion is not to

suggest that women's use of violence is increasing, that women are "equals" on the streets, or that gender does not matter. It does suggest that researchers should continue developing feminist perspectives to address the issue.

What is most notable about the current research is the incongruity between motivations and accomplishment of robbery. While a comparison of women's and men's motivations to commit robbery reveals gender similarities, when women and men actually commit robbery their enactments of the crime are strikingly different. These differences highlight the clear gender hierarchy that exists on the streets. While some women are able to carve out a niche for themselves in this setting, and even establish partnerships with males, they are participating in a male-dominated environment, and their actions reflect an understanding of this.

To accomplish robberies successfully, women must take into account the gendered nature of their environment. One way they do so is by targeting other females. Both male and female robbers hold the view that females are easy to rob, because they are less likely than males to be armed and because they are perceived as weak and easily intimidated. Janet Outlaw describes women's robbery of other women as "just a woman to woman thing." This is supported by Ne-Ne's description that her male friends do not participate with her in robberies of females, and it is supported by men's accounts of robbing women. While women routinely rob other women, men are less likely to do so, perhaps because these robberies do not result in the demonstration of masculinity.

At the same time that women articulate the belief that other women are easy targets, they also draw upon these perceptions of women in order to rob men. Two of the women describe committing robberies much in keeping with Maher's (1997) descriptions of "viccing." In addition, a number of women used men's perceptions of women as weak, sexually available, and easily manipulated to turn the tables and manipulate men into circumstances in which they became vulnerable to robbery—by flirting and appearing sexually interested in them. Unlike women's robberies of other women, these robberies tend not to involve physical contact but do involve the use of guns. Because they recognize men's perceptions of women, they also recognize that men are more likely to resist being robbed by a female, and thus they commit these robberies in ways that minimize their risk of losing control and maximize their ability to show that they're "for real."

West and Zimmerman (1987: 139) note that there are circumstances in which "parties reach an accommodation that allow[s] a woman to engage in presumptively masculine behavior." In this study, it is notable that while both women and men recognize the urban street world as a male-dominated one, a few of the women interviewed appear to have gained access to male privilege by adopting male attitudes about females, constructing their own identities as more masculine, and following through by behaving in masculine ways (see also Hunt, 1984). Ne-Ne and Janet Outlaw both come to mind in this regard—as women who completed robberies in equal partnerships with men and identified with men's attitudes about other women. Other women, such as Lisa Jones and Tish, accepted not only women's position as secondary, but their own as well. While Ne-Ne and Janet Outlaw appeared to draw status and identity from their criminality in ways that went beyond their gender identity, Lisa Jones and Tish used their gender identity to construct themselves as noncriminal.

In sum, the women in this sample do not appear to "do robbery" differently than men in order to meet different needs or accomplish different goals. Instead, the differences that emerge reflect practical choices made in the context of a gender-stratified environment—one in which, on the whole, men are perceived as strong and women are perceived as weak. Motivationally, then, it appears that women's participation in street violence can result from the same structural and cultural underpinnings that shape some of men's participation in these crimes, and that they receive rewards beyond protection for doing so. Yet gender remains a salient factor shaping their actions, as well as the actions of men.

Though urban African-American women have higher rates of violence than other women, their participation in violent crime is nonetheless significantly lower than that of their male counterparts in the same communities (Simpson, 1991). An important line of inquiry for future research is to assess what protective factors keep the majority of women living in under-class settings from adopting violence as a culturally legitimate response. While research shows that racial and economic oppression contribute to African-American women's greater participation in violent crime, they do not ensure its occurrence. Daly and Stephens (1995: 208) note: "Racism in criminological theories occurs when racial or cultural differences are overemphasized or mischaracterized and when such differences are denied." Future research should strive to strike this balance and attend to the complex issues surrounding women's participation in violence within the urban street world.

Discussion Questions

1. How can being female be used to complete a violent crime? Can gender be used as a criminal resource?

2. What are women's motivations to become involved in street violence? How close are these motivations to why men commit robbery?

3. How does the way female offenders approach their victims and negotiate differ by gender of the victim?

4. Compare and contrast the roles in crime from Chapter 9 (Alarid et al.) and Chapter 10 (Decker et al.) to the roles in robbery described in Miller's study.

5. What characteristics differentiate females who play primary roles in robbery from females who play secondary roles in the crime?

References

Agar, Michael H. 1977. Ethnography in the streets and in the joint: A comparison. In Robert S. Weppner (ed.), *Street Ethnography: Selected Studies of Crime and Drug Use in Natural Settings*. Beverly Hills, Calif.: Sage.

Ageton, Suzanne S. 1983. The dynamics of female delinquency, 1976–1980. *Criminology* 21 (4): 555–584.

Anderson, Elijah. 1994. The code of the streets. *Atlantic Monthly* 273: 81–94.

Baskin, Deborah, Ira Sommers, and Jeffrey Fagan. 1993. The political economy of violent female street crime. *Fordham Urban Law Journal* 20: 401–417.

Braithwaite, John and Kathleen Daly. 1994. Masculinities, violence and communitarian control. In Tim Newburn and Elizabeth A. Stanko (eds.), *Just Boys Doing Business?* New York: Routledge.

Campbell, Anne. 1993. *Men, Women and Aggression*. New York: Basic Books.

Chesney-Lind, Meda. 1993. Girls, gangs and violence: Anatomy of a backlash. *Humanity & Society* 17 (3): 321–344.

Chesney-Lind, Meda and Randall G. Shelden. 1992. *Girls, Delinquency and Juvenile Justice*. Pacific Grove, Calif.: Brooks/Cole.

Daly, Kathleen and Deborah J. Stephens. 1995. The "dark figure" of criminology: Towards a black and multi-ethnic feminist agenda for theory and research. In Nicole Hahn Rafter and Frances Heidensohn (eds.), *International Feminist Perspec-*

tives in Criminology: Engendering a Discipline. Philadelphia: Open University Press.

Decker, Scott and Barrik Van Winkle. 1996. *Life in the Gang*. New York: Cambridge University Press.

Federal Bureau of Investigation. 1996. *Crime in the United States, 1995*. Washington, D.C.: U.S. Government Printing Office.

Glassner, Barry and Cheryl Carpenter. 1985. The feasibility of an ethnographic study of adult property offenders. Unpublished report prepared for the National Institute of Justice, Washington, D.C.

Hill, Gary D. and Elizabeth M. Crawford. 1990. Women, race, and crime. *Criminology* 28 (4): 601–623.

Hunt, Jennifer. 1984. The development of rapport through the negotiation of gender in field work among police. *Human Organization* 43 (4): 283–296.

Joe, Karen A. and Meda Chesney-Lind. 1995. Just every mother's angel: An analysis of gender and ethnic variations in youth gang membership. *Gender & Society* 9 (4): 408–430.

Katz, Jack. 1988. *Seductions of Crime*. New York: Basic Books.

Kelly, Liz. 1991. Unspeakable Acts. *Trouble and Strife* 21: 13–20.

Laub, John H. and M. Joan McDermott. 1985. An analysis of serious crime by young black women. *Criminology* 23 (1): 81–98.

Maher, Lisa. 1997. *Sexed Work: Gender, Race and Resistance in a Brooklyn Drug Market*. Oxford, UK: Clarendon Press.

Maher, Lisa and Richard Curtis. 1992. Women on the edge of crime: Crack cocaine and the changing contexts of street-level sex work in New York City. *Crime, Law and Social Change* 18: 221–258.

Maher, Lisa and Kathleen Daly. 1996. Women in the street-level drug economy: Continuity or change? *Criminology* 34 (4): 465–492.

Mann, Coramae Richey. 1993. Sister against sister: Female intrasexual homicide. In C. C. Culliver (ed.), *Female Criminality: The State of the Art*. New York: Garland Publishing.

Messerschmidt, James W. 1993. *Masculinities and Crime*. Lanham, Md.: Rowman & Littlefield.

——. 1995. From patriarchy to gender: Feminist theory, criminology and the challenge of diversity. In Nicole Hahn Rafter and Frances Heidensohn (eds.), *International Feminist Perspectives in Criminology: Engendering a Discipline*. Philadelphia: Open University Press.

Newburn, Tim and Elizabeth A. Stanko (eds.). 1994. *Just Boys Doing Business?* New York: Routledge.

Oliver, William. 1994. *The Violent Social World of Black Men*. New York: Lexington Books.

Sampson, Robert J. and William Julius Wilson. 1995. Toward a theory of race, crime, and urban inequality. In John Hagan and Ruth D. Peterson (eds.), *Crime and Inequality*. Stanford, Calif.: Stanford University Press.

Sikes, Gini. 1997. *8 Ball Chicks: A Year in the Violent World of Girl Gangsters*. New York: Anchor Books.

Simpson, Sally. 1989. Feminist theory, crime and justice. *Criminology* 27 (4): 605–631.

——. 1991. Caste, class and violent crime: Explaining difference in female offending. *Criminology* 29 (1): 115–135.

Simpson, Sally and Lori Elis. 1995. Doing gender: Sorting out the caste and crime conundrum. *Criminology* 33 (1): 47–81.

Sommers, Ira and Deborah R. Baskin. 1993. The situational context of violent female offending. *Journal of Research on Crime and Delinquency* 30 (2): 136–162.

St. Louis Metropolitan Police Department. 1994. Annual Report—1993/1994.

Stack, Carol B. 1974. *All Our Kin: Strategies for Survival in a Black Community*. New York: Harper & Row.

Steffensmeier, Darrell J. 1983. Organization properties and sex-segregation in the underworld: Building a sociological theory of sex differences in crime. *Social Forces* 61: 1010–1032.

Steffensmeier, Darrell J. and Robert Terry. 1986. Institutional sexism in the underworld: A view from the inside. *Sociological Inquiry* 56: 304–323.

Watters, John and Patrick Biemacki. 1989. Targeted sampling: Options for the study of hidden populations. *Social Problems* 36: 416–430.

West, Candace and Sarah Fenstermaker. 1995. Doing difference. *Gender & Society* 9 (1): 8–37.

West, Candace and Don H. Zimmerman. 1987. Doing gender. *Gender & Society* 1 (2): 125–151.

White, Jacquelyn W. and Robin M. Kowalski. 1994. Deconstructing the myth of the nonaggressive woman: A feminist analysis. *Psychology of Women Quarterly* 18: 487–508.

Wilson, William Julius. 1996. *When Work Disappears: The World of the New Urban Poor*. New York: Alfred A. Knopf.

Wright, Richard T. and Scott Decker. 1994. *Burglars on the Job: Streetlife and Residential Break-Ins*. Boston: Northeastern University Press.

——. 1997. *Armed Robbers in Action: Stickups and Street Culture*. Boston: Northeastern University Press.

Excerpted from: Jody Miller, "Up It Up: Gender and the Accomplishment of Street Robbery." In *Criminology*, 36 (1): 37–66. Copyright © 1998 by American Society of Criminology. Used with permission. ✦

21
Women Who Kill in Drug Market Situations

Henry H. Brownstein
Barry J. Spunt
Susan M. Crimmins
Sandra C. Langley

Recent studies of women and homicide have shown that lethal violence by women is a more complex phenomenon than merely self-defense against abusive partners. In this chapter, the authors explore the ways in which changing drug markets may have influenced women's involvement in lethal violence. From open-ended and semistructured interviews with 215 women sentenced to prison in New York State for homicide, the authors identified 19 cases (or 8.8 percent of all the homicide cases) that involved a drug market situation. Through qualitative analysis of the narratives offered by these women to explain their involvement in the killing, the authors found evidence that women will use violence, as will men, to protect or augment an economic interest in a drug market. From further analysis, however, these researchers concluded that even in a clearly economic context in which women are able to acquire their own economic interest, some women will kill or participate in a killing in connection with their relationship with a male business or intimate partner. That is, women who kill in the economic context of a drug market may kill for economic reasons, but the specific circumstances of involvement in a drug market do not necessarily negate the significance of gender. Bear in mind that this study of homicide represents a small percentage of homicides and that women overwhelmingly kill in connection with victimization by horrific abuse or in self-defense situations.

The literature comparing homicides by women and by men has focused primarily on cases involving domestic situations. It has been suggested that women are more likely than men to have killed a relative, especially a spouse or partner and more likely to have killed in a domestic dispute. This statement may be statistically accurate, but it does not negate the fact that women also kill for reasons unrelated to concerns of the family or home.

Adler (1975) and Simon (1975) independently proposed a liberationist view that is useful for explaining the greater complexity in homicide by women. This liberationist perspective suggests that as women are "liberated" from the social and economic constraints of their traditional and historical role, they will become more like men in regard to their patterns of criminal offending (see Jurik and Winn 1990). This position has been widely criticized (Daly and Chesney-Lind 1988; Miller 1986; Smart 1978), but the question—whether women will follow men's patterns in pursuit of their own social or economic interests—remains (Simon and Landis 1991).

Critics of the liberationist perspective have argued that gender differences remain significant, even when women are given the same social and cultural opportunities as men (see Chesney-Lind 1993; Miller 1986). In regard to homicide by women, this argument suggests that women kill for gender-based reasons because of the nature of their personal and historical relationship as women to men.

In this [chapter] we examine women who have killed in circumstances related to a market economy rather than in a domestic setting. Through the experiences of women who have killed in an economic rather than a domestic context, we explore whether the significance of gender is altered by the specific circumstances of the economy of the situation. Specifically, we focus on women who have killed in drug market situations.

We selected drug markets as a focal point for two reasons, both related to the relatively recent introduction of crack cocaine to the drug market economy. First, studies of contemporary drug markets, particularly crack markets, have shown that lethal violence is used commonly by drug traffickers in the pursuit of their economic interests. Young men involved in the early crack trade were particularly likely to use lethal violence to protect their interests in disputes with other traffickers over market share and business practice (see Goldstein, Brownstein, and Ryan 1992; Goldstein et al. 1989). Second, crack is relatively easy to manufacture, can be packaged in inexpensive quantities, and has a high addiction potential. In addition, crack markets have high volume sales and high profit margins. Consequently the first crack markets could be opened independent of the social controls of established drug business hierarchies and of the law, thereby promising the opportunity for ownership, control, and autonomy to anyone who could afford to purchase even a minimum amount of cocaine.

Thus drug markets in the late 1980s provided women, at least in theory, with the opportunity for economic liberation in a social setting where problems of socioeconomic relationship were commonly resolved with violence. In this [chapter] we do not explore whether the crack market actually provided women with widespread economic opportunities. Rather, we examine situations in which women used lethal violence in relation to the drug market, and ask whether or not they killed in relation to an economic interest related to the market. Alternatively, even in a violent market situation, did these women kill for gender-based reasons?

Sample

As was true for drugs, the women in the sample were not strangers to violence. About one-third grew up in communities that they remembered as violent. As for their own use of violence, 65 percent said they had participated in violent activity (e.g., hitting others, robbery), and 64 percent said they had seriously harmed someone else (e.g., beating up, threatening with a weapon) when they were growing up. In discussing their own violent victimization, 58 percent said they had been the victims of serious physical harm as a child, and 79 percent said they had been the victims of such harm as an adult. In addition, 49 percent said they had been the victims of sexual harm (i.e., inappropriate touching or forced sexual penetration) as a child; 43 percent said they had experienced such harm as an adult.

Of the 205 women who reported that they had ever used any drug, including alcohol, 56 percent said that at least once their drug use was connected to violence. Of the 178 women who told the interviewer they had ever used any drug other than alcohol, 46 percent said that at least once the drug use was associated with violence.

Sixty percent of the 215 women told the interviewer that they were personally responsible for the homicide for which they were convicted and sentenced to prison. An additional 12 percent said they were accomplices, 2 percent said they were conspirators, and 10 percent said they were simply bystanders. The remainder said they were not present or not involved in the killing, could not remember, or did not want to discuss the event in detail.

Most of the killings took place in a residence (64%), usually that of the victim (24%) or a place shared by the victim and the respondent (26%). About one-third of the women used a knife or other cutting instrument to kill the victim; 28 percent used a gun. The victim was the respondent's spouse or partner in only 20 percent of the incidents; more often, the victim was a stranger (23%); and most often, an acquaintance (33%). Sixteen percent of the victims were the children of respondents, and 9 percent were other relatives. In 68 percent of the incidents the respondent said the killing was precipitated by the victim's actions or words, including threats, insults, and arguments.

Most of the respondents who described being present or involved in the killing (181) said they had used some drug on the day of the homicide. Sixty-four percent said they had used one or more drugs, including alcohol; 47 percent said they had used alcohol, 18 percent crack, 12 percent cocaine, 11 percent marijuana, and 10 percent heroin. Thirty-nine percent of the women said they were high at the time of the killing; 24 percent on alcohol, 8 percent on crack, 8 percent on cocaine, 3 percent on marijuana, and 5 percent on heroin.

All cases of homicide by women who were present or involved in the killing were classified in terms of the relationship between the killing and drugs. Sixty-six percent of these incidents were related to drugs in one way or another. Fifty-seven percent involved drug ingestion by the woman or her victim, 12 percent involved a compelling need by the woman or someone else to obtain drugs or money for drugs, and 11 percent involved the participation of the woman or her victim in the typically violent relationships of drug trade and traffic (for details about this classification scheme, see Brownstein and Goldstein 1990; Goldstein et al. 1989).

Motives of Women Who Kill

In any given year in the United States, the number of women who commit homicide is smaller than the number of men, and the number of women who kill for economic reasons is a small percentage of all female homicide offenders (Federal Bureau of Investigation 1994). In this section we discuss those women with economic motives for killing in order to study women who kill in situations related to social or economic interests.

Every homicide event is a complex social interaction between "an offender, victim, and possibly an audience" in what Luckenbill, almost two decades ago, called a "situated transaction" (1977: 176). As the event occurs over time and through the course of progressive interaction, individual motives are subject to change. Thus a single homicide event can have a variety of associated motives. . . .

Eight of the 13 killings were related to an attempt to get drugs or money for drugs. In Incident 099, for example, the respondent was involved in the killing of a taxicab driver to get money to repay drug money that had been stolen. In Incident 265, the respondent was collecting money from the spot where she sold drugs, and she shot and killed someone who tried to rob her. According to the respondent in that case,

> I went to collect some money from one of my [drug-selling] spots. I drove up, parked my car, and went to get the money. This guy from the neighborhood, a heroin user in fact, one of my customers probably, comes up to my car, pointed a gun at me, and demanded the money. I kept my own gun with me, and before he had a chance to shoot me, I shot him first. I was really scared. I thought he was going to kill me.

As described by the respondent, this case is a representative example of an incident that began with an economic motive and ended as a killing motivated by fear.

Of the remaining five of these 13 incidents, one was a case of someone being paid to kill, one involved getting money for something other than drugs, and three involved angry retaliation for "messing" with drugs or drug money. In one of the latter incidents, Number 433, the motivation was as close as possible to being purely economic. The respondent was the lieutenant in a drug-dealing operation, and she killed a worker who had run off with her boss's money.

Of the six drug market incidents that were coded as not having economic motivations, the respondents either claimed noneconomic reasons for their participation in the killing (four respondents) or stated that they had nothing to do with it (two respondents). One of the latter said she was too high to remember what happened; the other said she was just a bystander. The bystander, Respondent 078, was the girlfriend of a dealer and was present during a robbery of another dealer in a dispute over drug territory. The woman who was too high to remember what happened, Respondent 014, was convicted of killing a drug dealer she was robbing while he was picking up his money.

The respondent in Case 014 might not have been able to remember what happened, but the police produced three witnesses who said they did. The woman was 26 years old in 1986, when she was arrested for killing a man over crack and money. The police witnesses claimed they saw her get out of a car and shoot a man to get his money and his crack. They told her, she said to the interviewer, that the man was in the drug business and was in her building picking up his money.

The woman in Case 014 had been selling crack for about a year when the killing occurred. For $50 she bought crack worth about $100 on the street from a dealer who had several sellers working for him. In this case, she told corrections officials, the victim owed her money, and she was trying to scare him. Although she reports that she does not remember the killing, she knows, as she said to the interviewer, that "when using crack, I was always into fighting over anything and with anybody, especially men."

Among the four other cases involving women who killed in the context of the drug business but said they killed for other than economic reasons, two said they killed in self-defense, one was trying to scare the victim, and one was protecting herself from sexual attack. In the case involving a sexual attack (086), the respondent was the girlfriend of a major dealer who attacked her in part because on one occasion she refused to carry a package of drugs for him. The motivation for the killing clearly was not economic, but it was just as clearly connected with the drug business.

The boyfriend of the respondent in Incident 086 was much older than she and was well known in the neighborhood as a major heroin dealer. She worked for him as a carrier, delivering heroin to another part of the city. One night after midnight he asked her to go to pick up a package. She was afraid to go to that part of the city alone at that hour, and refused. He slapped her. A friend of his who was in the room held her down while he beat her. Then he ripped off her clothes and sodomized her. When he finished, he hit her again and sent her to bed.

While she lay in bed waiting for him, she kept thinking, "I'm gonna kill him." When he came to bed, she got up and went to get a gun that he always left under the dresser. She came back to bed and shot him twice. She took a handful of money and went to a shooting gallery where she "shot a lot." Then she turned herself in to the police.

Women and Crack Market Killing

The crack markets of the late 1980s and early 1990s represent what Johnson and his associates (1992) call the "free-lance" drug market model. Compared with the highly structured "business" market model, with its reliance on capital and its routinized and hierarchical relationships between employers and employees, the "free-lance" model involves "actors at all levels [who] work together without clear employee-employer relationships being established" (Johnson et al. 1992: 60). It is most likely to be found in open, unregulated markets where entrepreneurs with a small amount of product can establish themselves as drug dealers.

Because of the characteristics of the product and the market, as described earlier, crack cocaine was particularly well suited to the "free-lance" market model when it first appeared in urban communities in the United States. In later years the crack market saw the formation of "confederations" of free-lance dealers, and increasingly it came to resemble the "business" model. In the early days, however, it gave young, inexperienced individuals with as little as one or two grams of cocaine an opportunity to establish their own crack businesses independent of and in conflict with one another.

The early crack markets, then, provided opportunities for individuals who could afford even a minimal amount of cocaine to acquire a stake in a growing business (compare Belenko 1990; Spunt et al. 1989). For the young entrepreneurs who took this opportunity and acquired an interest or stake in the crack economy, violence became the means of protecting or defending that interest, and the means of acquiring the interests of others. With no recourse to the legal system but with easy access to weapons, they routinely used lethal violence to settle disputes over territory and money (Brownstein et al. 1992; Goldstein et al. 1989).

In theory, the same opportunities to gain an economic interest in the crack market should have been available to enterprising young women, who typically found opportunities only at the lower levels of the more firmly established drug markets (compare Brownstein et al. 1994; Fagan 1994; Inciardi et al. 1993; Sommers and Baskin 1992, 1993). As noted earlier, we do not attempt here to assess to what extent women took this opportunity and became active in the crack market. Rather, we focus on women who became involved in drug markets during this period, both as traffickers and as users, and we consider to what extent they engaged in lethal violence in pursuit of their social and economic interests. Given the central role of violence as a means of social control in the crack markets, we would expect that women who acquired a stake in the early crack markets would have engaged in market-related violence.

Of the 19 killings related to the drug market, 10 (53%) involved crack as the primary drug. All of these took place between 1986 and 1991. One involved a dispute over territory; one, the collection of a drug debt; four, the robbery of a drug dealer; one, the "messing up" of drug money; and three, other reasons.

We have hypothesized that women with their own economic interest in the crack market would use lethal violence to protect that interest. In six of the 10 incidents involving crack, the respondent herself was a participant in the drug trade. In one of these (250) she denied involvement in the killing, and in another (399) she was the codefendant. In the remaining four cases the respondent said she was the killer. One of these was Incident 014, described earlier, in which the woman killed another dealer for his money and crack. The circumstances of the other three are described below.

In Incident 223, in 1990 a woman in the drug business killed someone who was working for her. Originally she had her own business selling drugs on the street, and felt safe in her belief that being on the street made it easy to get away if the police came. One day, when she was short of money and was looking for a way to make some, a bigger dealer offered her an opportunity to work for him selling crack from an apartment. She disliked inside selling because it made her feel trapped, and she feared the beatings workers faced when they were accused (rightly or wrongly) of "messing up the money." Still, the bigger dealer was insistent and she needed the money.

At first, things went well. The respondent was able to control her own smoking while on the job and she showed herself to be a responsible worker, taking care of herself and her son and not "messing up the money." The bigger dealer saw this and set her up in her own business, selling his drugs and hers. She started to make $6,000 daily, but the money was "possessing" her, and she spent days locked in the apartment from which she sold the crack. She told the bigger dealer, "I got to go home and take care of my personal needs." He agreed, but she had to leave another woman locked in the apartment to take care of business.

After a day of shopping, being with her son, and sleeping, the respondent became worried about her money and the woman she had left in the apartment. At 10 that night she returned and found that the other woman had given the bigger dealer his share of the earnings but did not have the respondent's $6,000.

On the way to the apartment, regular customers stopped the respondent to complain that bottles were short. To keep her customers satisfied, she paid $200 to the people who had complained. She also sent someone up to the apartment to cop two bottles, to see if in fact they were short. They were, so she went home and got her gun.

In her anger, the respondent returned to the apartment and demanded her money. Because the apartment was locked from the outside and only the bigger dealer had the key, she could not get in and the woman inside could not get out. They argued. She called to the woman, "You don't have none of my money?" The woman responded, "I don't have nothing. I smoked it. I bought dope. I bought works. I bought cigarettes."

The respondent was enraged. As she left, the woman asked her if she would bring back a pack of cigarettes. That only made her angrier. She went to a liquor store and came back with a few dollar bottles of Bacardi. The apartment was lit with candles. She threw the Bacardi in and watched the apartment burst into flames while the other woman was locked inside. Before she walked across the street to watch, she said, "Smoke that."

In Incident 433 the respondent was a lieutenant in a crack dealing business. She killed a worker who had absconded with company funds. In 1989 a man who was working for her ran off with $8,500, and it was her job to notify the boss. He told her, "You're the lieutenant and you're responsible for it. Either you find him and get the money back or kill him, or I'll have to kill you."

When the respondent found the man, she did not ask any questions. She did not ask for the money; she simply shot him in the eye and killed him. She was not arrested until a year later.

Incident 405 involved a woman who was the girlfriend of a crack dealer and had worked in his drug business. She killed a man who tried to rob her. On an "average day" in 1992, she decided to go out to cop some crack. In the past she had taken her drugs from her boyfriend, but that arrangement had led to too many fights. She still worked for him occasionally, but now she mostly hustled on her own. On this occasion she robbed a house of a television set and a video recorder, and sold the television to buy some crack. After she smoked the crack she ran into a man who knew that her boyfriend was a dealer. He assumed she was carrying for her boyfriend, and demanded that she give him money or drugs. When she said she had none, he called her a liar and began fighting with her. He took a knife from his pocket, it fell to the floor, and she grabbed it and stabbed him in the chest. Respondent 405 was involved infrequently in dealing crack for her boyfriend; she killed the man who attacked her because he thought she had an economic interest in the boyfriend's business. Respondents 223 and 433 are examples of women who killed in defense of their own economic interest in the crack trade. Both of these women, however, were someone else's employees rather than owners of their own business. It could be argued that these two women killed not only to defend their own interests but also in the economic interest of or from fear of their male employers.

Of the two women who were in the drug business and were involved in killings related to the crack trade, but denied being the killers, one (399) was present when a male associate did the killing. The other (250) claimed in the interview that a man killed her drug partner, and stated in the EOC report that she killed her partner over a fight with her boyfriend. These cases are described below.

Incident 399 involves a woman who participated in 1991 in the robbery of a drug dealer, during which the dealer was killed. The dealer was a friend to whom she had loaned $1,500 to set up his own crack house. The friend had worked previously for Dominican dealers, who wanted to kill him because he owed them money. With her loan he was supposed to buy drugs from her son and her nephew, who were in business as distributors, and to use his profits to pay back the Dominicans and the loan from the respondent.

The respondent discovered that her friend was buying most of his drugs directly from the Dominicans and cutting out her son and nephew. Also, he was not paying back the loan. She and her nephew and son decided to rob him: she would get her $1,500 and they would keep the rest. Then he would be unable to pay the Dominicans, and they would likely kill him.

On the night of the planned robbery, the respondent went in to the dealer's apartment first to buy $10 worth of crack. She thought too many people were present, but her nephew and son came in anyway. An argument ensued, and the dealer pulled a machete and cut the nephew badly. The nephew and the son took out their guns, and ended up killing the dealer and two other people in the room.

In case 250, a 32-year-old woman describes the 1989 killing of another woman who had "a good package of crack." The respondent was on hand when it happened, but her role in the killing is uncertain. She had started using drugs (inhalants) at age 14, and by the time of the killing she believed she had been dependent on crack for six years. During the years before her arrest for the homicide, she had used and sold drugs with her boyfriend. Because he was always high, she "was always taking care of business." He smoked everything he had and then tried to take her drugs. He also tried to take her money. They fought often.

Respondent 250 first became involved in selling drugs when she was 21. She was very successful; customers came constantly. Sometimes people from other areas came to her territory and tried to sell their drugs there. Whenever she saw them, an argument started. So, as she said, "a lot of times I might pull out the gun [I carried] to scare them off." At other times she might get into fights with people whose drug stash she had stolen, or with someone whose money she had "messed up" after they had given her drugs on consignment.

The woman who was killed was the respondent's drug-dealing partner. The victim was stabbed 17 times and shot between the eyes. According to the respondent, they had a fight over drug money in a residence hotel room. Fighting was not unusual, but they were best friends, and the respondent knew that her partner was really looking out for their mutual interests. The respondent used to get high, smoking up their product, and her partner did not.

On this occasion they stopped fighting and the respondent went downstairs, where someone approached her about buying crack. He told her he had heard that her partner had a good package upstairs. She took the money and brought it back upstairs to the room where her partner was. She claims she knocked on the door and no one answered. It was unlocked, and she pushed it open. Her partner never left it unlocked. The respondent looked around but did not see her partner. When she looked into the bedroom, she saw a body and ran into the hall, screaming. She returned to the room with her boyfriend, and they called the police.

About a month later, the police arrested the respondent for the killing. She told the interviewer that she thought her partner was robbed and killed by the man who sent her upstairs to get the drugs for him to buy. She told corrections officials that she was guilty of the killing, but that she did it "in an attempt to intervene in an argument between the victim and [her own] boyfriend." The boyfriend denied being present at the time.

In the remaining four crack market cases, the respondents reported that they were not participants in the drug business, but in two of these cases they said they were the killers. In one case (340) the respondent killed a female crack dealer who repeatedly harassed her and threatened her family after she called the police about the crack traffic in the neighborhood. She stabbed the dealer to death during a fight on the street.

In the other case (295) a woman killed her cousin, who stole the crack she was holding for a male dealer. The dealer had promised the respondent a cut of the profits for watching his drugs. According to the EOC, this was her first encounter with the criminal justice system but not the first time she had killed someone. In 1988 the courts decided she was justified in stabbing her boyfriend to death after he attacked her during a drunken incident, and she was not prosecuted. She also claims she stabbed her stepfather once, but that was not reported.

Respondent 295 told the interviewer that she started using alcohol and marijuana when she was a teenager, but was still using only powder cocaine and crack at the time of the killing. She never was involved in dealing drugs or any other crime, except for the month when she tried prostitution. She did that to earn money for drugs. At the time of the killing, she was holding crack in her house for somebody else. As she told the interviewer,

> I had possessions of money and drugs in my house that belonged to somebody else. My cousin smoked at the time, and she stole it—the drugs and the money. The person that it belonged to came for the money, which I didn't have. He threatened my life and put a gun to my head. I told him I'd try to get the money back. My cousin came back about four days later and she wanted to go to sleep, and I told her no. She acted like she ain't did nothing wrong. So I threw her clothes out the house and she tried to force her way back in, and that's when I stabbed her.

The woman originally was holding the drugs because the dealer promised to give her a cut if she did so. Thus one could argue that fear of reprisal for losing the drugs might have been her main motive, but protecting her own economic interest was also a consideration.

The two other cases that were related to the crack trade involved women who said they were not drug dealers and did not commit the killings. In Incident 078, a woman was present in 1988 when her boyfriend, a crack dealer, shot and killed two men and wounded another in a dispute over drug business territory. Incident 401 involved a woman who was trying to sell a gun to a drug dealer. She denies responsibility for the killing, but that conclusion is uncertain even according to her account of the circumstances.

Respondent 401 was convicted and sentenced for shooting and killing a drug dealer during the course of her dealings in a business that was tangential to the drug trade: she was trying to sell a gun to a crack dealer. One day in 1991, she was smoking crack and drinking alcohol when she came into possession of a gun that she believed she could sell. She took it to a woman she knew, whose boyfriend was a crack dealer. She negotiated with the dealer until he agreed to buy the gun for $75. Then he decided he wanted his money back. He held the money and the gun, playing with the gun for about an hour before returning it.

Meanwhile a young boy who sold drugs for the dealer entered the building, and the respondent asked him if he wanted to buy the gun. He brought some friends to look at it. Suddenly the crack dealer asked to see it again. He took it, then slammed it into the respondent's hand. By her account, at the same time he turned the gun toward the boys and pushed the clip into it. The gun went off, and one boy was shot and killed. Then she remembers being beaten unconscious and left to take the blame for what she assumes was the punishment of a drug worker for "messing up the money."

Drug Market Killings and Economic Interests

Of the 19 women who killed in drug market situations, 10 killed in cases primarily involving the crack business, and only six of those were participants in the business. When all illicit drugs are considered, however, 11 of the 19 women were personally involved in the drug business. Beside the six who trafficked in crack, two were dealers of other drugs (045 and 265), two delivered drugs for someone else (086 and 441), and one guarded cocaine for a dealer (099). In addition, two women worked at an occupation that depended on the drug business for its profits; these women (369 and 440) were in the business of robbing cocaine or crack dealers. Thus 13 of the 19 women had an economic interest in the drug business.

Only one of the 13 women with an economic interest in the drug market killed for reasons that were clearly not economic. That was Respondent 086, who killed her dealer boyfriend. He raped her after she refused to carry drugs for him; the killing was in response to the abuse. In one other case (405), a woman killed someone who was trying to rob her, thinking she was running drugs or money for her boyfriend. According to her interview, she was more interested in defending herself than in protecting money or drugs—hers or her boyfriend's—so the significance of the economic interest is unclear.

The remaining 11 women clearly killed or participated in a killing to protect or enhance an economic interest. In four of these cases the economic interest was their own. Two reported that they were in business for themselves and did the killing on their own. Respondent 014, described earlier, told corrections officials that she was robbing a man of his money and crack to try to scare him into paying her the money he owed her for drugs. Respondent 265, also discussed earlier, was defending her own economic interest as a drug dealer when she shot and killed a man who tried to rob her while she was collecting money at her drug spot. A third respondent, 223, was employed by a male dealer but killed in her own interest. This woman set fire to a locked apartment from which another woman was selling drugs for her. The fourth respondent in this group, 045, was present when a male associate killed someone in her interest.

In Incident 045, the woman was a dealer who, in 1983, ran low on drugs and money while partying and getting high on cocaine, heroin, and marijuana. She remembered that a customer owed her $6,000 for cocaine she had sold him earlier in the week. She called him and asked:

> "You got my shit? You got my money and stuff?" So he starts giving me a song and dance routine and finally I'm like, "Look, forget about the bullshit, okay. It's over a week now. You said you was going to pay me in a week and I haven't heard anything." So he says, "Okay, come over. I'll have everything for you." I said, "Fine." Then when I come over to the house his girlfriend tells me that he left to go to Puerto Rico.

This made the respondent angry, especially because she recently had had to stop her people from killing his mother over a previous debt. She felt that "he played me for a fool." Her lover, who had accompanied her to get the money, was even angrier. He shot the woman who answered the door, the girl-friend of the man who owed the money.

The respondent claimed she was "shocked" when the killing took place. She said, "You know, being in the drug business you hear about people getting killed, and it's no biggie. But actually being there and witnessing it for yourself is totally different." The EOC, however, tells another story. According to corrections records, this woman was involved in at least one other killing earlier in the same year. She was present when a male acquaintance shot a Colombian man twice in the head during a robbery. The murdered man apparently was a partner of the woman in a cocaine trafficking business. According to the EOC, "The defendant felt that she had done nothing wrong in that she was merely a businesswoman, admittedly dealing in cocaine for profit and enjoyment."

Four additional women who had an economic interest in the drug market killed or participated in a killing related to their mutual interest with others in that market. One respondent, 250, was linked to the killing of her drug-dealing partner, with whom she had argued earlier over her personal use of their product and whom she told the interviewer she found dead when she went to her to pick up drugs for a male customer. Respondent 399 was present when her nephew and son shot and killed three people during the robbery of a drug dealer who she claimed owed her money. She had loaned him that money to buy crack from a distribution business run by her son and nephew; as noted earlier, the dealer had used the money to buy his drugs from their competitors.

In both of the above cases, the woman was a dealer whose shared interest in the drug market was at stake. In the other two cases involving women who killed to protect or augment a shared interest, the women were robbers rather than drug dealers. In both of these cases the woman was the killer.

The respondent in Case 369 was visited in 1983 by two friends, who offered her $500 to drive a car for them during a robbery. She accepted the job, saying, "Shit, I do that shit with my eyes closed." They left to rob a shooting gallery where heroin and cocaine were sold and used.

Their plan was to gain entrance to the apartment as if they were potential customers. When the first member of the team was denied admittance, the respondent was given a gun to hold in case she needed to scare anyone. She went upstairs with the woman who [had] not been admitted alone. When the people inside saw the respondent, they opened the door and admitted her and her partner.

For a while they stood around getting anxious, while other people sat around getting high. Her partner went off with someone and got high too. At that point the respondent got nervous and said to her, "Come on. Let's do this shit and get the fuck out of here." Then she pulled the gun and yelled, "Everybody against the wall. This is a fucking stickup." A man in the room laughed at her and told her to stop playing around with the gun, which was already cocked, and to try some cocaine. When he saw she was serious, he grabbed the money in the cash box. He started to stand up, and she saw the handle of his gun. She got scared and started to back up toward the wall. Her arm hit the wall, and the gun went off. The man fell dead. Her friends came up, and they took the money and ran.

The respondent in Case 440 went out with her brother late one night in 1990 to rob a "coke spot." When they arrived, she was high on alcohol and "hyped" by the situation. "I'm not a woman now," she said. "I'm a man."

When they got to the coke spot, they announced the robbery, and words were exchanged. As respondent 440 recalls,

> I had noticed one of the guys had been standing behind the scale went for his pocket, and I was always told, "Never allow anybody to move after the specific orders were given." By me being under the influence, I did what I did because of the simple fact [that] I didn't know what you were going in your pocket for 'cause I knew you was told "Don't nobody move, nobody get hurt." I told you not to get anything, just something in reach where I could see, but I didn't know what you had inside of your pocket. So when he went to go, I pistol-whipped him. When I pistol-whipped him, the bullet hit the next guy. Actually, the one I took his life, it wasn't called for. The bullet wasn't meant for him. The bullet wasn't meant for either one of them. It was to show [that] when orders are given, don't do nothing but what you are supposed to do.

As in the previous case, this respondent was a robber who shared her economic interest in the drug market with others with whom she preyed on drug dealers.

The three remaining women who were involved in killings related to drug market interests did not kill primarily in their own economic interests. Rather, they participated in killings in someone else's interest. Respondent 433, the lieutenant in a crack-dealing business, in 1989 killed a worker who had absconded with company funds. When she notified her boss, he told her it was her responsibility to get the money back or to kill the absconder. She killed him. A second case (099) involved a woman who was guarding drugs for a dealer; the third (441) a woman who was delivering drugs for a dealer. These two cases are described below.

According to the EOC, Respondent 099 killed a man to get money in 1983, at the dawn of the crack era in New York. She needed the money for a cocaine dealer who had threatened her with the loss of a leg unless she paid him. She and a male accomplice robbed and killed a cab driver. The EOC does not make clear who pulled the trigger.

In the story she told to the interviewer, Respondent 099 was only a bystander. She had been using a variety of drugs since she was a teenager, and sold drugs a few times when she was 19. She worked out of her home for her boyfriend, selling drugs to people she knew. He used to "sell weight" between New York City and Washington, DC. On the day of the killing, after using "a lot" of cocaine and crack, she was spending the evening with her boyfriend.

Besides her boyfriend, with whom she was living at the time of the killing, Respondent 099 had a husband. For some reason she did not explain, she had been forced into an arranged marriage to this man, which she now blames for all her troubles. One evening a few days before the killing, she was alone in the apartment when her husband, from whom she was estranged, came by and begged her to drive to his uncle's house with him. She finally agreed, and they walked to his car, which was parked in the dark under a tree. Two men jumped out and began yelling at her but not at him. When she heard them "speaking the same damn Jamaican language" as her husband, she guessed they were his friends. The two men forced them back to her apartment, where they stole whatever drugs and money they could find. Then they and her husband left her alone. She wondered what she would tell her boyfriend, to whom the drugs and money belonged.

Respondent 099 acquired a pistol, and looked for her husband for two days. When she finally found him at his girlfriend's house, she was ready to kill him. He grabbed a small girl and held her in front of him. The woman would not shoot the child. He talked to her until she agreed to go with him to find the men who had taken her boyfriend's money and drugs. On the way, they apparently shot a cab driver to get the money to give back to her boyfriend. In this case her motive was fear rather than money.

Respondent 441 was delivering angel dust for a dealer when she became entangled in an argument that resulted in a fatal stabbing. She claims she was only a bystander.

One day in 1991, the respondent took an order for $250 worth of angel dust to be delivered to an apartment in the building where she lived. Against the dealer's better judgment, she chose to make the delivery herself. She was surprised when the door was opened by an older woman whom she recognized as a churchgoer. The older woman invited her in but stalled when she was asked for the $250.

A man who was obviously high came out of a back room and began to argue with the respondent. He did not want to pay and refused to take the drugs. She told him, "This is a house call. First of all, I didn't even charge you for a house call, being that I know the project. Second of all, you have to pay for it even if you don't want to take it."

The older woman and the man began to argue. He hit her. The respondent intervened, asking to get her money so she could leave. Then she claims she fell and was knocked unconscious. When she awoke, the older woman was dead on the floor, and the man was standing over her, mumbling. He saw the respondent, and she claims he threw her from the window. She fell six stories and broke her ankle and hip.

Conclusion

From our analysis of 19 cases of women who killed in drug market situations, we cannot determine to what extent women gained greater access to positions in the violent free-lance drug market of the early crack era in New York. We made no attempt to do this. Rather, we used these data to examine whether the effect of gender on homicide is altered when women occupy positions in which men have been known to kill for an economic interest. Specifically, we asked whether women involved in homicides related to a violent drug market participated in those killings in relation to an economic interest associated with that market, or whether they killed for gender-based reasons even in the context of a violent drug market economy.

Our analysis shows that some of the women participating in a drug market economy killed to protect or extend their own interests in that economy. Of 10 killings committed in the especially violent crack market of the late 1980s and early 1990s, six involved women who were in the trade; five of those clearly killed for economic reasons. Among 13 cases of women who had a personal interest in the drug market economy involving any illicit drug, we found four in which the woman killed in her own economic interest, four in which she killed in a shared interest with a partner, and three in which she killed in someone else's interest.

Even the women who killed for obviously economic purposes, however, typically had other motives unrelated to the drug economy. Of the six who worked in the crack market economy and participated in killing someone in connection with that economy, in addition to their economic motive, three killed because they were angry and two killed in what they considered self-defense. Of the 11 women who were in the drug business and killed for an economic reason, five also killed because they were angry. Three were defending themselves, one was trying to scare someone, and one was trying to stop abuse.

Many of the respondents killed in the context of their relationship with a man, even among those who killed for primarily economic reasons. Three of the 19 women called themselves the girlfriends of dealers, and one the girlfriend of a drug hit man. Four of the women said they worked in the drug business for a man; four others said they were in business with male partners. Two women were present when a male partner killed someone who threatened his interests; two others were present when a male partner killed someone in their mutual interest. One woman killed specifically on a man's orders. Three killed because they felt threatened by a man; one had been raped earlier, and two killed men who were robbing them. Two women killed men who were defending themselves while the women were robbing them. Two women killed or participated in killing someone because of threats made by male drug dealers.

The gender-based argument suggests that women kill because of the nature of their relationship as a woman to a man. The liberationist argument, on the other hand, suggests that women kill for reasons independent of their gender. The traditional literature on women who kill has focused on domestic situations in which people turned to lethal violence to resolve problems in their home, family, and personal relationships. With its emphasis on the home and family, this literature offers gender-based explanations for homicide by women. In this [chapter] we intentionally focused on homicides by women that took place in a very different setting, one in which social relationships characteristically are based on economic rather than personal relationships. Specifically, we examined killings that occurred in drug market settings to learn whether killings in that context would support the liberationist viewpoint.

Our findings support the conclusion that in the economic context of drug markets, women who kill do so for purposes unrelated to their gender. We found evidence that in such circumstances, women kill to protect or enhance their own economic interests. Yet, we also found evidence to support the conclusion that even in a setting which gives women who kill the opportunity and the rationale to act in their own self-interest, they often act in terms of their relationship to a man, killing on behalf of a man or out of fear of a man. Thus in these cases, the effect of gender is not necessarily altered by the circumstances of the drug market economy.

Discussion Questions

1. What are the primary motive(s) of women who kill in drug market situations?

2. How many of the 19 women in this study acted in primary and/or secondary roles in the commission of the homicide? Do you feel that the liberationist viewpoint effectively describes women's participation in killing related to market situations?

3. If you were a judge, what kind of punishment would you give the women in this study? Would this sentence be different than for women who killed their abusers?

4. In the readings in this section, what crimes committed by women would rational choice theory best explain?

5. What reasons can you provide to explain gender differences in offending, or why there are more males arrested than females?

References

Adler, F. (1975) *Sisters in Crime: The Rise of the New Female Criminal*. New York: McGraw Hill.

Bannister, S. A. (1991) "The Criminalization of Women Fighting Back against Male Abuse: Imprisoned Battered Women as Political Prisoners." *Humanity and Society* 15: 400–16.

Belenko, S. (1990) "The Impact of Drug Offenders on the Criminal Justice System." In R. A. Weisheit (ed.), *Drugs, Crime and the Criminal Justice System*, pp. 27–28. Cincinnati, OH: Anderson.

Block, K. J. (1990) "Age-Related Correlates of Criminal Homicides Committed by Women: A Study of Baltimore." *Journal of Crime and Justice* 13: 42–65.

Browne, A. (1987) *When Battered Women Kill*. New York: Free Press.

Browne, A. and K. R. Williams (1989) "Exploring the Effect of Resource Availability and the Likelihood of Female-Perpetrated Homicides." *Law and Society Review* 23: 75–94.

Brownstein, H. H., H. R. S. Baxi, P. J. Goldstein, and P. J. Ryan (1992) "The Relationship of Drugs, Drug Trafficking, and Drug Traffickers to Homicide." *Journal of Crime and Justice* 15: 25–44.

Brownstein, H. H. and P. J. Goldstein (1990) "A Typology of Drug-Related Homicides." In R. A. Weisheit (ed.), *Drugs, Crime and the Criminal Justice System*, pp. 171–92. Cincinnati, OH: Anderson.

Brownstein, H. H., B. J. Spunt, S. Crimmins, P. J. Goldstein, and S. Langley (1994) "Changing Patterns of Lethal Violence by Women: A Research Note." *Women and Criminal Justice* 5: 99–118.

Canestrini, K. (1987) *1986 Female Homicide Commitments*. Albany: New York State Department of Correctional Services.

Chesney-Lind, M. (1993) "Girls, Gangs and Violence: Anatomy of a Backlash." *Humanity and Society* 17: 321–44.

Daly, K. and M. Chesney-Lind (1988) "Feminism and Criminology." *Justice Quarterly* 5: 497–538.

Daniel, A. E. and P. W. Harris (1982) "Female Homicide Offenders Referred for Pre-Trial Psychiatric Examination: A Descriptive Study." *Bulletin of the American Academy of Psychiatry and Law* 10: 261–69.

Ewing, C. P. (1987) *Battered Women Who Kill*. Lexington, MA: Lexington Books.

Fagan, J. (1994) "Women and Drugs Revisited: Female Participation in the Cocaine Economy." *Journal of Drug Issues* 24: 179–225.

Fagan, J. and K. Chin (1990) "Violence as Regulation and Social Control in the Distribution of Crack." In M. De La Rosa, E. Y. Lambert, and B. Gropper (eds.), *Drugs and Violence: Causes, Correlates, and Consequences*, pp. 8–43. Washington, DC: National Institute on Drug Abuse.

Falco, M. (1989) *Winning the Drug War: A National Strategy*. New York: Priority Press.

Federal Bureau of Investigation (1994) *Crime in the United States 1993*. Washington, DC: U.S. Department of Justice.

Goetting, A. (1987) "Homicidal Wives: A Profile." *Journal of Family Issues* 8: 332–41.

——. (1988) "Patterns of Homicide among Women." *Journal of Interpersonal Violence* 3: 332–41.

Goldstein, P. J., H. H. Brownstein, and P. J. Ryan (1992) "Drug-Related Homicide in New York: 1984 and 1988." *Crime and Delinquency* 38: 459–76.

Goldstein, P. J., H. H. Brownstein, P. J. Ryan, and P. A. Bellucci (1989) "Crack and Homicide in New York City: A Conceptually Based Event Analysis." *Contemporary Drug Problems* 13: 651–87.

Hazlett, M. H. and T. C. Tomlinson (1987) "Females Involved in Homicides: Victims and Offenders in Two U.S. Southern States." Presented at the annual meetings of the American Society of Criminology, Montreal.

Inciardi, J. A. (1989) "Beyond Cocaine: Basuco, Crack, and Other Coca Products." *Contemporary Drug Problems* 14: 461–92.

Inciardi, J. A., D. Lockwood, and A. E. Pottieger (1993) *Women and Crack Cocaine*. New York: Macmillan.

Jacobs, S. and R. A. Rosen (1983) *Homicide in New York State, 1981*. Albany: New York State Division of Criminal Justice Services.

Johnson, B. D., A. Hamid, and H. Sanabria (1992) "Emerging Models of Crack Distribution." In T. Mieczkowski (ed.), *Drugs, Crime, and Social Policy: Research, Issues, and Concerns*, pp. 56–78. Boston: Allyn and Bacon.

Jones, A. (1980) *Women Who Kill*. New York: Holt, Rinehart and Winston.

Jurik, N. C. and R. Winn (1990) "Gender and Homicide: A Comparison of Men and Women Who Kill." *Violence and Victims* 5: 227–42.

Luckenbill, D. (1977) "Criminal Homicide as a Situated Transaction." *Social Problems* 25: 176–86.

Mann, C. R. (1984) *Female Crime and Delinquency*. Tuscaloosa: University of Alabama Press.

——. (1986) "Getting Even? Women Who Kill in Domestic Encounters." Presented at the annual meetings of the American Society of Criminology, Atlanta.

Massing, M. (1980) "Crack's Destructive Sprint across America." *New York Times Magazine*, October 1, pp. 38, 40–41, 58, 60, 62.

Mercy, J. A. and L. E. Saltzman (1989) "Fatal Violence among Spouses in the United States, 1976–85." *American Journal of Public Health* 79: 595–99.

Mieczkowski, T. (1990) "Crack Distribution in Detroit." *Contemporary Drug Problems* 17: 9–29.

Miller, E. M. (1986) *Street Women*. Philadelphia: Temple University Press.

Office of the Attorney General (1989) *Drug Trafficking: A Report to the President of the United States*. Washington, DC: U.S. Department of Justice.

Rasche, C. E. (1990) "Early Models for Contemporary Thought on Domestic Violence and Women Who Kill Their Mates: A Review of the Literature from 1895 to 1970." *Women and Criminal Justice* 1: 31–53.

Reuter, P., R. MacCoun, and P. Murphy (1990) *Money from Crime: A Study of the Economics of Drug Dealing in Washington, D.C.* Santa Monica, CA: RAND.

Riedel, M., M. Zahn, and L. Mock (1985) *The Nature and Patterns of American Homicide*. Washington, DC: U.S. Department of Justice, National Institute of Justice.

Simon, R. J. (1975) *Women and Crime*. Lexington, MA: Lexington Books.

Simon, Rita J. and J. Landis (1991) *The Crimes Women Commit, The Punishments They Receive*. Lexington, MA: Lexington Books.

Smart, C. (1978) "The New Female Criminal: Reality or Myth.?" *British Journal of Criminology* 19: 50–59.

Sommers, I. and D. R. Baskin (1992) "Sex, Race, Age, and Violent Offending." *Violence and Victims* 7: 191–203.

——. (1993) "The Situational Context of Violent Female Offending." *Journal of Research in Crime and Delinquency* 30: 136–62.

Sparrow, G. (1970) *Women Who Murder.* New York: Tower.

Spunt, B. J., P. J. Goldstein, C. Tarshish, M. Fendrich, and H. H. Brownstein (1993) "The Utility of Correctional Data for Understanding the Drugs-Homicide Connection: A Research Note." *Criminal Justice Review* 13: 46–60.

Spunt, B. J., P. J. Ryan, P. J. Goldstein, and H. H. Brownstein (1989) "Current Research on the Drugs-Homicide Relationship." Presented at the annual meetings of the Academy of Criminal Justice Sciences, Washington, DC.

Swigert, V. Lynn and R. A. Farrell (1976) *Murder, Inequality, and the Law.* Lexington, MA: Lexington Books.

Totman, J. (1978) *The Murderess: A Psychological Study of Criminal Homicide.* San Francisco: R&E Research Associates.

Walker, L. E. (1989) *Terrifying Love—Why Battered Women Kill and How Society Responds.* New York: Harper and Row.

Ward, D., M. Jackson, and R. Ward (1979) "Crimes of Violence by Women." In F. Adler and R. Simon (eds.), *The Criminology of Deviant Women,* pp. 14–38. Boston: Houghton Mifflin.

Weisheit, R. A. (1984). "Female Homicide Offenders: Trends over Time in an Institutionalized Population." *Justice Quarterly* 1: 471–89.

Wilbanks, W. (1984) *Murder in Miami: An Analysis of Homicide Patterns and Trends in Dade County (Miami) Florida, 1917–1983.* Lanham, MA: University Press of America.

Wolfgang, M. E. (1958) *Patterns in Criminal Homicide.* Philadelphia: University of Pennsylvania Press.

——. (1967) "Criminal Homicide and the Subculture of Violence." In M. E. Wolfgang (ed.), *Studies in Homicide,* pp. 3–12. New York: Harper and Row.

22

Pathways Out of Crime

Crime Desistance by Female Street Offenders

Ira Sommers
Deborah R. Baskin
Jeffrey Fagan

This selection considers the role of life events among women and the relationship of cognition and life situations to the crime desistance process. The authors are concerned with whether one's social and the psychological processes experienced and the events leading up to a person's desistance from crime vary by gender. In other words, do men and women differ in the processes and events that bring them to the decision to give up crime? The authors constructed a sample of 30 women. Initially, 16 subjects were recruited through various drug and alcohol treatment programs in New York. An additional 14 women were accessed through a chain of referral process. The sample included women with at least one official arrest for a violent street crime and who had desisted from crime for at least two years prior to the study. Life history interviews were conducted by Sommers and Baskin, and each interview lasted approximately two hours. The subjects had engaged in a wide range of criminal activities. Eighty-seven percent were addicted to crack, 63 percent had been involved in robberies, 60 percent had committed burglaries, 94 percent had sold drugs, and 47 percent had at some time been involved in prostitution. The mean number of prior incarcerations was 3. The authors found that the reasons for the women's desistance from crime were remarkably similar to those found for men. Like desistance studies of male criminals, the women in this study had begun to take the threat of incarceration seriously and attempted to reestablish links with conventional society while severing relationships in the deviant subculture.

Studies over the past decade have provided a great deal of information about the criminal careers of male offenders. (See Blumstein et al. 1986 and Weiner and Wolfgang 1989 for reviews.) Unfortunately, much less is known about the initiation, escalation, and termination of criminal careers by female offenders. The general tendency to exclude female offenders from research on crime and delinquency may be due, at least in part, to the lower frequency and comparatively less serious nature of offending among women. Recent trends and studies, however, suggest that the omission of women may seriously bias both research and theory on crime.

Although a growing body of work on female crime has emerged within the last few years, much of this research continues to focus on what Daly and Chesney-Lind (1988) called generalizability and gender-ratio problems. The former concerns the degree to which traditional (i.e., male) theories of deviance and crime apply to women, and the latter focuses on what explains gender differences in rates and types of criminal activity. Although this [chapter] also examines women in crime, questions of inter- and intragender variability in crime are not specifically addressed. Instead, the aim of the [chapter] is to describe the pathways out of deviance for a sample of women who have significantly invested themselves in criminal social worlds. To what extent are the social and psychological processes of stopping criminal behavior similar for men and women? Do the behavioral antecedents of such processes vary by gender? These questions remained unexplored.

Specifically, two main issues are addressed in this [chapter]: (1) the role of life events in triggering the cessation process, and (2) the relationship between cognitive and life situation changes in the desistance process. First, the crime desistance literature is reviewed briefly. Second, the broader deviance literature is drawn upon to construct a social-psychological model of cessation. Then the model is evaluated using life history data from a sample of female offenders convicted of serious street crimes.

The Desistance Process

The common themes in the literature on exiting deviant careers offer useful perspectives for developing a theory of cessation. The decision to stop deviant behavior appears to be preceded by a variety of factors, most of which are negative social sanctions or consequences. Health problems, difficulties with the law or with maintaining a current lifestyle, threats of other social sanctions from family or close relations, and a general rejection of the social world in which the behaviors thrive are often antecedents of the decision to quit. For some, religious conversions or immersion into alternative sociocultural settings with powerful norms (e.g., treatment ideology) provide paths for cessation (Mulvey and LaRosa 1986; Stall and Biernacki 1986).

. . . A model for understanding desistance from crime is presented below. Three stages characterize the cessation process: building resolve or discovering motivation to stop (i.e., socially disjunctive experiences), making and publicly disclosing the decision to stop, and maintaining the new behaviors and integrating into new social networks (Stall and Biernacki 1986; Mulvey and Aber 1988). These phases . . . describe three ideal-typical phases of desistance: "turning points" where offenders begin consciously to experience negative effects (socially disjunctive experiences); "active quitting" where they take steps to exit crime (public pronouncement); and "maintaining cessation" (identity transformation):

Stage 1
Catalysts for change
Socially disjunctive experiences
- Hitting rock bottom
- Fear of death
- Tiredness
- Illness

Delayed deterrence
- Increased probability of punishment
- Increased difficulty in doing time
- Increased severity of sanctions
- Increasing fear

Assessment
- Reappraisal of life and goals
- Psychic change

Decision
- Decision to quit and/or initial attempts at desistance
- Continuing possibility of criminal participation

Stage 2
Discontinuance
- Public pronouncement of decision to end criminal participation
- Claim to a new social identity

Stage 3
Maintenance of the decision to stop
- Ability to successfully renegotiate identity
- Support of significant others
- Integration into new social networks

- Ties to conventional roles
- Stabilization of new social identity

Stage 1: Catalysts for Change. When external conditions change and reduce the rewards of deviant behavior, motivation may build to end criminal involvement. That process, and the resulting decision, seem to be associated with two related conditions: a series of negative, aversive, unpleasant experiences with criminal behavior, or corollary situations where the positive rewards, status, or gratification from crime are reduced. Shover and Thompson's (1992) research suggests that the probability of desistance from criminal participation increases as expectations for achieving rewards (e.g., friends, money, autonomy) via crime decrease and that changes in expectations are age-related. Shover (1983) contended that the daily routines of managing criminal involvement become tiring and burdensome to aging offenders. Consequently, the allure of crime diminishes as offenders get older. Aging may also increase the perceived formal risk of criminal participation. Cusson and Pinsonneault (1986, 76) posited that "with age, criminals raise their estimates of the certainty of punishment." Fear of reimprisonment, fear of longer sentences, and the increasing difficulty of "doing time" have often been reported by investigators who have explored desistance.

Stage 2: Discontinuance. The second stage of the model begins with the public announcement that the offender has decided to end her criminal participation. Such an announcement forces the start of a process of renegotiation of the offender's social identity (Stall and Biernacki 1986). After this announcement, the offender must not only cope with the instrumental aspects (e.g., financial) of her life but must also begin to redefine important emotional and social relationships that are influenced by or predicated upon criminal behavior. Leaving a deviant subculture is difficult. Biernacki (1986) noted the exclusiveness of the social involvements maintained by former addicts during initial stages of abstinence. With social embedment comes the gratification of social acceptance and identity. The decision to end a behavior that is socially determined and supported implies withdrawal of the social gratification it brings. Thus, the more deeply embedded in a criminal social context, the more dependent the offender is on that social world for her primary sources of approval and social definition. The responses by social control agents, family members, and peer supporters to further criminal participation are critical to shaping the outcome of discontinuance.

New social and emotional worlds to replace the old ones may strengthen the decision to stop. Adler (1992) found that outside associations and involvements provide a critical bridge back into society for dealers who have decided to leave the drug subculture. With discontinuance comes the difficult work of identity transformations (Biernacki 1986) and establishing new social definitions of behavior and relationships to reinforce them.

Stage 3: Maintenance. Following the initial stages of discontinuance, strategies to avoid a return to crime build on the strategies first used to break from a lengthy pattern of criminal participation: further integration into a noncriminal identity and social world and maintenance of this new identity. Maintenance depends in part on replacing deviant networks of peers and associates with supports that both censure criminal participation and approve of new nondeviant beliefs. Treatment interventions (e.g., drug treatment, social service programs) are important sources of alternative social supports to maintain a noncriminal lifestyle. In other words, maintenance depends on immersion into a social world where criminal behavior meets immediately with strong formal and informal sanctions.

Despite efforts to maintain noncriminal involvement, desistance is likely to be episodic, with occasional relapses interspersed with lengthening of lulls in criminal activity. Le Blanc and Frechette (1989) proposed the possibility that criminal activity slows down before coming to an end and that this slowing down process becomes apparent in three ways: deceleration, specialization, and reaching a ceiling. Thus, before stopping criminal activity, the offender gradually acts out less frequently, limits the variety of crimes more and more, and ceases increasing the seriousness of criminal involvement.

Age is a critical variable in desistance research, regardless of whether it is associated with maturation or similar developmental concepts. Cessation is part of a social-psychological transformation for the offender. A strategy to stabilize the transition to a noncriminal lifestyle requires active use of supports to maintain the norms that have been substituted for the forces that supported criminal behavior in the past.

Findings

Resolving to Stop

Despite its initial excitement and allure, the life of a street criminal is a hard one. A host of severe personal problems plague most street offenders and normally become progressively worse as their careers continue. In the present study, the women's lives were dominated by a powerful, often incapacitating, need for drugs. Consequently, economic problems were the most frequent complaint voiced by the respondents. Savings were quickly exhausted, and the culture of addiction justified virtually any means to get money to support their habits. For the majority of the women, the problem of maintaining an addiction took precedence over other interests and participation in other social worlds.

People the respondents associated with, their primary reference group, were involved in illicit behaviors. Over time, the women in the study became further enmeshed in deviance and further alienated, both socially and psychologically, from conventional life. The women's lives became bereft of conventional involvements, obligations, and responsibilities. The excitement at the lifestyle that may have characterized their early criminal career phase gave way to a much more grave daily existence.

Thus, the women in our study could not and did not simply cease their deviant acts by "drifting" (Matza 1964) back toward conventional norms, values, and lifestyles. Unlike many of Waldorf's (1983) heroin addicts who drifted away from heroin without conscious effort, all of the women in our study made a conscious decision to stop. In short, Matza's concept of drift did not provide a useful framework for understanding our respondents' exit from crime.

The following accounts illustrate the uncertainty and vulnerability of street life for the women in our sample. Denise, a 33-year-old black woman, has participated in a wide range of street crimes including burglary, robbery, assault, and drug dealing. She began dealing drugs when she was 14 and was herself using cocaine on a regular basis by age 19.

> I was in a lot of fights: So I had fights over, uh, drugs, or, you know, just manipulation. There's a lot of manipulation in that life. Everybody's tryin' to get over. Everybody will stab you in your back, you know. Nobody gives a fuck about the next person, you know. It's just when you want it, you want it. You know, when you want that drug, you know, you want that drug. There's a lot of lyin', a lot of manipulation. It's, it's, it's crazy!

Gazella, a 38-year-old Hispanic woman, had been involved in crime for 22 years when we interviewed her.

> I'm 38 years old. I ain't no young woman no more, man. Drugs have changed, lifestyles have changed. Kids are killing you now for turf. Yeah, turf, and I was destroyin' myself.

I was miserable. I was . . . I was gettin' high all the time to stay up to keep the business going, and it was really nobody I could trust.

Additional illustrations of the exigencies of street life are provided by April and Stephanie. April is a 25-year-old black woman who had been involved in crime since she was 11.

I wasn't eating. Sometimes I wouldn't eat for two or three days. And I would . . . a lot of times I wouldn't have the time, or I wouldn't want to spend the money to eat—I've got to use it to get high.

Stephanie, a 27-year-old black woman, had used and sold crack for 5 years when we interviewed her.

I knew that, uh, I was gonna get killed out here. I wasn't havin' no respect for myself. No one else was respecting me. Every relationship I got into, as long as I did drugs, it was gonna be constant disrespect involved, and it come . . . to the point of me gettin' killed.

When the spiral down finally reached its lowest point, the women were overwhelmed by a sense of personal despair. In reporting the early stages of this period of despair, the respondents consistently voiced two themes: the futility of their lives and their isolation.

Barbara, a 31-year-old black woman, began using crack when she was 23. By age 25, Barbara had lost her job at the Board of Education and was involved in burglary and robbery. Her account is typical of the despair the women in our sample eventually experienced.

. . . the fact that my family didn't trust me anymore, and the way that my daughter was looking at me, and, uh, my mother wouldn't let me in her house any more, and I was sleepin' on the trains. And I was sleepin' on the beaches in the summertime. And I was really frightened. I was real scared of the fact that I had to sleep on the train. And, uh, I had to wash up in the Port Authority.

The spiral down for Gazella also resulted in her living on the streets.

I didn't have a place to live. My kids had been taken away from me. You know, constantly being harassed like 3 days out of the week by the Tactical Narcotics Team [police]. I didn't want to be bothered with people. I was gettin' tired of the lyin', schemin', you know, stayin' in abandoned buildings.

Alicia, a 29-year-old Hispanic woman, became involved in street violence at age 12. She commented on the personal isolation that was a consequence of her involvement in crime:

When I started getting involved in crime, you know, and drugs, the friends that I had, even my family, I stayed away from them, you know. You know how you look bad and you feel bad, and you just don't want those people to see you like you are. So I avoided seeing them.

For some, the emotional depth of the rock bottom crisis was felt as a sense of mortification. The women felt as if they had nowhere to turn to salvage a sense of well-being or self-worth. Suicide was considered a better alternative than remaining in such an undesirable social and psychological state. Denise is one example:

I ran into a girl who I went to school with that works on Wall Street. And I compared her life to mine and it was like miserable. And I just wanted out. I wanted a new life. I was tired, I was run down, looking bad. I got out by smashing myself through a sixth-floor window. Then I went to the psychiatric ward and I met this real nice doctor, and we talked every day. She fought to keep me in the hospital because she felt I wouldn't survive. She believed in me. And she talked me into going into a drug program.

Marginalization from family, friends, children, and work—in short, the loss of traditional life structures—left the women vulnerable to chaotic street conditions. After initially being overwhelmed by despair, the women began to question and reevaluate basic assumptions about their identities and their social construction of the world. Like Shover's (1983) male property offenders, the women also began to view the criminal justice system as "an imposing accumulation of aggravations and deprivations" (212). They grew tired of the street experiences and the problems and consequences of criminal involvement.

Many of the women acknowledged that, with age, it is more difficult to do time and that the fear of incurring a long prison sentence the next time influenced their decision to stop. Cusson and Pinsonneault (1986) made the same observation with male robbers. Gazella, April, and Denise, quoted earlier, recall:

Gazella: First of all, when I was in prison I was like, I was so humiliated. At my age [38] I was really kind of embarrassed, but I knew that was the lifestyle that I was leadin'. And people I used to talk to would tell me, well, you could do this, and you don't have to get busted. But then I started thinking why are all these people here. So it doesn't, you know, really work. So I came home, and I did go back to selling again, but you know I knew I was on probation. And I didn't want to do no more time.

April: Jail, being in jail. The environment, having my freedom taken away. I saw myself keep repeating the same pattern, and I didn't want to do that. Uh, I had missed my daughter. See, being in jail that long period of time, I was able to detox. And when I detoxed, I kind of like had a clear sense of thinking, and that's when I came to the realization that, uh, this is not working for me.

Denise: I saw the person that I was dealing with—my partner—I saw her go upstate to Bedford for 2 to 4 years. I didn't want to deal with it. I didn't want to go. Bedford is a prison, women's prison. And I couldn't see myself givin' up 2 years of my life for something that I knew I could change in another way.

As can be seen from the above, the influence of punishment on these women was due to their belief that if they continued to be involved in crime, they would be apprehended, convicted, and incarcerated.

For many of the women, it was the stresses of street life and the fear of dying on the streets that motivated their decision to quit the criminal life. Darlene, a 25-year-old black woman, recalled the stress associated with the latter stage of her career selling drugs:

The simple fact is that I really, I thought that I would die out there. I thought that someone would kill me out there and I would be killed; I had a fear of being on the front page one day and being in the newspaper dying. I wanted to live, and I didn't just want to exist.

Sonya, a 27-year-old Hispanic woman, provided an account of what daily life was like on the streets:

You get tired of bein' tired, you know. I got tired of hustlin', you know. I got tired of livin' the way I was livin', you know. Due to your body, your body, mentally, emotionally, you know. . . . And I used to have people talkin' to me, "You know, you're not a bad lookin' girl. You know, why you don't get yourself together."

Perhaps even more important, the women felt that they had wasted time. They became acutely aware of time as a diminishing resource (Shover 1983). They reported that they saw themselves going nowhere. They had arrived at a point where crime seemed senseless, and their lives had reached a dead end. Implicit in this assessment was the belief that gaining a longer-range perspective on one's life was a first step in changing. Such deliberations develop as a result of "socially disjunctive experiences" that cause the offender to experience social stress, feelings of alienation, and dissatisfaction with her present identity (Ray 1961).

Breaking Away From the Life

Forming a commitment to change is only the first step toward the termination of a criminal career. The offender enters a period that has been characterized as a "running struggle" with problems of social identity (Ray 1961, 136). Successful desisters must work to clarify and strengthen their nondeviant identity and redefine their street experience in terms more compatible with a conventional lifestyle. The second stage of the desistance process begins with the public announcement or "certification" (Meisenhelder 1977: 329) that the offender has decided to end her deviant behavior. After this announcement, the offender must begin to redefine economic, social, and emotional relationships that were based on a deviant street subculture.

The time following the announcement was generally a period of ambivalence and crisis for the study participants, because so much of their lives revolved around street life and because they had, at best, weak associations with the conventional world. Many of the women remembered the uncertainty they felt and the social dilemmas they faced after they decided to stop their involvement in crime.

Denise: I went and looked up my friends and to see what was doing, and my girlfriend Mia was like, she was gettin' paid. And I was livin' on a $60 stipend. And I wasn't with it. Mia was good to me, she always kept money in my pocket when I came home. I would walk into her closet and change into clothes that I'm more accustomed to. She started calling me Pen again. She stopped calling me Denise. And I would ride with her knowing that she had a gun or a package in the car. But I wouldn't touch nothin'. But that was my rationale. As long as I don't fuck with nothin'. Yeah, she was like I can give you a grand and get you started. I said I know you can, but I can't. She said I can give you a grand, and she kept telling me that over and over; and I wasn't that far from taking the grand and getting started again.

Barbara: After I decided to change, I went to a party with my friend. And people was around me and they was drinkin' and stuff, and I didn't want to drink. I don't have the urge of drinking. If anything, it would be smokin' crack. And when I left the party, I felt like I was missing something—like something was missing. And it was the fact that I wasn't gettin' high. But I know the consequences of it. If I take a drink, I'm gonna smoke crack. If I, uh, sniff some blow, I'm gonna smoke crack. I might do some things like rob a store or something stupid and go to jail. So I don't want to put myself in that position.

At this stage of their transition, the women had to decide how to establish and maintain conventional relationships and what to do with themselves and their lives. Few of the women had maintained good relationships with people who were not involved in crime and drugs. Given this situation, the women had to seek alternatives to their present situation.

The large majority of study participants were aided in their social reintegration by outside help. These respondents sought formal treatment of some kind, typically residential drug treatment, to provide structure, social support, and a pathway to behavioral change. The women perceived clearly the need to remove themselves from the "scene" to meet new friends, and to begin the process of identity reformation. The following account by Alicia typifies the importance of a "geographic" cure:

> I love to get high, you know, and I love the way crack makes me feel. I knew that I needed long-term, I knew that I needed to go somewhere. All away from everything, and I just needed to get away from everything. And I couldn't deal with responsibility at all. And, uh, I was just so ashamed of the way that I had, you know, became and the person that I became that I just wanted to start over again.

Social avoidance strategies were common to all attempts at stopping. When the women removed themselves from their old world and old locations, involvement in crime and drugs was more difficult.

> **April:** Yeah, I go home, but I don't, I don't socialize with the people. I don't even speak to anybody really. I go and I come. I don't go to the areas that I used to be in. I don't go there anymore. I don't walk down the same blocks I used to walk down. I always take different locations.

> **Denise:** I miss the fast money; otherwise, I don't miss my old life. I get support from my positive friends, and in the program. I talk about how I felt being around my old associates, seeing them, you know, going back to my old neighborhood. It's hard to deal with, I have to push away.

Maintaining a Conventional Life

Desisters have little chance of staying out of the life for an extended period of time if they stay in the social world of crime and addiction. They must rebuild and maintain a network of primary relations who accept and support their nondeviant identity if they are to be successful (the third stage of this model). This is no easy task, since in most cases the desisters have alienated their old nondeviant primary relations.

To a great extent, the women in this study most resemble religious converts in their attempts to establish and maintain support networks that validate their new sense of self. Treatment programs not only provide a ready-made primary group for desisters, but also a well-established pervasive identity (Travisano 1970), that of ex-con and/or ex-addict, that informs the women's view of themselves in a variety of interactions. Reminders of "spoiled identities" (Goffman 1963) such as criminal, "con," and "junkie" serve as a constant reference point for new experiences and keep salient the ideology of conventional living (Faupel 1991). Perhaps most important, these programs provide the women with an alternative basis for life structure—one that is devoid of crime, drugs, and other subcultural elements.

The successful treatment program, however, is one that ultimately facilitates dissociation from the program and promotes independent living. Dissociation from programs to participate in conventional living requires association, or reintegration, with conventional society. Friends and educational and occupational roles helped study participants reaffirm their noncriminal identities and bond themselves to conventional lifestyles. Barbara described the assistance she receives from friends and treatment groups:

> . . . a bunch of friends that always confronts me on what I'm doing' and where I'm goin', and they just want the best for me. And none of them use drugs. I go to a lot like outside support groups, you know. They help me have more confidence in myself. I have new friends now. Some of them are in treatment. Some have always been straight. They know. You know, they glad, you know, when I see them.

In the course of experiencing relationships with conventional others and participating in conventional roles, the women developed a strong social-psychological commitment not to return to crime and drug use. These commitments most often revolved around renewed affiliations with their children, relationships with new friends, and the acquisition of educational and vocational skills. The social relationships, interests, and investments that develop in the course of desistance reflect the gradual emergence of new identities. Such stakes in conventional identity form the social-psychological context within which control and desistance are possible (Waldorf et al. 1991).

In short, the women in the study developed a stake in their new lives that was incompatible with street life. This new stake served as a wedge to help maintain the separation of the women from the world of the streets (Biernacki 1986). The desire to maintain one's sense of self was an important incentive for avoiding return to crime.

> **Alicia:** I like the fact that I have my respect back. I like the fact that, uh, my daughter trusts me again. And my mother don't mind leavin' me in the house, and she don't have to worry that when she come in her TV might be gone.

> **Barbara:** I have new friends. I have my children back in my life. I have my education. It keeps me straight. I can't forget where I came from because I get scared to go back. I don't want to hurt nobody. I just want to live a normal life.

Janelle, a 22-year-old black woman, started dealing drugs and carrying a .38-caliber gun when she was 15. She described the ongoing tension between staying straight and returning to her old social world:

> It's hard, it's hard stayin' on the right track. But letting myself know that I'm worth more. I don't have to go in a store today and steal anything. I don't deserve that. I don't deserve to make myself feel really bad. Then once again I would be steppin' back and feel that this is all I can do.

Overall, the success of identity transformations hinges on the women's abilities to establish and maintain commitments and involvements in conventional aspects of life. As the women began to feel accepted and trusted within some conventional social circles, their determination to exit from crime was strengthened, as were their social and personal identities as noncriminals.

Discussion

The primary purpose of this study was to describe—from the offenders' perspective—how women embedded in criminal street subcultures could end their deviance. Desistance appears to be a process as complex and lengthy as that of initial involvement. It was interesting to find that some of the key concepts in initiation of deviance—social bond, differential association, deterrence, age—were important in our analysis. We saw the aging offender take the threat of punishment seriously, reestablish links with conventional society, and sever association with subcultural street elements.

Our research supports Adler's (1992) finding that shame plays a limited role in the decision to return to conventional life for individuals who are entrenched in deviant subcultures. Rather, they exit deviance because they have evolved through the typical phases of their deviant careers.

In the present study, we found that the decision to give up crime was triggered by a shock of some sort (i.e., a socially disjunctive experience), by a delayed deterrence process, or both. The women then entered a period of crisis. Anxious and dissatisfied, they took stock of their lives and criminal activity. They arrived at a point where their way of life seemed senseless. Having made this assessment, the women then worked to clarify and strengthen their nondeviant identities. This phase began with the reevaluation of life goals and the public announcement of their decision to end involvement in crime. Once the decision to quit was made, the women turned to relationships that had not been ruined by their deviance, or they created new relationships. The final stage, maintaining cessation, involved integration into a nondeviant lifestyle. This meant restructuring the entire pattern of their lives (i.e., primary relationships, daily routines, social situations). For most women, treatment groups provided the continuing support needed to maintain a nondeviant status.

The change processes and turning points described by the women in the present research were quite similar to those reported by men in previous studies (Shover 1983, 1985; Cusson and Pinsonneault 1986). Collectively, these findings suggest that desistance is a pragmatically constructed project of action created by the individual within a given social context. Turning points occur as "part of a process over time and not as a dramatic lasting change that takes place at any one time" (Pickles and Rutter 1991, 134). Thus, the return to conventional life occurs more because of "push" than "pull" factors (Adler 1992), because the career of involvement in crime moves offenders beyond the point at which they find it enjoyable to the point at which it is debilitating and anxiety-provoking.

Considering the narrow confines of our empirical data, it is hardly necessary to point out the limits of generalizability. Our analysis refers to the woman deeply involved in crime and immersed in a street subculture who finds the strength and resources to change her way of life. The fact that all the women in this study experienced a long period of personal deterioration and a "rock bottom" experience before they were able to exit crime does not justify a conclusion that this process occurs with all offenders. Undoubtedly, there are other scenarios (e.g., the occasional offender who drifts in and out of crime, the offender who stops when criminal involvement conflicts with commitments to conventional life, the battered woman who kills) in which the question of desistance does not arise. Hence, there is a need to conceptualize and measure the objective and subjective elements of change among various male and female offender subgroups.

Furthermore, the evidence presented here does not warrant the conclusion that none of the women ever renewed their involvement in crime. Because the study materials consist of retrospective information, with all its attendant problems, we cannot state with certainty whether desistance from crime is permanent. Still, it is also clear that these women broke their pattern of involvement in crime for substantial lengths of time and have substantially changed their lives.

Discussion Questions

1. What might happen in a woman's life so that she ponders and then discontinues involvement in crime?

2. Is the desistance process gendered? If so, how? If not, why not?

3. How are the pathways *out* of crime and deviance related to the pathways that lead women *into* crime and deviance?

4. How is a woman's new "noncriminal identity" maintained?

5. How would you characterize women who commit crimes of rational choice?

References

Adler, Patricia. 1992. "The 'Post' Phase of Deviant Careers: Reintegrating Traffickers." *Deviant Behavior* 13: 103–126.

Anglin, Douglas, and George Speckhart. 1988. "Narcotics Use and Crime: Multisample, Multimethod Analysis." *Criminology* 26: 197–234.

Biernacki, Patrick A. 1986. *Pathways from Heroin Addiction: Recovery Without Treatment.* Philadelphia: Temple University Press.

Biernacki, Patrick A., and Dan Waldorf. 1981. "Snowball Sampling: Problems Techniques of Chain Referral Sampling." *Sociological Methods and Research* 10: 141–163.

Blumstein, Alfred, Jacqueline Cohen, Jeffrey A. Roth, and Christy A. Visher. 1986. *Careers and Career Criminals.* Washington, DC: National Academy Press.

Collins, J., R. Hubbard, and J. V. Rachal. 1985. "Expensive Drug Use and Income: A Test of Explanatory Hypotheses." *Criminology* 23: 743–764.

Cusson, Maurice, and Pierre Pinsonneault. 1986. "The Decision to Give Up Crime." In *The Reasoning Criminal: Rational Choice Perspectives on Offending,* edited by Derek Cornish and Ronald Clarke. New York: Springer-Verlag.

Daly, Kathy, and Meda Chesney-Lind. 1988. "Feminism and Criminology." *Justice Quarterly* 5: 101–143.

Faupel, Charles. 1991. *Shooting Dope: Career Patterns of Hard-Core Heroin Users.* Gainesville: University of Florida Press.

Goffman, Erving. 1963. *Stigma: Notes on the Management of Spoiled Identity.* Englewood Cliffs, NJ: Prentice-Hall.

Hirschi, Travis, and H. C. Selvin. 1967. *Delinquency Research: An Appraisal of Analytic Methods.* New York: Free Press.

Le Blanc, Marc, and M. Frechette. 1989. *Male Criminal Activity from Childhood Through Youth: Multilevel and Developmental Perspective.* New York: Springer-Verlag.

Matza, David. 1964. *Delinquency and Drift.* New York: Wiley.

Meisenhelder, Thomas. 1977. "An Exploratory Study of Exiting from Criminal Careers." *Criminology* 15: 319–334.

Mulvey, E. P., and M. Aber. 1988. "Growing Out of Delinquency: Development and Desistance." In *The Abandonment of Delinquent Behavior: Promoting the Turnaround* edited by Richard L. Jenkins and Wald K. Brown (pp. 99–116). New York: Praeger.

Mulvey, Edward P., and John F. LaRosa. 1986. "Delinquency Cessation and Adolescent Development: Preliminary Data." *American Journal of Orthopsychiatry* 56: 212–224.

Petersilia, Joan, Peter Greenwood, and Marvin Lavin. 1978. *Criminal Careers of Habitual Felons.* Washington, DC: Law Enforcement Assistance Administration, U.S. Department of Justice.

Peterson, M., and H. Braiker. 1980. *Doing Crime: A Survey of California Prison Inmates.* Santa Monica, CA: Rand.

Pickles, Andrew, and Michael Rutter. 1991. "Statistical and Conceptual Models of 'Turning Points' in Developmental Processes." In *Problems and Methods in Longitudinal Research: Stability and Change,* edited by D. Magnusson, L. Bergman, G. Rudinger, and B. Torestad (pp. 110–136). New York: Cambridge University Press.

Ray, Marsh. 1961. "The Cycle of Abstinence and Relapse Among Heroin Addicts." *Social Problems* 9: 132–140.

Shover, Neil. 1983. "The Latter Stages of Ordinary Property Offenders' Careers." *Social Problems* 31: 208–218.

——. 1985. *Aging Criminals.* Newbury Park, CA: Sage.

Shover, Neil, and Carol Thompson. 1992. "Age, Differential Expectations, and Crime Desistance." *Criminology* 30: 89–104.

Stall, Ron, and Patrick Biernacki. 1986. "Spontaneous Remission from the Problematic Use of Substances: An Inductive Model Derived from a Comparative Analysis of the Alcohol, Opiate, Tobacco, and Food/Obesity Literatures." *International Journal of the Addictions* 2: 1–23.

Travisano, R. 1970. "Alteration and Conversion as Qualitatively Different Transformations." In *Social Psychology Through Symbolic Interaction*, edited by G. Stone and H. Farberman (pp. 594–605). Boston: Ginn-Blaisdell.

Waldorf, Dan. 1983. "Natural Recovery from Opiate Addiction: Some Social Psychological Processes of Untreated Recovery." *Journal of Drug Issues* 13: 237–280.

Waldorf, Dan, Craig Reinerman, and Sheila Murphy. 1991. *Cocaine Changes*. Philadelphia: Temple University Press.

Weiner, Neil, and Marvin E. Wolfgang. 1989. *Violent Crime, Violent Criminals*. Newbury Park, CA: Sage.

Weis, Joseph G. 1989. "Family Violence Research Methodology and Design." In *Family Violence*, edited by Lloyd Ohlin and Michael Tonry (pp. 117–162). Chicago: University of Chicago Press.